RUTH B. RUSSELL

THE UNITED NATIONS
AND UNITED STATES SECURITY POLICY

THE BROOKINGS INSTITUTION
Washington, D.C.

© 1968 by

THE BROOKINGS INSTITUTION
1775 Massachusetts Avenue, N.W., Washington, D.C. 20036

Library of Congress Catalog Number 67-30602

THE BROOKINGS INSTITUTION is an independent organization devoted to nonpartisan research, education, and publication in economics, government, foreign policy, and the social sciences generally. Its principal purposes are to aid in the development of sound public policies and to promote public understanding of issues of national importance.

The Institution was founded on December 8, 1927, to merge the activities of the Institute for Government Research, founded in 1916, the Institute of Economics, founded in 1922, and the Robert Brookings Graduate School of Economics and Government, founded in 1924.

The general administration of the Institution is the responsibility of a self-perpetuating Board of Trustees. The trustees are likewise charged with maintaining the independence of the staff and fostering the most favorable conditions for creative research and education. The immediate direction of the policies, program, and staff of the Institution is vested in the President, assisted by an advisory council chosen from the staff of the Institution.

In publishing a study, the Institution presents it as a competent treatment of a subject worthy of public consideration. The interpretations and conclusions in such publications are those of the author or authors and do not purport to represent the views of the other staff members, officers, or trustees of the Brookings Institution.

The United Nations came of age in a world that has been almost constantly under threat of war since the Organization was born. Established "to maintain international peace and security," there has never been a final peace settlement of World War II for it to maintain. Formal acceptance by its Member states of the principles and purposes set forth in the Charter has not been reflected in their practical acceptance of the policies necessary to achieve those commonly declared, but variously interpreted, objectives. As one of the permanent members of the Security Council, the United States has played its anticipated leading role in the Organization; but the development of neither the United Nations, nor the American role therein, has fulfilled the more hopeful expectations of 1945.

Since international peace and security have not existed under the United Nations, many persons have sought in regional or bilateral arrangements the means to achieve world peace and national security. But none of the international arrangements utilized by governments in the conduct of their foreign affairs since World War II has given the world peace because the problem is not essentially one of international machinery. It is, rather, one growing out of the policies of governments: where there is inadequate national will to peaceful settlement of international differences, there is no way to maintain a condition of world peace and security through international organizations.

Permanent machinery of collective action, such as the United Nations, is still so new a diplomatic implement that governments are often reluctant to use it. When they decide to do so, they are not always skilled in using it to best advantage, even for their own purposes. The United States bears favorable comparison with most other Members in these respects. And in absolute terms its political and financial support of the Organization has been essential to its development. Washington, however, has had difficulties in attempting to develop a satisfactory place for United Nations activities within the general scheme of its national security policy.

Because of its position of world leadership and its enormous military power, the United States views its national security objectives not only in terms of safeguarding the national homeland but also in terms of maintaining international peace and preventing the outbreak of general nuclear war. Its national security policy is thus a combination of strategic military and foreign policies. The state of international peace that is the objective of the United Nations Charter is based on an even broader concept of the security to be maintained. Not only must the Member states forgo the use of force as an instrument of national policy (except in certain limited, defensive ways) and settle their disputes peacefully; they must also seek to ameliorate the underlying causes of conflict that, if allowed to fester, are likely to develop into the kinds of disputes that eventually threaten the peace.

The Organization, since its early years, has been the subject of numerous studies by the Brookings Institution. The present study examines the role of the United Nations in connection with United States security concerns since the end of World War II; and, as the obverse of the medal, the role the United States has played in the United Nations in many matters of international peace and security that have come within the purview of the Organization. The current volume complements a 1958 Brookings study by Miss Russell, *A History of the United Nations Charter: The Role of the United States 1940–1945*, in which she analyzed the evolution and negotiation of the United Nations Charter as part of American foreign policy during the war years.

No single study could do justice to the complex interplay of bilateral and multilateral diplomacy, political, military, and economic in character, that makes up the story of United States–United Nations relations. To facilitate understanding that interdependent experience as surveyed in Part Two of this volume, the chapters in Part One seek to provide some perspective on the general directions of United States policy and of United Nations activities over the past two decades. A final chapter considers the possible directions of future United States policies toward the world organization.

Miss Russell was a member of the senior staff of Brookings until 1966, when she joined the School of International Affairs at Columbia University as a Research Associate. The Institution joins her in expressing appreciation to Dean Andrew W. Cordier of the School for his generous understanding and support during her final revision of the manuscript. The author greatly benefited from the views of an advisory committee on the first draft of the study, which included Robert E. Asher, Lincoln P. Bloomfield, Benjamin V. Cohen, James N. Hyde, Ernest W. Lefever, and Anne Winslow, to all of whom special thanks are due. Messrs. Asher and Cohen and Miss Winslow read and commented also on the revised manuscript. The volume was edited by Evelyn Breck and the index prepared by Helen B. Eisenhart. The project was developed under the general direction of H. Field Haviland, Jr., Director of Foreign Policy Studies at Brookings.

This study is the final one in a series on the United Nations system that was initiated a number of years ago with the financial support of the A. W. Mellon Educational and Charitable Trust of Pittsburgh. On behalf of the Institution, I wish to express grateful appreciation to the Mellon Trust for the generous grants that made this series possible.

A study of this scope could not have been written without the cooperation of many people, too numerous to list, who are experts in one or another of the subjects covered in the present analysis. Some of the most helpful must remain anonymous because of their official status in the United States Government, national missions to the United Nations, or the Secretariat. The author, therefore, takes this opportunity to acknowledge gratefully their willingness to share their time and experience. The result has added immensely to the value of her study. Those who disagreed with her views, it should be noted, were as helpful as those who shared them in enabling her to gain a better perspective on many points. The interpretations expressed in the book, however, are solely the author's and do not necessarily represent those of her consultants or of the trustees, officers, or other staff members of the Brookings Institution or of the Mellon Trust.

KERMIT GORDON
President

January 1968
Washington, D.C.

CONTENTS

PART ONE

BACKGROUND

BACKGROUND

CHAPTER ONE

THE DIRECTION OF UNITED STATES
POLICY SINCE 1945

At the end of World War II, the United States stood without challenge as the strongest state in the world. Militarily it was armed with a monopoly of atomic power. Politically it headed the United Nations coalition that had just defeated the Axis powers. Under its leadership, the victorious Allies had agreed to the Charter for a permanent Organization through which they and other like-minded nations would seek to maintain international peace and security in the future.

The system provided for in that Charter could come fully into being, however, only as the Members of the United Nations fulfilled their commitments to its peaceful purposes and principles. Such a state of affairs did not obtain after the end of the war. Instead, the United States found the Soviet Union seeking to achieve atomic standing and to force world politics into a mold very different from that hoped for by the United States and outlined in the Charter. Lesser powers also complicated the picture with their own conflicts. Americans had therefore to learn to accept two frustrating conclusions: that the existence of the United Nations was insufficient in itself to bring about a world conforming to Charter standards; and that the possession of a monopoly of atomic power conferred no equivalent monopoly of political power on the United States.

Political conflict had been apparent among the major allied powers well before the end of the war in 1945, but it was kept subordinate to the need for military cooperation until hostilities were ended. When it became apparent that the degree of great-power cooperation essential to effective functioning of the United Nations security system was not going to develop, the United States had to adapt its political and military policies to fit the unfolding situation. In theory and in view of its prewar history the United States might have sought to return to a policy of isolation as a reaction against postwar developments. In fact, only a small minority of

3

Americans favored that general policy; the nation as a whole accepted the position of international leadership it had achieved during the war. It has, however, been divided between two approaches to the problem of maintaining national security and international peace in a world of political and ideological conflict between the holders of great military power. Those two approaches, described below as containment-confrontation versus containment-coexistence, view the United Nations and its role in relation to United States security in quite different lights.

The Containment-Confrontation Approach

If the United States had no intention of seeking a return to isolationism after World War II, neither did it have any desire to meet the widening Soviet Communist threat head-on, in an attempt to eliminate it by military threat or action. The country was not without some advocates of such a policy, however. In the early postwar period, the view was often and openly couched in terms of preventive war against the prime enemy, the Soviet Union. The position is not illogical, in fact, for those who see a monolithic communist menace as presenting the United States with an "absolute confrontation," allowing for neither reconciliation nor coexistence.[1] In more recent years, Peking has tended to become the main villain of this communist threat. Wherever its headquarters are considered to be, however, a faceless "international communism" constitutes the menace to United States security and world peace in the view of proponents of this school. They advocate "the utter rout of Communist imperialism and the liberation of all peoples who suffer under the yoke" as this country's ultimate aim; and a few would still have the United States undertake a strategy of military liberation, at least in the Far East, to achieve it.[2]

The advent of thermonuclear weapons systems and their attainment by the Soviet Union as well as the United States, plus some two decades of

1. Admiral Arleigh Burke, USN Ret., "Power and Peace," *Orbis*, Vol. VI (Summer 1962), pp. 187–88.
2. In *The Red China Lobby* (Fleet, 1963), pp. 271–72, for example, authors Forrest Davis and Robert A. Hunter went so far as to write a scenario for D-Day in mainland China, North Korea, and Laos, with U.S. air and naval forces used to transport and support the armed forces of Nationalist China, South Korea, and Thailand in simultaneous invasions. These "would topple the Red Regime" since they would result in an "attendant wholesale revolt of the Chinese masses." The quoted statement of U.S. objective is from the Foreword to their book, by Admiral Arthur W. Radford, USN Ret., p. xi.

official refusal in Washington to adopt such a draconian policy in practice, have blunted that approach—but without eliminating the underlying attitude, which is still held by many people. Rather than advocating what is now called preemptive military action, however, they more often argue that firm military deterrence under the threat of nuclear retaliation will eventually lead to the collapse of the communist system.

If the United States carried out this approach fully in a strategy of "protracted conflict," as it has come to be known,[3] its foreign policy would be shaped primarily by the military security needs of the anticommunist confrontation. An analysis of the nature of the communist threat by advocates of such a containment-confrontation policy and the kinds of action required to meet it were spelled out in 1965 by General Thomas S. Power, former head of the Strategic Air Command. His *Design for Survival* is based on the principle of deterrence through such superior military strength that the Soviet Union will never be tempted to precipitate general war in the belief that the odds would be heavily in its favor. If such a posture is sustained, the General maintains, the very nature of communism will "condemn it to slow but certain deterioration."[4]

At the same time, he considers the "communist system" both self-perpetuating and unchangeable. Any apparent change made by a new set of "rulers" would be deceptive. That is because the system is guided by the inflexible rules of the party, which aim at total conquest and therefore permit no compromise. Thus they cannot change. In this view of communism, coexistence does not "prevent Communist aggression, but at best postpones it and, in effect, lays the groundwork for it." The United States must therefore aim not to coexist with but to defeat the "Communist ideology" if it is to survive as a sovereign nation.[5]

General Power thinks that the communist military threat is relatively recent, not posing a danger to this nation's survival until several years after World War II. Communism presumably was able to become so dangerous primarily because "our national policy dictate[d] a purely de-

3. The term was given currency by Professors Robert Strausz-Hupé and Colonel William Kintner of the Foreign Policy Research Institute, University of Pennsylvania. It was suggested by the title of Mao Tse-tung's book, *On the Protracted War*. See Robert Strausz-Hupé and others, *Protracted Conflict* (Harper and Rowe, 1959), p. xii. For their views on the role of the United Nations in U.S. policy, see Franz P. Gross, ed., *The United States and the United Nations* (University of Oklahoma Press, 1964), "Introduction" by Strausz-Hupé, especially pp. 18–19, and "The United Nations Record of Handling Major Disputes," by Kintner, especially pp. 121–24.

4. Thomas S. Power, *Design for Survival* (Coward-McCann, 1965), pp. 46–47. The quotations from this book are reprinted by courtesy of General Power.

5. *Ibid.*, pp. 59–60, 68, 70, 184.

fensive military strategy . . . even where it meant serious harm to the cause of democracy"—as in the Korean, Hungarian, and Cuban episodes. The United States, he feels, could have used its strategic-strike capability (not necessarily with nuclear weapons) to crush "communism at its roots" in the early fifties. Hungary (in 1956) was perhaps the last chance to have dealt it a possibly "fatal blow," but this hemisphere's "festering cancer" of Cuba could still have been eradicated "without risk and without working up a sweat."[6]

Power's complex analysis of the situation stresses the following factors: (1) The tremendous expansion of Soviet (and, by extension, the potential expansion of Communist Chinese) military power can serve but one purpose: aggression. (2) Historical precedents demonstrate the improbability of the Soviet rulers indefinitely continuing to strengthen their gigantic military machine without using it for "some profitable objective." (3) "If the Soviets should become convinced that they cannot subdue the United States through their present strategy, they will have no choice but to resort to all-out military action," a contingency for which they have long prepared. (4) Despite "the ever-growing threat of nuclear war," the United States should be able to maintain peace on its terms if it pursues "a realistic and dynamic policy of deterrence against any and all aggressors, including Red China."[7] His grim prospect is for an unending succession of ever more complex weapons systems (including aerospace developments) in order to maintain the "war-winning capability" necessary to national survival.[8] Even if the communist threat should one day spend itself, "there will be other threats, and other ideologies, and other nations or alliances bent on aggression."[9]

It is hardly necessary to add that the only significant role for international organizations, within General Power's frame of reference, is in terms of security arrangements that can buttress the national strategy. Accordingly, he gives little attention to the United Nations; it clearly seems ineffective for accomplishing his purpose. On the other hand, he does give attention to another possible strategy involving international organization that he

6. *Ibid.*, pp. 50, 106.
7. *Ibid.*, pp. 49–50, 44–45.
8. "War-winning capability" has the following specific meaning in General Power's usage: All-out nuclear war would mean that neither side could "win" in the commonly accepted sense. "But if one side manages to retain sufficient military strength after the nuclear exchange to terminate hostilities on its terms and to force the surrender of the other side, it has gained what is called a 'military victory.' This is the kind of victory we must always be able to achieve if we want to deter aggression successfully." *Ibid.*, p. 126.
9. *Ibid.*, p. 216.

considers irreconcilable with his own position. That is the official United States outline for a "Treaty on General and Complete Disarmament" (GCD), which includes a three-stage plan for gradual disarmament with the concurrent development of international means to maintain the peace. The latter part of the plan involves the establishment of an International Disarmament Organization authorized to control the world's armaments and to prevent aggression, and enabled to do so through its own control of a United Nations Peace Force.[10] Power rightly considers that this plan, if carried out successfully, would logically end in world government; and that the "one world syndrome," as he diagnoses it, points in the opposite direction from his own approach. "Our citizens," he concludes, "must therefore select one or the other."[11]

No such definitive choice, however, has been made in fact by those determining United States policy since 1945. The international political spectrum has been found varied enough to allow a more flexible range of choice for the national strategy than between the black and white extremes of precarious deterrence, on the one hand, or complete disarmament on the other. In between, the picture has been much more complicated politically (at least as complex as the General's deterrent system). The general approach followed by the United States might be designated as "containment-coexistence," in contrast to the "containment-confrontation" school.

The Containment-Coexistence Approach

The historical method of succession to the position of dominant world power has traditionally been through militant conflict rather than through political accommodation. In this respect, the previous approach with its military emphasis has history in its favor if one concedes that the revolutionary technological, political, and social changes of recent years require no new doctrine. Rightly or wrongly, however, that solution did not appeal to most Americans as the cold war developed after 1945. They had little desire for a modern equivalent of the grand-imperial role of past centuries.

Depending on their temperament, people in the United States were

10. The U.S. plan is considered at greater length in Chapters 4 and 5. Text in *Arms Control and Disarmament Agency (ACDA), Documents on Disarmament, 1962,* Vol. 1, pp. 351–82 (U.S. Government Printing Office, 1963).

11. Power, *op. cit.,* p. 87.

more inclined to think of national security, right after the war, along either of two other lines: One considered that possession of the most powerful industrial economy in the world, along with the atom bomb and means of aerial delivery, would provide the nation with adequate security.[12] The other tended to assume that the existence of the United Nations and United States membership therein would satisfactorily maintain international peace, and thereby the national security also. The two views were not necessarily considered to be in conflict. President Truman, for example, shared the military view that the United States atomic monopoly guaranteed the national security; but he was also optimistic in 1945 about the possibilities of the United Nations replacing "the old power politics," of which he disapproved in typically American fashion.[13]

Both these assumptions, however, foundered on the fact of the developing cold war—even though it did not then represent a direct threat to the Western Hemisphere, nor an overt threat to most European states still outside the Soviet orbit. The United States atomic monopoly did not in itself discourage the economic, political, and covert military actions of Moscow and local communist groups in seeking to gain control of European and Near Eastern governments. Nor, in the Far East, did it help to cope with the internal Chinese struggle against communist factions.

At the same time, the United States had no intention of allowing the Soviet Union to take over the role of world dominance that it clearly sought in terms of its revolutionary ideology. But if the leading noncommunist power was not prepared to threaten the use of atomic weapons against the Soviet Union in the circumstances (as an indirect means of supporting noncommunist governments in such countries as Greece, Italy, and France), it then had to face the necessity for undertaking new direct responsibilities in the field of international politics. These included maintaining a capacity to make limited military responses in foreign areas not traditionally considered vital to its national security.

Strategic military thinking in the United States in the immediate post-

12. See, for example, General Maxwell D. Taylor, on the belief of many in 1945 that "our armed forces had in the air-delivered atomic bomb the absolute weapon which would permit the United States, its sole possessor, to police the world through the threat of its use." *The Uncertain Trumpet* (Harper, 1960), pp. 4–5.

13. See Harry S. Truman, *Memoirs* (Doubleday, 1955), Vol. 1, pp. 245–46. For the attitudes of many United States officials during World War II on "power politics" and its displacement by a world organization, see Ruth B. Russell, *A History of the United Nations Charter: The Role of the United States, 1940–1945* (Brookings Institution, 1958), pp. 181, 484, 490, 963.

war period, however, concentrated on the traditional aim of safeguarding the homeland and on preparing to fight a defensive war against the Soviet Communist threat—and on little else.[14] This position also had the domestic political virtue of requiring the least immediate sacrifice in men and money, compared to the costs of maintaining a more flexible military establishment geared to different levels of possible conflict in various parts of the world. These political-strategic ideas represented a curious return to the way of thinking of the prewar isolationist period, although combined with a widespread theoretical acceptance of the new role of world leadership that had fallen to the United States. Americans as a people, and sometimes as a government, found it easier to forswear old habits of thought than to forgo them in practice.[15]

Reluctantly, therefore, the United States began to cope with the fact that it would have to play the kind of "power politics" it was traditionally antipathetic to. It would have to take over where the Western European powers were being forced by circumstance to leave off. It began with the Truman Doctrine in 1947, justifying programs of aid to Greece and Turkey on the ground that "it must be the policy of the United States to support free peoples who are resisting attempted subjugation by armed minorities or by outside pressures . . . [to] assist free peoples to work out their own destinies in their own way."[16] For some time longer, however, the government hoped it could extend its assistance primarily in the form of economic and financial aid—that it could do the job the politically easy way, that is, mainly through giving money, equipment, and advice.

But Greek-Turkish aid and the Marshall Plan led, through the Berlin Blockade and the communist takeover in Czechoslovakia in 1948, to the North Atlantic Treaty Organization (NATO) in the West. In the East, although the "loss" of China in 1949 was a traumatic shock, the country did not face up to the serious international political-military issues in-

14. Even in 1964, the geographer of the State Department could note that: "So preoccupied are Americans with concern for the 'home base' and its preservation that this level of geopolitical thinking may not always progress apace with world development." G. Etzel Pearcy, "Geopolitics and Foreign Relations," U.S. Department of State, *Bulletin*, Vol. 50 (1964), p. 324.

15. See also Stanley Hoffmann's comment on "responses that at first might appear to be unprecedented," but which can be shown to be "nothing but the application of the old habits of thought and action to a new problem." "Restraints and Choices," in Wesley W. Posvar, ed., *American Defense Policy* (Johns Hopkins Press, 1965), pp. 448–49.

16. From statement to the Congress, March 12, 1947, text in Truman, *Memoirs*, Vol. 2, pp. 106–07.

volved. The search, instead, was for "who" lost China. It took the Korean War to bring about an acceptance *in practice* of a policy that the United States was not even yet prepared to accept *in principle*: that the military strategy of limited war was the natural accompaniment of a political strategy of containment. Yet, if the United States was not prepared to pay the price or accept the consequences either of the ultimate military confrontation or of Western submission to communist "burial," it had of necessity to accept this last approach—as in fact it did.

"Containment," however, has a defeatest sound to many Americans, who still prefer to talk about "victory"—meaning elimination of the problem—as the only patriotic objective. Military containment, alone, can indeed be a sterile policy. It must be accompanied by continuous effort to find other, political means that may force or persuade the communist powers to adopt more peaceful means to a more limited end than their unlimited objective of making the world over in their image. But most of those who advocate United States objectives that are superficially more conclusive and noble-sounding than containment also declare that they favor only peaceful means to reach them. They do not accept the full implications of a policy emphasizing military confrontation.[17] The difficulty with this attitude is that, unless one can also believe that the communist governments are going to collapse conveniently, or to concede all major American demands in relatively short order, the restriction to peaceful methods leaves no alternative but indefinitely to accept the hazards of the delicately balanced nuclear confrontation that most people want to escape. More consistent Americans, therefore, have accepted a policy consciously seeking to combine containment and coexistence.

Some have done so reluctantly and as the inevitable result of the rapid and relentless advances in modern weapons. More, however, have probably done so because they reject the analysis of the nature of the communist threat given earlier. They prefer the hazards of a search for gradual, responsible, and mutual accommodation as ultimately the means to the kind of international system that the United States would like to see prevail. In broadest terms, the contrast is between the approach that sees an unchanging and unchangeable threat to U. S. security and to world

17. Former Vice-President Richard M. Nixon, for example, has declared that: "Our goal must not be simply to keep freedom from shrinking, but to make it grow too. Our goal must be a free Cuba, a free Eastern Europe, a free Russia, a free China. And every policy must be directed to reach that goal through peaceful means." Quoted in *New York Times*, Oct. 6, 1963.

peace, which therefore requires an unceasing resistance on all levels; and that which seeks to maintain the deterring power of resistance to aggressive action, while seeking to influence the potential aggressors gradually out of their violent intentions through policies of constraint and collaboration. President Johnson declared the latter to be United States policy when he said "Our guard is up, but our hand is out."[18]

Neither the posture nor the policy is easy to maintain. Arnold Wolfers has noted: "Such a twofold policy presents the greatest dilemmas because efforts to change the intentions of an opponent may run counter to the efforts to build up strength against him."[19] The application of this approach was in some ways facilitated by developments in both the communist and noncommunist spheres during the second postwar decade, which modified the earlier bipolar world and changed the particular form of the cold-war threat. In the third decade, it has once again become more difficult to apply because of the rise of Communist Chinese expansionism and the increased United States involvement in conflict in southeast Asia. Even during the previous decade, steps toward détente with the Soviet Union made too little progress toward a less dangerous world from the American viewpoint.

To meet Washington's declared standards, an acceptable international society must be based on positive purposes and pluralistic principles of the kind that are formally accepted by all signers of the Charter of the United Nations, and institutionalized in the Organization based on it. This was the kind of world that President Kennedy referred to, in June 1963, when he answered his rhetorical question: What kind of peace do we seek?

Not a Pax Americana enforced on the world by American weapons of war. Not the peace of the grave or the security of the slave. I am talking about genuine peace . . . that enables men and nations to grow and to hope and to build a better life for their children. . . .

Some say that it is useless to speak of world peace or world law or world disarmament—and that it will be useless until the leaders of the Soviet Union adopt a more enlightened attitude. I hope they do. I believe we can help them do it. But I also believe that we must reexamine our own attitude, as individuals and as a nation, for our attitude is as essential as theirs. . . .[20]

18. "NATO, A Growing Partnership," U.S. Department of State, *Bulletin*, Vol. 50 (1964), p. 607.

19. Arnold Wolfers, " 'National Security' as an Ambiguous Symbol," *Political Science Quarterly*, Vol. 67 (December 1952), p. 497.

20. "Toward a Strategy of Peace," Address at American University, June 10, 1963. U.S. Department of State, *Bulletin*, Vol. 49 (1963), pp. 2, 3.

The attitudes to which the late President was referring were shaped by, and they shaped in turn, United States reactions to the pattern of events in the postwar period, which are considered in the chapters that follow. In general, the world environment has been one in which the pace of change has challenged the government to adjust to those outside forces it could not control and to adapt its policies to influence the forces amenable to United States power—whether political, military, economic, or ideological. In this revolutionary world, President Kennedy urged that Americans focus on attaining a peace based "not on a sudden revolution in human nature" but on the more practical approach of "a gradual evolution in human institutions—on a series of concrete actions and effective agreements which are in the interests of all concerned."[21]

International Organizations and United States Policy

In this broadly cooperative policy context, the role of international organization also becomes a more constructive one. Multilateral security arrangements continue to be a significant part of the machinery for maintaining deterrent strength against expansionist powers; but in addition the cooperative objectives of coexistence call for more broadly based organizations with more general political aims. In the speech by President Kennedy just quoted he thus advocated, as one of his specific aims, making the United Nations "a more effective instrument for peace."[22] The objectives of the Charter and the rules of the game it promulgates would clearly meet the United States purpose in the sense here considered. Dissatisfaction with the unpeaceful state of affairs that has marked the contemporary world has, however, led to much criticism of the United Nations for its presumed failure to maintain international peace and security, one of its chief purposes. This in turn led many to search for an alternative basis of international organization to serve as the multilateral mainstay of United States policy in its objective of promoting truly peaceful coexistence.

The search for alternatives to the United Nations stemmed in part from the feeling of many Americans that all the adaptations the United States has made to the postwar world, and all the contributions it has generously donated to militarily or economically threatened peoples,

21. *Ibid.*
22. *Ibid.*, p. 5.

should have brought about a safer and more comfortable world. As President Kennedy pointed out in an address shortly before his death:

Americans have come a long way in accepting in a short time the necessity of world involvement, but the strain of this involvement remains. . . . We find ourselves entangled with apparently unanswerable problems in unpronounceable places. We discover that our enemy in one decade is our ally in the next. We find ourselves committed to governments whose actions we cannot often approve, assisting societies with principles very different from our own.

The burdens of maintaining an immense military establishment, with one million Americans serving outside our frontiers, of financing a farflung program of development assistance, of conducting a complex and baffling diplomacy, all weigh heavily upon us. . . . The world is full of contradiction and confusion, and our policy seems to have lost the black-and-white clarity of simpler times. . . .

[But] if this nation is to survive and succeed in the real world of today, we must acknowledge the realities of that world. . . .[23]

WORLD GOVERNMENT

Not all the proposed alternatives to the United Nations do, in fact, acknowledge these complex realities of the present world. At the opposite extreme from those who have urged resolution of the problem of peace by the calculated risk of nuclear conflict, there has been a relatively small group of supporters of the idea of resolution by constitution-making for some form of world government.

Neither during the wartime preparations for the United Nations Charter nor at any time since has there been a significant body of official opinion, least of all in Congress, supporting *in fact* the yielding of United States sovereignty to some form of world federation. Nor has any other people appeared any more willing to lead the way to a voluntarily accepted system of world government. In the late forties, however, the superficial appeal of the world federalist idea had a fair number of followers among the public, including some legislators. Its supporters based their position essentially on the observable fact that major wars are normally fought between states, while peaceful conditions seem to be the more general rule within states. They then reasoned that, if the sovereign national units were "eliminated," through merger into a world federation, war would automatically be eliminated along with them. This simplistic reasoning tended

23. "Pioneers for Peace," Address at Salt Lake City, Sept. 26, 1963. U.S. Department of State, *Bulletin*, Vol. 49 (1963), p. 633.

to overlook all problems save that of writing the constitution for such a world government. It amounted to little more than a semantic solution of the problem of political conflict, in effect transmuting international war into civil war and then ignoring the latter subject.[24]

In recent years, proponents of federal or confederal world government have tended to base their arguments on somewhat more sophisticated approaches. They usually stress gradualism as their key, whether urging the "strengthening" of the United Nations into a world federation, or advocating the achievement of world peace through enforceable world law under some form of global supranatural authority.[25] There are, however, two prerequisites to the effective federation of existing states into a world government by peaceful means. One is a widespread willingness to accept such a fundamental political reorganization through the large-scale voluntary transfer of sovereignty by the world's independent states. The other is a practical prerequisite of similarly structured component political units. Neither prerequisite yet exists, nor seems likely to develop in the foreseeable future. It is therefore unnecessary to analyze further the shortcomings of this alternative, beyond noting that the real political problems in the way of achieving a world government cannot be overcome simply by describing them as strengthening the United Nations.

EXTENSION OF REGIONAL ORGANIZATIONS

In contrast to these proposals for achieving peace through tighter political organization of the world, others have argued that a looser regional organization is the better way to that end. The regional-security approach initially grew out of the cold-war experiences in the early postwar years that, as noted, led to NATO by 1949. The year before, the tradition of a special regional relationship in the Western Hemisphere had been formalized into the Organization of American States (OAS), including for the first time a regional security arrangement—the Treaty of Rio de

24. For further discussion, see Ruth B. Russell, "The Management of Power and Political Organization: Communication," *International Organization*, Vol. 15 (Spring 1961), pp. 630–32.

25. For completeness there should also be noted another approach to world government predicted by some who think it may come of necessity after nuclear crisis or war. This federation-by-fusion idea seems less "unthinkable" to the present writer than "un-thought-through." For further consideration, see in connection with some of the proposals for world police forces in Chap. 5. For the enforceable law approach, see Chap. 8 pp. 292–302.

Janeiro, signed in 1947.[26] In the view of the United States Government, this arrangement probably was considered more important in relation to an extra-Hemisphere communist threat than to any intraregional danger then perceived. To Latin American governments its importance lay in its expression of a "good neighbor" relationship to the United States, which was expected to serve as protection against Yankee imperialism.

In the Far East, on the contrary, the United States between 1945 and 1950 followed a policy of "neutralism" on the whole, outside of its direct obligations in Japan and certain Pacific islands. It avoided military commitment in either the Chinese civil war or in the Euro-Asian conflicts stemming from emerging nationalist forces in southeast Asia. It withdrew militarily from Korea. In part, this was a result of the degree of unilateral United States conventional disarmament, which was rationalized in the emphasis placed by prevailing military thought on the Soviet threat in Europe. Korea, for example, was characterized as of "insignificant" strategic and economic value.[27] Despite the shock of the communist conquest of mainland China, Washington did not then reverse its policy of avoiding the use of national combat forces in mainland Asia.[28] While continuing to recognize the Nationalist Government on Formosa as the legitimate government of all China, the Truman Administration at first decided that Formosa (like Korea) was not sufficiently important to the national security to justify the use of American forces in its defense.[29]

United States actions in the Far East thus spoke more loudly to the communists than the now-famous words of Secretary of State Acheson in January 1950. At that time, he reaffirmed the current military concept that immediate United States security concerns lay within a Pacific "defensive perimeter" running from the Aleutians to Japan, the Ryukyus, and the

---

26. The Rio Treaty was itself an outgrowth of Latin American determination at San Francisco to make the inter-American system the basis of enforcement action in the Western Hemisphere by limiting the authority of the Security Council to prevent regional action. Latin American efforts in this direction influenced the terms of Article 51 and Chapter VIII in the Charter, and extracted a promise from the United States to join in a regional security arrangement as well. See Russell, A *History of the United Nations Charter*, especially Chap. 27.

27. See for example, Secretary of War Patterson's view in 1948, in Walter Millis, ed., *The Forrestal Diaries* (Viking, 1951), p. 273.

28. See Tang Tsou, "Civil Strife and Armed Intervention: Marshall's China Policy," *Orbis*, Vol. 6 (Spring 1962), pp. 85–88.

29. See, for example, Truman's statement of Jan. 5, 1950: "The U.S. . . . . [has no] intention of utilizing its armed forces to interfere in the present situation." U.S. Department of State, *Bulletin*, Vol. 22 (1950), p. 79.

Philippines—omitting both Formosa and mainland Asia where no American troops were stationed. In the event of attack on areas outside the pale, he emphasized, reliance would have to be initially on self-defense "and then upon the commitments of the entire civilized world under the Charter. . . ."[30] When the attack did come from North Korea in June 1950, however, Washington immediately, almost instinctively, responded to the appeal of the South Koreans for help at the same time that it invoked the Charter.

Although the lightning had struck in the Far East rather than in Western Europe, as anticipated, the United States saw the attack in terms of its established interpretation of the general communist threat to its security and the possibility of a third world war. It mobilized the United Nations in a voluntary collective-security action, since the Charter provisions to make forces available for the mandatory application of sanctions had not been brought into effect.[31] Some rapid adaptation and improvisation resulted in a collective military operation under the aegis of the United Nations that probably resembled in many ways what might have happened had it been mounted originally as a collective-defense operation under Article 51.

The consequences of Korea for the United Nations are considered later.[32] The consequences for the United States, as a result of the ultimate stalemate in Korea and the eventual truce of 1953, were: widespread disillusionment with collective-security possibilities through the United Nations; an even greater concentration on "international communism" as the sole threat to world peace;[33] and the eventual development of further regional and special security arrangements that have since formed the chief bases of United States strategic policy. In the fifties, NATO and the OAS were supplemented by the Southeast Asia Treaty Organization (SEATO) and the Central Treaty Organization (CENTO) and by

---

30. "Crisis in Asia, An Examination of U. S. Policy," *ibid.*, p. 116.
31. See Chap. 5 for the failure of negotiations under Art. 43 between 1946 and 1948. See also Secretary Acheson's later statement of interpretation in U. S. Department of State Press Release 761 (Sept. 26, 1952).
32. See Chap. 5, pp. 122–30.
33. Secretary of State Dulles wrote, for example, in 1957: "United States foreign policy since 1945 has been forced to concern itself primarily with one major threat to the peaceful and orderly development of the kind of international community the American people desire"—that posed by the directors of the "totalitarian system of International Communism." "Challenge and Response in U.S. Policy," *Foreign Affairs*, Vol. 36 (October 1957), p. 26.

numerous bilateral accords, bringing over forty states into formal military alliance with the United States.

Although national security policy thus concentrated on the communist source of international violence, another major historical force had also been playing its part in forcibly reshaping the postwar world. It, too, first clearly emerged in the Far East and affected the development of regional arrangements. This was the vigorous anticolonial drive that, with unanticipated speed, brought over fifty new states into being by 1967.

The development of nationalist movements had been foreseen as a postwar political factor by United States leaders, although in general they underestimated its strength. The traditional United States policy, which favored national independence for all peoples wanting it, was normally qualified in administration pronouncements by the requirement that they be "prepared and willing to accept the responsibilities of liberty."[34] To advance this end during the war officials sought, unsuccessfully on the whole, to persuade their major European allies to follow (at least in their more advanced colonial possessions) the sort of policy whereby the United States prepared the Philippines for independence.

After the war, the shape of things to come first appeared in Indonesia, where conflict with the Netherlands flared violently by 1947. The United States, although unhappy about opposing a recent wartime ally, followed its traditional instincts and supported action through the United Nations on behalf of Indonesian independence. Simultaneously, it put political and economic pressure on The Hague to settle with the nationalists. In Indochina, on the other hand, where the French remained for some years dominant behind a façade of autonomous nationalists, communist influence became the evil genie to the United States after the Korean experience. By 1954, whatever hold France had been able to regain in its former colonies there had vanished, despite greater military efforts to maintain it—supported by massive material and financial aid from the United States—than had ever been necessary to establish it originally. Dien Bien Phu marked the failure of France to retain its influence in Southeast Asia. President Eisenhower's final decision, not to use United States forces directly in support of the French at that point, again made clear that it was not Washington's policy to commit combat units in main-

---

34. As stated by Secretary of State Cordell Hull in U. S. Department of State, *Bulletin*, Vol. 7 (1942), p. 642. For development of U. S. policy during the war period, see Russell, A *History of the United Nations Charter*, especially Chaps. 4, 13, and 23.

land Asia.[35] The episode, however, led to the great extension of regional and bilateral security pacts, already noted.

From the mid-fifties on, the sometimes conflicting factors of anticommunism and anticolonialism (with racism complicating the latter) presented the United States with some of its most agonizing foreign policy problems. As the increasingly numerous new states became Members of the United Nations, they naturally brought their chief concerns to that Organization. Moreover, they were encouraged by the Soviet Union, which sought to win friends and influence governments by claiming to be the leading anticolonial power. Torn by its conflicting objectives in frequently ambiguous specific situations, the United States tried to follow a "neutral" policy by abstaining in United Nations votes, especially on anticolonial resolutions involving European territories in Africa. This pleased practically no one, either at home or abroad. It became the focus of criticism both by those who condemned failure to oppose colonialism, and by those who condemned failure to support NATO allies against communist machinations in colonial areas.

During 1960, difficulties in the United Nations Congo operation and an increasing likelihood that Peking might be seated in the Organization intensified other frustrations for United States policy caused by the increasingly anticolonial majority of the General Assembly.[36] General de Gaulle's caustic reference to the "dis-United Nations" began to be echoed both by Americans who favored a stronger military confrontation policy with the communist powers, and by those who felt the Assembly was "irresponsibly" pressing for action, sometimes embarrassing to the United States, on issues of self-determination and racial oppression.

ALTERNATIVES TO THE UNITED NATIONS

By late 1961, the growing financial difficulties of the United Nations stemming from the failure of a number of members (most important, the Soviet Union and France) to pay for the unprecedentedly high costs of international peacekeeping operations in the Congo, led the Assembly to decide to issue $200 million worth of bonds as a temporary financing

35. For the President's account of his policy toward Indochina, see Dwight D. Eisenhower, *Mandate for Change* (Doubleday, 1963), Chap. 14.

36. Eighteen new states, all former colonies (17 in Africa) were admitted as Members in 1960. For a list of Members as of December 1967 see App. B.

measure.[37] The need to obtain congressional authorization for the Kennedy Administration's proposal to purchase half the issue brought into the open a series of complaints from a variety of sources about the world Organization, its shortcomings in maintaining international peace, and its relationship to the United States. The point of interest here is the concern displayed by such responsible critics as Senators Jackson and Fulbright, both administration leaders, that too much stress was being laid on the United Nations to the detriment of more constructive development of regional security organization.

Senator Jackson expressed a widely held concern, that the government might be "taking an exaggerated view of the United Nations' role" in maintaining peace, and allowing the United States delegation in New York to "operate as a second foreign office." In Jackson's view, however, peace in this divided world depended on "the power and unity of the Atlantic Community and on skillful direct diplomacy." Although he concluded that the United Nations should continue to be "an important avenue of American foreign policy," he also advocated a revision of attitude "in the direction of a more realistic appreciation of its limitations, [of] more modest hopes for its accomplishments."[38]

Senator Fulbright felt that the United States was bearing "a disproportionate share of the burden of world responsibility," despite the creation of "extensive international machinery since World War II"; and that "failures of the United Nations and of other international organs suggest that we have already gone beyond what was internationally feasible." What was needed, he argued, was "a dynamic 'concert of free nations' . . . through which [they could] advance their common interests" on a more coordinated basis:

It is clear [he declared] that the United Nations, although it was designed to form just such a concert, has fallen far short of the hopes which attended its creation; we must look elsewhere for a system that can unify the force of freedom effectively.

·   ·   ·   ·   ·   ·

A realistic "concert of free nations" might be expected to consist of an "inner community" of the North Atlantic nations and an "outer community" embracing much or all of the non-Communist world. The North Atlantic nations represent an almost-existing community and, because they do, they can press forward in the development of supranational institutions. . . . The "outer

37. For further consideration of this matter, see Chaps. 6 and 9.
38. Henry M. Jackson, "The U.S. in the U.N.: An Independent Audit," National Press Club address, press release (unnumbered), March 20, 1962, pp. 3, 8, 10.

community" poses much more difficult problems because it is [only] a *potential* community still far from realization. Our objective must be to bring it into existence. . . .[39]

Strong support for the "Atlantica" approach came also from the Republican side, as in an article of that title by former Secretary of State Herter in January 1963. Although protesting that there "ought not" to be any basic conflict between the world Organization and the Atlantic Community, his concept of a strong regional community appeared to lead, in fact, in the direction of weakening the global agency.[40]

None of these attempts to overcome the limitations of the United Nations by increasing dependence on less inclusive arrangements, unfortunately, provides a more sure means of attaining world peace on terms more to American liking. Senator Javits made this point forcefully:

Those who raise questions about the United Nations and suggest no answers, and then rush to cast their lot wholly with institutions less broad in purpose or coverage, fail to see beyond today's crises. I support alliances for security and regional cooperation—and so does the United Nations Charter. But we cannot fool ourselves into thinking that these alliances alone will fulfill our long range hopes and purposes. By the very nature of their limitations, they cannot. *They can and do play a vital role in maintaining some balance of power in a world which has not yet accepted the disciplines of the rule of law, but they cannot provide us with permanent peace other than the standstill of the balance of terror.*[41]

It is noteworthy moreover that, although the national strategy has placed great emphasis on those regional security arrangements to contain communist thrusts, they do not always serve either to resolve or contain various disputes involving their own members. The argument is sometimes made that the latter is not their purpose. But this overlooks the fact that conflicts involving such regional allies have frequently drawn the threat, if not the reality, of intervention by communist states. On occasion, such conflicts reach a crisis stage that leads to use of the United

---

39. J. William Fulbright, "For a Concert of Free Nations," *Foreign Affairs*, Vol. 40 (October 1961), pp. 2–3, 16–17.

40. Christian A. Herter, "Atlantica," *Foreign Affairs*, Vol. 41 (January 1963), pp. 299–310. A modified version of the world-government approach on a regional basis, in terms of the Clarence Streit "Federal Union" proposals for the Atlantic nations, still receives support also. Senator Frank Carlson (Kansas Republican), for example, has urged that the United States set a timetable for converting NATO into a full federal union. See *New York Times*, June 1, 1965.

41. Jacob K. Javits, "The U.S. and the U.N.: An Affirmative View," National Press Club address, press release (unnumbered), May 23, 1962, p. 3.

Nations to bring them under at least temporary control. Suez, the Congo, and Cyprus were all episodes of this nature, involving in one form or another failures of communication and coordination among NATO allies, and ultimately threatening to bring the Soviet Union into the conflict.[42]

The maintenance of peace requires more than manning the bastions against communist aggression, whether direct or indirect. So long as the objective of the United States remains the kind of peaceful world based on the ground rules of the Charter, the search for a more satisfactory alternative basis for the international organizational aspects of United States policy tends to ignore the fact that what makes the United Nations less than perfect in meeting American desires has little to do with its machinery and procedures, or even with the size of its membership. It has everything to do, on the other hand, with the politics of its member states, which would not be changed simply by bringing some under a different institutional canopy and excommunicating the rest.

Recent Policy Directions

The ideal of finding a more satisfactory international basis for the maintenance of peace and security through greater development of regional organization became less appealing, moreover, as difficulties within NATO intensified in the sixties. Hope for a détente with the Soviet Union also faded, and potential conflict came close to catastrophe in October 1962 over Cuba.[43] The shock of that encounter led to tacit accord with Moscow on the desirability of preventing nuclear war and to more cautious Soviet policies. It also facilitated such actions as minor moves in the direction of nuclear crisis control, partial nuclear test-banning, and limited cooperative measures within the United Nations. None of these small steps, however, was accepted without protest from some groups in the United States. They also objected to expanding trade and diplomatic relationships with communist governments on the part of various allied states—in particular, of France and Great Britain with China and Cuba, respectively.

Such developments tended to lead to a resurgence of resistance to the actual, if not always the declared, United States policy of seeking for points of accommodation with the Soviet Union, which all administrations have followed more or less consistently since the end of the Korean

42. See Chap. 6 below for discussion of U.N. operations in these cases.
43. See Chap. 4 below.

conflict. By the summer of 1964, that attitude was sufficiently strong to play some part in bringing about the nomination of Senator Goldwater as the Republican presidential candidate. His overwhelming defeat in November showed at least that there was no majority trend in the United States away from the predominant direction of postwar foreign policy, even though his view on the need for sterner resistance to all communist powers was not a determining factor in the election.

Only a few months later in February 1965, however, increasing difficulties in South Vietnam led the Johnson Administration to adopt a policy of "persuasive deterrence" such as advocated by General Power;[44] that is, the carefully planned and progressively heavier bombing of North Vietnam to interdict men and supplies moving south and to persuade Hanoi to accept negotiations for settlement in South Vietnam. Then, at the end of April 1965, the President ordered a military intervention in the Dominican Republic, eventually justified as necessary to prevent a communist takeover of the government.[45]

A year later, the situation in Santo Domingo was considerably easier; a free election was held in June 1966, and all foreign troops were withdrawn by September. Taken alone, therefore, the Dominican episode might have been considered the exception that proved the rule of the general United States policy of containment-coexistence during the twenty postwar years. On the other hand, United States involvement in Vietnam has steadily increased since 1965. Committed ground troops rose above 450,000 by mid-1967. Bombing of the North was irregularly intensified, while still avoiding heavy attacks on major cities and staying clear of Chinese territory. Nonetheless, efforts, including several bombing pauses of varying length, to get Hanoi to agree to negotiations continued to be unsuccessful.

The escalation of the Vietnamese conflict (on top of more direct controversies with Moscow, noted in Part 2) handicapped further efforts

---

44. Based on an analysis of the military problem in the South as being to cut off support of the guerrillas at its source, rather than to counter their activities on the local ground. He concluded: "Thus, within a few days and with minimum force, the conflict in South Vietnam would have been ended in our favor." *Op. cit.*, pp. 224–25. Two years later, Gen. Curtis LeMay, former Air Force chief of staff, denounced the gradualism of U.S. bombing policy: "The only way to win a war is to escalate it one way or another above what the enemy can take." In the event that such escalation resulted in Communist Chinese intervention, he argued, South Korea and Nationalist China—with U.S. air, naval, and logistical support—"should provide more than enough force to bring an unstable Red China to her knees." *New York Times*, Oct. 4, 1966, quoting from article in current *U.S. News & World Report*.

45. See Chap. 6 for discussion of Vietnam and the Dominican episode.

toward détente with the Soviet Union. President Johnson still maintains his policy of seeking for new points of accord with Moscow and the East European Communist governments, and declares the military policies being followed in the Far East have only peace as their objective. Although the split between Peking and Moscow has reached serious proportions, both support Hanoi as against Saigon and Washington. The latter has been the enemy to the Communist Chinese authorities since first frustrating their intended conquest of Formosa and seeming to threaten them directly in North Korea; the Vietnamese situation has, if possible, made a bad matter worse.[46] Given the complex interactions of great power policies, neither the United Nations, the Secretary General, the "Geneva" powers,[47] nor interested nonaligned governments has been able to play an effective role in bringing about negotiations for a ceasefire or a start toward peaceful settlement of a conflict that many fear may escalate beyond control at some point into a more general war.

Such broader world security problems have had both direct and indirect effects on the working of the United Nations, some of them serious enough to place its future role in some jeopardy. The application by the United States of an evolutionary policy of détente to particular political and security issues, within and without the Organization, is extraordinarily difficult in contemporary circumstances.

Nevertheless, so long as Washington is in fact searching for a world in which coexistence might some day in truth become peaceful in the Charter sense, an increased role for the United Nations should remain an objective also. This is because the Organization and its related group of specialized agencies still provide the best available means of expanding the areas of desired international cooperation on a global basis as the necessary will to cooperate is painfully cultivated. The relationship of the United States to the United Nations can therefore most usefully be viewed in a perspective of the best way to assist the Organization in overcoming the hazards that now prevent it from working as its Charter anticipates, as it would if its members carried out their Charter commitments. There is no other way to develop the kind of international system that remains the United States goal.

46. For further discussion of the Communist Chinese situation in relation to the United States and the United Nations, see below, Chaps. 4 and 9.

47. The states that met at Geneva in the two conferences on Far Eastern settlements —in 1954 on Korea and Indochina, in 1962 on Laos—including Great Britain and the Soviet Union as co-chairmen.

CHAPTER TWO

CHANGE AND THE CHARTER

In its twentieth year, the United Nations was partially stalemated by a constitutional crisis. It was no more profound, perhaps, than some earlier constitutional challenges the Organization had successfully survived through a process of informal Charter interpretation and institutional adaptation. The particular financial and peacekeeping difficulties that caused the 1965 crisis, however, reached the stage where formal confrontation of conflicting Charter interpretations could only be avoided by adopting a procedural device to evade decision that prevented the functioning of the General Assembly.

This was not the first time that a procedural device had been used to avoid pushing a bitterly divisive issue to the point of hard and fast decision—the question of Chinese representation in the Organization, for example, was postponed for years by such means. But in the nineteenth Assembly, the issue was whether the United States was going to push for a decision to deprive the Soviet Union, France, and some other Members of their vote under the penalty of Article 19. The refusal of those states to pay certain special assessments for peacekeeping operations had led to their being declared in arrears to an amount greater than two years of assessed contributions. The United States eventually decided not to force a showdown in the face of widespread opposition to such action; but the price of postponing that decision for some months had to be the avoidance of all voting in the Assembly in order to evade the critical issue.

The constitutional arguments are discussed later in this study. What is of interest here is that the major parties on both sides of the argument—the United States on the one hand, the Soviet Union and France on the other—all contended that, to resolve the problem, the basic necessity was a "return to the Charter." President Johnson found the United Nations problems traceable to violations "of either the spirit or the letter of the

24

Charter."[1] *Pravda* urged the "strict and unswerving" observance of the Charter,[2] and General de Gaulle called for the Organization to revert "to prudence and the Charter."[3] Because of these identical claims by governments that bitterly disputed the correct interpretation of that Charter, it will be well to begin with a look at the question as it appeared in 1945.

Interpretation of the Charter

"That we now have this Charter at all is a great wonder," President Truman reminded the final session of the United Nations Conference in June 1945.[4] The sessions at San Francisco had been marked by differences so strong that, more than once, they almost stopped the negotiations. The will to establish a successor to the League of Nations finally proved stronger than those substantive differences, but only at a cost in consensus that was, even in the euphoria of the V-E Day period, clearly visible to those with the will to see. Controversial issues were often resolved, not in favor of one side or the other, but by "fuzzing over" the controversy at the lowest common denominator of agreement and in language that was inevitably vague if not confusing. The outcome was a treaty committing its signers to act in pursuance of purposes and in conformance with principles that they understood in widely varying ways. Strictly speaking, all that was agreed by the San Francisco Conference was the form of the words that went into the Charter provisions—in five languages of equal authenticity[5] —and into certain official interpretations.

The linguistic puzzle was further complicated by lack of any provision for authoritative interpretation. Various delegations had favored making the new International Court of Justice or the plenary General Assembly authoritative in matters of interpretation. But by the time the issue came up near the end of the Conference, it was evident, from the number of disputes over the interpretation of wording then being written into pro-

1. President Johnson's press conference, Feb. 4, 1965, text in *New York Times*, Feb. 5, 1965.
2. *Pravda* article, in *Soviet News*, #5099, February 1965.
3. Gen. de Gaulle's press conference, Feb. 4, 1965, excerpts in *New York Times*, Feb. 5, 1965.
4. U.N. Information Organizations and U.S. Library of Congress, *Documents of the United Nations Conference on International Organization*, Vol. I (1945), p. 714. Hereinafter cited as UNCIO Documents.
5. Art. 11. For the text of the Charter, see App. A.

visions of the Charter, that it would be impossible to reach accord on any organ as the definitive interpreter. The adamant refusal of both the United States and the Soviet Union to countenance a Charter with compulsory jurisdiction for the International Court, for example, was alone sufficient indication of this;[6] but there were many others.

This left matters to the daily decisions necessary in the work of each organ, and to procedures for resolving differences over interpretation within or between organs. The latter might involve seeking advice from the International Court or from *ad hoc* jurists' committees, or the voluntary submission of questions for Court interpretation. But if such interpretations were not "generally acceptable," the Conference considered, they would not be binding and Charter amendment might then be required.[7]

A proposed amendment, however, can be blocked by any permanent member of the Security Council failing to ratify it,[8] leaving matters quite inflexible when any serious difference destroys unanimity among the major powers. That is likely to be the case on any important contentious issue. The procedural difficulty meant that, despite numerous constitutional disputes in the United Nations, no amendments were formally proposed until December 1963. Two were then adopted by the Assembly—to enlarge the Security and the Economic and Social Councils.[9] The changes had been desired for many years to make the Councils more representative of the enlarged membership of the Organization; but they had never been voted on before because of Soviet opposition to any structural change while Peking did not occupy China's seat in the Organization. After the Moscow-Peking split in the early sixties, the Communist Chinese—evi-

6. For action at San Francisco, see Ruth B. Russell, *A History of the United Nations Charter: The Role of the United States 1940–1945* (Brookings Institution, 1958), pp. 877–78, 884–90.

7. See report of the Committee on Legal Problems, *UNCIO Documents*, Vol. 13, pp. 709–10; also, Oscar Schachter, "The Relation of Law, Politics and Action in the United Nations," *Recueil des Cours de l'Academie de Droit International*, Vol. 2 (1963), pp. 185–90, 196–98.

8. Art. 108.

9. A/Res. 1991A and 1991B (XVIII), Dec. 17, 1963. The Security Council was to be increased to 15 members, 4 to be elected members. ECOSOC was to be enlarged to 27. The resolutions also provided that members be elected on the basis of the following geographic distributions: The Security Council nonpermanent members would include 5 from Africa and Asia, one from Eastern Europe, 2 from Latin America, 2 from Western Europe and other areas; ECOSOC membership would include the United States, 12 African and Asian states, 5 from Latin America, 3 from East Europe (including the Soviet Union), and 6 from Western Europe and other areas.

dently courting the neutrals—declared they were not against the proposed changes. The Soviet Union then reversed itself.[10]

To pacify somewhat the many delegations at San Francisco that were dissatisfied with various Charter provisions, the possibility of a general conference to review the entire Charter was also provided for.[11] No strong sentiment for convening such a conference has ever arisen, however. When the Members cannot agree on specific amendments to the Charter by the regular procedure, they are not likely to settle their differences by attempting a general revision of the document.

Had United Nations Members achieved effective consensus on either a strict or a liberal construction of the Charter, the Organization could have developed reasonably peacefully as either the relatively "static conference machinery" or the "dynamic instrument of governments," which Secretary-General Hammarskjold described as its future alternatives in his final annual report.[12] The informal kind of Charter interpretation that could then have become customary was shown early in 1946, when the Soviet representative announced he was abstaining from voting on, but not vetoing, a Security Council resolution.[13] This gave a desired flexibility to the rigidity of the literal meaning in the requirement of Article 27(3), that Council decisions must receive "the concurring votes" of all permanent members. It therefore became accepted practice[14] and avoided the need to reopen the Charter provision to amendment.

10. Once Moscow altered its opposition, it went the whole way and became the first permanent Security Council member to ratify the proposed amendments. Malaysia became the necessary 71st nonpermanent member to ratify before the end of May 1965. Although the United States Senate consented to ratification in June, its instrument of ratification was not deposited until Aug. 31, 1965, which brought the amendments into effect. See *UN Monthly Chronicle*, Vol. 2 (August-September 1965), pp. 24–25.

11. Art. 109.

12. *Introduction to the Annual Report of the Secretary-General on the Work of the Organization, 16 June 1960–15 June 1961*, U.N. Doc. A/4800/Add. 1, p. 1.

13. U.N., *Repertoire of the Practice of the Security Council, 1946–1951* (1954), p. 173.

14. It was never challenged until April 1966, when Portugal called for a ruling on the legality of Security Council Resolution 221 (1966) authorizing Great Britain to use force to prevent the shipment of oil to Rhodesia through Mozambique. The resolution had passed on April 9 unanimously, but with France and the Soviet Union abstaining. No "ruling" as such has been made. But an article by the U.N. Legal Counsel (although written in his personal capacity) may be taken to answer the challenge. See Constantin A. Stavropoulos, "The Practice of Voluntary Abstentions by Permanent Members of the Security Council under Article 27, Paragraph 3, of the Charter of the United Nations," *American Journal of International Law*, Vol. 61 (July 1967), pp. 737–52. He concludes that the interpretation, originated and applied consistently by the permanent members with respect to voluntary abstentions, "has been acquiesced in by other Members of the Organization and can now be considered a firm part of the constitutional law of the United Nations."

A later pragmatic adaptation, also generally accepted, was to split the two-year terms of elected Security Council members between two contestants when neither could command the requisite majority. This device resolved certain election difficulties and also permitted more states to participate as Council members. This partly compensated for the inability to enlarge that organ until after the membership had increased greatly.[15]

In the turbulent years after the Charter became effective, however, no across-the-board consensus was possible. The disputed document has therefore had to serve as the constitutional basis of an institution dedicated to the promotion of international cooperation but operating in a world of conflict. Some United Nations Members (led by the Soviet Union) saw their national interest in maintaining a strict construction of the Charter. Others, under United States leadership, strove for a liberal construction that would permit easier adaptability to changing circumstances. As a result, the United Nations has had its difficulties in interpreting and fleshing out in practice the skeleton of authority and principle contained in the Charter and in the machinery and procedures for the attainment of its objectives.

The record, in spite of the absence of broad consensus, has on balance been dynamic (in Hammarskjold's sense), especially in the great expansion of United Nations activities as compared with the League of Nations. Such expansion has marked nearly all its fields of interest; but, as will be noted, it has varied in pattern among the several areas. The different development patterns have reflected partly the continuation of fundamental conflicts of interest that made it difficult to negotiate the Charter in the first place; partly the inconsistency of member governments within the United Nations; and partly the increasingly rapid rate of change in the world that has brought about so many uncontrollable economic, social, political, demographic, and military results. These last have affected all governments individually and the United Nations as their Organization.

Patterns of Constitutional Change

The Charter embodied a flexible nucleus of authority and procedures that contemplated growth and development toward the completion of its proposed institutional system. It was therefore to prove adaptable to many of

15. Indonesia withdrew from the United Nations in January 1965, ostensibly because Malaysia took the Security Council seat it had agreed in 1964 to share with Czechoslovakia. (See U.N. Docs. A/5857 and A/5861, Jan. 21 and 25, 1965.) The objection was against Malaysia being in the Council, not against the principle of the split term.

the unforeseeable changes that have altered world political relationships during the past two decades. The changing nature of various international problems has inevitably been reflected in alterations of the scope and character of related activities carried on through the United Nations. The relative ease with which such changes have been achieved—especially in terms of a broader competence for the Organization in relation to national governments and of an increased operating role for the Secretariat as an executive agency of the collective United Nations—has varied greatly, however, from area to area. The main part of this study will deal with many of those changes in somewhat more detail; but it may be useful here to note briefly some of the fundamental shifts that they have brought about, in terms of the original concepts for which the structure of machinery and authority of the United Nations was originally devised. The degree of success of the Organization in adapting to revolutionary changes in an atmosphere of continuing political conflict is testimony to the flexibility of the Charter, as well as a reflection of the general desire of Member governments to maintain the United Nations as a going concern, though frequently for strongly opposed reasons.

MAINTENANCE OF PEACE AND SECURITY

In 1967, there was for all practical purposes a stalemate on the constitutional issue of the respective competence of the Security Council and the General Assembly in maintaining international peace. The basic point of conflict was over the extent of the Council's "primary responsibility for the maintenance of international peace and security."[16] Before and at San Francisco, the Soviet Union strove for an organization that would safeguard collective great-power control of international security through action by the Council alone. It only reluctantly accepted a grant of authority for the Assembly to discuss and recommend on matters of peace and security, which was included in Articles 10–12 and 14.[17] Because of the subsequent lack of great-power unanimity, the Security Council was unable to develop in practice the sort of collective enforcement system anticipated in the Charter provisions; but the Assembly's more limited authority proved flexible enough, when a sufficiently wide degree of support could be mustered behind its use, to fill some of the vacuum that would otherwise have been left by failure of the Security Council to operate.

16. Art. 24.

17. For background of the pertinent Charter provisions, see Russell, *op. cit.*, especially Chap. 29.

Minor innovations in procedure and major innovations in machinery were used, over the years, to expand the activities of the General Assembly in the peace and security field. Where the Council continued to act, moreover, it tended to concentrate on a peaceful-settlement (rather than an enforcement) approach to halting violence and promoting the restoration of peace in cases of serious conflict. In the first years, both major organs made recommendations for settlement on the merits of some cases. This tendency diminished, however, as the development of the cold war handicapped the Security Council and the increasing membership affected the Assembly, making it more difficult to mobilize the necessary majorities behind specific settlement terms. The result was to limit United Nations action in many disputes to mediatory efforts to get the parties to agree to halt violence and to settle their conflict by negotiation.

The most dramatic innovation in this process was the use of international military forces composed of national troop contingents under Secretariat command. They were not intended to enforce decisions by the international Organization, but primarily to assist the parties in a conflict to sustain the suspension of violence that they had agreed to. Arguments over the authority of the Assembly and the Secretary-General in connection with such operations—especially their financing—resulted in the 1965 constitutional crisis, which will be considered later in detail. Here it need only be noted that those details are basically manifestations of an underlying political conflict over the entire role of the United Nations in the maintenance of world peace and security.

ADVANCEMENT OF DEPENDENT PEOPLES

From a constitutional viewpoint, perhaps the most radical change during the first two decades of the United Nations has occurred in connection with the expansion of the Organization's relationship to dependent territories and peoples. The nature of the substantive political conflict that underlay constitutional developments in this area, moreover, brought about another and wholly unexpected revolution in the nature of the United Nations concern with human rights.

The viewpoints in conflict since 1945 were already in evidence before then. During the war, as noted in Chapter 1, United States leaders were convinced that the emerging nationalist demands of colonial peoples would be a major political factor in the postwar world. President Roosevelt's somewhat vague vision of an international trusteeship system was a projection of United States policy in the Philippines, the theme of which had been training for self-government and the establishment of target dates for independence.[18] But American officials failed to persuade their chief allies, the main European imperial powers, to "go and do likewise" in the interest of peaceful postwar decolonization.

By the time of the United Nations Conference, Washington's position had become somewhat ambivalent as a result of military insistence that the Japanese mandated islands be retained by the United States for security reasons.[19] At San Francisco, the other major powers divided on this issue along lines that were later to become familiar: Great Britain and France opposed any significant extension in the role of the United Nations beyond that of the League in the mandate system; while the Soviet Union and China pressed for greater international activity. Underlying these positions on constitutional issues of function and authority lay conflicting political judgments on the strength of the rising nationalist movements. The colonial powers as a group, time was to show, underestimated the effects of the war and wartime promises. Even those accepting the inevitability, if not the desirability, of political evolution in their dependencies generally misread the clock in thinking they could count on a lengthy period of evolutionary development toward autonomy or independence. But Under Secretary of State Sumner Welles was only relatively premature when he declared, in 1942, that: "The age of imperialism is ended."[20] The rhetoric of a conservative American diplomat was thus in accord with the doctrine of the communists—and the judgment of both was to be vindicated by the sweep of decolonization that, shortly after the war, began to transform the world and the United Nations.

In 1945, however, the provisions of the Charter had to be voluntarily accepted. The colonial powers were thus able, by threatening to reject any

18. Roosevelt, for example, told the Soviet Foreign Minister in 1942, that: "The white nations . . . could not hope to hold these [southeast Asian] areas as colonies in the long run"; and that, while each colony might require "a different time lapse before achieving readiness for self-government, . . . a palpable surge toward independence was there just the same." Until they were ready, perhaps in 20 years, "some form of international trusteeship" might be the best way to administer them. Robert E. Sherwood, *Roosevelt and Hopkins* (Harper, 1948), p. 573.

19. See Russell, *op. cit.,* Chap. 23.

20. U.S. Department of State, *Bulletin,* Vol. 6 (1942), p. 488. The Welles statement caused unfavorable repercussions among the colonial-power allies of the United States, leading to a subsequent reaffirmation of policy by Secretary of State Hull that included the traditional official qualifications. The United States favored independence, he said, for all peoples wanting it who were "prepared and willing to accept the responsibilities of liberty." *Ibid.,* Vol. 7 (1942), p. 642.

trusteeship provisions, to oppose the more extreme proposals then made to put all colonies in trust, if not to declare their imminent independence.[21] To forestall more drastic provisions, the metropolitan governments accepted a statement of principles applicable to all dependencies, which became the Declaration Regarding Non-Self-Governing Territories.[22] They praised its uniqueness as a joint statement of colonial policy. But they insisted on its form as a "declaration" supposedly not binding them beyond responsibility to promote the well-being of dependent peoples and voluntarily to transmit technical data, "for information purposes" only, on colonies of their own choosing.[23] In due course, eight Western Members of the United Nations listed seventy-four territories as in this class, indicating their self-confidence that the Charter contained adequate safeguards from their point of view against undue international "intervention."[24] The Soviet Union, on the other hand, although having taken over the Kurile Islands from Japan, neither listed them under Article 73 nor proposed to put them under a trust agreement, as the United States did with the former Japanese mandated Pacific islands.

The trusteeship provisions of the Charter[25] authorized a United Nations successor to the mandates system of the League, which was to give the Organization, through a Trusteeship Council, stronger powers of supervision than its predecessor had. The system, however, depended on states with non-self-governing territories voluntarily placing them in trust. It was generally understood at San Francisco that former mandates and any "detached" enemy territories would be included in the trusteeship system. The system was so permissive, however, that even the existence of the Trusteeship Council depended on the administering states taking this

21. Not all colonial powers were equally resistant. Australia and New Zealand, for example, favored Assembly authority to "specify territories in respect of which it shall be the duty of the states responsible for their administration to furnish annual reports to the United Nations upon the economic, social, and political development of the territories concerned." See *Report by the Australian Delegates on the UN Conference*, Australian Cmd Paper, No. 24 (1945) Group E–F. 4311, pp. 10, 22–24, 97.

22. Chap. XI of the Charter.

23. Art. 73e. The unusual "declaration" in the midst of a treaty was aimed to placate France, in particular, which did not want any such general statement of colonial accountability. It entered a formal reservation of its right to resort to Art. 2(7) in connection with this part of the Charter.

24. The self-defined "administering powers" were Australia, Belgium, Denmark, France, the Netherlands, New Zealand, the United Kingdom, and the United States. See U.N. Office of Public Information, *Everyman's United Nations* (1964 ed.), pp. 344–46, for listing of the seventy-four territories.

25. Chaps. XII–XIII.

action voluntarily, and in effect on their own terms, since the membership of the Council was to be evenly divided between "administering" and "nonadministering" powers.[26] This arrangement was intended to compensate the small number of members in the former group by practically guaranteeing a voting deadlock on contentious issues that would mean no action could be taken against the wishes of the trustee powers.

The potentials of the Charter for the development of a wide-ranging trusteeship system along Rooseveltian lines could only be realized, therefore, through the initiative of the imperial powers. This was not forthcoming. Only eleven territories were placed in trust: ten former mandates (all but South West Africa) and the former Italian colony of Somaliland. By 1965, the Trusteeship Council had about "withered away," as eight of its territories had become independent—all but the trust territories of New Guinea and Nauru (under Australia) and the Pacific Islands Trust (under the United States). To constitute the Trusteeship Council according to the terms of Article 86 in this strange situation, New Zealand and Great Britain must be counted as "administering authorities" along with Australia, which alone administers Nauru on behalf of the three. With the United States as a fourth administering power, and the remaining three permanent Security Council members automatically becoming nonadministering members, one state then remains to be elected to give the Trusteeship Council a balanced total of eight.[27]

The Charter also contained a time bomb, almost unrecognized in 1945, in the "principle of equal rights and self-determination of peoples" as the basis of "friendly relations among nations."[28] No one was prepared to oppose the principle, first suggested by the Soviet Union, but neither was there agreement on its meaning. The rights of revolution and secession were both debated inconclusively, and the result was one of the fuzziest terms in the Charter.[29] By 1960, however, it had been "defined" in practice, and embodied in an Assembly resolution (generally known as

26. Art. 86. For discussion of the negotiation of the pertinent Charter provisions, see Russell, *op. cit.*, Chap. 21.

27. If Australia and the United States alone were counted as administering members, then the requirement that all nonadministering permanent Security Council members must be included would give an automatic membership of two administering to four nonadministering states, making an evenly divided Council impossible.

28. Art. 1 (2).

29. See *UNCIO Documents*, Vol. 6, p. 455. The Soviet delegate left no doubt where Moscow stood on its meaning. "We must first of all see to it," he said at a press conference, "that dependent countries are enabled as soon as possible to take the path of national independence." *New York Times*, May 8, 1945, p. 15.

the "Declaration on Colonial Independence") as the right of colonial peoples to be freed from imperial rule.[30] The intervening years had been marked by failure to develop the potential of the trusteeship system through voluntary placement of more dependencies within its framework. The Assembly, under the vague terms of Article 73—especially of the obligation to transmit technical information on conditions in dependent territories—had developed in its stead numerous procedures, objectives, standards, and machinery for implementing United Nations concern with the progress of dependent peoples under Chapter XI.

Its organization for this purpose began with an "Ad Hoc Committee on Information Transmitted under Article 73e" (set up in 1946 with 16 members evenly divided between administering and nonadministering states), with practically no power but publicity.[31] By 1961, the Assembly was exercising its competence under a much stronger "Special Committee on the Situation with Regard to the Implementation of the Declaration on the Granting of Independence to Colonial Countries and Peoples," with 24 members, mostly noncolonial powers. The committee absorbed the functions of the original Committee on Information and several other intervening groups. The Assembly had established its right to determine which territories came under Article 73, the resistance of various colonial powers notwithstanding.[32] The Committee of 24 received petitions, heard individuals, made field investigations in connection with dependent areas (going to neighboring territories to hear petitioners when barred from admission to the territories under consideration), and in general was functioning in relation to non-self-governing peoples and to the Assembly in somewhat the way originally envisaged for the Trusteeship Council.

SELF-DETERMINATION AND HUMAN RIGHTS

In the course of this transformation of the Organization's concern with the colonial problem, the issue of national self-determination became mixed with that of individual human rights—in particular with the question of racial discrimination, a prevalent characteristic of colonialism whatever the legal regime. Human rights as a field of United Nations

---

30. A/Res. 1514 (XV), Dec. 14, 1960. Events leading to this resolution are considered in Chap. 7, pp. 250–56 below.
31. A/Res. 66 (I), Dec. 14, 1946.
32. See Schachter, *op. cit.*, p. 187.

activity was initially treated from a legal approach. With relative rapidity the Universal Declaration of Human Rights was agreed by 1948.[33] After that, the intended development of covenants specifying those rights in detail and making them binding, remained in the drafting stage until 1966. However, a political approach to the issue also appeared in 1946, when India complained against discriminatory treatment of Indians by South Africa as a violation of human rights. In 1952, the general problem of apartheid was added to the particular case, with the charge that race conflict also threatened the peace. This possibility had been recognized at San Francisco in 1945, largely as a result of the revelations of Nazi concentration camps then occurring.[34] The idea that domestic policies might threaten international peace was not so generally endorsed a few years later.

By 1960, the declaration on colonial independence pronounced colonialism a "denial of human rights." It incorporated the right of self-determination as defined in the draft human rights covenants, and admonished all states to observe the Human Rights Declaration and the Charter. Since then, denials of both self-determination and racial equality have been ever more strongly condemned as threats to the peace. The Security Council and Assembly have recommended certain diplomatic and economic sanctions and arms embargoes against South Africa and Portugal. Pressures have continued to mount for even stronger mandatory sanctions, which would seek to enforce the end of apartheid in the first, and the end of Portuguese rule in Africa in the second.

Before more general consensus on such enforcement action developed in the United Nations, however, the white minority government of Southern Rhodesia declared the country independent of Great Britain in November 1965, under a constitution discriminating against the African majority. London declared the action rebellious and instituted economic and financial sanctions against the illegal government. This led, by April 1966, to Security Council authorization for Great Britain to use force, if necessary, to prevent the importation of oil to Beira (Portuguese Mozambique) destined for Rhodesia. Military enforcement action under United Nations authority was thus initiated in a dispute that combined issues of self-determination and racial discrimination and whose "con-

33. A/Res. 217 (III), Dec. 10, 1948.
34. For further discussion, see Chap. 3.

tinuance in time," the Security Council unanimously found, "constitutes a threat to international peace and security."[35]

So long as the two group rights of self-determination and racial equality remain far from universal realization, pressures for their achievement will continue to take priority over any significant expansion of United Nations activity in other human rights areas. Indeed, even the end of both colonialism and racism might not see much greater concern with individual rights; for those touch on sensitive domestic policies of *all* countries, not just of a small minority of the Assembly—and few governments are yet prepared to be as liberal about their own policies as about those of others.

PROMOTION OF ECONOMIC AND SOCIAL WELFARE

In the great-power negotiating period before San Francisco, Moscow was largely uninterested in this subject. The influence of Washington and London was therefore predominant in determining the economic and social provisions of the Charter. The Soviet Union conceived the international security problems of a world organization in political-military terms only; but Great Britain and the United States felt strongly that in the long run world peace depended as much on removing the underlying nonpolitical causes of international conflict as on settling specific disputes and on meeting threats to or breaches of the peace. They were also agreed that such economic and social activities should be extended well beyond their growth in the League period.

Anglo-American postwar planning was developed around the objective of an expanding world economy. In brief, cooperative international efforts were to focus on stabilization of that economy against the effects of national boom-and-depression cycles such as marked the interwar years. The chief means employed would be the coordination of national "full employment" policies. In terms of postwar organization, Great Britain and the United States envisaged a series of global technical agencies with a central international economic organ that would both provide a coordinating mechanism and concentrate on the overall problem of maintaining full employment.[36]

35. S/Res. 221 (April 9, 1966). For further consideration of the Rhodesian case, see Chap. 5 below.

36. The general concept was outlined in a 1943 "Memorandum concerning the Washington Meeting between British and American Economic Experts," text in U.S. Department of State, *Postwar Foreign Policy Preparation, 1939–1945* (February 1950), pp. 562–64. See also Russell, *op. cit.*, pp. 72–74.

These objectives met with enthusiastic approval at San Francisco. The Charter accordingly authorized the United Nations, in general terms, to promote cooperation on "international problems of an economic, social, cultural, and humanitarian character." It also established the Economic and Social Council (ECOSOC) to carry out those responsibilities and to bring the specialized agencies "into relationship" with the Organization.[37] Overwhelming needs of the war-devastated areas had led, even before 1945, to the establishment of the United Nations Relief and Rehabilitation Administration (UNRRA) and to arrangements for several specialized agencies. The new ECOSOC was prompted by those same needs to form the regional Economic Commission for Europe (ECE) and a similar one for Asia and the Far East (ECAFE) in 1947. It also set up the functional economic, social, and human rights commissions provided for in Article 68. An Economic and Employment Commission was to be the main coordinating organ under ECOSOC. A wide-ranging International Trade Organization (ITO) would perform a similar function in aiming to liberalize restrictive national policies in related fields of trade, commodities, cartels, employment, investment, and development.

Agreements to establish the ITO and to undertake liberal economic policies were signed at a major United Nations Conference on Trade and Employment, held in Havana in 1948. The trade organization never came into being, however, nor did governments generally adopt the liberal policies hoped for.[38] What happened instead was epitomized in the title of the second trade meeting of the United Nations, held in Geneva in 1964: the Conference on Trade and Development (UNCTAD). Emphasis had switched from the "maintenance of full employment"—the chief concern of the industrialized countries—and had become centered on development of the underdeveloped areas as the focus for United Nations economic and social policies. This shift reflected the changing nature over time of an increased membership, an ever-increasing proportion of which consisted of economically weak states.

Development was always, of course, the chief economic concern of the

37. Art. 1(3); Arts. 55–72.
38. Although ITO never materialized, many of its commercial policy and commodity provisions have been applied through the General Agreement on Tariffs and Trade (GATT) and the Interim Coordinating Committee for International Commodity Arrangements (ICCICA), established in 1947 in connection with anticipated responsibilities to be included in the Havana Charter, and for which no other agency existed. See Robert E. Asher and others, *The United Nations and Promotion of the General Welfare* (Brookings Institution, 1957), pp. 240–65.

so-called less developed countries, which pressed from the start for attention to Charter provisions for promoting "economic and social progress
and development."[39] That objective called less for accord on harmonizing
separate national policies, than for direct assistance in meeting the lack of
technical skills and capital that accounted for much of the national under-
development. The Assembly, in 1946, ventured into this field by calling
on ECOSOC to study ways of extending expert advice about the requirements of economic development. It also unwittingly began the operational programs that have become a United Nations hallmark in this
area. It authorized the Secretary-General to continue for a short period
certain advisory functions in the social welfare field that had been instituted as part of the temporary United Nations Relief and Rehabilitation
Administration.[40]

In 1947–48, ECOSOC authorized the Secretariat to provide experts
and other resources to help members, and formalized a technical assistance
program with a small budget. Then in 1949, President Truman's "Point
IV" program for the United States inspired the Expanded Program of
Technical Assistance (EPTA), as a joint endeavor of the United Nations
and the specialized agencies.[41] The scope of technical assistance activity
was significantly extended a decade later with the establishment of a
second major operational program, the U.N. Special Fund, to sponsor
preinvestment projects in less developed countries. In 1965, the two were
combined in the interests of efficiency into a United Nations Development Program.[42]

The Special Fund itself was one result of continuous pressure by the
less developed countries from the early days of the United Nations for the
establishment of a large-scale capital development fund within the Organization itself. The International Bank for Reconstruction and Development (IBRD), a specialized agency, had been negotiated before the
end of World War II for the purpose of financing both postwar reconstruction and longer-term development needs. It was required to lend on
economically sound terms, and its policies were to be determined by a
voting system proportionate to the capital subscription of the members.
This gave the United States, as the major subscriber, a dominant role in

39. Art. 55.
40. A/Res. 57 (I) and 58 (I), Dec. 14, 1946. These supposedly short-term "Advisory Social Welfare Services" still continue.
41. E/Res. 180 (VIII), March 4, 1949.
42. A/Res. 1240 (XIII), Oct. 14, 1958; A/Res. 2029 (XX), Nov. 22, 1965.

deciding the Bank's policies. The developing countries, however, wanted larger investment funds to be made available on easier terms or as outright grants by wealthier governments. They wanted them provided through an agency controlled not by the major capital contributors, but by majority voting of the Members; hence, their pressures within the Assembly for establishing a subsidiary Special United Nations Fund for Economic Development (SUNFED). Although resisting SUNFED in principle, the more advanced states eventually agreed to setting up two affiliates of the IBRD in order to increase available capital resources on easier terms. The International Finance Corporation (IFC) was established in 1956, to facilitate loans for private investment; and the International Development Association (IDA) in 1960, to lend on "softer" terms than is possible for the IBRD.

Those two agencies, however, are controlled like the IBRD by a voting system related to the capital subscriptions of participating members. Both EPTA and the Special Fund, on the other hand, are financed on the basis of voluntary contributions pledged each year at a special conference of all interested states. But the voluntary nature of those national contributions also leaves the major donors in a position to determine (negatively) the nature of the two programs. None of these agencies or programs, therefore, met the demand of the developing countries for a SUNFED under Assembly control. As the Assembly majority of developing states increased in size, they succeeded by 1963 in obtaining a resolution instructing the Secretary-General to submit to the forthcoming UNCTAD meeting a report on means to transform the Special Fund into a full-fledged Capital Development Fund.[43] Although 1965 saw only the merging of EPTA and the Special Fund, ECOSOC authorized a special committee to draft a statute for the desired investment fund. In 1966 the Assembly "decided to bring into operation" the United Nations Capital Development Fund as a subsidiary organ on the basis of the committee's proposals.[44]

The capital-producing states continue to oppose its establishment, even though the statute provides for voluntary financing (except for the agency's administrative expenses). However, it also provides that the fund be directed by an intergovernmental Executive Board of 24, including both developed and less developed countries, which will report an-

43. A/Res. 1936 (XVIII), Dec. 11, 1963. UNCTAD in turn recommended the early establishment of a Capital Development Fund, with first consideration to be given to transforming the Special Fund so as to meet that objective.

44. A/Res. 2186 (XXI), Dec. 13, 1966 (includes text of articles of establishment).

nually to the Assembly through ECOSOC. The voting system in connection with its disbursements will thus not be weighted in terms of the relative capital contributions received from the advanced countries.

The increased influence of the development theme was also important in the extension of the regional economic commissions. The European and Far Eastern Commissions (ECE and ECAFE) were originally intended to be temporary agencies for coping with postwar emergencies; but they proved adaptable to newly felt needs once the worst of reconstruction was over. The suitability of the regional approach for many developmental problems led to the formation in 1948 of a third one for Latin America (ECLA).[45] The three were made permanent in 1951. The resulting decentralization of ECOSOC, unforeseen at San Francisco, was further increased when the Economic Commission for Africa (ECA) was set up in 1958, even before the great surge of new African states on the scene. Meanwhile, reflecting in an opposite manner the change of emphasis in ECOSOC's work, the Economic and Employment Commission was allowed to expire, leaving no general economic commission under the Council. Instead, new machinery has been established under the Assembly in the field of industrial development and for trade and development matters.[46] The explosion of new agencies has made the task of coordination (in theory, the function of ECOSOC) almost hopelessly complex.

EXPANDED SECRETARIAT ROLE

The technical activities of the numerous specialized agencies have combined with the economic and social programs of the central Organization in greatly extending the scope of field operations conducted by inter-

45. Latin American dissatisfaction with OAS economic machinery was also a factor in the establishment of ECLA. Another U.N. commission was contemplated in the late forties for the Middle East but never materialized due to the Arab-Israeli conflict.

46. In 1960, a Committee for Industrial Development was established under ECOSOC, which set up a Center for Industrial Development in 1961. As with the financial institutions, demands of the developing countries were not satisfied by the efforts of these agencies. Pressure continued for the replacement of the Center by a specialized agency for the field, and in 1965 the Assembly approved the establishment of "an autonomous organization" within the United Nations to be known as "the U.N. Organization for Industrial Development." (A/Res. 2089 (XX), Dec. 20, 1965.) IDO was set up in 1966.

UNCTAD was made a permanent organ of the Assembly and will meet periodically; while a 55-member Trade and Development Board was established as an interim authority between sessions of the full conference. A/Res. 1995 (XX), Dec. 30, 1964.

national secretariats. These now go far beyond mere administrative and servicing duties for international bodies composed of government representatives, which was the more typical League of Nations relationship. The performance of technical tasks by international experts has marked a quiet revolution, since 1945, in the degree to which governments that represent a wide spectrum of political shadings now accept action by international institutions with, and even within, national states. The United Nations Resident Representative, who may advise on country programing, and OPEX officials[47] who fill government posts while training replacements, are illustrations of how these activities have practically obliterated the traditional distinctions in the economic and social field between "domestic" and "international" jurisdictions.[48] The very success of the technical assistance programs—at first castigated by communist spokesmen as an economic sheepskin on the imperialist wolf—in time brought about a diminution of their polemics and even some limited contributions from communist governments.

In the less concrete political area, the role of the Secretary-General and Secretariat staff as executive agents of the Security Council and Assembly has also increased in importance over the years. This was seen most dramatically in the innovation, in 1956, of international military forces composed of national contingents of troops under United Nations command. The kind of peacekeeping service performed by them, however, has also been carried out by smaller groups of international military or civilian personnel and by individual Secretariat officials on numerous other occasions. To some extent, this increasing Secretariat role in the political field has reflected a change in the nature of the international activity concerned, as it has in the economic and social field. The requirements for manning field activities continuing over a period of time are likely to be met better by the services of technical experts from (or seconded to) the Secretariat, than they are by the assignment of diplomatic officials (remaining responsible primarily to their own governments) for temporary duty on international committees or commissions.

In the more traditional diplomatic activities of good offices and mediation—usually of shorter duration and less likely to involve extended field operations—there has also been a trend to accept the services of the Secretary-General in a way that never developed under the League of Nations.

47. Recruited by a program for providing "operational, executive, and administrative personnel."
48. See also Schachter, *op. cit.*, pp. 235–38, 242–45.

In this case, however, the expanded role of the international official has reflected less a change in the nature of the activity than an inability of governments, in contemporary circumstances, to function more effectively through the political organs of the United Nations. When conflict among the permanent members in the Security Council resulted in stalemating that organ, the first reaction by those Members wanting to use the international Organization was to turn to the Assembly as an alternative. When controversy within the enlarged Assembly became too acute for effective political decision-making, the tendency was to turn to the Secretary-General and Secretariat to fill the impending political vacuum. "Let Dag do it," became a handy device which could work for both Security Council and Assembly, when there was a generally agreed policy and a sufficient degree of willingness to use the Organization, and inadequate agreement only on the procedures to be applied. In time, the habit of accepting such Secretariat diplomatic intervention made it relatively easy for Members to request assistance from the Secretary-General in other cases, sometimes even without going through the political organs of the United Nations. When the policies to be executed became contentious, however, and the Secretary-General found it impossible to maintain an accepted "third-party" posture between the contending Members, the limitations on the Secretariat in an executive role became predominant over the technical possibilities of expanding that role.[49]

LAW AND CHARTER INTERPRETATION

As a result of the serious political conflicts that have marked the period since the United Nations was established, adaptation by the Organization to change in the international scene, as noted earlier, has tended to be made more through informal Charter interpretation and usage than through formal interpretation or amendment of the basic treaty. The degree of conflict itself reflects the transitional nature of the period. Traditional international law is no longer authoritative, while new law awaits the development of a greater degree of international community, which is only painfully being developed by contemporary political experience.

The International Court of Justice, although one of the principal organs of the United Nations,[50] has consequently been less used than was the Permanent Court under the League of Nations. The International

49. For further discussion, see Chap. 6.
50. Art. 7(1).

Law Commission, established by the Assembly to help carry out the latter's responsibility for "the progressive development of international law and its codification,"[51] has been limited by its primary preoccupation with the preparation of draft treaties in a period when the lack of general consensus makes that approach relatively unrewarding. In the circumstances, therefore, there has been less development of law under the United Nations through the work of its chief legal organs than through the development of customary law by the practices of its political organs.[52] The degree to which such development has been possible has varied, of course, from field to field. It is perhaps least in security matters. The cold war has prevented consensus on the development of the collective enforcement system of the Charter, and events leading to the constitutional crisis over peacekeeping halted the development of usages that had seemed to presage the emergence of some customary rules in this field.[53]

Despite this experience, whenever there has been effective consensus of the Members, the doctrine of implied powers has provided adequate rationale for dynamic institutional adaptation within the flexible terms of the Charter. The controlling factor in the future will continue to be the effectiveness of that collective consensus. It must encompass both the positive consent of the required voting majority, including those states with means to implement a particular decision, and the "negative consent" of abstinence on the part of those in the minority with power to prevent implementing action. The peacekeeping crisis demonstrated that such power, either to prevent or to implement, may be psychological and political, as well as financial or military.

51. Art. 13(1a).

52. See Rosalyn Higgins, *The Development of International Law through the Political Organs of the United Nations* (Oxford University, 1963), Introduction. For further discussion of legal issues, see Chap. 8 below.

53. See below, Chaps. 5, 6, and 9. Also, Ruth B. Russell, "Development by the United Nations of Rules Relating to Peacekeeping," American Society of International Law, *Proceedings*, Vol. 58 (1964), pp. 53–60.

PART TWO

THE UNITED STATES
AND THE MAINTENANCE OF PEACE
THROUGH THE UNITED NATIONS

CHAPTER THREE

THE UNITED NATIONS
SECURITY SYSTEM

The United Nations was born in a world exhausted by years of devastating warfare and with an overwhelming desire for assured peace, assured security, and assured stability. Americans were not the only people looking for a panacea at that time. Because the United States had so recently doffed the cap of isolationism for a position of world leadership, however, people were perhaps too ready to assume that the United Nations would keep the hard-won peace without much effort on the nation's part beyond participation in the Organization.

Uninformed enthusiasm marked the attitude of the general public, which was glad to have the war over and to leave to the new international agency the job of keeping the peace. In a sense, those Americans reversed the process that had occurred after World War I. They subconsciously thought the United States, by joining the United Nations, could isolate itself psychologically from the problem of maintaining the peace as a national burden. When the next few years did not in any satisfactory sense bring peace and security, this large group reasoned along the following lines: the United Nations having been established to maintain the peace, and the peace not being maintained, therefore the Organization was useless for that purpose and the United States could expect little from it.

It was more serious that many better informed persons, despite a general awareness of the complexity of the problem of maintaining peace when the major military powers are antagonists, should also have subscribed to a kind of myth-making about the United Nations. This grew out of natural disappointment, even dismay, at the rapid development of the cold war and the re-creation of international tensions after the victory of 1945.

What occurred was the reverse of the danger Senator Fulbright later warned against: instead of basing policy on "old myths rather than new realities,"[1] there developed a persistent desire to explain the imperfections of the United Nations Charter in the simplified terms of new myths.

Myth and Reality in the Charter

The realities inherent in that most complex of international political objectives, the maintenance of peace among nations, were more difficult to face. Almost as soon as problems outside the Organization began to be reflected within it—especially given the way the Soviet-Western conflict hampered the functioning of the Security Council—two charges of lack of foresight on the part of the founding fathers gained wide currency as explaining the inability of the United Nations to overcome this handicap.

The first related to the veto. Government officials and academic experts were sometimes among those who discovered that the authors of the Charter had "assumed" that the great-power permanent members of the Security Council would cooperate, as required by its voting procedures. Else, it was explained, the unanimity requirement would not have been written into the Charter. The second charge was that the document was "pre-atomic"—and that, had atomic warfare been foreseen, the Charter would have been differently and more effectively written.[2] Those who make this charge have not come up with specific proposals for another voluntary international institution that would better fit the nuclear age. Some of them have, however, proceeded from this reasoning to advocate proposals for some form of world federation, on the ground that only a governmental, rather than an intergovernmental, authority can meet the requirements of the time.

These charges, which miss the real reasons for the final terms of the Charter security system and the structure of the institution based on it,[3] seem to have developed from some misconception of the functional limitations of international organization in general, and from failure to consider the particular historical background out of which the Charter grew.

1. J. William Fulbright, *Old Myths and New Realities* (Random House, 1964).
2. John Foster Dulles, for example, wrote in 1950 (not long before becoming Secretary of State): "The bomb fell on Hiroshima . . . about six weeks after the San Francisco Conference was over. If it had been dropped during instead of just after the . . . Conference, Article 11 might have been drawn differently and more positively." *War or Peace* (Macmillan, 1950), p. 208. Just what that might have involved in Charter terms, he did not further explain.
3. See discussion of world government plans, Chap. 1, pp. 13–14.

All assumptions of the founding fathers about a postwar security organization started from the existence of a state of war; and their plans had to be based on the fact that the terms (but not necessarily all the signatories) of any charter would have to assume the continued cooperation of a great majority of members if its system was to function. In this respect, the obvious appears to be too often overlooked: namely, that it would be impossible to negotiate an agreement for an international organization based on fundamental disagreement. The foundation of any institution has to be general accord on its purposes, principles, and procedures—even when there may be important mental reservations, doubts, or outright fraud behind the formal acceptance.

The Charter did not establish an independent, fully operational security system. It did provide the principles, procedures, and machinery whereby the member states could, to the extent they agreed, complete such a system.[4] It gave the means, in short, through which they could operate collectively—or, as one of its stated purposes declares, it provided "a center for harmonizing the actions of nations in the attainment" of their common ends.[5] Yet, in spite of the fact that the Charter makes clear that the Organization is essentially a means of collectively channeling the policies and power of its Members, the tendency to discuss it as though it were an independent entity with power of its own is so widespread as almost to constitute another myth.

The defining of precise security commitments by the member governments was postponed, especially regarding the military forces and facilities they would make available to the Security Council for enforcement purposes (under Article 43) and future measures of arms control and disarmament. The Charter was negotiated while the allies were exerting every effort to increase the strength of their armed forces and armaments in order to win the war. An attempt to agree on specific military commitments and disarmament measures for an uncertain future arrangement would have been distracting at best. Moreover, the principle of the

4. The British delegate at San Francisco, Lord Halifax, noted the advantage of not "trying to govern the actions of the members and the organs of the United Nations by precise and intricate codes of procedure; [instead], we have preferred to lay down purposes and principles under which they are to act. And, by that means, we hope to insure that they act in conformity with the express desires of the nations assembled here, while at the same time we give them freedom to accommodate their actions to circumstances which today no man can foresee." *UNCIO Documents*, Vol. 6 (1945), p. 26.

5. Art. 1(4).

"French thesis"[6] is implicit in the Charter: arms reductions are clearly envisioned as dependent on the concurrent development of a system of international security enforcement and controls, so that governments would not be expected to decrease their national protection before an international system was able to safeguard their vital interests.

The Charter therefore committed its signers simply to the principle of armaments regulation in Article 26, and to the consideration of disarmament plans later to be formulated by the Security Council and submitted for their approval. No other sort of commitment could have been negotiated successfully during the course of the war, even if the nature of atomic weapons had been known. The machinery provided in the Charter was, in any event, flexible enough to adapt to the needs of the nuclear age.

The concerns of the great powers that led to an enforcement system with veto privileges for the permanent Security Council members were based on fear that they might *not* always cooperate, rather than on any easy assumption that they generally would—whatever optimistic hopes may have been entertained at the time. The atmosphere of enthusiasm that enveloped the successful end of the San Francisco Conference is sometimes cited in support of the "assumption" myth. But this overlooks the fact that, long before the Conference began, the major Allies were having difficulties in agreeing both on joint military policies and on collective decisions affecting the postwar period. While their disagreements may not have been fully visible to the general public, since every effort was made to subdue them in the interests of the military alliance, they were well known to government officials responsible for planning the postwar Organization. The constant bickering over the future of Poland, for example, became so acute in the spring of 1945 that the country was not represented at San Francisco because London, Washington, and Moscow could not agree on an acceptable Polish government.

A corollary myth implies that the Western powers accepted the voting procedure of the Security Council because they did not realize how Soviet abuse of its privilege would hamstring the operation of that organ. On the contrary, they realized that the veto privilege placed a premium on inaction at precisely the most critical point of great-power disagreement. Long and fruitless efforts were therefore made by American experts in the period leading up to Dumbarton Oaks to devise some method of decision-

6. The principle of interdependence between the development of an international enforcement system and the reduction of national armaments was most strongly promoted by France during the League period, so that it became widely known as the "French thesis."

making on security issues that would allow the Council to override the negative vote of at least one permanent member. All such formulae, however, collapsed before the dominating political fact that the administration was not prepared to allow American armed forces to be ordered into some unknown future military action without United States consent. Even had Executive officials felt less strongly on the question, they would never have assumed that Congress could be persuaded to relinquish so much authority to an untried international organization. The United States therefore could not ask other powers to make a greater commitment than it would undertake; moreover, it rightly thought that the other major powers would feel similarly. Although there was disagreement with the Soviet Union on the voting system, the argument was one of degree not of substance—important though that degree was.

Developing the Charter Concept of Security

In terms of history rather than myths, officials in the United States concerned with planning for the post-hostilities period began with the realization that at the end of the war the military power of the world would be concentrated primarily in the hands of the leading victors. Ways would have to be sought both to prevent the enemy states from again becoming aggressive and to organize future relations among allies so as to facilitate their cooperation in keeping the peace—and in keeping it according to the principles and purposes repeatedly expounded from the Atlantic Charter to the United Nations Charter.

The emphasis on enforcement grew directly out of experience with the Covenant of the League, which had made no specific provision for enforcement procedures. The effects of unilateral disarmament by the democratic powers during the thirties, while the Axis states had armed heavily, were also an influential element. As a result, during the interwar period a concept of collective security had developed based on the belief that the most effective way to maintain peace would be for the international community to mobilize strong countermeasures against any state that resorted to war:

The essential and indispensable feature of such a system had to be certainty in the operation of sanctions; for without certainty, deterrence could not be assured . . . [This idea] arose primarily from the endeavor of France and her allies to convert the League [designed to ensure the observance of settlement procedures] into a system which would . . . guarantee . . . the maintenance of the territorial settlement in Europe. . . . The immediate preoccupations of France . . . were translated into general terms such as the defining of aggression

and the designation of the aggressor . . . [and the] organization of collective security in the sense of automatic application of sanctions against aggression.[7]

This became the "French thesis" when rounded out with the idea that any move toward disarmament, which would weaken the capacity of a state to defend its territorial integrity, must be balanced by the development of a system of international military sanctions.

In planning for the United Nations, as a result, the idea of a system of collective sanctions was combined with these more particular lessons derived from the League and World War II.

COLLECTIVE ENFORCEMENT

The first assumption in that planning was that all the great powers would have to participate in any postwar security arrangement if it was to be effective. That would not necessarily mean their formation of a general international organization, since they could continue the wartime alliance and, if they so agreed, largely impose whatever conditions of peace they wanted. The privileged position of the permanent members of the Security Council has, indeed, been seen in just that light; but that is part of the myth, not the history, of the Charter.

Such a solution was in effect advocated by some, including Walter Lippmann in 1944, who wanted the victorious powers to undertake enforcement of the peace treaties against the Axis powers outside of any permanent international organization. Lippmann then proposed to replace the League by a purely consultative institution, one not authorized or given means of action to enforce the peace generally.[8]

7. William M. Jordan, "Concepts and Realities in International Political Organization," *International Organization*, Vol. 11 (Autumn 1957), pp. 589–90.
   The semantics of "collective security" cause certain difficulties. Two studies, after considering the question at exhaustive (and exhausting) length, conclude that the term, along with "balance of power," really has no agreed meaning. (See Inis L. Claude, Jr., *Power and International Relations*, Random House, 1963, and Roland N. Stromberg, *Collective Security and American Foreign Policy*, Praeger, 1963.) The logical conclusion would seem to be to avoid using it; but continued usage prevents this sensible solution. Therefore, the present study seeks to avoid the theoretical controversy by explicitly referring to the specific concepts of Covenant and Charter.
   8. The chief argument for such a dual arrangement seemed to be a feeling that Congress would go along with both separate undertakings but would probably be less willing to commit the country to membership in an international organization endowed with military enforcement power. See Walter Lippmann, *U.S. War Aims* (Atlantic Monthly Press, 1944), pp. 157–69.

The United States government, however, considered that arrangements to control the enemy states would not alone suffice to guarantee peace and security. Recognizing that peace could be maintained only if the great powers cooperated, State Department officials thought that such cooperation was more likely to develop within a general security system than in connection with the more limited objective of surveillance over the former enemy.[9] They intended that system, moreover, to encompass "security" in the broadest sense, as will shortly be noted; not, as the Soviet Union proposed at Dumbarton Oaks, to be confined to peace-enforcement functions, with other kinds of international collaboration organized separately, if at all.

In practical terms, therefore, the enforcement issue remained primarily a question of what the major military powers were prepared to do. If they could not agree to use their power collectively to maintain the peace, there was not much hope that the United Nations agency would be more effective than the League. As far as the great powers themselves were concerned, on the other hand, if one of them turned aggressive, that state could only be resisted effectively by the combined weight of the others. That, unfortunately, would mean another all-out war, Charter or no Charter.

The Soviet Union made another proposal at Dumbarton Oaks that threatened to abort the entire project for postwar organization. It insisted on an absolute veto for the great powers in the voting system of the Security Council. This would have meant that no decision of the Council, even the most mild recommendation, could be taken against the wish of any permanent member. The United States and Great Britain felt, however, that while the lesser powers would accept a privileged position for the major ones in the decision to undertake military enforcement, they would not submit to complete great-power hegemony in the guise of an international institution.

The issue stalemated Dumbarton Oaks and was not settled until Yalta, by a compromise that can only be understood in relation to the problem of settlement as well as that of enforcement.

9. See a memorandum for Secretary Hull in Ruth B. Russell, A *History of the United Nations Charter: The Role of the United States, 1940–1945* (Brookings Institution, 1958) pp. 395–96.

ENFORCEMENT AND SETTLEMENT

Although history gave little cause for optimism that an organization to maintain the peace could succeed if based essentially on the commitments of member states to settle their disputes by peaceful means only, there was no other ground on which a voluntary international institution could be established.[10] The Charter system therefore began with a pledge by members to refrain from the threat or use of force except in accordance with United Nations purposes. It moved through the voluntary undertaking of pacific settlement by parties in conflict, to Assembly or Security Council consideration and recommendatory action of various kinds, depending on the degree to which peaceful relations appeared threatened by any dispute. Only as the last resort, when the threat to or violation of peace had been determined, could mandatory sanctions be ordered by the Council, and then only by the qualified-majority voting system that gave the permanent members their veto.[11]

Although the other members were bound to carry out such enforcement decisions of the Council, they were thus assured that they would not be asked to act against the will of any great power. Moreover, they could then be required to contribute only such armed forces, facilities, or other assistance as they had specifically undertaken to make available through separate agreements with the Security Council.[12] The extent of the latter's mandatory power was therefore significantly limited.

The United States originally thought that the Council's decisions on settlement terms should also be given mandatory effect. That is, if proposed terms of settlement of some dispute were not accepted and obeyed, the Council should then be empowered to enforce them. The state's act of disobedience would be considered to constitute a justifying breach of the peace. This idea ran into difficulties, however.

The Security Council could obtain the necessary means of military enforcement only from the governments possessing the world's armed forces and facilities. It was evident that the strongest powers would refuse to

10. Practically all the states of the world, including the United States, had been parties to one or more of the main prewar multilateral instruments binding the signatories to the pacific settlement of their international disputes: the League Covenant, the General Treaty for the Renunciation of War (the Kellogg Pact, 1928), and the Saavedra-Lamas Pact (1933). There were, besides, hundreds of bilateral treaties for pacific settlement between the parties.

11. Arts. 2(3), 33–42.

12. Arts. 25 and 43.

commit their national forces to collective use unless they had individual controlling votes in any such Council decision. That meant that any one of them could block action it opposed, against either itself or any other state it was interested in. Such inequity, it was therefore argued, was inevitable if those powers were to accept a collective enforcement system. On the other hand, the Soviet Union's additional demand for a similar right of veto on *all* substantive decisions of the Council, though a logical extension of the above reasoning, would have too flagrantly violated the Western tradition against self-judgment. It would also have discriminated too heavily against all the other states.

The compromise finally reached at Yalta was written into the Charter in the voting formula of Article 27(3), which permits the permanent members a complete veto only on decisions under Chapter VII. Their veto on pacific-settlement decisions is limited to those cases in which they are not themselves involved. Moreover, the force of all such settlement decisions is limited to recommendation. It was necessary thus to separate the Security Council's arbitral function from its enforcement authority, and to weaken the force of the former, before agreement could be reached on the provision that no party to a dispute, even a permanent Council member, could vote on settlement issues.[13]

This compromise was rationalized at the time on the ground that sanctions would be necessary only to stop aggression; but it also constituted recognition that the permanent members would not give up their right to veto even a settlement decision unless they could be assured that it would not be enforceable against themselves. At the same time, it removed the fear of "another Munich" on the part of the smaller states. Some of them feared the possibility of unjust settlement decisions by a Security Council dominated by the major powers, which could then have been enforced with all the authority of the Charter.

Paralleling the political-settlement provisions, the authority of the International Court to settle legal disputes was similarly confined to voluntary jurisdiction. This was decided against a strong majority sentiment at San Francisco in favor of compulsory jurisdiction. Both the United States and the Soviet Union, however, were adamantly opposed to such authority for the Court, and they won out after practically issuing an ultimatum.[14]

13. A fuller discussion of these issues, both before and at San Francisco, appears in Russell, *op. cit.*, Chaps. 19, 21, 24, and 26.

14. See *Ibid.*, pp. 884–90.

Settlement authority in the Charter is distinguished in another significant way from enforcement power. The Covenant seemed to emphasize unduly machinery and procedures for settlement. The Charter therefore deliberately left in general terms the means and modalities to be used in promoting pacific settlement and political adjustment by Security Council and Assembly. The two bodies were given the right to consider any potential or actual conflict, to take action of a recommendatory nature, and to establish subsidiary organs. This would give them all the authority they needed to move effectively when there was sufficient agreement on any particular action. Procedural details were left to Council or Assembly decision, although always within the framework of the Charter's purposes and principles.

It was possible to take this flexible approach precisely because there had been so much experience in the methods of conciliation, mediation, and arbitration. In the matter of international enforcement through the agency of a world organization, however, the very novelty of the undertaking required spelling out in more detail the machinery to be used and the kind of commitments to be asked of the national governments. This was especially true with regard to the idea of pledging contingents of national armed forces to future action through the international Organization; but in that instance, as already noted, the commitments were left open-ended and subject to subsequent voluntary agreement by all Members.

The Charter provisions for an international enforcement system were thus embryonic in nature. In the event of serious disagreement among the permanent Security Council members, the voting arrangement would likely make collective decisions impossible, both on the commitments to supply the Council with means of enforcement and on action to be taken against a threat to or breach of the peace. To avoid the potentially stifling effects of that situation, which might well result in the breakdown of the Organization at a critical point of great-power disagreement, Article 51 was written into the Charter as a possible way out of the dilemma. It recognized the inherent right of self-defense by each Member state (and by extension the right of "collective self-defense" by groups of governments) in the event the Security Council did not act to preserve or restore the peace. Such action was authorized, however, only until the Council was able to take over; and the governments concerned were obligated to act within the framework of purpose and principle binding all United Nations Members. Such an escape valve, it was hoped, would enable collective action to be undertaken by regional agencies or by such governments as favored it, so that Council inaction would not necessarily mean the destruction of the Organization.[15]

PEACE AND POLITICAL CHANGE

The Charter system does not view the maintenance of peace as confined to such settlement of acute disputes and the taking of enforcement action against aggressive states. It considers that an integral part of the problem of international security lies in easing less acute differences before they become potential threats to the peace. This is seen as a problem of peaceful change in the broadest sense, involving any contentious question—such as dissatisfaction with treaty restrictions, or with existing borders, or by a dependent people with its political status—that might be resolved by political adjustment and compromise on all sides. In addition, commitments to and machinery for harmonizing the efforts of governments to ameliorate the deeper-lying sources of conflict, in the domestic as well as the international realm, were also written into the Charter as necessary to the long-term maintenance of a just and peaceful world. Economic and social welfare, living standards and employment, human rights and political development were recognized as factors that play their parts, directly and indirectly, in the larger problems of peace and change.

The rationale justifying limitation of United Nations authority to recommendation in matters of political settlement and adjustment was that, with violence temporarily contained by agreement of the parties or by international intervention, the forces of persuasion, compromise, and cooperation could be brought into play to pacify the situation on a more permanent basis. That this has not occurred in many cases is obvious. Truces are not settlements, even when maintained for more than a dozen years (as in Korea), and time is not necessarily on the side of the peacemakers (as witness Kashmir, sixteen years after the 1949 cease-fire). Yet the political factors still hold that led, in 1945, to the decision not to make mandatory the settlement authority of the Organization. At the same

15. The Assembly, it was anticipated in 1945, would have pacific-settlement functions supplementary to those of the Security Council, but it was not then thought of as a possible substitute for the Council in enforcement matters. The extension of the Assembly's recommendatory authority in the enforcement field at the time of Korea, however, provided an alternative way around a stalemated Council. See Chap. 5 below for further discussion.

time, the terrifying weapons developments of recent years make national resort to the arbitrament of force as in the past too dangerous to countenance.

Revolutionary political and social change exacerbated by the speed of technological developments and population growth have prevented traditional international law from being adapted to change through legal evolution. The letter of the law has been too often used to justify making the status quo into a storm cellar, while the winds of change mount steadily to hurricane force.

Recognition of the need for peaceful adjustment to political and social change is evident throughout the Charter, beginning with its incorporation as an essential principle and prerequisite to attainment of the objectives of the Organization. The spelling out of those objectives and the development of agreement on their substantive content and on means to achieve them through international action was in large part left to the Organization to work out in practice. The Charter provides some of the machinery, as in the Economic and Social Council (ECOSOC), and some of the practical standards, as in the Declaration Regarding Non-Self-Governing Territories.[16]

There has not in fact been such a smooth development toward agreement because of violent opposition between the forces of change and those of resistance—in spite of the lip service universally paid to the maxim that, if evolutionary change is prevented, revolutionary change becomes inevitable. Unfortunately, evolutionary progress depends on wide acceptance of common economic, social, and political standards, which permit the development of procedures and machinery to meet, at least minimally, the demands for change. Only then can legal norms be effectively revised and institutionalized in an international order under law. "What is needed," as one United Nations report pointed out, "is readiness to understand the new forces in the world, courage to accept change, and wisdom to formulate and pursue viable means towards an enduring peaceful solution."[17] Such acceptance, however, depends not only on courage, but on greater ideological agreement than prevails in the contemporary world, and without which accord on "enduring peaceful solutions" too often proves impossible.

The demands for change usually begin reasonably enough, on a small

16. Art. 60; Chaps. X and XI.
17. S/4993 (Nov. 27, 1961), Report of the Sub-Committee on the Situation in Angola, para. 479.

scale and in terms of specific measures requested to meet specific needs formerly not felt, or not felt to be amenable to public action—in the present case, to United Nations action. When justifiable in terms of the objectives and principles spelled out in the Charter, when they have reflected deeply felt needs, and when they have not been met at least to an extent sufficient to satisfy reasonable hopes for progress in the desired direction, the pressures for change have continued to mount even in the face of strong resistance. Sometimes the continuing differences have intensified to the point of becoming violent disputes, when there is usually wide agreement that they threaten the peace. Sometimes, specific demands for change have developed through a lengthy period of more general dispute over the standards of definition to be given to the generalities of principle and purpose in the Charter. The clamor for "self-determination" and human rights, for example, illustrates how this kind of abstract difference can become a specific dispute in concrete political terms when there has not been rapid enough acceptance of new norms.[18]

The Charter sought to provide against these hazards through provisions for international cooperation in the many fields of economic, social, and human rights endeavor. It not only listed them among the purposes and principles of the Organization about to be established but, in Article 14, implicitly recognized their interrelationships.

PEACE AS AN INTEGRAL PROBLEM

The ever-increasing "togetherness" of the modern world results in ever-increasing pressures. Matters that long were considered purely domestic are now, in varying degree, accepted as legitimate subjects of international concern. The issue of degree, however, is frequently a contentious one. In this connection, the decisions at San Francisco on the terms of the domestic-jurisdiction reservation in the Charter[19] become of considerable interest.

Because the subjects of concern to the new Organization were so broadly stated in the Charter, and because there were considerable differences over the desirable degree of authority to be developed by the new Organization, most governments were wary of giving it too broad powers. Voluntary jurisdiction for the Court, limitation to recommendatory authority for Assembly and Security Council save in specific exceptions, and

18. See Chap. 7 below for further consideration.
19. Art. 2(7).

voluntary application of the trusteeship system, all reflected this attitude. In addition, the general reservation of domestic jurisdiction was written in unconventional terms that have ever since been the source of persistent disputes concerning the competence of the United Nations.

The United States led a drive to change the language of an equivalent provision in the Covenant of the League, which had referred to "matters that by international law [are] solely within the domestic jurisdiction" of states.[20] Consistent with their joint opposition to granting the Court compulsory jurisdiction in disputes over questions of international law, the United States and the Soviet Union succeeded in getting the phrase altered to "matters which are *essentially* within the domestic jurisdiction" of any state, and omitting any reference to the standard of international law. Article 2(7) also specifies that the Organization is not authorized to "intervene in" such matters, nor the members required to submit them to settlement. At the same time, it declares that the principle is not to "prejudice the application of enforcement measures under Chapter VII."

The intent of the United States delegation in 1945 was to widen the area of national reservation, as it feared possible congressional reaction to the broad international concern with economic, social, and cultural activities being written into the Charter. The objection to the standard of "international law" as the determinant of domestic jurisdiction was undoubtedly related to United States and Soviet wariness of Court authority in this field; but the argument formally used for deleting it was that: "The body of international law on this subject is indefinite and inadequate. To the extent that the matter is dealt with by international practice and by text writers, the conceptions are antiquated and not of a character which ought to be frozen into the new Organization."[21] Developments since 1945, however, have made those words true in a sense almost the opposite of the United States intention at that time. The traditional concepts of domestic jurisdiction have been overturned, but in the direction of narrowing rather than widening the extent of the national reservation.

Soviet-American resistance to use of the standard of international law was widely opposed in the San Francisco Conference; but the desire to limit the exemption from Security Council action to enforcement mea-

---

20. Art. 15(8) of the Covenant.

21. U.S. Department of State, *Charter of the United Nations: Report to the President on the Results of the San Francisco Conference, by the Chairman of the United States Delegation, the Secretary of State*, Publication 2349 (June 26, 1945), p. 45.

sures only, was almost universally supported at San Francisco. Norway alone, sturdily and consistently, opposed the moves of great and small powers alike to circumvent in their own interests the competence of the Organization by widening the area of domestic jurisdiction. The Norwegian delegate sardonically pointed out:

Some delegations now insist that the Security Council shall not in any circumstances, when investigating a dispute or situation, or when tendering its good office for the investigation and composition of a dispute or situation, touch upon any matter belonging essentially in the domestic jurisdiction of a party. This is . . . tantamount to saying that we are in favor of the Council maintaining or restoring the peace, but we will have it do so only on our own conditions.[22]

The general willingness to permit enforcement action by the Council, even if the threat to peace originated in a matter normally considered domestic, was in part a reflection of the horror felt at the revelations coming to light as Allied armies overran the infamous Nazi concentration camps. There was wide support for the idea that such inhuman persecution could constitute a threat to international peace and should not, therefore, be outside the scope of United Nations action under any domestic-jurisdiction claim. France, for example, proposed to add to the draft text of the domestic-jurisdiction reservation: "unless the clear violation of essential liberties and of human rights constitutes in itself a threat capable of compromising peace."[23] The idea was, however, considered already included in the final clause of Article 2(7), which was intended to cover any internal source of disorder that might threaten international peace.

The United Nations and Threats to International Peace

Thus, in scope, the concept of the peaceful world that is the United Nations objective was an inclusive one. In character, it was an integrated one, going far beyond the control of serious disputes and violence, and encompassing the underlying causes of events leading ultimately to such need for enforcement. So much was clear despite numerous ambiguities

22. U.N. Information Organizations and U.S. Library of Congress, *Documents of the United Nations Conference on International Organization*, Vol. 6, p. 431. (Hereinafter cited as *UNCIO Documents*.)

23. *UNCIO Documents*, Vol. 3, p. 386. For fuller background of the final Conference action, see Russell, *op. cit.*, pp. 898–910.

in the Charter. Time, as the following chapters illustrate, has tended to bring many of those underlying sources of international conflict within the competence of the United Nations in practice, as well as in theory—but often in ways that could hardly have been anticipated in 1945.

The Organization has faced political and military conflict in all parts of the world, ranging from purely local quarrels to the threat of general thermonuclear war. Conflicts between the two extremes are internationally less dangerous in themselves than in the possibility that, through escalation, they may involve the nuclear giants in action that would tip the uneasy "balance of terror" into the dreaded nuclear conflict.

The problems at these various levels that confront both the United States and the United Nations in the search for peace fall into various categories: (1) the control of nuclear crises, and the control and reduction of the armaments that make the thermonuclear threat so terrible; (2) the management and reduction of all other armaments, which reflect as well as exacerbate political conflict and the costs of which hinder more rapid economic and social development in all countries; (3) the "fire-brigade" job of preventing or containing the use of nonnuclear armed force with its indirect threat to the uneasy equilibrium of the nuclear powers themselves; (4) the settlement of political conflicts, and the submission to adjudication of legal disputes, before they give way to military action or after armed violence has been suspended; (5) the minimal meeting of the social and national demands for change encompassed in the numerous "revolutions of rising expectations," so that they do not end in violent efforts to upset the status quo.

The turmoil caused by this last factor in particular underlies many of the individual conflicts that threaten the peace, from relatively minor situations of tension to the newest version of the balance-of-power conflict, the thermonuclear confrontation. It has also helped change the basic form taken by those threats: from the traditional pattern of organized military threats by one government against another's national security and territorial integrity, to that of revolutionary and subversive activity that runs rampant around the globe while President Kennedy's "nuclear sword of Damocles" hangs heavy over our heads.[24]

The new pattern of security problems did not develop overnight, nor could it be foreseen when the United Nations Charter was negotiated. The prevailing version of collective security written into the Charter

24. "Let Us Call a Truce to Terror," address before the U.N. General Assembly, Sept. 25, 1961, U.S. Department of State, *Bulletin*, Vol. 45 (1961), p. 620.

emphasized, as described, a police concept of enforcing the peace that the new Organization was designed to maintain. But successful police enforcement depends both on the existence of a generally acceptable state of law and political affairs and on the overwhelming weight of the community behind that police power. There has never been a final settlement of World War II that could be a starting point in this sense. The maintenance of international peace under the revolutionary conditions that have dominated so much of the postwar world—to anticipate one of the conclusions of this study—would appear to be more akin to the problem of maintaining civil order when the state of public law and affairs is challenged by a significant group, and when the means of lawful change are inadequate to their demands. Disorder can be suppressed in those conditions, provided there is enough police power and the will to use it— as the Soviet Union showed in Hungary, in 1956. But peaceful and constructive change cannot be imposed by such an application of force; it must grow from within. The difficulties of maintaining peace in the struggle for civil rights within the United States, for example, may thus shed light both on the nature of the broader international problem and on the difficulties of finding a way to handle it.

The relationship of the United Nations to United States policy for maintaining national security and international peace in these circumstances has been an irregular one. Given the nature of the Organization, its direct role in the calculations underlying national security is necessarily limited. As a voluntary agency for international cooperation operating in a situation of political conflict between the holders of great military power, its function has been both less than, and different from, that hoped for by more optimistic individuals in 1945. Even had the cold war not developed so acutely, however, the United Nations role could not have become central in national policy determination until major advances toward true community under the Charter had been achieved. The actual interplay of national policy and international organization has been so complex and uneven that the influence of the United Nations cannot be weighed with any certitude. To do so would first require knowledge of what would have happened had the Organization never been founded. This negative circumstance in itself would have reflected the existence of a different, presumably even less cooperative, relationship among the powers than prevailed in 1945.

Although the Member governments retained their national control of all significant political authority when establishing the world Organization, the latter became something more than (not something different from) the collectivity of its Members. Unlike a temporary international conference, but like the League, the United Nations is a continuing institution. Its procedures and machinery permit it to delegate, to a permanent international staff, continuing responsibilities beyond those actions taken by the Members' representatives in its political organs. But under contemporary conditions, the Members have been unwilling to delegate any great degree of such responsibility. The fact that the Organization has nonetheless extended its competence far beyond that of the League may be more significant, in the long run, than that it has not yet become a "strong" factor in the world of great power relationships. Weakness does not necessarily connote lack of significance, moreover: the weakest link in a chain can be the most important one. It depends on the function being performed.

The important point concerning the United Nations is that it has become an integral part of the complex of means whereby governments seek to deal with the various problems of conflicting interest that face them. Where the Organization has been successful (or unsuccessful) in "handling" some problem, it has been so because the Member governments were also using (or failing to use) their other available foreign policy instruments in support of the same end.

CHAPTER FOUR

THE UNITED NATIONS
AND ARMS CONTROL

Governments formerly sought preponderant military strength in the hope that conclusive evidence of superior armaments would lead to political accommodation by their enemies without the test of battle; but the risk of war was accepted and was internationally permissible. Today, the Soviet Union and the United States are in the unprecedented position of accumulating ever more overwhelmingly destructive power for the declared purpose of preventing its use. Their willingness to engage, as a last resort, in mutual devastation with their nuclear arsenals is publicly maintained to sustain the credibility of their deterrents. This element of irrationality in their posture, as President Kennedy declared in 1961, puts "every man, woman, and child . . . under a nuclear sword of Damocles, hanging by the slenderest of threads, capable of being cut at any moment by accident, miscalculation, or madness."[1] The weapons of war, he continued, "must be abolished before they abolish us." Six years later, nonetheless, arsenals had increased to an even higher level. The resulting delicate and unstable political equilibrium has been described by President Johnson as an "uncertain and unsatisfactory balance of terror," which will become "all terror and no balance" should possession of these weapons spread to "dozens of nations, large and small," each with its own "nuclear trigger."[2]

In rational terms, therefore, the avoidance of nuclear war has become an imperative of policy. Nuclear weapons, unlike troops or warships, are not themselves direct instruments for the achievement of the purposes of

1. John F. Kennedy, address of Sept. 25, 1961 to the General Assembly, U.S. Department of State, *Bulletin*, Vol. 45 (1961), p. 620. See also Secretary McNamara: "The mere fact that no nation could rationally take steps leading to a nuclear war does not guarantee that a nuclear war cannot take place." U.S. Department of Defense Press Release 980–62, June 16, 1962, p. 7.
2. White House press release, Jan. 21, 1964, p. 1.

national policy. They are, rather, sanctions enjoining on their possessors restraint in the pursuit of conflicts between them lest holocaust result. In that situation, concern ought logically to focus on steps to help avoid thermonuclear war, at least as intensively as on how best to conduct such a conflict. The former requirement is clearly a matter within the sphere of interest of the United Nations. Yet, the nature of the problem is such that bilateral accord between the United States and the Soviet Union is indispensable to progress on any significant scale. There is thus a tendency to overlook, if not to deny, possibilities of constructive action through the Organization that might help alleviate the dangers inherent in any direct confrontation of the nuclear giants. As an organizational entity, the United Nations can obviously neither control nor eliminate the situation that threatens disaster, but it has nonetheless functioned in various constructive ways in the course of disarmament negotiations.

Both the dangers of existing arsenals and the consequent desire to reduce them have increased throughout the postwar period. Neither element, however, has been strong enough to overcome the combination of fear and suspicion that still prevents agreement on a system of control acceptable to both sides in the cold war, and without which no significant measure of armaments reduction can be anticipated. Negotiations on the subject have continued since 1946, however, with only occasional lulls—now within, now without the United Nations, the locale and format making no effective difference.

The Negotiating Minuet, 1946–62

Although twenty years of arms negotiation have achieved little in the way of control and nothing in the way of reduction, the very act of negotiating has been one element in the total political situation that has so far helped to avoid the ultimate outbreak of nuclear war. As Secretary-General Hammarskjold once said, in answer to a question about the impossibility of disarmament before political conflicts are resolved:

It is quite true that there is an interplay between political factors—the political atmosphere—on the one side, and disarmament on the other. But, when people say, in those simple terms, that if the political situation improves, disarmament will follow and that, for that reason, it does not make sense to discuss disarmament, they overlook one essential factor; that the very study of disarmament may be the vehicle for progress towards greater international understanding. That is to say, disarmament is never the result only of the political situation; it is also partly instrumental in creating the political situation.[3]

More concretely, the negotiations and the preparations for them have resulted in an extensive body of the technological and political knowledge that is essential to any significant advances. It proved helpful in the case of the partial test-ban treaty, for example, which was technologically feasible by the time it became politically possible in 1963.

The pattern of negotiations over all, nonetheless, has been well described as a frustrating minuet—"advancing and retreating, but never meeting."[4] It is oversimplified, but not inaccurate, to say that a basic reason for Soviet refusal over the years to accept United States proposals for either test bans or broader armaments regulation was that they were postulated on maintaining relative American supremacy; while Soviet proposals were rejected by the United States precisely because they sought to undermine that position.[5] Moreover, the general political situation did not remain the same over the years, despite the continuing cold war; and some of its changes significantly affected the course of disarmament negotiations.

Vacillations and sudden policy reversals at times marked both Soviet and Western positions. With the United States, these sometimes reflected domestic or interallied difficulties, sometimes differences with the Soviet bloc. Moscow's more glaring contradictions are harder to assess as representing either "sham or vacillation."[6] Neither Moscow nor Washington could steer a consistent course through the complexities of modern international politics, hampered as they were by a heritage of suspicion and hesitation due to what each side considered proof positive of the hostile intentions of the other. Thus, the back-and-forth pacing of the negotiations minuet. Nonetheless, certain net advances were made.

3. Wilder Foote, ed., *Dag Hammarskjold: Servant of Peace* (Harper and Row, 1962), p. 132.

4. Anne Winslow, ed., in Preface to Lawrence S. Finkelstein, "Arms Inspection," *International Conciliation*, No. 540 (November 1962), p. 1.

5. See, e.g., Matthew B. Ridgway, *Soldier: The Memoirs of Matthew B. Ridgway* (Harper, 1956), pp. 171–72, for the American attitude in the early postwar period. For a survey of the course of negotiations during the first 15 years, see Bernhard G. Bechhoefer, *Postwar Negotiations for Arms Control* (Brookings Institution, 1961).

6. Sir Michael Wright (chief British negotiator for several years), *Disarm and Verify: An Explanation of the Central Difficulties and of National Policies* (Praeger, 1964), p. 115. He suspends judgment, but notes that: "A Russian 'never' should never be taken to mean never." p. 116.

In the first years, the Soviet Union concentrated largely on propaganda efforts to "ban the bomb" (which it did not yet possess) or to obtain commitments to large-scale, general arms reductions without verification or controls of any sort. The main effort of the United States, in the Baruch proposals for complete control of atomic energy at all stages, was both detailed and free of propaganda broadsides. It depended, however, on strong safeguards against violation, which would have eroded Soviet secrecy (a major element of Soviet military strength, as well as an obsessive concern throughout the communist system); and it failed to provide in equal detail for the elimination of nuclear weapons. It thus offered an inadequate return to the Kremlin.

Until the Korean war, the United States was greatly inferior in conventional armaments, having unilaterally disarmed in this area. By the end of the conflict, the West had rearmed; but also, by then, the Soviet Union had achieved atomic capability. No serious disarmament negotiations were possible during the Korean conflict; but in that period the Western allies developed the basis of a comprehensive program for controlled disarmament by stages.

The death of Stalin in 1953 allowed a relaxation of earlier Soviet rigidity, and Moscow began to show an interest in Western proposals. With the approach of a relative nuclear stalemate, about 1955, reappraisals were required. The Soviet Union was now more aware of, and began to admit, the catastrophic implications of general nuclear war. It called for comprehensive disarmament on lines of the earlier Western proposals and even accepted the principle of partial disarmament measures as a first step toward the ultimate goal.

Negotiations were broken off again in 1957, however, at a time of worsening East-West relations. Substantive differences on disarmament issues, moreover, had been complicated by Western insistence that its proposals, constituting a considerable package of partial measures of interest to the West, be accepted on an all-or-nothing basis. At the same time, the West offered no concessions on foreign bases or the reduction of occupying forces in Europe, which were of greatest importance to the Soviet Union.

Pressure from the lesser powers for the renewal of negotiations began at once.[7] This opened the way to the start of correspondence between

7. Prime Minister Nehru, for example, appealed to both Moscow and Washington, "to stop all nuclear test explosions and thus to show the world that they are determined to end this menace and to proceed also to bring about effective disarmament." Quoted in Bechhoefer, *op. cit.*, p. 444.

President Eisenhower and the Soviet leaders, resulting in a voluntary cessation of testing by both powers and two technical conferences in 1958. One conference, on the avoidance of surprise attack, failed shortly as Soviet and Western views were irreconcilable.[8] The other, seeking a full test-ban treaty, led to further three-power talks which made little progress for several years. At the end of 1959, moreover, President Eisenhower ended the informal test moratorium and declared the United States free to resume testing—although it did not do so.

At the General Assembly that same year, Khrushchev again proposed negotiations looking toward "general and complete disarmament" (GCD), but now recognizing the possibility of starting with partial steps.[9] Great Britain also made comprehensive proposals. The major powers, in addition, agreed on a new Disarmament Committee of ten members, evenly divided between the two "sides," in the hope of facilitating negotiations. They undertook to "explore" all types of controlled disarmament measures and to inform the United Nations of the results, which would thus provide "a useful basis for consideration" of the question in the Assembly.[10] Negotiations ran from March to June 1960, then broke down once more after the U-2 episode and the collapse of the Paris summit meeting that summer. Soviet tactics in the Congo, Berlin, Laos, and elsewhere subsequently became increasingly aggressive. In spite of the growing tensions, however, a degree of consensus was reached during 1961 by the two nuclear powers on the principles necessary to the development of any effective disarmament system.

DEVELOPMENT OF UNITED STATES POSITION, 1961

During the presidential campaign of the previous year, Kennedy had criticized the Eisenhower Administration for a lack of serious effort in

8. To the West, "measures against surprise attack meant inspection to cover all strategic air bases and missile sites, as well as large troop movements. To the Soviet Union, it meant specifically the so-called Rapacki Plan, originally presented by the Foreign Minister of Poland, to establish a nuclear-free zone in Central Europe." Bernard C. Bechhoefer, "The Test-Ban Treaty; Some Further Considerations," *Bulletin of the Atomic Scientists* (May 1964), p. 26. For discussion of nuclear-free zone, see below, pp. 98–99.

9. Khrushchev's plan for GCD "appropriated almost literally but without attribution large portions of" a 1952 U.S. proposal. Bechhoefer, *Postwar Negotiations for Arms Control*, p. 183. A summary of the 1952 proposal is on pp. 178–81.

10. Four-power communiqué in U.S. Department of State, *Bulletin*, Vol. 41 (1959), pp. 438–40. The committee included Canada, France, Italy, Great Britain, the United States, Bulgaria, Czechoslovakia, Poland, Rumania, and the Soviet Union.

the disarmament field. He did not believe arms control would come about "in a romantic moment of human redemption"; but because of the mutual interest of the two nuclear powers in preventing nuclear war, it might come with the development of "careful, detailed, and well-staffed proposals."[11] The new administration's subsequent approach in 1961,[12] therefore, took account of the frustrations caused by the Soviet theory of total disarmament by a single agreement and by the new factor of the intercontinental ballistic missile system. Its central concept was that of "stable nuclear deterrence": the situation in which surprise attack by one side could not prevent retaliation by the other. Neither side, then, would rationally initiate an attack that could only result in its own destruction. Such a system, moreover, should make it possible to limit the size of the deterrent and thereby to halt the nuclear race. Considering total disarmament as currently irrelevant, the administration proposed stable deterrence as the best way to create an atmosphere in which reduced tensions might lead to progressive agreement on further arms-control measures. Eventually, it could even lead to the desired total disarmament. The ultimate objective was thus reconciled with the interim needs of national security.

On the basis of such thinking, the government established the Arms Control and Disarmament Agency (ACDA),[13] its title reflecting the official approach and its formation emphasizing the importance the President gave to the question. During the spring and summer of 1961, intensive work developed on a new negotiating proposal.[14] It provided, on the basis of stabilized deterrence and arms control, for progressive reduction (while maintaining the balance of deterrence at each stage) and eventual abolition of national armaments and armed forces beyond those needed for internal security. Parallel development of international settlement and enforcement machinery was to make that final stage possible.

11. Quoted in Arthur M. Schlesinger, Jr., A Thousand Days: John F. Kennedy in the White House (Houghton Mifflin Co., 1965), p. 469.

12. Described by Schlesinger as "the Charles River doctrine," see Ibid., pp. 470–72. This referred especially to the thinking developed by a group headed by Drs. Jerome Wiesner (to become Scientific Adviser to the President), Thomas C. Schelling, and Henry Kissinger.

13. Formalized by statute in September 1961, 75 Stat. 631.

14. See Schlesinger, op. cit., pp. 472–86; also Arthur H. Dean, Test Ban and Disarmament: The Path of Negotiation (Harper and Row, 1966), pp. 6–9, 25–27, 30–33.

An exchange of views with the Soviet Union on reopening negotiations was undertaken. Moscow finally agreed to consider a statement of general principles which was negotiated in time to be presented to the General Assembly in the fall.

Increasing tension over Berlin, a resumption of Soviet nuclear testing in September, and the United States decision to respond with tests of its own, raised some question whether President Kennedy should present the new disarmament proposal personally. Hammarskjold's tragic death settled any doubts that he should. Also, as a presidential aide pointed out, Moscow's resumption of testing put it "on the defensive re disarmament, an issue devoid at this point of any practical negotiating possibilities but of tremendous psychological significance, particularly as the world moves closer to the brink on Berlin."[15] The President accordingly announced the United States plan. Declaring that the goal of disarmament was no longer a dream, but "a practical matter of life or death," he urged that negotiations continue "without interruption until an entire program for general and complete disarmament" had been agreed on and achieved in actuality.[16] In addition, the two powers presented as planned their agreed statement of principles on which disarmament should be negotiated. The Assembly unanimously endorsed it and also called for a treaty to ban nuclear tests under effective measures of verification and control.[17]

GUIDING PRINCIPLES FOR DISARMAMENT

The first principle declared the goal of negotiations to be the achievement of a program to ensure general and complete disarmament (GCD), plus the replacement of war as a means of settlement by "the establishment of reliable procedures" for pacific settlement of disputes and the maintenance of peace.[18] Within the context of United States official thinking just described, however, GCD still remained more of a distant dream than a practical objective of policy. This was especially true in the theoretical terms of principle 2, which foresaw the reduction of national

15. Quoted in Schlesinger, *op. cit.*, p. 484.
16. U.S. Department of State, *Bulletin*, Vol. 45 (1961), p. 622.
17. A/Res. 1722 (XVI), Dec. 20, 1961.
18. Text of principles is in Arms Control and Disarmament Agency (ACDA), *Documents on Disarmament*, 1961 (August 1962), pp. 360–61.

arms to the level of internal-policy requirements. That objective would be made possible by providing for the development of adequate international institutions for settlement.

The third principle spelled out what GCD would signify by way of disbanding armed forces, eliminating stockpiles of weapons, abolishing military institutions, and so forth; while number 4 provided for implementing the program "in an agreed sequence, by stages," each one appropriately verified.

The fifth point established the critical principle of balance: "All measures of general and complete disarmament should be balanced so that at no stage of the implementation of the treaty could any State or group of States gain military advantage and that security is ensured equally for all." This is the central problem that still thwarts any real progress on specific technical measures, which almost inevitably appear to result in some military advantage for one party. Moreover, if an elaborate scheme for controlled disarmament on these terms will ensure "the security of all," the question may well be asked why the present balance does not already so ensure it. The answer to that conundrum was dramatically illustrated by the Cuban crisis of 1962: it involves both the frighteningly delicate balance of the nuclear deterrent, in spite of any "stable deterrence" doctrine, and the perennial problem of verification.

The sixth principle dealt with that last issue, declaring that all disarmament measures were to be carried out under "strict and effective international control," in order to guarantee compliance; and providing for an international disarmament organization, "to implement control over and inspection of disarmament." At the same time, this statement was supplemented with an exchange of letters "on the question of control"— meaning that the two governments disagreed in principle.[19] The United States insisted, in effect, on inspection of all armaments (those remaining, as well as those eliminated, at each stage); while the Soviet Union "resolutely" opposed the former (which it calls "control over armaments," rather than over "disarmament").

Principle 7 provided that steps in disarmament be accompanied by "measures to strengthen institutions for maintaining peace," and to ensure the "settlement of international disputes by peaceful means." These would include the eventual establishment of an international peace force whose nature was not clearly defined in spite of its importance in the scheme. Moreover, the chance of achieving it appears practically non-

19. See Dean, *op. cit.*, pp. 32–33, for U.S. insistence on the exchange.

existent, if one defines it by logical extensions of the brief Outline Plan.[20]

The final principle, number 8, calls on participating states to seek "the widest possible agreement at the earliest possible date," so that even limited measures might serve to advance the total program.

THE EIGHTEEN-NATION DISARMAMENT COMMITTEE

The Assembly resolution also accepted an accompanying proposal for an Eighteen-Nation Disarmament Committee (ENDC) to be the negotiating organ in Geneva. It added eight nonaligned governments to the five states on each "side" of the disarmament conflict, which had made up the earlier negotiating committee.[21]

The United States accepted this membership with little enthusiasm, insisting on the unbalanced number of neutrals to avoid an appearance of adopting the Soviet "troika" principle. In fact, however, the specific designation of unaligned and cold-war groups recognized the three-way division of the world seen by Soviet spokesmen. The middle group not only represented the interest of nearly all members in the goal of disarmament,[22] but also an increasing awareness that this interest could "best be pursued . . . through agreement between the opposing sides rather than excessive pressure on either."[23]

ENDC negotiations have proved valuable from the United States viewpoint in spreading greater appreciation among the United Nations membership of the extraordinary complexity of the technical problems involved in armaments regulation. The unaligned "Eight" generally support the United States effort to bring the always oversimplified Soviet proposals down to discussion in more practical terms, while seeking on their own to obtain clarification of technical ambiguities from both sides.[24] The negotiations also provide an opportunity to make clear to

20. This question is considered at greater length in Chap. 5 below.

21. The Western "side" includes the United States, Great Britain, Canada, Italy, and France, although the last refuses to participate, maintaining that disarmament negotiations should be limited to members of the "nuclear club." The Eastern "side" includes the Soviet Union, Bulgaria, Czechoslovakia, Poland, and Rumania. The Eight include Brazil, Burma, Ethiopia, India, Mexico, Nigeria, Sweden, and the U.A.R.

22. See Dean, *op. cit.*, p. 13.

23. Catherine Manno, "Weighted Voting in the United Nations: A Study of Feasibility and Methods," unpublished Ph.D. thesis, American University, 1964, p. 186.

24. See, for example, the Burmese member's opening statement, quoted in M. Samir Ahmed, "The Role of the Neutrals in the Geneva Negotiations," *Disarmament and Arms Control*, Vol. 1, No. 1 (Pergamon Press, Oxford, Summer 1963), p. 24.

other Members the implications for their own military status of any significant moves to implement either the Soviet or the American plan for GCD. In their emotional concern with thermonuclear dangers, the smaller powers have too frequently overlooked this latter aspect. Since many of them are more pacifist in their demands on the great powers than they are in the use of military means themselves, such an awareness may have salutary effects in time on the reasonableness of their expectations.

1962 NEGOTIATIONS

Following the President's address to the Assembly in September 1961, the United States officially submitted a draft "Declaration on Disarmament: A Program for General and Complete Disarmament in a Peaceful World."[25] Expanding on the agreed principles, this organized the results in a sketchy outline of a three-stage disarmament program, calling on the Members to develop it "into an agreed plan for general and complete disarmament and to continue their efforts without interruption until the whole program has been achieved."[26] The Assembly referred this proposal to the new negotiating committee.

At the initial session of the ENDC, in March 1962, the Soviet delegate unexpectedly produced a complete draft disarmament treaty. Based on earlier Soviet plans, it was ostensibly designed to bring about GCD in three stages over four years' time, but contained no particulars on the method of transition. The United States, in return, hastily formalized its own earlier proposal into an "Outline of Basic Provisions of a Treaty on General and Complete Disarmament in a Peaceful World," which it presented to the committee in April.[27]

This outline plan was all to the good to the extent that, for all its brevity, it made far clearer than Soviet delegates had ever admitted the technical and political complexities of any serious disarmament program. Despite the amount of study that had gone into the preparation of the "Draft Declaration" on which the outline was based, however, there remained a good deal of vagueness in the concepts underlying the second and third stages of the plan. There was also a great amount of internal dis-

25. U.S. Department of State, *Bulletin*, Vol. 45 (1961), pp. 650–54.
26. *Ibid.*, p. 651.
27. Text in ACDA, *Documents on Disarmament, 1962*, Vol. I (November 1963), pp. 351–82.

agreement, in both the administration and the Congress, especially over the proposed longer-term political institutions.[28]

In April 1962, the Eight submitted a memorandum of their own on principles for a test-ban treaty, thus reflecting the prevailing concern of the nonnuclear majority of the Assembly. It was "accepted" by both the East and West "sides," which kept the appearance of test-ban negotiations going; but actually it did nothing to reduce the real differences between the major powers. In fact, no significant advance was made in 1962 on any of the technical issues of disarmament, despite the new plans. The artificiality of the performance at that time was indicated by Washington's public warning in April that, unless an effective test-ban treaty were signed by the end of the month (an obvious impossibility), it would renew atmospheric tests as a military necessity in light of the 1961 Soviet series.

This it did; which led in turn to another Soviet round of tests, including some multimegaton explosions, and then to a supplementary American series in October. The Eight renewed efforts to bring about a definitive halt to the tests. They proposed the end of 1962 as a cutoff date and the acceptance of a ban on tests in other environments, pending solution of the problem of verifying underground tests. A partial ban on Soviet tests appeared by then more valuable to the United States than continued testing, so it agreed to accept the cutoff date, provided one of the draft treaties before the ENDC was first adopted.[29] Before any progress was made in that direction, however, the crisis over Soviet attempts to emplace long-range missiles in Cuba came to a head, climaxing increased conflicts in other areas, especially Berlin.

The 1962 Cuban Crisis

The intangibles of political life are as important and as impossible to weigh with any accuracy in the international as in the national sphere. In considering the role of the international Organization in the Cuban crisis,

28. See Chap. 5 below, especially pp. 138–48. "Some of these questions." Arthur H. Dean (who worked on them at the time) has written, "were in pioneer territory and we succeeded only in mapping their main features." *Op. cit.*, p. 25.

29. The United States and Great Britain had offered either a complete test-ban with modified control machinery or, alternatively, a partial ban with no international verification required. National methods of detection and identification were by then considered adequate to determine any violations occurring in outer space, the atmosphere, or under water.

that brought the world to the brink of nuclear conflict, only a few points can be made without argument. First, that the resolution of the impending conflict without war depended basically on the actions of both major antagonists. Secondly, that the obvious role of the United Nations as a forum was useful in rallying the moral support of other governments in favor of peaceful settlement; and that its somewhat less obvious role, operating especially through the Secretary-General, was even more useful in allowing the nuclear dialogue to be reopened without either side appearing to concede its case.

THE COURSE OF EVENTS

The United States was aware, by September 1962, that Soviet aid to Cuba included certain surface-to-air missiles, but Washington considered them essentially defensive in nature and not threatening to this country. Then the potentialities of a new agreement between the two communist states alarmed the government, which warned against Soviet emplacement in Cuba of any long-range, surface-to-surface missiles with offensive capabilities. It also instituted intensive air and sea surveillance of the island. A secret build-up of sites for such offensive missiles and for jet bombers began nonetheless in October, but was discovered before the weapons were fully emplaced. President Kennedy reacted with a restrained policy combining national and international action and bringing into play a whole series of political, legal, and limited military measures.

The President, in a radio address on October 22, charged that the Soviet purpose could be "none other than to provide a nuclear strike capability against the Western Hemisphere." Calling the Soviet action "a deliberately provocative and unjustified change in the *status quo*," he declared it could not be "accepted by this country if our courage and our commitments are ever to be trusted again by either friend or foe. . . . Our unswerving objective, therefore, must be to prevent the use of these missiles . . . and to secure their withdrawal or elimination from the Western Hemisphere."[30] He accordingly ordered a military alert, threatened retaliation against the Soviet Union were any nuclear missile launched from Cuba against any place in the Hemisphere, and called for meetings of the OAS and the Security Councils. On the 23d, the OAS Council demanded immediate withdrawal of the contentious weapons. It also recommended

30. Text in U.S. Department of State, *Report to the People*, Publication 7449 (October 1962), pp. 1, 6.

that all OAS members take steps to prevent delivery of further missiles and to keep the ones already in Cuba from becoming an active threat. Kennedy thereupon proclaimed a quarantine, effective October 24.

On October 23 also, the Security Council met. Draft resolutions—by the United States on the one hand and by the Soviet Union and Cuba on the other—each condemned, and demanded the revocation of, the actions of the opposite party. Both drafts also, and significantly, urged the Council to call on the parties to enter into negotiations to "remove the existing threat" to peace or to "reestablish a normal situation."[31] They were, in short, seeking a means of escape from an apparently closed situation. The Security Council members provided one by hearing the parties and then adjourning without voting on any resolution. This allowed the start of direct negotiations by the Soviet and American delegates under the Council's aegis and in consultation with U Thant.

The Secretary-General, meanwhile, had appealed to both Kennedy and Khrushchev to refrain from aggravating the situation. To facilitate negotiations, he proposed the voluntary suspension of Soviet shipments, of American quarantine measures, and of Cuban construction of installations. The President declared, however, that only removal of the weapons causing the crisis could bring about a peaceful solution.

The Secretary-General then proposed (October 25) that, to permit discussions, Soviet ships for the next few days should stay away from the announced interception areas; and that United States vessels should avoid direct confrontation with Soviet ships. On October 26, the Soviet Premier told U Thant that he had so ordered Soviet ships; and the President, that American vessels would do everything possible to avoid confrontation if the ships stayed away.[32] Work on the missile sites continued to aggravate the situation. Between October 26 and 28, a number of messages crisscrossed between President and Premier. The end result was an undertaking by Khrushchev to dismantle the offending weapons and return them to the Soviet Union, subject to United Nations verification; and by Kennedy that, if these commitments were implemented and no further weapons introduced (subject to verification), he would lift the quarantine and give assurances against any invasion.

In early January 1963, the two governments informed the Secretary-

31. Texts in *United Nations Review* (November 1962), pp. 6–7.
32. Texts of letters in *New York Times*, Oct. 27, 1962. Summary of events from U.S. Senate Foreign Relations Committee, *Events in U.S.-Cuban Relations: A Chronology, 1957–1963*, 88 Cong. 1 sess.

General that they had reached a "degree of understanding" that made it "unnecessary for this item to occupy further the attention of the Security Council." In a simultaneous message, Cuba "deplored" the fact that negotiations had not been successfully ended and reserved its right to possess "pertinent" arms. As there was no agreement on safeguards against reintroduction of the weapons or on international inspection, the United States in turn gave no commitments against invasion and continued its surveillance of Cuba.

ROLE OF INTERNATIONAL ORGANIZATION

Political scientists devising an experiment in nuclear crisis in circumstances least attendant with fatal possibilities might well have prescribed the Cuban situation. Moscow and Washington were able to control the development of the crisis as they alone willed. Confrontation took the form of naval vessels operating on the high seas and asserting a right of search against commercial vessels. The possibilities of accident, the danger of spontaneous military escalation, the injection of complicating local partisan activity, were all excluded by the special circumstances.[33] The relative superiority of American power, furthermore, was strengthened by the fact that the critical confrontation occurred far from the Soviet base.

Even in these comparatively favorable circumstances, however, the possibility of nuclear war was considered dangerously close, since it could as easily escalate from a Soviet countermove in some other tense spot, such as Berlin, as from action directly related to Cuba. Some melancholy satisfaction may therefore be derived from the skillful performance by both sides of the diplomatic *danse macabre* which "maintained the options"— in Secretary McNamara's phrase. But the statesmanship then exhibited extended only to the immediate objective of getting the weapons removed while avoiding thermonuclear war. Indeed, the necessity arose because of the prior inability of statesmen of the great powers to reach any equivalent meeting of minds on measures to control—much less to eliminate— their doomsday weapons.

The danger was considered so great that diplomatic consultations with allies were short-circuited. Although the United States had for years been

33. See also, William M. Jordan, "Political Role of the United Nations," in Richard N. Swift, ed., *Annual Review of United Nations Affairs, 1962–1963* (Oceana, 1964), pp. 4–5.

cultivating regional security arrangements in both Europe and the Western Hemisphere, their inherent weakness in the situation of transregional confrontation was illustrated thereby. The political value of OAS procedures to the United States was considerable, however, given success in avoiding holocaust. Had the United States not been able to mobilize the other OAS members and convince them of the reality of the threat, the political aftermath of the episode might well have been, on balance, merely an increase in the Latin American suspicion of the Yankee colossus, which the 1965 Dominican Republic crisis so quickly resuscitated.[34]

In the United Nations, the Security Council could only provide a forum, but U Thant became a focal point of the world's expectations. Although his initial proposals were not acceptable, his offer of conciliatory services was; and his second suggestion—that Soviet and American ships should deliberately avoid confrontation—was quickly adopted. How is this activity to be evaluated?

The Secretary-General modestly described his intervention as "useful" in view of "the somewhat rigid" initial positions of the chief antagonists.[35] But Ambassador Stevenson placed a higher value on the Secretary-General's action in reporting to the Senate Foreign Relations Committee: "At a critical moment—when the nuclear powers seemed to be set on a collision course—the Secretary-General's intervention led to the diversion of the Soviet ships headed for Cuba and interception by our Navy. This was an indispensable first step in the peaceful resolution of the Cuban crisis."[36] Many consider this an exaggeration; but it was no doubt easier for Khrushchev to accept a proposal formally made to both parties than to back down publicly in the face of United States obduracy alone.[37] It might also be pointed out that not so many years earlier such a novel diplomatic troika as the consultations between the Secretary-General and the Soviet and American delegates in New York would have been inconceivable as one of the means to be used in resolving a near-catastrophic crisis between Washington and Moscow.[38]

34. See Chap. 6 below.

35. *United Nations Review* (January 1964), p. 5.

36. *Review of United States Participation in the United Nations*, Hearing before the Subcommittee on International Organization Affairs, Senate Foreign Relations Committee, 88 Cong. 1 sess., March 13, 1963, p. 7.

37. See also Averell Harriman's advice on providing an "out" for the Premier, in Schlesinger, *op. cit.*, p. 821.

38. For the very different reception given Trygve Lie's efforts at the time of the 1948 Berlin blockade, see his *In the Cause of Peace* (Macmillan, 1954), Chap. 12.

It is, of course, impossible to measure the influence either of the existence of the United Nations or of the unique office of Secretary-General in the situation. To do so would first require knowledge of what would have happened had neither element been present in the complex of factors that marked the Cuban crisis. While not exaggerating the intangible international influence, it is also necessary to avoid the other fault of retrospectively depreciating the danger that did not eventuate.

It has been argued, for example, that the issue was simply one of the relatively greater importance of Cuba to the United States, which also possessed more relevant power, so that Khrushchev, in consequence, had to "back down." But if this impersonal mathematical computation, or the even simpler explanation that Moscow will always retreat when confronted by superior power, were adequate to account for the American success, there would have been little need for the elaborately cautious procedures followed, after October 22, in bringing the situation under control. And subsequent statements of various actors in the melodrama (Khrushchev and Kennedy included) about the imminence of catastrophe would have to be attributed more to political rhetoric tinged with hysteria, than to sober evaluation of the situation. Both words and deeds during the critical period, on the contrary, seemed to sustain the implications of Kennedy's earlier Damocletian warning.

Even accepting the "mathematical" approach in purely political-military terms, it assumes a total absence of unpredictable human factors. Yet, "there is always some so-and-so who doesn't get the word"—as the President remarked when a U–2 from Alaska inadvertently entered Soviet air space in the middle of the crisis.[39] Perhaps today technical accidents can be eliminated, as between the Soviet Union and the United States; and, for the sake of argument, irrationality can also be counted out (though neither history nor contemporary politics gives any reason for so doing). But the element of misjudgment remains as essentially the cause of the crisis[40] and always a hazard to the power-politics calculation.

As President Kennedy wrote to Premier Khrushchev October 28, both had become "aware that developments were approaching a point where

39. Quoted in Schlesinger, *op. cit.*, p. 828.

40. "Each side apparently made the mistake of identifying its opponent's mode of calculation with its own." Fred Greene, "The Intelligence Arm: The Cuban Missile Crisis," in Roger Hilsman and Robert Good, eds., *Foreign Policy in the Sixties* (Johns Hopkins Press, 1965), p. 138. See also Kennedy's comments, in Schlesinger, *op. cit.*, pp. 830–32.

events could have become unmanageable." He therefore suggested: "Perhaps now, as we step back from danger, we can together make real progress in this vital field. I think we should give priority to questions relating to the proliferation of nuclear weapons, on earth and in outer space, and to the great effort for a nuclear test ban."[41] The Cuban episode had also illuminated another danger: the slowness of communicating through regular diplomatic channels which involved coding and decoding of messages and transmission through foreign offices. Such delay proved intolerably slow at the height of the crisis, and unconventional channels were resorted to by both sides.[42]

1963: The Year of "First Steps"

The influence of the recent experience was seen in 1963 in the achievement of a few first steps in the field of nuclear control after so many years of futile arms negotiations. The initial move, immediately after the crisis had passed, was to undertake to establish a direct communications link between the heads of the two superpowers—a "hot line," as it was called.

THE "HOT LINE"

Such a line had been urged unofficially for some years, and the idea was included in the official United States outline plan as a first-stage measure to reduce the risk of war. Yet it was another ten months before Washington and Moscow completed negotiations and opened the line in August 1963.[43] The occasion was a remarkably quiet affair, without even an exchange of official messages. The Defense Department merely announced that the line was "now operational."[44]

41. ACDA, *Documents on Disarmament*, 1962, Vol. 2 (1963), pp. 1000–01.

42. On October 28, for example, Khrushchev made an open broadcast of his message to the President. Kennedy responded "at once, . . . even though the official text has not yet reached me." *Ibid.*

43. The complicated equipment used (known as "one time tape system encoding equipment") is employed by commercial as well as military communications systems, so no military secrets had to be divulged when using it in the Soviet Union. The system is considered virtually "breakproof," and makes possible an exchange of messages between the President and the Soviet Prime Minister within minutes. *New York Times*, Aug. 31, 1963.

44. Washington sent a "message used by Teletype operators to test whether a circuit is operating—'The quick brown fox jumped over the lazy dog's back 1234567890.' " Back from Moscow came a similar test message in Russian, which was completely unintelligible to the United States operators, but at least showed that all the characters on the Teletype were working correctly." *Ibid.*, Aug. 31, 1963.

To be used only in time of emergency for exchange between the two heads of government, it was recognized that the value of the line would be only as an instrument to control a highly critical situation. Its one use so far was in fact just that: when the United States heard, during the Arab-Israeli hostilities in June 1967, of an attack by an as yet unidentified source on the communications ship, the USS Liberty, in the eastern Mediterranean, Washington advised Moscow (whose ships were observing the U.S. Sixth Fleet movements) that its carrier-based planes were scrambling into action for the sole purpose of assisting the damaged Liberty.[45] The line cannot in itself prevent such a situation from developing. A hesitant, if indirect, step toward that latter goal was also achieved in 1963, when the partial nuclear test-ban treaty earlier discussed was signed on August 5.

PARTIAL TEST-BAN TREATY

Negotiations between the Soviet Union, the United States, and Great Britain had been renewed after the crisis, and the cessation of testing that had in fact followed the 1962 series of experiments was tacitly continued. The agreement, therefore, formalized rather than changed in any significant way the existing situation between the parties. By restriction to the three environments where international verification was not necessary, the thorny issue of inspection was avoided. The step could be taken, moreover, without disturbing the military balance in the eyes of either side.

The psychological significance of this first small step in the field of nuclear arms control lay in helping to reduce international tensions, as was emphasized by the great fanfare over formal signature of the treaty in Moscow.[46] The immediate practical effect lay in stopping further increase of atmospheric pollution by signatory states. More importantly, it was also expected to slow down nuclear proliferation by increasing the difficulty and the costs of achieving an independent nuclear capability. The

45. *Ibid.*, June 9, 1967.
46. The three Foreign Ministers signed in the presence of the Secretary-General, who was especially invited for the occasion, and the agreement was opened to adherence by all states, including Communist China. The United States made a point of explaining that common signature, by "an ingenious system of multiple depositaries," would not signify its recognition of the East German regime or of Peking, had it signed. See Schlesinger, *op. cit.*, p. 908.

greatest value of the treaty, it was hoped, would be in the precedent set, as "a shaft of light [cutting] into the darkness."[47]

To obtain Senate consent to ratification, however, the fears had to be overcome of those who failed to see the treaty as a step toward stabilizing the international power balance and who therefore opposed even this limited restriction on the arms race. The administration gave assurances that the agreement would not halt underground testing or other weapons development, nor affect the United States defense posture in any way.[48] It also announced arrangements for resumption of testing in the event of any Soviet violation, and perhaps overstressed that the limitations should be more useful to the United States than to the Soviet Union. The same arguments in reverse were used by Moscow—the last, especially, probably felt to be necessary in light of the Sino-Soviet split. Significantly, no official notice was taken by either side of these mutually exclusive claims.

Even this success was not complete, however. France, which had not participated in the ENDC because insistent on developing its own nuclear power, consistently refused to sign the treaty. The Communist Chinese also rejected it, as did Albania and Cuba.[49]

The Chinese argument, stripped of its vitriolic vocabulary, was essentially the inverse of that used by American opponents of the accord, leading to the ironic absurdity of American conservatives and Communist radicals joined in opposition.[50] The treaty was mere deception, according to Peking, and would only put off genuine disarmament. In a move reminiscent of Soviet ban-the-bomb campaigns before Moscow developed its own nuclear arsenal, Communist China formally called for a world conference for the "complete, thorough, total, and resolute prohibition or

47. Kennedy, statement Aug. 6, 1963, U.S. Department of State, *Bulletin*, Vol. 49 (1963), p. 234.

48. For the assurances and senatorial arguments, see ACDA, *Review of International Negotiations on the Cessation of Nuclear Weapons Tests: September 1962–September 1965* (May 1966), pp. 62–66.

49. In all, the treaty had been signed by 112 countries by mid-December 1967.

50. "I will vote against this treaty," declared Senator Goldwater, "because it preserves the enemy's advances in high-yield weaponry while freeing them to overtake our lead in low yield research. We pay a price; they do not." Senator Russell also felt that the Soviet Union signed the ban only to retain a nuclear lead, and denounced the treaty as "a step toward unilateral disarmament." Peking, in a 10,000-word statement, declared that: "The essence of the matter is that the United States is in the lead in the field of underground testing," which the treaty will help it to "maintain and improve." (*New York Times*, Sept. 18 and Sept. 20, 1963.) The Chinese statement was quoted in *The Washington Post*, Sept. 9, 1963.

destruction of nuclear weapons" by all states.[51] Pending such a total ban, the Chinese argued that they were the ones most in need of an "independent deterrent," which "must be" purely defensive for a socialist country and was essential to "prevent the imperialists from launching a nuclear war."[52]

As the Assembly began in September 1963, talks between the Soviet, United States, and British foreign ministers continued to reflect the improved atmosphere. But they took no "second step" in the direction of a full test ban. An effort to move toward that desired end was made by the nonaligned Eight in the ENDC, who drafted a mild resolution calling for early agreement to ban underground tests.[53] To obtain Soviet acceptance, it made no mention of on-site inspection, which made it unacceptable to the Western powers. Its reference to earlier resolutions mentioning the need for international control, on the other hand, displeased the Soviet Union. Still wearing their cooperative "new look," the Soviet and United States delegations jointly offered in its stead a deliberately noncontroversial resolution that avoided the touchy inspection issue and was confined to the formality of getting negotiations resumed. This annoyed some of the Eight, who felt the Disarmament Committee was being bypassed.

Nonetheless, the Assembly adopted essentially that innocuous draft in October—without a dissenting vote, although France abstained. It called on all states to adhere to the partial test-ban treaty and urged the ENDC to strive to "achieve the discontinuance of all test explosions of nuclear weapons for all time."[54]

INSPECTION IN ANTARCTICA

The inspection issue continued to prevent further progress in that direction. This situation may have influenced the United States announcement, in September 1963, of its intention to undertake a first inspection in Antarctica in the 1963–64 austral summer season (November-March), as provided for in the 1959 Antarctica Treaty.[55]

51. *New York Times*, Aug. 5, 1963.

52. Quoted in Joan Robinson, on Chinese attitudes as of the summer of 1963, in "The Chinese Point of View," *International Affairs*, Vol. 40 (April 1964), pp. 243–44.

53. See M. Samir Ahmed, *The Neutrals and the Test Ban: An Analysis of the Unaligned States' Efforts, 1962–1963* (Carnegie Endowment for International Peace, February 1967), Occasional Paper No. 4.

54. A/Res. 1910 (XVIII), Oct. 31, 1963.

55. U.S. Department of State Press Release 469, Sept. 13, 1963.

Article VII of the 1959 treaty had been hailed as a "first" in providing for a ban on all military measures and for mutual inspection on an optional basis, in order to verify compliance by the signatory governments, of each other's installations in the region.[56] Agreement to these provisions had been possible only because the continent is so remote, so inhospitable to regular settlement, and of so little security concern to any of the major powers. In no other region, therefore, have similar straightforward obligations been possible without—in the words of the United States original note on Antarctica—"being hampered or affected in any way by political considerations."[57]

Soviet acceptance of the inspection provision was technically the first exception to its persistent refusal to agree to any sort of international inspection involving itself. In the cooperative atmosphere following the partial test-ban treaty, and possibly also to help reassure senatorial objectors to that treaty,[58] Washington announced its intended undertaking. It also declared that its action was not "based on any anticipation that there have been any treaty violations by any signatory powers." The United States, the State Department informed the other treaty signatories, would "welcome inspection of its stations"; and was confident that the operation would "in fact reinforce the basis of mutual confidence that

56. The 12 nations participating in cooperative scientific research in the Antarctic during the International Geophysical Year agreed, at United States suggestion, to the accord as a means to "further the purposes and principles" of the United Nations Charter. Article I of the treaty declared unequivocally: "Antarctica shall be used for peaceful purposes only. There shall be prohibited, *inter alia*, any measures of a military nature, such as the establishment of military bases and fortifications, the carrying out of military maneuvers, as well as the testing of any type of weapons." Text in ACDA, *Documents on Disarmament, 1945–1959*, Vol. 2, pp. 1550–56. The U.S. note to the other participants is in *Ibid.*, pp. 1020–23. The states concerned were Argentina, Australia, Belgium, Chile, France, Japan, New Zealand, Norway, Union of South Africa, U.S.S.R., and Great Britain.

57. A Soviet delegate to the 1959 negotiating conference later wrote that the Soviet Union could agree to inspection in Antarctica, "where inspections cannot be used against national security." Quoted in James Simsarian, "Inspection Experience under the Antarctic Treaty and the International Atomic Energy Agency," *American Journal of International Law*, Vol. 60 (1966), p. 509.

58. At the time of ratification of the Antarctic Treaty, the State Department had given a pledge to the Senate Foreign Relations Committee to conduct such inspections, which it had not yet undertaken. Preparatory work had been slow, partly because of technical difficulties under the physical conditions of the region, and partly because of the sheer novelty of the operation.

prevails in Antarctica." It even offered logistical assistance to any government wishing to accept the invitation.[59]

Everything went smoothly in this international pioneering effort, possibly leaving some puzzlement but no hard feelings among personnel of the Soviet stations, who showed no interest in making any inspections themselves.[60] The United States inspected nine stations and made one overflight, covering operations by six governments. New Zealand, Australia, and Great Britain inspected United States stations as well as each other's. An additional inspection by Argentina of a United States installation was made in 1965.

The success of the effort, however, led to no direct follow-up in the field of arms control. At most, it may have facilitated agreement on a first joint international inspection in 1965 of Soviet and United States fishing vessels under the International Commission for the Northwest Atlantic Fisheries to verify compliance with catching and processing regulations.[61]

NUCLEAR WEAPONS IN OUTER SPACE

One other "first step" in line with Kennedy's letter to Khrushchev was also accomplished in the fall of 1963, after unsuccessful discussions in previous years. The two governments agreed on a joint statement of intent not to orbit weapons of mass destruction in outer space. This was then combined, in a General Assembly resolution, with a call for continued abstention in the future.[62] The resolution seems to have been achieved both because of its limited scope and because neither Washington nor

59. U.S. Department of State Press Release 469, Sept. 13, 1963. Some thought had been given to the possibility of joint inspections. But with a dozen countries involved, some with overlapping territorial claims and none with any experience in the field, the logistical and political problems of internationally organized inspections seemed too great to tackle all at once.

60. The U.S. decision to inspect had been made over strong objections by some government scientists, who feared that it might adversely affect the excellent international scientific cooperation then existing. No such untoward reaction occurred. In May 1966, the leader of the Soviet expedition in Antarctica (in a radio interview with Moscow) "emphasized that international agreements . . . were being successfully fulfilled, setting an example in fruitful, peaceful coexistence. All the scientific work . . . was international in character and the results of observations were available to the scientists of all countries." *Soviet News*, No. 5272, May 10, 1966, p. 4.

61. A team of three Russians and three Americans inspected seven Soviet and five U.S. vessels. *Washington Post*, May 24, 1965.

62. A/Res. 1884 (XVIII), Oct. 17, 1963.

Moscow was required to stop any existing activity. Moreover, it did not take treaty form, apparently because the administration felt that the Senate was not prepared to accept another treaty (after the test-ban) without verification arrangements.[63]

Ambassador Stevenson pointed out, in Committee I of the Assembly, that the action confirmed a policy already adopted by both countries, giving "international recognition that the arms race . . . must not be extended into this new environment."[64] The reasoning behind the American (and presumably also the Soviet) policy was that, although either country could place thermonuclear weapons in orbit, such action would not be "a rational military strategy for either side for the foreseeable future." It would be irrational because it is cheaper, easier, and at least equally accurate to launch such weapons from existing earth stations. However, this technological situation could change, as Stevenson also noted, and "if events as yet unforeseen [should] suggest the need for a further look at this matter, we would acquaint the United Nations with such events."[65]

Although the hoped-for "second steps" of a formal agreement on the subject did not soon materialize after 1963, in May 1966 President Johnson proposed a treaty "to insure that explorations of the moon and other celestial bodies will be for peaceful purposes only," and that no country should be "permitted to advance a claim of sovereignty." Most importantly, perhaps, he also proposed to prohibit the stationing of "weapons of mass destruction on a celestial body," and to guarantee access by each party to installations of the other—provisions reminiscent of the Antarctic Treaty.[66] Within a month, the Soviet Union made a parallel proposal of its own, similar to both the Antarctic Treaty and the Johnson proposal. A treaty was negotiated on these lines during the following weeks in the Outer Space Committee at Geneva and completed at the twenty-first Assembly in New York.[67] The final text was unanimously "commended"

63. Alton Frye, " 'Gobble'uns' and Foreign Policy: A Review," *Conflict Resolution*, Vol. 8 (September 1964), p. 319.

64. U.S. Department of State, *Bulletin*, Vol. 49 (1963), p. 753.

65. The Deputy Secretary of Defense, quoted in *Ibid*.

66. U.S. Department of State, *Bulletin*, Vol. 54 (1966), pp. 900–01.

67. A/Res. 2222 (XXI), Dec. 19, 1966. On its negotiation and terms, see Goldberg's statement before the Senate Foreign Relations Committee, March 7, 1967. United States Mission to the United Nations, Press Release 23, March 7, 1967. Difficulties of translating some technical terms into Chinese delayed official signature of the treaty for a month. The Mission is hereinafter cited as USUN.

by that body and opened for signature by all states. The Assembly also expressed its hope for "the widest possible adherence." The United States ratified the accord in April 1967, the Soviet Union in May.

Almost as much praise was heaped on this accomplishment as had been bestowed on the partial test-ban treaty in 1963. President Johnson called it "the most important arms control development since" that earlier treaty;[68] but like it, the new one promised no direct international control of nuclear proliferation and no degree of disarmament. Moreover, as the Secretary-General noted "with regret . . . the door is not yet barred against military activities in space. The crux of the difficulty is that space activity is already part of the arms race, a fact which we have to reckon with. . . ."[69] What he was referring to, of course, were the Soviet and American efforts to achieve manned space vehicles. In this country, they are headed by the $1.5 billion Air Force program for developing a Manned Orbiting Laboratory (MOL).

1964: No Collateral "Second Steps"

In January 1964, President Johnson sent a message to the resuming ENDC session, praying that future generations would mark the year "as the one when the world turned for all time away from the horrors of war and constructed new bulwarks of peace."[70] Such hopes were in vain, although 1964 did prove to be "the year of the mutual example"[71]—but the examples were only in the field of minor measures collateral to an arms control program.

In January, both the President and Khrushchev announced modest reductions in their respective military budgets. On a small scale, such budgetary restrictions do not effect any significant diminution of the enormous American and Soviet arms supply and do not raise the issue of verification. Any important moves in the direction of budgetary controls, at whatever level, would, on the other hand, raise both the verification issue and that of maintaining the balance between the Soviet Union and

68. *New York Times*, Dec. 8, 1966.

69. Press release, GA/3312, Dec. 20, 1966, p. 2.

70. Text of message of Jan. 22, 1964 in Arms Control and Disarmament Agency, *Agenda Item-Peace*, Publication 23 (July 1964).

71. Arthur H. Dean, "The War on Weapons," *Saturday Review*, March 19, 1966, p. 23.

the United States, with all their attendant difficulties. There is, therefore, little possibility such moves will be made in the near future.

The President also called on the ENDC to undertake a verified agreement to halt all production of fissionable materials. This supplemented a step taken unilaterally in 1964. By then Uranium 235 was in surplus production in the United States and plutonium potentially so, and President Johnson had ordered a 25 percent reduction in enriched uranium production and the closing of several plutonium production centers.[72] In February, the United States took the initiative in placing one of the large reactors it was shutting down under the control of the International Atomic Energy Agency (IAEA).[73] The Soviet Union did not follow suit in this last respect, nor did it respond to the ENDC proposal involving international inspection. But in April, simultaneous announcements were made in Washington and Moscow of further intended national cutbacks in weapons-material production over the next few years.[74] No suggestion of international inspection was included.

Other United States proposals at Geneva in the direction of possible "second steps" were for a verified freeze on vehicles to carry nuclear weapons, which would hinder the increase in strategic armaments; and for a verified "bonfire" of certain obsolete bombers by the nuclear states, which would eliminate their possible acquisition by smaller states that now receive such second-hand arms.[75] International verification in the latter case, at least of actual destruction publicly announced, it was thought might be easier to agree to than the proposed "freeze." Moreover, since the B–47 and TU–16 bombers had similar strategic roles and

72. Great Britain shortly followed suit, announcing it had sufficient fissionable material for all foreseeable requirements.

73. IAEA initially was authorized to inspect and control only small reactors in which U–235 produces only neutrons for research. In 1963, with Soviet support, the IAEA Conference authorized the agency to extend its safeguards to large reactors put under its supervision by participating nations.

74. The independent announcements resulted from confidential correspondence between Khrushchev and Johnson. Dean, *Test Ban and Disarmament*, p. 112.

75. The bonfire idea was first proposed informally by the United States in 1963. It was then raised in another version in 1964 at Geneva by the Soviet Union, which proposed the destruction of all bombing planes as obsolete in the missile age. This all-or-nothing response seemed more a return to earlier GCD extravagances than a serious offer, especially as its acceptance would presumably increase the Soviet disadvantage in missiles.

the two governments possessed "roughly comparable numbers" of them, the United States delegate pointed out, destruction in equal numbers would not alter significantly the military balance between the superpowers. It would thus avoid difficulties over the fifth principle, which declares that balance must be maintained.[76]

Another type of collateral measure that the United States sought to promote, both before and after 1964, was the possibility of reducing the fear of surprise attack through the stationing of observers on both sides of the Iron Curtain in Europe (or farther afield). The Soviet Union has insisted, however, that such an accord must be accompanied by the withdrawal of troops from foreign countries, the dismantling of foreign bases, and the creation of appropriate denuclearized zones. These moves have been resisted in turn by the Western powers, as seeking to "bring about the deployment of forces in a manner which would obviously benefit the Soviet Union" and would therefore violate principle 5.[77] The particular proposals and objections on both sides are equally applicable to many other phases of the arms-control negotiations. They also illustrate the point made by Hedley Bull:

In all serious arms control negotiations, the proposals of any power express a closely reasoned (though not necessarily correct) estimate of its military interests. Thus . . . the United States, decisively inferior in military intelligence, gives priority to the idea of inspection; the Soviet Union, suffering from her encirclement by the Western system of alliances, gives priority to the abolition of foreign military bases.[78]

Nineteen-sixty-four had thus shown no visible progress either in the ENDC or by way of mutual example, when Khrushchev was deposed in October, which increased the uncertainty of future Soviet attitudes, and Peking exploded its first "nuclear device." The experiment had been anticipated, and from the viewpoint of the United States, in any event, one bomb did not a weapons system make.[79] Nonetheless, the political

76. Statement by Ambassador William C. Foster, Jan. 31, 1964, in U.N. Doc. DC/214/Add. 1, pp. 9–11.

77. Ambassador Foster, U.N. Doc. DC/PV. 82, May 17, 1965, p. 26.

78. Hedley Bull, *The Control of the Arms Race*, Institute for Strategic Studies (Praeger, 1961), p. 68.

79. For a survey of the initial official and unofficial reactions to the Chinese achievement, see Ralph L. Powell, "China's Bomb: Exploitation and Reaction," *Foreign Affairs*, Vol. 43 (July 1965), pp. 616–25. The author finds the political and psychological "impact" was "less than had been expected" without explaining what had been expected.

fallout from the explosion was considerable. In particular, it added to other elements in the world picture, especially to the increasing conflict in southeast Asia, that promised to make arms-control measures even more difficult to achieve.

The combination of these political hazards to further progress, and the technical hazards involved in the related principles of verification and the maintenance of the military balance (principles 6 and 5 of the 1961 agreement), almost guaranteed for the foreseeable future the failure of serious efforts at control of either nuclear or conventional arms by the superpowers. This conclusion applies, whether the measures in question are of a collateral nature or deal with more central issues in the proposals for GCD—as a practical matter, with the proposals for Stage I in either disarmament plan.

The Verification Issue

Over the years, every proposed technical measure of arms control or reduction has been blocked, sooner rather than later, by the problem of verification, which the Soviet Union has not opposed in principle, but denied in practice. What seems a reasonable precaution to Americans as well as the *sine qua non* for any arms control or reduction agreements—that the fulfillment of any undertaking should be verified by inspection—has been consistently resisted by Soviet officials as an attack in disguise on the heart of their closed system. Moscow declares, for example, that it will allow inspection of actual measures of *disarmament*, but rejects the verification of declarations concerning retained arms. Khrushchev once justified the position in these terms: "Control over remaining weapons is bound to be reconnaissance, an attempt to ascertain whether the balance of forces has changed as a result of the cut in armaments, and whether it is not possible to take advantage of a change to launch an attack. No self-respecting country can accept such control."[80]

Moreover, the precise Soviet meaning of permissible inspection under its own proposals has never been spelled out in terms of a detailed system of verification. The argument, as a result, has been more a battle of slogans than of substance. On the substantive side, the complexity of the technical

80. Quoted in ACDA, *Documents on Disarmament,* 1962, Vol. 2, p. 643.

problem necessitates such an intrusive inspection system that it becomes unacceptable as between suspicious adversaries.[81]

Since this perennial issue is still central to the opposing Soviet and Western positions on disarmament proposals, no significant agreement on specific weapons controls or reductions can be anticipated in the near future. It is therefore unnecessary, for purposes of this study, to consider further the technical military details of the two major plans for GCD. In the past few years, however, a few faltering steps have been taken that may hold the promise of ameliorating the inspection and control problem itself.

A COMPLETE TEST BAN?

In the first place, technological progress has reduced in limited respects the size of the problem, by making some verification possible without formal inspection. The partial test-ban treaty first reflected this situation, when the main adversaries became satisfied that they could detect and verify any violation of the ban in the three environments covered. Since 1963, intensive scientific research has considerably improved United States capacity to differentiate other underground explosions from earthquakes.

On the ground that such advances had already made some progress possible, the extension of the test ban to underground tests above a certain kiloton range (4.7 is usually proposed for this "threshold" approach) was suggested by Brazil in the ENDC meetings of 1964. The idea would be to extend the ban progressively as further scientific progress is made.[82] The proposal was supported by other neutrals at Geneva. Some American

81. The problem has been succinctly described as follows:

"The nature of the inspection mechanism depends upon what is being inspected. A good model in one instance might be a poor one in another. Nor can the extent and depth of inspection be necessarily correlated with the gravity of the threat posed by a particular object.

"Even an inspection system that is highly satisfactory when it is devised is unlikely to remain so. There is a never-ending race between the perfecting of detection and anti-detection devices. . . . Furthermore, the objects covered by an inspection agreement may become more or less central to national security. . . .

". . . An inspection net adequate to determine that there were no hidden stockpiles or armaments and that materials used for peaceful purposes were not being diverted to weapons manufacture, would require an invasion of sovereignty at almost every point in society. In the current climate of distrust this appears unthinkable." Winslow, ed., in Finkelstein, *op. cit.*, p. 2. See also, Dean, *Test Ban and Disarmament*, Chap. 3.

82. See ACDA, *Review of International Negotiations on the Cessation of Nuclear Weapons Tests: September 1962–September 1965*, Publication 32 (May 1966), pp. 80–83.

scientists went even further, arguing that little was to be gained by underground testing so that a comprehensive treaty might be risked without provision for on-site inspections.[83]

In 1965, Senator Robert F. Kennedy suggested that the ban could be extended to "certain types" of underground tests "without jeopardizing our security." But even in 1967, United States officials were still unwilling to forgo all on-site inspections.[84] Formally, their attitude rests on still-existing scientific limitations, but it is reinforced by political caution. Senator Frank Church, after a visit to the ENDC session in May 1966, made the latter point explicit:

As for a comprehensive test-ban treaty, it seemed obvious to me that Europeans are not sufficiently aware of the political problems that would arise in the United States if the Senate were asked to ratify a comprehensive test-ban treaty which did not include the right to on-site inspection. Consequently, our reluctance to drop our insistence on inspection—that is, our refusal, as they see it, to accept a small risk for large political gains—is considered in some quarters to be an indication of the dominance of military influence over U.S. policy. This is all the more regrettable because, to many at Geneva, a comprehensive test ban agreement is considered to be the most effective nonproliferation measure, for nations are apparently unable, at present, to develop nuclear weapons without testing them.[85]

Although the Soviet Government at one time declared itself willing to permit a few such inspections annually, it later withdrew the offer. A technological breakthrough may yet be made in this field, however, that could eliminate the need for ground inspection altogether.[86] On the other

83. J. B. Wiesner and Herbert York, "National Security and the Nuclear Test Ban," *Scientific American* (October 1964), pp. 27–35. See also recommendation of the National Citizens' Commission [International Cooperation Year], "Report of the Committee on Arms Control and Disarmament" (Dr. Wiesner, Chairman), White House Conference on International Cooperation, November 1965 (UNA reprint), p. 5: "A comprehensive nuclear test ban treaty adequately verified, perhaps utilizing recent improvements in national detection systems making it possible to rely on challenge inspections or to otherwise bridge the gap in acceptable numbers of on-site inspections that appeared to prevent agreement in 1963."

84. Address by Kennedy, in *New York Times*, June 24, 1965. See Foster statement in Committee I, Nov. 22, 1966, reiterating this position. USUN Press Release 4982, Nov. 22, 1966.

85. Frank Church, *Europe Today, Report to the Senate Foreign Relations Committee on a Study Mission to Brussels, Paris, London, Bonn, Berlin, and the Eighteen-Nations Disarmament Conference at Geneva*, 89 Cong. 2 sess. (May 1966), p. 5.

86. ACDA commented hopefully at the start of 1966: "Recent progress in seismology, together with work done in coordination with the Department of Defense on inspection techniques, may introduce a new flexibility into the presently stalemated negotiations on a comprehensive test ban treaty." *Fifth Annual Report*, p. 13.

hand, in the course of 1966, both Moscow and Washington stepped up their underground testing on a larger scale than ever, presumably aiming to develop warheads for antimissile missiles,[87] and certainly indicating no military interest in a complete test ban for the time being. In June 1967, in fact, the two powers, although still unable to agree on terms of a nonproliferation accord, joined in rejecting an Indian suggestion at Geneva that the ENDC devote one meeting weekly to the question of underground tests.[88]

EXTENSION OF INTERNATIONAL ATOMIC ENERGY AGENCY CONTROLS?

In the second place, although there was no direct follow-up to the initial Antarctic inspection, some advances have been made in the area of safeguards against the diversion to military purposes of nuclear facilities and materials intended for peaceful uses. The United States originally hoped that its bilateral safeguards procedure would be replaced by an international system under IAEA responsibility; but this has not yet occurred on a significant scale.[89] Development of international controls has been primarily through a system of bilateral agreements between the few exporters of nuclear reactors and fissile material (the United States, the Soviet Union, Great Britain, France, and Canada) and their customers. Initially, this was inevitable, since IAEA was not even operating until 1956 and required time to find its footing. Then various recipients—such as India and the United States allies in the European Atomic Energy Community (Euratom)—objected to being "discriminated against" by subjection to international inspection, while the nuclear powers themselves were not so inspected.

With nuclear power rapidly attaining competitive economic status, and more countries approaching the point of producing enough by-product plutonium from nuclear power reactors to sustain weapons programs, the concern for safeguards increased. In 1963, as already noted, both the United States and the Soviet Union supported an extension of authority for the IAEA, so that its safeguards could be applied to large reactors. In 1964, Washington began a more active policy of urging countries receiving

87. See, for example, Finney dispatch, *New York Times*, Dec. 21, 1966 p. 16.
88. *Ibid.*, June 7, 1967.
89. For background, see John A. Hall, "Atoms for Peace or War," *Foreign Affairs*, Vol. 43 (July 1965), pp. 602–16.

its assistance in this field to submit the arrangements to IAEA safeguards, but it met considerable resistance.[90]

In the spring of 1965, the United States sought to persuade its Western allies to join in an agreement that, in all foreign sales of reactors and fuels, they would require inspection by the IAEA.[91] In September, an expanded and improved system of IAEA safeguards was approved by the agency's general conference. But voluntary submission to these international controls is still resisted by national governments—to such an extent that the United States originally omitted a binding obligation to accept the IAEA safeguards from its "Draft Treaty to Prevent the Spread of Nuclear Weapons."[92]

This failure disturbed members of the Joint Congressional Committee on Atomic Energy, which must pass on United States bilateral agreements involving the transfer of atomic materials for peaceful use and which has become increasingly insistent on the application of international controls. In 1966, agreements with both Great Britain and France, among others, came up for renewal. The administration found them still resistant to its proposal to shift from bilateral to IAEA or Euratom controls in the new arrangements.[93] In February, the IAEA agreed on procedures for inspecting plutonium reprocessing plants (in addition to reactors); and in April, Washington invited the agency to inspect such a plant in New York State. At Geneva, the director of ACDA said the offer would contribute to the "development of safeguard procedures and for the training of IAEA inspectors."[94]

90. See *Ibid.*, pp. 611, 613, and Simsarian, *op. cit.*, pp. 503, 506.

91. In June, Canada announced new restrictions on all export sales of uranium, requiring verification and control of its use for peaceful purposes; and Great Britain put its own largest nuclear power plant under IAEA inspection. *New York Times*, June 4 and 17, 1965.

92. The problem of nuclear proliferation is considered below. The U.S. delegate told the ENDC, when presenting the Draft Treaty (Aug. 17, 1965): "We have drafted the provision [Article III] in its present form to take account of the views of all countries, including those which are not prepared at this time to commit themselves to accept IAEA safeguards in all applicable circumstances." Quoted in ACDA, *To Prevent the Spread of Nuclear Weapons*, Publication 26 (September 1965), p. 5. Text of Draft Treaty, *Ibid.*, pp. 14–16.

93. See, for example, "Allies Resist U.S. on Atom Controls," *New York Times*, Jan. 16, 1966; also, Jo Pomerance, *Halting the Spread of Nuclear Weapons* (Committee for World Development and World Disarmament, 1966), p. 4.

94. Quoted in *Washington Post*, April 29, 1966. The major nuclear powers and India alone possess such plants, but plans were under way for others in Japan, Italy, West Germany, and Pakistan.

DEVELOPING CONTROL TECHNIQUES

The difficulty of moving toward the desired objective of wider and more thorough controls on the peaceful uses of atomic energy, even among countries allied with the United States,[95] serves mainly to underscore how much greater are the practical and political difficulties hampering agreement on inspection and verification directly related to arms control measures. Even if agreement were reached with the Soviet Union to inspect some significant disarmament undertaking, it is doubtful that personnel of any international agency would be competent, without considerably more preparation, to handle the technical requirements, let alone to satisfy the chief powers on both sides that they could be trusted politically. In this sense, had Castro concurred in the Soviet proposal for United Nations verification of its weapons removals from Cuba in 1962, the undertaking might well have created as many problems as it would theoretically have solved.[96]

Some mixture of international machinery combined with reciprocal "adversary" inspection—that is, direct participation by the major powers concerned in order to satisfy themselves of compliance with important commitments—will probably have to be developed if any significant progress is to be made in this field. Experience has already been gained, in military fields other than that of armaments regulation, with various types of international observation and control machinery,[97] which might prove

95. It was reported that the question of international controls had also become an issue in the negotiations for "a record-breaking sale" of plutonium for peaceful development by the United States to the European Atomic Energy Community: "Euratom fears that the United States will attempt to use the sale as a lever to get European acceptance of controls by the IAEA—a step thus far resisted by the European organization." *New York Times*, May 9, 1966.

96. Khrushchev's commitment was to withdraw his missiles from Cuba and to permit United Nations inspection of the island to confirm the withdrawal. In appearance, Castro was able to oppose the inspection of the missile sites, although not the withdrawal of weapons; but it seems unlikely that the little dictator compelled the two great powers to abandon against their will this part of the initial agreement. It would not have been too difficult for them to utilize the machinery of the Security Council, under Article 41 or 34, to impose their joint will with all the sanction of international law. The fact that the U.S. did not insist on so verifying the removal of the weapons probably meant that it could satisfy itself by other methods of their withdrawal. Meanwhile, nonfulfillment of the inspection undertaking allows the U.S. to hold in suspense its contingent commitment not to invade Cuba. The Soviet Union certainly had no real interest in extending international authority in this field, as it has shown by its general opposition to inspection proposals.

97. See Chap. 6 below.

useful if and when the nuclear powers agree to promote the necessary specialized training in international arms-control activities.

Restraints on Nuclear Proliferation

Neither a complete test ban nor the significant extension of controls over the peaceful uses of atomic energy would greatly advance the objective of bringing nuclear arms directly under international control; but both, if achieved, would prevent "self-help" development of nuclear arms production by signatory governments not already engaged in manufacturing them. The measures would probably not be accepted by, and therefore would not slow down the ability of, France and Communist China to improve their present status as second-rate nuclear powers—that is, having nuclear capacity, but not yet possessing operational nuclear weapons systems. Neither measure, however, would affect the transfer of such weapons, or of the know-how to manufacture them, from one of the present members of the "nuclear club" to other governments.

Even finding successful methods to ban the further proliferation of nuclear weapons would not in itself mean further control over existing weapons, or, necessarily, the cessation of further production by present powers, or any reduction in the existing supply that now sustains the delicate balance of terror. Faced with the impossibility of achieving more substantive arms control measures, and alarmed by the potential threats inherent in further spread of nuclear weapons, however, both the superpowers and many other states have given increasing attention in the last few years to antiproliferation measures, including the complete test ban. The uncertainties implicit in the rapidly expanding number of countries with the near capability of producing nuclear weapons are so great that the proliferation issue has become the center of current negotiating efforts. When combined with new technological possibilities in the field of antiballistic missile (ABM) systems, ". . . the spread of nuclear weapons has already threatened to spark a second problem by encouraging one or both of the major nuclear powers to seek protection from less powerful nuclear states in antiballistic-missile systems quite capable of catalyzing a new round of offensive weapons. . . . [A] U.S. or Soviet ABM system would almost certainly induce both superpowers to step up their strategic weapon programs in an effort to ensure their respective 'deterrent' capabilities."[98]

98. "Report of the Committee on Arms Control and Disarmament," *op cit.*, pp. 9, 16.

The renewal of testing in 1961, after a three year moratorium, revived concern with nuclear prohibitions. In the General Assembly, Ireland took the lead in proposing a resolution to prevent further nuclear dissemination. Its key elements have since been the basis of all negotiations to that end: (1) all states, particularly the nuclear powers, would undertake to refrain from giving control of nuclear weapons or transmitting necessary information for their manufacture to states not possessing such weapons; (2) while the latter would undertake not to manufacture or otherwise acquire control of the weapons.[99]

NUCLEAR WEAPONS AND THE SUPERPOWERS

The Soviet Union and United States draft plans for GCD, in 1962, both contained provisions against transfer or acquisition of nuclear weapons. No progress having been made on terms for the general treaty, in 1965 both powers submitted specialized draft treaties to prevent proliferation—spurred no doubt by the first Chinese nuclear explosion of October 1964.[100] Considerable progress on this narrower accord, after a slow start, was made during 1966 in negotiations between the Soviet Union and the United States—but final success continued to be thwarted by the close relationship of an agreement to the broad political issues of NATO and Germany, which have always divided the communist-noncommunist alliances in Europe.

Soviet policy makers remain obsessed by fear that West Germany may become a nuclear power through acquisition from the United States or through getting "a finger on the trigger" of American arms stationed in the area. In 1957, the Rapacki Plan (named for the Polish Foreign Minister who submitted it) proposed to avoid either possibility by prohibiting such nuclear weapons in a nuclear-free zone covering the two Germanies, Poland, and Czechoslovakia.[101] In 1959, the Soviet Union suggested similar bans on atomic weapons in a Balkan-Adriatic and a Baltic-Scandinavian zone.[102] As explained by the Soviet Union in a memorandum to the United Nations: "In the view of the Soviet Government, the need to establish denuclearized zones is particularly acute and urgent in those regions of the world where substantial quantities of nuclear weapons are

99. A/Res. 1665 (XVI), Dec. 4, 1961.
100. Text of U.S. proposal is in ACDA, *To Prevent the Spread of Nuclear Weapons*, pp. 14–16.
101. For proposal, see ACDA, *Documents on Disarmament, 1945–1959*, Vol. 2, pp. 944–48.
102. See *Ibid.*, pp. 1423–26, 1434–39.

concentrated and there is great danger of the outbreak of nuclear conflict."[103] Reasonable as that argument might seem in the abstract, from the point of view of Washington such weapons are essential to Western defense against communist nuclear threats. As the Department of State replied, to another Soviet denuclearizing proposal in 1963 (to cover the Mediterranean area where Polaris submarines had been introduced), the United States "was compelled to strengthen the security of its Allies in the Mediterranean only after their security had been directly threatened by the Soviet Union's deployment of an extensive array of missiles[104] aimed at countries in the area...."

In the disarmament negotiations, the West has claimed that such nuclear-weapon bans would upset the existing balance of power to its disadvantage (disarmament principle 5), by taking "certain weapons away from certain states under piecemeal arrangements in the absence of general disarmament."[105] More specifically, and more frankly, it has claimed that the Rapacki Plan (and a subsequent version, the Gomulka Plan)[106] would effectively eliminate United States tactical nuclear strength from Europe, "while not affecting those nuclear weapons or missiles inside the U.S.S.R. still fairly close to [and aimed at] NATO countries."[107] The Western conclusion, therefore, has been that denuclearization should not be attempted in regions of confrontation between the great powers, where nuclear weapons are already a vital part of the military balance that is not to be disturbed by the process of arms reduction.

In itself, objection to the nuclear-free-zones approach need not have hampered agreement on halting further proliferation. But the Central European situation, which initially brought forth the Rapacki proposal, also became the main stumbling block to a nonproliferation treaty through the related issue raised by United States proposals for a multilateral nuclear force (MLF) within NATO.[108] This sought to give West Germany a means of participation in NATO's nuclear defense system, through "mixed manning" of naval vessels; but without allowing it any control over the weapons, which would remain in American hands. The

103. Memorandum of Dec. 7, 1964, U.N. Doc. A/5827, p. 5. Resubmitted on April 28, 1965, as U.N. Doc. DC/213/Add. 2.

104. U.S. Department of State *Bulletin*, Vol. 49 (1963), p. 83.

105. The Turkish delegate in the United Nations, quoted in *United Nations Review* (December 1962), p. 50.

106. The Gomulka Plan, also named for its Polish sponsor, would have frozen, rather than eliminated, such weapons in Central Europe.

107. Dean, *Test Ban and Disarmament*, p. 39.

108. Also by a later British version, called the Atlantic Nuclear Force (ANF).

Soviet Union opposed the whole concept of the multilateral force as violently as it opposed the possibility of any extension to Germany of the "double-key" system (whereby nuclear weapons, stationed in other NATO countries, can be fired only with the joint consent of the United States and the national government). Moscow insisted that the MLF proposal meant Bonn would gain control through access to nuclear weapons. Washington's response was that, on the contrary, the plan would prevent the weapons from passing into the "national control" of any state not already possessing them and thus would actually restrict nuclear spread.[109] Moscow remained adamant, however, that the MLF must be abandoned before any nonproliferation agreement could be considered. The 1964 session of the ENDC consequently made no progress on this issue or on any other "measures aimed at the lessening of international tension."[110]

The NATO allies (except for West Germany) had given only lukewarm support to the MLF proposal, especially as it became apparent that control of the weapons would in fact remain with Washington.[111] By 1965, with external pressures for a nondissemination accord mounting, especially as an increasing number of states reached the point of near-nuclear capacity, the administration began to let MLF quietly but not officially recede.[112] Then in September, as noted, the United States produced its draft treaty on nonproliferation. Its provision against transfer was rejected again by the Soviet Union, in spite of its careful wording:

1. Each of the nuclear States Party to this Treaty undertakes not to transfer any nuclear weapons into the national control of any nonnuclear State, either directly or indirectly through a military alliance; and each undertakes not to take any other action which would cause an increase in the total number of States and other Organizations having independent power to use nuclear weapons.[113]

109. The United States' ultimate control was to be exercised through a "governing body on which all members would be represented in accordance with control arrangements consistent with principles of non-dissemination." U.S. Department of State Press Release 382, Aug. 28, 1964. See also, statement of Feb. 6, 1964 in U.S. Department of State, *Bulletin*, Vol. 50 (1964), p. 378.

110. *Report of the Conference of the Eighteen-Nation Committee on Disarmament*, U.N. Doc. A/5731, Sept. 22, 1964, p. 5.

111. Dean, *Test Ban and Disarmament*, pp. 131–33.

112. This was managed over a period of time by letting the initiative for further development of a MLF go to the European members of NATO, who have not produced an alternative proposal. For a picturesque account of "How Johnson Judo Put MLF Issue in Its Place," see Philip Geyelin in the *Washington Post*, June 5, 1966, p. E–5.

113. Text in ACDA, *To Prevent the Spread of Nuclear Weapons*, pp. 14–16.

At the General Assembly, shortly afterwards, the Soviet Union produced its own draft treaty. It would have made German participation impossible, not only in an MLF, but even in anything like the alternative arrangements then being considered by the West for a consultative planning group.

In March 1966, at the ENDC, the United States amended its definition of "control" in the draft treaty, to make explicit its intention to maintain a veto over the use of its nuclear weapons.[114] The Soviet Union was not impressed. In May, the session adjourned (again, with nothing to show for its efforts) just as the Chinese exploded their third nuclear device. Nevertheless, by mid-1966, it seemed that the United States and the Soviet Union might be coming within sight of agreement.

Other events, however, had not been suspended during this period of stalemate over the significance of MLF for nuclear proliferation, including the Chinese achievements and the escalating conflict in southeast Asia. One result of these international developments was a growing hesitation by some of the nonnuclear powers, especially several with the capability of producing nuclear weapons themselves, to accept a simple nondissemination agreement without some accompanying steps by the superpowers to halt the arms race. This led one observer to point out:

If these [demands of the nonnuclear powers] are meant at all seriously, they offer a gloomy prospect for the future. It does not seem too much to say that a pointless and irrelevant Soviet-American debate about multilateral forces has given such nonnuclear powers as India the opportunity to develop a strong diplomatic position from which to resist formal nonnuclear status.[115]

NUCLEAR WEAPONS AND NEAR-NUCLEAR POWERS

It is therefore a critical question how much longer such potential nuclear powers as India, Japan, Sweden, and Israel may be willing to accept the kind of simple and complete ban embodied in the Irish Resolu-

---

114. ENDC/PV.250 (March 1966), p. 11. Art IV (c) was amended to read: " 'Control' means right or ability to fire nuclear weapons without the concurrent decision of an existing nuclear-weapon state." Another amendment had been to alter the terms "nuclear" and "nonnuclear" states to read: "nuclear-weapon" and "non-nuclear weapon" states. The U.S. delegate referred to states with "important programs for peaceful uses of nuclear energy," which had "wisely chosen to refrain from manufacturing or acquiring nuclear weapons." The Indian delegate had evidently first used the new terms informally. *Ibid.*, pp. 12–13.

115. Leonard Beaton, *Must the Bomb Spread?* Institute for Strategic Studies (Penguin Books, 1966), p. 133.

tion, which would make it difficult to "go nuclear" in future. As the Canadian Foreign Secretary had already pointed out, in 1965:

[T]here has been a growing awareness that it may not be practicable to try to prevent the spread of nuclear weapons through the agency of a nonacquisition agreement in those areas of the world where nonnuclear states are apprehensive of the aims of a neighboring nuclear—or potential nuclear—power.

Accordingly, it may be necessary first—or simultaneously—to guarantee the security of such . . . states, at least against nuclear attack by the nuclear state concerned, if they are to be expected to forego the option of becoming nuclear powers. Collective security arrangements have already provided in large measure a guarantee of this nature for allies of the great nuclear powers. The nonaligned and neutral nations do not enjoy similar guarantees, and it is within their ranks that the spread of nuclear weapons is more likely to take place within the next decade.[116]

At the time of the first Chinese explosion (October 1964), President Johnson had declared that United States support would be available against any "threat of nuclear blackmail," to nations not seeking "national nuclear weapons."[117] The nonaligned states, however, would prefer a multilateral guarantee involving all the nuclear powers; a guarantee by only one raises obvious difficulties, putting the nonallied in the position of receiving protection in the same way as the allied. A joint Soviet-United States guarantee, on the other hand, while the cold war remains chilly and the Vietnam situation continues to escalate, must seem tenuous reassurance at best to a country like India. Although the combined strength of the two giants could provide theoretical protection against blackmail by other nuclear powers of nonnuclear governments, there is no sign as yet of the superpowers being either willing or able to "put their common interest ahead of their traditional rivalries and loyalties."[118]

In the general debate at the nineteenth General Assembly, Ireland proposed a treaty of guarantee ratified by as many nuclear powers as possible; while India thought a "joint declaration by all major nuclear powers might act as a disincentive to nonnuclear countries."[119] Another approach

116. Paul Martin, address of May 3, 1965, in Canadian Department of External Affairs, *Canadian Weekly Bulletin*, Vol. 20, May 5, 1965, p. 5.

117. U.S. Department of State, *Bulletin*, Vol. 51 (1964), p. 613.

118. Beaton, *op. cit.*, p. 131. See, for example, a report from India that Moscow declined to join in a guarantee against China because that would put an end to what little relations still exist with Peking. Warren Unna dispatch, *Washington Post*, May 13, 1966.

119. Quoted in Richard N. Swift, ed., *Annual Review of United Nations Affairs*, 1964–1965 (Oceana, 1966), p. 24.

suggested has been that the United Nations might call on the nuclear powers to guarantee a provision, in the hoped-for nondissemination treaty, that the nuclear states would protect all signatories against attack. But as Kenneth Younger has pointed out:

Guarantees of this kind cannot be usefully generalised. If they were, they would add nothing to the existing general obligations which members of the United Nations have to one another. Since they can only be given by the nuclear powers, it would be necessary for these to be ready to negotiate from time to time with any government requiring protection as the price of abstaining from a nuclear arms program of its own.

If they were required to act together as a consortium in all cases, the system would inevitably break down, if indeed it ever got under way. For it would be subject to all the disabilities which have already made it impossible for the Security Council to offer adequate protection to all members of the United Nations.[120]

When the nineteenth Assembly could not continue disarmament discussions in the First Committee because of the Article 19 crisis, the Disarmament Commission[121] was called into session on Soviet initiative. There, in May 1965, India declared that the guarantee desired by the nonaligned states should be within a United Nations framework in spite of the disadvantage just noted.[122] That may have indicated in fact a loss of interest by India in the basic policy of accepting protection from nuclear governments and a growing concern to "maintain the options" for itself on going nuclear. India, moreover, was not the only unaligned delegation at the meeting to declare that the nuclear giants themselves would have to take firmer steps toward a full test ban and some reduction in their own nuclear arsenals, at least to the extent of a freeze on further production and means of delivery and a cut in stockpiles.[123]

This "package" approach, applying to partial measures the same principle of balance that has been so deadly in connection with GCD negotiations, was carried over to the next ENDC session in the fall of 1965, as noted earlier. When the superpowers once again failed to make any progress in their own negotiations toward a nonproliferation accord, the Eight

120. "The Spectre of Nuclear Proliferation," *International Affairs*, Vol. 42 (January 1966), p. 18.

121. The commission includes all U.N. Members. It had not met since 1960.

122. Disarmament Commission statement May 4, 1965, *New York Times*, May 5, 1965.

123. See James L. Bodnar, *Report on the Debate in the U.N. Disarmament Commission, April 21–June 16, 1965*, pp. 12–21, for further discussion of the "package" approach at that meeting.

issued a "Joint Memorandum on Non-proliferation of Nuclear Weapons." Placing their "basic approach" on record, they declared:

A treaty on non-proliferation of nuclear weapons is not an end in itself but only a means to an end. That end is the achievement of General and Complete Disarmament, and, more particularly, nuclear disarmament. The eight delegations are convinced that measures to prohibit the spread of nuclear weapons should, therefore, be coupled with or followed by tangible steps to halt the nuclear arms race and to limit, reduce, and eliminate the stocks of nuclear weapons and the means of their delivery.[124]

Since neither GCD, nor even nuclear disarmament, is remotely likely, "to link the two is to ensure that the nonnuclear powers will avoid formal commitments."[125] Sweden, moreover, specifically urged early agreement on a full test ban, even ahead of a nonproliferation accord, on the ground that it would require the nuclear powers also to sacrifice some nuclear potential. The Eight called in addition for an immediate suspension of all nuclear tests and urged international cooperation in seismic detection work as a help toward a full ban. At the twentieth Assembly, these positions were effectively incorporated in resolutions, along with a ritual repetition of the importance of continuing efforts through the ENDC toward the achievement of collateral measures and of GCD under international controls.[126] The committee sessions of 1966 were as void of achievement as ever, although concurrent negotiations in the Outer Space Committee laid the foundation for the space treaty and Assembly endorsement noted earlier.[127]

The twenty-first Assembly again passed the ritualistic resolutions by overwhelming majorities, urging completion of the full test ban and the nonproliferation treaty.[128] Then, early in 1967, it appeared that the United

124. Report of the Eighteen-Nation Committee on Disarmament, U.N. Doc. A/5986, DC/227 (Sept. 22, 1965), p. 18.

125. Beaton, op. cit., p. 136.

126. A/Res. 2028 (XX), Nov. 19, 1965, non-proliferation of nuclear weapons; A/Res. 2031 (XX), Dec. 3, 1965, question of general and complete disarmament; A/Res. 2032, Dec. 3, 1965, urgent need for suspension of nuclear and thermonuclear tests.

127. Supra, pp. 87–88.

128. A/Res. 2149 (XXI), Nov. 4, 1966, and A/Res. 2153A (XXI), Nov. 17, 1966, both on nonproliferation of nuclear weapons; A/Res. 2162 (XXI), Dec. 5, 1966, question of GCD; A/Res. 2163 (XXI), Dec. 5, 1966, urgent need for suspension of nuclear and thermonuclear tests. In addition, A/Res. 2153B (XXI), Nov. 17, 1966, provided for a conference in 1968 of the nonnuclear weapons states to consider safeguards for their security. It was adopted by a vote of only 48–1 (India)–59, the abstentions including the United States, the Soviet Union, France, and most of the near-nuclear states as well.

States and the Soviet Union might finally be on the verge of agreement on treaty terms. At this point, ironically, the nonnuclear NATO allies, in particular West Germany and Italy, began to raise difficulties over intended provisions inhibiting the development of "peaceful" atomic explosives and for the inspection of nuclear industries by the IAEA.[129] They were soon joined by Brazil, which also objects to any prohibitions on its right to conduct atomic explosions for peaceful purposes.

It appeared, moreover, that the danger of another upward spiral in the nuclear arms race might be approaching in the form of an antiballistic-missile (ABM) competition. In November 1966, Secretary McNamara reported considerable evidence of Soviet deployment of a limited ABM defense system around some major cities. Early in the new year, President Johnson proposed that the two powers agree to a moratorium on such missile defense systems, which would not increase their security but simply raise the level of insecurity at fantastic cost to both sides.[130] The Soviet Union was not interested in such discussions on defensive systems only; but did agree to discussions that would link them to a ceiling on offensive weapons as well (in which the United States has a commanding lead).[131] Neither completion of the nonproliferation treaty nor a beginning of the talks on a missile freeze had, however, occurred by August 1967. It is generally considered, moreover, that if a renunciation of the ABM spiral cannot be achieved, the nonproliferation treaty will also be ruled out.[132]

129. The Europeans feared such provisions might hinder development of atomic industries and raised the specter of industrial espionage by communist inspectors. The United States considers this fear exaggerated and, as this study went to press, was trying to work out a system that would also utilize Euratom inspection. On the prohibition of "peaceful" explosives, however, the U.S. position remained firm, on the ground that there is no difference in technology between peaceful explosions and those intended for military purposes.

130. See J. I. Coffey, "The Anti-Ballistic Missile Debate," *Foreign Affairs*, Vol. 45 (April 1967), pp. 403–13.

131. See statement at Presidential press conference, March 2, 1967. *New York Times*, March 3, 1967.

132. See Alastair Buchan, ed., *A World of Nuclear Powers?* (Prentice-Hall, 1966), for an excellent discussion of many of these issues. Lord Chalfont (British Minister for disarmament) is among those who think deployment of an ABM defense system would "almost certainly kill the possibility of a nonproliferation agreement . . . and would in fact encourage the spread of nuclear weapons" (p. 135). Urs Schwartz presents a contrary view, but admits it would require the development of devices preventing the use of ABMs as MRBMs (p. 151).

Moving in a different direction from the near-nuclear powers, the smaller states in Africa and Latin America have sought to increase their security by finding effective means to ban nuclear weapons from their regions, even without the conclusion of a general nonproliferation accord.

NUCLEAR WEAPONS AND NONNUCLEAR POWERS

In 1961, not unconnected with the fact that France was about to test in the Sahara, a number of African states first proposed an Assembly resolution to that effect. It invited all states to respect their continent as a denuclearized zone, and called on the nuclear powers not to station, transport, or test weapons in Africa.[133]

The United States, for somewhat obvious reasons, argued that it was not appropriate for the United Nations to initiate recommendations to particular areas for disarmament measures, by means of declarations alone. Only after the African states had themselves arrived at pertinent "regional agreements or arrangements," should the Organization be asked to request all members to cooperate in their fulfillment. Moreover, the United States would not approve an uninspected, unverified moratorium on testing, although it was ready to sign "immediately an effective treaty, with international controls," to ban all further testing in any part of the world.[134]

The states of the region formed the Organization of African Unity (OAU) in 1963; and at the first session of its Assembly of Heads of States and Governments, in July 1964, declared their readiness to undertake, in a treaty under United Nations auspices, to refrain from manufacturing or acquiring control of nuclear weapons.[135] Their declaration calling on all states to respect the status of Africa as a nuclear-free zone was endorsed by the neutral conference at Cairo in October 1964 and by the General Assembly in 1965.[136] The latter resolution called on all states to refrain from testing, manufacturing, using, or deploying such weapons on the continent, and from transferring them (or any knowhow for their manu-

133. A/Res. 1652 (XVI), Nov. 24, 1961.

134. Quoted in U.S. Department of State, U.S. *Participation in the U.N.: Report by the President to the Congress for the Year 1961*, Publication 7413 (1962), p. 31. The novelty of the issue was reflected in the voting on the resolution. It was unanimously adopted, but only by a 55–0 vote (with communist support), and with 45 abstentions, including the United States.

135. Issued as U.N. Doc. A/5975, Sept. 23, 1965.

136. A/Res. 2033 (XX), Dec. 3, 1965. It passed by 105–0–2 (France and Portugal).

facture) "to the national control of any [African] state." It also hoped that those states would initiate studies through the OAU to implement denuclearization, but such action has not yet followed.

Greater progress has been made in Latin America where, in the midst of the 1962 Cuban crisis, Brazil proposed that Latin America become a denuclearized zone. The idea did not then have solid Latin support, however, and it was opposed by the United States because of Cuban demands. The latter declared that, in addition to self-denying undertakings by the Latin American republics,

The nuclear powers too must provide guarantees that they would not employ their nuclear weapons against that part of the world. Furthermore, the principle of denuclearization should be applied to Puerto Rico and the Panama Canal Zone, which were part of Latin America. Finally, all military bases in the region should be eliminated, including in particular the Guantanamo base....[137]

The General Assembly deferred the subject for later consideration. Brazil subsequently rallied broader hemispheric support for a new resolution that it presented in November 1963 to the Assembly. This urged the Latin American states to study measures through which they could agree "not to manufacture, receive, store, or test nuclear weapons" and trusted that, "after a satisfactory agreement has been reached, all States, particularly the nuclear Powers," would cooperate in carrying out its aims.[138] Brazil also indicated that any agreement reached should meet conditions previously announced by the United States as necessary to a denuclearization accord, namely, that all states in the region voluntarily accept it, that it include an adequate inspection system, and that it maintain the general military balance.[139] The Soviet Union, however, refused to support the

137. See *United Nations Review* (December 1962), p. 51.

138. Passed as A/Res. 1911 (XVIII), Nov. 27, 1963, by a vote of 89–0–14. Brazil was joined by 10 other states: Bolivia, Chile, Costa Rica, Ecuador, El Salvador, Haiti, Honduras, Mexico, Panama, and Uruguay. The resolution was based on a Declaration of the preceding April by the Presidents of Brazil, Bolivia, Chile, Ecuador, and Mexico, announcing readiness to sign such an agreement. Text in U.N. Doc. A/5447/Addendum 1, Aug. 12, 1963. See also Alfonso García Robles, *The Denuclearization of Latin America* (Carnegie Endowment for International Peace, 1967), especially Pt. 2, International Documents, Nos. 12 and 13.

139. The British delegate elaborated the last concern: "The creation of a nuclear-free zone," he said, "must not . . . conflict with one of the cardinal principles of disarmament—namely, that the existing military balance, which helps to preserve world peace, should not be disturbed. Otherwise, the effect of a nuclear-free zone might well be to increase insecurity rather than to reduce tension." *New York Times*, Nov. 19, 1963.

resolution since the debate showed that Cuba's earlier conditions would not be included in the proposed agreement. It passed without a negative vote, nonetheless.

Mexico then took leadership in setting up a Preparatory Commission for the Denuclearization of Latin America, which met in Mexico City in March 1965. It was ready with draft provisions a year later. There were several points at issue, however, which its 1966 session did not resolve; and the opposing views were therefore incorporated in the official "Draft Treaty on the Denuclearization of Latin America."[140] This was circulated to all concerned governments—which included the nuclear powers that were to be asked to undertake to respect the nuclear-free status of Latin America; and those states outside the treaty zone but having territories within the applicable geographical area, that were to be asked to accept the status for such territories.[141]

One of the major unresolved issues in 1966 was whether all states within the treaty zone must sign and ratify the accord before it would become operative. Brazil led the Latin American states favoring this requirement. But a larger group joined Mexico in wanting the treaty to become effective for ratifying states as soon as a minimum number deposited their instruments of acceptance. The absence of Cuba from all the proceedings of the commission was crucial in this respect.[142]

The United States, in a commentary of December 1965, considered it "important that all states in the area should participate. The refusal of certain states to participate would lead us to consider whether their exclusion might render the agreement ineffective or meaningless, or whether the agreement would still be worthwhile.[143] At the same time, the United States opposed an equally inclusive obligation on the part of extra-zonal states with "de jure or de facto" international responsibility for territories in the region covered, whereby they would undertake to apply the denuclearized status to those territories. Washington "did not wish to have included" either the Virgin Islands or Puerto Rico, since in the case of both

140. Text included as an annex to Res. 14 (III), May 4, 1966, of the Preparatory Commission. This is part of the Final Act of the Third Session (April 19–May 4, 1966), issued as U.N. Doc. A/6328, May 12, 1966, pp. 13–30.

141. Text in U.N. Doc. A/6663, Feb. 23, 1967. Additional Protocols of Guarantee, Annex 2, pp. 1–3.

142. The other 19 Latin American states participated in the Preparatory Commission, plus Jamaica and Trinidad-Tobago from the Third Session on.

143. Quoted in subsequent commentary of Aug. 29, 1966, text in García Robles, *op. cit.*, p. 150.

areas it "must deal with disarmament policies affecting other nuclear powers." On the other hand, the United States would not object to inclusion of the Panama Canal Zone (its transit rights remaining unaffected), nor of Guantanamo if Cuba participated.[144]

Washington's reasoning proved unconvincing. The geographic limits of the nuclear-free zone finally incorporated in the treaty run from the limits of the Antarctic Treaty area—60° south latitude—to 35° north latitude. This included all of Mexico, but specifically excluded continental United States and its territorial waters. At the end of the negotiating sessions, Great Britain was offended by passage of a resolution providing that, for purposes of representing territories subject to disputes or claims, "the Preparatory Commission . . . recognizes the law of the Latin American States." This appeared to imply support for Argentine claims to the Falkland Islands and Guatemalan claims to British Honduras.

Another issue unsettled in 1966 related to whether the treaty should prohibit the development of all nuclear explosives, as well as of weapons. The United States made clear its position (as explained above in connection with the nonproliferation treaty negotiations) and suggested that the treaty be worded in all appropriate places to apply to "nuclear weapons or other nuclear explosives."[145] This explicit reference was not used in the final text. At first the United States, in a statement to the final Preparatory Commission meeting, evidently found the treaty language adequate to meet its concerns; but later, Secretary Rusk stated that "we cannot except peaceful explosions from such a treaty."[146] The Soviet Union disliked the language from the start.[147]

A last critical issue from 1966 also related to the conditions to be met before the treaty would become effective. In addition to the question whether all participating states had to ratify (already noted), there were differences over whether the guarantees by the extraterritorial states, in

144. In commenting on the Draft Treaty of 1966, the United States declared: "While the United States favors in principle the placing of appropriate territories in the Nuclear-Free Zone, we do not believe it is necessary to make this an all-inclusive policy. In some cases, existing political and international considerations could create difficulties in seeking to include territories. We believe the states concerned should be invited to place territories in the Nuclear-Free Zone." *Ibid.*, pp. 151–52.

145. *Ibid.*, p. 148.

146. U.S. Department of State Press Release 35, Feb. 14, 1967; and *U.S. Armament and Disarmament Problems*, Hearings, Subcommittee on Disarmament, Senate Foreign Relations Committee, 90 Cong. 1 sess. (1967), p. 153.

147. Soviet objections reported in Henry Giniger dispatch, *New York Times*, Feb. 13, 1967.

two protocols covering the nuclear powers and those with dependencies in the region, must also first come into force, and whether bilateral agreements with the IAEA required under the safeguards system must first be concluded. An elaborate compromise was worked out that allows the treaty to come into force for signatory countries choosing to waive the formal requirement of prior treaty ratification by all participating countries, protocol ratification by all the extrazonal states involved, and the conclusion of the safeguards agreements, when eleven governments deposit declarations of waiver with their ratifications.

Although all commission participants approved the Final Act, only fourteen Latin American states signed the treaty on February 14, 1967.[148] Neither Brazil nor Argentina was among them. The two protocols, according to news dispatches, were not even presented for signature at the time. China had already refused to have anything to do with the project, on the ground that it was negotiated under United Nations auspices.[149] The United States, Great Britain, and the Soviet Union have all taken exception to various provisions. The Brazilian representative on the ENDC has since declared that his government would renounce its right to produce nuclear explosives for peaceful purposes only if an international organization was given the monopoly of manufacturing all such explosives.[150] The British observer at the Preparatory Commission meetings was reported to have suggested that the resolution so offensive to his country might be "a 'devious device' designed to prevent the treaty from ever coming into effect."[151] It is not beyond the realm of possibility that some of the treaty provisions fall into that classification also.

NUCLEAR WEAPONS AND THE "NEW" CLUB MEMBERS

Both France and Communist China have continued to develop their own nuclear weapons. Neither has signed the partial test-ban treaty nor participated in any other control negotiations. Development of the small French nuclear capacity is not yet a matter of serious concern to the other club members; but in 1966 its planned tests for the Pacific brought forth

148. The signers were Bolivia, Chile, Colombia, Costa Rica, Ecuador, Guatemala, Haiti, Honduras, Mexico, Panama, Peru, Salvador, Uruguay, and Venezuela.

149. García Robles, *op. cit.*, p. 157.

150. *New York Times*, March 31, 1967 and July 5, 1967.

151. *Ibid.*, Feb. 12, 1967.

protests from various Latin American states, as its earlier testing in the Sahara had done from African states.[152] Annoyance has been the general reaction to French efforts in this field; but increasing alarm has been the reaction to the speed of technological advance registered by the successive Chinese tests, especially in view of the truculent political stance maintained by Peking.

When the Second Conference of Heads of Government of Non-Aligned Countries was held in Cairo in October 1964, at the time of the first Communist Chinese explosion, it urged that "the convening of a world disarmament conference under the auspices of the United Nations to which all countries would be invited, would provide powerful support to the efforts which are being made to set in motion the process of disarmament. . . ."[153] The conference participants were to take steps toward that end at the forthcoming General Assembly. That was impossible at the nonvoting nineteenth Assembly, but the resurrected Disarmament Commission endorsed the Cairo proposal in June 1965, a month after the second Chinese blast. The commission recommended a world disarmament conference to the twentieth General Assembly for "urgent consideration."[154]

The Assembly in due course considered it favorably. But because Albania had declared that Peking would not participate in any conference under United Nations auspices until its demands for the Chinese seat had been met, a resolution was adopted which left vague who was to do what, when, and how, in setting up the preparatory committee for "a world disarmament conference not later than 1967."[155] It was understood that the most interested neutrals would take the initiative in seeking Chinese acceptance; but there had been no sign that Peking would accept such an

152. Chile, Colombia, Ecuador, and Peru registered complaints with Paris, and New Zealand barred any French ships and aircraft carrying test equipment. *Washington Post*, April 21, 23; May 17, 18, 20; *New York Times*, May 1, 1966.

153. From declaration adopted by the conference, quoted in Bodnar, *op. cit.*, App. 12, p. 111.

154. U.N. Doc. DC/224, June 15, 1965.

155. A/Res. 2030 (XX), Nov. 29, 1965. Paragraphs 2 and 3 read:

"2. *Urges* that the necessary consultations be conducted with all countries for the purpose of establishing a widely representative preparatory committee which will take appropriate steps for the convening of a world disarmament conference not later than 1967;

"3. *Urges further* that all countries be kept informed, as appropriate, of the results achieved by the preparatory committee in accordance with paragraph 2 above."

The Chinese representation issue is discussed below, in Chap. 9.

officially "un-U.N." invitation by mid-June 1967, when it conducted the sixth explosion of its series, which was a hydrogen bomb. The point to such a general conference would not in any case be the resolution's rhetorical goal of progress toward controlled GCD. Rather, it would be to bring together all the significant military powers in hope of at least reducing world tensions, if not world armaments, by reducing Peking's isolation.

Meanwhile, in Warsaw periodic talks between United States and Communist Chinese representatives had proved fruitless over the years, the stumbling block (according to American sources) being the constant Chinese demand that the United States withdraw recognition from the Nationalist regime and yield on Formosa. With its first nuclear explosion, Peking repeated the call for a world conference to ban and destroy all nuclear weapons, which it had made when rejecting the partial test-ban treaty. This was dismissed as merely a propaganda ploy by Washington. The communists continued to press for such a conference after each of the first four explosions; but not after the last two, in December 1966 and June 1967. After all of them, however, Peking has repeated: "China's sole purpose in developing nuclear weapons is defense, and its ultimate aim is to eliminate nuclear weapons. We solemnly declare once again that at no time and in no circumstances will China be the first to use nuclear weapons."[156] On the occasion of the third explosion in May 1966, that formal statement was immediately followed by Premier Chou En-lai's disclosure that China had proposed at Warsaw after its initial test that all nuclear governments pledge not to be the first to use atomic weapons.[157] Washington had rejected the proposal because, as the State Department explained in acknowledging its earlier action, "such a pledge, without controls to enforce it, would be useless and would not contribute to disarmament."[158] To reporters' queries on how controls could be devised to enforce such a no-first-use pledge, the department spokesman "provided no explanation. Instead, reading from a 'position paper,' he went on to contend that China had shown no 'constructive interest in' disarmament steps involving controls and verification."[159]

The disclosure drew senatorial criticism of the administration's failure to use the Peking offer as at least an opening for further exploration. Sena-

---

156. Translation of official statement, *New York Times*, May 10, 1966.

157. A no-first-strike pledge had been proposed on various occasions also by the Soviet Union.

158. *New York Times*, May 12, 1966, p. 10.

159. *Ibid.*

tor Robert F. Kennedy suggested, for example, that the State Department might have inquired whether China would stop testing in return for a United States no-first-use pledge.[160] Secretary Rusk, a few days later, amplified that the Chinese had not "responded constructively" to other disarmament issues raised in the bilateral Warsaw talks, nor shown any willingness to be associated with the preparatory committee for the proposed 1967 world disarmament conference.[161]

By early June, however, the State Department let it be known that the United States Ambassador at Warsaw had been instructed to inquire whether Peking would sign the test-ban treaty along with a no-first-strike pledge.[162] At the same time, it called attention to a 1962 letter on such a treaty from Secretary Rusk to the Secretary-General. The United States, he had said, would "offer fullest assurance that it will never use any weapon large or small with aggressive intent;" and he had pointed out that "the Charter makes a distinction not between one weapon and another, but between the use of force for aggression and for self-defense. This distinction is critical." The surest way to remove the threat of nuclear weapons, he concluded, is by general and complete disarmament under effective international control.[163] This brought the issue full circle round.

In spite of State Department reticence, however, it is clear that the government is concerned politically by the rapid advances of the Communist Chinese in nuclear technology,[164] in combination with their belligerent revolutionary policies and their obsessive antagonism toward the United States as the main enemy that has frustrated the achievement of their political goals.[165] It is not impossible that the escalating war in Viet-

160. *Ibid.,* May 18, 1966. The Senate also passed a resolution (84–0) commending the President's efforts to reach an accord on non-proliferation.

161. U.S. Department of State Press Release 114, May 17, 1966, pp. 9–10. The Secretary added: "We are prepared to sit down with them, as we have said many times, to talk about disarmament, . . . but we can't take up these great issues of war and peace solely on the basis of unverified declarations which may or may not mean anything."

162. *Washington Post,* June 4, 1966, p. 10. This announcement followed by a few days a statement by Senator Albert Gore that he had told a private international meeting (including communists) that "in his view" the U.S. would be willing to enter into a no-first-strike treaty if China would adhere to the test-ban treaty. *Ibid.*

163. Quoted in *Washington Post,* June 4, 1966.

164. See, for example, Hanson W. Baldwin, "China Is Maturing Fast as a Nuclear Power," *New York Times,* May 15, 1966, p. 4–E.

165. Secretary McNamara expressed such concern in March 1966, for example. China will soon have the nuclear capacity to send missiles against states 5–700 miles beyond its borders, he said, and may be "moving to support [its] aggressive talk." Statement, Senate Foreign Relations Committee, *Hearings,* March 8, 1966.

nam is also causing concern to officials in Peking, in spite of their bellicose talk. In the latter case, the move to make public the no-first-strike offer might have indicated an opening for further involving the Chinese in international negotiations. If the neutrals could make the projected world conference look non-United Nations enough to satisfy Peking, or if the ENDC invited the Chinese to join their discussions, an acceptance might come in time (and in spite of the Formosa issue) if the communist authorities were in fact becoming interested in reentering the international community. The French approach—that the five "nuclear club" members should conduct summit negotiations to resolve some of these problems— seems increasingly impracticable. For if membership in "the club" thus becomes officially the badge of international leadership, it is inconceivable that India, for one, would not promptly pay its membership dues.

If Peking continues to maintain its demands without any concessions, and the war in Vietnam continues to escalate, the school that favors stronger bombing measures against North Vietnam will no doubt become even more outspoken. Proposals to bomb China, especially its nuclear facilities, have been made before now as one means of preventing proliferation, as well as of cutting aid to Hanoi.[166] This approach has been rejected by the administration so far. But it has as yet made only the most hesitant steps toward a more positive policy of seeking to diminish Chinese bellicosity by indirect political means (direct ones seem still infeasible without abandonment of the Nationalist Chinese) that might bring Peking back into international society on truce terms, at least, if not on a truly peaceful basis. This is a broader issue than just the nuclear-threat aspect, urgent though that may become.[167]

Arms Control and Smaller Countries

In the ever-increasing obsession with the nuclear threat, great and small powers alike have tended to ignore the problems of conventional arms control at lower levels in relation to international security. At the 1965

166. See, among others, former Senator Goldwater's comment: "I rather pray that Red China would give us provocation to attack her military and atomic installations," with "sufficient provocation" defined as sending "troops into South Vietnam or materiel in massive quantities." (*Washington Post*, April 28, 1965.) And more recently, Gen. Curtis LeMay's recommendation that "if the Chinese come in [to Vietnam] to fight us, use it [the bomb]." *New York Times*, April 2, 1967.

167. It is considered at greater length in Chap. 9, pp. 368–86.

meeting of the Disarmament Commission, with international measures so far beyond the limits of accord, the United States made another effort to promote some arms reduction through unilateral actions (taken in the hope of Soviet emulation) to destroy, or forego construction of, certain military aircraft. Ambassador Stevenson, warning that there were limits to such unilateral action without reciprocity, continued:

We believe that all nations should exercise restraint in the armament field. Indeed, we believe it might be well for each nation to ask itself whether or not it could profitably engage in constructive discussions with its neighbors, either regionally or under other arrangements, to restrain the temptation for competition in arms.[168]

Secretary Rusk has pointed out, for example, that some seventy United Nations Members have voted unanimously for disarmament in the Assembly, while simultaneously asking for military aid from the United States.[169] If the use of such arms by the less-developed countries resulted only in disorders and instability within the confines of their own areas, it would be bad enough; but, as subsequent chapters illustrate, under present-day conditions great-power involvement in small-power conflicts becomes almost inescapable—thereby increasing the hazards of escalation toward the dreaded nuclear outbreak. The countries of Africa and Latin America have taken the first steps toward some sort of control over nuclear diffusion in their regions; but, as already shown, both the United States and the Soviet Union, in different ways, have found reasons to refrain from wholehearted support of the more advanced effort in the Western Hemisphere.

So long as political tensions are high, moreover, it will remain difficult if not impossible to develop enough cooperation among the arms-exporting countries to make feasible regional systems of control over the acquisition of sophisticated, offensive weapons. They are more likely to continue the pattern of competitive sales.[170] For one thing, the smaller states are not always willing to forego arms beyond the level needed for internal security

168. Statement of April 26, 1965, U.S. Department of State, *Bulletin*, Vol. 52 (1965), p. 774.
169. U.S. Department of State, *Bulletin*, Vol. 52 (January 1965), p. 69.
170. An example occurred in connection with Iran. After lengthy negotiations in 1966, the United States agreed to sell some advanced jet fighters to Iran (a CENTO member), lest it turn to Moscow for missiles to defend the Persian Gulf, where the government fears the potential threat from Soviet-armed U.A.R. Even so, early in 1967, it was disclosed that Iran had also signed a military aid agreement with Moscow. *New York Times*, dispatches, Dec. 14, 1966 and Feb. 8, 1967.

purposes, even when such arms are too costly for poor governments professedly concerned with the development and modernization of their countries. Either reasons of prestige or the demands of some local conflict appear sufficiently important to those governments to warrant or require additional armaments. Nor, in this situation, can it be said that the great powers themselves provide a good example of the spirit of accommodation that alone makes possible the resolution of political conflicts without recourse to force or the fear of it, which stimulates the desire for arms. "Perhaps the most important single reinforcement of a regional approach to security through arms control would be evidence that the great powers were pursuing with equal vigor measures of arms control applicable to themselves."[171]

Although that point seems still far off, an initiative to encourage the smaller states to consider such possibilities, at least as regards weapons commonly considered to be sophisticated and offensive, was made at the start of 1966, in President Johnson's message to the reconvening ENDC. The one new point touched upon by the President was an indication that the United States would support regional limitations on conventional arms if the interested countries could agree on them.[172] Nothing happened at Geneva that year; but in February 1967, after considerable effort, the administration succeeded in obtaining Latin American consent to place the subject of arms-spending controls on the agenda of the hemisphere summit meeting scheduled for April.[173] The move may have been made in response to senatorial charges that the Defense Department had been following a policy of "aggressively" promoting arms sales. According to a staff study for the Senate Foreign Relations Committee:

Over the past four years there has been a basic change in the composition of American military assistance. The sale of arms has now replaced the giving of arms as the predominant form of U.S. military assistance. . . . In Europe, American arms salesmanship has often been zealous to the point of irritation, and overpowering to the point of encouraging Europeans to compete more aggressively for the arms markets in the underdeveloped regions of the world. In some underdeveloped regions . . . notably Latin America and the Middle East, where there are no significant balance of payments incentives, the United

171. Lincoln P. Bloomfield and Amelia C. Leiss, "Arms Control and Developing Countries," *World Politics*, Vol. 18 (October 1965), p. 19. This article provides a good survey of the variety and complexity of arms-control problems throughout the developing regions.

172. Reported in *Washington Post*, Jan. 28, 1966. U.S. Department of State, *Bulletin*, Vol. 54 (1966), p. 264.

173. *New York Times*, Feb. 22, 1967.

States, when faced with tough decisions as in Iran and Argentina, seems to be drifting into a policy of preemptive selling rather than the more difficult alternative of arms denial.[174]

The subject became of particular interest later in the year, with the renewal of hostilities in the Middle East (where all the parties were using foreign manufactured arms).[175] This development coincided with congressional consideration of the administration's request for foreign aid appropriations and for an extension of the Export-Import Bank's lending authority. The latter had been quietly used by the Pentagon to help finance arms sales to a number of countries.[176] Congressional hostility was reflected in demands for an investigation of the whole issue. And in late July, the Senate Committee on Foreign Relations voted to place restrictions on arms sales to underdeveloped countries, as well as to propose severe cuts in the Defense Department's original request for military grant aid of $590 million.

The subject needs to be pursued more vigorously, even though current political tensions do not augur well for the effort. The following chapters will throw some light on whether a reduction in tensions, such as might assist in a forward movement throughout the entire field of arms control, is likely to be any easier to achieve than progress on armament problems seems to be. For as Hedley Bull has pointed out:

. . . [It] is just at the point where a nation has been brought to the verge of defeat in the pursuit of its policy by other means that it resorts to violence. If an attempt is to be made to stabilize the arms race, such a policy must be accompanied by one of attempting to stabilize the whole field of political relations between the two antagonists.[177]

174. U.S. Senate Foreign Relations Committee, *Arms Sales and Foreign Policy*, 90 Cong. 1 sess. (1967), p. 12. See also *New York Times*, Jan. 30, 1967. The study recommended, inter alia, that the forthcoming meeting of Hemisphere heads of government might consider agreements for "a Latin American conventional weapons 'free zone'." *Ibid.*, p. 13.

175. On this aspect, see Alastair Buchan, "Arms Nobody Wants to Control," *Current* (December 1965), pp. 24–26.

176. See, for example, Neil Sheehan dispatch, *New York Times*, July 31, 1967.

177. Hedley Bull, *The Control of the Arms Race* (Praeger, 1961 ed.), p. 205.

CHAPTER FIVE

LIMITATIONS
OF COLLECTIVE ENFORCEMENT
THROUGH THE UNITED NATIONS

The Charter system for peace enforcement is often criticized in retrospect for having ignored too many obvious warnings of future difficulties. Yet its very incompleteness, as already noted, was a result of considerable awareness of those incipient hazards, as well as of the sheer impossibility of negotiating the details of future enforcement procedures in the midst of war. Time has confirmed that without basic cooperation among the major military powers, an effective enforcement system could not be developed. At the same time, the Charter has proved more adaptable than might have been thought possible to the development of more limited kinds of collective action on behalf of international peace.

Such limited measures were confined at first to small-scale pacific settlement actions, such as in Greece and Kashmir. Then, in Korea, a sanctions operation was undertaken in circumstances quite different from those anticipated in Chapter VII of the Charter. The collective United Nations operation enormously increased in size, taking the form of a large-scale military combat force. The undertaking did not, however, triumphantly vindicate the enforcement authority of the Organization, but ended in a less-than-satisfactory armistice in 1953. As a result, the United Nations was relegated by the United States to an unimportant place in its strategic thinking, far behind the proliferating regional collective-defense arrangements. But in 1956, the earlier type of United Nations pacific settlement activity was renewed and enlarged in scope if not essentially changed in function. It now took the form of a new type of international noncombat armed force. This was mistakenly seen by many as a substitute for—or at least as the first step toward—the originally conceived sanctions forces. The difficulties of maintaining the peace satisfactorily through use of such limited, noncombat United Nations forces later became all too apparent, however, in the Congo episode.[1]

1. See below, Chap. 6, for discussion of these developments.

In spite of earlier sobering experience, the sixties saw a return to the concept of military sanctions in two quite different connections: one, as part of the United States Outline Plan for a Treaty on General and Complete Disarmament (GCD);[2] the other, in connection with the persistent drive for sanctions against the "white" governments of southern Africa. The latter is presently most acute in connection with the case of Rhodesia, where selective economic sanctions are already being applied. A review of the reasons for failure in 1946–47 to implement the Charter scheme for collective military arrangements may therefore be useful in evaluating problems likely to arise in any attempt to carry out these new proposals for military enforcement.

Attempt To Implement Article 43

The composition of the Security Council and its advisory Military Staff Committee (representatives of the Chiefs of Staff of the five permanent members), partly institutionalized the pattern of wartime strategic direction. Then the political reins had been in the hands of the major allied leaders, advised and assisted by the chiefs of their armed forces. In Charter enforcement terms, the same kind of predominance, given the collective-security ideas then prevailing, was inevitable, because it was necessary to the carrying out of any large-scale sanctions operations by the Council. The main military forces at its disposal would have to come from the major powers and thus justified their claim to direct any required sanctions. The smaller powers were, however, safeguarded against complete great-power domination in two ways. Although the permanent members could *stop* enforcement action individually by their veto rights, they could *initiate* action only with the concurrent consent of at least two nonpermanent members, representing in this respect the general membership. More important, as a practical matter, those elected members were only committed to support even unanimous Council decisions with such men and facilities as they had undertaken to provide in agreements made under Article 43.

The first step in setting up this proposed system, it was agreed by the permanent members, was for the Military Staff Committee to decide on the contributions to be pledged by those governments—which would de-

2. See above, Chap. 4, pp. 72, 74–75 for bases of plan.

termine the general nature and size of the overall forces available to the Council. In this process, the first order of business was to work out the principles to govern the organization and command of those collective forces. The Staff Committee was accordingly instructed by the Council in February 1946 to develop the bases for negotiating the system of Article 43 agreements. Unfortunately, the cold war had already set in; and the mutual suspicions of the United States and the Soviet Union were reflected in the barrenness of the committee's discussions. In April 1947, the military group reported its still divergent views to the Security Council, which had no better success in reaching accord.

MILITARY STAFF COMMITTEE DIFFERENCES

The critical issues, and the Soviet and American positions on them—the two extremes—were roughly as follows. The Soviet Union argued that collective forces need not be large since the enemy was already disarmed and United Nations Members anticipated reducing their own arms. Contributions by the permanent members, moreover, should be equal in size and composition. This attitude was consistent both with the idea of small total forces and with the Soviet concern to preserve the identical status of the permanent members. The Soviet view was also consistently restrictive on such matters as the basing of pledged contingents on national territory until called for by the Council and on their immediate withdrawal to home bases after any sanctions action. These positions followed logically from the negative Soviet attitude toward international cooperation in general and its suspicions of American military aims in particular.

The United States proposed relatively large total forces, with emphasis on air and naval arms and with the composition of national contingents to be decided on the principle of comparable contributions depending on the relative capacity of each country. The Soviet Union saw this as giving the United States predominance in the air and naval components of any future forces, which might then be used against its interests.[3] The United States

3. "The acceptance of this principle," the Soviet delegate said on one occasion, "might lead to the organization of the armed forces being used in the interests of powerful states and to the detriment of the legitimate interests of other countries." U.N. Security Council, Second Year, *Official Records*, No. 44 (June 6, 1947), p. 968.

For an interpretation of U.S. views, see Matthew B. Ridgway, *Soldier: The Memoirs of Matthew B. Ridgway* (Harper, 1956), 169–70.

position was inconsistent with the practical limitations imposed by the Council's voting system, which did not permit action against any of the great powers. It was, however, consistent with the possibilities of Article 51, as the British representative once explained:

Any one of the permanent members by exercising its vote could arrest the movement of the United Nations forces. There is, unfortunately, no way out of that. The only answer—and it is admittedly only a partial answer—is provided by Article 51. . . . If any one of the permanent members were to call a halt to the United Nations force, the remainder of the United Nations would be entitled . . . to take action against that Member. Their forces, already made available to the Security Council, could legitimately be jointly employed to that end for so long as the Security Council failed to take the measures necessary to maintain international peace and security.[4]

Great Britain, France, and China were in the middle, proposing relatively small contingents (probably reflecting their own weakness, as well as recognizing the practical effects of the veto), but advocating that national contributions be made on an equivalent rather than identical basis. They also opposed the rigid Soviet views on basing and training, favoring principles permitting considerable flexibility in operating the contingents as a joint force.

Meanwhile, first efforts were also being made to establish the principles on which arms control and disarmament might proceed, and by which an international control might be established over atomic energy. United States military officials, involved in all three of these activities, saw Soviet moves to prohibit the use of atomic and other weapons of mass destruction as coordinated with its position on limiting the size of forces to be available to the Security Council; and both, as aimed at "the unilateral disarmament of the U.S., under the guise of a plea for general regulation and reduction of armaments by all nations."[5] Under the cold-war conditions of the summer of 1947, the conflicting Soviet and United States views were clearly irreconcilable. Neither government wanted to implement Article 43, in effect, and each sought to blame the other for the stalemated situation in the Council. For all practical purposes, this was the effective end of official United Nations consideration of the problem of making forces available under Article 43.

4. U.N. Security Council, Second Year, *Official Records*, No. 45, June 10, 1947, pp. 994–95.
5. Ridgway, *op. cit.*, p. 172.

LIE'S PROPOSAL FOR A PALESTINE FORCE

One last effort to rescue something from those futile discussions was made behind the scenes, however, by Secretary-General Lie. As events in 1947–48 moved toward the critical moment when Great Britain would end the Palestine mandate, local Arab-Jewish violence was increasing. Despite the failure of the Military Staff Committee, Lie suggested to Great Britain and the United States that there had been sufficient accord to permit a land force to be established out of "the minimum units which the Big Five were committed to placing at the Security Council's disposal," and which would be "more than adequate" to keep the peace in Palestine. But both governments rejected the proposal, so Lie did not present it to the Council.[6]

In terms of the international mobilization of military forces, the United States turned in the direction of regional arrangements, spurred by the Berlin blockade and the communist takeover in Czechoslovakia. NATO was formally established in 1949, as a collective defense arrangement under Article 51 of the Charter. In theory, NATO might initiate action under that article, but would be subject to subsequent Security Council direction if that organ could take over. But in fact, it was generally considered as an alternative necessitated by the failure of the Organization to cope with Soviet aggressiveness in Europe and to establish its own collective security system. In either view, NATO could be seen, as Canadian Prime Minister Lester B. Pearson later described it, as "a practical and regional means of cementing cracks which had appeared in the Charter security system."[7]

United Nations Forces in Korea

When the avalanche of armed communist aggression finally descended in June 1950, however, it was on Korea rather than Europe. The United States interpreted the aggression as an attack by "international commu-

6. Trygve Lie, *In the Cause of Peace* (Macmillan, 1954), pp. 164–70. Hanson Baldwin commented at the time: "There is, in fact, very little chance of setting up an 'international police force' in the terms so far discussed, now or in the near future, despite the urgency of the Palestine situation. The last thing the United States wants is Russian troops in Palestine, and presumably Russia feels the same way about American troops in Palestine." *New York Times*, Dec. 28, 1947, Sec. IV, p. 4.

7. Address of May 7, 1964, Press Release (unnumbered), Office of the Prime Minister, Ottawa, p. 4.

nism" against the noncommunist world as a whole—one that was simpler to react against than the probings and subversive actions in Europe. It had to be stopped, therefore, as much in the interest of the European citadel as of Korea.

No forces were available, of course, for the Security Council to send to the rescue of South Korea; and little thought had been given to procedures that might be followed should the Council decide on sanctions before the Article 43 agreements were concluded. With the Soviet representative boycotting the Council because of its refusal to seat the Peking government in place of Nationalist China, the danger of a veto was removed. Moreover, the United Nations Commission on Korea[8] was able to report immediately from the scene and convinced the Council that North Korean forces had in fact invaded the South.

INITIAL STAGES

The United States took the initiative in proposing a procedure suitable to these irregular circumstances. The Security Council, after initially calling for a cessation of the North Korean actions,[9] more specifically recommended (when the first resolution was ignored) that members "furnish such assistance to the Republic of Korea as may be necessary to repel the armed attack and to restore international peace and security in the area."[10] By this approach, the United States "brought its own action within the framework of the United Nations," thus obtaining "broad support for specific measures which it probably would have felt impelled to take in any case."[11]

American responsibilities in South Korea and the presence of its military forces in Japan made immediate political and military action possible.

8. A temporary commission had been appointed in 1947 by the Assembly to facilitate establishment of a single Korean Government through national elections. Although failing in that task, it was replaced in 1948 by another U.N. Commission on Korea instructed to continue the effort toward reunification. That group also failed, but it was later (1949) assigned to observe developments that might lead to armed conflict in the peninsula.

9. S/Res. 1501, June 15, 1950.

10. S/Res. 1511, June 27, 1950. The United States also considered the possibility that the Soviet Union might return to the Council to veto these resolutions. It was therefore prepared to request Lie "to summon a special session of the Assembly the following day." Ernest A. Gross, *The United Nations: Structure for Peace* (Council on Foreign Relations, 1962), p. 57.

11. Leland M. Goodrich, "Efforts to Establish International Police Force down to 1950," in Wm. R. Frye, *A United Nations Peace Force* (Oceana, 1957), p. 185.

A Military Assistance Group (developing defensive security forces for the Republic) was already in this sense in charge of Korean forces. Initial American air, sea, and ground units ordered to Korea came from the Far East Command under General MacArthur, and the first British Commonwealth units were also placed under his command.

The Secretary-General was anxious to keep the United Nations "in the picture." He informally suggested that the Security Council might request the United States to direct the international forces in Korea, with a "Committee on Coordination of Assistance for Korea" to promote and supervise United Nations participation in the military action. The Europeans liked the idea, but the United States "promptly turned thumbs down."[12] In view of the military facts of the situation, the Council had no real alternative to accepting Washington's ideas on the subject.

The Security Council accordingly established a United Nations Unified Command and requested the United States to designate the commander and to report to the Council, "as appropriate, on the course of action taken under" the command.[13] The request for reports was the only provision for any United Nations "supervision" of the operation in its name, a weakness undoubtedly stemming from knowledge that the Pentagon opposed any formal element of direction by the Organization. General MacArthur's chain of command was through the Chief of Staff (U.S. Army) to the Joint Chiefs of Staff, to the Secretary of Defense, to the President. His reports to the international Organization were subject to revision by his superiors in Washington before being transmitted to the Security Council by the United States political representative. According to Lie:

Later it even proved a bit difficult to arrange that reports of the United Nations Commander in Korea should be officially transmitted to the Security Council before being released to the press by American attachés in Tokyo. As the Korean War developed, Washington complained, and had reason to complain, that the United States was carrying too much of the burden; but its unwillingness, in those early days when the pattern of the police action was being set, to accord the United Nations a larger measure of direction and thereby participa-

12. The committee would have included initially the United States, Australia, New Zealand, Great Britain, India, France, Norway, and Korea, plus the Secretary-General as *rapporteur*, with other states furnishing assistance to be added later. Lie, *op. cit.*, p. 334.

13. S/Res. 1588, July 7, 1950. The resolution was passed July 7, 1950, by a 7–0 vote, Yugoslavia, Egypt, and India abstaining. President Truman appointed General MacArthur as Commander, U.N. Forces.

tion, no doubt contributed to the tendency of Members to let Washington assume most of the responsibility for fighting.[14]

In spite of American predominance and control, the collective operation was nonetheless internationalized to a degree that was politically important by offers of ground, naval, or air forces from twenty-two governments (of which fifteen were accepted), and by significant contributions of ancillary support, such as shipping, medical facilities, and supplies.[15]

The Unified Command generally insisted that minimum national contingents should be of reinforced battalion strength with adequate supporting artillery and reinforcements. While contributing to military efficiency, such standards discouraged broader participation by governments either unable or unwilling to contribute on that scale. The Secretary-General therefore suggested forming an international brigade of volunteers from countries not sending organized contingents. They might be enlisted for two to three years, he proposed, bear the United Nations name, wear its uniform, and be at the disposal of the Security Council. As a practical matter in 1950, however, such a brigade would have had to be financed and organized by the United States. Washington was unenthusiastic.[16]

THE 38TH PARALLEL REVISITED

Until September 15, the American monopoly of control created no serious problem, since all energies were bent to halt and repel the North Korean attack. The success of the Inchon landing and the breakout from

14. Lie, *op. cit.*, p. 334; see also, pp. 335–37. The Secretary-General also suggested unsuccessfully that a joint command be established to include officers from countries contributing substantial assistance. Even a proposal to designate the Korean headquarters of the U.S. Eighth Army (operating headquarters for all ground forces) as headquarters of the "First U.N. Army" was rejected, although this was where the multinational character of the operation was most apparent. *Ibid.*, p. 338.

15. For fuller discussion of the international operation, see Leland M. Goodrich, *Korea: A Study in U.S. Policy in the United Nations* (Council on Foreign Relations, 1956); also Ruth B. Russell, *United Nations Experience with Military Forces: Political and Legal Aspects* (Brookings Institution, 1964), pp. 28–33.

16. Lie later wrote: "It would, they acknowledged, facilitate the participation of small countries in the United Nations effort. But special United States legislation would be required; perhaps the job might better be left to Canada. They wondered what might be done with the troops if the Korean fighting ended in 1950, and I responded that they could be used for police duties there. To this they agreed; but they doubted whether volunteer forces could be moulded into combat units in time for the Korean fighting." Lie, *op. cit.*, p. 339.

the Pusan perimeter then radically changed the situation, requiring a decision on whether to cross the 38th Parallel. That military decision would have far broader political implications in terms of the objectives of the collective-enforcement action as defined by the Security Council: to repel the attack and to "restore international peace and security in the area."

The latter phrase had been generally understood, in Secretary of State Acheson's terms, as intended "solely" to restore "the Republic of Korea to its status prior to the invasion," and to reestablish "the peace broken by that invasion."[17] There were, however, two ways to view the situation.

The one view was that the prime object should be to end hostilities. The system of collective security had been vindicated. The chances were that future aggressors would be adequately deterred by what had already happened . . . it should be [made] crystal clear that the motives of the United Nations were above reproach or suspicion. No other intention—ulterior intention—must be mixed with the single grand intention of demonstrating that aggression does not pay.
. . . But the view on the other side . . . said that the aggression by North Korea could not be regarded as ended when the United Nations forces reached the Parallel, but only when the North Korean Government surrendered and its army was disbanded. The arrival of the United Nations forces at the Parallel was no more than a sign that military operations were going well. If their progress was now halted, the North Koreans would wait their time to renew their offensive to better advantage . . . At the very least, to leave Korea still divided was to leave the seed of inevitable future struggle.[18]

There was no precedent to fall back on in making this choice, for Korea was not only the first United Nations collective military action; it was the first war in history fought specifically in the name of a collective security organization. Moreover, the issue could not be decided in the abstract, in isolation from the fact that Korea was not a peninsula unto itself, but bordered on the north by both Communist China and the Soviet Union.

The intention to keep the operation localized had been officially proclaimed. Many United Nations Members shared the American view that aggression must be stopped before peaceful-settlement possibilities could be discussed; but others, led by India, believed that the possibility of negotiation and settlement should not be precluded at any stage, in view

17. U.S. Department of State, *Bulletin*, Vol. 23 (1950), p. 46.
18. Guy Wint, *What Happened in Korea? A Study of Collective Security* (Greenfield, Middlesex, England: Batchworth, 1954), pp. 37–38. It should be noted that this is a British study. In the United States, the second view was so heavily predominant as to be practically the only one considered.

of the dangers inherent in an expansion of the conflict. The Secretary-General had privately circulated to a few leading Members, in the early fall, a paper on "Suggested Terms of Settlement of the Korean Question." It proposed that the Assembly demand acceptance by the North Koreans of a cease-fire, entry of United Nations political and relief personnel into the North, and a United Nations supervised election within a year. On that basis, the de facto jurisdiction of the North Koreans would be recognized until after the election, and United Nations troops would not cross the 38th Parallel until then, when authority would be handed over to a new all-Korean government. If the North Korean authorities refused these terms, the Assembly should then recommend that United Nations forces proceed to eliminate them and occupy the area until an election could be held for the entire country.[19]

Lie dropped his proposal, however, in the face of strong United States objection. Washington anticipated a decisive military result that would in turn permit a satisfactory resolution of the whole Korean problem in terms sought by the Assembly since 1947. It accepted MacArthur's evaluation that the Chinese threats to intervene if the parallel was crossed need not be taken seriously. While evidently feeling that the Unified Command had sufficient authority to decide militarily on its own, the United States wanted a collective endorsement that would strengthen its political force. Since the Soviet return to the Security Council in August had deadlocked further decisions there on the Korean military operation, the Assembly became the focus of further political action when it reconvened in September. In the atmosphere of optimism then prevailing, there was little open opposition outside the communist bloc to a resolution recommending "all appropriate steps" to ensure conditions of stability and the establishment of a unified government, the objective of the Assembly.[20]

These objectives, in the United States view, would necessitate crossing the parallel to destroy the North Korean forces. Although open opposition was small because of the desire to avoid public controversy with Wash-

19. Lie, *op. cit.*, pp. 344–45.
20. A/Res. 376 (V), adopted Oct. 7, 1950, 47–5 (the Soviet bloc), with 7 abstentions (and Indonesia not participating). The abstaining states were: Yugoslavia, which argued that an attempt to change the status quo ante, rather than merely restore it, could set an unfortunate precedent for intervention in domestic affairs; India, which took Peking's warnings seriously and continued to urge that the 38th Parallel not be crossed before trying to get a negotiated settlement; and five Middle East states—Egypt, Saudi Arabia, Yemen, Syria, and Lebanon—no doubt less concerned about the unwisdom of the resolution than about its possible precedent as an action to enforce U.N. settlement terms, specifically in Palestine.

ington, considerable misgivings had been privately expressed. The United States therefore sought to reassure other members with its estimate that Chinese or Soviet intervention was unlikely. It undertook, in carrying military operations north of the 38th Parallel, to construe most conservatively such "appropriate steps" as were necessary. To many others, that meant going only far enough to establish the best line of defense. The Assembly resolution also incorporated a declaration of limited intentions to reassure the communist governments: United Nations forces would remain in Korea only until stability was reestablished and national elections held.

The politically significant parallel was accordingly crossed. MacArthur, however, did not stop at the narrow waistline of Korea, probably the most defensible line, but undertook to march to the Yalu. Neither the military nor political results were as predicted by the United States. Massive Chinese intervention did occur and, as MacArthur described it, created "an entirely new war" that changed both the balance of power in Korea and the essential nature of the conflict. From being primarily a collective enforcement action against a single minor government, it became in effect a clash between the major powers; and the need to prevent its spread beyond the limited war in Korea became the overriding aim. The military setback to United Nations forces enhanced the now obvious unwillingness of most Member states to run the risk of a broader war; while the Truman Administration became convinced that Korea was "the wrong war, at the wrong place, at the wrong time, and with the wrong enemy."[21]

When United Nations forces recovered from their retreat and again moved toward the 38th Parallel, Washington was accordingly prepared to issue a policy statement in agreement this time with the other governments fighting in Korea. It was to have declared:

> The aggressors have been driven back . . . to the general vicinity from which the unlawful attack was first launched last June. There remains the problem of restoring international peace and security in the area in accordance with the terms of the Security Council resolution. . . . The spirit and principles of the Charter require that every effort be made to prevent the spread of hostilities and to avoid the prolongation of the misery and loss of life.[22]

21. Gen. Omar Bradley, head of the Joint Chiefs of Staff, in *Military Situation in the Far East*, Hearings before the Senate Armed Services and Foreign Relations Committees, 82 Cong. 1 sess., Pt. 2, p. 732.

22. Harry S. Truman, *Memoirs* (Doubleday, 1956), Vol. 2, p. 439.

It would also have invited the communists to agree to a cease-fire and negotiation on political issues. General MacArthur successfully forestalled
that declaration, however, by publicly making one of his own threatening
direct military action against China. This insubordination soon led to his
dismissal, but it also confused the situation internationally and further
delayed United Nations cease-fire efforts. Ultimately, the cease-fire was
arranged, and the painful process of armistice negotiations began, finally
resulting in an agreement in 1953.

The course of events as they related to United States strategic and
foreign policies—in particular, the complicating factor of American
domestic political difficulties over the dismissal of MacArthur and over
China policy generally—increased the ambivalence created by the revision,
and then the reversal, of position on the objective of the collective-enforcement operation. The question of appropriate criteria for relating the element of military enforcement to the requirements of political settlement
in any collective-security action thus remained unanswered.

Although it is never possible to know what would have happened had
the attempt been made to initiate action for settlement before the march
to the Yalu, it is possible to point out that even if military events had
ended as they did, the United Nations would have gained its point without suffering such losses. Official declarations that the collective-enforcement objective had been achieved would have been true in 1950, rather
than poor concealment for a sense of defeat in 1951. The case for restoration of the status quo, as the legitimate "victory" in the military part of a
collective-security action, would have been accepted in terms Secretary
Acheson later used during the MacArthur hearings in 1951:

> Our objective is to stop the attack, end the aggression on [South Korea],
> restore peace, providing against renewal of aggression. These are the military
> purposes for which . . . the United Nations troops are fighting.
>
> The United Nations since 1947 has . . . stood for a unified, free, and demo-
> cratic Korea. That is still . . . [its] purpose . . . not sought to be achieved by
> fighting, but . . . by peaceful means, just as was being attempted before this
> aggression.[23]

On the other hand, given both the state of United Nations fortunes when
the parallel was first crossed, and American strategic concepts as then

---

23. *Military Situation in the Far East*, Hearings, Pt. 3, p. 1729. The National
Security Council, in May 1951, also described the military, as distinct from the political, aim in similar terms. See Truman, *Memoirs*, Vol. 2, p. 456.

applied to the cold war and the Soviet threat, the policy followed was understandable, if not inevitable.

"Uniting for Peace": An Attempt at Institutionalization

The Soviet Union returned to the Council in August 1950 and Secretary Acheson proposed to the Assembly, in September, that it "organize itself to discharge its responsibility [for collective security] promptly and decisively if the Security Council is prevented from acting." Declaring that the Council action of June 25 had "marked a turning point in history, for it showed the way to an enforceable rule of law among nations," the Secretary claimed that when the Council is "obstructed" by one member, "the Charter does not leave the United Nations impotent," nor do the obligations of members to maintain the peace disappear. Articles 10, 11, and 14, he argued, also vested in the Assembly "authority and responsibility for matters affecting international peace."[24]

The basis for so organizing the Assembly was laid out by the United States in what ultimately became the Uniting for Peace Resolution, adopted in November.[25] John Foster Dulles, then United States representative in Committee I, argued that:

Korean events have dramatized organizational weaknesses which, in future, could prevent the will and capacity of the member states finding timely collective expression. If the United Nations is really to be formidable enough to deter those who plot aggression, these organizational weaknesses must be corrected.[26]

The resolution accordingly sought to provide for Assembly supervision of military sanctions within the limits of its recommendatory authority, while giving full recognition to the primary responsibility of the Council so long as it could act. Whenever a veto prevented it from acting, however, a special emergency Assembly session could be convened within twenty-four hours by a procedural vote of any seven Members. Although involving only a procedural change, the chief importance of this resolution

24. U.S. Department of State, *Bulletin*, Vol. 23 (1950), pp. 524–45.
25. A/Res. 377 (V), Nov. 3, 1950, by a vote of 39–5 (the Soviet bloc).
26. U.S. Department of State, *Bulletin*, Vol. 23 (1950), p. 651. The U.S. draft text is on pp. 655–56; the final text in *ibid.*, pp. 823–25. The formal move from the Council to Assembly on enforcement questions also came in November, when the Soviet Union vetoed a six-power resolution against the Chinese intervention.

lay in marking a psychological change of attitude toward the political role of the Assembly.

The main institutionalizing provisions recommended that all Members earmark units of their armed forces to be maintained in readiness for future use under either Council or Assembly resolutions; authorized the Secretary-General to appoint a panel of military experts to advise governments, on their request, about setting up the earmarked national units; and established a fourteen-member Collective Measures Committee to study further methods to improve the ability of the United Nations to meet future cases of aggression. These arrangements would provide the elements of a sanctions-force-in-readiness, on a voluntary basis and along lines generally equivalent to those laid down in the Charter. Instead of commitments through Article 43 agreements, the Member governments were unilaterally to designate forces for United Nations use on call of the appropriate political organ. Instead of the Military Staff Committee, professional advice would come from the panel of experts.

The thinking behind this system was a natural outgrowth of the particular circumstances in which the resolution was proposed: the failure to maintain the peace in Korea, the suddenness of the act of aggression, and the general unpreparedness of the Organization to mobilize effectively the power of the general membership. The presence of the Temporary Commission on Korea, as noted, had served to clarify opinion on the *fact* of aggression. The Uniting for Peace Resolution therefore established a permanent agency to fill this role in future, a fourteen-member Peace Observation Commission (POC),[27] to serve either the Council or the Assembly by reporting on the situation in any area threatened by international tensions.

THE COLLECTIVE MEASURES COMMITTEE

Despite the overwhelming majority which passed the Uniting for Peace Resolution, few governments followed their own recommendations. The communist states considered the whole thing illegal; but many others indicated a lack of sympathy. The majority, while favorable to the resolution's purpose, were not willing to make specific commitments. Only Thailand, Greece, Denmark, and Norway made relatively unconditional

---

27. The POC was also related to the U.N. Commission on the Balkans (UNSCOB) which was felt to have operated successfully in connection with the Greek border troubles, and which is considered further below. See Chap. 6, pp. 163, 165–66.

offers of national troop contingents, totaling about 6,000 men; and Uruguay offered two destroyer escorts. Neither they nor any other government ever requested advice from the panel of military experts.

One reason, perhaps, for the poor showing in general was that the United States in particular reneged on its proposal. On the excuse of current commitments in Korea, Washington earmarked neither troops nor facilities—the result, according to one source, of a conflict between the State and Defense Departments. The Defense Department "did not believe the UN could or should be relied on, even in part, for United States security."[28]

The Collective Measures Committee, meanwhile, had begun its studies of the principles and procedures to be used by the Assembly or Council in taking collective action against aggression. In two reports, it largely spelled out lessons already learned from Korea and from smaller-scale experience with Council and Assembly field missions.[29] Because these were largely common-sense proposals, they paralleled in substance the same common-sense principles of Articles 43–47, in providing for the mobilization of national support for international military measures.

Defining the nature and functions of the panel of military experts, the committee recommended, in effect, formalizing an already developed custom of using military officers seconded by governments to United Nations duty, as in Kashmir and Palestine. These panel members would be "in no sense representatives of their countries, and [would] not be instructed by

---

28. Frye, *op. cit.*, p. 60.

29. For example, the committee recommended that, pending conclusion of Article 43 agreements:

"(i) States should take further action to maintain elements in their armed forces so trained, organized, and equipped that they could promptly be made available, in accordance with their constitutional processes, for service as United Nations units;

(ii) States should take [necessary] steps . . . to enable them to provide assistance and facilities for United Nations forces. . . .

(iii) States should examine their legislation and administrative regulations to ensure that they can carry out promptly and effectively, United Nations collective measures, in accordance with their constitutional processes;

(iv) States should continue to survey their resources to determine the nature and scope of the assistance that they may be able to render in support of United Nations collective measures."

U.N. General Assembly, Sixth Session, *Official Records*, Supplement 13. *Report of the Collective Measures Committee*, p. 33. Text of the second report is in *Ibid*, Seventh Session, *Official Records*, Supplement 17. Although a third report was made in 1954 only the first two are of substantive interest.

their governments or report to them," but would, on the contrary, have the privileges and immunities of regular Secretariat employees.[30]

Even these mild proposals for improving the potential availability of national forces were watered down considerably through "interpretation" by the Assembly—for example, that each government would be the sole judge of its capacity to contribute. After a third report in 1954, the Assembly put the committee on a stand-by basis, urging governments to study its recommendations. It does not appear that any of them did even that much. This lack of enthusiasm was succinctly explained by one of the Secretary-General's chief aides in this matter:

The absence of unanimity among the Great Powers on collective security arrangements, present [1953] world tensions, acts of localized aggression, and guerilla activity in areas of instability make it entirely unrealistic for the United Nations to attempt to pin its hopes on advance pledges of specific forces.[31]

PROPOSAL FOR A UNITED NATIONS LEGION

Although it did not get beyond preliminary consideration in the committee, a proposal for a "United Nations Legion" submitted by the Secretariat should also be noted briefly. This was an adaptation of the Lie suggestion for an international volunteer brigade in Korea. Conceived, again, as a minor supplement to basic forces that would be made up of self-contained national contingents, the Legion would have consisted of volunteers from countries not in position to set aside special United Nations units of their own. It would not operate independently of the national contingents nor be, in size or composition, an international army. Its primary purpose would be to facilitate support from smaller states, rather than leave "the extent and nature of their contributions to await detailed negotiation at the outbreak of an aggression."[32] Such states might jointly support an organized United Nations volunteer reserve, or they might enlist individuals in their military establishments, who would undertake to be trained and held in reserve for use in the volunteer reserve.

The Collective Measures Committee took no formal action on this

---

30. *Ibid.* Earlier experience in utilizing seconded national military personnel in U.N. missions is considered further in Chap. 6, pp. 164–66.

31. Col. Alfred G. Katzin, "Collective Security: The Work of the Collective Measures Committee," in Clyde Eagleton, ed., *Annual Review of United Nations Affairs,* 1952 (Oceana, 1953), p. 206.

32. Katzin, *op. cit.,* pp. 212–13.

plan. Secretary-General Lie himself informed the group that he did not wish it to proceed further with the proposal, thus yielding "to the dual pressures of the depreciation or disinterest of Members, and the doubts of his Secretariat colleagues most closely concerned."[33]

Collective Enforcement Proposal at Suez

The growing disinterest in preparations for United Nations mobilization of military enforcement measures matched the gradual recession of East-West tensions that followed the Korean truce of 1953, the Geneva Conference of 1954, and the summit meeting of 1955. It also reflected an increasing American reliance on the development of further regional security arrangements in the Far and Middle East. SEATO and CENTO were established in 1954–55, although conditions in both their areas bore little, if any, resemblance to the situation in Europe that had made NATO an effective military barrier to Soviet expansion. In any event, Korea, as became apparent in the perspective of time, also marked "the end of communist gambling on *direct* aggression in areas of Great Power interest."[34] Instead, communist subversion and guerilla activities were intensified; they were less susceptible to the use of large-scale military forces.

Moreover, the next international crisis brought on by aggression in the form of an organized military invasion of one country by another, the invasion of Egypt in 1956, was a Western responsibility. The affair was marked by the formation of the United Nations Emergency Force (UNEF)—a new kind of international military force for peace-observation, rather than peace-enforcement, purposes—which is considered in Chapter 6. The decision on UNEF, however, was preceded by a Soviet Union proposal for further collective enforcement measures.

When Great Britain, France, and Israel did not comply with the initial United Nations call for a cease-fire and withdrawal, the Soviet representative demanded another Council meeting to discuss "immediate steps to

33. Stephen M. Schwebel, "A United Nations 'Guard' and a United Nations 'Legion'," in Frye, *op. cit.,* p. 216. The plan is summarized in *ibid.,* pp. 209–12; full text in the second report of the Collective Measures Committee, *op. cit.,* p. 29.

34. Lester Pearson, May 7, 1964. Text in Andrew W. Cordier and Wilder Foote, eds., *The Quest for Peace: The Dag Hammarskjold Memorial Lectures* (Columbia University Press, 1965), p. 102.

halt the aggression" of the three governments. He submitted a draft resolution for the agenda urging all members to give military and other assistance to Egypt, including military support under Article 42. Moscow also
suggested that Washington and itself, as permanent members with readily
available air and naval forces, should jointly take the lead in initiating such
assistance on the expiration of a twelve-hour ultimatum to the three invaders to cease their military action against Egypt.[35] The proposed pattern
of action thus adapted to the occasion the form of initial action undertaken by the United States in connection with Korea.

Washington, however, wanted neither to join in any such move, which
would bring Soviet forces into the Middle East under United Nations
auspices; nor to leave Moscow in the position of Egypt's best "friend in
need"; nor to counterbalance Soviet support of Egypt by even counte-
nancing the current invasion of which it disapproved in principle as well
as because of the risk of escalation inherent in it. Considerable behind-
the-scenes diplomatic pressure was brought to bear on the British and the
French, the Secretary-General supporting the United States and Canadian
efforts. Combined with a deep split in British political circles, a run on
sterling of heavy proportions, and public Soviet threats against Great
Britain and France, this sufficed to extract Anglo-French agreement to
cease hostilities before the Council reconvened. Their commitment was
made contingent on Egyptian-Israeli acceptance of a peacekeeping United
Nations Emergency Force, originally proposed by the Canadian Foreign
Minister, to separate the combatants until satisfactory settlements were
reached on the Arab-Israel and the Canal disputes. The acceptances were
obtained, and implemented through the Assembly, so that an actual cease-
fire was imminent when the Security Council met. It was therefore possible to defeat the Soviet draft resolution, thus giving the United States
an escape from the dilemma posed by the Soviet proposal for joint enforcement action.[36]

The abortive Soviet proposal to the United States marked the end of
collective-enforcement discussions on the public agenda for some years.

35. The exchange of messages between Washington and Moscow is in Paul Zinner,
ed., *Documents on American Foreign Relations, 1956* (Harper, 1957), pp. 355–58.
36. The resolution was defeated, 3 in favor (U.S.S.R., Iran, Yugoslavia), 4 against
(U.S., U.K., France, Australia), and 4 abstentions (Belgium, China, Cuba, and Peru).
For further discussion of UNEF, see below, Chap. 6, pp. 173–74.

When the subject came up again in the sixties, it was in a new guise as part of the Soviet and United States disarmament plans.

Collective Enforcement in a Disarmed World

The goal of the disarmament negotiations, as set forth in the joint Soviet-American set of principles endorsed by the Assembly in 1961, is to agree on a program for general and complete disarmament (GCD), under which states would then dispose, individually, only of forces necessary to maintain internal order. The process of disarmament is to be "accompanied by the establishment of reliable procedures for the peaceful settlement of disputes and effective arrangements for the maintenance of peace in accordance with the principles of the United Nations Charter."[37] Those "effective arrangements" are to include a "United Nations Peace Force" as an enforcement agency. The character of that force is not further described in the principles, except that the disarmed states will "support and provide agreed manpower" for it.

SOVIET VERSION OF THE PEACE FORCE

When the Soviet Union presented its disarmament treaty draft to the ENDC in early 1962, it contained no detailed specifications on the means whereby it expected to bring about GCD in three stages over four years. A proposed peace force was included in general terms only, except for being clear that it would operate under the Security Council and thus be subject to the veto. Moscow has consistently held to this doctrinal position, that any use of military personnel through the United Nations is illegal except under Council authorization, control, and command and with advance commitments to be made only through Article 43 agreements.[38]

The Soviet draft did not include machinery for maintaining peace and security under conditions of GCD, so Western disarmament negotiators persistently queried the sort of international force Moscow envisaged to keep the peace if the world really disarmed. Occasional Soviet responses were in line with its basic doctrine, and emphasized, as Khrushchev noted

37. Text in Assembly resolution of endorsement, A/Res. 1722 (XVI), Dec. 20, 1961. The principles were considered at greater length in Chap. 4, pp. 71–73.

38. In practice, however, it has been somewhat less consistent, as is shown in the following chapter.

on one occasion, that such forces would be used only for "international" peacekeeping, not to intervene in domestic affairs, nor to "suppress" forces struggling for colonial "liberation" or social revolution.[39]

Then in February 1964, at Geneva, the British Foreign Minister advocated that a few modest measures be taken in the near future to improve planning for, and the conduct of, the current type of nonsanctions peacekeeping forces. Support for such activities, he said, would be a "good measure of the true desire of states to achieve general and complete disarmament." While that was a broad jump to make from such a narrow base, general (especially Soviet) agreement to support even such mild measures would of course indicate an improved political atmosphere that might bode well for arms control talks also.

Little chance even of that seemed likely, however, as the Soviet delegate made it clear that his government felt no urgency about establishing international forces. He acknowledged that a regular force would be necessary at "a certain stage of GCD in order to protect States against possible violations of such disarmament [and] against possible acts of aggression"; and advocated that it be formed of police or militia contingents made available by members to the Council when needed. Their command should be composed of "an equal number of representatives from each of the three groups of States, and decisions adopted by agreement among them." That would

preclude the possibility of these international forces being used by any particular . . . States for aggressive purposes and to the detriment of the national independence and sovereignty of other countries. . . .

It is our profound conviction [he concluded] that the establishment of international armed forces at the present time, outside the framework of a treaty on general and complete disarmament, might give rise to great difficulties and seriously complicate the international situation.[40]

But in July, Moscow reversed that position with a new proposal for the establishment of regularized United Nations "armed forces" in the near future,[41] of which more will be said shortly. It followed the usual Soviet plan and thus, although presented outside the GCD framework, might logically be seen as the beginning of the kind of permanent force, in a disarmed world, that Soviet interpretations of their draft treaty suggest.

39. Quoted in Alexander Dallin, *The Soviet Union at the United Nations* (Praeger, 1962), p. 138.

40. ENDC/PV. 169, Feb. 25, 1964, p. 26.

41. U.N. Doc. A/5721, July 13, 1964 (also issued as S/5811): "Memorandum of the Government of the USSR regarding certain measures to strengthen the effectiveness of the United Nations in the safeguarding of international peace and security."

UNITED STATES VERSION OF THE PEACE FORCE

In the outline plan, which it submitted in response to the Soviet move of 1962, Washington proposed that a sanctions-type United Nations Peace Force would have to be an integral part of its three-stage measures for armaments control and reductions. The force would ultimately be equipped with "agreed types of armaments necessary to ensure that the United Nations can effectively deter or suppress any threat or use of arms."[42]

In Stage I of the plan, the parties would examine United Nations experience with international forces, including new consideration of the possibility of concluding Article 43 agreements. They would also agree on the establishment of the peace force in Stage II, defining its "purpose, mission, composition, strength, disposition, command and control, training and logistical support, financing, equipment, and armaments." The force would then come into being in Stage II on the agreed bases, "and would be progressively strengthened." In Stage III, it would be further strengthened "until it had sufficient armed forces and armaments so that no state could challenge it." In each stage, the growth of the force would be accompanied by the progressive development of related peacekeeping machinery for the pacific settlement of disputes, the codification of "rules of international conduct related to disarmament" (including means to assure states against "indirect aggression or subversion"), and the investigation of any threat to or breach of the peace by a Peace Observation Corps.

In general, these latter provisions do not appear to go beyond the possibilities of the existing United Nations system. Specifically, however, the "unchallengeable" peace force implies an "international" system that would, in reality, have supranational control over the military enforcement power. For its military and political command would have to be independent of any national control (either positive control or negative control through the ability to prohibit action by some version of a veto right). It would have to be independently maintained, that is, on a *standing* rather than *stand-by* basis, or a strong state could presumably challenge the force by withholding its contribution, whatever the legal status of the parties' obligations. The command element alone is sufficient to show that the parties would have to yield critical sovereign rights to some supranational

42. "Outline of Basic Provisions of a Treaty on General and Complete Disarmament," in ACDA, *Documents on Disarmament, 1962*, Vol. 1 (November 1963), pp. 51–82. Quotations below from this text.

rather than international political organ. Considered simply in terms of the technical requirements of mounting a sanctions force of this type, the same conclusion seems inescapable. As one private study indicates:

In order to maintain a standing force capable of fielding even a division-level expeditionary force, the United Nations would require legal, political, and financial means to requisition and control property, facilities, supplies, and services, in addition to an assured source of and command of personnel, plus certain extraterritorial rights.

And even if all these requirements could be met, it points out, "the problems of maintaining such a force in combat readiness appear insurmountable."[43]

That is not the official interpretation of the GCD plan, however. The United States declares the "overall goal" to be the establishment of "a free, secure, and peaceful world of *independent* states adhering to common standards of justice and international conduct and subjecting the use of force to the rule of law."[44] It is argued that in the far-distant, disarmed, and peaceful world in which Stage III of the Outline plan will become applicable, such a sanctions force and even so strong an international organization would in fact be acceptable.[45] But this is simply to give a new twist to the old fallacy already noted in Chapter 1, which has long bedeviled the argument for world federation as the sure means to world peace.

In that context, the means proposed to eliminate war between states is by federating the states into a world government with monopolistic power to police the peace against any aggressive component unit. Such a federation, however, could not be successfully imposed by constitutional fiat on states in a condition of conflict. It would have to be based on a

43. Institute for Defense Analyses, *National Armaments and International Force*, (Study DAIS, Final Report R–101, July 1963), pp. 58–59. These factors had obviously not been considered by Senator Albert Gore when he proposed a novel version of the U.N. force idea, in February 1967, at Hearings of the Senate Disarmament Subcommittee on the Soviet-American undertaking to begin talks on freezing the ABM situation (see Chap. 4). Gore suggested the possibility of an international force to shoot down any missiles crossing the north polar ice-cap, for which purpose it should be equipped to launch defensive missiles. From *New York Times*, Feb. 4, 1967.

44. ACDA, *Questions and Answers on Arms Control and Disarmament*, prepared for the House Foreign Affairs Committee, 88 Cong. 1 sess., July 11, 1963, p. 7.

45. *Ibid.*, p. 5, for example, recognizes that the disarmed world is a long-term goal, not achievable in today's conditions because it necessitates "major changes in outlook toward world affairs by many nations, including the Soviet bloc countries"; and because the United States would not enter into the final Stage III "unless such changes had occurred."

sufficient community of interests among its member units to guarantee their continued peaceful cohesion. Formal federation, in those circumstances, might further cement a community of interests and standards among states already at peace among themselves; but it could not in itself be the cause of their peaceful relations.

In the context of the GCD plan, the weakness of the argument lies in its concentration on the structure of the technical enforcement machinery, rather than on the controlling political institutions.[46] In the state of GCD defined in the United States outline, the achievement of Stage III is contingent on the successful working of institutions for peaceful settlement and arms control. But independent states that had developed such friendly political relations (the modern Scandinavian states, for example) could, presumably, also succeed in operating an international militia[47] or disarmament-control force through machinery based on principles similar to those of the Charter or assumed by the Soviet approach.

On the other hand, the experience of recent efforts to achieve even the beginnings of nuclear control seem to this writer to make it sheer fantasy to assume that a state of GCD can somehow be brought about between nations still in a serious adversary relationship. More specific difficulties in evolving any kind of permanent sanctions force during the transitional stages en route to GCD, as noted below, also show the need for greater attention to developing political accord and the will to peaceful settlement among governments, rather than continuing the tendency to concentrate on the provision of technical machinery for international settlement and enforcement.

DEVELOPMENT OF A FORCE DURING DISARMAMENT

The examination of experience in Stage I, in order to "strengthen United Nations forces for keeping the peace," will show that such current "United Nations forces" are not sanctions forces writ small, but observer groups or truce supervision teams writ large. As such, they are not prototypes of the desired United Nations Peace Force of Stage III; but should rather be considered as forerunners of the military aspects of the permanent Peace Observation Commission also proposed in the outline.

46. For an interesting speculation on what the GCD proposal would require in the way of political commitments, see Lincoln P. Bloomfield, "Arms Control and World Government," *World Politics*, Vol. 14 (July 1962), pp. 633–45.

47. The Scandinavians already have organized an international "fire brigade" for possible U.N. use. See Chap. 6, p. 214.

Given their small size and peaceful function, they are capable of being organized and used on an ad hoc basis even in contemporary conditions of conflict; and presumably could be institutionalized on a more regular basis should international political relations improve even to a limited degree.

The inherent limitations of these "forces" are frequently not recognized by proponents of GCD.[48] Their tendency is to "fuzz over" the situation by vaguely implying that some long-term process of evolution will somehow transform the current type of peacekeeping force without sanctions into the desired United Nations Peace Force of a disarmed world. Even official statements do not make clear whether that is the implication of the proposed examination and "strengthening" of such forces under the official plan. The political characteristics of the two types of forces are so fundamentally different, however, as to preclude this apparently facile means of evolving a sanctions force.

As part of the transitional machinery of the United States plan, the companion proposal to reconsider negotiating agreements under Article 43 must be supposed to aim at the beginnings of an enforcement system. Both logic and the experience of the Military Staff Committee show that the essential commitments cannot be agreed upon by the major military powers when they are fundamentally disagreed on the nature and standards of international peace and security that are to be maintained by the future force. The conclusion of such agreements along the lines originally anticipated—that is, for sanctions forces—therefore, seems impossible under contemporary political circumstances, especially when the agreements must be concerned with such delicate political issues as command and control.

A sanctions force to prevent or repel conventional acts of military aggression is at least a fairly clear concept in terms of traditional collective-security ideas. The nature and function of sanctions machinery geared to prevent the violation of disarmament agreements is vague to the point of confusion. The United States negotiator at Geneva declared in 1964, for example, that the gradual strengthening of effective peacekeeping and verification machinery was important because the threat posed by hidden nuclear delivery vehicles and weapons would increase as both sides approached "zero" level. Consequently, he concluded, means other than

48. An example of this confusion is to be found in the classification of articles on "peacekeeping forces" (in the majority-U.N. sense) under "Procedures of Coercive Settlement," rather than under "Procedures for Pacific Settlement," in Richard A. Falk and Saul H. Mendlovitz, eds., *The Strategy of World Order* (World Law Fund, 1966), Vol. 3, *The United Nations*, pp. 526–74.

national forces would have to be established for ensuring the peaceful settlement of disputes which might arise.[49] What those means might be, he did not specify, but his argument seemed to assume that substantial progress could be made toward a disarmed world while an adversary relationship continued between the nuclear powers. The unreality of this assumption becomes clear, however, if one tries to work out in concrete terms what the planned stages of disarmament would be likely to mean on that basis.

One such unofficial estimate of conditions at a halfway point in the proposed disarming process (according to the United States plan) in fact makes it clear that, long before reaching a state of GCD, the results would, given conventional military concepts, seriously restrict the national ability to maintain American security interests. It finds, for example, that:

There would still be a wide range of threats to peace and to U.S. interests. Everything from minor border clashes to a nuclear war would still be possible. And in one respect, at least, the U.S. would be more vulnerable than in the present armed world: it would have a reduced capacity to protect geographically distant interests....

In the half-disarmed world the U.S. would be less able to prevent the use of an IMF [International Military Force] against its wishes ... because the U.N. would have increased military capability ... and would not be as dependent upon the U.S. logistically as it is today ...

Further, in terms of relative military capability U.S. allies and friends on the periphery of the Communist world would face a dangerous, perhaps their most dangerous, period in the disarming process. Their own capabilities for defense would be substantially reduced and U.S. ability to assist them would also be diminished. At the same time, the capacity of the Communist powers for aggression against neighboring territories would not have been significantly reduced. This added hazard to U.S. interests could not be offset by any IMF believed to be within the realm of political and military feasibility.[50]

To talk about developing "international" sanctions forces while strategic thinking continues along the above lines is surely a waste of time. This is not to deny the "French thesis" in general terms: that national disarmament will be possible only as an international system is developed that will safeguard nations against aggression. This is also implicit in the Charter. It is, however, to point out that more than the current lip-service will have to be given to the need for increasing political will to peaceful settlement as the major element in any collective security system.

49. Ambassador Foster, in ENDC/PV 165, Feb. 11, 1964, p. 24.
50. Institute for Defense Analyses, *National Armaments and International Force*, Report R–101 (July 1963), pp. 98–99.

Moreover, the *political* problem of transition (from the present situation of unregulated national armaments to the establishment of some permanent international force to safeguard world peace) also tends to be overlooked. Little or no attention is normally given, either to the international political system of which the force would form a part, or to the problem of obtaining the political consent of existing national governments to the commitments necessary for the effective working of the desired system.

The most carefully constructed of such unofficial plans, the well-known *World Peace Through World Law* proposal, tackles the details both of its United Nations Peace Force and of the greatly altered international political system in which it is planned to function. But even it appears to assume that by some great collective act of will humanity (or at least the leaders of the major nuclear powers) will accept and put into effect within a short time the necessary international agreements on Charter revision, GCD, and new institutions that are to bring world peace into being.[51] The costs of modern nuclear weaponry and the dangers of holocaust no doubt *ought* to make mankind more willing to act rationally to maintain peaceful international relations—in the Clark-Sohn, or any other sensible pattern of cooperation. History, however, is not encouraging in this respect.

It has been suggested, on the contrary, that man's incapability, rather than his rationality, might lead him in the end to such a comprehensive plan as that of Clark and Sohn. On this basis, Herman Kahn has written of "what could happen." He imagines an accidental firing of missiles by the Soviet Union or the United States, with reprisal from the other side; but with the accidental nature of the attack soon discovered (presumably via the "hot line") so that more massive attacks are prevented after "only" some five to ten cities on each side have been destroyed—a blow both countries would survive:

One could confidently predict [he continues] that the morning after this event there would be a deeply felt conviction among all nations, but particularly the two antagonists, that deterrence and anarchy were not a good way to run affairs, that we simply could not go back to the old precarious balance of terror and assume the same risks over again. Under these circumstances, it would not be at all surprising to find the United States and the Soviet Union ready to sign something resembling the Clark-Sohn proposals within a few

51. Grenville Clark and Louis Sohn, *World Peace Through World Law* (Harvard University Press, 1960 ed.). Inherent in the plan is the conviction that important political settlements will be impossible without a prior agreement for comprehensive disarmament as part of a more comprehensive security plan.

days. It would be realized that unless an agreement were made within days, that is, before the dead were buried, one side or the other would quite likely try to exploit the common danger for unilateral advantage. . . . Black as this prospect is, a war or crisis is the most likely route by which we shall achieve a more stable world order.[52]

History counsels against expecting easy acceptance of any such full-coverage insurance plans for instant peace. The psychology of politics, moreover, is equally against counting on the kind of national self-control necessary for working out the practical political commitments (including the consent of the Senate in this country) that would have to follow such a tenuous U.S.-Soviet accord, signed over the unburied bodies of un-counted dead! Unlike the optimistic Mr. Kahn, the present writer would indeed be "surprised" by the advent of utopia through such a nuclear "crisis."

One of the few attempts to deal with this problem of transition on some level between that of vague evolution and apocalyptic revolution is in a study by the (British) Institute for Strategic Studies.[53] Starting with the "facts" of the technological impossibility of enforcing an abolition of nu-clear weapons and the existence of "unorthodox delivery systems" (for ex-ample, airliners), the report reached the almost standard conclusion that nuclear disarmament will be possible therefore "only where an interna-tional force can deal with any secret nuclear force which might still exist." To give universal security, the argument went, it would have to be "mili-tarily effective against a great power" and adequate "to deter the use or threatened use of a clandestine nuclear force." But then, the Institute noted:

The fundamental problem . . . is that the origins of the authority of this force have never been clearly defined and there is no obvious international instrument which is likely to command general acceptance. Through their insistence on a continuing veto, the Russians are making it clear that they do not expect any force of this kind to exercise effective control over any power which may remain in the West when the treaty comes into force. The United States and others would be as free to exercise a veto as the Soviet Union. To achieve a disarmament programme which it can claim will lead to general and

52. Herman Kahn, "The Arms Race and World Order," in Morton A. Kaplan, ed., *The Revolution in World Politics* (Wiley, 1962), p. 351. For a more realistic discus-sion of the kind of "negotiation" that is possible with nuclear weapons, see Thomas Schelling, *Arms and Influence* (Yale University Press, 1966), pp. 260–86.

53. Institute for Strategic Studies, *Disarmament and European Security: The Effect of Implementing the First Stage of the Soviet Draft Treaty and the U.S. Proposals* (August 1963); excerpts below from Vol. 1, pp. 69–71.

complete disarmament in the world as it is today, the Western powers must clear their minds about what is acceptable as a world authority.

In the end, it is possible that such an authority might be created through the commitment of national forces to a unified command in the manner foreseen for the more limited purposes of the NATO. This system allows countries such as the United States and the United Kingdom to take part in a unified system while remaining secure in the knowledge they have in the hands of their own officers weapons which can, if necessary, be used under the orders of their own chiefs of staff.

To adapt the NATO command system as here proposed, to the requirements of a disarmed world under the apparent assumptions of the GCD plan, however, would be to try to set up a force that would seek to unify powers presumably still in enough of an adversary relationship for each to fear the possibility of concealed nuclear forces being held by the other party. It is hardly possible, on the other hand, to imagine the allied command of NATO functioning without a degree of trust among its members that exceeds anything even remotely conceivable in the foreseeable future in United States relations with the Soviet Union or Red China. The Institute pointed out that such an international "peacekeeping" authority would, in fact, be "much closer to what the Russians are proposing than what the West appears to be proposing," and would give

the appearance of disarmament without for many years abandoning the reality of national power. But with this security, national military systems would erode away, like the methods of personal and local self-protection in the old American West. The political framework of a disarmed world could be created and could, through custom and acceptance, be relied on increasingly to carry the burden of security.

It would, it should be noted, seem possible to bring such a "political framework" and international enforcement agency into existence under the authority and procedures already existing in the Charter. The problem of *initiating* the joint commitments among states viewing themselves as opponents rather than allies would remain, of course. But if it can be overcome by the development of a greater degree of détente, perhaps something like the Soviet Union's proposal of July 1964[54] would be as workable as any of the more elaborate proposals for establishing an international force in the face of strong political antagonism.

The Soviet memorandum was not geared, however, primarily to a force related to some arms control system, but to the kind of sanctions force

54. Text in U.N. Doc. A/5721, July 13, 1964. Quotations below are from this source. See also *supra*, p. 137.

under Article 43 arrangements that Moscow had originally expressed interest in. Moscow argued that, in cases where the peace is threatened or breached by an act of aggression, it would be "rightful for the Security Council [first] to adopt enforcement measures of a non-military character" under Article 41; but that "situations may [also] arise where the only way to prevent or stop aggressive acts and protect the sovereignty and territorial integrity of a victimized state" is to employ force under Article 42:

Decisions of this kind should be taken, however, only as a last resort and after all the relevant facts have been carefully weighed, for it must be kept in mind that the use of any foreign troops including those of the United Nations to settle conflicts, indeed their very presence in foreign territory, may, as experience has shown, lead to the very opposite result, i.e. to interference in the domestic affairs of States, to grave international complications, to a heightening of tensions.

There followed the usual Soviet argument that only the Security Council is authorized to act to maintain or restore peace, including the power to establish, operate, control, and finance United Nations armed forces. Moreover, to ensure that any United Nations application of sanctions "corresponds solely to the interests of peace and not to the unilateral aims of any particular States or groups of States," such forces should include contingents from "socialist," Western, and neutral countries. "Representatives of the socialist countries" should also be in the command structure. Contingents from any of the permanent members of the Security Council, however, would be "inadvisable." Advance planning, the memorandum continued, should be done by the Military Staff Committee under Articles 46–47, with the Secretary-General "contributing" to the execution of Council decisions "as the chief administrative officer" of the Organization.

The costs of armed sanctions should be reimbursed by the responsible "aggressor States." Emergency conditions might require Member states to "take part in defraying" expenditures, however; and—a new note:

In such future cases when the Security Council adopts decisions to establish and finance United Nations armed forces in strict compliance with the provisions of the Charter, the Soviet Union will be prepared to take part with other States Members . . . in defraying the expenditure involved. . . ."

To facilitate the availability of such forces, the Military Staff Committee should draft the main provisions of appropriate Article 43 agreements for approval by the Security Council; and Members desiring to contribute contingents should then enter into such agreements with the Council.[55]

Thus, in spite of its "troika" twist and its limitation on participation by the permanent members in the proposed forces, the Soviet proposal would, in effect, bring the Charter system of sanctions forces into being.

In August, London replied to this proposal.[56] The British noted that Moscow had ignored the current noncombat type of peacekeeping force with which the United Nations had "fortunately" found means to

contribute to the maintenance of international peace and security by the provision of forces bearing arms, which have entered the territory of the States concerned with the consent of their Governments. Her Majesty's Government hope the Soviet Government have no intention of excluding the possibility of these valuable activities which are clearly in accordance with the United Nations Charter.

The note also expressed London's interest in learning "at an appropriate time" Soviet views on "how and when to resume" Article 43 negotiations. No direct response was made by Moscow. In 1965, however, it resubmitted its memorandum to the Special Committee on Peacekeeping Operations.[57]

In terms of the near future, the most interesting part of the Soviet memorandum was its discussion of the possible application of force in connection with southern African disputes.

The Soviet Union . . . has repeatedly expressed in the Security Council her support of the African countries in their demand that [nonmilitary, yet forcible] measures [under Article 41] be applied to the Union of South Africa, whose quite inhuman *apartheid* policy is threatening the peace of the continent, and to Portugal, which is conducting a colonial war against the people of Angola and adjacent territories.

. . . At the same time, however, the Soviet Government does not deny the possibility of a situation arising where the United Nations has no other choice than resorting to force, according to Article 42 . . . to prevent or stop military aggression or to protect the sovereignty and territory of a country. In the latter, exceptional cases it will be best for United Nations purposes to deploy its military forces to the troubled area.

55. In November and December 1964, Czechoslovakia and Bulgaria offered to make contingents available under Article 43 agreements. See U.N. Docs. S/6070, Nov. 27, 1964, and S/6120, Dec. 18, 1964.

56. U.N. Doc. A/5726, Aug. 5, 1964.

57. See Chap. 10 below, pp. 405–06 for possibility of using Art. 43 to negotiate preparatory arrangements for noncombat peacekeeping forces.

This evokes not Soviet ideas on an international force under some disarmament plan, but Soviet efforts to have the Congo Force used to overcome Katangese resistance to the Leopodville government.[58] It reinforces Soviet support for African attempts to have stronger sanctions voted by the Security Council against Rhodesia, as well as in the longer-term South African and Portuguese cases. Even if the Soviet position were accepted and armed forces provided for through Article 43 agreements, however, the Security Council (complete with veto) would control their utilization, thus guaranteeing Moscow's ability to avoid, when it wishes, the implications of its proposal. That it might so wish began to appear with the Rhodesian case and took a surprising turn during Assembly consideration of the South West African question after the Court's refusal to decide on the merits of the case in 1966 as will shortly be seen.

Collective Enforcement and Political Change

Perhaps no development in the United Nations has been more striking than the broadening concept, epitomized by recent African events, of what constitutes a threat to the peace—and thereby becomes subject to possible enforcement action through the Organization. Article 2(7) made the domestic-jurisdiction reservation inapplicable to "enforcement measures under Chapter VII"; and the San Francisco Conference recognized that internal sources of disorder could come to threaten international peace. France, as noted, even wished to specify that "the clear violation of essential liberties and of human rights" might in itself constitute "a threat capable of compromising the peace."[59]

For some years, however, "threats to the peace" continued to be considered, in the traditional way, as involving hostilities across national borders—by organized guerillas if not by national military forces. Controversies over demands of colonial peoples for independence and those protesting discriminatory racial treatment on a serious scale were either disqualified as domestic issues by the "Western-minded" majority of the United Nations, or at most were treated as issues for peaceful settlement.

As the rising forces of nationalism began to undermine the traditional colonial empires, however, the issues of national self-determination gradually became interwoven with those of human (especially racial) rights,

58. See Russell, *op. cit.*, pp. 86–126.
59. *UNCIO Documents*, Vol. 3, p. 386.

wherever peaceful evolution to independence or majority rule did not occur. By the sixties, the number of new Member states that were also newly emerged from colonial status began to have a telling effect on Assembly voting. The end of apartheid in South Africa, of colonial rule in South West Africa and the Portuguese colonies, and of racial discrimination and white government in Southern Rhodesia were all found by overwhelming majorities to be legitimate objectives of United Nations concern.[60]

When Assembly recommendations failed to bring about changes of policy in those hard-core cases, African Members, enthusiastically supported by the communist states, took the issues to the Security Council as constituting threats to the peace. While the vast majority of Members were willing to put political pressures on the three resistant governments to accept change in the direction of self-government and majority rule, in the form of Assembly and Council resolutions calling for new standards of human and political rights, they were more reluctant to consider collective action to enforce such changes.

By 1962, however, the temper of the Assembly resulted in a resolution recommending that all Members, "separately or collectively," apply a diplomatic and commercial boycott to South Africa in an effort to secure that government's compliance with earlier anti-apartheid resolutions.[61] In 1963, the Security Council passed resolutions recommending arms embargoes against Portugal and South Africa, plus a boycott on the latter's products and a ban on exports to it of "strategic materials of direct military value."[62] Through 1964 and 1965, the two states continued to ignore all United Nations calls for policy changes on their part. Further resolutions were passed by both the Assembly and the Council along similar lines, becoming increasingly stronger in tone; but the Council never went to the extent of finding that Portugal or South Africa threatened the peace or of deciding to order sanctions. Although the Soviet Union encouraged more radical language, Western efforts kept the resolutions technically within nonmandatory limits. Then, in late 1965, developments in Southern Rhodesia, which had been following somewhat parallel lines since 1962, suddenly reached a climax ahead of either the South African or Portuguese cases. The territorial government declared its independence of Great

60. See below, Chap. 7, for further consideration of decolonization issues.
61. A/Res. 1761 (XVII), Nov. 6, 1962, passed 68–16–23.
62. S/Res. 5481, Dec. 11, 1963, passed 10–0–1 (France); S/Res. 5386, Aug. 7, 1963, passed 9–0–2 (France, Great Britain).

Britain, and the affair led to the first mandatory Council action under Chapter VII of the Charter.

THE CASE OF RHODESIA

In 1953, in spite of opposition by African political groups in both North and South Rhodesia and in Nyasaland, Great Britain set up a loose Central African Federation of the three colonies. The British hoped that its economic advantages would, in combination with progressive multiracial advances, win over African nationalist leaders. The racial policies of Southern Rhodesia, a "self-governing colony," made little advance, however, and African opinion became steadily more antifederation. In 1960, a conference to consider modifications in the original federation plan was stalemated by the opposing views of Sir Roy Welensky, premier of the federation, and the African leaders of the two protectorates. In 1961, Southern Rhodesia adopted a new constitution, with voting qualifications that Africans felt were aimed to perpetuate the system of white domination. Repressive measures against nationalist political parties and leaders enhanced their fears.

Early in 1962, the newly established U.N. Special Committee to promote implementation of the 1960 declaration on colonial independence found, and the Assembly later accepted its findings, that Southern Rhodesia was "a Non-Self-Governing Territory in the meaning of Chapter XI of the Charter. . . ." The Assembly also requested Great Britain to take steps to set aside the 1961 constitution and to convene a conference representative of all political parties in the territory to formulate a new constitution ensuring the equal rights of the majority.[63] New measures against African political organizations in Southern Rhodesia led to another resolution in October, deploring such actions as endangering "peace and security in Africa and the world at large."[64] The African sense of urgency was based partly on fear that, when the 1961 constitution became effective, the white government would assume all powers and declare the territory's independence. Although London maintained that Southern Rhodesia was neither sovereign nor independent, it was unwilling to call the proposed constitutional convention or otherwise intervene beyond efforts to persuade Salis-

63. A/Res. 1747 (XVI), June 28, 1962, adopted 73–1 (South Africa)–27 (United States), Portugal and Great Britain not participating.
64. A/Res. 1755 (XVII), Oct. 12, 1962, adopted 83–2 (Portugal and South Africa)–11 (United States), Great Britain not participating.

bury to reverse its policy for one of progressive racial and political liberalization.

During the next three years, after the new constitution came into effect, the situation continued to worsen from the African viewpoint. The Central African Federation was dissolved in 1963, and the other two members achieved independence (as Zambia and Malawi) in 1964. Discussions between Salisbury and London on independence for Southern Rhodesia deadlocked, however, over the issues of minority rule and racial policies. While Great Britain continued to refuse repeated calls from the United Nations for more direct intervention, it did make clear in 1964 that it would not agree to independence without political changes leading toward majority rule and racial equality.

Growing resistance in Salisbury made a "unilateral declaration of independence" (UDI) seem more likely. In May 1965, therefore, an African group requested the Security Council to consider the situation. By 7–0, the Council adopted a resolution[65] "approving" the opinion "of the majority of the population of Southern Rhodesia" that Great Britain should convene a fully representative constitutional conference, and "requesting" London to take any necessary action to prevent UDI. The Soviet Union abstained, obviously feeling the resolution did not go far enough; Great Britain, France, and the United States abstained also, presumably for the opposite reason. London continued to limit its efforts to persuasion, the Assembly to repeat its calls for action in ever stronger terms.

On November 11, all discussions failed and Salisbury issued its UDI. London declared this constituted rebellion and announced economic and diplomatic sanctions aimed to end it. Both the Assembly and the Security Council promptly condemned the UDI and called on all states not to recognize the "illegal racist minority regime."[66] A more detailed Council resolution the following week described the situation as "extremely grave" and declared that "its continuance in time constitutes a threat to international peace and security." Great Britain was called on to "quell this rebellion" and to bring the regime "to an immediate end." The Council also reaffirmed its earlier call for diplomatic sanctions and for a general arms and economic boycott, including specifically "an embargo on oil and

65. S/Res. 202 (1965), May 6, 1965.
66. A/Res. 2024 (XX), Nov. 11, 1965 and S/Res. 216 (1965), adopted Nov. 12 by vote of 10–0–1 (France).

petroleum products"; and urged Great Britain to enforce "with vigor" the economic and other measures it had instituted to end the rebellion.[67]

London opposed African pressures to get it to employ military force against the Rhodesian regime, depending on its nonmilitary measures to bring about the collapse of the illegal government. But Prime Minister Wilson's optimistic view, that nonmilitary sanctions would succeed within a short time, proved false. Pressures for stronger sanctions therefore continued in the United Nations, especially as oil shipments across South Africa and Mozambique thwarted the embargo. The situation came to a climax in April 1966, when a Greek-flag tanker entered Beira, Mozambique, with oil for Rhodesia. (The ship had been intercepted by a British naval vessel off the coast, which failed to persuade the tanker's master not to continue to that port.) The British Government requested Security Council authority to use force to halt any such tankers. The Soviet Union, Bulgaria, and the African members of the Council (Mali, Nigeria, and Uganda) sought a stronger resolution, which would have called for British use of armed force to prevent oil imports into Rhodesia from any source (that is, South Africa as well as Mozambique) and to bring down the Salisbury regime.[68] The Council, however, rejected their proposed amendments in favor of the British proposal to follow a step-by-step approach, confined for the moment to halting tankers approaching Beira. That went beyond the resolution of the previous November in making a clear determination that the "situation constitutes a threat to the peace," and in authorizing Britain to use force if necessary to prevent tankers with contraband oil from arriving at Beira.[69]

Although less than the Africans wanted, the resolution marked a significant breach in London's policy (supported by the United States) of avoiding the invocation, even indirectly, of military force by the United Nations. Portuguese authorities finally took over the vessel a few days later, its oil still unloaded. A second vessel, intercepted by the British Navy on April 10, changed its destination to Durban, South Africa, where it was

---

67. S/Res. 217 (1965), adopted Nov. 20, 1965, 10–0–1 (France).
68. S/Doc. 7243, April 9, 1966, amendment to British draft resolution by Mali, Nigeria, and Uganda.
69. The main operative paragraph read: "5. Calls upon the Government of the United Kingdom to prevent by the use of force if necessary the arrival at Beira of vessels reasonably believed to be carrying oil destined for Rhodesia, and empowers the United Kingdom to arrest and detain the tanker known as the Joanna V upon her departure from Beira in the event her oil cargo is discharged there." S/Res. 221 (1966), adopted April 9, 1966, 10–0–5 (Soviet Union, France, Mali, Bulgaria, Uruguay).

refused permission to off-load. In spite of these measures, African and communist pressures for stronger international action never let up.

The next act took place in London. On April 27, the government announced that it would resume talks with Salisbury in an effort to resolve the conflict peacefully. This was treated by the anticolonialists as a betrayal of the British pledge to end the rebellion. (Prime Minister Wilson had originally declared that he would never negotiate with the Ian Smith government.) Rejecting British efforts to dissuade them, thirty-one African delegations requested another Council meeting, writing to U Thant that:

> We are convinced that any arrangements arrived at between the United Kingdom Government and the Salisbury racist regime, during any negotiations envisaged by the two parties, which excluded the genuine representatives of the people of Zimbabwe [Rhodesian Africans] and which failed to guarantee the rights of the majority would only aggravate an already explosive situation and would thus lead to racial conflict that would envelop all Southern Africa.
>
> Our Governments consider that the Security Council should devote the closest attention to this new situation, which constitutes a threat to international peace and security, and should examine, under Chapter VII of the Charter, the necessary measures to establish majority rule in Southern Rhodesia in accordance with the declaration set forth in General Assembly resolution 1514 (XV).[70]

Their proposed draft resolution would have specifically called on Great Britain to take, among other steps, measures under Chapter VII "in order, by the use of air, sea, or land forces, to prevent any supplies, including oil and petroleum products, from reaching Southern Rhodesia."[71]

In the Council on May 18, Lord Caradon (the British delegate) opposed such action as prejudicial to a peaceful settlement through the talks then going on, which he pledged would not betray African interests.[72] The British have maintained that they will grant independence only on the basis of six principles: (1) unimpeded progress toward majority rule; (2) immediate improvement in the political status of Africans; (3) no retrogressive amendment of the constitution; (4) progress toward the end of racial discrimination; (5) a basis for independence acceptable to all Rhodesians; and (6) guarantees against oppression by either majority or minority of the other. If the talks should fail, Caradon argued, stronger measures could be considered. Ambassador Goldberg supported this posi-

---

70. S/7285, May 10, 1966, pp. 1–2. Res. 1514 is the Declaration on Colonial Independence.
71. S/7285/Add. 1.
72. *New York Times*, May 19, 1966.

tion, pointing out that "to fall apart would only give support to the Smith regime." It was, moreover, the "main objective" of the Organization "to bring about the solution of international problems by peaceful, not violent, means."[73]

Against these efforts to persuade the Africans not to press their resolution, communist influence worked to reinforce fears that the British-Rhodesian talks indicated a sellout and that British-American cooperation represented collusion against African interests. A vote was eventually demanded, but the resolution failed of adoption (May 23) due to the large number (8) of abstentions: Great Britain, the United States, France, the Netherlands, China, Japan, Argentina, and Uruguay.[74] A British veto was not necessary, therefore.

Anglo-Rhodesian talks continued, with intermittent pauses, through the fall of 1966, in spite of increasingly gloomy prognostications and intensifying suspicions on the part of the African states. In September, Prime Minister Wilson promised the Commonwealth Prime Ministers that he would ask the United Nations to authorize mandatory economic sanctions if settlement efforts failed. In December, the efforts collapsed.[75] Wilson immediately requested the Security Council to declare the situation a threat to the peace and to order sanctions against a selected list of exports and of military imports.

Its failure to propose a complete embargo (especially the omission of oil) brought forth denunciations from African and communist delegations. The British eventually gave way in part on the import issue. They accepted a provision to embargo all oil products, and added nonmilitary "aircraft and motor vehicles" to the list. But they successfully opposed

73. U.S. Department of State, *Bulletin*, Vol. 54 (1966), p. 991.

74. Only New Zealand voted against the resolution. The six votes in favor were cast by Mali, Uganda, Nigeria, Jordan, Bulgaria, and the Soviet Union. *New York Times*, May 24, 1966.

75. Texts of statements at the time talks were broken off are in the *New York Times*, Dec. 6, 1966. In October and November, the Assembly had passed resolutions expressing "grave concern" over the "talks about talks," and condemning in advance "any arrangement" between London and Salisbury that might transfer power to "the illegal racist minority regime . . . on any basis." The second also called for a complete economic embargo and for Great Britain to "take all necessary measures, including in particular the use of force . . . to put an end to" the Rhodesian regime. See A/Res. 2138 (XXI), Oct. 22, 1966 by vote of 86–2 (Portugal and South Africa)–18 (including the United States, which objected to the harshness of the indictment of Great Britain and to the call for the use of force); and A/Res. 2151 (XXI), Nov. 17, 1966 by a nonroll-call vote of 89–2–17.

other amendments that would have called on them to prevent, by force if necessary, the transport of the banned items through South Africa or Portuguese territory. The Security Council's resolution "decided" that "all Member States . . . shall prevent" the various prohibited actions, including: "participation in their territories or territories under their administration or in land or air transport facilities or by their nationals or vessels of their registration in the supply of oil or oil products to Southern Rhodesia."[76]

The United States supported the British position on Rhodesia. Ambassador Goldberg, noting that Great Britain had granted independence to twenty-eight former colonies, especially urged the Council to recognize that government's constitutional responsibility for Rhodesia. This was an important point in the United States view, as the Ambassador indicated in answer to certain criticisms from American sources. It is argued, he said,

that the application of mandatory sanctions to Rhodesia constitutes a dangerous precedent for similar action wherever any violations of human rights may be involved. This argument overlooks a number of unique elements in the Rhodesian situation. Here we have witnessed an illegal seizure of power by a small minority bent on perpetuating the subjugation of the vast majority. Moreover, in this situation the sovereign authority with international responsibility for the territory has asked the United Nations to take measures which will permit the restoration of the full rights of the people of this territory under the Charter.

.   .   .   .   .   .

Law in the United Nations, as in our own society, is often developed on a case-by-case basis. We should analyze each action of U.N. political organs with due regard for the facts of each case and be careful of hasty generalizations. Because the Security Council considers the situation in Rhodesia, with its unique legal and factual elements, as constituting a threat to the peace requiring the application of mandatory sanctions, does not absolve it from an independent exercise of judgment in different situations.

76. S/Res. 232, Dec. 16, 1966, passed 11–0–4 (Soviet Union, Bulgaria, Mali, and France). Ambassador Federenko explained Soviet abstention as due to the defeat of five African amendments that would, in addition to that noted above, have deplored British refusal to use force against the Smith regime, condemned South Africa and Portugal for assisting it, and have sought to enforce a wider trade embargo and the formal withdrawal of British offers of settlement terms to the rebel government. (See U.N. Security Council, Twenty-first Year, *Official Records*, Meetings, December 8–16, 1966, for the draft proposals and debate.) The Rhodesian exports ban covers asbestos, iron ore, chrome, pig iron, sugar, tobacco, copper, meat and products, hides and leather products.

Moreover, each of the Permanent Members of the Security Council has the power to prevent the use of enforcement measures in other situations where it may deem them to be inappropriate.[77]

The implications of his remarks were obvious for the other southern African cases in which the African and other anticolonial states have long sought mandatory sanctions. In the case of South West Africa, it had been hoped that the Court's decision might provide another channel through which the enforcement of political change could be brought about, namely in terms of implementing a Court decision.[78] This was not to be the case.

SOUTH WEST AFRICA

Without reviewing the lengthy tale of United Nations concern with South West Africa, suffice it to note that South Africa, alone of the League mandatory powers, failed to place its mandate under the trusteeship system of the United Nations. This led to persistent efforts, through the Assembly and through advisory opinions of the Court, to pressure Pretoria into accepting the supervisory authority of the world Organization. In time, the mandate problem became intertwined with the apartheid issue in South Africa itself, leading in 1960 to Liberia and Ethiopia (former League members) bringing the problem to the International Court as a contentious case. After six years (a lengthy period even for the Court), that body declined in July 1966, to give judgment on the status of the territory or the obligations of South Africa.[79]

South Africa interpreted the refusal as vindication of its position; but practically all other governments were as shocked as they were surprised by the decision. Inevitably, South West Africa received priority attention from the Assembly in the fall, with the anticolonial powers generally demanding an immediate confrontation with South Africa. The United States and Great Britain, strongly opposed to such a policy, led an opposition sufficient to get a compromise resolution adopted almost unanimously.[80] This terminated the forty-six year old mandate of South Africa

77. U.S. Department of State Press Release 304, Dec. 29, 1966, pp. 6–7.

78. Art. 94 (1) makes the Court's decision legally binding, while 94(2) authorizes the Security Council, "if it deems necessary [to] make recommendations or decide upon measures to be taken to give effect to [its] judgment."

79. See South West Africa, Second Phase, Judgment, *I.C.J. Reports*, 1966.

80. A/Res. 2145 (XXI), Oct. 27, 1966, adopted 114–2 (Portugal and South Africa)–3 (France, Britain, Malawi) and 2 absent (Botswana, Lesotho).

and declared South West Africa "under the direct responsibility of the United Nations." It also set up an Ad Hoc Committee for South West Africa "to recommend practical means" for administering the territory so the people might "exercise the right of self-determination and achieve independence." It was instructed to report to a special Assembly session by April 1967. The United States became a member of the fourteen-nation committee; but Great Britain declined to serve.

Not surprisingly, the Ad Hoc Committee proved unable to agree on a single set of recommendations to the Assembly. Instead, it submitted three draft resolutions: (1) A group of African states proposed to establish a United Nations commission and council for direct administration of the territory, with a call for the application of forcible sanctions under Chapter VII if necessary to remove the area from South African control. (2) A Latin American submission also called for direct United Nations administration but stopped short of specifically calling for enforcement measures. (3) Canada, Italy, and the United States suggested the appointment of a special representative (on nomination of the Secretary-General) and a United Nations Council for South West Africa (three or more members to be designated by the Assembly President), to which the former would report. He would survey the entire situation, "consult with all representative elements" in the territory, and determine the conditions necessary to establish "a nucleus of self government ... as soon as possible" and the achievement of "self-determination and independence."[81] The U.S. representative stressed that their proposal sought peaceful means for implementing the intentions of the Assembly resolution of the previous October.[82]

The stalemate in the Ad Hoc Committee was repeated in the fourth special Assembly in April-May, forcing a number of compromises in the draft resolution finally adopted. This was essentially a merging of the Afro-Asian and Latin American positions and was sponsored by seventy-nine states. It established an eleven-member council for South West Africa responsible to the Assembly, to administer it until independence (if possible, to be attained by June 1968). The council, to be based in South West Africa, is to "enter immediately into contact with the authorities of South Africa" to arrange for the transfer of administration, the withdrawal of South African police and military forces and other personnel. The resolution also provided for a U.N. Commissioner as an execu-

81. U.N. Doc. A/AC. 129/L.6, March 15, 1967.
82. USUN Press Release 26, March 20, 1967.

tive-administrative officer of the Council and requested the Security Council "to take all appropriate measures to enable the . . . Council for South West Africa to discharge [its] functions and responsibilities . . ."[83] South Africa, as expected, refused to recognize any United Nations competence in the matter.

There were thirty abstentions in the voting, which included all the permanent Security Council members except China. The continued objections of the United States and Great Britain are not surprising in view of Washington's insistence on an initial attempt to establish a dialogue with Pretoria looking toward peaceful solution.

I do not know [said Ambassador Goldberg during the debate]—nobody can know—whether such a dialogue would be fruitful. But I do know that public opinion in my country, and indeed in many parts of the world, would not understand a policy which seems ready to resort to immediate coercion rather than explore the possibilities of peaceful progress. . . . What is needed now is not confrontation, but consultation.[84]

But if the resolution was too strong for the United States, it was too mild for the Soviet Union and other communist states. They had argued that the Assembly demand immediate South African withdrawal from the territory and speedy independence for South West Africa without any kind of United Nations trusteeship or other presence. The communist states endeavored to soften their refusal to support African desires for collective action against South Africa by suggesting that the Organization of African Unity (OAU) should become involved in assisting the territory—a proposal that the Ivory Coast delegate found "not very fortunate" —and to evade the issue by declaring that South Africa could defy the United Nations only because of the support it received from the Western powers.

WIDER IMPLICATIONS OF RHODESIA AND
SOUTH WEST AFRICA

In the United States, the application of a U.N. recommended arms embargo against South Africa has caused no public difficulty; but no action has been taken by the government to apply financial or economic

83. A/Res. 2248 (S-IV), May 19, 1967, adopted 85–2 (Portugal and South Africa)–30. In June, the Council members were elected: Chile, Colombia, Guyana, India, Indonesia, Nigeria, Pakistan, Turkey, U.A.R., Yugoslavia, and Gambia.
84. USUN Press Release 49, April 26, 1967.

restrictions similar to its regulations against trade with Rhodesia (which were extended after the Security Council's action in December 1966). South Africa, although to a lesser extent than Portugal, which is a member of NATO, is considered by many to have strategic value as part of the Western anticommunist system, its apartheid and South West African policies notwithstanding. American investment in, and trade with, the country are large and have been growing in recent years, although they are still far smaller than British interests there. As a result of the Rhodesian experience, moreover, the effectiveness of economic sanctions to bring down a stubborn government is more than ever in question, unless a full-scale blockade could be instituted. This could be seen as the beginning of the more direct military sanctions demanded by more militant anti-colonial states. Even if American opinion developed in favor of such drastic action, the increasing strains of the Vietnamese conflict would make it difficult to assign sizable United States forces for the purpose.

Such favorable opinion does not, in late 1967, seem likely to develop. It is doubtful that most Americans are even aware of the way in which the issues are developing in southern Africa. It is fairly certain that neither Congress nor the public would be willing, in effect, to go to war for the Africans' right to vote. The administration has had enough trouble trying to explain why Americans should pay such a high price to support the South Vietnamese right to self-government, as part of a United States policy of resisting communist expansion. It would no doubt have even more difficulty in explaining why the use of force in support of African nationalists' right to self-government should be undertaken as a matter of principle. There must still be many who would agree with one journalist's description of the Security Council's action against Rhodesia, in April 1966, as "cracking down on a country at peace" while the United Nations ignored "Red aggression in Asia."[85]

As for the Soviet Union, although it had written in March 1966 to the Secretary-General to declare its support for "the most determined measures, including force, against the South African Government in order to compel it to apply the principles of the [1960 Declaration] to South West Africa,"[86] in 1967 it abstained in the voting on Resolution 2248, as noted. Nevertheless, it is still possible in theory to imagine a situation where, if

85. "Double Standard for UN? Action on Rhodesia and Vietnam," *U.S. News & World Report*, April 25, 1966, p. 50. See below, Chap. 6, for further discussion of Vietnam and the United Nations.

86. Quoted in *Soviet News*, #5256, March 25, 1966, p. 4.

Great Britain or the United States vetoed a Security Council call for sanctions against South Africa, the Soviet Union might accept an Assembly recommendation as a legitimate basis for action. In practice, however, it is difficult to imagine Moscow deliberately leading the militant Africans in such an international enforcement measure. Southern Africa presumably remains peripheral to its interests, and assistance to subversion is infinitely cheaper than large-scale sanctions.

Most Americans, even if visualizing future conflict, do not understand the African viewpoint, which sees a clear and present danger in the current policies of the three white governments. African states also see, in British reluctance to attack the Rhodesian and South African regimes forcibly, a "white" double standard, since no such reluctance was formerly displayed in putting down colonial rebellions where the defiance of authority was displayed by black Africans. Unless greater consensus can be developed on the criteria of what constitutes a threat to the peace, therefore, the United Nations will probably see a continuation of the flow of strong resolutions that fail to induce action by the powers most capable of implementing them. It is an ironic reversal of situation for the United States from 1950. Indulgence in mutual recriminations about double standards will probably also continue, which will not improve the Organization's already threatened capacity for peacekeeping. Meanwhile, the rebellious government in Salisbury continues as unyielding as in 1965, and the resistant one in Pretoria defies the United Nations and continues to strengthen its defenses, economically and militarily.

CHAPTER SIX

PEACEKEEPING
AND THE PROCESSES OF SETTLEMENT

The uncertainty and confusion that mark the present state of peace enforcement are also characteristic of the current state of "peacekeeping." The term itself, widely used since the Suez crisis of 1956, was formalized only in February 1965, in the title of a Special Committee on Peace-Keeping Operations established by the General Assembly. Its meaning was then haggled over for some months, but the committee reported back to the Assembly in August without agreement on what the term "peacekeeping" involved.

The *concept* of peacekeeping and its practice, on the other hand, have been evolving throughout the life of the United Nations—with little dispute during the first fifteen years. Accepted as an adjunct to the more traditional pacific settlement procedures within the chambers of the Organization and through regular diplomatic channels, it takes the form of related field operations to help effect the suspension of actual or incipient international violence. It is thus a device to give the forces of negotiation and settlement time to pacify and resolve a conflict situation.

There was little or no concern for many years over precise definitions, until the relatively large-scale peacekeeping operations in Egypt and the Congo came under fire for external political reasons. Politics then led, in the next few years, to the serious financial and constitutional crises that paralyzed the nineteenth General Assembly and still hold in thrall the future of the Organization.

Although debated in terms of the proper scope of "peacekeeping," the underlying political controversy is a fundamental one over constitutional authority and institutional means, understandable only in light of the earlier experience of the United Nations in promoting pacific settlement. More than is usually recognized, cases handled by the United Nations in its early years set the patterns of peacekeeping that have recently come under attack. Articles 106 and 107 of the Charter envisioned a postwar transitional period during which the great powers would direct the security tasks involved in ending the conflict and deciding the peace settlements (much as they were then directing the war). Meanwhile, the new world Organization would acquire its political sea legs, possibly even before the end of hostilities. World War II came to a close unexpectedly soon, however, before the Charter was ratified. Moreover, it proved impossible for the major allies to agree fully either on transitional arrangements or on a satisfactory permanent settlement. The maintenance of the latter had been expected to "provide an initial community of interest" to the permanent Security Council members.[1] The United Nations itself, however, became involved in numerous issues relating to the establishment of that postwar status quo, as well as in all the types of international security problems that were to plague the future: those concerned with still pending peace settlements, with the emergence of nationalist forces, and with subversive communist efforts to seize governments.

United Nations Settlement Patterns: 1945–50

The Security Council was hardly organized, in January 1946, when it began to receive charges and countercharges about the continuing presence of major power troops in foreign countries after the end of hostilities. Its first case was Iran's complaint against the failure of the Soviet Union to withdraw its troops. This was met by retaliatory communist charges against the continued presence of British troops in Greece and Indonesia. Syria and Lebanon, in turn, soon complained of the British and French troops that remained in their countries. Council hearings and discussions led, in the first and last cases, to accords between the parties on withdrawals that were shortly effected. The Council refused to act on the Greek and Indonesian cases, where charges against the British military presence were brought by the Soviet Union and the Ukraine, not by the countries concerned.

Many subsequent complaints to the Security Council have also been handled by such conciliatory and mediatory actions. Its discussions have sometimes led to formal recommendations, sometimes merely to dip-

1. Statement of John Foster Dulles in connection with U.S. proposal to establish the Interim Committee of the General Assembly, text in U.S. Department of State, *Bulletin*, Vol. 17 (1947), pp. 671–72.

lomatic "assumptions" of cooperation, which the parties then implemented. Similar settlement procedures were usual in the League, and have
been continued by the United Nations, supplemented by behind-the-
scenes negotiations and by supporting diplomacy outside the international
institution. They have often proved adequate to subdue the international
tensions that made a situation appear potentially dangerous to peace.

Action beyond Council discussions and direct negotiations, however,
was also called for when disputes involved violence. In December 1946,
for example, the Security Council first utilized a subsidiary investigatory
committee to check Greek complaints that border violations by its neighbors constituted threats to the peace. When Soviet vetoes blocked further
consideration of the case in 1947, it was removed from the Council's
agenda and taken up by the Assembly.[2] That organ in turn established its
first subsidiary field group, the Special Committee on the Balkans
(UNSCOB), to observe the situation and assist the parties in reaching
settlement. Similar field operations were authorized by the Security
Council between 1947 and 1949, in connection with cease-fire and truce
agreements between the Netherlands and Indonesia, between India and
Pakistan over Kashmir, and between Arabs and Jews in Palestine. In the
last case, the Assembly was cooperatively and contemporaneously involved
with the Security Council in support of mediatory and truce-observation
activities.

Besides supplementing the Council, the Assembly also played an active
role of its own in the pacific-settlement field. Governments unable to make
headway by more traditional means in a difficult situation turned to the
plenary body in numerous cases. In 1947, for example, Great Britain
called for the first Special Assembly, to deal with the future of Palestine
after the end of the British mandate. The Assembly proposed a solution by
partition, as recommended by its Special Committee on Palestine; but was
unable to implement it, especially after the proclamation of independent
Israel and its immediate recognition by the United States.[3] The Assembly

2. This was not the first time a case blocked in the Council was subsequently taken
up by the Assembly. In December 1946, Poland had asked the latter to recommend
diplomatic sanctions against Franco Spain, after the Soviet Union had vetoed a Council
resolution because it was too weak in finding the Franco regime merely a "potential"
threat to peace, and because it wrongly suggested that the Assembly (rather than the
Council) should recommend severance of diplomatic relations unless the regime was
replaced.

3. See Trygve Lie, *In the Cause of Peace* (Macmillan, 1954), pp. 166–70, for an
account of the controversy over proposed enforcement of the Palestine plan.

then created another subsidiary "organ," the United Nations Mediator in Palestine, to work both with the Truce Commission established by the Security Council and with the local authorities in an attempt to bring about a political settlement.

By 1947 also, the United States was deadlocked with the Soviet Union over jointly establishing a provisional government for Korea. Washington took the problem to the General Assembly, but in Korea—unlike Palestine —the submitting party did not control the entire area for which the Assembly was asked to make recommendations. The latter created a Temporary Commission on Korea to help arrange for elections and the establishment of a national government; but that effort also failed, the crucial problem being inability to reach an agreement acceptable to both sides on who would be allowed to vote.

Greater success was achieved in other cases, however. The Security Council was made guarantor of the independence and integrity of the Free Territory of Trieste (although it never performed the function because the plan for the territory eventually foundered). The disposition of the Italian colonies was referred to the Assembly in 1948, as agreed in the Italian Peace Treaty, in the event that the four powers had not decided the issue within a year. In this instance the Soviet Union may have been willing to accept United Nations intervention because it would not otherwise have been involved in the final decisions, inasmuch as it controlled none of the territories in question. In 1949, consequently, the Assembly decided that Somaliland should become sovereign after ten years under a trusteeship administered by Italy; that Eritrea's future would be decided only after a five-member commission ascertained local wishes more fully; and that Libya should become independent by 1952, meanwhile being aided by a United Nations commissioner to draw up a constitution and establish its government.[4]

COMPOSITION AND FINANCING OF
SUBSIDIARY MISSIONS

The early subsidiary missions, following League of Nations precedent, were composed of diplomatic officials of the states named as members. When necessary, those delegates used military officers (also provided by

4. For this story, see the forthcoming study by Adrian Pelt, *Libyan Independence and the United Nations: Planned Transition from Colony to Statehood* (Carnegie Endowment for International Peace, 1968).

their governments) to carry out some types of field work, such as observation of cease-fire or withdrawal agreements or investigation of alleged border violations. Such national personnel came, in time, to be seconded to the United Nations Secretariat while on their international missions—a practical development since their service was often prolonged.

Utilization of military personnel was most striking in connection with Security Council-Assembly cooperation on Palestine. After Count Bernadotte was appointed United Nations Mediator by the Assembly, he requested "some military personnel to assist him in truce control functions," on which he was cooperating with the Truce Commission.[5] The governments on the commission seconded some fifty military officers for duty as United Nations observers. Not long afterwards, Bernadotte also asked for "50 guards to assist the military observers in their truce control functions." Secretary-General Lie appealed for volunteers from the Headquarters guard and Secretariat staff, who were promptly flown to Palestine. There, "unarmed and with the United Nations uniform as their only protection," they did guard duty, provided transport, and performed other essential chores.[6] The number of professional military observers was eventually increased to some 700, after armistice agreements were concluded in 1949 between Israel and its four Arab neighbors, Egypt, Jordan, Lebanon, and Syria. The observers were continued by the Security Council to help implement the agreements. They were formalized as the United Nations Truce Supervision Organization (UNTSO) and operated with four mixed armistice commissions under a Chief of Staff. Thus, a practice begun of necessity and "almost by accident" in 1947 had evolved into accepted usage by 1949.[7]

The Secretariat's relationship to the field missions changed with the passage of time. Originally, in Indonesia and Greece, Secretariat members performed only a limited servicing function. This reflected basically a lack of capacity in the Secretariat resulting from both inexperience and the distrust of Member governments, who tended to view it in a passive role such as that played by the League Secretariat. In 1947, in the Indonesian case,

5. The commission was set up by the Council in April 1948, when Arab-Jewish violence increased as the end of the mandate approached. It was to include those members with consuls in Jerusalem: Belgium, France, the United States, and Syria. The last refused to participate, however, which meant that the commission did not include nationals of one of the subsequent combatants.

6. Trygve Lie, *op. cit., pp.* 187–88.

7. Brian E. Urquhart, "U.N. Peace Forces and the Changing United Nations," *International Organization*, Vol. 17 (Spring, 1963), p. 341.

the Security Council had to resolve formally that the Secretary-General should act as "convenor" of the Good Offices Committee it had appointed and arrange for the organization of its work. The Assembly committee on the Balkans (UNSCOB) planned to use seven observation groups on Greece's borders and requested operating funds from the Secretary-General so as to "safeguard" their international character. But the request so greatly exceeded the Assembly's appropriations for UNSCOB, that a major part of its expenses—such as for salaries, transport, and equipment—had to be provided by the participating governments.[8] The United States supplied logistical support for the missions, thereby instituting what was to become a customary American role in United Nations peacekeeping activities.

Secretariat services for the Palestine Commission in 1948 were headed by Dr. Ralph J. Bunche as "principal secretary." When the commission was replaced by a mediator, Bunche became head of Count Bernadotte's staff as Secretary-General Lie's "personal representative." When Bernadotte was assassinated in September 1948, Lie named Bunche as Acting Mediator, and the Security Council ratified his action. It did not accord Bunche the full title of Mediator, however, although he carried out the function until armistice arrangements were completed in 1949, the first Secretariat member to serve in such a role.

The habit of always naming government representatives as members of the field missions was thus slowly eroded in favor of Secretariat membership in civilian as well as military phases. The drawn-out nature of the more serious conflicts made the continuity of the Secretariat, in dull times as well as in crises, a more efficient basis of organization and reporting once the members accepted it as a normal channel. But it took time to develop such acceptance on the part of governments jealous of their prerogatives or simply habit-bound. It is still far from full-fledged, as witness the Soviet complaints in 1965—in line with habitual communist resistance to extended third-party activity by the Secretariat—against "excessive" activity by U Thant in the Kashmir crisis.

The financial pattern that was later to cause much difficulty also became well established in this first period. Initially, each government delegation on a field mission met its own expenses, with only the few United Nations personnel paid from the Organization's budget. Supplies and equipment were of necessity largely provided on loan or as contributions by the participating Members or the parties. The salaries of nationals seconded to

8. *United Nations Yearbook, 1947–48,* pp. 298–99.

the United Nations missions were usually continued by their governments, with an additional per diem paid by the Organization. Thus a mixture of charges on the international budget and of contributions from the national governments became an established method of financing such operations.

FAILURE TO INVOLVE COMMUNIST STATES

Where the activities of subsidiary organs would have taken them into communist-controlled areas, they were invariably met by refusals. Albania, Bulgaria, and Yugoslavia, for example, would not allow UNSCOB to enter their territories from Greece. The Soviet Union rebuffed both the Korean Commission and one to investigate conditions for holding free elections precedent to the unification of Germany. The forum of the Assembly provided some means of highlighting Western grievances against Soviet policies and of giving some vocal support to the United States declared "liberation" policy for the "captive peoples" of eastern Europe. In the Security Council, too, cases like the Berlin blockade of 1948 or the communist coup in Czechoslovakia served political purposes even when action was prevented by Soviet vetoes.

The 1947 peace treaty with Italy, as noted, led to some constructive United Nations action in Western-controlled territories; but those with Bulgaria, Hungary, and Rumania provided no equivalent means of effectively putting the Organization into the communist picture when the Assembly in 1949 sought ways to activate the commissions of settlement provided for in the event of disputes over treaty terms. Attempts to bring legal complaints to the International Court likewise ran into communist rejection of its jurisdiction—a perfectly legal position in view of the Court's lack of compulsory jurisdiction.[9]

ATTEMPTS AT INSTITUTIONALIZATION

Paralleling these ad hoc political developments, attempts were made to formalize new rules and to create new machinery through which the pacific-settlement authority of the Security Council might be regularized

9. The United States suffered from this situation on three occasions—when it sought to bring communist governments before the Court in connection with "aerial incidents" (involving American aircraft and crews) in Hungary, with Czech aircraft over the U.S. zone of Germany, and with Soviet aircraft over Japanese territory. On each occasion the other government maintained that there was no reason the Court should deal with the question; and the Court consequently ordered the cases removed from its list.

and the General Assembly might act more effectively on settlement cases when the Security Council was stymied by a veto.

The United States took the initiative in the Assembly's establishment in November 1947, after transfer of the Greek cases to that organ, of an Interim Committee to function between regular Assembly sessions.[10] It was intended to serve, in the political field, much as the Economic and Social Council and the Trusteeship Council acted to give preparatory consideration to issues in their fields.[11] It was boycotted as illegal by the Soviet bloc, however, so it could take no effective action on matters requiring communist cooperation, that is, on any significant matters. Its chief activity was to make some interesting studies and recommendations intended to liberalize the Security Council voting system and to improve pacific settlement machinery.[12] Its efforts became of relatively less interest after the outbreak of the Korean episode; and after a decline in activity, it was adjourned sine die in March 1952.

In an attempt to diminish the effect of the veto, the Interim Committee recommended that the Security Council consider as procedural thirty-five types of decisions in pacific-settlement cases, such as sending fact-finding or observation missions to troubled areas, and that the permanent members agree among themselves not to exercise the veto in such decisions when seven favorable votes were cast. It also proposed that the Council adopt the League practice of using one of its members to act as a rapporteur in each case (with agreement of the parties to the dispute). He would attempt informal conciliation before the Council became formally embroiled in the merits of the dispute. In response to other recommendations, the Assembly changed some rules of procedure and established a

10. This was a committee of the whole, more popularly known as the "Little Assembly," A/Res. 111(II), Nov. 13, 1947.

11. The Security Council had been intended, in effect, to "screen" items in the political-security field by seizing itself of the more important ones, which the Assembly could not act on while they were under Council consideration (Art. 12). The Soviet Union had originally proposed that the Assembly should not be able to consider any question until the Council gave it permission to do so. Ruth B. Russell, *A History of the United Nations Charter: The Role of the United States, 1940–1945* (Brookings Institution, 1958), p. 441.

12. See James N. Hyde, "Peaceful Settlement Studies in the Interim Committee," in *International Conciliation*, No. 444 (1948), pp. 531–59; "Issues Before the Fourth General Assembly," *Ibid.*, No. 453 (1949), pp. 535–39; "Issues Before the Fifth General Assembly," *Ibid.*, No. 463 (1950), pp. 372–74.

panel for inquiry and conciliation. Each member was invited to designate to the panel persons who, "by reason of their training, experience, character, and standing" would be "well-fitted to serve as members of commissions of inquiry or conciliation."[13] None of the recommendations to the Council was ever adopted in practice, nor has the panel for inquiry and conciliation ever been actively used.

In an effort to extend the usefulness of the improvised field guard sent to the Palestine Mediator, Secretary-General Lie proposed in 1948 that the Assembly create a United Nations Guard Force of some 800 men, "entirely non-military in character," to provide support for field missions and protection to their personnel and property. The guards were to have no police powers, to be armed only with personal defense weapons, and to accompany any mission only with the consent of the government of the country concerned.[14] The proposal was strongly opposed by the Soviet Union, which maintained that no United Nations "armed forces" could be organized except under Article 43, that Lie had already violated the Charter in improvising his team for Palestine and only wanted to legitimize his action. Other governments accepted the legality of the plan but raised questions of costs, size, or the guard's relationship to local forces. The Secretary-General subsequently reduced his proposal to a small unarmed Field Service, to perform abroad only the functions of the Headquarters Guard in New York. In 1949, the Assembly found his authority already adequate to allow recruitment of such a Field Service as part of the regular Secretariat.

It also approved the compilation by the Secretary-General of a Field Reserve Panel, of persons nominated by Members, to be available for such observation or truce functions as the Assembly or Council might require. The Soviet Union protested that the panel, too, infringed on the Security Council's functions. The panel, however, like that for inquiry and conciliation, was by-passed in practice in favor of more effective and speedier direct consultation by the Secretary-General with interested Member governments whenever special military or civilian personnel were needed to augment the regular Secretariat staff. The Field Service alone, of all these

13. A/Res. 258 (III), April 28, 1949. The Secretary-General has accordingly maintained the panel of names so submitted by relatively few states.

14. U.N. General Assembly, Third Session, *Official Records*, Pt. 2, Annexes, 1948 (A/656), Sept. 27, 1948.

early measures, proved itself in practice because in effect it did no more than extend accepted machinery in meeting an immediate practical need.

Action and Reaction, 1950–56

The Peace Observation Commission (POC), established as part of the Uniting-for-Peace Resolution, had also been influenced by the satisfactory Western experience with UNSCOB in Greece. Like the Field Service, it was an attempt to make permanent an ad hoc device that had already proved useful. When UNSCOB reported in 1951 that external aid to small guerilla groups in Greece still constituted a threat, the Assembly substituted for the earlier body a Balkan Subcommission of the POC with similar powers.[15] Subcommission observers continued to report on the Greek situation until 1954, when the group was withdrawn at Greek request. Since then, the POC has remained in existence—but unhonored, unsung, and unused.

The efforts to provide, through the Assembly, alternate means to overcome the rigidities and limitations of the Security Council in the pacific-settlement field were thus almost as unrewarding as those subsequently made, through the Uniting-for-Peace Resolution, to turn the Korean pattern of military enforcement into a permanent system of Assembly machinery and procedures. In reaction to United Nations limitations in the Korean case, as seen by American military strategists, the United States extended its regional and bilateral accords to form a global security system against "international communism." The policy, characterized as "pacto-mania" by unsympathetic observers, may have deterred Soviet aggression; but it did not bring about any noticeable international pacification. The cold-war atmosphere of the period also handicapped the United Nations as an instrument of pacific settlement and its formal machinery was less extensively employed in that area as well.

In 1954, however, the office of the Secretary-General began to be more actively used in this field. In connection with efforts to obtain the release

15. The 14-member POC included the 5 permanent members, Colombia, Czechoslovakia, India, Iraq, Israel, New Zealand, Pakistan, Sweden, and Uruguay. (A/Res. 377A [V], Nov. 3, 1950.) The Balkan Subcommission included Colombia, France, Pakistan, Sweden, and the United States. (A/Res. 508–B [VI], Dec. 7, 1951.) The POC was the only part of the Uniting-for-Peace Resolution that the communist bloc would have anything to do with.

of American airmen held by Peking after the Korean armistice, Dag Hammarskjold undertook his first personal mission of a mediatory character.[16] The success of his unorthodox approach, which resulted in the release of the airmen (as a unilateral Chinese act) later in 1955, was to lead to an ever-increasing role for the Secretary-General.

The first half of the fifties also saw the development of three factors—racism, self-determination, and an increasing number of weak new states in the Assembly. In combination these helped to create a new series of United Nations peace and security cases eventually involving the Organization in another expansion of pacific-settlement activities. Earlier charges by India against South Africa for its treatment of people of Indian origin, for example, gave way in 1952 to a broader attack in the Assembly on the question of racial conflict resulting from the policy of apartheid. The Assembly set up a commission to study the situation.[17] It was refused admission by South Africa, which declared the question ultra vires. Two other issues that were to remain long with the United Nations were also brought before the Assembly in the early fifties: Indonesia (in connection with West Irian) and Greece (in connection with Cyprus) appealed for action on the ground of national self-determination rights of the claimant party. Nothing much but talk happened at that time.

In 1955, however, a cold-war stalemate that had prevented the admission of a long list of applicant states was resolved by a political horse-trade whereby sixteen new members, both communist and noncommunist, were admitted simultaneously.[18] While most of them were not "new" nations, this break in admissions also opened the way for the relatively facile admission policy that shortly thereafter began to expand the Organization's membership by the rapid influx of newly independent former colonies. Their interests then began to shape the Assembly and to influence Security Council actions.

Late 1956 saw this influence begin to make itself felt with the outbreak of military violence in Egypt. On November 4, the Assembly passed reso-

16. The United States initiated Assembly action on a resolution (A/Res. 906 [IX], Dec. 10, 1954), declaring the detention of the airmen a violation of the Korean Armistice, condemning their trial as spies, and requesting the Secretary-General to seek their release "by the means most appropriate in his judgment." For an account of this mission, see Joseph P. Lash, *Dag Hammarskjold: Custodian of the Brushfire Peace* (Doubleday, 1961), pp. 56–65.

17. A/Res. 616A (VII), Dec. 5, 1952.

18. The states admitted were: Albania, Austria, Bulgaria, Cambodia, Ceylon, Finland, Hungary, Ireland, Italy, Jordan, Laos, Libya, Nepal, Portugal, Rumania, and Spain.

lutions authorizing the Secretary-General to take action in connection with invasions of both Egypt and Hungary.[19] The two issues had earlier been vetoed in the Security Council, then transferred to the Assembly, which had called for cessation of hostilities and withdrawal of foreign troops. There the parallels between the two cases diverged.

The Hungarian case did not lead beyond limited international action, since the Soviet Union never conceded its use of force was in violation of the Charter nor did it heed the efforts of the Organization to get it to withdraw. The new government installed in Budapest refused to admit either a United Nations investigatory mission sent by Hammarskjold or the Special Committee on Hungary which the Assembly then set up. The latter was limited to acting outside the country. Even so, the United Nations passive measures of condemnation and exposure, its assistance to escaping victims, and facts that were brought before the world in the report by the committee[20] tarnished the Soviet reputation and may, for all anyone knows, have inhibited any tendency to repeat the procedure.

The episode dramatized the limits of either United Nations or regional security action when the major members of an international agency are unwilling to apply their collective military power for enforcement purposes. The United States, theoretically, might have sought to mobilize the majority of the international community, which had voted for the condemnatory resolution, in an operation under Article 51. Or it might have sought to oppose the Soviet action through NATO, but that agency was in disarray over the concurrent Suez crisis. In the circumstances, however, Washington was prepared neither to lead such collective actions nor to act on its own in line with its declared "liberation" policy.

Military Peacekeeping Operations

The situation in Egypt developed quite differently and resulted in the formation of the first United Nations military peacekeeping force. The welter

19. A/Res. 998 (ES–I) requested him to submit a plan for setting up, with the consent of the nations concerned, a United Nations Emergency Force to "secure and supervise the cessation of hostilities" already agreed to in Egypt by Israel, France, and Great Britain. A/Res. 1004 (ES–I) requested him to investigate the situation in Hungary following the outbreak of fighting between Soviet armed forces and Hungarians. A/Res. 1000 (ES–I), Nov. 5, 1956, established the U.N. Command for UNEF.

20. *The Report of the Special Committee on the Problem of Hungary, June 12, 1957*, U.N. Doc. A/3592.

of inter-Arab rivalries, Arab-Israeli conflict, and Arab-Anglo-French controversies that had beset the Arab world from the Atlantic to the Persian Gulf ever since the end of the war, erupted in political cataclysm in November 1956, with the Israeli invasion of Egypt. British and French invasions followed almost immediately on the plea of protecting the Suez Canal. Turning to the United Nations in the situation was almost inevitable, if only because of the long history of the Organization's concern with Palestine and of its more recent involvement in problems resulting from Egyptian nationalization of the Canal. In addition, however, the United States did not want to get involved directly, especially against its NATO allies and Israel, and especially not in company with Khrushchev[21] and Colonel Nasser. It wanted even less to see the Soviet Union come to the rescue of Egypt, which appeared at least possible. Washington therefore joined in promoting the use of a new style peacekeeping force, which the Canadian representative, then Foreign Minister Lester B. Pearson, first formally proposed.[22]

Both the United States and the Soviet Union were in fact willing to accept this international means of restoring the status quo, and the three invaders, Great Britain, France, and Israel, were susceptible to their diplomatic and not-so-diplomatic pressures for a cease-fire and withdrawal. The great majority of smaller powers also favored it, although from a multiplicity of motives.

UNITED NATIONS EMERGENCY FORCE (UNEF)

The United Nations Emergency Force was accordingly authorized by the Assembly, which also endorsed the guiding principles proposed by the Secretary-General to govern it.[23] Those were subsequently summarized by Hammarskjold as follows:

[Any] such force, unless it were to be called into being by the Security Council under Chapter VII of the Charter, must constitutionally be a non-fighting force, operating on the territories of the countries concerned only with their consent and utilized only after a decision of the Security Council or General Assembly regarding a specific case, for those clearly international purposes

21. See above, Chap. 5, pp. 134–35 for the Soviet proposal for a joint enforcement action.

22. For a detailed account of UNEF, see Gabriella Rosner, *The United Nations Emergency Force* (Columbia University Press, 1963). See also Lester B. Pearson, "Force for U.N.," *Foreign Affairs*, Vol. 35 (April 1957), pp. 395–404.

23. The Secretary-General made two reports on the proposed force: texts in U.N. Doc. A/3289, Nov. 4, 1956 and U.N. Doc. A/3302, Nov. 7, 1956, U.N. General Assembly *Official Records* (ES-1), Agenda Item 5.

relating to the pacific settlement of disputes which are authorized by the Charter.[24]

UNEF's particular purpose was to help maintain quiet during the agreed troop withdrawals and to secure compliance with other Assembly directives, although it had neither strength nor authority to enforce them. Far larger than any preceding United Nations peacekeeping mission, its function was nonetheless politically similar and its organization was adapted from earlier patterns. A commander, Lt. Gen. E. L. M. Burns, was drawn from the nearby UNTSO and various Members contributed men, equipment, and facilities, not least of which was the logistical support provided by the United States. The 6,000 troops of UNEF were supplied by ten governments in organized national contingents. It was a true armed force (rather than a paramilitary force, strictly speaking),[25] but could use its arms only in self-defense. That was interpreted in United Nations terms to mean never initiating the use of force, never applying more than the necessary minimum, and then only when all efforts at peaceful persuasion had failed. Nevertheless, the sheer novelty of seeing an international military force commanded in the name and under the flag of the United Nations, by Secretariat officials under Assembly direction, was so great that its limited authority and its strictly pacific-settlement function were widely overlooked.

The financing pattern also followed precedent, combining voluntary contributions of nonreimbursable services from participating governments with payment for other expenses from the Organization's budget. Because of the emergency situation and the unusual size of the operation, the Secretary-General recommended setting up a separate account of $10 million for initial outlays. The Assembly accepted this, eventually apportioning it according to the 1957 budget scale; but it decided that additional expenses should be financed by voluntary contributions. By October 1957, little more than half of the assessed $10 million had been received; and only six states had even pledged contributions toward the extra costs ($3.8 of an estimated $6.5 million), of which some $600,000 was paid in. This pattern of inadequate contributions, both assessed and voluntary, was to set a precedent for the future.

24. *Introduction to the Annual Report of the Secretary-General on the Work of the Organization, 16 June 1957–15 June 1958,* U.N. Doc. A/3844/Add. 1, p. 2.

25. See Lt. Gen. E. L. M. Burns, *Between Arab and Israeli* (Ivan Obolensky, 1963), p. 313.

SUBSEQUENT MILITARY OPERATIONS

The same basic characteristics have applied to subsequent peacekeeping operations involving the use of military personnel, regardless of their varying sizes, mandates, and details of organization and operation.[26] These included an observation group in Lebanon (1958); a second United Nations Force in the Congo (ONUC, 1960–64); a small security force in West Irian (1962–63); a minor observation mission in Yemen (1963–64); another substantial force in Cyprus (UNFICYP, since 1964); an expanded India-Pakistan Observation Mission in Kashmir (UNIPOM), which in 1965 supplemented the earlier United Nations Observer Group of 1949; and the handful of observers sent to the Suez Canal area in July 1967 (under the Chief of Staff of UNTSO) after the renewed Egypt-Israel hostilities had been ended with a cease-fire in June.

Only ONUC became critically contentious in regard to its functions and its methods of carrying out its mandate.[27] Because it was extraordinarily large and costly in United Nations terms—including over 20,000 troops at its height and costing over $100,000,000 annually—the political controversy over its operation was reflected in more widespread failures by Members to pay their assessed costs and to make voluntary contributions. The financial deficit of the Organization mounted rapidly after 1960.

Among the sources of ONUC's difficulties were: (1) a lack of clarity in the resolutions of Security Council and Assembly on the authority granted the force, to do what, and how; and (2) the fact that so many governments (including the Congolese), in one way or another and at one point or another, actively opposed ONUC in spite of their Charter obligation to give it at least passive support. External forces of opposition sought to turn the force to the ends of whatever factions within the Congo they were supporting; and the internal factions each opposed, at various times, ONUC's efforts to keep from becoming party to their internal conflicts—that is, to follow its instructions "not to enforce any specific political solution of

26. See Ruth B. Russell, "Development by the United Nations of Rules relating to Peacekeeping," *American Society of International Law, Proceedings* (1965), pp. 53–60.

27. For a fuller account of the ONUC military operation, see Ernest W. Lefever, *Crisis in the Congo: A U.N. Force in Action* (Brookings Institution, 1965).

pending problems or to influence the political balance decisive to such a solution."[28] The internal situation might have been managed without the complicating foreign factor that made a clear, consistent mandate to the force impossible. External attempts to control domestic political factions might have been resisted had any effective Congolese government existed.[29]

ONUC nevertheless managed for nearly four years to carry out the various mandates given the force: to monitor the withdrawal of Belgians, eliminate the foreign mercenary element, deter civil war, and maintain a modicum of law and order throughout a territorially integrated Congo. Its conciliatory political efforts eventually brought about the establishment of a generally recognized central government once more. Its technical assistance and crash training programs produced some Congolese able to conduct the government and economy. Unfortunately, the force was unable to fulfill the security goal of the assistance program—to retrain the Congolese army into a respectable, nonpolitical force. Leopoldville refused to allow the United Nations to undertake this basic retraining. It insisted on bilateral military assistance, which ONUC's presence, in turn, prevented. ONUC was not an occupying army, however, and United Nations officials considered that they lacked both authority and means to act without the government's cooperation.

In mid-1964, in spite of growing internal disorder, the ONUC force was withdrawn, its international mission (if not its internal one) largely accomplished. Although Chinese communist influences were known to be behind various rebel groups in the Congo, the "foreign factor" was no longer either overt or "colonial," as in 1960. The apparent domestic nature of the current conflicts, especially in combination with other difficulties of the world Organization, resulted in general political disinterest in the Congo and even greater financial resistance to further support for the United Nations peacekeeping operation.

In spite of the strains of the Congo experience, however, several smaller undertakings were initiated during the life of ONUC, as already noted. These later operations were better able to maintain their status as impartial adjuncts to pacific-settlement endeavors through the Organization.

28. Hammarskjold's joint report to the Security Council on the force, July 18, 1960, U.N. Doc. S/4389, para. 13.

29. See Robert C. Good, "The Congo Crisis: A Study of Post Colonial Politics," in Laurence W. Martin, ed., *Neutralism and Non-Alignment* (Praeger, 1966), especially pp. 40–45.

The most successful operation politically, the Security Force in West Irian, achieved this rating because the political conflict between the Netherlands and Indonesia, which gave rise to it, was resolved even before the force went into action as part of the general settlement terms.[30]

The small group of observers sent to Yemen in 1963, which had literally no mandate beyond that of observation, was technically successful; but since the parties in conflict (Egypt and Saudi Arabia) failed to carry out their commitments to cease their intervention in the Yemeni civil war, the international presence in itself did not lead to settlement of the original dispute. Nor was outside diplomatic influence (especially that through the Arab League) any more successful. The United Nations mission was subsequently reduced, then finally withdrawn in 1964.

When the Kashmir cease-fire collapsed in the fall of 1965, it was restored by the Security Council after the cessation of all aid from the United States and with the assistance of Soviet conciliation at Tashkent. An additional group of observers was required to supplement the original United Nations Mission in supervising the restoration of order. Neither the Council nor the persuasions of the great powers, however, was able to move the parties beyond withdrawal of their forces to earlier positions and on to some step toward political settlement.

UNEF conducted its border patrols until May 1967. Egypt then dramatically demonstrated how fragile any peacekeeping operation is[31] when not sustained by a strong degree of political accord. President Nasser formally demanded the withdrawal of UNEF only after moving elements of his army into positions that, as a practical matter, destroyed the usefulness of the force as a buffer.[32] The subsequent renewal of fighting between Israel and Egypt, Syria, and Jordan also disrupted the functioning of the

30. See Ruth B. Russell, *United Nations Experience with Military Forces: Political and Legal Aspects* (Brookings Institution, 1964), pp. 126–32.

31. See *United Nations Emergency Force: Report of the Secretary-General*, U.N. Doc. A/6672, July 12, 1967, pp. 5–10 for general observations on the peculiar limitations of peacekeeping operations.

32. His prompt acceptance of the withdrawal demand caused considerable criticism of U Thant, for acting on his own initiative and for not resisting the Egyptian demand and taking the issue to the Security Council or the Assembly. The criticism is hardly valid in light of the complex facts of the situation (many of which were not publicly known at the time). See the detailed *Report of the Secretary-General on the Withdrawal of the United Nations Emergency Force*, U.N. Doc. A/6730/Add. 3, June 26, 1967.

UNTSO groups throughout the area of hostilities. When the Security Council, after difficulties, managed to obtain a cease-fire, the inadequately staffed UNTSO was brought back into service. As the new Israel-Egypt cease-fire line on the Suez Canal was not covered by the 1949 armistice arrangements, however, a new Council decision was required to extend United Nations observation there—where the forces of Egypt and Israel faced each other, and the cessation of hostilities was most tenuous. Political differences between the Soviet Union and the United States—as well as between the parties to the conflict—severely handicapped agreement in this instance. It was not until July 10, therefore, that the Council approved a "Consensus expressed by the President," to the effect that the Secretary-General should proceed as he had suggested in statements before the Council, on July 8 and 9, 1967, to request the Chief of Staff of UNTSO, General Odd Bull, to work out with the two governments the necessary arrangements to station United Nations observers in the Suez Canal sector.[33] The planned total of observers at this strategic point was only thirty-two men, but continued disputes between the parties delayed full implementation of the arrangement beyond the end of July.

The Cyprus Force (UNFICYP) continues to maintain a modicum of order in the island, although near breakdown was threatened by Turkish air attacks in the summer of 1964, in retaliation for Greek-Cypriot destruction of two Turkish-community villages. UNFICYP was extended for the eleventh time in June 1967 (until December 26), with the usual expression of hope "that sufficient progress towards a solution by then will make possible a withdrawal or substantial reduction of the Force."[34]

The Inter-American Peace Force

Meanwhile, in 1965, the United Nations became involved for the first time with a regional peacekeeping force, the Inter-American Peace Force in the Dominican Republic. As both the United States and the United Nations were involved in the Dominican affair, it will be considered briefly.[35]

33. U.N. Doc. S/8047, July 10, 1967.
34. S/Res. 238, June 19, 1967.
35. For an excellent survey of UN-OAS relationships to 1964 see Inis L. Claude, Jr., "The OAS, the UN, and the United States," *International Conciliation*, No. 547 (March 1964).

The Charter, Article 52(3), clearly encourages pacific settlement through regional organizations.[36] The situation is less clear-cut when a dispute becomes violent enough to involve military activity and when the distinctions among pacific settlement, self-defense, and enforcement action may be ambiguous. Difficulties arise both from the terms of the Charter and the character of existing regional organizations. For the three general regional organizations share a common characteristic in that, in each area, the majority of member states have declared their opposition to common membership with (even to the continued existence of) certain other governments, which would normally be considered natural members: the Organization of African Unity (OAU) against the "white European" governments of Africa, the Arab League against Israel, and the Organization of American States (OAS) against communist or communist-supported governments in the hemisphere. Since Article 53 declares regional agencies should not undertake "enforcement action" without Security Council authorization, disagreement has been endemic for years over the meaning of enforcement in relation to peace and security actions by the OAS.

Both the United States and the Latin American governments have shown ambivalent attitudes toward the regional-world relationship. A preference exists for keeping regional quarrels within the regional framework; but because of historical antipathy toward United States hegemony, the Latin Americans also regard the United Nations as a hedge against too much Yankee domination. When intra-American cases have been brought before the Security Council, however, the United States (with a certain amount of diplomatic pressure) has usually been able to obtain Council concurrence in recognizing OAS authority to handle the particular disputes, because it has secured the support of its other allies as well as of the majority of Latin American governments.

Within the hemisphere, the major security issue between the United States and the other governments has been the nature and intensity of the communist threat. The critical issue is the point at which radical leftist movements in Latin America become the "Marxism-Leninism" which

36. "Regional organizations" is here used to denote the three general agencies: the OAS, the League of Arab States, and the Organization of African Unity (OAU). These are the only ones that comprise both security and nonsecurity functions, and aim to maintain the peace among their members, as well as to provide for collective defense against external threat. They are, in that sense, roughly equivalent regionally to the United Nations.

the Ministers of Foreign Affairs in 1962 declared "incompatible with the inter-American system." They then urged OAS members to "strengthen their capacity to counteract threats or acts of aggression, subversion, or other dangers to peace and security resulting from the continued intervention in this hemisphere of Sino-Soviet powers. . . ."[37] This referred primarily to Cuba which was "excluded" from "participation in" the OAS.

Washington's fears of further communist takeovers influenced its interpretation of an outbreak of revolutionary violence in the Dominican Republic in April 1965. The fighting caused a serious breakdown of internal order, leading to a threat to the safety of foreigners in Santo Domingo, to a request from Dominican "military authorities" for United States assistance and, on April 28, to a military intervention in response, which Washington claimed was solely a rescue mission.[38] Controversy still rages over whether the subsequent enlargement and transformation of the United States military action into an occupation operation, in effect, were justified by the claim of imminent communist success in overturning the military junta then asserting control.[39] Suffice it here to note that the United States sought shortly to justify its action in terms of the OAS resolutions against communist intervention, and to mollify the general hue and cry over Yankee intervention by offering to transform its unilateral military force into an inter-American peacekeeping force through action by the OAS.

OAS ACTION

The United States had acted originally without consultation through the regional body, thus enhancing Latin suspicions of its offer to "transfer its responsibility to the OAS at the earliest possible moment."[40] The OAS consultative meeting, however, quickly called for a cease-fire, appealed for establishment of an international neutral refuge zone, and sent a Special

37. Eighth Meeting of Consultation, Ministers of Foreign Affairs, Punta del Este, Uruguay, January 1962. Text in U.S. Department of State, Bulletin, Vol. 48 (1962), p. 278. The resolution was the chief concern of the United States at the meeting, while economic aid programs were the main interest of the Latin Americans.

38. Ibid., Vol. 52 (1965), p. 738.

39. See, for example, Sen. J. William Fulbright's speech in Congress on Oct. 22, 1965, as contrasted with the Department of State's "white paper": The Dominican Crisis: The Hemisphere Acts, Publication 7971, October 1965.

40. Ambassador Bunker's statement, text in U.S. Department of State, Bulletin, Vol. 52 (1965), p. 740.

Committee to the island to offer good offices, investigate the situation, and make recommendations for future action. But Latin American governments remained so opposed to the military intervention, as violating Articles 15 and 17 of the OAS Charter,[41] that it took a full week to marshall the necessary two-thirds majority (14 votes) to establish the inter-American force proposed by Washington.[42]

The Inter-American Peace Force differed in certain important respects from the standards of United Nations peacekeeping forces described above. Although based on voluntary contributions of national military and police contingents and operating under an international agency, its "Unified Command" was not established by the OAS Secretary-General but was worked out between the Special Committee in Santo Domingo and the commanders of the national contingents. The command was reminiscent of Korea; but the chief of the Brazilian contingent, rather than the head of the twenty-times-larger United States contingent, was made commander.[43] Moreover, only when the Unified Command determined the force to be "adequate" was it permitted to take responsibility from the United States forces for keeping the peace. It is not surprising that the "inter-Americanness" of the command was widely considered more a matter of form than of substance.

41. Art. 15. "No State or group of States has the right to intervene, directly or indirectly, for any reason whatever, in the internal or external affairs of any other State. The foregoing principle prohibits not only armed force but also any other form of interference or attempted threat against the personality of the State or against its political, economic and cultural elements." Art. 17. "The territory of a State is inviolable; it may not be the object, even temporarily, of military occupation or of other measures of force taken by another State, directly or indirectly, on any grounds whatever. No territorial acquisitions or special advantages obtained either by force or by other means of coercion shall be recognized."

42. The resolution was adopted 14–5 (Chile, Mexico, Uruguay, Peru, Ecuador), Venezuela abstaining. U.S. Department of State, *Bulletin*, Vol. 52 (1965), text in Annex A. To obtain that vote required the support of the peace mission in Santo Domingo, plus the vote of the Dominican representative of a presumably nonexistent government, plus a commitment by President Johnson to withdraw unneeded U.S. troops whenever the "unified [OAS] command . . . determines that the Inter-American Armed Force is adequate for its assigned purposes." (The title of the force was subsequently changed to "Peace Force.") Withdrawal of the force was to be determined by the Consultative Meeting of the OAS. *Ibid.*, p. 862.

43. Brazil and four Central American states contributed contingents, only the first of significant size, and the force was activated on May 23. Some 1,700 Latin Americans (1,000 Brazilian) replaced an equal number of withdrawn U.S. troops. Improved conditions shortly allowed the U.S. to reduce its own forces, from a high of about 25,000 men, to some 11,000 in July; and again to 6,800 by December 1965.

The most important difference from United Nations peacekeeping operations was to be found in the political purposes of the OAS Force. Washington claimed that neither its forces nor the Inter-American Peace Force was intervening in an "enforcement action," in the sense of Article 53 of the United Nations Charter, because they never aimed at "asserting any authority to govern any part of the Dominican Republic" but were intended to "preserve for the people . . . their right to choose their own government free of outside interference."[44] Nevertheless, both the United States and the OAS actions set political (noncommunist) limits within which the Dominican factions had to act in finally agreeing on a new government, aided by the mediatory efforts of the OAS group. The United Nations operations have sought to remain completely neutral in treating local factions. Their successes (as in Lebanon and Cyprus) only underscore the political dangers that resulted from the inability of ONUC to maintain that standard in the unique circumstances that applied to the Congo.

Latin objections to the force were due not only to general suspicions of Washington but also to the broader implied doctrine that foreign intervention is justified when a communist takeover is said to be threatened.[45] Latin Americans were divided among themselves on the interpretation to be given the OAS resolutions against communist influence in the hemisphere. These divisions affected, in turn, the fate of the Dominican question in the United Nations.

UNITED NATIONS ACTION

The Soviet Union promptly brought the Dominican case before the Security Council, condemning Washington's "armed intervention" as in violation of the Charter. It demanded immediate withdrawal of United States forces, and later also denounced the Inter-American Force as illegal. Ambassador Stevenson recognized the Security Council's right to concern itself, but questioned both the need and wisdom of its intervention, which

44. Under Secretary Thomas C. Mann, *New York Times* (May 19, 1965), p. E–3. The resolution authorizing the Inter-American Peace Force declared "its sole purpose" to be "in a spirit of democratic impartiality," to cooperate "in the restoration of normal conditions in the Dominican Republic, in maintaining the security of its inhabitants and the inviolability of human rights, and in the establishment of an atmosphere of peace and conciliation that will permit the functioning of democratic institutions."

45. A Montevideo dispatch, for example, reported concern that Brazil might attempt to invoke the Dominican crisis as a precedent for intervention in Uruguay. *New York Times*, June 9, 1965, p. 14.

would "complicate" the effective OAS activities. Uruguay, which had voted against the force in the OAS, worked in the Council for a compromise that would insert that organ into the situation, without condemning the regional activity. Lacking strong Latin American support, the United States therefore accepted a resolution that described the Security Council as "deeply concerned at the grave events in the Dominican Republic," called for a strict cease-fire, and "invited" the Secretary-General to send a representative to "report" on the "present situation" to the Council.[46]

The few United Nations officials (including the Secretary-General's Military Adviser) sent in response to this resolution had such a weak mandate that there was no question of any direct conflict with the Inter-American Force or the conciliation commission. Since all were concerned with the same objectives, theoretically they should have been able to cooperate in their activities. But in practice, especially at first, there was apparently more competition than cooperation between the two missions, in part because there was no speedy resolution of the internal political controversies. Neither international mission had notable success in resolving Dominican difficulties, nor did further debates in the Security Council and the OAS Meeting of Consultation result in rapid progress toward political pacification within the Dominican Republic.

Space does not permit detailing the complicated events of the following year; but in spite of resistance to the program of the Provisional Dominican Government, especially from rightist military elements, and of sporadic outbursts of violence, the promised national elections were held on June 1, 1966, and a moderate constitutional government was elected. All three presidential candidates were united in calling for withdrawal of the Inter-American Force, whatever else they disagreed on. Toward the end of June the first troops (United States) were accordingly withdrawn as a symbolic gesture before the inauguration of President Joaquin Balaguer. The end of the force was marked on September 20 by the departure of its Brazilian commander after a farewell ceremony.[47] In October, the Dominican Government expressed its appreciation for the United Nations interest, but declared the objectives of the Security Council had been accomplished and it would therefore be advisable to withdraw the U.N. mission —which was forthwith done.[48]

46. S/Res. 203, May 14, 1965. Text also in U.S. Department of State, *Bulletin*, Vol. 52 (1965), pp. 869–85 with U.S. statements in the Council.

47. *New York Times*, Sept. 21, 1966.

48. See U.N. Press Release M–1709, Dec. 31, 1966, p. 7.

Thus another peace-keeping operation appeared to be concluded by the resolution of the political problem underlying it. The regional aspect, however, raised a broader problem, as the Secretary-General pointed out. While not questioning the competence of regional agencies to function in the field of peace and security in accordance with their constitutions, U Thant raised the problem of:

the functioning of regional organizations vis-à-vis the United Nations . . . under the Charter. . . . If a particular regional organization, under the terms of its own constitution, deems it fit to take certain enforcement action in its own region, it naturally follows that other regional organizations should be considered competent, because of the precedent, to take certain enforcement action within their own regions.

And he specifically mentioned the Organization of African Unity and the League of Arab States as coming under this generalization.[49]

Current pressures for United Nations sanctions against the southern African "white" governments have made all too apparent the implications of U Thant's comment in that continent; and in their efforts, the African states already have the moral support of the Soviet Union, as noted in Chapter 5. The implications for the Arab-Israeli disputes are equally obvious. Both raise problems for direct United States policy interests in those areas and the question whether Washington would willingly accept the development of regional forces elsewhere than in the Western Hemisphere. While that may not seem an immediate practical issue, especially with regard to the weak African states, it can hardly be ignored for the longer term.

Diplomatic Peacemaking Efforts

The record of military peacekeeping has thus been a mixed one. Successful operations, in the sense that the underlying political controversy was settled and the field group could wind up its work, as in the Lebanon or West Irian cases, tend to be forgotten. Where the basic political conflict has continued unabated or even re-exploded and the peacekeeping operation has had to be maintained over a lengthy period, its dramatic visibility and continuing cost raise questions about its "failure" as a means of settlement. The military presences themselves, however, were not intended to

49. U Thant address (May 27, 1965), in *UN Monthly Chronicle*, Vol. 2 (June 1965), p. 69.

bring the parties in conflict to a settlement, although the military personnel involved have often done yeomen service as conciliators in the practical day-to-day work of keeping the lid on an explosive situation. In addition, the military groups have often been supplemented by political presences with more responsibility for getting at the underlying political difficulties. The record of achievement of the latter has also been a mixed one.

In 1958, in Lebanon, for example, the activities of the Observer Group (UNOGIL) were interrupted by the landing of United States Marines in that country and of British troops in Jordan, at the request of those governments. (Their fear of subversive activities, stemming primarily from the United Arab Republic [UAR], was triggered by a bloody revolution in neighboring Iraq.) The United States and Great Britain eventually accepted an Assembly finding that United Nations activity made their continued military presence unnecessary in the area, and the Secretary-General was requested to make "such practical arrangements as would adequately help in upholding the purposes and principles of the Charter in relation to Lebanon and Jordan," thereby facilitating "early withdrawal of the foreign troops."[50] A peaceful election in Lebanon made withdrawal of UNOGIL also possible before the year's end. To Jordan, which would not accept another observer group, Hammarskjold sent a "Special Representative" whose presence facilitated withdrawal of the British troops and whose office was maintained there subsequently.

In West Irian, in 1962, the Secretary-General was requested to assist in fulfilling the role assigned to the United Nations by the Dutch-Indonesian agreement, which had been concluded only after considerable diplomatic persuasion by both the United States and the Secretary-General. The United Nations was to establish a Temporary Executive Authority under the Secretariat (including the security force noted earlier). It would administer the territory on an interim basis and later transfer it to Indonesia.[51]

In 1963, similar diplomatic pressures by Washington and the Secretary-General finally achieved the agreement of Saudi Arabia and the UAR to disengage from their involvements in Yemen, with a United Nations

50. A/Res. 1237, Aug. 21, 1958. For further consideration of these events, see Russell, *United Nations Experience with Military Forces*, pp. 71–77.

51. Text of Assembly resolution granting the necessary authorization, in U.N. Doc. A/5170, Aug. 20, 1962, Annex A. U Thant was also requested to send observers to the area at once to assist in execution of the cease-fire accord, which he did without further formal authorization.

observer group to check on fulfillment of the undertakings. But whereas the Dutch Indonesian accord was fully observed and the peacekeeping operation was therefore a simple and successful one, the Yemen accord was flouted by the UAR, in particular, and the observation mission, as earlier noted, could only observe its nonfulfillment. As a result, in November 1963, U Thant withdrew most of the mission, leaving a few observers and appointing a civilian head to emphasize the need to work toward settlement. Neither he nor inter-Arab efforts had any success. The Secretary-General withdrew the mission in September 1964, since the parties had not met their obligations.

The conflict in Cyprus was as much internal as international. Dissension over the Congo operation and increasing financial problems made it very difficult, in early 1964, to obtain enough Security Council agreement to inaugurate a peacekeeping operation in Cyprus. When finally achieved in March it involved the establishment, not only of another force, but also of a special mediator to assist in finding a political solution of the basic controversy.[52] The hope that this greater attention to political requirements would avoid a prolonged military operation has not worked out in practice, as already noted. The demands of the parties in conflict—Greece, Turkey, and the two Cypriot communities—remain irreconcilable as of 1967, and UNFICYP remains on duty in spite of constant difficulties in finding the voluntary funds to finance it.[53]

The renewal of large-scale hostilities in Kashmir, in August 1965, was matched by a renewal of interest in attempting to resolve the basic dispute between India and Pakistan.[54] The latter insisted that progress toward resolution of the political conflict had to be made if it was to abide by any Council agreement. All that could be achieved in the Council, however, was a cease-fire accord, which a new group of United Nations observers had some difficulty in persuading the parties to carry out.[55]

52. S/Res. 5575, March 4, 1964.
53. In a letter of May 8, 1967, U Thant estimated that the deficit as of June 26, 1967 would amount to more than $6.6 million. *UN Monthly Chronicle*, Vol. 4 (June 1967), p. 49.
54. The expansion of violence in Kashmir had been preceded by an outbreak of fighting in the Rann of Kutch area in April 1965. Cease-fire and withdrawal of troops were not agreed to until June 30 (text in U.N. Doc. S/6507, July 7, 1965) after strenuous British and Commonwealth diplomatic efforts. If the border dispute could not be settled by the parties within the next two months, a three-man arbitral tribunal was authorized to make final determination. The reopening of Kashmir fighting broke off these arrangements.
55. See S/Res. 211, Sept. 20, 1965 and S/Res. 215, Nov. 5, 1965.

At that time, both the Soviet Union and the United States wanted to keep the violence from spreading; but Communist China supported Pakistan's truculence and accused Moscow of conspiring with Washington to dominate the world through the United Nations. The withholding of foreign economic and military aid from both parties succeeded in forcing an end to the fighting before a military decision. (Although India appears to have been leading at the time, both sides later claimed to be winning.) Perhaps to avoid the Chinese charges, the Soviet Union offered its good offices to the two governments in direct negotiations. President Ayub and Premier Shastri accepted, meeting in Tashkent in November 1965 with Premier Kosygin. This effort resulted in a formal accord, most importantly to withdraw to military positions held prior to the outbreak of hostilities; but politically little was accomplished except to open a door through which further negotiations might be undertaken.[56] Unfortunately, the sudden death of the Indian Prime Minister, immediately after signature of the agreement, made further progress more difficult. Certain measures to restore economic relations were about all the advance made.

In contrast to this great-power cooperation in Kashmir, the renewal of Middle East hostilities, in June 1967, found the Soviet Union strongly behind the Arab demand for a finding of aggression against Israel, while the United States backed an impartial, mediatory role for the Security Council. On June 6, the Council called for "an immediate cease-fire,"[57] but several days passed before it became effective. An impasse was reached over further steps. Moscow and the Arabs continued to demand that Israel, as the aggressor, yield its territorial gains and withdraw all its troops behind the armistice lines. Tel Aviv demanded direct negotiations with the Arab states for a settlement. Washington proposed that the call for withdrawal of Israeli troops be combined with arrangements for discussions looking toward longer-range settlement, the parties to be assisted by the United Nations or some other third party. But that would have involved at least practical acceptance by the Arabs of Israel's sovereignty and their relinquishment of claims to the rights of belligerency—"unilateral belligerency," as it came to be called—which they refused to consider.

Beyond the cease-fire calls, therefore, the Council could agree only on a resolution calling on Israel to ensure the safety of inhabitants of the

56. Text in *New York Times*, Jan. 11, 1966.
57. S/Res. 233, June 6, 1967.

occupied areas and to facilitate the return of those who had fled in the path of hostilities.[58] A Soviet draft resolution failed of adoption and the United States did not press for a vote on its resolution. The Council then adjourned without setting another meeting date.

The day before, however, the Soviet Union had requested the Secretary-General to convene an emergency Assembly session to consider the situation created by continuing Israeli "defiance" of the Council and to "adopt a decision designed to bring about the liquidation of the consequences of aggression and the immediate withdrawal of Israeli forces behind the armistice lines."[59] The Assembly accordingly met on June 17, and largely repeated the charges and countercharges that had bedevilled the Council. A Soviet draft resolution would have condemned "Israel's aggressive activities," demanded unconditional withdrawal to the armistice lines, required it to "make good in full . . . all the damage [it had] inflicted," and appealed to the Security Council to act to "eliminate all consequences of the aggression. . . ."[60] The United States submitted a draft proposal that, after calling on the parties to respect the cease-fire, would have endorsed the objective of "a stable and durable peace in the Middle East," to be achieved through "negotiated arrangements with appropriate third-party assistance," and to be based on: (a) mutual recognition of the political independence and territorial integrity of all countries in the area; (b) freedom of innocent maritime passage; (c) a solution of the refugee problem; (d) limitation of arms shipments to the area; and (e) "recognition of the right of all sovereign nations to exist in peace and security."[61]

In addition, an Asian-African group's draft resolution concentrated on getting an Israeli withdrawal, after which the Security Council should be asked to seek a peaceful solution. A Latin American draft combined the request for withdrawal with acceptance of an end to the state of belligerency and of nonrecognition of forcible territorial acquisition, and requested the Council to continue working toward these ends. An Albanian proposal went beyond the Soviet one in demanding that the Assembly condemn the United States and Great Britain also for aggression, and that Israel withdraw unconditionally.

After more than two weeks of heated and repetitious debate, the Soviet

58. S/Res. 237, June 14, 1967. The resolution also called on all the governments to respect the humanitarian principles of the Geneva Conventions.

59. U.N. Doc. A/6717, June 13, 1967.

60. U.N. Doc. A/L.519, June 19, 1967.

61. U.N. Doc. A/L.520, June 20, 1967.

draft failed of adoption.[62] The Albanian resolution was defeated, 71–22–27. The nonaligned group's draft obtained less than the required two-thirds majority (53–46–20); and the Latin American resolution suffered a similar fate (57–43–20).[63] After defeat of its resolution and that of the nonaligned group, the Soviet Union negotiated behind the scenes with the United States on a milder resolution that might at least conclude the Assembly by pointing toward a settlement. This would have linked Israeli withdrawal with "acknowledgement by every United Nations Member in the area that each enjoys the right to maintain an independent national state . . . and to live in peace and security," and with a renunciation of "all claims or acts flowing from an asserted state of belligerency."[64] But the Arab states categorically refused to go along with the compromise, and the Soviet Union therefore did not submit it to the Assembly.

The Assembly managed to agree on little more than the Security Council earlier had done. It passed a more detailed resolution dealing with "humanitarian assistance,"[65] and one calling upon Israel to "rescind all measures already taken . . . to alter the status of Jerusalem."[66] After Soviet failure to obtain Arab acceptance of the idea of submitting a compromise resolution on the lines noted above, the Assembly passed an innocuous resolution calling for a "temporary adjournment." The issue was returned to the Security Council for further consideration "as a matter of urgency."[67] Lack of political accord had once again prevented effective United Nations peacekeeping action.

Political Efforts in Southeast Asia

Possibly Hammarskjold's success in the Near East, in 1958, influenced Thailand and Cambodia to request the Secretary-General later in the year

62. It was voted on by paragraphs, none of which was adopted. The resolution was therefore not voted on as a whole.

63. In an unusual compilation, the *UN Monthly Chronicle*, Vol. 4 (July 1967), sec. 1, pp. 78–79, gives the record of the roll-call votes on all the resolutions in the fifth Emergency Special Session.

64. USUN, Press Release 127, July 27, 1967, address by Ambassador Goldberg; and *New York Times*, July 23, 1967.

65. A/Res. 2252 (ES–V), July 5, 1967.

66. A/Res. 2253 (ES–V), July 5, 1967. The Secretary-General reported on the situation a week later, leading to a reiteration of the above call, in A/Res. 2254 (ES–V), July 14, 1967.

67. A/Res. 2255 (ES–V), July 21, 1967.

directly to assist in settling their differences over possession of a border temple. He sent another special representative, as in the case of Jordan, who eventually brought about restoration of relations between the two countries and submission of their dispute to the International Court of Justice.[68]

Another kind of mediatory Secretariat mission was used in 1963 to settle whether the people of North Borneo and Sarawak really approved joining the then-proposed Malaysian Federation. President Sukarno (Indonesia possesses most of the island of Borneo) violently opposed the political merger and instituted a "confrontation" program similar to the policy that had brought him satisfactory results in West Irian. He agreed to accept the findings of a United Nations mission made up of Secretariat personnel; but when they were favorable to the Federation—especially as formation of the Federation was declared before the mission's findings were issued—Indonesia rejected them and the confrontation continued.

In 1964, Indonesian guerilla activity led Malaysia to complain to the Security Council. But Djakarta's intransigence, with Soviet backing, meant another failure of the Council to take action on behalf of settlement. Even a compromise resolution, merely calling on the parties to respect each other's political and territorial integrity, was vetoed. The conflict indirectly led to Indonesia's withdrawal from the United Nations in January 1965, on the ground that Malaysia was seated as a Security Council member. The "confrontation" pattern of infiltration and violence by Indonesia continued until the anticommunist revolution changed control of the government. The change in the government permitted a resolution of the conflict in 1966.

In the former Indo-Chinese area of Southeast Asia especially, United Nations efforts to influence peaceful settlement have in general been unsuccessful because of the widespread unwillingness of the governments concerned to accept the Organization in any mediatory capacity. When conflict in the area was primarily an anticolonial war against France, the latter opposed any United Nations meddling in its "domestic" conflict. After the Korean affair gave added emphasis to United States views of the dominant communist influence in the nationalist movement, Washington supported Paris heavily with economic and materiel aid up to the

---

68. Further conflict over the award in 1962 led to another request for mediation to the Secretary-General. His second special representative continued in the post through 1964, when the mission was withdrawn by agreement of both countries.

defeat at Dienbienphu. The United States then refused to sign the Geneva accords in 1954, as did South Vietnam. Although for some years Washington gave only limited (mainly economic) support to Saigon, it was undoubtedly influential in the failure of South Vietnam to hold the elections provided for in the 1954 agreements. The international commissions for supervising implementation of the Geneva undertakings did not work satisfactorily after the initial period of disengagement and regroupment of military forces in the two zones.[69] Subversive conflict continued, and not only in Vietnam.

In 1959, perhaps also influenced by recent United Nations peace-keeping successes, Laos requested the Security Council to send a border observation force to act as a buffer against infiltration from North Vietnam in support of antigovernment elements. Over Soviet objection, the Council by a procedural vote sent a fact-finding subcommittee of four members to Laos. Refused admission to North Vietnam, it could only report the "appearance" of foreign intervention from across the border. When the Council proved unable to vote further action, the Secretary-General stepped in to accept a "long-standing" invitation to visit Laos. He subsequently sent other special representatives to supervise a program of technical assistance, as a means of maintaining some United Nations presence in the country. The device did not succeed in quieting the political situation in that effectively divided country, however, as it had elsewhere.

In South Vietnam, as the situation deteriorated in the late fifties, the United States showed no more interest in bringing the problem to the United Nations than France had earlier. With increased guerilla activities, the use of Cambodian "corridors" by Vietcong infiltrators from the North became the source of numerous border incidents. These often involved the United States through the presence of American equipment or military advisers. In May 1964, Cambodia first formally complained to the Council against "repeated acts of aggression by United States-South Vietnamese forces."[70] A small investigatory subgroup was sent by the Council to the area, which recommended that an observer group be

69. The commissions were composed of Canada, India, and Poland. Their mandate extended only to the cease-fire agreements, not to the political arrangements that accompanied them.

70. U.N. Doc. S/5697, May 13, 1964.

sent to watch the frontier and a mediator be appointed to assist in reestab-lishing diplomatic relations between the parties.[71] The United States sup-ported the idea, but no action followed. Cambodia, which favored a strengthened International Control Commission for the purpose, and South Vietnam, which proposed an international force, could not agree on acceptable modalities, so the problem of a possible Soviet veto did not materialize.[72]

The Council turned instead, in August 1964, to a more serious crisis. The United States announced that North Vietnamese torpedo boats had attacked American naval vessels in the Tonkin Gulf and that it had accord-ingly taken "defensive measures."[73] Council consideration of that situa-tion quickly petered out as Hanoi (backed by Peking) refused an invita-tion to present its case.

The political and military situation in South Vietnam steadily worsened after that episode. The United States began selective bombing of North Vietnamese military targets and supply lines in early 1965, in an effort to interdict the southward movement of men and supplies and to force Hanoi to the conference table. Although not wanting to take the issue to the Security Council, President Johnson on various occasions urged other United Nations Members to exert their influence on North Vietnam to bring about "unconditional negotiations," proclaimed as the American aim in April.[74] A first bombing "pause," of a few days in May, brought no response. At the end of the year, a much longer one of thirty-seven days was initiated, which was also accompanied by a vigorous diplomatic "peace

71. U.N. Doc. S/5832, July 27, 1964, p. 15.

72. See U.N. Doc. S/5921, Aug. 31, 1966 (South Vietnamese communication) and U.N. Doc. S/6092, Dec. 8, 1964 (Cambodian letter) on their differences. In 1966, border difficulties flared up strongly once again, including an incident in April when U.S. forces fired across the frontier. After numerous complaints, Prince Sihanouk again suggested that the ICC be strengthened to improve border supervision. While warn-ing that U.S. troops might cross the line in hot pursuit of attackers, Washington also offered to pay for expanding the ICC. No response appears to have been made to the offer, perhaps not surprisingly in view of the accompanying "hot pursuit" warning. See *New York Times,* June 16, 1966.

73. USUN Press Release 4424, Aug. 5, 1964 for Stevenson's statement. At about the same time, the Council was also occupied with a Turkish "defensive action" of retaliatory air attacks, after Greek Cypriots had attacked two Turkish Cypriot fishing villages.

74. Text of Presidential address of April 7 sent to Security Council, see U.N. Doc. S/6278, April 9, 1965, with a request for circulation "for the information of all mem-bers of the United Nations."

offensive."[75] It, too, failed to affect Hanoi's persistent refusal to accept negotiations on United States terms.

The air attacks were renewed at the end of January 1966, and the United States simultaneously took the dispute to the Security Council, urging that it "exert its vigorous endeavors and its immense prestige to find a prompt solution to it."[76] This juxtaposition of actions struck many as being either a propaganda "ploy" to assuage domestic opponents of resumed bombing, or an attempt to line up the nonaligned Council members behind the United States position, rather than as a genuine effort to see United Nations intervention as an impartial third party. The impression was reinforced by the terms of Washington's proposed draft resolution that would have called for "immediate discussions without preconditions at . . . on . . . among the appropriate interested governments to arrange a conference looking toward the application of the Geneva Accords of 1954 and 1962 and the establishment of a durable peace in Southeast Asia." The first order of business of such a conference would be to arrange a cease-fire "under effective supervision," with the services of the Council offered to achieve these purposes "by all appropriate means, including the provision of arbitrators or mediators."

The reference to "arbitrators" clearly referred to an appeal by the Pope (January 29), in which he suggested that "an arbitration of the United Nations confided to neutral nations might tomorrow . . . resolve this terrible question." Secretary Rusk answered a press conference question on the point by declaring:

It may be that this [arbitration] is one of the things which might come out of Security Council consideration.

I am not at all sure that His Holiness was talking in the most technical sense when he used the term "arbitration." But a role for neutral countries to explore the possibilities of peace would be entirely agreeable and welcome by the United States.[77]

75. Personal or written contacts were made with "more than 115" governments (communist and neutral as well as allied), the International Red Cross, the Pope, NATO, the OAS, and the OAU. Rusk statement, Jan. 31, 1966. U.S. Department of State, *Bulletin*, Vol. 54 (1966), pp. 223–24.

76. Goldberg letter calling for meeting, in U.S. Department of State, *Bulletin*, Vol. 54 (1966), pp. 229–30. See *Ibid.*, pp. 222–23, for President Johnson's statement at the time. Draft resolution submitted by the United States, S/7106, Jan. 31, 1966.

77. *Ibid.*, p. 229. It is extremely doubtful that the United States, any more than the communist countries, would be prepared to accept binding arbitration—or could agree with the other side on arbitrators, as the necessary preceding step. Nonetheless, the results of a poll question, on how people would feel about "turning over the entire Vietnam war to a special three-man U.N. committee for arbitration and a decision binding on all parties," were two-to-one in favor of such an approach.

The meetings showed the almost unanimous reluctance of the other Council members to become involved in a conflict that, by early 1966, was widely seen by the majority as a confrontation of the giants, with the United States behind South Vietnam on one side and the Soviet Union and China (albeit engaged in their own controversy) uneasily harnessed behind North Vietnam on the other. Their reluctance also reflected the view of many that the Organization cannot handle a dispute in the absence of one of the parties. The desire to avoid consideration of the issue was so strong that the Council almost refused to place the item on its agenda. After finally agreeing to that, on February 2, the Council then promptly adjourned to permit private consultations by the President on the best method of dealing with the subject.

Toward the end of the month, the outgoing President (Japan) sent the members a letter on his consultations, summing up what he "detected" as "a certain degree of common feeling": that the "termination of the conflict . . . should be sought through negotiations in an appropriate forum . . . to work out the implementation of the Geneva accords"; and that it would be "inopportune for the Council to hold further debate at this time."[78] Mild though that might seem, the Soviet Union, France, Bulgaria, and Mali rejected the letter as written on the President's personal authority alone.[79]

The reaction, from one point of view, might be considered as simply recognizing a fact which various crises have made clear: namely, that effective action is almost impossible against the strong opposition of any one of the major powers except at serious risk to the Organization itself. Washington, however, has been reluctant to accept that limitation as inherent in the voluntary nature of the international institution. Thus, Ambassador Goldberg told an audience in March 1966 that:

Nothing would be more heartening . . . than to have the international community—acting through the United Nations—accept the responsibility for the most immediate of our aims—that of checking the resort to violence against South Vietnam. . . .

But it would be unrealistic not to recognize that the membership of the

78. U.N. Doc. S/7168, Feb. 26, 1966.
79. U.N. Doc. S/7173, Feb. 28, 1966 (French view that "since there had been no discussion . . . no conclusion should be put forward"). U.N. Doc. S/7174, March 3, 1966 (Bulgarian return of President's letter). U.N. Doc. S/7175, March 2, 1966 (Soviet letter declaring the statement "illegal"). U.N. Doc. S/7176/Rev. 1, March 3, 1966 (Mali's "most express reservations . . . for as no discussions have been held . . . there can be no grounds for claiming to detect any common feeling . . .").

United Nations is not yet prepared to accept [that] responsibility. And one should recall that the only occasion on which the membership accepted an equivalent responsibility was in Korea in 1950 when the Soviet Union was temporarily absent from the Security Council and when the membership did not yet include a host of newly independent countries who. . . . hesitate to take sides in issues where the Great Powers strongly disagree.

With more realistic recognition of the possibilities of future international peacekeeping action in Vietnam, he added that the United States interest would be met if the United Nations took over "some, if not all, the responsibility for seeing to it that, once this intolerable use of force is abandoned, the people of South Vietnam are, through impartial and effective policing and supervision, guaranteed the physical security necessary to permit a free choice concerning their own government and their own future."[80]

By the spring of 1966, Washington and Saigon were placing more emphasis than ever before on the domestic Vietnamese aspects of the war, including preparations for the election in September of a constituent assembly. While the internal political dilemmas of South Vietnam cannot be considered here, it should be noted that Saigon requested the Secretary-General to provide impartial observers to check on the validity of the proposed elections. Washington not only supported the idea, it publicly declared its willingness to "accept and abide by the results of the elections—as well as the reunification elections contemplated by the Geneva agreements—whatever these results may be."[81] U Thant, however, replied to a press inquiry that he could not at that time see such a role for the United Nations in supervising the South Vietnamese elections.[82]

At the end of June 1966, another step in military escalation occurred,

---

80. USUN Press Release 4825, March 24, 1966, pp. 6–8.

81. See, for example, Goldberg speech, June 5, 1966. U.S. Department of State, *Bulletin,* Vol. 54 (1966), p. 1028. Also Secretary Rusk, to a subcommittee of House Appropriations Committee on May 11. Quoted in *Washington Post,* Aug. 4, 1966, p. D14.

82. Press Conference in Canada, May 28; summary in UN *Monthly Chronicle,* Vol. 3 (June 1966), p. 33. Earlier in the month, U Thant had reiterated that, "at least for the moment," the Organization could not "and should not be effectively involved in peacekeeping operations in Vietnam," partly because only one of the participants "directly involved" was a U.N. member. But a "more basic" reason was because of "the disagreement among the big powers regarding the projected U.N. involvement in Vietnam in the field of peacekeeping. . . . The Soviet Union and France are against [such] involvement . . . and I have very good reason to believe that the United Kingdom would be very reluctant to get the United Nations involved in any sort of peacekeeping operation in Vietnam." *Ibid.,* p. 31.

when the United States extended bombing to include fuel installations near Hanoi and Haiphong. Ambassador Goldberg notified the Security Council that the action was necessitated by "the increased intensity of North Vietnam's aggression" against the South, in spite of "repeated and increased efforts" to open negotiations. He concluded: "A peaceful solution to the problem must be found. This could be accomplished through reconvening the Geneva Conference in order to reaffirm and revitalize the Geneva agreements of 1954 and 1962 as the basis for peace in Southeast Asia, or in some other forum."[83] The letter was circulated as a Council document. Ten days later, the Soviet Union formally rejected it, charging it was a "maneuver" to justify the expansion of the "shameful war."[84]

At about the same time, President Johnson proclaimed, more explicitly than ever, American "determination . . . . to meet our obligations in Asia as a Pacific power." That meant, among other things, the need "to prove to aggressive nations that the use of force to conquer others is a losing game," and that "guerilla warfare, inspired by one nation against another, cannot succeed." The war would continue "until the Communists in North Vietnam realize the price of aggression is too high—and either agree to a peaceful settlement or to end the fighting."[85]

The war has since continued its unconventional way into 1967, the United States still limiting its territorial and political objectives against the external enemy in Hanoi, but maintaining its unlimited internal objective of eliminating militant communist opposition to Saigon. Washington also continued to profess its desire to halt hostilities and institute negotiations on the basis of the Geneva accords, and to urge U Thant to continue his efforts to persuade Hanoi to accept such proposals. In spite of its professions, however, the administration has continued to reject the Secretary-General's repeated insistence that an unconditional cessation of bombing is a prerequisite to any chance of negotiations. In March, for example, the President declared:

The problem is a very simple one. It takes two to negotiate at a peace table and Hanoi has just simply refused to consider coming to a peace table. . . .

We are prepared to go more than half-way and to use any avenue possible to encourage such discussions . . . But reciprocity must be the fundamental principle of any reduction in hostilities.[86]

83. U.N. Doc. S/7391, June 30, 1966.
84. U.N. Doc. S/7401, July 11, 1966.
85. *Washington Post*, July 13, 1966.
86. Speech at the joint session of the Tennessee State Legislature, March 15, 1967, U.S. Department of State, *Bulletin*, Vol. 56, pp. 538, 539.

While U Thant, in July, once again drew attention to "the fact that Hanoi refuses to negotiate with Washington while the bombing of North Vietnam is going on, and Saigon will not negotiate with the National Liberation Front under any circumstances."[87]

By mid-summer 1967, the strains of the Vietnam conflict were becoming more sharply reflected in domestic affairs. On the one hand, the failure either to force or persuade Hanoi to the negotiating table led some to advocate escalation to the point of military victory, while on the other the intensification of the war and its increasing demands on American manpower and resources led others to press for de-escalation—to minimize the chances of Communist Chinese intervention as well as to enhance those for negotiation. The outbreak of racial violence in numerous urban areas of this country occurred just when the President was considering greater commitments to Vietnam (and contemplating higher taxes to pay for them). The confluence of all these factors was reflected in congressional reactions on both sides: for escalation and de-escalation,[88] and in the latter case for renewed attempts to bring the United Nations into the picture.

Secretary McNamara reiterated that the first position ignored United States objectives in the air campaign against the North, which were not to destroy it, but to "avoid unnecessary devastation and civilian casualties . . . and to avoid action which carried with it the risk of widening the war with all that implies."[89] Senators Mansfield and Cooper, in bipartisan agreement, considered that it was already moving dangerously in that very direction. Rather than intensification, therefore, they urged the administration to renew its January 1966 effort to place the issue before the United Nations—"without any reservations whatever."[90] They proposed that Hanoi, Saigon, the Vietcong, and Peking all be invited to send representatives to a Security Council debate, while bombing of the North was halted and military operations in the field confined to defensive actions

---

87. U.N. Press Release SG/SM/782, July 28, 1967, p. 8.

88. House Minority Leader Ford demanded the removal of all restrictions on bombing targets in the North before more troops were sent to Vietnam. "Our Navy and Air Force," he declared, "have clear superiority in the air over North Vietnam and its coastal areas. They have the weapons and resources they need" to impose a military solution on Hanoi. (*New York Times*, Aug. 8, 1967.) Senator Stennis, chairman of the Senate Preparedness Investigating Subcommittee, and members of the subcommittee also urged an end to the restrictions and opposed any bombing suspension as "a tragic and perhaps fatal mistake." *Ibid.*, Aug. 10, 1967.

89. *Ibid.*, Aug. 9, 1967.

90. *Ibid.*, Aug. 8, 1967.

against supply lines and infiltration routes. Were the government prepared to act on these terms, it might indeed become feasible for the
United Nations at last to influence the cessation of hostilities and for the
Geneva Conference to be reconvened.[91] All such proposals, however,
assume that both South Vietnam and the United States would be willing
to reverse policies that, in the one case, have been considered as essential
to the very existence of the state, and in the other must increasingly be
seen as affecting the 1968 elections. The issue remains a "cliff-hanger" as
the present study goes to press.

Development of the Constitutional Crisis over Peacekeeping

Although peacekeeping operations initiated after 1960 were financed
mainly on an extra-budgetary basis, the Organization's financial deficit
continued to increase, in particular for the duration of ONUC (withdrawn in mid-1964). UNEF continued to be financed only in part by
annual assessments, and expenditures for the Cyprus Force were not
covered by the voluntary contributions requested by the Secretary-
General. In addition, the Organization had postponed an immediate
crisis in 1961, by means of a $200 million bond issue;[92] and assessments
for interest and amortization on the bonds, which began in 1963, were
also rejected by the same states that had refused to pay the earlier peacekeeping assessments. By the time the nineteenth Assembly met in December 1964, the financial situation of the United Nations had reached a point
that also brought to a head wider constitutional issues with regard to the
authorization and direction of peacekeeping activities, as well as to their
financing. Article 19 was the catalytic agent.

THE ARTICLE 19 CONFLICT

Article 19 provides that any member in arrears in payment of "its financial contributions to the Organization shall have no vote in the General
Assembly if the amount of its arrears equals or exceeds" two full years'

91. Also see Prof. Leo Gross's suggestions for the Secretary-General to take the
initiative in bringing the issue to the Council under his Art. 99 powers. Letter in *Ibid.*,
July 2, 1967.
92. See Chap. 9 below, for further consideration of the financial problem.

assessments.[93] By the end of 1964, the Soviet Union, France, and ten other states were sufficiently in arrears, according to the way deficits were calculated through the years, to be threatened with application of the Article 19 sanction. But the legality of the majority interpretation was itself in dispute.

From the start of UNEF, the Soviet Union had maintained that all costs should in principle be borne by the "aggressors." A good many others, the Latin American states in particular, argued that they should at least not be considered normal operating costs (and thereby to be included in the regular budget, apportioned by the Assembly under Article 17), and in any event should not be considered as coming within the scope of Article 19. In 1961, therefore, the Assembly decided to ask the International Court for an advisory opinion to help straighten out some of these legal issues in dispute. The question presented was whether, as the majority of Members maintained, the share of UNEF and ONUC costs that had been budgeted and assessed against the full membership were properly "expenses of the Organization" in the meaning of Article 17(2).[94]

The Court found, 9–5, that the peacekeeping expenditures did constitute expenses under Article 17(2); and to give the opinion greater legal force, the Assembly formally "accepted" it, by a vote of 76–17–8.[95] Although the majority accepting the Court opinion was well above the necessary two-thirds, it was considerably less than unanimous, thus leaving in

93. It should be noted that the penalty of Art. 19 in no way guaranteed that a member in arrears would pay up. It was not restricted in any other organ of the U.N. A member could keep its seat in the Assembly and even participate up to the point of voting. The "slap on the wrist" sanction was written into the Charter in hopes that the new Organization might improve on the poor collection record of the League of Nations, which had no sanction against defaulters. It was considered a minor matter at San Francisco and adopted without controversy. Then the unanticipated expansion of relatively expensive U.N. executive operations, which also became politically controversial, brought the constitutional issues of peacekeeping to a head in the form of a financial crisis.

94. France had protested that the Court should first be asked for its opinion on whether the Assembly recommendations authorizing expenditures for the two forces were themselves in conformity with the Charter, before deciding whether the costs were valid expenses under 17(2). See International Court of Justice, "Certain Expenses of the United Nations (Article 17, paragraph 2, of the Charter), Advisory Opinion of 20 July 1962," *ICJ Reports*, 1962, especially pp. 156–57 and 180–81 on the rejected French amendment; pp. 155–80 for the majority opinion.

95. A/Res. 1854 (XVII), Dec. 19, 1962.

question whether it constituted a "generally acceptable" interpretation of the disputed point.[96]

A number of states accepted the legal determination and paid assessments they had previously held not to be binding; but the major states in arrears denied any binding force in *either* the advisory opinion or the Assembly's acceptance. They continued to refuse payments for costs of the two forces, and the deficits continued to mount. The Court had expressed no opinion about the application of Article 19 in relation to any failure to pay those expenses, but most members inferred that arrears in payment of the peacekeeping accounts could be included as part of the deficit that would bring the Article 19 sanction into effect.

The United States had taken the lead in promoting the extended peacekeeping activities under the Secretariat that were the cause of the financial crisis, and it took the most advanced stand on their legitimacy. Washington maintained (1) that the various operations were properly initiated in terms of the authority of the Assembly, as well as of the Security Council, to recommend measures and to establish subsidiary organs for the maintenance of peace; (2) that Article 17 clearly authorized the Assembly to assess Members for legitimate "expenses of the Organization," which the International Court confirmed applied to costs of both UNEF and ONUC; (3) that once so assessed, those expenses were binding on the Members and properly included in the total due for purposes of determining the applicability of Article 19; (4) that the Assembly had therefore followed correct procedure in levying the disputed assessments and authorizing the bond issue; and (5) that its subsequent acceptance of the Court opinion by "an overwhelming majority" properly made that the law of the Charter.[97]

The major Soviet contentions against the validity of the UNEF and ONUC assessments were: (1) that only the Security Council had authority to take action for the maintenance of peace and security; and that its exclusive authority extended to the means of financing operations it authorized—hence both forces and the assessments for their costs were illegal; (2) that Article 17 (and by extension Article 19) applied to the

---

96. See above, Chap. 2, p. 26.

97. The U.S. arguments are spelled out at length in a Memorandum of Oct. 8, 1964, text in U.S. Department of State, *Bulletin*, Vol. 51 (1964), pp. 681–90. It also summarizes and answers the main arguments in a Soviet memorandum of Sept. 11, 1964. The U.S. memorandum called forth another Soviet one on Nov. 7, 1964, which is in U.N. Doc. A/5777, Nov. 9, 1964.

administrative budget of the Organization only, and that those ordinary expenses alone were binding and assessable—hence the question of applying Article 19 was irrelevant; and (3) that the Court opinion and the Assembly resolution accepting it had only recommendatory effect in any case, and did not bind dissenting Members. French refusal to pay for ONUC[98] was based chiefly on the last two points. Both countries, however, went along passively for years, as the majority authorized and assessed payments for various smaller peacekeeping activities in ways they now rejected as illegal.

Although numerous states were in some arrears in practice, the great majority always accepted the legality of the operations undertaken, the principle of collective financial responsibility for them, and the binding character of Assembly assessments.[99] By the opening of the nineteenth Assembly, they had also come to think it would be a mistake, in view of the dispute among the great powers over Charter interpretation, to push that principle too far. An attempt to apply Article 19's sanction to the twelve members sufficiently in arrears, so as to deny them the right to vote in the Assembly, came to seem to the majority more likely to result in disrupting the United Nations than in obtaining payment of the arrears. As the Nigerian delegate, Chief Adebo, succinctly expressed their attitude: "Nobody is prepared to blow up the world Organization on the altar of a principle founded upon Charter provisions of an admittedly ambiguous character."[100] The majority recognized, in short, that the United States effort to "strengthen" Charter law in the direction of collective financial responsibility for the disputed peacekeeping assessments had passed the point where the development of international political cooperation could sustain it. A compromise seemed essential.

THE NINETEENTH ASSEMBLY

Given the positions of the major antagonists, however, compromise appeared almost impossible in the fall of 1964. The United States insisted

98. France paid its UNEF assessments but argued that its payment was voluntary.

99. They had sought, however, for a special scale of assessments for the more costly operations, under which the permanent members in particular would be allocated higher proportions than in the regular budget. The United States resisted that approach in favor of the system of partial assessments plus requests for supplementary voluntary contributions. See below, Chap. 9, pp. 338–43.

100. U.N. Doc. A/AC. 121/PV. 5, April 29, 1965, p. 17.

that the loss-of-vote sanction became applicable at the time of the first vote in the approaching Assembly. The Soviet Union threatened to walk out of the Organization if the Assembly "illegally" rescinded its vote.[101] There was just enough consensus to agree on an effort to resolve the question by outside negotiations while the Assembly carried on the opening debate without voting. Diplomatic negotiations failed to break the stalemate before the general debate ended.

The United States was not prepared to give up its position on Article 19, but in view of the widespread opposition to a "confrontation," as it came to be called, Washington hesitated to force a showdown on the issue —which might have meant its defeat, for one thing. Neither did the Soviet Union want to force the issue. It probably did not wish to go against the majority's "passionate determination to avoid a decision";[102] but, in addition, a partially paralyzed Assembly that could take no action in the security field was from the Soviet's point of view not undesirable in any event.[103]

Albania, however, nearly upset the applecart on February 16, 1965 when the Assembly—to help "ensure as soon as possible the normalization of its work"—was about to accept by consensus a resolution establishing a Special Committee on Peacekeeping Operations. The group was to undertake "a comprehensive review of the whole question . . . in all [its] aspects, including ways of overcoming the present financial difficulties."[104] At that point, the Albanian delegate demanded that the Assembly return at once

101. The controversy over the procedure to be followed if the issue were pushed to the point of decision was also significant. The United States maintained that the sanction automatically went into effect on notification by the Secretary-General that a state was in arrears to the pertinent amount. The Soviet Union argued that loss of vote would be an "important question," requiring a two-thirds majority decision by the Assembly in each case alleged to be in default.

102. Assistant Secretary of State Harlan Cleveland's description of the state of mind of the Assembly in February 1965. See U.S. Department of State, Bulletin, Vol. 52 (1965), pp. 380–81.

103. Some of the inconvenience of an inactive Assembly was overcome by convening, in the spring of 1965, the Disarmament Commission (including all members) which had not met since 1960. It served as a general political forum, as well as for the discussion of disarmament issues. It also used normal voting procedures, in spite of being a subsidiary of the Assembly.

104. Finally adopted as A/Res. 2006 (XIX), Feb. 18, 1965. The nonvoting consensus was more apparent than real, since decisions on matters such as authorizing budgetary assessments were essential to carrying on the Organization. The device used was to have Members register their positions in off-the-record and off-the-scene balloting

to its regular business and normal procedures. The resulting frantic and unsuccessful effort to get him to withdraw his proposal (which would have required a vote) resembled a scene from the theater of the absurd. The President, under his general powers, therefore simply announced pontponement of the session for two days.[105] On February 18, the United States announced it would permit one procedural vote without compromise to its position on Article 19. Over the protests of Albania, the Assembly then voted to rule voting out of order.[106] After authorizing the special committee, without a vote, the Assembly adjourned until September.

SPECIAL COMMITTEE ON PEACEKEEPING OPERATIONS

The new committee (of 33 members) proved as incapable as any previous forum of resolving the basic differences within the United Nations over the constitutional and financial questions.[107] Those had continued unchanged in substance from the beginning, and they remain unsettled in 1967. The point of no return had evidently been reached on the Article 19 confrontation, however, and the United States decided, in August 1965, to accede to the general feeling of the membership. It agreed to refrain from raising the sanctions issue when the Assembly next met, but reserved its legal position.[108] That move allowed the committee to report, to a final session of the nineteenth Assembly on September 1, that it had reached consensus on two points: (1) that the new Assembly should return to normal procedures, to permit which "the question of the applicability of Article 19" would not be raised with regard to UNEF and ONUC; and

---

in the office of the Assembly President. In a subsequent plenary session, the President would announce what draft resolution was before the Assembly, then add something like: "If I hear no comments, I shall take it that the General Assembly accepts this draft resolution without objection." The record would later show: "It was so decided."

105. See U.N. General Assembly, Nineteenth Session, Plenary, *Official Records*, 1329th Meeting, Feb. 16, 1965.

106. *Ibid.*, 1330th Meeting, Feb. 18, 1965, p. 7. Albania and Mauritania voted against nonvoting. The favorable vote was 97, with 13 abstentions and 2 nonparticipations.

107. Summary records of the committee meetings are contained in annexes to the Special Committee's two reports, U.N. Docs. A/5915 and Add. 1, June 15, 1965 and A/5916 and Add. 1, Aug. 31, 1965.

108. For Ambassador Goldberg's statement, see U.N. Doc. A/Ac. 121/PV. 15, Aug. 16, 1965, pp. 7–10.

(2) that the current financial difficulties of the Organization should be solved by voluntary contributions.[109]

On the substantive constitutional questions, however, the committee failed to resolve its conflicting viewpoints on the related issues of authorization, control, and financing of "peacekeeping operations." It could not, therefore, reach a generally accepted definition of the term. This had been clear by June, when it submitted a series of "guidelines" (derived from its discussions) for the views of all Members on their suitability as guiding principles for future United Nations operations.[110] These sought to present the rather thin areas of agreement in terms most hopeful for further negotiation of some compromise on the basic issue of the degree of the Security Council's "primary responsibility" for the maintenance of peace and security. That, in turn, would determine the key questions noted above of peacekeeping authority and procedures.[111]

As the comments on the guidelines came in from Members other than those in the Committee of 33, the position of the committee majority seemed to be sustained by a majority of the responding governments. That position accepted past experience as the criterion for the future, in the terms in which peacekeeping operations have been described in this chapter: that is, essentially voluntary undertakings, requiring consent of the countries involved, noncoercive in nature, not constituting a pretext for foreign intervention, and, where military personnel might be utilized, limited to a highly restricted and self-defensive use of force. Such operations might include frontier observation, truce supervision, investigatory or mediatory missions, and other similar functions.[112] The primary responsibility of the Security Council in the field was recognized, but the Assembly's right to make recommendations on the maintenance of peace was also endorsed, including the initiation of voluntary peacekeeping operations as "subsidiary organs" under Article 22, as in the past.

109. U.N. Doc. A/5916, Aug. 31, 1965. For Assembly adoption of the report, see U.N. Doc. A/PV. 1331, Sept. 1, 1965, p. 2.

110. The Secretary-General and President of the committee (the Assembly President) presented a summary interim report to the committee on its discussions, in U.N. Doc. A/Ac. 121/4, May 31, 1965, including the "guidelines" on pp. 25–26. The committee then made its report to the Assembly, asking for more time for study, in U.N. Doc. A/5915, June 15, 1965.

111. On the two fundamental questions, the guidelines noted: (1) that the functions and powers of Council and Assembly should be "understood as complementary and not as contradictory"; and (2) that financing should be "in conformity with the provisions of the Charter," with Council and Assembly "cooperating" in this respect.

112. See, for example, the speech of the Swedish Ambassador in U.N. Doc. A/Ac. 121/PV. 3, April 23, 1965, pp. 3–11.

The Soviet Union stuck to its position that only the Security Council can "act" to maintain or restore peace and security; that the involvement of military personnel is not only the determining factor in any definition of "peacekeeping," but also automatically brings the matter under Chapter VII. It granted the Assembly only such "responsibilities in accordance with the Charter" as do not extend to "action." In the event of Council failure to act, the Assembly might reconsider a question, but only "in order to adopt new recommendations based on [its] terms of reference" under the Charter.[113]

The committee had stressed the fact that the roles of Council and Assembly were to be considered "as complementary, and not as contradictory"; but the crux of the authorization issue lay in the scope and nature of the recommendations the Assembly might make under Articles 10, 11(2), or 14 and on the steps it might take in the event the Council proved unable to act in some case. The Soviet Union criticized the guidelines for what it called an attempt to "define" those Council-Assembly relationships "on the basis, not of the Charter, but mainly of the past practice of these organs when violations of the Charter were allowed to occur." And it reiterated that the principles listed were "at variance with the Charter," which makes the Council "the only organ empowered to take action" on peace and security.[114]

The twentieth Assembly continued unable to break the logjam of these conflicting viewpoints. The Special Political Committee remitted the whole problem to the Committee of 33 again,[115] which found itself, in the spring of 1966, with practically no place to go since the ground had been thoroughly covered the preceding year.

In an effort to get the discussion off the sterile constitutional issues, the Swedish representative pointed out that:

It may reasonably be asked what purpose would be served by laying down, in advance, more precise rules governing the problems of competence. As experience has shown, there is a need for the organs of the United Nations, when

---

113. U.N. Doc. A/Ac. 121/PV. 2, April 22, 1965, pp. 7–10. The Soviet memorandum of July 13, 1964, U.N. Doc. A/5721, which was noted above in Chap. 5, p. 137, was resubmitted to the Special Committee on Peacekeeping Operations.

114. U.N. Doc. A/AC. 121/5, Aug. 5, 1965, pp. 17–19.

115. A./Res. 2053 (XX), Dec. 15, 1965. One proposal, submitted by Ireland, was specifically recommended for consideration by the committee. It proposed to recognize the Assembly's right to authorize a peacekeeping operation when action by the Council was vetoed and to establish a complicated financing system. The latter was its most significant suggestion. The proposal is therefore discussed in Chap. 9, below. For text, see U.N. Doc. A/5966/Rev. 2, Sept. 13, 1965.

called upon to adopt measures for the preservation of peace to take into consideration the particular requirements of the political situation then prevailing. They are likely to continue to interpret the Charter in the way that is peculiar to sovereign political bodies, namely through action.[116]

Canada and Sweden both suggested that the Committee of 33 therefore concentrate on the technical details of organization, administration, and financing of peacekeeping operations, which aspects required agreement regardless of the final resolution of the constitutional issues. They were only partially successful. The majority of members continued to support greater United Nations activity in (including preparations for) peacekeeping, but the Soviet Union and France continued adamantly opposed to practically all proposals. At the end of summer, the Secretary-General noted, in his annual report, the lack of agreement and hoped that Members might

find it possible, within the Charter, to agree upon the procedures to be followed in launching such [peacekeeping] operations, the responsibility of the various organs in their actual conduct, and the financial arrangements by which the expenditures involved may be met. . . . The peacekeeping activities of the United Nations, perhaps more than any other part of its work, have enabled the Organization to gain a measure of public confidence which is in danger of being lost if the Member States remain deadlocked on the constitutional and financial questions involved.[117]

In the Special Political Committee at the twenty-first Assembly, numerous draft resolutions and amendments thereto finally jelled into four main proposals. A new version of the earlier Irish resolution concerning financing methods[118] passed by a narrow majority in the committee, but was withdrawn in the plenary, since it would have failed to receive the necessary two-thirds vote. A three-power resolution (India, the United Arab Republic, and Yugoslavia) would have continued the Special Committee on Peacekeeping, instructing it to report to the next Assembly; and would have recommended that the Security Council also study means to improve preparations for peacekeeping, in particular the possibilities of agreements to be made under Article 43, and that it inform the following Assembly of steps taken.[119]

116. U.N. Doc. A/AC. 121/WG/PV. 1, May 10, 1966.
117. *Introduction to the Annual Report of the Secretary-General on the Work of the Organization, 16 June 1965–15 June 1966*, U.N. Doc. A/6301/Add. 1, p. 13.
118. *Comprehensive Report of the Whole Question of Peacekeeping Operations in All Their Aspects: Report of the Special Political Committee*, U.N. Doc. A/SPC/L. 129, Nov. 17, 1966.
119. *Ibid.*, U.N. Doc. A/SPC/L. 138, Dec. 8, 1966.

After the defeat of a UAR motion to give priority in voting to this proposal, the draft resolution was withdrawn by its sponsors. A Jamaican draft that concentrated on a recommendation to the Security Council to prepare to discharge its responsibilities under Articles 42 and 45, in particular that it negotiate arrangements under Article 43,[120] was adopted in committee by the curious vote of 20–5–80. The large number of abstentions evidently reflected a mixture of dissatisfaction with the narrow scope of the resolution and uncertainty of what its adoption might therefore imply.

The major draft proposal came initially from Canada although finally sponsored by seven powers. It combined reaffirmations both of the principle of collective financial responsibility (with a presumptive scale of apportionment) and of the residual authority of the Assembly to act when the Security Council is unable to do so. It, too, took note of the Soviet Union's repeated proposals for reexamination of the possibility of negotiating Article 43 agreements, recommending in this connection that the Council study all means of improving preparations for peacekeeping operations of a "nonenforcement nature." And it requested the Special Peacekeeping Committee and the Security Council to report on their investigations to the twenty-second Assembly.[121] Over communist opposition, it was accepted in the Special Political Committee by a 52–14–42 vote. The resolution was therefore recommended for adoption to the Assembly,[122] and it was generally anticipated that it would receive the necessary two-thirds vote in the plenary session.

The Soviet Union and France apparently also feared that result, for they both took strong stands in the Assembly against any vote on the recommended draft. The former went so far as to declare: "No one is entitled to change the provisions of the United Nations Charter concerning the use of armed force for the maintenance of peace." The Special Political Committee action, therefore, could not "and cannot have any force." Moreover, if proposers of the "illegal" resolution succeeded in "foisting it on the General Assembly," the Soviet Union declared, they would create "a situation that will be fraught with serious consequences for the United Nations."[123]

Despite an Italian refutation of the Soviet allegations, in a paragraph-

---

120. *Ibid.,* U.N. Doc. A/SPC/L. 133/Rev. 1, Dec. 8, 1966.
121. *Ibid.,* U.N. Doc. A/SPC/L. 130/Rev. 4.
122. *Ibid.,* U.N. Doc. A/6603, Dec. 15, 1966, pp. 12, 16–18.
123. U.N. Doc. A/PV. 1497 (Prov.), Dec. 17, 1966, pp. 113–15.

by-paragraph analysis of the Canadian resolution, the Franco-Soviet threats had their effect. A new resolution (to replace the Special Political Committee recommendations) was presented two days later, given priority in voting, and adopted.[124] By it, the Assembly postponed further action on the Canadian proposal, referring the committee report to the special Assembly already called for April 1967 on the South West African problem. It also continued the Committee of 33.

In 1967, the renewed discussions of the Committee of 33 were essentially repetitive of the previous year in their failure to move any closer toward agreement on the bases for future peacekeeping activities—constitutional, technical, or financial. The Soviet position hardened, if possible, on the exclusive role of the Security Council: "As far as the Charter . . . is concerned," the Soviet representative declared, "the use of United Nations forces is possible only on the basis of Chapter VII and only in those cases where the need arises to avert or put an end to armed aggression against the independence and territorial integrity and sovereignty of a given country."[125] In line with this approach, emphasis was placed on the earlier Czechoslovakian proposal for a renewed effort to negotiate the agreements called for by Article 43. The United States constitutional position continued to be shared by the majority. But because it met with such adamant rejection by the communist states in particular, none of the suggested proposals for compromise approaches—either to technical problems of peacekeeping arrangements or to procedures for future financing—were acceptable even as the basis of further study. In addition, bickering over the question of contributions to the rescue fund by the Soviet Union and France, on the one hand, and the United States, on the other, became a prominent part of the proceedings, as will be noted in Chapter 9. The end result, once more, was inability of the committee to make any recommendation to the Special Assembly, followed by another Assembly resolution that merely reiterated earlier calls for voluntary financial contributions and requested the Special Committee on Peacekeeping Operations to continue its studies and report again to the twenty-second Assembly in September 1967.[126]

124. U.N. Doc. A/PV. 1499 (Prov.), Dec. 19, 1966, pp. 7–10. The vote on priority issue was 49–41–27. That on the resolution, 56–36–25. Final resolution text, A/Res. 2220 (XXI), Dec. 19, 1966.

125. U.N. Doc. A/AC. 121/PV. 23, Feb. 16, 1967, pp. 18–20.

126. A/Res. 2249 (S–V), May 23, 1967, adopted 90–1 (Albania)–11. See also U.N. Doc. A/6654, May 17, 1967, the report of the Special Committee.

Little change, if any, in the situation seemed likely even then. A compromise of basic differences between the major antagonists is clearly not in the cards while other international tensions remain so high. It is probably unnecessary as a practical matter in any event. Should the Security Council fail to act in some threatening situation, whether the Assembly undertakes to authorize another peacekeeping operation will continue to depend, as it did in the past, on the extent of the Members' willingness to support the particular action, rather than on any formal resolution of constitutional arguments. The Soviet Union's willingness to resort, in effect, to the Uniting for Peace procedures in the recent Middle East crisis—although not working out as Moscow obviously anticipated—reinforces that judgment, even though the Soviet draft resolution proposed to return the responsibility for "action" to the Security Council.

"Strengthening" International Peacekeeping Capacity

The weaknesses of "peacekeeping," however it is defined, as a means of controlling violence and leading to the settlement of disputes are obvious. The nature of the difficulties and the means of correcting them are less so.

TECHNICAL VERSUS POLITICAL DIFFICULTIES

There has been a tendency to propose means to improve the standards of authorization, operation, or administration of the missions concerned, as though their too-frequent failure to bring about final solutions of the political disputes that called them into being were primarily the result of technical weaknesses.[127] Difficulties in the Congo, for example, brought forth recommendations that future United Nations forces should receive clearer mandates, without adequate recognition that in a situation of acute political conflict it is usually impossible to obtain the necessary votes in the Security Council or the Assembly for a precise definition of an agreed political goal. Cyprus soon showed this once again. Imprecision, in short, may be the price of any operation through an international organization.

In any event, precision itself is not always the key. The mandate for the

127. See Ruth B. Russell, "Development by the United Nations of Rules relating to Peacekeeping." American Society of International Law, *Proceedings*, Vol. 59 (1965), pp. 57–58.

Yemen Observation Mission (UNYOM) was quite clear: the group was to observe an agreed-upon disengagement of the UAR and Saudi Arabia from their respective involvements in the Yemen civil war. The less visible aid from Saudi Arabia may or may not have ceased; but the highly visible Egyptian troops were clearly not withdrawn. In the end, the UNYOM was withdrawn instead of the troops, but it had fulfilled its mandate by observing the failure of the parties to comply with their undertakings.

Technical improvements, especially in deploying relatively large peace-keeping missions, are important, of course, to the efficiency of such operations. They are also far easier to grasp in concrete terms of men, machinery, and procedures, and hence they receive the greater part of official and unofficial attention in the many proposals to "strengthen" the peace-keeping capacity of the United Nations. But even if all the technical improvements were put into practice tomorrow, the toughest problem—the political problem—would remain. This is not so much a question of strengthening the ability of the *Organization* to promote peacekeeping and, even more important, peaceful settlement. It is rather a matter of overcoming the resistance of the *Members* to making the political concessions required to settle their disputes. The history of the United Nations demonstrates that only to the degree that the will to settlement exists, can a way to settlement be found.

For the effectiveness of all pacific-settlement endeavors can be said to be in almost mathematical proportion to the degree of political accord underlying them. When accord is strong enough, parties in dispute will accept binding arbitral or judicial means of settlement if they are unable to resolve their conflict by direct negotiations. When accord is weak or nonexistent, they may be willing to resort to violence to avoid settlement against their conceived interests, or even to impose settlement on their own terms. In contemporary circumstances, fear of the unknown consequences has at times sufficed to bring about enough political consensus to stop open violence and even to maintain a neither-war-nor-peace situation for years on end, as in Palestine and Korea, for example. But the political problem of moving from that state of suspended violence to a settlement bringing peaceful change instead of mere pacification, still escapes us. The proposals surveyed briefly below, which have been aimed at improving United Nations "capacity" to keep the peace through the various means of peaceful settlement, must be judged in relation to the achievement of that ultimate goal, as well as to their immediate application to weaknesses of the Organization's procedures and machinery.

TECHNICAL IMPROVEMENTS IN INTERNATIONAL
PEACEKEEPING

Although most proposals to "strengthen" peacekeeping by the United Nations have been in terms of the larger and more complex operations involving the use of armed forces, the same principles would also apply (with appropriate adaptations) in seeking to improve the smaller field missions. Moreover, national units or resources held ready to participate in international peacekeeping could be made available to either the world Organization or regional bodies.

The *technical elements* of the task of mobilizing and deploying field missions are largely the same, regardless of the size or political objective of the undertaking: personnel in sufficient numbers, of acceptable nationalities, with the right training and temperament for the anticipated tasks to be performed; adequate supplies, equipment, transportation, and administrative facilities to meet foreseeable needs; sufficient legal and political authority to carry out their missions effectively. Where a combat-sanctions force need worry about legal consent only when dealing with friendly governments, peacekeeping missions of any size have always operated on the basis of consent because of their neutral, mediatory role. In connection with the larger United Nations forces, the most unusual military aspects also follow from that role: their limitation to the use of minimal force in self-defense alone, and their consequent requirement for guaranteed freedom of movement throughout the area.[128]

The limitations that apply to military peacekeeping operations are an adaptation of the requirements for any effective political action of a third-party, mediatory kind. United Nations forces, in short, are not sanctions forces writ small, but observer groups writ large; and when active opposition to their impartial, third-party role becomes serious, as it did in the sometimes chaotic Congo situation, their political effectiveness as well as their efficiency may be destroyed.

128. "There is no enemy, there is no one to be defeated, there is no intention of eliminating and . . . it is not enough to neutralize one opponent—it is necessary to neutralize all belligerents without using force, solely by being present. Freedom of movement throughout the area occupied by both sides is therefore necessary." Lt. Gen. Indar Jit Rikhye, "Preparation and Training of United Nations Peace-Keeping Forces," in Per Frydenberg, *Peace-Keeping: Experience and Evaluation—The Oslo Papers* (Norwegian Institute of International Affairs, 1964), p. 191. This report of an unofficial conference on U.N. forces includes papers and discussion on many of these technical problems and on steps that might be taken to improve preparations for future operations.

United Nations experience is now extensive enough to make clear the practical requirements for achieving a more efficient state of readiness to undertake new operations, and for conducting them once they are authorized.[129] Ideally, such requirements should be determined and coordinated by a headquarters staff militarily and politically adequate to handle the technical requirements. It need only be conceived in small-scale terms for the foreseeable future, as there is widespread agreement on one important point: namely, that improvements in the military area will apply at most to a system of national contingents available for call-up when needed, rather than to any form of permanent international standing force.[130] Official proposals looking toward such advance planning and preparations began to be made almost as soon as the success of UNEF became evident, generating considerable enthusiasm on the part of the United States, Canada, and the Scandinavian governments in particular, for this "new" international device to control the outbreak of international violence.

OFFICIAL PROPOSALS FOR PERMANENT FORCES

In 1957, congressional resolutions were introduced in support of the idea of developing a permanent United Nations police force of a kind similar to UNEF. The Secretary-General felt encouraged to draw up a report for the 1958 General Assembly based on that experience, which he thought the plenary body might endorse and thus regularize the basic legal principles and certain practices so as to ensure more efficient mobili-

129. For a brief summary of generally accepted recommendations along these lines (accepted, that is, by those who favor extending U.N. capabilities in this field), see Lefever, *op. cit.*, pp. 154–59, 162–69. For Canadian statements suggesting what might be done along such lines, see the Canadian Ambassador's remarks in the Committee of 33, U.N. Doc. A/AC. 121/WG. B/PV. 1, April 4, 1967, pp. 13–23; and address by the Secretary for External Affairs, Paul Martin, "Canada's Role in Supporting UN Peacekeeping Efforts," Canadian Mission to the U.N. Press Release 12, April 26, 1967, especially pp. 7–12.

130. There is, nonetheless, no end of proposals for permanent peacekeeping forces, as well as for the sanctions type forces considered in Chap. 5 above. For example, the Report of the Committee on Arms Control and Disarmament of the national Citizens' Commission for the White House Conference on International Cooperation, advocated the creation of both a U.N. Peace Observation Corps and a U.N. Peace Force composed of national standby units plus "a small elite force of about one or two thousand men . . . as a 'fire prevention brigade'." (UNA Print, pp. 27–28.) For a summary of some other plans for international police forces, before as well as after World War II, see D. W. Bowett, *United Nations Forces* (Praeger, 1964), Chap. 9. His own proposal is in the "Conclusions."

zation and conduct of possible future undertakings.[131] But any chance there might have been of institutionalizing the new mode of peace-keeping, even to this mild degree, was destroyed by the American and British troop landings in Lebanon and Jordan in the summer of 1958.

All the "anti-imperialist" fears endemic to the region flared up, aided and abetted by the Soviet Union. In the emergency Assembly shortly called as a result of these events, President Eisenhower's personal sponsor-ship of a noncombat type of "Standby United Nations Peace Force" amounted to the kiss of death.[132] The hostility generated by immediate events was reinforced by longer-range concerns of various states. India, for example, had earlier rejected Commonwealth suggestions that an interna-tional force might pacify Kashmir and supervise the agreed plebiscite; other states, chiefly Latin American, objected to the implied expense of such measures. It was clear that no resolution of approval could be passed in view of such hostility, even in the limited terms contemplated by Ham-marskjold. The whole matter was therefore shelved by the Special Political Committee, along with a much reduced United States proposal for simply a planning staff in the Secretariat.

With the successful but hectic launching of ONUC in 1960, again almost from scratch, there was another renewal of interest in improving advance preparations for probable future needs. The Secretary-General reiterated his conviction that a standing United Nations force would be both unnecessary and impractical; but added that it would be "an entirely different matter" if governments that were able would also be willing to "maintain a state of preparedness to meet possible" United Nations de-mands, and if the Organization were better prepared to deal with "the crucially important first stages" of organizing and deploying a properly authorized force.[133]

The United States again strongly supported this earmarking approach. The President assured governments receiving American military aid that it

---

131. See *Summary Study of the Experience Derived from the Establishment and Operation of the United Nations Emergency Force,* U.N. General Assembly, Thir-teenth Session, *Official Records,* Annexes, Agenda Item 65, U.N. Doc. A/3943, 1958. See also H. Con. Res. 373 (85 Cong. 2 sess.), Aug. 12, 1958, and Lester B. Pearson, "Force for U.N.," *Foreign Affairs,* Vol. 35 (April 1957), pp. 395–404.

132. For a brief account of these episodes, see Russell, "United Nations Experience with Military Forces," pp. 71–79. For the U.S. proposal, see U.S. Department of State, *Bulletin,* Vol. 39 (1958), pp. 337–42; 527.

133. *Introduction to the Annual Report of the Secretary-General on the Work of the Organization,* 16 June 1959–15 June 1960, U.N. Doc. A/4390/Add. 1, p. 4.

might be used to maintain earmarked contingents in a state of readiness for possible international use and committed the United States to maintain "substantial air and sea transport facilities on a standby basis to help move contingents requested by the United Nations."[134] President Kennedy repeated the urging in 1961. With increasing difficulties in the Congo, however, it was impossible to create any significant international interest in systematically developing standby arrangements. And as the political controversy over that operation became reflected in the financial and constitutional crises of the Organization, not even the mildest proposals for Headquarters improvement commanded support.

NATIONAL SUPPORT FOR THE ORGANIZATION

A few countries, Canada and the Scandinavian governments foremost among them, proceeded to improve their own preparatory arrangements. By 1962, the latter were ready to inform the Secretary-General that they would undertake to establish a joint force of some 4,000 men (organized in nationally self-sufficient units, as well as an international whole), which would be available for the kind of nonfighting political function that had become the standard of United Nations peacekeeping.[135] In spite of the difficulties within the Organization, efforts along these lines have continued to be made by a small group of concerned governments. Canada, Denmark, Norway, Sweden, Finland, the Netherlands, Iran, and Italy have made specific commitments to hold personnel in readiness; and Great Britain, to provide "logistic backing for a United Nations force of up to six infantry battalions."[136]

Less formal efforts to improve future peacekeeping undertakings have also been made, the most significant of which was "an informal, working-level conference" called by the Canadian Foreign Secretary in November 1964:

to enable countries with experience in United Nations peacekeeping operations to compare notes, to identify and survey the technical problems that have been encountered, to pool our experience in meeting those problems and to

134. Text in U.S. Department of State, *Bulletin*, Vol. 43 (1960), p. 554. The commitment was subsequently confirmed in a letter from the Secretary of State.

135. See Per Haekkerup, "Scandinavia's Peacekeeping Forces for the U.N.," *Foreign Affairs*, Vol. 42 (July 1964), pp. 675–81.

136. United Kingdom Mission to the U.N. Press Release 12, Feb. 23, 1965.

see how, individually, we might improve our response to the United Nations in future situations requiring the services of an international Force.[137]

Even with its strictly limited scope, which specifically excluded consideration of "questions relating to the authorization, control, or financing of peacekeeping forces," the proposed meeting brought Soviet charges that it envisaged "the creation of a military apparatus on a collective basis by a number of states members of military blocs with the aim of conducting military operations in the interests of this group of states under the cover of the United Nations flag."[138] As a result, the Secretary-General felt that his staff could neither participate in, nor endorse, Ottawa's modest effort at coordination and organization.

UNITED STATES PROPOSAL FOR AN INTER-AMERICAN FORCE

The United States has confined its official commitments to the United Nations to promised logistical support, since direct participation by troops of a permanent Security Council member is normally excluded by the politics of peacekeeping. Washington has apparently not tried systematically to use its military aid program to assist some additional smaller governments to prepare special units for possible international call-up, although the training in police and communications techniques for international purposes could benefit the national security system as well. Military aid programs in Latin America might seem a logical point of departure for offering this kind of support. An abortive attempt by Washington in May 1965, however, to promote the development of a regular inter-American force after the initiation of the ad hoc force in the Dominican Republic diminished for the time being the chances of favorable Latin American reception of United States assistance offers on behalf of any international forces.

At that time, the United States proposed that arrangements should be made for a permanent inter-American force on a call-up basis as, in the President's words, "a stronger shield against disaster" in view of "new

137. Canada, Department of External Affairs, Statements and Speeches, No. 64/32, Paul Martin, "Peacekeeping: Some Prospects and Perspectives," Nov. 21, 1964, p. 4.
138. *Ibid.*, p. 5.

realities."[139] Although there was practically unanimous agreement among the American governments that some major reorganization of the OAS was in order, there was profound disagreement over whether it should be politically in the direction of strengthening its "peacekeeping" powers or its "nonintervention" standards. Since the intervention in Santo Domingo, Latin American opposition to any permanent machinery for peacekeeping forces has become even more pronounced.

A regular meeting of Foreign Ministers, which had been scheduled for May 1965, was twice postponed until November because of the difficulties in Santo Domingo. By the time it took place in Rio de Janeiro, Secretary Rusk did not specifically propose an inter-American force, but spoke in general terms of "the question of joint action." In both the Cuban missile crisis and the Dominican "situation," he said:

> The discharge by the OAS of its responsibilities involved not merely the assumption of political responsibility but also the employment of units of the armed forces of various member states . . . contributed voluntarily and operated collectively under a combined command. . . .
> The United Nations has, of course, had much more experience than has the OAS in this type of multilateral peacekeeping force. Many of your countries have made personnel available for both United Nations observation and military operations in several crisis situations. It may, therefore, be useful for us to examine, in the light of experience and the nature of our collective responsibilities for peace and security in the hemisphere and elsewhere, the desirability of establishing these voluntary contributions to international peacekeeping operations on a more orderly basis in advance of their possible future use by the OAS or by the U.N.[140]

The Foreign Ministers were not prepared to make any kind of commitment, however. No specific mention was made of the subject in the guidelines given a special committee set up to prepare "a preliminary draft proposal on amendments to the [OAS] Charter." (In contrast, the committee was instructed to include in its draft a lengthy list of "additional" economic and social standards to be included in the Charter.)[141]

By way of postscript, when the special committee met in Panama in March 1966, the United States failed again on a proposal for draft amend-

139. He emphasized the need for new international machinery "geared to meet fast-moving events. When hours can decide the fate of generations, the moment of decision must become the moment of action." U.S. Department of State, *Bulletin*, Vol. 52 (1965), p. 990.

140. Text in U.S. Department of State, *Bulletin*, Vol. 53 (1965), pp. 993–94.

141. Texts of *Act of Rio de Janeiro: Amendments to the Charter of Bogotá* in *Ibid.*, pp. 996–98; and of the *Economic and Social Act of Rio de Janeiro*, pp. 998–1001.

ments that would have given the OAS Council and its Secretary-General some extended powers in the field of peacekeeping and anticommunist activities. In February 1967, another Foreign Ministers' meeting defeated, by 11–6 (the United States abstaining), an Argentine suggestion for a permanent defense advisory committee that would have done little but put the Inter-American Defense Board under the OAS. The arguments against it were that it might open the door to possible military interventions or transform the OAS into "a military alliance."[142]

THE UNITED STATES AND UNITED NATIONS FORCES

In spite of the discouraging record, and an international situation in the spring and summer of 1966 that negatively affected all attempts to improve political cooperation, the United States maintained its efforts in the United Nations to promote a favorable resolution of the peacekeeping controversy. "The capacity of the United Nations to help in keeping the peace must not be weakened," Ambassador Goldberg declared in April, "it must be made stronger. . . ."[143] Some members of Congress went even further, optimistically submitting proposals for United States support to implement that objective. The Republican Coordinating Committee, for example, endorsed a plan, originated in 1965 by a group of Republican representatives, for a volunteer "First Brigade" of 1,000 American non-combatant logistical experts and other technicians to be maintained for call-up by the United Nations.[144] Nothing was said in either the original proposal or the subsequent endorsement about whether an equivalent group of Soviet military technicians would be acceptable in a United Nations Force at some future time. It seems doubtful that the Republican group would welcome such a parallel development, although it would presumably have to be willing to see a communist offer made also.

In June 1966, a bipartisan group of some sixty congressmen introduced identical concurrent resolutions reaffirming earlier support by Congress (as embodied in the 1958 H.Con. Res. 373) "for a permanent United

142. *New York Times*, Feb. 23, 1967. Dislike of the military regime in Buenos Aires was also considered a contributing cause.

143. U.S. Department of State, *Bulletin*, Vol. 54 (1966), p. 750.

144. Original proposal printed in *Congressional Record*, Vol. 111, Pt. 10, 89 Cong. 1 sess. (1965) pp. 13826–27. Report of the Republican Coordinating Committee's Task Force on the Conduct of Foreign Relations, *The United Nations*, July 11, 1966, p. 4 (mimeo.). The committee also advocated an expansion of the Military Advisor Group in the office of the Secretary-General.

Nations peacekeeping force," and urging the United States delegation to present a plan to the twenty-first General Assembly for the establishment of such a United Nations "World Peace Force" on a permanent basis and for rules to govern the proper and effective use of such a peacekeeping force and provisions to train, equip, and finance it.[145] Representative Schweiker argued that

With the heightening of international fears over the war in Vietnam, . . . the Congress, speaking for the Nation, ought at this time and in this manner to emphasize our interest in peace and in strengthening the organizations which might help to achieve peace.

It is important also to point out to the world that the American eagle holds an olive branch as well as a sheaf of arrows and that we want to do everything possible to strengthen the peacekeeping operations of the United Nations.[146]

In view of the peacekeeping deadlock at the United Nations, the State Department discouraged any such extensive proposal. No hearings were held at the time, but the subject remains of interest to the Congress. In addition to the interest in the House of Representatives, promotion of the idea may be one of the activities of a bipartisan group of senators and congressmen formed in October 1966 as the "Members of Congress for Peace through Law."[147] They plan to press for, among other goals, the establishment of a permanent United Nations peace force, presumably along lines similar to the one advocated in the concurrent resolutions.

The sincerity of the congressmen is not in question; yet, if the analysis of this chapter is valid, their timing must be faulted. This is hardly the moment to press for a permanent system of earmarked national contingents. The very issues that would have to be solved, in order to organize and maintain such forces on a cooperative basis among any substantial number of Members, are those that were still hamstringing the Special Committee on Peace-Keeping Operations in the fall of 1967. Nor

145. The original group of draft resolutions are numbered H.Con.Res. 683–746, June 9, 1966. Rep. Schweiker made the formal introduction on behalf of 50 members, his own being H.Con.Res. 690. Five Republican members added to their resolutions provision for "an unqualified offer" of the 1,000-man noncombatant brigade noted above. See *Congressional Record*, Vol. 112, June 9, 1966, 89 Cong. 2 sess., pp. 12291–93.

146. *Ibid.*, p. 12291.

147. The group is under the leadership of Sen. Joseph S. Clark, with a steering committee including Sens. Jacob K. Javits, Robert F. Kennedy, Eugene J. McCarthy, George McGovern, and Reps. Jonathan B. Bingham, Donald M. Fraser, James G. Fulton, Robert W. Kastenmeier, Patsy T. Mink, F. Bradford Morse, Benjamin S. Rosenthal, and Richard C. Schweiker. *New York Times*, Oct. 30, 1966.

would it be easy to separate the constitutional and technical issues of establishing such a system on a permanent basis from questions of its financing, as well as from the more immediate problem of making the Organization solvent once more. The significance of the proposals, for present purposes, lies in their illustration of a widespread American tendency to concentrate on the procedures and machinery required for an effective system of United Nations operations, almost to the exclusion of consideration of the basic problem of how to develop the necessary political cooperation that will allow any machinery and procedures to be developed and paid for.

Manifestations of good will toward the United Nations are important, but they do not compensate for lack of a realistic understanding of the causes of its difficulties. Canada's General Burns, out of his wealth of personal experience in peacekeeping operations, has succinctly summarized the crux of the matter. It will not be possible, he points out, to put even reasonable suggestions into effect, "while the U.S.S.R. is so adamantly opposed to the use of United Nations forces in any other manner than that provided in the Charter." Any plan for a United Nations force would require the cooperation of the Secretariat, but, "as events since 1960 have demonstrated, the Secretariat must maintain neutrality as between the power blocs, if the United Nations is to continue in being."[148]

Peacekeeping and Settlement

The control of international violence is fundamentally a function of the will to peaceful settlement. Once a dispute has reached the stage of open hostilities, the first step toward peaceful resolution of the dispute is to bring the violence under control. On this, United Nations peacekeeping has not done too badly.[149] Charter theory anticipated that then, with

148. Lt. Gen. E. L. M. Burns, in a review of Lincoln P. Bloomfield, ed., *International Military Forces* (Little, Brown and Co., 1964), in *American Journal of International Law*, Vol. 59 (1965), p. 978. See also Burns, *Between Arab and Israeli* (Ivan Obolensky, 1963) for an account of his experiences in United Nations Truce Supervisory Organization (UNTSO) in Palestine and in UNEF.

149. Adlai Stevenson suggested that the record of "violence without wars" indicated an "imperceptible" movement into "an era of peaceful settlement of disputes—or at least . . . of ceasefires while disputes are pursued by other than military means." "From Containment to Cease Fire and Peaceful Change," in Andrew Cordier and Wilder Foote, eds., *The Quest for Peace* (Columbia University Press, 1965), p. 59. The latter more accurately describes the state of affairs today.

violence halted, the processes of adjustment and settlement could be made operative. Practice has fallen considerably short of that in many cases. Something more is needed, clearly, than merely the availability of means, if settlement is to be achieved.

At the White House Conference on International Cooperation in November 1965, the "Report of the Committee on Peaceful Settlement of Disputes" recommended "continuing study under the auspices of the General Assembly of the process of peaceful settlement as a Charter obligation." It reemphasized the Members' obligation to seek solution by the various procedures of settlement listed in Article 33, but then admitted:

There remains the hard question of settlement of a dispute when the policy of one party involved is to keep the dispute unresolved, to apply the direct or covert use of force or subversion, or to dictate a unilateral solution. The [conventional] procedures outlined do not of themselves provide response to such a policy.

This led the committee also to suggest that "a learning process about the need for peaceful change could demonstrate the common interest of states, even those with differing values, in this process over the long run."[150]

The atmosphere of 1966–67 has not been conducive to progress in this field, whether through United Nations machinery or by some of the other means frequently recommended. Joint commissions, for example, have been proposed as the basis for more direct negotiations between the disputants—by the report just noted, for one—as a possible supplement to United Nations action. Another oft-repeated suggestion has been for the use of rapporteurs (in League of Nations fashion) to facilitate settlement by the Security Council. New machinery to improve and encourage fact-finding as a means toward settlement was suggested by the Netherlands delegation in the United Nations.[151] Referred to the Sixth Committee, the subject has been reported and commented on for the past three years, only to be continued each time on the agenda of the next Assembly.[152]

Great Britain introduced, in the twentieth Assembly, a proposal to establish a special committee to study the problem of peaceful settlement

150. ICY National Citizens' Commission, "Report of the Committee on Peaceful Settlement of Disputes," 1965, pp. 1–2 (multilithed).

151. Background for the proposal was explained by the Netherlands Permanent Representative, Ambassador Carl W. A. Schurmann, in *A Center for International Fact Finding: A Review and a Proposal*, Columbia University, School of International Affairs Occasional Paper, July 1963.

152. See, for example, U.N. Doc. A/6547, Dec. 7, 1966, pp. 43–44.

of disputes in all its aspects.[153] But with the Rhodesian situation coming to a head in late 1965, the proposal encountered heavy opposition to the principle of peaceful settlement by many of those who were more interested in the application of forcible means to settle that particular dispute. They therefore charged that the British were motivated by a desire to avoid sanctions in Rhodesia. The Assembly accordingly decided to adjourn discussion of the item and remit it to the next session.

At the twenty-first Assembly, in December 1966, Great Britain reverted to its suggestion for a study committee. It argued in the Special Political Committee that it was not proposing any new machinery at that stage, nor recommending specific use of any existing machinery, nor advocating anything in conflict with the Charter or the powers of the principal organs. The Netherlands suggested that, although time did not permit thorough study until later, states might be invited to submit suggestions to the Secretary-General for strengthening the means of peaceful settlement and encouraging recourse to them, with the item to be placed on the agenda of the following session.[154] Opposition to consideration of methods of peaceful settlement continued to be strong, however. The Guinean delegate put the argument most bluntly: the Charter provided adequately for pacific settlement of disputes until the decolonization task was completed in Africa, Asia, and Latin America. Only after ending rebellion in Rhodesia, solving the South West African issue, and eradicating apartheid in South Africa "would the United Nations be able to perform its peacekeeping function effectively."[155]

The Special Political Committee ended by adjourning debate on the issue[156] and the Assembly merely noted the committee's report.

A somewhat more novel approach than any of the above has been suggested by Professor Swift: to adapt to political questions the new conciliation procedures devised for UNCTAD that are available for use before voting on matters affecting the members' economic and financial inter-

153. U.N. Doc. A/5964, Aug. 20, 1965.
154. A draft resolution (U.N. Doc. A/SPC/L. 144) to this effect was sponsored by the Netherlands, Afghanistan, Argentina, Iran, Jamaica, Malta, and Sweden.
155. U.N. Doc. A/SPC/SR. 548, Dec. 16, 1966, p. 7.
156. On the ground that there was not enough time for full consideration of the question at that session, Tanzania first proposed to defer the item to the next Assembly. Then, after adjournment for consultations, the Tanzanian delegate took advantage of a procedural rule to adjourn the debate. The motion carried, 50–26–6, despite considerable protest against the method used. U.N. Doc. A/6617, Dec. 17, 1966.

ests. [157] Recognizing that it is too early to know how effective the new procedures will be and that it would be more difficult to apply similar ones in the political field, he nonetheless argues that:

These procedures actually could result in a new criterion for the success of an international organization: not merely whether a state can mobilize a majority for its point of view, but whether all the Members can arrive at a workable consensus that will not destroy the organization itself . . . UNCTAD has now devised an institutional way, not now required under existing U.N. procedures, to force delegates to think about the consequences of their actions . . . [and] establishing these procedures . . . requires only a change in Assembly rules, not an amendment to the Charter. . . .
. . . Under such arrangements, the test for U.N. action would become effectiveness, i.e., how best to influence a situation the majority wanted to change, instead of best to force an issue to a vote for the record.

All these proposals, however, assume at least a minimum willingness to accommodate and cooperate on both sides; whereas we live today in an age of the "just war" rather than of willingness to make the compromises and exhibit the patience essential to peaceful settlement. The inability to make the slightest progress toward any settlement of the Arab-Israeli conflict since 1949 is a depressing reminder of this fact. The renewal of hostilities in 1967 merely made acute once again the issues that have been lying semidormant for years; and the Arabs have been able to maintain their refusal of the slightest political concession toward Israel in spite of their military defeat, as noted earlier, in part because of the lack of accord between the two superpowers. A commentary by the Iraqi representative on Lester Pearson's proposal in 1957, that withdrawal of Israeli troops from the Gaza Strip should be followed by United Nations administration of the area (in addition to the posting of UNEF on the armistice line), will serve equally well to explain the difficulties of pacific settlement today, and not only in the Middle East.

Mr. Pearson [he said] has two weaknesses in all his thinking on Palestine. . . . The first is that he has never been in the Middle East nor has he had, as far as I know, any serious discussions with Middle Eastern statesmen . . . his knowledge is only on the side of Zionist propaganda. But ignorance is not the only cause, and we come now to the other one. *Mr. Pearson thinks that compromise and expediency are the road to peace in international affairs* . . . A man with these—shall I call them—vacuums in his knowledge and experience cannot be a fair judge or mediator in the Palestine issue.[158]

157. Richard N. Swift, "San Francisco Revisited: The Dilemma of Intervention," *The Correspondent,* No. 34 (Spring-Summer 1965), pp. 62–68.
158. Quoted in Terence Robertson, *Crisis: The Inside Story of the Suez Conspiracy* (Atheneum, 1965), p. 331. Italics added.

To progress beyond a system of cease-fires and the suspension of violence, Adlai Stevenson once pointed out, would require "a reliable system of order with the capacity to induce peaceful change where change is needed." To achieve that, he recognized, United Nations Members would not only have to improve the machinery of settlement but also cultivate the profession of peacemaking.[159]

On the basis of the record here surveyed, if greater progress is to be made toward an orderly and peaceful world, it would appear that the "cultivation of peacemaking" must begin at an earlier stage in the development of conflict than that of the settlement of disputes. It must start at the stage of peaceful adjustment and change, rather than only when a conflict of interests has reached the stage of being a "dispute or situation . . . likely to endanger the maintenance of international peace and security," in Charter terms. For it is axiomatic that if peaceful change is not permitted, violent change will sooner or later occur. None of the disputes that led to the peacekeeping forces or the less dramatic United Nations measures considered in this chapter was a sudden affair—only the final outbreak of violence appeared sudden. All had backgrounds of controversy providing ample warning signs that preventive diplomacy looking toward settlement was called for. Yet they were not heeded. The next chapter will examine why.

159. Stevenson, "Strengthening the Machinery for Peace," U.S. Department of State, *Bulletin*, Vol. 50 (1964), pp. 969–70.

CHAPTER SEVEN

PEACEFUL ADJUSTMENT AND
POLITICAL CHANGE

A major obstacle in the way of any deliberate broad-scale attack by the United States Government on the problems of preventive peaceful change has been the very human one of "not troubling trouble, until trouble troubles you." Throughout the entire postwar period, there have been troubles enough and to spare, not only for Washington as a newcomer in the field of international leadership, but also for the world at large. From the viewpoint of the United States, the immediate difficulties have been only too real: the danger of communist aggression has always been present and nationalist aspirations have often reached the explosive point. Preoccupied with the resulting acute problems and the improvisation of efforts to contain incipient or actual violence, the government has understandably paid less attention to the less demanding, longer-term problems, even when it was evident that they would probably worsen with time.

The impatient American temperament, moreover, is not given to viewing events in the long perspective, either historically or into the future. On some occasions, circumstances do not allow the luxury of happy policy solutions to both short- and long-run aspects of a complex problem or give time to weigh them carefully and seek some satisfactory compromise when the solutions may be in conflict. Or the longer-run elements may present so uncertain a picture as to lead to serious controversy over the best policy to pursue. In these cases, the long-run interest perforce takes second place to short-run demands. On other occasions, even though time may not be so pressing, the lack of any long-run perspective, even of any long-run interest, may lead to faulty diagnosis of the problem, with consequent danger of a wrong or at best inadequate prescription for cure.

Since history unfortunately "does not disclose its alternatives," it is extremely difficult to demonstrate precisely how another policy, or the same policy applied sooner, or in larger doses, or with more skill, might have worked better in particular cases. On the broad world canvas since 1945, however, the two major historical forces for change that have affected United States foreign-policy directions—communism and emergent nationalism—could be seen clearly at an early stage, even seen to present conflicting policy problems to Washington. The precedence originally given to the need to contain the communist thrust was both logical and necessary, in view of its immediacy as a threat in the early postwar years. It is impossible to say when the second thrust became strong enough to warrant much greater consideration in policy analysis and planning. But hindsight makes it clear that prevailing opinion in the government was too slow to recognize the need for an attempt to find ways to reconcile, when they were in conflict, policies of resistance to communist expansionism with policies aimed to promote political adjustments in the interest of international peace and security.

The Nature of the Contemporary Problem

The content of the problem of peaceful change has itself changed from the League of Nations period, when the term gained currency as referring primarily to change in territorial status or treaty obligations; change, that is, in the legal status quo.[1] By definition this would not be obtainable through resort to judicial organs or appeals to international law. Article 10 of the Covenant committed the League members to "preserve, as against external aggression," each other's political independence and territorial integrity; but Article 19 empowered the Assembly "from time to time" to advise on reconsideration of "treaties which have become inapplicable" and to consider international conditions that might become dangers to peace. Even this mild recognition of the need for peaceful change became a dead letter in practice, however, while Article 10 was invoked to justify resistance to demands for political adjustments in response to altered conditions.[2]

1. The League, it has been pointed out, was "based upon the theses that states were easily identifiable and that the activity of the League would relate mainly to conflicts about the borders between defined states—concepts which had guided the discussion on defining aggression." W. M. Jordan, in Richard N. Swift, ed., *Annual Review of United Nations Affairs*, 1963–64 (New York University Press, 1965), p. 45. See also Frederick S. Dunn, *Peaceful Change: A Study of International Procedures* (Council on Foreign Relations, 1937), especially pp. 106–11.

2. See Pitman B. Potter, *Article XIX of the Covenant of the League of Nations*, Geneva Studies, Vol. 12 (Geneva Research Center, 1941).

At San Francisco, the same two principles were again in conflict: the need for sanctity of the pledged word if any international order is to have stability, and the need for peaceful evolution if it is to avoid change by violence. League experience led to a deliberate avoidance of any formal commitment by the United Nations similar to Article 10: that is, to preserve the status quo to be established in the anticipated peace settlements after 1945. Instead, Article 2 (4) of the Charter bound individual members not to threaten or use force against "the territorial integrity or political independence of any state." As noted in Chapter 3, Article 14 then recognized more broadly the need for the "peaceful adjustment of any situation, regardless of origin" which might impair friendly international relations. The Organization was left procedurally as flexible as possible in promoting peaceful adjustment of difficulties. At the same time it was to observe the standards incorporated in the purposes and principles of the Charter. In a curious compromise of the conflict over treaty maintenance versus treaty modification, the principle of "respect for obligations arising from treaties and other sources of international law" was spelled out only in the normally less binding Preamble; but the Preamble was then declared to be as binding as the rest of the document.[3]

The concept of change envisaged in general terms in Article 14 was given more detailed substance in the provisions for economic and social advance, the promotion of human rights, and the political evolution of dependent peoples. The possibility that the problems of change in this broad context might become sources of threats to international peace and security (even when originating within a nation) was foreseen in 1945. Before long, it became the actuality in various cases that came before the United Nations and in many that did not. Internal conflicts (including what used to be described as "colonial rebellions") and social as well as political revolution have been among underlying causes of all the peacekeeping conflicts just considered. And because of the cold-war situation between the major powers, those conflicts became involved in greater or less degree with that overlying problem.

None of these manifold underlying sources of conflict has received anything like the systematic attention (in the context of peacekeeping requirements) given to the more obvious immediate causes of violent dispute, with the significant exception of the field of economic development.

3. This controversy at San Francisco is described in Ruth B. Russell, *A History of the United Nations Charter: The Role of the United States 1940–1945* (Brookings Institution, 1958), Chap. 29, especially pp. 750–76.

In previous eras, development, in the sense of the growth of the human community in its economic, social, and political forms, moved generally at an evolutionary pace in relation to the individual's life span. Now, population and technological pressures force movement at revolutionary speed in the economic and political fields as well, and give new urgency to the problems thereby caused.

DEVELOPMENT AND CHANGE

Economic development was seen by the United States in the early post-war period as the means of meeting the "revolution of rising expectations" in a material sense. The satisfaction of rising standards of living, it was supposed, would counteract the appeal of communist aims and methods. Nonetheless, assistance for development purposes as such has generally been considered by Washington as second in urgency to programs of aid—military, economic, or political—given in the cold-war context.

With time, there has come greater comprehension of the need for con-current political and social development of the weaker states (whether new or old) if economic modernization is not to result in instabilities that threaten their capacity to resist subversive communist influences as well as more obvious military threats. As experience has pointed up the full complexity of the problem and its long-term nature, Americans increasingly understand the need for development assistance on a far larger scale and over a far broader field than originally anticipated. Development is seen to require investment in the economic and social "infrastructure" of a country (to use the lingo that has accompanied awareness of the problem) as well as in the direct improvement of agricultural and industrial output. It also calls for deliberate effort to broaden the social distribution of the product, if there is to be any chance of achieving political stability and progress toward minimally representative forms of government, along with growth of the national product as reflected in economic statistics.

In its contemporary manifestation, this is a new field of public endeavor. Even now, the complex interconnections just noted receive more lip service than implementation on the necessary scale or with the necessary urgency to keep resource development and the national product ahead of the population threat in many areas.[4]

---

4. For example, see statements on "The World Food and Population Crisis," by the Vice President and the Secretaries of State and Agriculture, U.S. Department of State, *Bulletin,* Vol. 55 (1965), pp. 199–212.

There is no general agreement on the most effective "mix" of public and private means to carry out such a program under a pluralistic system; on the most effective order of priorities for its various components; on the most effective division of labor between bilateral and multilateral channels for carrying out the programs decided on; nor even on the best way to use multilateral organizations in applying the resources eventually allocated to those institutions. Most important of all, there has never been developed, there has never been seriously sought, a general policy capable of harmonizing and harnessing the rising winds of political change in the colonial world with the rising expectations of economic and social change in all the underdeveloped lands. Perhaps that was inherently impossible, although we could not know without trying. Yet, if containment of communist expansion militarily is not accompanied by a more positive development and stabilization of the weaker states, it will fail to produce the peaceful world order that is the aim of the United States.

Although agreement on these many aspects of economic development aid has not yet been reached, the concept itself has long been an integral part of United States foreign policy. In contrast, American military thought has only in the sixties embraced any equivalent concept in relation to the Third World, separate from its preoccupation with strategic deterrence. A doctrine of counterinsurgency (CI) was developed during the Kennedy Administration in recognition that nuclear deterrence alone failed to answer the problem of communist expansion in underdeveloped countries through subversive internal activities, including guerilla warfare.[5] The program incorporates such military elements as antiguerilla pacification operations and civic-action projects, which may contribute to nonmilitary aspects of the modernization process in weak and unstable countries, as well as counter communist subversion and insurgency more directly. By the mid-sixties:

The rationale for CI [was] provided by a State Department white paper called "U.S. Overseas Internal Defense" ..., which defines Communist insurgency as an attempt to interfere with the modernization process. Any insurgency is dangerous because all insurgency provides the Communists with a foothold, although the Government insists that it is not opposed to noncommunist revolutions. Insurgency is seen on three levels: inactive, a situation

5. For a description of the origins and development of the CI program, see Roger Hilsman, *To Move a Nation: The Politics of Foreign Policy in the Administration of John F. Kennedy* (Doubleday, 1967), especially Chap. 28, "Subterranean War."

in which the U.S. concentrates on "nation-building" and equipping local forces to deal with future insurgency; existent, when the U.S. effort has a higher military content, but the emphasis is still on nation-building and self-help; and active, when the U.S. response is almost entirely military, as in Vietnam.[6]

There are two hazards to the CI doctrine within this framework, however. One lies in the difficulty of distinguishing between communist and noncommunist insurgency, with the danger that the program may end in being used to suppress dissidence and maintain in authority governments that, for all their lip-service to the objective of modernization, are unable or unwilling to carry through the domestic reforms required to achieve it. United States intervention in the Dominican Republic in 1965 has been criticized as a case in point.

The second hazard lies in the manner in which the military and non-military aspects are related in the course of applying the general counter-insurgency concept. On this, there has been a deep split in official thinking. In the first two stages of subversion, as described above, the military role remains subordinate to and supportive of the political, economic, social, and administrative programs that are essential in any case to the development process. In the stage of active insurgency, however, the official position—that the response must be mainly military—was not the basis on which the CI doctrine was originally conceived in relation to Vietnam, in particular, in the Kennedy Administration. Rather, it had been intended to follow the principles advocated by Robert Thompson (the British official responsible for much of the success of a prototype program in Malaya), especially that of giving priority "to defeating the political subversion, not the guerillas," in the insurgency as well as in the build-up stages.[7] But in practice, "the United States effort lacked both the 'unified civilian, police, and military system of command and control' and the 'subordination of civic, police, social, and military measures to an overall counter-guerilla program' that were the first principles of the strategic concept that had been worked out."[8] On the contrary, the view expressed by General Earl Wheeler in 1962 won out: "The essence of the problem in Vietnam is military."[9]

6. Arthur Herzog, *The War-Peace Establishment* (Harper and Row, 1965), pp. 133–34.

7. Robert Thompson, *Defeating Communist Insurgency: Experiences from Malaya and Vietnam* (Chatto and Windus, 1966), pp. 55–56.

8. Hilsman, *op. cit.*, p. 442.

9. Quoted in *Ibid.*, p. 426.

This is not the place for a disquisition on the problems of military aid in the development process generally, but two points need to be noted here. First, unless the United States can reconcile its CI doctrine with the violence inherent in the modernization process even without the communist threat, it is not likely to achieve that security against communism which it theoretically recognizes must flow, not "out of the barrel of a gun," but out of reasonably stable, developing political societies. More will be said of this in the final chapter. The second point to be made here relates more immediately to the theme of the present chapter. Until now, Western governmental policies with regard to these interrelated aspects of political, economic, administrative, and military change and conflict in the Third World have on the whole tended to "jes' grow," individually, like Topsy. The communists, on the other hand, have always seen "capitalist-imperialism" as a single evil, no less in their attacks on the post-1945 status quo than in their theoretical doctrine.[10]

CHANGE AND COMMUNISM

As would be expected from the nature of its ideology, "change" in the communist lexicon is practically synonymous with "revolution." The very concept of international, as well as domestic, change through compromise and peaceful adjustment is incompatible with the authoritarian doctrine and practice of communism. In the first years of the United Nations, communist opposition to the development of those cooperative relations that would make peaceful change possible often took the form of proposed cold-war resolutions in the General Assembly on broad questions of peace and security. They stressed outlawing atomic weapons and reducing armaments, or denounced "inciters of war" and "criminal propaganda" for war. Later, as the Soviet Union acquired nuclear weapons and as more new states achieved membership, emphasis shifted toward anti-colonialism as a central Soviet theme and the stick with which Moscow could beat all the capitalist-imperialists, including the United States.

In 1960, Khrushchev presented the Soviet position in a typical draft

10. A Soviet pamphlet on the United Nations, for example, emphasizes the fact that the "Decree on Peace and the Declaration on the Rights of the Working and Exploited People" were the "very first decrees of the Soviet state"; and that it had ever since been "waging a consistent struggle for the liberation of all peoples from colonialism." G. Morozov and E. Pchelintsev, *The United Nations—Twenty Years of Failures and Successes* (Novosti Press Agency, 1965), pp. 21–22.

declaration favoring immediate independence for all dependent peoples. His argument went as follows: (1) The "struggle of the peoples for their liberties . . . is a great historical process, one of ever-growing and invincible power." (2) As feudalism gave way to "the bourgeois order of things," so capitalism is giving way to socialism today, and "colonial slavery" to freedom. (3) If, "instead of plundering and exploiting" their colonies, the metropolitan states had really been guided by the interests of their colonial peoples, the latter would have developed uniformly with the imperial power. Instead, they enriched themselves from their dependent peoples, who can only escape from "want and arbitrary rule" through "liquidation of the colonial system of government." (4) This is what, in effect, occurred in the Soviet Union. Remote areas of the Tsarist empire, like colonies, were "cruelly exploited"; but after the October Revolution, their peoples obtained "complete freedom" and quickly improved their economic, cultural, and social condition. Thus, Soviet experience proves that it is "perfectly possible for the countries of the East to do away with backwardness, poverty, diseases, and ignorance within the lifetime of one generation and to rise to the level of economically advanced countries."[11]

In short, and in communist terms, if the "Third World" does not achieve, under American leadership of a cooperative international system, the global political and economic revolution that it has set as its goal, the dissatisfied peoples have only to turn to the communists who promise what they want under an authoritative system. The superficial appeal of these extravagant terms has constituted a serious difficulty for the former imperial powers—the advanced Western nations—to overcome in dealing with the more anticolonial states. In less distorted terms, this is also the contemporary problem of "peaceful change" that challenges the United States. It is change in the broad sense of Article 14, which can only be met by "creative acts of peaceful policy"[12] and the ameliorating effects of evolutionary political adjustments *before* the minor sources of friction grow into major disputes, when the time for peaceful settlement is usually past.

11. U.N. Doc. A/PV. 869 (Sept. 23, 1960), pp. 70–78.
12. Max Huber, "The Role of International Law," *Perspectives on Peace, 1910–1960* (London: Carnegie Endowment for International Peace, 1960), pp. 157–58. "Preventive diplomacy" would be a most useful term to describe the need; but, thanks to its use by Secretary-General Hammarskjold in describing U.N. activities to prevent breakdowns of peace in several concrete disputes, it has come to imply "preventive" primarily of actual hostilities.

CHANGE AND UNITED STATES POLICY

Soviet recovery from the devastation of World War II and its achievement of atomic weapons meant that it became a greater military threat to
the United States and could also influence other governments in areas
beyond its military control. At first, this was done chiefly through political
subversion, with but little effort through economic means. After the isolationism of the Stalin era, however, the Soviet Union also sought to compete in technical assistance and aid programs as part of an overall effort to
destroy the *status juris* of the Western-dominated, nonwestern world,
while defying Western attempts to alter the status quo within the Soviet
orbit.[13]

The most dramatic aspect of political change in the postwar period has
been the revolutionary sweep of decolonization around the globe. To a
large extent, this was achieved by relatively peaceful means, with the
imperial governments soon recognizing the demand for independence—
as in Burma. But where independence came only after violent revolution
against the legal and political authority of the metropole, the communists
often made political gains from the resulting virulent anticolonial sentiments. The presence of this communist element inclined Washington to
view the consequent difficulties for its own policy aims as primarily a part
of its strategic problem of containing militant communism. The government's preoccupation with that latter threat hindered greater efforts to
promote a more cooperative evolution of the colonial and semicolonial
world into the kind of international order outlined in the Charter.

Concentration on the immediate threat perhaps also reinforced an
assumption that because peaceful adjustments with the communists
themselves were so patently impossible, there was little that could be done
elsewhere. But the communist and noncommunist worlds have presented
two quite different aspects of the problem, and lack of progress in one
should not have stifled initiative in the other. In itself it probably would

13. See also W. W. Rostow, "The Third Round," *Foreign Affairs*, Vol. 42 (October 1963), p. 5: "There is no doubt that Moscow came to believe that it had deeply
rooted advantages in seeking to expand Communist power and influence in these
[underdeveloped] regions at the expense of the West by orchestrating flexibly the devices of subversion and guerilla warfare; trade and aid; appeal to anti-colonialism and
nationalist sentiments; and by the claim that communism was not merely the fast-
closing rival of the United States, but the possessor of a method for the more efficient
—even if ruthless—modernization of an underdeveloped region."

not have done so, because the United States has in general had an "anti-colonial" attitude. But the major European imperial powers were all NATO allies as well, and the anticolonial drive soon expanded to include an intensive Soviet drive against "imperialistic" foreign (including United States) military bases, especially in dependent territories.

It was not long, therefore, until the wartime concern in Washington to develop a broad program of colonial evolution toward self-government (through the United Nations trusteeship system) gave way before demands of national and allied security policy. The trend was reinforced, moreover, when some of the new governments turned out to be less than democratic in political makeup, avowedly socialistic in economic philosophy, and more interested in avoiding involvement in the cold war than in joining an alliance against communism. Could the United States have considered alone either the short-term or the long-term requirements of the resulting complex of problems, policy decisions would have been much simpler. But the conflict of principles involved was of such a nature that there seemed to be no solution that could satisfactorily encompass both time phases. Consequently, the government tended to swing from favoring one aspect of the problem to the other, or it followed a relatively neutral course that satisfied proponents of neither side.

The inability to move more peacefully toward self-government and to develop more satisfactory relations among the new states and between them and the older powers, meant the diversion, into controversy over nationalist claims, of vast energy and resources that might otherwise have gone into political and economic development of a more constructive sort. The price that has been paid, to the degree that peaceful change was not the rule, has therefore been enormous, although by its nature unmeasurable. The noncommunist world, as a consequence, still confronts the United States with one of its most difficult tasks of leadership: finding a policy of reconciliation between the conflicting interests of the "allied" and "neutral" states that comprise it.

The most complex manifestation of those conflicts, what has come to be called the "decolonization" movement, has been the main problem of peaceful change in the postwar period. The major problem for the foreseeable future in this area will be to complete that process as peacefully as possible and to evolve more satisfactory relationships between the stronger and weaker states, regardless of their age. This must be seen as a problem with two facets, which have already overlapped in time and in substance. The ramifications of the problem extend far beyond the issues of legal and constitutional status.

Decolonization and the Trusteeship System

After pointing out that we "have made progress in recent years, halting and limited, if you will, but some progress toward the prevention of war by collective action," Prime Minister Lester Pearson asked, some years ago: "Why have we been unable to make even the same amount of progress in assisting the growth to national independence from colonial status by planned collective action and by international support for the emerging States on a broad and acceptable basis?"[14] He found part of the answer in the unwillingness of the colonial powers to use the United Nations trusteeship system to this end for their own possessions, and in the suspicion of the newer nations that an extension of that system might become a cloak for a return to imperialism. Had the colonial governments ever seriously sought to utilize the possibilities of the trusteeship machinery and procedures along lines envisioned by Franklin Roosevelt and Cordell Hull, however, it is arguable that such an honest international effort to assist "the growth to national independence" might have resulted in less suspicious reactions and more willingness to make speed slowly on the part of the still-dependent peoples. Such an approach was urged, in vain, by Secretary-General Lie in 1950, as part of his twenty-year program for peace:

I firmly believe, [he declared] that such great changes as have been taking place since the end of the war—fundamental changes in the relationships of whole peoples and even continents—can be prevented from tearing the world apart only by using the universal framework of the United Nations to contain them within peaceful bounds . . . This opportunity [through the Trusteeship and other Charter provisions on dependent territories] needs to be more fully used. . . .[15]

FROM TRUST TO INDEPENDENCE

In practice, however, as noted in Chapter 2, only a small segment of the dependent world of 1945 was placed under the limited authority of the

14. In the Foreword to Alastair Taylor, *Indonesian Independence and the United Nations* (1961), p. xvi.

15. U.N. General Assembly, Fifth Session, *Official Records*, 308th Meeting, Nov. 17, 1950, p. 440.

Trusteeship Council, and the future of a few Italian colonies was later arranged through the Assembly only because the major allied powers could not agree on what to do with them in the Italian peace settlement.[16] The results of this limited international supervision do not compare unfavorably with the results of the surge to national independence that occurred outside the area of United Nations direct influence.

Somaliland and seven former mandates—Tanganyika, both French and British Togoland and Cameroons, Ruanda-Urundi, and Western Samoa —had become independent states by 1962. Only Nauru (Australia), New Guinea (Australia on behalf of itself, New Zealand, and Great Britain), and the Pacific Islands Trust (United States) remained in trust status by 1967. The way in which some trusts became new states is perhaps the most significant aspect of the system, especially in contrast with decolonization patterns elsewhere.

British Togoland, after a plebiscite in 1955, opted to become part of Ghana, when the former Gold Coast became independent in 1957. The French mandates elected to become independent Togo and Cameroon in 1960; but the following year, after Assembly debates had "produced a consensus" that the two parts of the British Cameroons did not constitute a viable entity, it was decided that each should elect to join one of its neighbors. As a result, the south voted to join Cameroon, and the north to become part of the Federation of Nigeria; while "the presence of United Nations observers at the plebiscite ensured the legitimacy of the outcome and enabled the world community to withstand the pressure of

16. In 1947, all the former B and C mandates except South West Africa were placed under trusteeship by agreements that made the former mandatory (Great Britain, France, Australia, Belgium, or New Zealand) the new administering authority. The Japanese mandated islands became the Pacific Islands Trust Territory, with the United States as trustee, under the Security Council as the only strategic trust.

In 1949, the former Italian Somaliland was designated a trust territory by the Assembly, with Italy as the administering authority. It was given the target date of 1960 for independence; and an Advisory Council of three states (Colombia, Egypt, and the Philippines) was established to assist Italy in its administration. The Assembly also decided that Libya should become independent by 1952, with a U.N. Commissioner (an Assistant Secretary-General) assisting the Libyans to draw up a constitution and establish their government. In 1950, the Assembly adopted the proposed plan of an investigatory commission to make Eritrea an autonomous unit federated with Ethiopia, again assisted by a U.N. Commissioner.

Although Art. 81 provided that the U.N. itself might become a trustee, it has never been made one. It was virtually so for a short period in both Libya and West New Guinea, and has theoretically assumed such a role in relation to South West Africa.

those who wished to reopen the question."[17] Italian Somaliland became independent in 1960, in accordance with the Assembly's 1949 decision, and was joined by British Somaliland to form Somalia; but it remains at odds with Ethiopia and Kenya where groups of Somalis agitate for their incorporation in the new state, and with France over the future of French Somaliland. In March 1967, an "independent referendum" in this last territory resulted in a majority for continuation of French rule, considered to have been cast largely by the nomadic Afars. The minority Somalis, in response, erupted in violent rioting in the capital of Djibouti. Ruanda-Urundi, after considerable debate between the United Nations and Belgium over the form its independent successors should take, emerged as the two states of Rwanda and Burundi in July 1962, leaving some dire prophecies of "another Congo" unfulfilled. At the start of that year, Western Samoa also gained independence, after a plebiscite supervised by a United Nations Commissioner elected by the Assembly. Alone of the group (and indeed, alone of all the new states) Western Samoa voted for a constitution that allowed New Zealand, its former "trustee," to continue handling its foreign affairs and defense, and it did not seek membership in the United Nations.[18]

In short, the degree of both international supervision and of international consultation of the people in the process of self-determination was greater in connection with the trust territories than with other dependent areas. The results of the plebiscite in the British mandates of Togoland and the Cameroons left Professor Emerson with "an inescapable sense of doubt as to whether other peoples in Asia and Africa might not have chosen different destinies than those assigned to them if they had been given the chance."[19]

The history of the Trusteeship Council has not been an altogether happy one, in spite of accomplishing so much of its assigned task. Its even division of membership (between administering and nonadministering

17. Joseph E. Johnson, "Helping to Build New States," in The United States and the United Nations, Francis O. Wilcox and H. Field Haviland, eds. (Johns Hopkins Press, 1961), pp. 9–10.

18. The same general procedure was followed by New Zealand in connection with the attainment of self-government by the Cook Islands. See below, pp. 285–86.

19. Rupert Emerson, "Colonization, Political Development and the UN," International Organization, Vol. 19 (Summer 1965), p. 492. The author recognizes the instances in which elections or other forms of consultation were held prior to independence in numerous colonies, but points out that they were run by, and on the terms of, the administering governments rather than under third-party United Nations supervision.

governments) led within a few years to impasses in the Council and, consequently, to conflict with the Assembly as a whole where the noncolonial members were heavily preponderant. Nonetheless, compared to the Mandates Commission of the League of Nations, the Trusteeship Council's greater authority—especially to send visiting missions to the territories and to hear petitioners—enabled it to press effectively for movement toward independence for all the trusts. The frequently heard objection from administering powers that the Council or Assembly pressed with undue haste for decolonization before the dependent trust or colony was "ready" for self-government, must be weighed against claims in the other direction: that the administering governments failed to act energetically to prepare their dependent peoples for self-government.

One ironic example of the difficulty of making clear-cut judgments in this matter can be seen in the fate of a recommendation in 1954, by the Trusteeship Council's visiting mission to Ruanda-Urundi. The mission expressed "faith in the possibility" that Ruanda-Urundi could become self-governing "in 20 to 25 years."[20] Belgium was highly critical of the whole idea at that date, only to agree to complete independence in 1962.

Greater use might have been made of joint development projects (even if aimed short of full administrative union) between trust territories and neighboring dependent areas—such as the East African Territorial Organization (EATO) for administering certain common public services among Tanganyika, Zanzibar, Uganda, and Kenya.[21] But such plans would have required the imperial governments to initiate more of them in areas where there was no fear of political domination by white settlers, and to show more willingness to place the larger territorial groups under the trusteeship system. However, proposals by administering authorities to create almost any kind of administrative union were generally regarded with great suspicion by the noncolonial governments. They saw union as a device remi-

20. Quoted by Emil J. Sady, in Robert E. Asher and others, *The United Nations and Promotion of the General Welfare* (Brookings Institution, 1957), p. 986. The United States joined India and El Salvador in this majority view; New Zealand opposed the idea of setting the time limit in years as neither helpful nor possible on available evidence. See also Carlos P. Romulo, "Whither, Submerged Millions?," *Journal of International Affairs*, Vol. 9 (1955), p. 22.

21. The EATO was part of the East Africa High Commission established in 1948. After the independence of Tanganyika, but while the other colonies were still dependent, the function was continued under the East African Common Services Organization, which came into effect in December 1961. Considered by many the hopeful forerunner of an East African political federation, by 1966 the common services appeared in danger of complete dissolution.

niscent of Class C mandates, aimed primarily to take the trusts out from under the United Nations safeguards.[22]

Nor were the colonial powers much interested in any joint political action on behalf of their trusts and other dependencies, even in cases where close geographic or cultural relationships might have made something of the sort seem logical. In 1947, for example, leaders in the Western Samoa Trust Territory requested the Trusteeship Council to leave the political status of the islands in abeyance "until a meeting can be arranged between Eastern and Western Samoa."[23] American Samoa was outside the Council's jurisdiction, although the United States could on its own have acted with New Zealand. There appears to have been no move in the direction of such consultation, however. The Navy then governed American Samoa with unlimited executive authority (until 1951) and presumably would have been even more opposed to such a proposal than it was to Samoan requests in 1945–46 for full American citizenship under an organic act.[24]

THE FATES OF NEW GUINEA

In 1949, Australia formed an administrative union of the Trust Territory of New Guinea and its colony of Papua. That year, the Netherlands recognized full Indonesian independence and undertook further negotiations on the political status of the remainder of New Guinea, known also as West Irian. Dutch New Guinea had been administratively separated from Indonesian territory under Dutch rule; but claimed by Djakarta as inheritor of all the Netherlands East Indies. The two governments failed to reach agreement in their negotiations. The Hague accordingly declared it would exercise sovereignty "until the right of self-determination is utilized by the population of New Guinea."[25]

The dispute continued throughout the fifties. Although informal suggestions were apparently made to the Dutch that it might be good diplomacy to place the territory under United Nations trusteeship, they never

22. See Sady, *op. cit.*, pp. 979–82, for a general discussion of the administrative-unions issue.

23. Quoted in Benjamin Rivlin, "Self-Determination and Dependent Areas," *International Conciliation*, No. 501 (January 1955), p. 229.

24. See Whitney T. Perkins, *Denial of Empire: The U.S. and Its Dependencies* (Leyden: A. W. Sythoff, 1962), p. 285.

25. Taylor, *op. cit.*, p. 441.

responded favorably.[26] It was not until 1961 that the Netherlands set up a Legislative Council in its territory and offered to relinquish control to a United Nations administration that would prepare the Papuans for self-determination during an interim period. But the hour was too late.

Indonesia, after periodically but unsuccessfully seeking General Assembly support for its claims to sovereignty, had already accepted Soviet military aid and inaugurated a "confrontation" policy over West Irian. Concerned at the Soviet intrusion into the picture and the possibility of a wider war developing, the United States and the Secretary-General made strenuous diplomatic efforts to bring about a Dutch-Indonesia agreement, which succeeded in 1962. In effect, the Netherlands turned the territory over to Indonesia by means of an interim United Nations Temporary Executive Authority (UNTEA), which administered the area until May 1963.[27] The agreement also included a commitment by the Indonesians to hold a plebiscite before 1970 to determine the wishes of the Papuans on their future.[28] It seemed of dubious value at the time and was later rescinded by Sukarno. After the violent upheavals of 1966, however, the new government informed the Secretary-General that it would comply in 1969 with the original undertaking. This involves appointment of a United Nations representative to advise on the arrangements for the act of self-determination.[29]

Meanwhile, although Australia was concerned lest the status of the western part of the island be changed, it paid little if any attention (at least publicly) either to the question of self-determination for its own areas or to the possibility of joint measures with the Dutch. Only after 1960, when the broader issue of decolonization became so important in the United Nations, did Canberra take more active steps to hasten the

26. Australia having favored Indonesian independence after the war, the consequent strained relations between it and the Netherlands would probably have made impossible the theoretical possibility of organizing a single trust arrangement for the whole island in the interests of Papuan self-determination. It seems never to have been considered, in any event, although if tried early enough might have outweighed the emotional and legalistic claims of Djakarta.

27. UNTEA employed the small U.N. Security Force (referred to in Chap. 6) in its administration. For a brief account of the background, see Justus M. van der Kroef, "The West New Guinea Settlement: Its Origin and Implications," *Orbis*, Vol. 7 (Spring 1963), pp. 120–49; Ruth B. Russell, *United Nations Experience with Military Forces: Political and Legal Aspects* (Brookings Institution, 1964), pp. 126–34.

28. Text in U.N. Doc. A/5170, Aug. 20, 1962, Annex A.

29. *Introduction to the Annual Report of the Secretary-General on the Work of Organization 16 June 1966–15 June 1967*, U.N. Doc. A/6701/Add. 1, p. 1.

economic and political development of its New Guinean dependencies. Their future has been discussed, however, only in terms of the alternatives of statehood as part of Australia or of independence, and whether the goal decided on should be sought on a unitary or some sort of federal basis.[30] Theoretically, since the Papuans in West Irian are to be consulted in 1969, it might be possible to envisage some political solution at that time in terms of the whole island. Such a move appears virtually impossible in practice, however.

TRUST TERRITORY OF NAURU

Australia is also responsible for the Trust Territory of Nauru, 1,300 miles to the north, a coral peak of 8.25 square miles, with some 5,000 people (1964), about 2,700 of them Nauruans. Technically under the joint administration of Great Britain, New Zealand, and Australia, the last acts for all three. Famous phosphate deposits are the only resource of the island and will be exhausted in the foreseeable future. Initially, the sensible solution appeared to be to resettle the Nauruans, and Australia undertook to provide another island for them.

Agreement proved impossible. The province of Queensland would not relinquish an apparently satisfactory one; Canberra refused to cede sovereignty over a close offshore island; while the Nauruans refused to become Australian. Home rule in Nauru was inaugurated in 1966, but control of the phosphate industry, defense, and foreign affairs remained in the hands of the Administering Authority. The Nauruans demanded independence by January 31, 1968, control of the industry and the replacement of exported phosphates with an estimated 35 million tons of fertile soil. The General Assembly supported them, requesting the Administering Authority "irrespective of the cost involved" to take immediate steps to restore the island "for habitation by the Nauruan people as a sovereign nation," and to fix "the earliest possible date, but not later than January 31, 1968," for independence.[31] In 1967, Australia agreed with Nauru on inde-

---

30. See F. J. West, "The New Guinea Question: An Australian View," *Foreign Affairs*, Vol. 39 (April 1961), pp. 504–11. New Guinea political leaders were publicly criticizing the Australian Government by 1966 for not being clear on its future plans. See "New Guinea Asks Independence Action," *New York Times*, May 1, 1966.

31. A/Res. 2111 (XX), Dec. 21, 1965, and A/Res. 2226 (XXI), Dec. 20, 1966.

pendence in 1968 (with the land rehabilitation issue left open) and the General Assembly was about to end its trust status as this study went to press.

PACIFIC ISLANDS TRUST TERRITORY

The United States may some day find itself in the position of last trustee. There has been such a complex interplay of problems for Washington in its combination role as colonial governor of Guam and American Samoa and as trustee of the former Japanese mandated islands conquered during World War II, that the Trust Territory cannot be considered by itself.[32] Most importantly, the Trust Territory shares United States military-security concerns with the other two. It also provides an interesting example of how the pressures to "do something" to advance the political development of the Trust Territory, because of the United Nations spotlight on it, also speeded up United States concern for the welfare of the rather neglected Guam and Samoa, so they would not be left too far behind.[33]

Over the years, United States administration of the territory has received on the whole not unfavorable assessment by the Trusteeship Council and the Assembly.[34] The most widely publicized criticism had to do with nuclear tests in the area, which resulted in fallout damage from the

32. The Trust Territory comprises the Caroline and Marshall Islands, and all the Marianas except Guam (which has been a U.S. possession since 1898). It consists of more than 2,000 "islets," forming 96 "island units" (single islands or groups), and containing only 687 square miles of land spread over some 3,000,000 square miles of ocean. Population in 1966: 92,373, compared to 88,215 in 1964. At the current rate of expansion, population will be over 150,000 by 1980.

33. In October 1945, President Truman constituted the Secretaries of State, War, Navy, and Interior a committee to make recommendations on the future government of all three Pacific territories. According to Perkins, *op. cit.*, 285–86, quick agreement was impossible because the military departments were anxious to preserve as much authority as possible. For the intragovernmental controversy in Washington during the war years over the future of the Japanese mandates and the development of a trusteeship system for the United Nations, see Russell, *A History of the United Nations Charter*, pp. 336–46 and 573–87. The strategic trust (Article 82) was devised to allow the Trust Territory to be under Security Council rather than Assembly supervision (and thus subject to the veto) and to permit the closure of areas under national security claims.

34. Recent American writers have been more harshly critical of U.S. policy. See, for example, Willard Price, *America's Paradise Lost* (John Day, 1966).

hydrogen bomb tests of 1954.[35] The main regular criticisms were of inadequate political and economic progress in the islands and, in particular, of the peculiar administrative arrangements that prevailed until the sixties.

Because of military emphasis on the strategic aspects of the Trust Territory, administration of the islands was left under the Navy until 1951, then shared with the Interior Department. In 1953, Washington told the Trusteeship Council that a territorial site had been selected for a permanent government headquarters as soon as funds were available; but it remained in Honolulu until 1954, then in Guam until 1962.

It was probably not purely coincidental that the United States, like Australia, began to take a closer look at all its Pacific possessions after 1960. In 1962, Washington put the entire Trust Territory under civil administration, moved its headquarters within the territory (to Saipan), more than doubled the annual congressional appropriation for the islands, and reversed an earlier policy of discouraging private investment and development. Although further increases in appropriations have been sought in recent years, the authorized amounts have seldom been met by Congress. Even the authorized amounts were inadequate to replace capital destruction of the war period, let alone to promote economic development. Political development was also slow. Only in 1965 did an elected territorial legislature, the Congress of Micronesia, replace an advisory council as the main organ of self-government. In May 1966, the Interior Department submitted a five-year $172 million development program for the Trust Territory, and Ambassador Goldberg announced that hundreds of Peace Corps volunteers would be sent there.[36] The development plan, however, was considered too ambitious by Congress, which replaced it with a scaled-down two-year program.[37]

Samoa and Guam have also made economic and social gains and advanced toward internal self-government. The General Assembly included them in 1965 in a general "reaffirmation" of "the inalienable right" of the peoples of small island territories freely "to decide their constitutional

35. It took the administration until February 1966 to obtain the money from Congress and make payment totaling $1 million for damage claims, although the extent of injuries suffered "has never been accurately determined." *Washington Post*, Feb. 26, 1966.

36. See *New York Times*, May 21, 1966, and *Washington Post*, May 7 and June 2, 1966.

37. See Senator Mansfield on congressional inaction, *Congressional Record*, daily ed., July 18, 1967, pp. 9795–96.

status in accordance with the Charter" and various Assembly resolutions.[38] The aspirations of the islanders appear more inclined to favor closer association with the United States, rather than independence.[39]

By 1966, some political leaders in Guam were not only demanding more internal self-government and closer integration with the mainland, but also were urging a merger of the Trust Territory with Guam.[40] A natural geographic and ethnic association of Guam and the Pacific Islands Trust was reflected in the fact that the former was administrative headquarters for the Trust for some years, and also in a provision of the trusteeship agreement authorizing such an administrative union or federation. Guam is located in the heart of the area physically and is the natural commercial, transportation, and cultural center for the whole vast ocean region. Although administrative unions earlier developed a bad odor with the Trusteeship Council, conditions in recent years in the decolonization sphere have so changed that measures toward some form of integration might be acceptable if linked with rapid advances toward full self-government and with plebiscites overseen by some United Nations presence.

Another approach, less likely to receive approval (either by the islanders or the United Nations), was that proposed by Senator Hiram Fong of Hawaii: for Congress to consider whether it would be feasible for Hawaii to annex all the island territories.[41] The wishes of those directly concerned would be ascertained by plebiscites in the territories and a vote in Hawaii, before action to enlarge the present state would be asked of Congress. The idea was promptly opposed by Guam's representative in

38. A/Res. 2069 (XX), Dec. 16, 1965, adopted 91–0–10.

39. See comment by Assistant Secretary of State Harlan Cleveland, "Reflections on the Pacific Community," U.S. Department of State Press Release 156 (March 28, 1963), p. 8. A resolution of the Committee of 24 referring to the Guamanians' "inalienable right to self-government and independence" called forth as one example a protest from the Guam Chamber of Commerce. This declared that "the primary goal of the people of Guam is closer association with their fellow citizens on the United States mainland, not disassociation." U.N. Doc. A/AC. 109/PET. 363, April 13, 1965, p. 2.

40. See *New York Times*, March 20, 1966. In November 1965, the Saipan (District) Legislature petitioned a visiting congressional delegation on behalf of withdrawing the Mariana Islands from the Congress of Micronesia (and to have its distinct legislature raised accordingly) and of conducting a plebiscite on their "reintegration" (i.e., with Guam) and subsequently becoming "part of the United States." The petition was sent to the Trusteeship Council also. U.N. Doc. T/PET. 10/L. 11, Jan. 20, 1966.

41. *Washington Post*, July 21, 1965, p. A–19. Senator Ernest Gruening (Alaska) seconded the Fong proposal in Congress and wrote that he had originated the idea as a way for the United States to "get rid of the stigma of practicing colonialism" and to free the islands "from its evils, if they so desired." *Ibid.*, Aug. 4, 1965.

Washington, who protested that incorporation as part of Hawaii would simply mean another form of "absentee government." He called instead for uniting Guam and the Trust Islands.[42]

Lack of agreement on a common future of some sort will inevitably mean increasing pressure from United Nations bodies for full independence. It will also put the emphasis on the separate units, if only because that is the way they have come to be handled within the organs of the world Organization, and the United States itself has failed to develop a longer-range, overall policy.

The Soviet Union has been especially emphatic in promoting the separate independence of each small political unit, supposedly in the sacred name of self-determination. It has also proposed in the Trusteeship Council that the Security Council should examine the situation of the Pacific Islands Trust, charging that the United States has failed to comply with its trusteeship commitments and that: "The United States is continuing a policy of actual annexation of the Pacific Islands, using Micronesia as a military reservation and an American base."[43]

This was part of a broader Soviet campaign of long standing against American and allied bases abroad. It came to a head in regard to dependent areas in 1965, when the Assembly passed a contentious resolution in favor of dismantling bases in colonial territories by an even more contentious vote.[44] The action made no difference in United States policy toward the island territories of the Pacific, simply adding to American annoyance at other "irresponsible" Assembly actions. The military attitude of 1945—that strategic needs demanded the retention by the United States of full control of all the islands—had no doubt already been confirmed by their usefulness in terms of the Vietnam fighting. Washington has never actively sought to develop any political unity among the array of islands, in spite of its attitude toward their military value. Yet, as Harold Jacobson wrote in 1960: "If both we and the Micronesians desire some form of lasting association, such as exists between the United States and Puerto Rico, for example, steps should be taken before the political climate becomes so

42. *Ibid.*, July 23, 1965.

43. Quoted in *Soviet News*, #5155, June 22, 1965. In view of the U.S. veto in the Security Council, nothing practical could come of the Soviet proposal there; but it might well be made as a propaganda gesture.

44. See below, p. 282. A similar paragraph in the equivalent 1966 A/Res. 2232 (XXI), Dec. 20, 1966 declared the establishment of military bases therein to be "incompatible with the purposes and principles of the Charter."

set that this kind of solution would provoke an untoward reaction in the United Nations."[45]

Congress, however, made no move looking toward possible changes in the status of the islands until 1967—and then only in connection with the Trust Territory. In response to a request by the Congress of Micronesia in 1966, Representative Bingham and Senate Majority Leader Mansfield introduced similar joint resolutions to create a "Commission on the Future Political Status of the Trust Territory of the Pacific Islands (Micronesia.)"[46] The proposed group would study how the wishes of the people of the Territory could be ascertained as to their political future and then recommend how Congress should give effect to them.

Complete independence would clearly have to be one of the alternatives presented to the voters, along with some form of association with the United States, such as those mentioned above. The former would undoubtedly be met by objections from military officials, especially in view of the Territory's geographic relation to Guam.[47] Strategic arguments may therefore be used to delay congressional action on the Mansfield-Bingham resolutions. No hearings had been scheduled by August.

Decolonization in a Broader Framework

Failure to develop any effective supervision of the decolonization process within the framework of the trusteeship system, plus the fact that the forces of emergent nationalism were far stronger than the imperial powers judged them to be in 1945, made it inevitable that decolonization would proceed apace through other channels. It was not inevitable, however,

45. Harold Karan Jacobson, "Our 'Colonial' Problem in the Pacific," *Foreign Affairs*, Vol. 39 (October 1960), p. 66.

46. H. J. Res. 594, 90 Cong. 1 sess., May 24, 1967, for a commission of 9 members; and S. J. Res. 96, 90 Cong. 1 sess., July 18, 1967, for a commission of 15. It was reported in late August that the President had also asked Congress to appoint such a study commission on the desirability of a plebiscite before 1972. *New York Times*, Aug. 22, 1967.

47. Vietnam may not be the only cause for military concern with the Pacific Islands. *U.S. News & World Report*, July 30, 1967 reported rumors that the Pentagon was contemplating removal of its bases in Okinawa and Japan to the islands as a security measure in view of the developing Communist Chinese nuclear capacity. There were prompt denials from both Defense and State Departments; and Japanese reactions were reportedly unfavorable, in spite of Tokyo's desire to reclaim jurisdiction over Okinawa. *New York Times*, Aug. 10, 1967.

that the process follow the particular course it did over the next two decades.

There would, of course, have been no need for any sizable international program aimed to smooth the transition to the postcolonial period had the imperial governments developed national programs capable of keeping pace with the legitimate political demands of dependent peoples. Even recognizing the great variations among the administering powers, both in willingness to prepare their dependencies for self-government and in the degree of success their former colonies have had as independent states, the fact remains that in terms of international repercussions the best was not good enough to compensate for the worst.

Judgment can only be based on the results seen in the legacy of new states that emerged from dependencies for which the major imperial powers—all NATO allies—were responsible. Robert C. Good has written:

> As the Western colonial system was unprecedented in scope, unprecedented too has been the impact of its collapse; . . . for the postcolonial era marks at the same time the death of Western colonialism and the universalization of the Western state system—if not as accomplished facts, then as generally accepted goals and norms.

The postcolonial heritage has thus been the form of the state as a "recognized legal entity"; but often without its practical and political prerequisites. For the colonial powers "were often unwilling, and indeed in large measure unable, to bequeath the capacities of statecraft or the qualities of the modern nation."[48] The resulting gap between expectation and realization, between aspiration and capability, provides one of the fundamental sources of tension in the contemporary world.

It must be remembered, in considering the international security problems which have grown out of this legacy, that the results of the inadequacies of the former mentors of the new states have been compounded by the mud-stirring efforts of the communists and by the instability of the conflict-ridden world. They have also been compounded by the fact that Western imperialism in general "asserted a racial superiority," and that colonial nationalism developed against that assertion in particular.[49]

48. Robert C. Good, "Colonial Legacies to the Postcolonial States," in Roger Hilsman and Robert C. Good, eds. *Foreign Policy in the Sixties* (Johns Hopkins Press, 1965), pp. 35–36, 46, 37.

49. Richard Harris, *Independence and After: Revolution in Underdeveloped Countries* (Oxford University Press, 1962), p. 2; and Joseph E. Johnson has noted: "The age of 'tutelage' is passed and, if truth be faced, we of the West who believed ourselves qualified to teach made very little use of the opportunity while we had it." *Op. cit.*, p. 5.

The colonial powers might have attempted to develop some other international approach than through the United Nations system, one by which they would have sought collectively to safeguard their own needs for political stability and security against communist expansion, while providing for more rapid political advance of their colonies. One observer's comment on Africa is equally applicable to the rest of those vast regions that have become known as the Third World:

In retrospect, it will surely seem little less than suicidal for the Western nations to [have met] the forces released by one of the great revolutions of history with so little preparation, so little consultation, so little planning and thought and, at times, so little sense. What [was] surely needed [was] some permanent machinery among the nations of the Western alliance to consult, to pool ideas, to plan a strategy for the cold war in Africa. This [had] to be fought, whether we like[d] it or not. It might as well [have been] fought effectively, not at halfcock.[50]

No attempt was made by the colonial powers as a group, however, to develop any such broad international program aimed at eventual self-government within a strongly democratic frame of reference. The few cooperative efforts made were minor at best, were limited to a regional approach, and deliberately avoided dealing with political development in the dependencies concerned.

During the war years, an Anglo-American Caribbean Commission (established when American bases were set up in leased areas of British islands) was gradually expanded to include the Netherlands and France and, in 1946, was renamed the Caribbean Commission. Although the activities and membership of the commission were later extended to include other countries of the region, its functions remained wholly within the economic and social spheres. Similarly, a South Pacific Commission for economic and social cooperation was established after the war, initially by the colonial powers in the area. Another regional Commission on Cooperation in Technical Matters in Africa South of the Sahara (the CCTA) was established in 1950 by six "white" governments (the four colonial powers plus South Africa and Southern Rhodesia), but it did not go even as far as the earlier two in the scope of its activities. One result of its colonially minded approach was the subsequent transformation of the agency as independent African states joined, beginning with Ghana in 1957. By 1962, Portugal and South Africa had been expelled, other found-

50. Elspeth Huxley, "The Next-to-Last Act in Africa," *Foreign Affairs*, Vol. 39 (July 1961), p. 669.

ing members reduced to nonvoting "associate" status, and northern African states added.[51]

Within the United Nations framework, technical assistance and economic and financial development activities were not without their influence on programs in the colonial areas; but normally the metropolitan governments maintained responsibility for direct arrangements with the United Nations or specialized agencies, even when the particular projects related to dependent areas. The regional economic commissions (for Latin America, Asia and the Far East, and Africa) have included not only independent countries of each region but also the extraregional powers with territorial holdings there and some dependencies as associate members. Although the commissions might thus have provided excellent means of preparatory training for self-government in the technical governmental functions of concern to them, they have been described as "almost untapped organs" in relation to meeting the needs for modernization and economic development even of the independent member states: " . . . The Commissions have been greatly hampered by the marked coolness displayed toward them by the West, which has preferred ECOSOC, presumably because it has greater relative power there."[52] In terms of education and preparation for independence, therefore, such benefits as flowed to the dependent peoples from activities of any of these regional economic and social agencies appear to have been largely incidental.

The rising tide of nationalism, as a result, was in no sense organized—in terms of either its sources or its international development—except insofar as the communists sought to influence the disparate colonial developments into their own preconceived channels of historical inevitability. The communists were by no means the only anticolonial states even in 1945, as events at the United Nations Conference demonstrated.[53] And after the inauguration of the new Organization, the Assembly provided another outlet for nationalist efforts when the Trusteeship Council's balanced membership and limited powers thwarted faster progress toward their goal.

51. "Technical Cooperation Planning among African States," *World Today* (May 1962), pp. 179–81. See also Assistant Secretary G. Mennen Williams' address in U.S. Department of State, *Bulletin*, Vol. 46 (1962), p. 846.

52. Johnson, *op. cit.*, pp. 18–19. By 1963, non-African powers, "on ceasing to have territorial responsibilities in Africa," were also to cease to be associate members of the Economic Commission for Africa. See E/CN. 14/Res./69 (V), Feb. 23, 1963.

53. See Russell, *A History of the United Nations Charter*, Chap. 31.

Because events within the United Nations received the spotlight of world attention, there has been a tendency to blame the Organization for having influenced the decolonization movement more than it reasonably could. As Professor Emerson has remarked: "Dependent peoples who receive an international hearing usually [have been] those who have resorted to self-help."[54] But in the United Nations, the metropolitan powers had to give public account of their responses to the emerging nationalist forces, even if only in the negative form of resisting the claims of accountability put forth by other members. In those terms, the intangible influence of the Organization was more important than any evidence of measures taken directly in response to resolutions of the Assembly or recommendations of the Trusteeship Council. The way in which the Assembly's role developed is significant in this respect.

The Assembly and Article 73(e)

The traditional colonial powers generally considered that the provisions of Chapters XI–XIII guaranteed them a voluntary system, both in establishing trusteeships and in reporting technical data for information purposes only. But others argued that, by placing their principles of colonial policy on record in a general treaty, they had "made the whole colonial system a subject for international consideration." Article 10, therefore, "clearly" gave the Assembly competence to discuss it and make recommendations.[55] On that reasoning, the Assembly early called attention to its awareness of "the political aspirations of the peoples who have not yet attained a full measure of self-government and who are not directly represented here," and declared the obligations of Chapter XI to be "already in full force."[56]

The Western colonial states (except Spain and Portugal, which were not yet Members) voluntarily listed seventy-four non-self-governing territories under their administration for which they would transmit informa-

54. Rupert Emerson, *From Empire to Nation* (Harvard University Press, 1959), p. 399.
55. See Wilfred Benson, "Non-Self-Governing Territories," in Clyde Eagleton, ed., *Annual Review of United Nations Affairs, 1949* (New York University Press, 1950), p. 196. See also "The United Nations and Non-Self-Governing Territories," *International Conciliation*, No. 435 (November 1947), pp. 712–14.
56. A/Res. 9(I), Feb. 9, 1946.

tion under Article 73(e).[57] But most of them did not expect to have it submitted to any special examination, certainly not to any judgment of the submitting government's administration.

The Soviet Union, however, neither put under trusteeship the former Japanese territories it had "detached . . . as a result of the war" (in the language of Article 77) nor listed them for reporting under Article 73(e). It has nonetheless escaped the pressures of the anticolonial states, partly because the voluntariness of the system really held in the early years (so that action was sought only in relation to the already listed territories); and partly because historical tradition and recent nationalist movements alike have since concentrated attention on the Western European empires. This was especially true of areas directly involved in World War II. Communist delegations, as ardent supporters of the move to establish machinery under the Assembly for exercising international concern in the advance of other governments' dependent peoples toward self-government, also served to divert attention from their own postwar territorial acquisitions.

THE COMMITTEE ON INFORMATION

After prolonged argument, the Assembly set up an *Ad Hoc* Committee on Information Transmitted under Article 73(e), balanced (like the Trusteeship Council) between administering and nonadministering states.[58] Great Britain, France, and Belgium energetically opposed making the committee a permanent organ, which would imply their acceptance of the principle of accountability. They failed, however. It was first made a "Special Committee" (1947); then extended periodically until 1961, when it became "permanent"; only to be absorbed shortly by the Special

---

57. Britain listed 43 territories; France, 16; the Netherlands, 3; Australia, 2; Belgium, 1; New Zealand, 1; Denmark, 1; and the U.S. 7: Alaska, American Samoa, Guam, Hawaii, Panama Canal Zone, Puerto Rico, and the Virgin Islands. (It also reports to the Security Council on the strategic Pacific Islands Trust Territory.) Panama promptly protested this inclusion of the Canal Zone, to which the Republic of Panama retained titular sovereignty. The United States agreed its transmission was in error and ceased to include information on the Zone. There was some congressional objection to including Hawaii and Alaska, with their clear destination as states of the Union; but the administration hoped its broad interpretation of Art. 73(e) might encourage other states to follow suit in reporting on "any territories administered by a Member . . . which do not enjoy the same measure of self-government as the metropolitan area of that Member." (See Sady, *op. cit.*, pp. 889–93.) Its example was not generally followed, however.

58. A/Res. 66 (I), Dec. 14, 1946.

Committee of 24, of which more is said below. Its authority was kept limited primarily by threats of nonparticipation from the administering states if it adopted various policies they objected to.[59]

From the beginning there were arguments over, initially, whether the metropole alone could determine which territories came under 73(e); and later, over who had authority to decide when transmission of information should cease on the ground that a territory was no longer non-self-governing. The political issue behind these technical questions was whether the domestic-jurisdiction provision of Article 2(7) safeguarded the metropole from interference by the United Nations in its colonial administration. From the viewpoint of the anticolonial states, the issue appeared in the guise of whether the metropolitan states unjustifiably used domestic-jurisdiction claims to conceal failure to meet their Charter obligations or to deny the right of self-determination.[60]

The dispute was most heated over the "factors" that should be taken into account to determine whether a territory was non-self-governing. Belgium in particular insisted that governments administering tribal groups (the Naga in India, for example) or minority peoples (such as non-Russians in the Soviet Union) should also report under Chapter XI. It was especially scornful of the "salt-water fallacy"—that is, that rule over an alien people is somehow more "colonial" when they inhabit noncontiguous territory than when they live in an area contiguous to the metropole; and that therefore in the former case they are more properly subject to international concern. But this "Belgian thesis" could only have been persuasive about other governments had Belgium itself been less resistant to all efforts to enlarge the Organization's competence in relation to the Congo, already listed under Chapter XI. In the circumstances, its contentions were clearly aimed to justify Belgian noncooperation, rather than to promote the extension of United Nations competence; and the chief argument in favor of what later became known as the "geographic principle" was the fact that the traditional colonial powers had in effect applied it themselves in 1946.

During the first decade of the United Nations, to oversimplify highly complex developments, the trend in the Committee on Information (and

59. Belgium refused to participate in 1953, for example, and France and Britain refused to discuss a resolution concerning self-determination.

60. For a discussion of this conflict over domestic-jurisdiction interpretation, see Rosalyn Higgins, *The Development of International Law through the Political Organs of the United Nations* (Oxford University Press, 1963), Pt. 2, "The Concept of Domestic Jurisdiction in United Nations Practice."

subsequently in the Fourth [Trusteeship] Committee and the Assembly),
as in the Trusteeship Council, was for the administering powers to resist
every attempt of the nonadministering states to increase the Organization's concern in their policies. Communist opposition was steady from
the beginning; but elsewhere, extreme begot extreme. The more resistant
in principle the colonial states were to attempts to broaden the area of
international accountability, the more the anticolonial governments
tended toward the communist end of the scale. Enormous amounts of
time and energy were consumed in fruitless contests over jurisdictional
questions—fruitless in the sense that the underlying issues of self-
determination and domestic jurisdiction were thereby neither settled nor
subdued. By 1954, one perceptive observer could prognosticate:

> One does not have to be clairvoyant to realize that the colonial peoples are
> on the move. . . . The Soviet Union, for whom these disturbances in the West-
> ern World are tailor-made, sees them also. . . . Yet despite the fact that the
> colonial issue has become part of the Cold War, the colonial powers . . . have
> tended to lay the blame on the United Nations alleging that its interference
> has aggravated the problem.[61]

BANDUNG AND AFTER

The mid-fifties marked a turning point on the colonial issue. The shape
of things to come was clearly foreshadowed at the Bandung Conference
in 1955, which condemned colonialism in any form as an evil that should
be speedily ended. The Anglo-French invasion of Egypt in 1956 confirmed
that attitude.[62] The United Nations was then also about to begin its great
expansion in membership.

In 1955, Spain and Portugal (the last of the "old" colonial powers)
were admitted with fourteen other states, after several years' deadlock
between communist and noncommunist governments over the admission
of new members. Portugal in particular was to exacerbate the anticolonial
conflict quite as much as any communist or neutral new state. In 1951, it
had followed French footsteps and proclaimed all its colonies "overseas
provinces" with the same political status as the metropolitan territory.
After being "colonies" for some four centuries, their switch in status

---

61. Benjamin Rivlin, *op. cit.*, pp. 269–70.
62. An illuminating example of the failure of colonial powers to comprehend contemporary anticolonial attitudes is given by former Prime Minister Eden. He wrote, in
1960: "The dispute over Nasser's seizure of the Canal had, of course, nothing to do
with colonialism, was concerned with international rights." *The Memoirs of the Rt.
Hon. Sir Anthony Eden: Full Circle* (Cassell, 1960), p. 499.

impressed most governments as aimed to enable Portugal to resort to the domestic-jurisdiction clause to escape United Nations concern.[63]

The dramatic emergence of independent states and new United Nations Members exploded in 1960, with the French grant of independence to a dozen African governments and the admission of seventeen more members to the Organization.[64] Such an increase in Members that had shortly before been dependent territories soon had repercussions, intensifying the already well-developed anticolonialism of the Assembly. In 1959, a Special Committee of Six had been established to study the principles to guide Member states in determining whether they were obligated to transmit information under Article 73(e).[65] This action resulted from the failure of either Spain or Portugal to respond to the Secretary-General's routine inquiry of the two new Members (in 1955) as to whether they administered any non-self-governing territories. In 1960, the Assembly accepted the committee's list of twelve applicable principles, many of which applied to Portugal in particular.[66] A companion resolution specifi-

63. The timing of the colonies "promotion" also made clear that the legal fact was largely a political fiction, a view substantiated by failure to integrate various aspects of European-Portuguese and overseas-Portuguese life—the exchange control between Angola and Portugal, for example. See Hamilton Fish Armstrong, "The Bell Tolls in Angola," *New York Times Magazine*, May 21, 1961, p. 86.

64. These were Cyprus and 16 African states: Cameroon, Central African Republic, Chad, Congo (Brazzaville), Congo (Leopoldville), Dahomey, Gabon, Ivory Coast, Madagascar, Niger, Somalia, Togo, Upper Volta, Mali, Senegal, and Nigeria.

65. A/Res. 1467 (XIV), Dec. 12, 1959, passed 54-5-15. This was not the first committee to go into the question; two Ad Hoc Committees on Factors had earlier been appointed when various administering states had announced they would no longer transmit information on certain territories. In 1953, after considerable discussion by the committees, the Assembly adopted a resolution to guide Members and the Organization, listing a number of factors to be considered in such determination. A/Res. 742 (VII), Nov. 27, 1953.

66. A/Res. 1541 (XV), Dec. 15, 1960. In the present context, the most significant principles listed were:

"I. The authors of the Charter of the United Nations had in mind that Chapter XI should be applicable to territories which were then known to be of the colonial type."

"IV. *Prima facie* there is an obligation to transmit information in respect of a territory which is geographically separate and is distinct ethnically and/or culturally from the country administering it.

"V. Once it has been established that such a *prima facie* case of geographical and ethnical or cultural distinctness of a territory exists, other elements may then be brought into consideration. . . .

"VI. A Non-Self-Governing Territory can be said to have reached a full measure of self-government by:

(a) Emergence as a sovereign independent State;
(b) Free association with an independent State; or
(c) Integration with an independent State."

cally criticized Portugal for neglecting its obligation to transmit information under Article 73(e) and listed nine "territories" on which it should report under the standards of the first resolution.[67]

The Declaration on Colonial Independence

The climax of Assembly action in 1960, however, came with the "great debate" on colonialism in general, when Soviet Premier Khrushchev, as already noted, introduced a draft resolution favoring the immediate grant of "complete independence and freedom" to all colonies, trust territories, and other non-self-governing areas, and the elimination of "all strongholds of colonialism" in the shape of possessions and leasehold areas, or of "any special rights or advantages" in the territories of other states. This would cover, among other items, all American military bases abroad and the Panama Canal Zone. He combined this, moreover, with the customary Soviet attack on alleged American preparations for war, emphasizing the recent "perfidious invasion" of Soviet air space by the U-2 plane shot down by the Russians.[68]

In the ensuing Assembly debate, the uncommitted states echoed communist arguments in varying degree; but they accepted a more limited declaration in the interests of gaining Western support. A new draft resolution, sponsored by forty Afro-Asian Members, contained sweeping language in the introductory paragraphs that proclaimed the "end of colonialism in all its manifestations"; but was somewhat more restrained in the wording of its operative paragraphs. As finally adopted (90-0-9), the resolution, which came to be known as the Declaration on Colonial Independence, read:

1. The subjection of peoples to alien subjugation, domination and exploitation constitutes a denial of fundamental human rights, is contrary to the Charter of the United Nations and is an impediment to the promotion of world peace and cooperation.

2. All peoples have the right of self-determination; by virtue of that right they freely determine their political status and freely pursue their economic, social, and cultural development.

3. Inadequacy of political, economic, social, or education preparedness should never serve as a pretext to delay independence.

67. A/Res. 1542 (XV), Dec. 15, 1960. The territories included: Angola, Cape Verde archipelago, Goa and dependencies, Portuguese Guinea, Macao and dependencies, Mozambique, São João Batista de Ajuda, São Tomé and Príncipe, and Timor and dependencies.

68. U.N. Doc. A/PV. 869 (Sept. 23, 1960), pp. 68-84.

4. All armed action or repressive measures of all kinds directed against dependent peoples shall cease in order to enable them to exercise peacefully and freely their right to complete independence, and the integrity of their national territory shall be respected.

5. Immediate steps shall be taken, in trust and non-self-governing territories or all other territories which have not yet attained independence, to transfer all powers to the peoples of those territories, without any conditions or reservations, in accordance with their freely expressed will and desire, without any distinction as to race, creed or colour, in order to enable them to enjoy complete independence and freedom.

6. Any attempt aimed at the partial or total disruption of the national unity and the territorial integrity of a country is incompatible with the purposes and principles of the Charter of the United Nations.

7. All States shall observe faithfully and strictly the provisions of the Charter of the United Nations, the Universal Declaration of Human Rights and the present Declaration on the basis of equality, noninterference in the internal affairs of all states, and respect for the sovereign rights of all peoples and their territorial integrity.[69]

To the consternation of many delegations, the resolution passed with the United States among the abstainers. By officially joining Great Britain, France, Belgium, Portugal, Australia, Spain, and South Africa, in abstaining, Washington had apparently placed itself where communist speakers had always said it was—on the side of the "colonialist-imperialist exploiters."[70] During debate on the resolution, the United States delegation had indicated that it would vote in favor if certain language changes could be worked out, which had appeared not too difficult. The last-minute change in position was made on White House orders, the result of a direct plea by Prime Minister Macmillan to the President.[71] It was evidently made on the general ground of support for the NATO allies, particularly

69. A/Res. 1514 (XV), Dec. 14, 1960. Only France opposed the resolution outright, as constituting an interference in domestic affairs despite the disclaimer in paragraph 7. In view of the adherence to domestic-jurisdiction claims by the colonial states generally, it is curious that not one of them voted against the declaration, which was passed with 9 abstentions (Australia, Belgium, Dominican Republic, France, Portugal, Spain, South Africa, Great Britain, and the United States). A similar reluctance to declare public opposition had been seen in 1948, in the vote on the Declaration of Human Rights: 48–0–8 abstentions (the Communist states, South Africa, and Saudi Arabia) and 2 absences (Yemen and Honduras).

70. Later in the session, the United States announced that it had changed its position and wished to be associated with the declaration. See Edward T. Rowe, "The Emerging Anti-Colonial Consensus in the United Nations," *Conflict Resolution*, Vol. 8 (September 1964), p. 227.

71. Even so, the delegation was split on the issue. See Sen. Wayne Morse's supplementary report on *The United States in the United Nations, 1960—A Turning Point*, U.S. Senate Foreign Relations Committee, 87 Cong. 1 sess. (February 1961), pp. 5, 20; see also, *New York Times* and *Washington Post* accounts, Dec. 15, 1960.

for Great Britain, which was then in the midst of negotiations on the future of the Central African Federation—a situation in which self-governing Southern Rhodesia faced London with a dilemma on racial discrimination not dissimilar to that facing Washington in the South.

As the declaration showed, within the United Nations the issues of national self-determination and the racial aspect of human rights—the issues of national and individual equality, in other words—had by 1960 become inextricably intertwined. From the point of view of the United States, moreover, they had also become irrevocably tangled with issues of national security.

Decolonization and United States Interests

During the fifties, Washington had been unable to find a satisfactory resolution of the conflicting interests of its imperial NATO allies and those of the majority of United Nations Members with a concern for the rapid end of colonialism. After the difficulties in the Assembly in 1960, another attempt was made at the December meeting of the NATO Council to agree on common and progressive decolonization principles. Such a policy might have enabled the West to meet legitimate demands in this field with some hope of greater reasonableness, in consequence, on the part of the noncommunist anticolonial states; but the attempt again failed. President-elect Kennedy, however, had earlier expressed himself publicly on the "anticolonial" side of the question, and a shift in American policy was therefore anticipated.[72] It occurred in March 1961, after the flames of nationalism from the Congo had fired unrest in Angola and violent racial clashes. The situation brought a Liberian complaint to the Security Council that Portugal's suppression of human rights constituted a threat to international peace.

DEVELOPMENTS IN 1961

Over bitter Portuguese protest that the question was a domestic affair, the United States supported placing the Angola problem on the Council's agenda. It argued that unless remedial measures were promptly undertaken by the metropole, there would be more disorders; the important

72. See Arthur M. Schlesinger, Jr., A Thousand Days (Houghton-Mifflin, 1965), pp. 551–60, for the President's attitude.

thing was to avoid "another Congo" in Angola by an accelerated movement toward self-government.[73]

Portugal was not the only colonial "sinner," of course; nor Africa the
only area where conflicts of principle and policy created such problems
for Washington. Moreover, the cumulative effects of controversy over all
the territories created an impact in 1961 that in itself was a major factor in
the resultant increase in general political tensions. Space does not permit
more than a brief note on some major aspects of the anticolonial drive
within the United Nations during that year, which culminated in the
establishment in November of the "Special Committee on the Situation
with regard to Implementation of the Declaration on the Granting of
Independence to Colonial Countries and Peoples."[74]

The Congo situation had its effects not only on Angola, but also on
other controversies over African colonial issues of longer standing: with
South Africa, in terms of both its South West African and apartheid
policies; with France over Algeria, a conflict that continued after the grant
of independence in 1959 to former French Equatorial Africa; and with
Great Britain over the Central African Federation. When the Angolan
resolution failed in the Council and disorders continued in the territory,
an Afro-Asian group took the question to the Assembly in April where a
resolution was passed establishing an investigatory subcommittee.[75] After
Portugal refused to admit the group to Angola, the Afro-Asians returned
to the Security Council in June with further charges of a threat to the

73. Stevenson speech, U.N. Security Council, Sixteenth Year, *Official Records*,
946th Meeting, March 15, 1961, p. 19. The American policy switch was so marked as
to give rise to some feeling that the new administration might have taken its decision
without full realization of the strain it would put on relations with its European allies,
especially if carried into other aspects of the colonialism issue. But any such impression
was promptly removed by a formal delegation explanation that: "The United States
decision to vote for the resolution was made only after thorough consultation . . . and
after approval by the Secretary of State and the President. . . . Our allies were informed
in advance. We have a deep and continuing common interest with them. The difficulty
and complexity of African questions are, however, such that there are and may continue
to be differences in approach on some of them." U.S. Department of State, *Bulletin*,
Vol. 44 (1961), p. 498.

74. A/Res. 1654 (XVI), Nov. 27, 1961. This is the Special Committee of 24
referred to earlier. See also Chap. 2, pp. 33–34. The committee is discussed below in
more detail.

75. A/Res. 1603 (XV), April 20, 1961, adopted 73–2. The United States voted
with the majority, as also on a resolution criticizing South Africa for not permitting
another subcommittee to investigate the administration of South West Africa.

peace. This time they obtained a resolution describing the situation as "likely to endanger the maintenance of international peace and security," and hoping that "a peaceful solution" would be found in accordance with the Charter.[76] Portugal continued to ignore the committee, and disorders continued in Angola. Meanwhile, the U.S. Joint Chiefs of Staff had "declared the Azores base essential to American security in case of trouble over Berlin."[77]

In July 1961, with de Gaulle attempting to negotiate with the National Liberation Front (FLN) in Algeria, Tunisia sought to drive the French from the base they had retained at Bizerte when recognizing that country's independence in 1956. France responded with a strong military attack, and Tunisia appealed to the Security Council. That organ could agree only on an interim resolution calling for a cease-fire. Both a Soviet-supported draft resolution calling for negotiation of the withdrawal of all French forces from Bizerte and a mild resolution (favored by the United States) calling on the parties to negotiate a peaceful settlement directly, failed to pass. France also broke off the negotiations with the FLN about this time. In August, the Afro-Asians brought the resolution calling for withdrawal of French forces before a Special Assembly. This time the United States abstained, fearing possible effects on de Gaulle's shaky position in France.[78]

In September, the British Foreign Secretary told the Assembly that his government's "process of creating new nations" was so "right," that London was "now" ready to provide political information to the United Nations on its remaining non-self-governing territories: " . . . You will recognize," he added, "that this is a decision of the first importance. There is nothing in the Charter which requires us to submit political and constitutional information."[79] Although factually and legally correct, any bloom left on this British concession with its condescending tone un-

76. S/4835, June 9, 1961, passed 9–0–2 (Great Britain and France). Although defeating a Soviet amendment to condemn Portugal for waging a colonial war, the Council called on Lisbon to "desist forthwith from repressive measures," as well as to admit the Assembly committee. Great Britain abstained on the ground that such a conclusion should not have been drawn before the subcommittee recommendations were received; France, because of its consistent opposition to U.N. "interference" in domestic affairs.

77. Schlesinger, *op. cit.*, p. 562.
78. *Ibid.*, p. 561.
79. Lord Home, Sept. 27, 1961. Text in *New York Times*, Sept. 28, 1961.

doubtedly vanished when it turned out that Southern Rhodesia was not included in the list, on the ground that it was a self-governing colony.

In November, the committee on Angola reported that Portuguese policy frustrated the desire of the people for self-determination, and the Assembly declared that the Colonial Declaration had been carried out in only a few cases. It therefore set up the Special Committee[80] to foster implementation of the declaration, with all remaining dependent territories under its mandate. Previous practice, in line with the wishes of the administering powers, had been to establish special committees only to investigate particular colonies—as in the case of Angola. The United States at first joined the traditional imperial governments in opposing the new committee. Its spokesman told the Assembly: "Where the responsible [colonial] parties falter or fail in their duties, we have a duty to press for action. Where problems are being solved in good faith, we must respect the work that is being done. And where all our appeals are met with stubbornness and defiance, let us stand and work for the right until the right can prevail in peace."[81]

The winds of change had become too strong by that time, however, to permit any "standing." The United States, recognizing this, ended by voting with the 97–0 majority in favor of establishing the Special Committee. Great Britain, France, Spain, and South Africa abstained; Portugal did not participate.[82] The first three powers had accepted in principle the objective of colonial emancipation, although disputing the degree of legitimate international concern in the process; their abstention from voting thus had a certain logic. But South Africa and Portugal, whatever their legal arguments for abstaining or not participating, by their inaction allowed the majority thereafter to point out that not a single vote was cast against either the 1960 declaration or the establishment of the Special Committee.[83]

---

80. A/Res. 1654 (XVI), Nov. 27, 1961. The original 17 members were: Australia, Cambodia, Ethiopia, India, Italy, Madagascar, Mali, Poland, Syria, Tanganyika, Tunisia, U.S.S.R., the United Kingdom, the United States, Uruguay, Venezuela, and Yugoslavia. The membership later expanded to 24.

81. USUN Press Release 3851, Nov. 22, 1961, p. 9.

82. For a summary of the debate, the draft resolutions, and voting details, see Lincoln P. Bloomfield, "The New Diplomacy in the United Nations," Wilcox and Haviland, eds., *op. cit.*, pp. 53–58.

83. This weakened the case of states like France which argued that such resolutions could not "re-interpret" the Charter without the acceptance of the original signatories, as in any other treaty. See, e.g., Swift, ed., *op. cit.*, pp. 15–16.

THE CASE OF GOA

Anticolonial events in 1961 reached their peak on December 17, when India invaded Goa, which had been a disputed issue with Lisbon since 1947. At that time the political, although not the legal, situation had also changed in relation to Goa and other, even more minuscule, pieces of the Indian subcontinent that had remained under Portuguese rule for centuries—not by virtue of the strength of Portugal, but by sufferance of the British. Portugal now lacked the means to maintain its position by force. India had both the means and, in its own eyes, sufficient motive to warrant its claim to the area. With the rising tide of nationalism in the fifties, with the Soviet Union encouraging India, with the United States having no intention of getting involved either to maintain the status quo or to break it forcibly, it is difficult to think of a clearer case for the application of preventive diplomacy in the interests of peaceful change.[84]

Yet the only "change" in the situation was Portugal's proclamation that Goa had become an "overseas province." When the Goa kettle began to simmer in the mid-fifties, its NATO allies accepted Portugal's legalistic definition of Goa's status as a "province" rather than risk any jeopardy to the Azores air and naval base. Only when conditions became critical in December 1961, did the United States go beyond its pattern of fruitlessly urging restraint on both sides and offering its unacceptable good offices. At that late date, it appears, an unsuccessful attempt was initiated by United States Ambassador Kenneth Galbraith to suggest a substantive compromise of the quarrel along the following lines: "India should guarantee Portugal that her Goan iron mines would not be nationalized, that her economic interests would be preserved, that Portuguese could still be taught in the schools. Portugal, in turn, would yield its sovereignty to the territories." Although the Ambassador was scheduled to present his proposal to Prime Minister Nehru, the State Department decided that "his plan could not be put to Portugal, [which] would never accept it."[85] It was therefore never formally presented to India either.

84. Even France, not notably perceptive in these matters, had surrendered control in 1954 over its tiny coastal enclaves in India (Pondichery, Karikal, Make, and Yanaon). A formal treaty was signed in 1956; but opposition by deputies representing French interests there delayed ratification until 1962. The Foreign Office won parliamentary ratification by arguing that it had a much better chance of negotiating various judicial and cultural guarantees for French-speaking people in the areas after ratification, than with the treaty still pending. See *New York Times,* July 14, 1962.

85. Reported by Bernard D. Nossiter, in the *Washington Post,* Jan. 22, 1962. See also Schlesinger, *op. cit.,* p. 562, on the "Europeanists" vs. the "Africanists" and the U.N. Mission vs. the Pentagon over the Portuguese colonial issues in general.

The situation in New Delhi had also hardened by that time, however. Portugal's last-minute proposal for a peace-observation group was unacceptable to India.[86] As Prime Minister Nehru wrote to President Kennedy, ten days after the invasion, public feeling against Portugal had risen to a pitch of angry resentment: "Year after year we tried to control these feelings and to prevent any popular action, but during the last two years this situation grew progressively more difficult. Then came the Angola tragedy, which had powerful reactions in India as elsewhere. In our minds, Goa and Angola became parts of a single problem."[87]

Pressures rose to the boiling point, with allegations of Portuguese firing on Indian fishing craft, of Indian retaliations, of troop reinforcements, and so forth. India invaded to settle the matter by force. Portugal immediately complained to the Security Council, where it was supported by its NATO allies in a call for cease-fire and withdrawal. Ambassador Stevenson initially declared:

It is clear as crystal on the basis of the facts and the complaint that the issue . . . is not the right or the wrong of Portugal's colonial policy; it is the right or the wrong of one nation seeking to change an existing political and legal situation by the use of armed force. That is expressly forbidden in the Charter. There are no exceptions, except self defense. . . .

. . . The Charter does not say all members shall settle their international disputes by peaceful means except in cases of colonial areas. Its says again and again . . . that the basic principle of the United Nations is the maintenance of peace . . . peace everywhere.[88]

But the issue was not really so crystal clear. The Indian position (aside from dubious evidence as to who was guilty of greater proximate provocations) was based on the countercharge that "colonialism is permanent aggression," in Krishna Menon's phrase.[89] In more legal terms, the Indian

---

86. David W. Wainhouse and associates, *International Peace Observation: A History and Forecast* (Johns Hopkins Press, 1966), p. 545.

87. Text in Selig D. Harrison dispatch, "How Nehru Saw Goa a Year Ago," *Washington Post*, Dec. 22, 1962. See also article by a former Indian Ambassador to the United States, G. L. Mehta, "West Sees Goa as a Precedent: An Indian Viewpoint," in *Washington Post*, Jan. 14, 1962 and Quincy Wright, "The Goa Incident," *American Journal of International Law*, Vol. 56 (July 1962), pp. 617–32, for a legal analysis and a discussion of the political and moral arguments of the Asian-African states.

88. U.N. Security Council, Sixteenth Year, *Official Records*, 988th Meeting, Dec. 18, 1961, pp. 19, 21.

89. Menon started invoking the concept en route to the Security Council meeting. As Ali A. Mazrui points out: "This idiom may have started as a merely figurative use of the word 'aggression,' but it would not be the first instance in which a figurative use of a given term later took on a literal meaning as well." "The United Nations and Some African Political Attitudes," *International Organization*, Vol. 18, No. 3 (Summer 1964), pp. 505–06.

argument in the Council was that the tenet of international law which gave colonial powers sovereign rights over territories conquered in Asia and Africa was no longer applicable. The initial occupation of Goa by Portugal was illegal 450 years ago and therefore was still illegal; Portugal had consistently refused to negotiate surrender of the territory to India, as was now specifically required by the 1960 declaration.[90] Ceylon introduced a draft resolution rejecting the charge of aggression, declaring the enclaves in question to constitute a threat to international peace, and calling on Portugal to terminate hostile action and negotiate with India on their transfer.[91]

Both draft resolutions failed of adoption by 7–4 votes. Voting split along the same lines as in the Bizerte dispute; but in this case it was the Soviet-led four who did not want Council action, and the Western-led seven who did. No attempt was made to take the issue to the Assembly, partly because Indian control of Goa was a fait accompli in a few days; but chiefly because it would have been a futile gesture in light of the other colonial developments of 1961 reviewed above.

Moreover, before the Assembly adjourned on December 21, Ambassador Stevenson had acknowledged another Charter obligation, not mentioned in his earlier Council statements: Taking Goa "as a laboratory case, rather than as a political act in itself," he said, India had "tried to negotiate for fourteen years and then they resorted to force. Now, if you are going to freeze the right of these people to assert their force, . . . you have got to open up a channel more fully and firmly on negotiations."[92] This

90. Wright points out, however, that India had never placed the matter before the U.N. under Art. 14, although the Assembly had already passed several resolutions pressing Portugal to abandon colonialism: "While the General Assembly . . . could not decide on the transfer of the territory, it seemed likely . . . that India could have obtained more than a two-thirds vote against Portuguese colonialism in Goa [which] might have brought effective pressure on Portugal. In view of these possibilities, it can hardly be said that India had exhausted peaceful methods." He suggests that India may have been reluctant to press for a U.N. resolution that, "instead of urging transfer of Goa to India, might have urged 'self-determination' for Goa, a principle which India has refused to apply in Kashmir." Wright, *op. cit.*, pp. 626–27."

91. The draft resolution was submitted by Ceylon, Liberia, and the UAR (S/4032, Dec. 18, 1962). Debate summarized in *US Participation in the UN . . . 1961*, pp. 101–06. See U.N. Security Council, Sixteenth Year, *Official Records*, 988th Meeting, Dec. 18, 1961, para. 99 for Indian case.

92. USUN Press Release on press conference of Dec. 21, 1961. There is reason to believe that the Ambassador had proposed to say something along this line in the Security Council, but that Washington did not consent.

channel the anticolonial nations were to seek to open up through the newly formed Special Committee, which began its work early in 1962.

The Special Committee of 24

Great Britain, supported by the United States, would have liked the Special Committee to be little more than a new version of the old Committee on Information. But by 1962, that was a lost cause. The anticolonial neutral majority was now in the saddle, and its desires for a more active program were encouraged by the communist states.[93] The new Members made their weight felt in terms of their own national interests, just as the older powers of all political leanings had always done. Moreover, international organization was an accepted norm when the new states were set up; and by 1963 the new African states had formed not only their own regional Organization of African Unity (OAU), but also numerous smaller experimental groupings among themselves. In some ways, accordingly, they found it easier to adapt themselves and their needs to the workings of the United Nations than did other governments, which had to "unlearn" many fixed habits when operating through the world Organization.

As a result, developments outside the United Nations in this general field were quickly brought within the framework of its Special Committee. As those developments did not move rapidly enough in the direction of fulfilling the independence goals of the 1960 declaration, the Assembly in 1962 enlarged the committee from 17 to 24 members.[94] It also broadened the committee's interests and its activities to the annoyance, if not the dismay, of the remaining colonial powers, including the United States. The trend of events outside the Organization is well known: in all the "hard-core" areas of southern Africa, the situation moved from bad to worse in the view of the Afro-Asian governments. The first resolution of

93. For an account of the controversy over the procedures and mandate of the Committee of 17 (and later of 24), see Taieb Slim (Tunisian Delegate), "The Work of the Committee of 24," in Swift, ed., *op. cit.*, pp. 1–9.

94. A/Res. 1810 (XVII), Dec. 17, 1962. The new members were Bulgaria, Chile, Denmark, Iran, Iraq, Ivory Coast, and Sierra Leone. The committee also eventually superseded the Special Committees on Portuguese Territories and for South West Africa, and the Committee on Information Transmitted under Article 73(e).

the new OAU in 1963 was a strong one against colonialism, illustrating its priority in African thinking.[95]

Their attitude was reinforced by the course of events in the Congo, which moved through a period of increasing tensions over the ONUC operations, until the attempted secession of Katanga was overcome; and then into a period of growing reluctance to support and pay for the international force, until ONUC was finally withdrawn in mid-1964.[96] In other parts of the world, it was much the same story of failure to find any way to reconcile the opposing forces that sought to maintain or to alter the status quo so that the end result would be agreed directions, methods, and rates of change. In the West Irian, Yemen, Malaysia, and Cyprus disputes, the United Nations became operationally involved when the disputes broke into open violence of varying intensity; in Africa, UNEF and ONUC played similar roles. In other decolonization cases, the activities of the Committee of 24 to some extent became a political equivalent of those peacekeeping missions.

The South West African dispute was taken to the International Court, which finally refused in July 1966 to rule on the merits of the case.[97] Other controversies, however, tended increasingly to pass through the committee and the Assembly to the Security Council, where a threat to the peace was usually charged on the basis of failure to fulfill obligations under both the Declaration of Human Rights and that on Colonial Independence. By the end of 1965, arms embargoes and diplomatic sanctions had been recommended against Portugal and South Africa, although neither have been effectively carried out. Mandatory sanctions against both have been sought by the African states, supported by the Soviet Union (until its reversal of position in the South West African case), but opposed by Great Britain and the United States. In the case of Rhodesia, of course, the three permanent Security Council members were on the same side. With that degree of great-power accord, as noted earlier, it was

95. Text in *Organization of African Unity: Basic Documents*, published by the Provisional Secretariat of the OAU, Addis Ababa (undated). The OAU also appointed four foreign ministers to speak on behalf of the membership in the Security Council, before which it planned to bring the hard-core cases, and created a coordinating committee to handle a special fund for assistance to liberation movements in the remaining colonial and "nonindependent" territories.

96. For an account of the ONUC military operation, see Ernest W. Lefever, *Crisis in the Congo: A U.N. Force in Action* (Brookings Institution, 1965).

97. *I.C.J. Reports 1966*, South West Africa, Second Phase; Judgment.

relatively simple to initiate economic and diplomatic sanctions, but they have failed to provide a solution as of this writing.

In the Portuguese case, perhaps more acutely than anywhere else, the United States has been caught in a dilemma caused by its conflicting security and political concerns. The underlying problem, however, has been common to Washington's relations with the other NATO imperial powers.

The NATO Allies

Serious discrepancy in NATO views on decolonization and racial conflicts has not been confined to United States opposition to the colonial policies of some of its allies. The Scandinavian members, for example, also sought to promote more progressive policies on the part of the resistant European governments and took initiatives in seeking a breakthrough in the South African impasse. They also joined the United States in various votes against the positions of the imperial governments, after a period of abstention brought no visible signs of progress.

In the present context, however, only the conflict between the United States and the major colonial allies was significant. Its repercussions have affected the smooth functioning of the military alliance on more than one occasion; and because the colonial issue is the source of so many disputes before the world Organization and the focus of the noisiest arguments in the General Assembly, it has served to spotlight the dilemma of United States allied relationships. For this reason, the Assembly debates have been blamed for exacerbating, if not causing, the problem and have led to criticism of the United Nations as handicapping the achievement of a strong allied security policy. Former Secretary of State Dean Acheson, for example, declared on one occasion:

At every session of the General Assembly some issue arises between a nationalist group in a colonial area and one of our European allies. These issues are rarely resolved, they are usually exacerbated, by the debates and resolutions of the Assembly. If one is interested in making orderly progress toward movement from a dependent position toward responsible and, possibly, competent government by the consent and the choice of these peoples, one must look elsewhere. If, on the other hand, one regards these proceedings as a useful goad to progress by the colonial power, they will occur without the United States taking positions which strain and embitter the alliance, whatever fleeting popularity they may gain for us in other quarters.[98]

Mr. Acheson, however, did not specify where "else" one might look for more orderly progress.

U.S. POLICY EVOLUTION

So long as the direct military confrontation with "international communism" was considered of primary importance in determining United States policy for maintaining world peace, the colonial policy adhered to rather consistently in the years following the formation of NATO and the stalemate in Korea was a logical choice for the United States. Although nominally neutral,[99] in effect it subordinated the American desire for more effective and speedier colonial progress toward autonomy whenever that desire weakened accord with the metropolitan powers. The policy was followed publicly, both within the United Nations (as in the case of Algeria) and outside it (as in Indochina); although it was evidently accompanied by continued private diplomatic efforts to persuade the imperial powers to reach agreement with their subject peoples on effective measures of political development. For their part, the NATO allies generally supported the United States on such issues as Korea and the seating of Communist China.

In the late fifties, the United States, as noted, moved first to a clearer neutralism, and then to frank support of anticolonialism, even when abstaining from voting for some of the more extreme resolutions. Where the earlier policies had been criticized by the anticolonialists, the shift brought forth criticism from the other side. This was often expressed in terms of the naïveté of Washington in trying to cultivate popularity with the new and uncommitted governments, or of the inexperience of Americans who did not understand the complexities of liquidating the colonial system peacefully. Even when not going to the extreme of accusing Washington of undermining NATO or the national security by its disregard of the interests of its allies, critics frequently charged that the United States

---

98. Text in *Vital Speeches*, Vol. 29 (Jan. 1, 1963), pp. 165–66.

99. The standard public declaration of policy in that period (as during World War II) was dedicated to "the goal of self-government and independence of all countries whose people desire and are capable of sustaining an independent existence." "Joint Declaration of the President of the United States and the Prime Minister of the United Kingdom," U.S. Department of State, *Bulletin*, Vol. 34 (1956), p. 231.

pushed the metropolitan governments too fast.[100] In view of the history of the fifties, however, the United States could argue that the violence attending the reshaping of the United Nations world was due at least as much to failure by the colonial powers to judge the strength of nationalist forces and to develop policies capable of turning them into more evolutionary channels. In short, the issue was not one of getting out too soon, but of not getting on with the political training of dependent peoples as fast as the colonial powers might reasonably have done after 1945. As a former United States delegation member wrote in 1961:

Of course, if Sir Pierson Dixon [British delegate at the United Nations], President de Gaulle, and Dr. Salazar are right, the alternatives are correctly posed as a choice between supporting debate [in the Assembly] or supporting our friends. It is, however, just as easy—and much closer to the truth—to state the matter the other way round. If the approach of our friends is wrong, it is they who face a choice of either accepting debate or undermining our common interest.[101]

The problem seldom came up in this clearcut "either-or" form, however. At home, the administration had to pick its way between contrary advice from those whom Arthur Schlesinger has described as the "Europeanists" and the "Africanists" in the State Department, or between the politically oriented advice of the State Department and the mission to the United Nations and the militarily oriented advice from the Defense Department.[102] Abroad, it had to support both its policies toward the newer, unaligned countries (where it was concerned to counteract communist political influences) and those toward its allies, which it was concerned to keep against the communist military threat. On self-determination and decolonization in particular, the United States has, along with practically every other government but Portugal and South Africa, accepted in principle the objectives of the 1960 Declaration on Colonial Independence. The issues in relation to the other colonial powers, therefore, have tended to center on the timing of the grant of self-government

100. Elspeth Huxley, for example, wrote in 1961: "That Belgium, one of the NATO powers, should have acted as she did in the Congo, without any consultation whatever with allies who have been seriously embarrassed by the consequences of her acts, seems in the highest degree irresponsible. This irresponsibility was displayed not by the Belgians alone. One of the reasons behind their panicky withdrawal was the constant sniping at colonialism in which some of her NATO partners had indulged." *Op. cit.*, p. 668.

101. Ernest A. Gross, "Shifting Institutional Pattern of the United Nations," in Wilcox and Haviland, eds., *op. cit.*, pp. 84–85.

102. See Schlesinger, *op. cit.*, pp. 560–63.

and the degree to which the world Organization should supervise, set standards for, or even participate directly in the process. The resistance of Portugal to any such political evolution resulted in an acute dilemma for United States policy both because of the importance attached to maintaining the Azores base, and because of Washington's reluctance to approve the use of sanctions to enforce change.

PORTUGUESE POLICY DILEMMA

The incident of Goa gave a foretaste of General Assembly attitudes toward Portugal's major colonial territories in Africa. A Special Committee on Portuguese Territories was set up, with which Portugal refused to cooperate on the ground that Chapter XI was inapplicable to its overseas provinces. Lisbon ignored the committee's 1962 recommendations for sweeping policy reforms, those of a subcommittee on Angola in particular. In December, the Assembly in turn requested all Members to ban arms shipments to Portugal, and the Security Council to "take all appropriate measures to secure the compliance of Portugal with" the resolutions.[103]

At that stage, the United States remained with the opposition, voting against such strong resolutions. It had, however, been attempting to make the Portuguese see light on this matter during the preceding months. It had succeeded in obtaining Lisbon's consent to admit an Assembly representative to visit Mozambique and Angola and then report on conditions to the next (Eighteenth) Assembly. But what might have been considered a significant advance earlier—as the first United Nations presence admitted to any Portuguese territory—was inadequate in the final days of 1962. The Afro-Asian group insisted that three-man committees should be sent to the territories and report back to the Special Committee. That would have brought the matter under Chapter XI, however, which made it unacceptable to Portugal. Washington's efforts thus proved abortive, and it withdrew a proposed draft resolution along the original lines.[104]

These almost desperate efforts by the United States to restore negotiations between Lisbon and the African states reflected the fact that the

103. A/Res. 1809, (XVII), Dec. 14, 1962, on Portuguese territories in general. A similar resolution, 1819 (XVII), Dec. 18, applied to Angola in particular. A/Res. 1809 (XVII) also dissolved the Special Committee on Territories under Portuguese Administration.

104. See U.S. Department of State, *U.S. Participation in the U.N.: Report by the President to the Congress for the Year 1962*, pp. 61–63.

question of the American base in the Azores was also at a critical stage in 1962. The 1957 base agreement was due to expire at the end of the year, and negotiations for renewal had been going on for several months without success. Military facilities there represented an investment of hundreds of millions of dollars, and the Pentagon was reported to believe "that the United States should seek to use its Azores complex for at least five more years."[105] Loss of the base rights would involve massive rerouting of military air traffic and, presumably, further expenditures to establish new facilities elsewhere. Negotiations for renewal of the agreement had clearly run into trouble over the African situation.

Washington had supported (or abstained on) various United Nations resolutions calling on Portugal to accept the "jurisdiction" of the Organization; it had made several strong protests before obtaining assurances that Lisbon would not use any American military equipment against insurgents in Angola;[106] and it had refused Portuguese demands for more arms. Its backing of Portugal's position on Goa did not, in the view of Lisbon, balance its actions in the African situation. Lisbon claimed American support as a NATO ally and on the contention that the troubles in Angola stemmed from communist-inspired terrorism. That view was not only oversimplified; it led to more positive ill effects. As the Congolese delegate declared in the Security Council debate on Angola: Africans seeking independence of Portugal "are not fighting under the banner of communism, but simply demanding something that is ours by right. If communism is the only path of liberation against colonialism, then, indeed, we are true communists without having known that fact ourselves."[107]

Because Portugal also would clearly lose a great deal by closure of the American facilities in the Azores, these difficulties were not allowed to wreck the base arrangements. Face was saved in 1962 by a "temporary" extension of the accord until the "current" negotiations were concluded.[108] The situation has since continued on this informal basis.

105. *New York Times,* June 27, 1962.
106. American officials subsequently declared that the assurances were being honored, but African delegates were openly skeptical of the claim. In any event, if American arms were not used in Africa, they released other equipment for use there, which was "the same difference," so far as African nationalists were concerned.
107. Quoted in *Washington Post,* June 9, 1961.
108. See Patricia Wohlgemuth, "The Portuguese Territories and the United Nations," *International Conciliation,* No. 545 (November 1963), for a more detailed account of these developments.

United Nations controversies with Portugal continued along the same contentious lines after 1962, with the Assembly and Security Council annually passing ever stronger resolutions of condemnation.[109] The United States continued to press the Portuguese to consider policy changes, but to no avail. Assistant Secretary of State Williams described official policy in 1963:

On the question of the Portuguese territories, we believe the principle of self-determination must be applied to those territories and that Portugal has a continuing role to play in Africa. We believe that Portugal should take rapid steps to prepare the peoples of those areas for self-determination. Our policy toward the Portuguese African territories has been consistent for some years. We are encouraging the Portuguese to undertake necessary reform. We believe the Portuguese recognize the firmness of our policy, and the need for reform in the African territories . . . We continue to be hopeful that rapid progress can be made in the Portuguese territories.[110]

So far as Lisbon's policies were concerned, the wish was father to American thought.[111] Washington had somewhat greater success in 1963, in its efforts to get the African states into discussions with Portugal. A group of nine Africans was named through the Committee of 24 to discuss matters with the Portuguese Foreign Minister under the auspices of the Secretary-General. The talks broke down shortly, however, on irreconcilable differences over the meaning of "self-determination" as applicable to Portuguese territories.

Since 1963, the Portuguese situation in the United Nations has steadily deteriorated. Although Lisbon has undertaken various economic, social, and political reforms in its territories that go considerably beyond its previous accomplishments, they fail to meet the sine qua non of self-government with the right to self-determination which is demanded by the Assembly. The Committee of 24 considers the policies of Portugal, South Africa, and the rebellious government of Rhodesia equally intolerable. The Security Council declared in November 1965, that "the situation resulting from the policies of Portugal . . . seriously disturbs international peace and security," and renewed its request to all Members to take

109. The Portuguese view is given in Franco Nogueira (Foreign Minister), *The United Nations and Portugal: A Study in Anti-Colonialism* (London: Sidgwick & Jackson, 1963).

110. U.S. Department of State, *Bulletin*, Vol. 48 (1963), pp. 604–05.

111. Lisbon's attitude toward U.S. policy was reflected in a report that the Foreign Minister was claiming the Angolan revolt was an American-financed plot to replace Portuguese by American influence in Africa. See *Washington Post*, Oct. 31, 1963.

measures to prevent the supply of arms to Lisbon.[112] In December, the Assembly recommended that all states "render to the people of the [Portuguese] territories the moral and material support necessary for the restoration of their inalienable rights." It specifically urged members "separately or collectively" to break diplomatic relations with Portugal, apply shipping and air transportation embargoes, and "boycott all trade with Portugal." It also specifically called on the NATO powers to ban arms sales and any other assistance to Lisbon, and requested the Security Council to consider sanctions for the enforcement of its resolutions.[113]

More of the same in slightly stronger language was adopted by the twenty-first Assembly, since there had been little change during 1966 in terms of practical implementation of the earlier resolutions.[114] Guerilla warfare continues in the Portuguese African territories, inhibited but not defeated by relatively large numbers of Portuguese troops. It is not likely that the United States will soon change its policy of resisting the application of sanctions in this case. Its position has been (as in the case of South Africa) that, undesirable as the situation is, it does not constitute a threat to the peace in the meaning of Chapter VII of the Charter.[115] As a practical matter, moreover, with the drain of Vietnam on United States resources and with the complications of Rhodesia burdening the British, the two essential countries in any strong drive for either economic or military sanctions against Portugal or South Africa are in no position to give a lead even if they wanted. The Soviet Union, although strong in words against Portugal, is similarly unenthusiastic when it comes to initiating action. "For the time being, Lisbon escapes greater pressure from the United Nations, where attention is centered on the Rhodesian and South West African situations; and in Africa, it manages to hold its own, though feeling the strain of supporting some 120,000 troops against the nationalist guerillas."[116]

112. S/Res. 218 (Nov. 23, 1965).

113. A/Res. 2107 (XX), Dec. 21, 1965. Few states outside of Africa have complied.

114. A/Res. 2184 (XXI), Dec. 12, 1966, adopted 70–13 (U.S. and U.K.)–22.

115. In January 1967, Ambassador Goldberg reiterated U.S. "unequivocal support" for self-determination for the peoples of Angola and Mozambique, but insisted that: "The first step, in our view, is for the parties to commence a genuine dialogue on the basis of recognition of the principle of self-determination. This is the indispensable way to a peaceful solution of the troubles which afflict these two territories." USUN Press Release 5, Jan. 27, 1967, p. 3.

116. See Tad Szulc dispatch, *New York Times*, June 25, 1967.

THE BROADER PROBLEM OF BASES

The Azores base not only has a special relevance to United States policies toward Portugal, it is also representative of a wider problem. The rising tempo of nationalism in the postwar period has been used by the Soviet Union to attack the United States and its NATO allies through all their colonial and foreign base holdings. Some of the bases have, directly or indirectly, led to major international crises involving the United Nations, such as Suez in 1956 (despite the earlier withdrawal from the British base) and Cyprus in 1964. Sometimes bases have complicated the decolonizing process by increasing the reluctance of the sovereign to grant independence either rapidly or completely, as illustrated by the French retention of Bizerte in Tunisia and the British of a huge base in Aden.

The United States has been involved as the administering authority of the strategic Pacific Islands Trust Territory; as the historic holder of territorial rights in Cuba and Panama; as the indeterminate holder of certain Japanese islands for bases; and as the temporary holder of base rights negotiated since World War II in Libya, Spain, Turkey, the Philippines, and elsewhere. In some of these countries, the local government has wanted the base and the American commitment it represents, so that its maintenance has created no serious difficulty from the point of view of United States bilateral policy. But as the Azores and Cyprus (in connection with Turkish bases) show, even bilaterally successful military-aid policies may create other kinds of multilateral policy difficulties. In other newly independent countries that were uncommitted so far as the anticommunist cold war is concerned—especially where United States base rights were negotiated with the former imperial power, as in Morocco—communist arguments have often had telling effect on the national desire to banish foreign bases. The problem created for United States security policy has thus varied according to time and place.

Technological advances in weaponry have radically changed strategic concepts, including the purposes for which and the locations where bases may be useful. Nonetheless, so long as a "forward strategy" guides United States military policy, foreign bases will continue to provide vantage points for limited-warfare use and thus will constitute potential points of political conflict. There can be no fixed criteria for determining the point at which a base becomes more of a political liability than a military advantage, because individual cases vary enormously in their political circumstances and in their military value over time.

In some cases, withdrawals have been negotiated without much difficulty or apparent hazard to American security interests when the initiative was taken by the foreign government, for example, in Morocco. In others, the nationalistic desire to get rid of the foreign base has conflicted with other interests of the local government—with economic concerns, in the case of Libya, which for a time simplified the problem of maintaining the United States base there. At other times, maintenance of a base may be no longer vital militarily, but withdrawal may conflict with the interests of the foreign government, give the impression of a lessening of interest by Washington in its ally, or look like backing down in the face of communist demands. This might have appeared to be the case if withdrawal from the Turkish bases had been agreed with the Soviet Union as a quid pro quo for Soviet withdrawal of its missiles from Cuba, even though the United States had been considering removal of the Jupiter missiles for some time.[117]

In the last circumstance, military-political judgment may be distorted by emotion, as it also tends to be in connection with bases held for a relatively long period of time, such as Guantanamo. Of these cases, the Panama Canal Zone is perhaps the best example. Americans are prone to take the status quo for granted, or as an inalienable right, although the development of nationalism in the postwar world has been most effectively arraigned against precisely that type of nineteenth and early twentieth century imperialist acquisition. In fact, Washington's relations with Panama over the Canal Zone illustrate in miniature nearly all the problems of peaceful change that have been the burden of this chapter; and the United States officially has often been as obtuse about Panama as it once considered Great Britain and France to be over Suez. "If the United States had to defend their treaty rights in the Panama Canal," wrote Anthony Eden in his *Memoirs*, "they would not regard such action as colonialism; neither would I."[118] But Panamanians did, which was the significant point in the present context.

THE CASE OF PANAMA

Space does not permit detailing the tale of bickering between the two governments over Panama's perennial efforts to obtain modification of the Hay-Bunau Varilla Treaty of 1903, whereby complete control of the

117. See, for example, Schlesinger's account of the debate, *op. cit.*, pp. 807-19.
118. Eden, *op. cit.*, p. 499.

Canal Zone was conceded by the fledgling Panama to the United States, "as if it were sovereign of the territory. . . ."[119] In the Good Neighbor era, protectorate status was terminated in a separate treaty; and a decade after World War II, various economic concessions were made in another accord by Washington. Annual payments to Panama were also greatly increased in 1955, but revision of the basic treaty was refused. Recognition of Panamanian "titular sovereignty" by the United States was not sufficient to cancel out the political effects of Washington's refusal to fly the Panamanian flag in the Zone.

Nasser nationalized the Suez Canal in 1956. This inevitably had its repercussion in Panama, despite Washington's efforts to avoid invidious comparisons.[120] By 1958, the political temperature in Panama was near the boiling point, especially over the flag issue. Milton Eisenhower, the President's brother, and the State Department proposed to counter simultaneously the effects of Castro-nationalist agitation against the "Yanqui colonialism" of the Zone, and of Castro-communist agitation against the social abuses and poverty in Panama, where an oligarchical controlling group opposed modernization. They urged a program of economic and social assistance to the Republic, combined with concessions in the Zone, to minimize the military accent on the United States presence, but without damaging any vital security interests of this country. Important congressional and military elements, however, were opposed to any treaty concessions or to tying together policies toward Panama and toward the Zone.[121]

119. Text of the treaty in 33 Stat., Pt. 2, p. 2208.

120. Robert D. Murphy, then Under Secretary of State, describes Secretary Dulles as taking "pains to explain the difference between the legal status of the Suez and Panama canals. Egypt retained sovereign rights in the Suez area, even though traffic was controlled by a privately owned company according to international agreement. The Panama Canal Zone, on the contrary, was 'leased in perpetuity' to the United States and therefore was an American, not an international, waterway." *Diplomat Among Warriors* (Doubleday, 1964), p. 385. See also Eden, *op. cit.*, pp. 434–38; Lincoln P. Bloomfield, "The United Nations and National Security," *Foreign Affairs*, Vol. 36 (July 1958), p. 602; and Milton S. Eisenhower, *The Wine Is Bitter: The United States and Latin America* (Doubleday, 1963), p. 226.

121. The kind of concession proposed, for example, was to appoint a civilian rather than the traditional military officer to the governorship and to meet, at least symbolically, the flag demand. The *New York Times* later reported, in 1960, that such proposals by the State Department were still being assailed as "soft" by Army authorities, in particular, who favored a "firm" policy of unequivocally retaining complete control over the Zone and the Canal. "These officials fear," it said, "that any more concessions, in view of the mounting demands of the Panamanians would merely encourage more

A year later the situation boiled over in riotous demonstrations, including tearing down the United States flag before the United States Information Office in Panama. A reporter then asked President Eisenhower's
opinion of suggestions that the Canal might be internationalized. He
replied:

As to the internationalizing of the Panama Canal, that is something that as
of this moment I would not even think of. We have got a specific treaty with
Panama. We have scrupulously obeyed its provisions for fifty years, most of our
relationships with Panama have been a model and I believe that this particular
incident that is so disturbing is really only an incident and should not be looked
at as giving us a real reason for breaking up a relationship which has worked so
well.[122]

Refusing concessions while "under attack," the administration waited
until calm prevailed and then gradually put into effect some of the earlier
rejected economic and social proposals. Most important, in September
1960, it authorized the flying of Panama's flag alongside the stars and
stripes at one entrance to the Zone. This raised another tempest in Con-

---

claims and perhaps nurture a demand for Panamanian control of the Canal" (July 10,
1960).

In February 1960, the fact that the department was again considering the flag concession led the House of Representatives to resolve (382–12) that it was the sense of
Congress that Panama's emblem should not be flown unless the 1903 treaty was modified, which would require Senate approval. *New York Times*, Feb. 3, 1960; *Congressional Record*, Vol. 106, Pt. 2, 86 Cong. 2 sess. (1960), pp. 1808–09. The House also
added an amendment to the appropriation for the Canal barring the use of any funds
to erect flagpoles or other devices for displaying the Panamanian flag. Rep. H. R. Gross
of Iowa offered the flagpole amendment, because: "I don't want the flag of Panama
flying over sovereign territory of the United States." There was "no audible opposition"
on the voice vote, according to *The Washington Post* (Feb. 10, 1960).

122. White House Press Conference, Nov. 4, 1959. (*Washington Post*, Nov. 5,
1959.) There have been various proposals to internationalize control of the Canal
under either the U.N. or the OAS, which are not described here because they have
never been seriously considered by the United States Government. The U.N. has been
favored by some on the grounds that the Canal's importance is worldwide and that the
chief shipping nations are not in the OAS. The latter has been supported with the argument that inter-American control would carry out U.S. pledges of hemispheric cooperation. The proposals were equally unlikely to win Panamanian support; nor would that
Republic have considered others along the lines of making Panama a state of the Union
or for having the United States purchase the Zone outright. For discussion of some of
these proposals see: Martin B. Travis and James T. Watkins, "Control of the Panama
Canal: An Obsolete Shibboleth?," *Foreign Affairs*, Vol. 37 (April 1959); Lincoln P.
Bloomfield, *United Nations and U.S. Foreign Policy* (Little Brown, 1960), pp. 164–
66; Milton S. Eisenhower, *op. cit.*, pp. 226–27; and the Republican Citizens' Committee, Critical Issues Council, *Panama: A Realistic Appraisal* (April 1964), p. 7.

gress and the Pentagon, so further State Department proposals were again dropped.

The demands from Panama continued, however, leading to the appointment of a joint commission in June 1962, by Presidents Chiari and Kennedy, to hold "discussions" on "points of dissatisfaction."[123] In the course of the following year, the commission announced various economic concessions, mainly affecting the employment of Panamanians in the Zone; but the only political one was an increase in the sites where Panama's flag might fly: at the Thatcher Ferry Bridge (built by the United States under the 1955 treaty, to connect the two parts of Panama across the Canal) and elsewhere "on land . . . where the flag of the United States is flown by civilian authorities."[124]

"Zonians" by this time (July 1963) were as emotional over the flag dispute as were Panamanians; and after considerable delay in implementing the decision, the Governor decided that no flags, rather than two, would be flown in front of the schools after the Christmas holidays of 1963. American students at one school (supported by adult organizations) defiantly raised their flag without the Panamanian one. A counterdemonstration by students from the Republic, endeavoring to raise their own banner, triggered large-scale rioting and sabotage on January 9, 1964. This was communist assisted, if not inspired, and resulted in twenty-six fatalities, including three U.S. soldiers, and hundreds of injured.

Initial official reactions were promising. Presidents Johnson and Chari at once agreed on halting the violence and asking the Inter-American Peace Committee to resolve the dispute.[125] By mid-January peace was

123. The official communiqué announced agreement on the principle that: "When two friendly nations are bound by treaty provisions which are not fully satisfactory to one of the parties, arrangements should be made to permit both nations to discuss these points of dissatisfaction." Text in U.S. Department of State, *Bulletin*, Vol. 47 (1962), pp. 81–82.

124. U.S. Department of State, *Bulletin*, Vol. 48 (1963), p. 172. The formal dedication of the bridge, as a result of Washington's refusal to name it the Bridge of the Americas (which had been widely proposed, including by the Panamanian Assembly), was boycotted by most of the diplomatic corps in Panama. Latin American diplomats and the papal nuncio refused to attend because their invitations did not come through official Panamanian channels; only the representatives of Great Britain, Italy, West Germany, Spain, and Nationalist China were present. Jeering student groups with Cuban revolutionary flags were out in force, however. *New York Times*, Oct. 7 and 13, 1962.

125. Panama also brought charges in the Security Council. The latter adopted Brazil's suggestion, that an appeal by the Council President to both sides to end the violence would be sufficient United Nations action. The appeal was of course promptly accepted.

restored and a binational commission was dealing with the emergency maintenance of order. The two governments agreed to renew diplomatic relations and to discuss "without limitations all existing matters of any nature" affecting their relations.[126]

But then a dispute arose over the use of "discuss" in the English text of the OAS communiqué announcing the agreement, in contrast with terms for "negotiate" in the Spanish text. The old issue of renegotiating the 1903 treaty was renewed in full force: Panama rejected anything less than the promise of a new treaty; the United States refused to admit publicly that an undertaking to discuss any subject might cover renegotiation of the treaty. A succession of OAS groups failed to break the deadlock until April 1964, when the two governments jointly agreed to appoint special ambassadors. They were to "seek the prompt elimination of the causes of conflict between the two countries, without limitations or preconditions of any kind," and to endeavor to reach "a just and fair agreement . . . subject to the constitutional processes of each country."[127]

The month before, however, the Departments of State and Defense had asked the Congress to authorize studies for a new sea-level canal, either across the isthmus or possibly further north in Nicaragua or Mexico.[128] The need for a new waterway had been apparent for some time: the present channel is unable to take the largest vessels, general traffic will probably increase beyond its capacity by 1970, and the complicated engineering works make it vulnerable to sabotage or bombing. The departmental request therefore emphasized that a new canal would be considered on its merits, and not in connection with the current difficulties in Panama. That statement met with general skepticism.

Special ambassadors were duly appointed to inaugurate the discussions provided for in the April 1964 agreement, but nothing visible resulted from their talks. They were recessed between October and early December.[129] With student groups planning another demonstration in Panama

126. U.S. Department of State, *Bulletin*, Vol. 50 (1964), p. 156.

127. *Ibid.*, p. 656.

128. Mexico announced it would not accept international financing and that its own resources were inadequate for the job. It was consequently not included in a presidential message (Dec. 18, 1964) that later referred to "four possible routes—two in Panama, one in Colombia, and one . . . which goes through Nicaragua and possibly Costa Rica as well." (Text in U.S. Department of State, *Bulletin*, Vol. 52, 1965, pp. 5–6.) Nicaragua had earlier repudiated the Bryan-Chamorro Treaty of 1914, which granted the United States perpetual rights to build an interocean canal there, on the ground that it violated the 1911 constitution.

129. The inauguration of a new Panamanian President, Marco A. Robles, took place in October; the U.S. elections in November.

on the anniversary of the 1964 riots, President Johnson announced two unilateral decisions in December: (1) to press forward, "with Panama and other interested governments, in plans . . . for a sea-level canal in this area"; and (2) "to propose to . . . Panama the negotiation of an entirely new treaty on the existing Panama Canal." There were, however, qualifications. The President explained:

In such a treaty, we must retain the rights which are necessary for the effective operation and protection of the Canal, and the administration of the areas necessary for these purposes. Such a treaty would replace the treaty of 1903 and its amendments. It should recognize the sovereignty of Panama. It should provide for its own termination when a sea level canal comes into operation. It should provide for effective discharge of our common responsibilities for hemispheric defense. Until a new agreement is reached, of course, the present treaties will remain in effect.[130]

The statement was not only unilateral; it made no reference to the bilateral talks, but only to "this Government's" intensive review of the problem as the basis of its new policy decisions. Moreover, by tying renegotiation of the 1903 treaty to consideration of possible sites for the new canal outside of Panama, the administration, as one headline described it, put the "squeeze" on Panama.[131] All this may have seemed necessary in domestic political terms; but it also roused Panamanian jingoism and radical demands for an immediate end to the "accursed treaty" and for elimination of any United States military presence and bases in Panama and the Zone.

By August 1965, serious unrest was again mounting in Panama over delay in the bilateral talks. In September, therefore, President Johnson announced, this time simultaneously, though not jointly, with President Robles, various "areas of agreement" that had been reached on the contents of a new treaty: (1) abrogation of the 1903 treaty; (2) effective recognition of Panamanian sovereignty over the Zone; (3) termination of

130. U.S. Department of State, *Bulletin*, Vol. 53 (1965), p. 6. Another paragraph in the announcement clearly reflected administration concern to forestall too much nationalistic criticism: "These decisions," the President declared, "reflect the unanimous judgment of the Secretary of State, the Secretary of Defense, and the Joint Chiefs of Staff. They are based on the recommendations of Ambassador Robert Anderson [U.S. special negotiator, formerly Eisenhower's Secretary of the Treasury], Secretary Stephen Ailes [Army], Secretary Thomas Mann [State] and Ambassador Jack Vaughan [in Panama]. They have the full support of Mr. Truman and Gen. Eisenhower. They have been reported to—and in most instances sympathetically received by—the leadership of the Congress." *Ibid.*

131. *Washington Post*, Dec. 20, 1964, column by Dan Kurzman: "New Canal Plan Puts Squeeze on Panama."

the new treaty "after a specified number of years" or when the sea-level canal opens, whichever is first; (4) "appropriate political, economic and social integration of" the canal-operating area with the rest of Panama: "Both countries recognize that there is a need for an orderly transition to avoid abrupt and possibly harmful dislocations. We also recognize that certain changes should be made over a period of time. The new canal administration will be empowered to make such changes in accordance with the guidelines in the new treaty"; (5) appropriate arrangements to safeguard the rights and interests of employees "of all nationalities" serving in the canal operation. But then the next paragraph (not numbered as an "area of agreement") added: "The new treaties will provide for the defense of the existing canal and any sea-level canal which may be constructed in Panama. United States forces and military facilities will be maintained under a base-rights and status-of-forces agreement."[132] Although President Johnson considered this "very fine progress," the December 1964 statement had already declared most of the general points to be United States policy, and the 1965 announcement left most of the difficult details still unagreed—especially the issue of military rights. Formal proposals were presented by Washington in January 1966. The Panamanians took until June to ready their position for negotiations.

Panamanian impatience with the slowness of the negotiations was reported in December, but the anniversary of the January riots passed off with only nonviolent demonstrations in 1967. In the spring, the chairman of the House of Representatives Subcommittee on the Panama Canal (Congresswoman Leonor K. Sullivan) disclosed that the negotiations contemplated the establishment of a binational authority to operate the waterway[133]—an idea long advocated by many (including Milton Eisenhower), but heretofore rigidly rejected by dominant opinion in this country. Then, on June 26, a joint announcement was made in Washington and Panama City that accord had been reached by their negotiators on "the form and content" of three agreements.[134]

The "proposed texts," which had still to be submitted to "their respective governments" for Presidential approval and legislative consideration before ratification, were not released at the time. The reasons for this withholding are not clear—the danger of renewed Panamanian demonstrations has been suggested. But the result seems to have been to stimulate criti-

---

132. U.S. Department of State, *Bulletin*, Vol. 53 (1964), p. 625.
133. *New York Times*, Dec. 11, 1966; April 28, 1967.
134. U.S. Department of State, *Bulletin*, Vol. 57 (1967), p. 65.

cism based on fears of national disadvantage (in the legislatures of both Panama and the United States), which supporters of the new policy were not in a position to answer effectively.[135] On the brighter side, General Eisenhower reversed his 1959 position (noted above), which may indicate that others, too, have come around to Secretary Rusk's view that: "After all, there is a difference between 1903 and 1967 . . . and we must take those differences (sic) into account."[136]

The texts were soon leaked, nonetheless, and printed in the *Congressional Record*.[137] The major treaty will concern the canal, supplanting the 1903 agreement and providing for a transition that will permit the Zone to be integrated into Panama. The existing canal will become the property of a United States-Panamanian Canal Authority.[138] Panama will share in the operation and the tolls, but will no longer receive an annual payment from the United States. A separate treaty will cover canal defense bases and its neutrality. The third will provide Washington with an option to construct the anticipated new sea-level canal in Panama.

STRATEGY, POLITICS, AND BASES

Strategists have long pointed to Soviet efforts to eliminate Western control of all such vital "bottlenecks" as the Dardanelles, Suez, and Panama or, at the least, to shift control to "friendly" neutrals. They have argued with respect to the Panama Canal, for example:

> that the political and psychological effects of internationalization or transfer to Panamanian control would have disastrous repercussions on the entire structure of United States bases around the world, particularly in the Caribbean and Latin America. Bases such as Guantanamo Bay in Cuba, and Chaguaramas in Trinidad, might be lost, imperiling the control of the Caribbean that is considered essential to United States security.[139]

135. See, for example, *New York Times* dispatches of the following dates: July 7, 1967: "Treaty Protests Begin in Panama"; July 14, 1967: "Canal Pacts Face Snags in Panama"; Aug. 9, 1967: "150 in House Oppose 3 Panama Canal Treaties."

136. U.S. Department of State Press Release 164, July 19, 1967, pp. 26–27. General Eisenhower urged the Senate to approve the proposed treaties, while expressing concern that they might face tough opposition. *New York Times*, July 27, 1967.

137. See *Congressional Record*, daily ed., July 10, 17, 21, 1967, pp. S 9266–67; S 9708–16; and S 10027–32.

138. A news dispatch from Panama reported that Panama had suggested that the binational authority should be composed of an equal number of Panamanian and U.S. citizens, plus an additional member to be designated by the United Nations Secretary-General. *New York Times*, Aug. 19, 1967.

139. Hanson Baldwin, *New York Times*, Jan. 16, 1964.

Military and some congressional opposition to any relaxation of sole United States control of the Canal Zone has previously been strong enough so that any concession in the direction of binational control could be successfully opposed as a "victory" for Castro-communism in Latin America. At the same time, any attempt to diminish the potential of communism in the area by anticipatory measures—such as the Milton Eisenhower-State Department recommendations well before the 1959 violence—has been equally spurned by the standpatters, although one of the dangers of most concern to military officials has been communist influence in Panama.

How much official opposition to Panamanian demands has amounted to emotional nationalism, and how much to valid security concerns, is impossible for the outsider to assess. Clearly, the military value of the Canal is different, at least, from what it was before the day of nuclear weapons, of the two-ocean Navy, of carriers that cannot transit it, of air-cargo fleets, and of the possibility of a sea-level canal that would be easier both to defend and to operate. But the United States military viewpoint has always emphasized the Canal's continued value as a transportation artery in limited-war circumstances, such as those in Vietnam. Since Panamanians have generally seen United States insistence on maintaining a military presence in the Zone as an excuse to hold the area against their will, the issue of base rights in the new treaties may be as crucial to ratification by Panama as the "sovereignty" issue is likely to be in Washington.

Continued sole control by the United States after 1959 did little to eliminate the covert communist threat exercised through nationalist groups in the Republic; and, even if it simplified operation of the Canal, left Washington in an unsatisfactory relationship with Panama, official statements to the contrary notwithstanding. Presumably, realization of such factors led the administration to chance a binational approach.

While one may doubt that the horrendous results for United States security anticipated by more fearful Americans will automatically follow from the proposed loosening of Washington's traditional control over the Canal and Zone,[140] the interpretation of Soviet aims against Western

140. Donald M. Dozer, for example, thought that if the Canal were "lost" the U.S. would "suffer irreparable harm throughout Latin America. It will lose whatever support it still retains in this hemisphere." The Canal must therefore continue to be "controlled, maintained, operated, sanitated, and protected by the United States." "The Interoceanic Canal and Hemispheric Security," in Norman A. Bailey, ed., *Latin America: Political, Economic, and Hemispheric Security* (Praeger, 1965), pp. 69–70.

foreign military bases in general is certainly valid. So also is concern with the way in which the communists' strategic objective (considered in relation to disarmament) has been able to benefit from the wider anticolonial sentiment. As earlier noted, the twentieth Assembly brought this issue to a head.

The Fourth Committee recommended a draft resolution on twenty-six island territories (including Guam and American Samoa), which contained two paragraphs declaring that: (1) "the existence . . . of military bases constitutes an obstacle to the freedom and independence" of the territories; and (2) requesting "the administering Powers to dismantle the existing bases and to refrain from establishing new ones."[141] In the Plenary, those paragraphs failed to obtain the required two-thirds majority and were excluded from the final resolution text.[142]

Four days later, the second paragraph was passed on the basis of a simple majority vote, as part of a broader resolution on the implementation of the Assembly's general policies on decolonization.[143] The United States protested against the motion by Mali to that effect, declaring that any question relating to peace and security was an "important" one, requiring a two-thirds majority under Article 18. However, Article 18 also provides for simple-majority determination of "additional categories" of questions to be decided by a two-thirds majority. On the ground that the resolution dealt with colonial matters (not specified in Article 18 as requiring the larger majority), the Mali motion was approved 59–45–4. The United States later declared that the procedure used violated the Charter and rendered the provision on military bases null and void.

The answer to this extremely complex problem (if there is one) does not lie in resisting the pressures for change—even when it is possible "at any given moment," as Professor Michael Howard has pointed out in connection with British base problems east of Suez, to produce "unanswerable" reasons for not seeking new approaches.[144] Attempting to con-

141. U.N. Doc. A/6160, Dec. 13, 1965. The two paragraphs, on separate votes, were adopted 50–26–23 and 50–27–22 in committee, where a simple majority sufficed.

142. A/Res. 2069 (XX), Dec. 16, 1965.

143. A/Res. 2105 (XX), Dec. 20, 1965, adopted 74–6–27. The United States joined Great Britain, Australia, New Zealand, Portugal, and South Africa in voting against the resolution. Paragraph 12 on bases, adopted 49–37–18.

144. "Irony comes too easily. . . . So does the wisdom of hindsight, which asks why we could not have foreseen 15 years ago that the political problems caused by large fixed bases in developing countries would increase as fast as their military utility, in the nuclear age, would diminish; and why a long-range policy of developing a base in

fine the problem within the old framework, so far as concerns the small dependent areas with significant strategic value to the major Western powers, adds one more complication to those that already mark the problem of the "bits-and-pieces" remnants of colonialism.

The Bits-and-Pieces Problem

Aside from the major "hard-core" African cases, where racism and anti-colonialism have combined to transform issues that began as matters of political change into disputes that are now debated in terms of collective enforcement, the remainder of the decolonization problem per se is largely confined to the small, frequently insular, imperial remnants. The frustrations of the hard-core cases have operated to intensify the concern of the Committee of 24 with these small units, which would in any event have drawn increasing attention as the more important colonial territories gradually achieved independence. On the other hand, the strategic aspects of many of these minor dependencies reinforce the colonial powers' denial in principle of competence to the Committee of 24 or the Assembly majority with regard to their future.

The last two Assemblies demonstrated how far that claim of competence has gone. The general resolutions on the implementation of the 1960 Declaration on Colonial Independence, both in 1965 and 1966, declared the continuation of colonial rule and the practice of racial discrimination to be crimes against humanity and threats to international peace. In addition to provisions already noted above, they also recognized "the legitimacy of the struggle of the peoples under colonial rule to exercise their right to self-determination and independence." Moreover, they urged "all states to provide material and moral assistance to the national liberation movements in colonial Territories," as well as to withhold all assistance from Rhodesia, Portugal, and South Africa. On the present subject, they invited the Special Committee to "pay particular attention to the small Territories" and to "recommend to the General Assembly the most appropriate methods as well as the steps to be taken to enable the

---

Northern Australia and a carrier task force for the Indian Ocean was not then set on foot to take their place. But at any given moment the reasons for not doing so seemed unanswerable." Michael Howard, "Britain's Strategic Problem East of Suez," *International Affairs*, Vol. 42 (April 1966), p. 181.

populations of those Territories to exercise fully their right to self-determination and independence."[145]

The Assembly also passed more specific resolutions on a group of twenty-six small island territories that referred to their inalienable right to "self-determination and independence" and "decided" that the United Nations "should render all help to the peoples of these Territories in their efforts freely to decide their future status."[146] The sentiment of the majority clearly interprets that status to require independence. Its actions in regard to Nauru also showed an indifference to any minimum size requirement (either territorially or in population) for statehood.

The number of small colonies that have gained independence, despite their size and political weakness as separate states, and become United Nations Members has already altered the character of the Assembly, shifted its voting balance, and changed the direction of its interests. These tendencies will probably be increased as the remaining minor dependencies follow the precedent of moving toward individual independence. The changes raise serious questions for the future of the Organization to the extent that the pattern set by the resolution on military bases in dependent territories noted above might in time lead to a trend away from the United Nations by the out-voted Western powers. While that likelihood may provide a good argument against the rapid grant of independence to the remaining territories, it is likely to be an academic one in present circumstances. None of the permanent Security Council members has been prepared as yet to veto the admission to the United Nations of what one observer has rather disdainfully called these "small and unfinished states,"[147] although the reasons for communist and noncommunist acceptance of their applications are patently different. For the moment, however, we are only concerned with the preliminary problem of the form their internal political development is likely to take.

145. A/Res. 2105 (XX), Dec. 20, 1965, and A/Res. 2189 (XXI), Dec. 13, 1966.
146. A/Res. 2069 (XX), Dec. 16, 1965, and A/Res. 2232 (XXI), Dec. 20, 1966. The Territories concerned are: American Samoa, Antigua, Bahamas, Bermuda, British Virgin Islands, Caymen Islands, Cocos (Kroling) Islands, Dominica, Gilbert and Ellice Islands, Grenada, Guam, Mauritius, Montserrat, New Hebrides, Nine, Pitcairn, St. Helena, St. Kitts-Neola-Conquilla, St. Lucia, St. Vincent, Seychelles, Solomon Islands, Tokelau Islands, Pacific Islands Trust, Turks and Edicos Islands, and U.S. Virgin Islands.
147. F. H. Hinsley, *Power and the Pursuit of Peace* (Cambridge University Press, 1963), p. 343.

In this connection, New Zealand showed, in the Cook Islands, a possible way to meet the United Nations assertions of competence to consider the fate of "all territories that are not yet independent," as the 1960 declaration put it, without inevitably leading to immediate independence and an application for United Nations membership.

New Zealand (in a novel move concerning a nontrust territory) requested the appointment of a United Nations representative to supervise the 1965 elections to establish full internal self-government in the Cook Islands. When the islanders accepted their constitution, they followed the precedent of Western Samoa (which had been a New Zealand trust) in deciding to leave the conduct of defense and foreign affairs to Wellington. Since the right of reclaiming the direction of those policies is inherent in the arrangement, the requirements of the Committee of 24 for self-determination of "constitutional status" were fully met. Nonetheless, the anticolonial states' suspicions of any status short of independence (and perhaps the committee majority's desire for a more important role) came through in the Assembly resolution accepting the new status of the islanders. It declared that transmission of information under Article 73(e) would no longer be necessary, but added that the Assembly: "Reaffirms the responsibility of the United Nations under General Assembly resolution 1514 (XV) to assist the people of the Cook Islands in the eventual achievement of full independence, if they so wish, at a future date."[148]

Anticolonial suspicions were not the only ones to surface in the course of this episode. The New Zealand request for United Nations supervision of the election came before the nineteenth Assembly, which could not discuss and vote on it under normal procedures, through a memorandum from the Secretary-General. By the "no-objection" method, the Secretary-General was therefore authorized to appoint a commissioner. The Soviet Union, evidently wishing neither to oppose the step nor to raise the Article 19 issue, nevertheless registered its disapproval of the procedure followed (presumably because of the Secretary-General's initiative). The

148. A/Res. 2064 (XX), Dec. 16, 1965. The chairman of Committee IV later asked rhetorically: "How should the results of such an experiment be appraised? Could it serve as a model for future action or, on the contrary, would it be necessary for such experiments to be accompanied in future by additional preparations and guarantees in order the better to protect the sacred right of a people to self-determination?" See U.N. Doc. A/C. 4/664, Dec. 30, 1965, p. 5. For a discussion of the U.N. debate, see Philip M. Allen, "Self-Determination in the Western Indian Ocean," *International Conciliation*, No. 560 (November 1966), pp. 40–49.

Soviet representative wrote to the Assembly President, "not supporting" the proposal without "due consideration" by the plenary organ. In addition, letters from the representatives of Australia, Great Britain, the United States, and France solemnly reserved their governments' positions: in effect, that the action did not constitute a precedent or create any obligation of "general applicability."[149] Since the action was taken at New Zealand's request, they could hardly have objected. Their motivations no doubt combined a general rejection of any United Nations participation with more particular concern about future intervention in their own strategically located dependencies.

The United States Government has been concerned with this issue on both legal and security grounds, since its remaining dependencies consist only of strategic Pacific and Caribbean island territories. In addition, it has with Puerto Rico a unique "commonwealth" relationship (developed to meet the particular situation of that island) that is not in practice essentially different from the New Zealand-Cook Island relationship. It has, however, had some difficulty in obtaining agreement of the Committee of 24 that the island is self-governing.

In 1953, the Assembly approved the cessation of information transmission under Article 73(e) and, by implication, endorsed the commonwealth status as being a fully self-governing one. There is no problem of "denying" full independence to the Puerto Ricans. Those in favor of that status have never been of political consequence in the island; but they have made considerable noise, especially in terms of petitions to the United Nations. Consequently, Puerto Rico not being as "yet independent," the Committee of 24 in recent years has evinced renewed interest in its status although not including it on the agenda for recommendatory action. The United States, in the spring of 1967, succeeded in obtaining an adjournment *sine die* of committee debate on whether to include the island on its agenda—which it interpreted as: "a de facto finding that . . . the question of Puerto Rico is not an appropriate item for the agenda of a Committee which deals with 'decolonization'."[150] On July 23, in a refer-

---

149. U.N. Docs. A/5885, Feb. 16, 1965, A/5893–5895, Feb. 18, 1965, and A/5907, March 9, 1965. The New Zealand request is in U.N. Doc. A/5880, Feb. 9, 1965, and the Secretary-General's memorandum in U.N. Doc. A/5882, Feb. 9, 1965. The Assembly's authorizing action is in A/Res. 2005 (XIX), Feb. 23, 1965. On Dec. 16, 1966 the four joined the communist states in abstaining from the vote on the resolution accepting the results, A/Res. 2064 (XX), which was passed 78–0–29.

150. USUN Press Release 45, April 19, 1967.

endum on the future of their island, Puerto Ricans chose to retain the commonwealth status by a wide margin.

Decolonization and "Neo-Colonialism"

"Colonialism, except in the Russian empire, is transient and after a few more years of emotionalism it should not longer distort the outlook of the United Nations," the British Foreign Secretary optimistically predicted at the end of 1961. If the analysis of this chapter has any validity, however, that rosy estimate is unlikely to prove accurate.

Even in the narrowest constitutional sense, the hard-core African cases seem sure to give plenty of difficulty for some time longer. Blame for the increasing difficulties over Portuguese, Rhodesian, and South African policies (as well as for the many less significant cases) has often been laid by Western officials on the communists, working subversively and aided and abetted by "irresponsible" anticolonial states in the United Nations. But the order of events in colonial areas, or in such places as Panama, makes it evident that the spread of communist influence has been more the consequence than the cause of nationalist movements. Communists, true to their tradition, have been alert to muddy the waters wherever an unstable situation provided an opening, whether before or after independence. And Western powers have been so cooperative, on occasion, as to reinforce the usefulness of their "capitalist-imperialist" propaganda by blaming all nationalist unrest on communist agitation.

The colonial powers have also been offended by the continuous pressures on them in the United Nations to hasten the day of independence, especially when viewed against what seems to them the indifference of many delegations to the "colonial" sins of the communists. The British Foreign Minister, for example, complained in December 1961 that whereas "the Russian empire . . . is ruled by fear," the British were moving, "perhaps faster than in prudence we ought in the direction in which the new countries want to go"; yet the United Nations "seldom condemn the Russians and constantly harass us."[151]

There are two main reasons the Western effort to tag the communists with a colonial label has failed to impress most of the newer states. First

151. Lord Home, speech at Berwick-upon-Tweed, excerpts in *New York Times*, Dec. 29, 1961.

is the language in which the attack is couched. In the great debate of 1960, for example, it was the Soviet bloc, not the uncommitted delegations, which responded with angry outbursts to any reference to communist "colonialism."[152] The United States referred to the Soviet Union's absorption of East European states, such as Estonia, and to its domination of other nominally independent governments, as the "new colonialism" that denies its subjects both self-determination as nations and personal rights as individuals;[153] but none of this carried much apparent weight.

For one thing, the percentage of Nigerians aware of Estonia, as an example, must be at least as low as the percentage of Americans aware of the difference between Niger and Nigeria. But more significant is the fact that such cases as Poland are not colonies from the point of view of delegates from a former "true" colony, in the sense of having been legally subordinate and governed by people of another color. Communist governments have the trappings of independent sovereign states; their representatives sit in the Assembly and noisily protest the Western claims; they often exchange diplomatic missions and carry on negotiations, trade, and even aid programs. Russians dominating Czechs thus do not meet the traditional requirements of the hated imperialism; while Soviet control of the Kurile Islands is not evident to delegates preoccupied with active petitioners from all sorts of other nonindependent areas, including Puerto Rico, for example.[154]

Secondly, as noted earlier, a more effective approach through attacking Soviet policy in relation to properly "colonial" areas, such as the Kurile Islands, has been foreclosed to a great extent because the Western colonial states originally objected to any international concern with their possessions. Having insisted on an essentially voluntary system to start

152. Khrushchev's famous shoe-thumping histrionics was in reaction to a suggestion by the Philippine delegate that the Soviet draft resolution should also cover "the inalienable right to independence" of Eastern Europeans "swallowed up, so to speak, by the Soviet Union." This set in motion a series of manifestations of displeasure by desk-thumping East European delegates, culminating in the Khrushchev performance.

153. Similar language was used by President Kennedy in addressing the Assembly in 1961. See U.S. Department of State, *Bulletin*, Vol. 45 (1961), p. 622.

154. On one occasion, the Japanese representative requested circulation, as an official committee document, of his memorandum taking issue with a Soviet declaration that Japan had relinquished all rights and claims to the Kurile Islands, and had been unwilling to conclude a peace treaty. "The fact is," the memorandum declared, "that Japan has consistently sought the return of territories that are inherently Japanese, while the Soviet Union has persistently refused to negotiate . . . on the pretext that the territorial issues are already settled." U.N. Doc. A/AC. 109/109, Nov. 20, 1964, p. 3.

with, then listed most of their possessions as dependent territories and fought the extension of United Nations concern in respect to them, they have not been in the best position to benefit from Soviet failure to acknowledge its own postwar territorial acquisitions. Time has changed many things, however, including the relative "voluntariness" of the metropole's situation in relation to the world Organization—as Portugal and South Africa so dramatically show. Providing the remaining colonial powers were willing to accept greater United Nations participation in their own affairs, therefore, they would have a stronger talking point about the "reactionary" policy of the communists. As one experienced observer of these developments commented some years ago: "In the not distant future, it is possible that it will appear paradoxical that states with colonial interests should have tried to narrow the competence of United Nations organs by an expansive interpretation of the reservations contained in Article 2(7)."[155]

On "Neo-Colonialism"

If the newer states have been generally indifferent to Western charges of a new "Soviet colonialism," they seem to many Western governments to have been deplorably susceptible to Soviet charges that the leading Western powers are shifting from the old imperialism to a predominantly economic form of colonialism. "Neo-colonialism," as it has been dubbed by the communists, is a relatively new term; but the concept is a familiar one to the United States, which has been accustomed to similar accusations of "dollar diplomacy" within the Western Hemisphere since before the days of communist challenges. There is, however, an additional modern slant to the new phrase:

The genesis of "neo-colonialism" might be described in horsebreeding terms as by Communism out of Embarrassment. It was Lenin's argument that capi-

155. Benjamin V. Cohen, *The United Nations: Constitutional Developments, Growth and Possibilities* (Harvard University Press, 1961), p. 27. Western criticism of the Committee of 24 is also heard in terms of its alleged indifference to claims of self-determination and human rights other than in connection with the colonial relationship. On one occasion, for example, when the committee was criticized for not concerning itself with "problems such as the Somali-Ethiopian-Kenyan dispute," as it did with the defense of "the Africans in Southern Rhodesia against the perpetuation of white supremacy," its then Chairman argued that "the alleged duality of approach" was nonexistent. "The Committee's mandate was to deal with dependent territories, and not with independent countries. It therefore had to limit itself to the question of outside domination." See Swift, ed., *op. cit.*, p. 21.

talist countries depended economically on the exploitation of colonial territories. Thus if colonies freed themselves of the imperialist yoke, the economies
of the ex-colonial powers would collapse. But as, one after the other, colonial
territories in Africa and Asia achieved independence, the predicted collapse
of the "exploiters" did not follow. Hence, the embarrassment. A reason had to
be found for this unfortunate defiance of what in the Communist canon was a
natural law. The reason must be that the capitalist powers were still, by subtler
means, exploiting the former colonies. So "neo-colonialism" was born.[156]

Marxian dialectics aside, however, the shift in terminology reflects a
shift in attack from political to economic factors in the colonial relationship and in the character of relationships between the weak new states and
the strong imperial powers. In connection with both the hard-core cases
and the remaining small dependencies, for example, the Assembly's resolutions in the past few years have tended to give increased and condemnatory attention to

the activities of those foreign financial and economic interests in colonial
Territories, in particular in South West Africa, Southern Rhodesia, and the
Territories under Portuguese domination, which support colonial regimes and
thus constitute a serious obstacle to the implementation of the [1960] Declaration . . . , and [to call] upon the Governments concerned to take the necessary
measures to put an end to these activities.[157]

As the old colonial system moves off the scene, it is being succeeded by
new relationships involving a multiplicity of weak, politically unstable,
and economically undeveloped states, with a resulting international dis-
equilibrium that, as many have noted, has led to most of the threats to
peace and the outbreaks of violence discussed in this study. The future
problem of peaceful adjustment and change will therefore be as much a
matter of the internal development and modernization of those new and
weak states as of the stabilization of relations among them, or between
them and the more powerful states. Peaceful adjustment in the interests
of political change, as this chapter has shown, has been almost as difficult
to bring about (from the viewpoint of the United States) in dealing with
allies and with the uncommitted states as in negotiating with the communists. It is not likely to become less so in the foreseeable future, within
the framework of either the end of the imperial, or the beginning of the
post-imperial, world.

156. NATO Letter, October 1965, p. 29, review of Brian Crozier, Neo-Colonialism
(London: The Bodley Head, 1964).
157. A/Res. 2189 (XXI), Dec. 13, 1966. The resolution also put an item on such
activities on the agenda of the 22nd Assembly.

CHAPTER EIGHT

THE "RULE OF LAW"
AND THE CONTROL OF FORCE

A "world community under law," the "rule of law," "world peace through world law," "world order under law," or "enforceable world law"—the manifold expressions of the goal, it has been pointed out, fail to identify its meaning: "The people of the United States are often favored with flights of oratory extolling the 'rule of law' among the nations, but practical action to achieve it has largely remained grounded. One reason is a lack of agreement as to the meaning of the phrase. Is it an objective, a program of action, or merely a slogan?"[1] It is an elucidation of the obvious to point out that "rule of law" in the international context is not synonymous with a legal order in the national sense (that is, complete with legislative and executive organs as well); that the applicability of law to settle disputes is much narrower in the international, than in the national, area; and that the problems of extending its rule are quite different in nature. Yet many who are aware of those differences, including some members of the legal profession, are advocates of plans for vast extensions of the rule of law as the means to a peaceful world community. Internationally, as nationally, however, law operates in the community. It does not create it.[2]

As noted in Chapter 2, the development of law under the United Nations has been least in the field of international peace and security. Until there is more consensus on the political objectives to be sought, and

1. Ernest A. Gross, *The United Nations: Structure for Peace* (Harper, 1962), p. 117.
2. "The essence of the rule of law ideal lies . . . not in technical law as such, but rather in the supremacy of certain ethical convictions, certain rules of decency prevalent in the community, and in the psychological fact that those who are at the apex of power share those convictions and feel bound to conform to them. A duly enacted statute to liquidate H.M.'s Opposition would violate 'the rule of law,' not because it would not be lawyers' 'law,' but because it isn't Britishers' 'cricket.'" Julius Stone, *Quest for Survival: The Role of Law and Foreign Policy* (Harvard University Press, 1961), p. 4.

on the standards of conduct to be enforced, international law cannot, in Ambassador Goldberg's words, "tame the forces of change and keep them peaceful."[3]

It is not the purpose of the present chapter to examine systematically how international law has (and has not) developed over the past twenty years. Other chapters have illustrated some of those legal developments and some of the areas where the existence of fundamental controversy still impedes the growth of accepted rules. The pages that follow discuss other aspects of law and the maintenance of international peace that seem especially pertinent to this study of United States-United Nations relations. For that reason, the failure of the United States, among others, to accept the compulsory jurisdiction of the International Court of Justice without qualifications is discussed. Also considered are the broader issues concerning the extension of an international juridical regime and the changing substance of international law. The effectiveness of the Court is not necessarily correlative with the rule of law; but such rule would necessarily include an effective court. Unwillingness by states to accept the Court's jurisdiction, therefore, may be taken as an indication of lack of willingness to submit to the much broader rule of third-party settlement that is implied in the ideal of world order under law.

Jurisdiction of the International Court

One of the main purposes of the United Nations is formally declared to be "to bring about by peaceful means, and in conformity with the principles of justice and international law, adjustment or settlement of international disputes or situations which might lead to a breach of the peace." To achieve this end, the International Court of Justice was established as a principal organ, its Statute was made "an integral part" of the Charter, and all Members of the United Nations ipso facto became parties thereto. The Members in turn were reminded that "legal disputes should as a general rule be referred by the parties to the International Court," in accordance with this Statute. The General Assembly was to encourage "the progressive development of international law and its codification" through studies and recommendations, the approval of draft conventions for submission to Members, and its own general declarations of principle.[4] All

3. U.S. Department of State, *Bulletin*, Vol. 54 (1966), p. 937.
4. Arts. 1(1); 7, 92, 93; 36(3); 13(1a).

of these would enlarge the body of agreed jurisprudence. Moreover, the Organization and the specialized agencies, through their cumulative bodies of practice and precedent, would directly add to the substance of law and custom.

Despite the United Nations machinery, the commitments of Members, and the extraordinary increase in treaties and agreements in force,[5] the hope that the new Court would move beyond the advances of the Permanent Court of International Justice has not been fulfilled. Relatively few cases have been submitted to the International Court, most of them unimportant. Resort to it for advisory opinions on legal aspects of disputes before the political organs has not been frequent, nor have the opinions always served to facilitate settlement of the disputes.[6]

The reason for this paradoxical situation—the declining application of international law at a time of greater commitment to its development than ever before—must be sought fundamentally in the revolutionary nature of the times. As former Secretary of State Dean Acheson has pointed out: "Withdrawal of the legal order occurs in all revolutionary situations. People are no longer content to 'pursue and realize values in an orderly way.' They are in a hurry. They pursue and realize new values in a disorderly way. Order has become an impediment. The sanction for law has disappeared."[7] This situation is currently reflected in a broad refusal to accept many of the conventional legal standards that prevailed during the League period, while there has as yet been no development of generally agreed new standards. A consequence of this situation is that states reject broader jurisdiction for the Court in the settlement of disputes because the uncertain "content of international law in a rapidly changing world . . . often makes international litigation . . . into a game of chance."[8] The problems of jurisdiction and of substance are thus interdependent; but they are discussed separately here because of the particular United States position on compulsory jurisdiction.

5. Secretary Rusk referred, for example, to the "4300 treaties and international agreements" to which the U.S. is signatory, of which "three-fourths . . . were signed in the past 25 years." U.S. Department of State, *Bulletin*, Vol. 53 (1965), p. 693.

6. See Shabtai Rosenne, "The Court and the Judicial Process," *International Organization*, Vol. 19 (Summer 1965), pp. 522–26 and 530–32 for discussion of the use of advisory competence in the development of U.N. law.

7. Dean Acheson, "The Lawyer's Path to Peace," Lecture at University of Virginia, May 7, 1966, p. 4 (mimeo.).

8. Stone, *op. cit.*, p. 17.

COMPULSORY JURISDICTION AND
THE CONNALLY AMENDMENT

The San Francisco Conference, in the face of Soviet and American adamant opposition to compulsory jurisdiction, adopted an optional jurisdiction system for the International Court of Justice.[9] At the same time, however, it recommended that Members individually and as soon as possible accept the compulsory jurisdiction of the Court in legal disputes, through adherence to the optional clause of Article 36 of its Statute.[10] Although a majority of delegations at San Francisco had favored compulsory jurisdiction for the Court, only forty-four states had accepted such jurisdiction by 1967. And many of those (including the United States) had qualified their declarations of acceptance by serious reservations.

Senate reluctance to accept Court jurisdiction in the limited area of legal disputes under paragraph 36(2) went back to nationalistic fears arising out of misunderstanding of the powers of the Permanent Court of International Justice to "intervene" in domestic affairs. These fears had defeated every effort to gain United States adherence to the Statute of that Court. As those efforts had been initiated by the Executive branch (under both Democratic and Republican administrations), the fears had combined with congressional jealousy of its powers vis-à-vis the Executive, more specifically, with Senate suspicion of the President's treaty-making power.

Senator Arthur Vandenberg, thinking back to earlier Senate refusals to adhere to the Statute of the Permanent Court, had argued at San Francisco that "any form of compulsory jurisdiction might endanger American ratification" of the Charter.[11] The Senate's qualified acceptance of the

9. For events at San Francisco, see Ruth B. Russell, *A History of the United Nations Charter: The Role of the United States, 1940–1945* (Brookings Institution, 1958), pp. 877–88, 884–90.

10. Art. 36(2) obligates states to accept the Court's jurisdiction "in relation to any other state accepting the same obligation" in all legal disputes concerning: "(a) the interpretation of a treaty; (b) any question of international law; (c) the existence of any fact which, if established, would constitute a breach of an international obligation; (d) the nature or extent of the reparation to be made for the breach of an international obligation."

Art. 36(6) declares: "In the event of a dispute as to whether the Court has jurisdiction, the matter shall be settled by the decision of the Court."

11. Arthur H. Vandenberg, Jr., ed., *The Private Papers of Senator Vandenberg* (Houghton Mifflin, 1952) p. 164.

optical clause in 1946 showed that it had not advanced beyond the fears of the 1930's. The significant reservation, sponsored by Senator Tom Connally, provided that the Court's jurisdiction should not automatically apply to: "(b) disputes with regard to matters which are essentially within the domestic jurisdiction of the United States of America as determined by the United States of America."[12] Practically speaking, this self-judging clause negated the United States commitment in principle.

After World War II, fear of Executive treaty authority was manifest in Senator Bricker's proposed amendment to declare ineffective any "provision of a treaty which conflicts with" the Constitution; and to subject treaties and executive agreements, before becoming effective as internal law in the United States, to "legislation which would be valid in the absence of a treaty."[13] Such limitations on the treaty-making power were resisted by both the Truman and Eisenhower administrations, yet the Bricker amendment was defeated in 1953 by only one vote.[14] In such an atmosphere, the Executive made no further attempt to obtain repeal of the Connally reservation until 1959, after subsidence of the xenophobia of the McCarthy era.

Even so, in the 1960 hearings on a resolution of repeal, the testimony, "inaccurate to the point of misrepresentation," showed the continuing prevalence of an almost pathological fear among many urging retention of the reservation, lest "unlimited power" be vested in a "communist infested World Court" that could jeopardize the security of the nation.[15]

12. S. Res. 196 (79 Cong. 2 sess.), Aug. 2, 1946. Reservation (a) was unexceptionable, simply reserving disputes "the solution of which the parties shall entrust to other tribunals." Reservation (c) excepted disputes "arising under a multilateral treaty, unless (1) all parties . . . affected by the decision are also parties to the case before the Court, or (2) the U.S.A. specifically agrees to jurisdiction." This was offered by Vandenberg primarily to prevent any dispute under an inter-American treaty from being brought before the International Court without U.S. consent. In 1946, the postwar inter-American treaty system had not yet been developed, but it was clear that basic reorganization was in the offing. The reservation was probably intended as a broad, safeguarding general reservation, rather than being related to any specific situation. Whatever the original intent, it had no subsequent use or even notice of any kind.

13. S.J. Res. 1, *Congressional Record*, Vol. 99, Pt. 1, 83 Cong. 1 sess. (1953), p. 160.

14. For an account of the episode, see Marquis Childs, *Eisenhower: Captive Hero* (Harcourt, 1958), p. 184.

15. See Herbert W. Briggs, "Confidence, Apprehension, and the International Court of Justice," American Society of International Law, *Proceedings*, Vol. 54 (1960), p. 29; also *International Court of Justice, Compulsory Jurisdiction*, Hearings before the Senate Foreign Relations Committee, 86 Cong. 2 sess. (1960).

Former Senator Connally personally denounced the idea of repeal as a "propaganda device," designed "to win an international popularity contest."[16] Despite strong administration support for repeal, vocal public sentiment remained largely hostile.

No direct action on the repeal resolution was taken, therefore, in 1960. The Senate's attitude was indicated in May, however, when it consented to ratification (77–4) of four conventions resulting from the United Nations Conference on the Law of the Sea, held in 1958.[17] An "Optional Protocol of Signature concerning the Compulsory Settlement of Disputes" in addition provided for the jurisdiction of the Court in disputes arising under the conventions or, at the parties' preference, for submission to conciliation or arbitration procedures. This the Senate rejected (49–30), on the ground that it failed to contain the Connally reservation.[18] With contentious political issues omitted from the accords, it did indeed seem, as the Washington Post put it, "inconceivable that issues arising under the law of the sea could be reasonably considered domestic."[19]

The issue has not been formally raised again by the Executive branch, although both the Kennedy and Johnson administrations have followed the path of their predecessors in informally favoring repeal of the Connally amendment. Secretary Rusk has also regretted the reluctance of United Nations Members to accord the International Court of Justice compulsory jurisdiction to settle disputes arising from treaties concluded under the auspices of the United Nations.[20] Nonetheless, the Legislative branch, determining United States policy in this case, puts members of the Executive branch in an awkward position when advocating in the abstract extended resort to the Court.

In view of official policy, it is ironical to note that a case between France and Norway provided the occasion for the Court to turn the American safeguard into a boomerang, by finding that on the basis of

16. New York Times, Feb. 18, 1960.

17. None covered the controversial issues of breadth of the territorial sea or of fishery limits, on which the conference could reach no agreement. Congressional Record, Vol. 106, Pt. 19, 86 Cong. 2 sess. (1960), p. 11192.

18. Ibid., p. 11193.

19. News item, May 28, 1960. It is also communist policy to sign conventions that provide for Court settlement of disputes over their terms with a reservation rejecting that provision. See Rosalyn Higgins, Conflict of Interest: International Law in a Divided World (Dufour, 1965), p. 154.

20. Comments on presentation of the Manley O. Hudson medal to International Court Judge Philip C. Jessup, American Society of International Law, Proceedings (1965), p. 259.

reciprocity both parties are entitled to invoke a self-judging reservation even if only one has formally so qualified its acceptance of the Court's jurisdiction.[21] Thus, a reservation aimed to keep other governments from taking the United States into Court can be used by the other party to avoid jurisdiction whenever Washington wants to submit some dispute of its own.[22] As the United States Solicitor General declared in 1960, the Court's decision had "materially changed" the situation originally contemplated by the Senate:

It is now apparent that the reservation cannot be effective for its purposes and will be most damaging to the proper protection of the interests of the United States and its citizens in dealing with other nations and their nationals. It is time that we recognized the need to eliminate the [Connally] reservation as France did in its own interests. Prompt action might avoid serious embarrassment to our position in support of the rule of law and at the same time gain the protection the Court can afford to both the country and its people.[23]

The argument clearly did not impress the senators that year.

Repeal of the Connally reservation would thus remove a conflict between United States precept and practice, and would increase its ability to give effective leadership in trying to extend the sway of the Court, in the limited area under Article 36 of the Statute, among basically likeminded states. As Secretary of State Dulles said, when preparing to urge Congress to remove the Connally limitation:

There is serious need for all of us to develop a respect for law as a basis for stability and confidence. Those nations which do have common standards should, by their conduct and example, advance the rule of law by submitting

21. France had copied the U.S. (Connally) reservation in its acceptance of compulsory jurisdiction. Norway claimed peremptory domestic jurisdiction in this case, although it had not made a general reservation of its own. The Court found Norway equally entitled to invoke the right and therefore that it had no jurisdiction (*I.C.J. Report* 9, 1957). As a consequence of this case, France later withdrew its earlier reservation and in 1959 deposited a new one reserving only "disputes relating to questions which, by international law, fall exclusively within domestic jurisdiction."

22. The United States has suffered from this situation on three occasions when it sought to bring communist governments before the Court in connection with "aerial incidents" (involving American aircraft and crews): (1) in Hungary; (2) with Czech aircraft over the U.S. Zone of Germany; and (3) with Soviet aircraft over Japanese territory. On each occasion, the other government maintained the Court should not deal with the question; and the Court consequently removed the cases from its list. Since Washington knew this would be the result, its actions were presumably taken primarily for propaganda effect rather than with any expectation of judicial results.

23. Excerpts from speech by J. Lee Rankin, *Washington Post*, July 5, 1960.

their disputes to the International Court of Justice, or to some other international tribunal upon which they can agree.[24]

At the same time, it must be recognized that cleaning our own hands (if and when we do so) would not suddenly change the now well-established habit of undue reservations, nor eliminate the even more resistant differences among nations over the content of that international law which the Court must apply. Moreover, the likelihood of repeal seems as remote as ever at this writing, which should give Washington pause before criticizing other governments that may not always support its moves to "strengthen" international law, as in the peacekeeping case.[25]

EXTENSION OF JURISDICTION

There are various ways in which the Court's jurisdiction in legal matters might be extended. If the United Nations itself is, as Adlai Stevenson characterized it, the "first step toward a world under law,"[26] a logical second step would be the fulfillment of the San Francisco Conference recommendation (renewed by the Assembly in 1947) urging universal acceptance of compulsory jurisdiction. No Charter or Statute amendment would be required to achieve this aim, which is a matter of persuasion.[27]

One objection raised to such a general acceptance of compulsory jurisdiction, especially by many new states, is that they cannot submit to adjudication on the basis of substantive rules of law that they have not expressly recognized or did not participate in developing. As Denmark noted a few years ago, however:

Without expressing an opinion on the general merits of [the above] argument, the Danish Government wishes to point out that [it] cannot reasonably be applied to rules of law elaborated within the framework of the United Nations, particularly as part of the general work of codification.

It is therefore with considerable concern that the Danish Government has seen two successive United Nations conferences—that in 1958 on the Law of the Sea, and that of 1961 on Diplomatic Intercourse and Immunities—reject

24. U.S. Department of State, *Bulletin*, Vol. 40 (1959), p. 259.
25. See Chaps. 6 and 9.
26. U.S. Department of State, *Bulletin*, Vol. 45 (1961), p. 68.
27. It has also been suggested, however, that the end might be attained through changing the Statute to give the Court jurisdiction, on the application of one party, in all international legal controversies that diplomacy fails to settle. This does not seem very realistic: Why would it be simpler than a Charter amendment making compulsory jurisdiction of the Court standard? Or than general acceptance of the optional clause? See Arthur N. Holcombe, Chairman, Commission to Study the Organization of Peace, *Strengthening the United Nations* (Harper, 1957), pp. 82, 91.

proposals for the compulsory judicial settlement of disputes arising out of the interpretation and application of the conventions adopted by these conferences, and relegate the clauses on compulsory jurisdiction to optional protocols which have been signed by a limited number of States only and which, by their optional character, are the very negation of a general compulsory system of judicial settlement.[28]

As already noted, the United States and the Soviet Union joined the newer states in thus helping to "negate" the extension of the Court's jurisdiction. The new states also join the communist countries in a widespread feeling that the Court is "a western-dominated or at least 'unrepresentative' body"[29]—a feeling that can only have been enhanced by the judgment of the Court in 1966 on the South West African case.

Another step advocated to promote the habit of utilizing the Court is that both Security Council and General Assembly should make greater use of its advisory authority. The number of advisory opinions requested has not been large—twelve, three of them dealing with the international status of the former League mandate of South West Africa—and, unlike experience with the Permanent Court, "the advisory competence has not been employed as part of the procedure for the pacific settlement of disputes." It has, rather, been used to elucidate "a series of major issues of constitutional interpretation" and the clarification of various legal questions.[30] This trend has not met with universal approval, Shabtai Rosenne noting for example that:

In retrospect it seems that some of the advisory opinions, which related to highly controversial situations, were put to the Court with excessive enthusiasm. . . . Until [the constitutional principles can be more firmly drawn] . . . it may be hoped that recourse to the advisory competence will be limited to those situations . . . in which the legal factors predominate over the political and where the immediate controversy is not too strident. . . .[31]

28. U.N. Doc. A/4796/Add. 1, July 26, 1961, pp. 7–8.

29. Edward McWhinney, "The 'New' Countries and the 'New' International Law: The United Nations Special Conference on Friendly Relations and Cooperation among States," *American Journal of International Law*, Vol. 60 (January 1966), p. 81.

30. Rosenne, *op. cit.*, p. 524.

31. *Ibid.*, p. 532. Secretary Rusk, on the other hand, has spoken approvingly of this role of the Court as "especially valuable and effective. . . . There has developed, though not fully enough, a tradition of referring constitutional issues arising under the charters of international organizations to the Court for adjudication. And more important, there has arisen also a tradition of accepting the Court's opinions as law and acting upon them." The Secretary's remark was made in November 1964, however, well before the United States changed its position on applying Article 19 in the peacekeeping expenses case. In view of the aftermath of the opinion in this case, more frequent recourse to advisory opinions is unlikely in the near future.

There is some feeling in areas outside of Europe that the International Court is too remote from the contending parties. Establishment of regional courts is therefore sometimes proposed to facilitate use of an international tribunal. If inaccessibility were the crucial difficulty, however, presumably states that avoided the World Court would tend to agree to arbitral arrangements for the settlement of disputes. But such a development has also been notable for its absence in the postwar world. It is, once again, the substance rather than the machinery of the law that is considered inadequate by many governments. Sufficient means exist to establish courts (on a regional or any other specialized basis) whenever the desire for them is felt. This was the case with the European Court of Human Rights under the European Convention on Human Rights, and the Court of the European Communities under the Treaty of Rome. When other groups of states reach the same degree of common consent that the members of these European Courts have attained, further development along such lines may be looked for. This does not seem likely in the near future.

ENFORCEMENT OF COURT DECISIONS

Because of the essentially voluntary jurisdiction of both the Permanent Court and the International Court, the problem of enforcement has never been a serious one. Parties in dispute have not taken their more difficult controversies to the Courts; and in less controversial cases, those willing to submit to judicial decision also tend to give effect even to an unfavorable award, which is binding. It has been pointed out, however, that:

Should there be a wider acceptance of compulsory jurisdiction—as through compromissory clauses in treaties or declarations under Article 36, paragraph 2, of the Statute—the chances of nonperformance would almost certainly increase; for it is evident that a state would not then be as prepared to accept an adverse decision as where it had agreed to the submission of a particular dispute.[32]

In any event, although judgments may not be challenged openly, they have not always been executed in full compliance with their terms.

32. Oscar Schachter, "The Enforcement of International Judicial and Arbitral Decisions," *American Journal of International Law*, Vol. 54 (1960), p. 5. See also R. P. Anand, "Execution of International Judicial Awards: Experience since 1945," *University of Pittsburgh Law Review*, Vol. 26 (June 1965), pp. 674–75.

In earlier days, international law permitted the use of force by one state to compel another to adhere to what the latter might consider an arbitral award against its interests. The Covenant empowered the Council of the League of Nations to propose steps, if necessary, to give effect to a decision of the Permanent Court. At San Francisco, the obligation of states to comply with decisions of the International Court was written into the Charter without opposition. But beyond that, difficulties emerged over proposals to authorize the Security Council to enforce the execution of Court decisions.

Even a permissively worded proposal by China was originally opposed by the Soviet Union and the United States.[33] Their position was consistent with their opposition to any equivalent grant of authority for the political organs to "impose" other forms of peaceful-settlement decisions in connection with political disputes and situations. To have made the Security Council an enforcement agency for the Court, moreover, would seem to have given the Organization a supranational aspect inconsistent with 1945 concepts of the nature of the United Nations system. At the same time, the Charter would no longer allow the use of force to states for the purpose of national enforcement of Court decisions. The right of resort to the Council by an aggrieved state was therefore written into Article 94(2), in terms essentially those of the permissive Chinese proposal. Enforcement action by the Council was made discretionary, the implication being that it would be considered necessary only when failure to execute a Court judgment created a threat to the peace; but refusal to comply with a court decision in a case with highly contentious political overtones, such as that of South West Africa, would undoubtedly be considered by many Members action constituting a threat to the peace. That need not lead to Security Council action, of course, as the decision would be subject to the veto, which might be applied for purely political reasons. The Court's decision in the South West African case, as previously noted, avoided the merits of the case, so that the possibility of testing the issue of enforcement awaits another day.

What is more serious is that the nature of the Court's action will in all probability have "unhappy consequences from the point of view of the

33. "If any party to a dispute fails to comply with the judgment of the International Court of Justice, the Security Council may, upon application by the other party or parties concerned, take such action as it may deem necessary to give effect to the judgment." Quoted in Russell, *op. cit.*, p. 892.

progressive development of the rule of law in the international field."[34] This will be true politically, in spite of the fact that the judgment was of such limited scope that it did not touch on the legal issues of South African policies in the mandate. It therefore did not, in the view of the Department of State, diminish the "legal authority" of earlier advisory opinions. In those, the Court established that:

> The Mandate continues in effect and that South Africa cannot alter the status of the Territory without the consent of the United Nations, that South Africa continues to be bound under the Mandate to accept United Nations supervision, to submit annual reports and to forward petitions to the United Nations General Assembly, as well as to "promote to the utmost the material and moral wellbeing and the social progress of the inhabitants."

Although the United States declared it would "continue to support the authority of the Opinions and Judgments of the Court as to those questions on which it has passed,"[35] the political problem of how to enforce the legal obligations South Africa now ignores remains as difficult as that of applying the political decisions of the Assembly.

Proposals To Extend the Rule of Law

Turning from the problems of extending the jurisdiction of international judicial organs in legal matters, we find two categories of proposals to expand the rule of law in the sense of achieving an orderly world under law. Going beyond the strictly legal area in the search for peace through judicial means, one kind of proposal would provide for the compulsory settlement by a court of political, as well as legal, disputes. The other approach finds the existing international legal system inherently so inadequate to the needs of a peaceful world, that it proposes a complete and radical replacement.

COMPULSORY SETTLEMENT OF ALL DISPUTES

Proposals to expand the rule of law by extending the jurisdiction of judicial or arbitral tribunals on a compulsory basis may seek, in effect, to

34. Prime Minister Lester B. Pearson, Aug. 9, 1966 address to American Bar Association, *New York Times,* Aug. 10, 1966.

35. U.S. Department of State Press Release 176, July 27, 1966, "Statement Concerning the South West Africa Case Judgment of the International Court of Justice of July 18, 1966."

cover all political disputes, as well as legal ones; or, on a somewhat narrower basis, to bring at least all disputes growing out of treaties under similar jurisdiction through individual treaty provisions to that end.

In the League period, the effort to guarantee peaceful settlement of all disputes came to a head in 1928, in the "General Act for the Pacific Settlement of International Disputes."[36] This was a model treaty draft for the settlement of all disputes by any of several methods (conciliation, arbitration, and judicial settlement), which states could subscribe to in order to improve the system for preserving peace.[37] The General Act, however, was not widely accepted and was therefore of little practical value. In 1949, in an effort to encourage wider use of pacific-settlement means, the General Assembly restored the General Act to its original efficacy and opened it again to accession by states. It is no more effective under the United Nations than it was under the League.

The year before, the Ninth Inter-American Conference sought to apply the same approach within the Western Hemisphere. The "Pact of Bogota"[38] provided that any dispute between countries of the region not settled by adjudication or some agreed procedure, should be submitted to compulsory arbitration. The Latin American governments, however, also managed to incorporate, in Article VII, the "Calvo doctrine."[39] This climaxed a long-fought legal controversy with the United States over the traditional doctrine enabling foreigners to claim greater rights than nationals in the protection of private investment.[40] Article VII would

36. It had been preceded in 1924 by the "Protocol of Geneva," which sought to provide for compulsory adjudication, arbitration, or settlement by the League Council of all disputes not resolved through diplomacy. The protocol failed of ratification.

37. Drawn up in the same year as the Kellogg-Briand Pact, in which states renounced force as an instrument of national policy except in self-defense, the two theoretically provided a logical and complete system for maintaining the peace.

38. Text in U.S. Department of State, "Report of the Delegation of the U.S.A.," *Ninth International Conference of American States*, Bogota, Colombia, March 30–May 2, 1948, Publication 3262 (November 1948), p. 188.

39. Under the "Calvo Doctrine," developed by Latin American states, foreign investment becomes domesticated on entry into the country, entitled only to equal treatment with local investment if expropriated, and without legal standing to invoke diplomatic protection by the investor's government. To retain full freedom of action on a matter of internal policy, according to their way of thinking, Latin American governments have generally refused to make international commitments inconsistent with this conception, even when in practice they have treated such investments satisfactorily. See Stanley D. Metzger, "The Nature and Extent of Legal Limitations upon a Nation's Freedom of Action," *Wisconsin Law Review* (March 1961), pp. 287–88.

40. In the heyday of "dollar diplomacy" such protection, sanctioned by international law, might include military intervention or foreign fiscal control in countries deemed by the United States to be delinquent in some respect.

thus have meant an unacceptable change in the legal rule still upheld by Washington. The United States objected that the subject was irrelevant to the treaty and, by entering a reservation against the article when signing, effectively destroyed its value for the other American governments.

In view of League and United Nations experience, it is doubtful that the Pact of Bogota, even without Article VII, would have brought about an era of pacific settlement throughout the hemisphere. In any event, the treaty was not submitted to the Senate in this country, for consent to ratification, nor did it fare much better with other OAS members.

In neither a regional nor universal framework have such generalized commitments to compulsory arbitration of nonjusticiable disputes been effective. This is because, as Professor Stone has succinctly pointed out: "In its main meaning a dispute is nonjusticiable if in the view of one or both of the disputant States, the interests at stake are so important as to override any condition of the law."[41] Proposals attempting to force such vital-interest disputes into a legal mold also overlook a point made by Judge DeVisscher: "There is no doubt that a part of the present disappointment with regard to international justice is due to the survival of a state of mind which has exaggerated the possibilities of recourse to courts for the maintenance of peace."[42] Such "exaggerated possibilities" are clearly reflected in the hortatory school of rule-of-law proponents.

LAW BY EXHORTATION

Most advocates of rapid and radical expansion of the dominion of international law within the near future base their optimistic proposals on the pessimistic assumption that, since war is now horrible beyond contemplation, law is therefore the only alternative. Supreme Court Justice William Douglas, for one, argues that:

The tools with which we can evolve a "rule of law" into a more mature system are at hand [if there] is only the will to use them. Why do nations hold back? Why are we not willing to take the lead in inaugurating a truly golden age for international law? We could, I think, do it, if we asserted the moral leadership of which we so often boast. We need more commitment and less lip service. World opinion is ready to be marshaled. Small nations quiver on the sidelines as they watch giant rivals spar, threaten, and shake their nuclear fists. The

41. Stone, *op. cit.*, p. 8.
42. Charles DeVisscher (formerly on the International Court), "Reflections on the Present Prospects of International Adjudication," *American Journal of International Law*, Vol. 50 (July 1956), p. 471.

world is filled with such a sense of insecurity that for the first time in history solid foundations for a "rule of law" can be laid.[43]

This school more commonly, however, considers existing machinery (both legal and political) inadequate and therefore advocates radical innovations in, as well as expansion of, legal machinery and jurisdiction. Starting from the conviction that the "key to war prevention is disarmament, general and complete," the rationale of this viewpoint is, in brief, that: "To attain the kind of peace for which the peoples of all nations yearn, we must achieve in the near future both world-wide disarmament and world law to enforce it. The two are inseparable. Disarmament won't work unless there is law to enforce it. . . ."[44]

The most systematic exposition along this line—that of Clark and Sohn —has already been noted in connection with its proposed enforcement machinery.[45] The "peace force" for that purpose would form but one part of their "comprehensive plan for total and universal disarmament and for the necessary world institutions to make, interpret, and enforce world law in the field of war prevention."[46] They consider it possible to draft and have ratified within a dozen years the necessary international treaties to bring all aspects of the plan into effect. Such rapid accomplishment will supposedly result from increasing popular pressures on governments to lighten the arms burden and to remove the "risk of world catastrophe from continuance of the arms race and a continuing lack of effective world machinery to settle international disputes by peaceful means." As previous chapters have shown, however, no such overwhelming pressures appear to be at work as yet; nor, if the present analysis is correct, is there any reason to anticipate that world law will thus descend upon us as a benison from Heaven.[47]

43. William O. Douglas, *The Rule of Law in World Affairs* (Center for the Study of Democratic Institutions, 1961), p. 27.

44. Senator Joseph S. Clark, Washington Conference on World Peace Through Law, address to Panel Session 5, Sept. 15, 1965, pp. 2, 1 (mimeo.).

45. See Chap. 5, p. 143.

46. Grenville Clark and Louis B. Sohn, *World Peace Through World Law* (Cambridge, 1960 ed.), pp. xliii–iv, xlvi, xlviii. A new edition (1966) retains the basic plan of the earlier versions, but makes a number of detailed changes, such as to reduce the strength of the proposed peace force and to lengthen the period required for the completion of the disarmament plan.

47. "In [the contemporary] world situation, the slogan, World Peace Through World Law, seems inadequate, if not sardonic. To call it idealistic too often means only that it sounds better than it is likely to work out." Acheson, *op. cit.*, p. 6.

Such exaggeration of the virtues of the rule of law tends, on the contrary, to create its own barriers to more effective understanding of the proper role of law in support of international peace. Judge DeVisscher might have had the radical innovators in mind when he urged putting aside "slightly messianic views" of the importance of nineteenth century arbitral decisions, in favor of reality:

To contemplate in its concrete realities the importance of the respective values of the arbitrations of the last century and those of recent arbitral or judicial decisions, it is evident that the comparison is not to the detriment of the latter. ... The reality is that today, as formerly, the international tribunal is generally only given jurisdiction of minor conflicts where the interests involved are limited. This does not prevent diplomatic action, impelled by the desire for even occasional agreement, to broaden at times the customary framework in order to submit to the Court serious disputes, even those which would put the national honor in issue. It has been properly noted that in such cases *the agreement to arbitrate had greater value to peace than the decision itself.* One need only recall the highly political significance of the Corfu Channel Case before the International Court of Justice.[48]

For the settlement of international disputes to be brought increasingly under the influence of law depends, not on restructuring the machinery for its application, but on finding means to broaden the accepted substance of that law.

The Changing Substance of International Law

The problem is often put in terms of the fact that the major international conflicts of today are not so much legal as political in nature, and are therefore not justiciable disputes. But even if they are not so vital in the view of the disputants as to fit Professor Stone's definition, serious political controversies also arise in areas where there is no applicable law, or where existing law is itself in controversy.

In historical perspective, the situation can be seen as a case where revolutionary change has outrun the politico-legal bases of a preceding period of relative stability. Yet the situation is also new in that it applies to revolution, not only within the traditional dominion of the state, but also in the contemporary international community, which is not yet a community in the political sense and has no generally accepted legal system. The problem therefore should be defined in terms of the attempt to

48. DeVisscher, *op. cit.*, pp. 471–72. Italics added.

build an international community of interests out of a world of nation-states, most of which are experiencing rapid change internally, and in many of which such change is accompanied by externally influenced violence.

Those states are legally independent, but in every other way interdependent. The realization of this fact justifies the effort to construct a stable world community founded on law—that is, on generally accepted standards of behavior—out of such elements of common interest as exist among the nations, lest the inherent instability of the situation suddenly end—to paraphrase—"not with a whimper, but with a bang." Only as such community develops in practice will a more acceptable, and hence more effective, legal system also develop, although the relationships are inter-acting, rather than simple cause-and-effect.

Underlying the extreme instability of the contemporary legal situation is the fact that the previously predominant system has been undermined from two directions at once. The most fundamental attack comes from the basic ideological conflict of the age: that of whether the world of government and diplomacy is to be based essentially on coercion or consent. This conflict, epitomized by the cold war although it is broader than the communist-anticommunist confrontation, penetrates every aspect of international relations. It may be more violent in the politico-military sphere, but it is no more fundamental than in the legal one.

The second attack, while conceptually less fundamental, is hardly less upsetting to the traditional system in practice. It arises from the legal concepts held by many smaller powers, which differ from the traditional system, and constitutes a search for equality on the part of the newer and less-developed states. The two assaults together might be characterized as conflicts in kind and in degree. While they can be separately defined, they are closely interrelated at many points.

CONFLICT IN DEGREE

Some of the less developed states fall into the communist bracket and hence are part of the conflict in kind; but most of them are still in the process of "finding themselves," of identifying their national interests and constructing modern national systems. The more recently independent ones will probably develop many of the attitudes of the older, non-industrialized countries represented by the Latin American states, with which they share many interests, especially as against those of the great powers.

They already reflect the general attitude described by the Mexican jurist, Jorge Castañeda, that the international law of today, "molded by a practice repeated a thousand-fold throughout the last century and a half," was often created against the interests of the weaker capital-importing countries; and that "the inequality of states in respect to power was [thus] translated in practice into inequality of rights." Few participated in the systematic development of juridical institutions and rules of law in the nineteenth century. Many didn't even exist then as independent states; some, indeed, lost their independence in that period. Castañeda continues:

The political mechanics of the nineteenth century and the concomitant method of creating international law, based on the order resulting from the Congress of Vienna, on the doctrine of the balance of power, and on the recognized supremacy of the states that formed the Concert of Europe, naturally resulted in according a comparatively minor role to the smaller states. Under the most favorable circumstances, when the interests of the great powers failed to coincide fully, as happened in the case of the law of the sea . . . the principles that were gradually consolidated, while they did not run directly counter to the aspirations of the small countries, did not fully reflect their future needs.[49]

Legal inequality was perforce accepted by the weaker states while the general international system permitted the direct enforcement of legal rights by powerful claimant states. Now, the effort to spread the "rule of law" (in traditional terms) by means of international commitments against the use of force as an instrument of national policy can, from one point of view, be seen as contributing instead to its breakdown. Thus, Julius Stone notes:

The enthusiastic efforts to ban all use of force in relations between states, except in defense of one's own territory against armed attack, have had the ironic effect of weakening international law. Formerly . . . small powers favored third-party settlement because equality before the law was better than inequality on the battlefield. But when atomic weapons are obviously too formidable to use in vindicating most kinds of legal rights, and when the opposed military bloc threatens nuclear retaliation against pressure exerted even by conventional forces (as the Soviet Union did in the Suez and Cuban crises), plausibility is given to the notion that force is out of the question even for defense of legal rights. When it begins to appear that small states can vio-

49. Jorge Castañeda, "The Underdeveloped Nations and the Development of International Law," *International Organization*, Vol. 15 (Spring 1961), p. 39.

late with impunity the rights of big states, the interest of the small ones in third-party settlement understandably diminishes . . . [and] the effect is to undermine the modest binding power which international law enjoyed in the old-fashioned days before the League of Nations and the United Nations.[50]

The above is more descriptive of contemporary political habits than it is accurate in attaching blame therefor to the Charter ban on unilateral force in defense of legal rights. Neither the nature of nuclear weapons nor the fact that force in support of nationally determined international legal rights has been proscribed accounts for the greater liberty of action now enjoyed by weaker states against the stronger. Basically, it is the deep-seated conflict between the great powers that gives the former their present advantageous position; for were today's superpowers agreed (to the extent that the Concert of Europe powers were agreed) on the standards of law to be enforced, they could use their nonnuclear weapons in collective defense of that law against weaker states without danger of escalation toward nuclear conflict. Moreover, given the political as well as military influence of the great powers, there seems little doubt that standards acceptable to them would also become the standards of law under the United Nations, much as the standards of the European Concert became the conventional law of an earlier period.[51]

Thus protected and given a disproportionate weight by the cold war, the smaller states are not in their view so much "violating with impunity the rights of big states," as seizing the opportunity to reject rules created by and for the purposes of their adversaries. The controversy over British Honduras (Belize), governed by international law in effect in the nineteenth century, illustrates these conflicts perfectly:

Great Britain proposes that the matter be submitted to the International Court of Justice so that the Court may resolve the controversy according to international law. Guatemala rejects the offer but, in turn, proposes that the matter be submitted to the same Court, not for decision on the basis of inter-

50. "Law, Force, and Survival," *Foreign Affairs*, Vol. 39 (July 1961), pp. 553–54. Not all "traditional" international lawyers support this interpretation of the law of the Charter and its effect. See, for example, Benjamin V. Cohen, *The United Nations: Constitutional Developments, Growth and Possibilities* (Harvard University Press, 1961), pp. 38–46.

51. R. P. Anand also points out that great-power rivalry, by destroying the unanimity of the permanent members of the Security Council and shifting international action to the Assembly, enhances the political power of the weaker states through their concerted action. See "Attitude of the Asian-African States toward Certain Problems of International Law," *International and Comparative Law Quarterly*, Vol. 15 (January 1966), pp. 55–75.

national law, but *ex aequo et bono*. This example could not be more elo-
quent.[52]

It is not, in short, so much the basic nature of the international legal
system that these countries now oppose, as the content of presently applicable law. According to Anand, "they accept everything that does not
smell of 'colonialism and imperialism,' [and they are] attempting to shape
international law according to their own interests."[53] For as Ambassador
Goldberg has also pointed out:

One of the dominant facts of the emerging world community is that the
majority of its members are still extremely poor and still have vivid recollec-
tions of what it is like to live under colonial rule. They are preoccupied with
economic and social development and with human rights. Their commitment
to the law of nations, and to the peace which it seeks to build, will deepen only
as the law helps them to realize these legitimate aspirations.[54]

New law that meets these demands, however, can either "be laid down
by the party wielding the greatest power in the social organism or it can
be the result of agreement between the parties."[55] Given the cold-war
effects noted above, the "greatest powers" cannot in this sense lay down
an agreed law. The problem then is to reach new agreements "whose
observance rests on the continuing self-interest of the parties and not
merely on coercion."

Difficulties in doing this arise from two main sources. On the one hand,
there is the resistance to change by states most satisfied with the existing
legal order. As one observer noted of two conferences (in 1958 and 1960)
on the law of the sea: "Too often delegates of satisfied states would not
even concede any necessary relationship between law and politics."[56] This
problem is essentially part of the larger problem of change considered in
Chapter 7. Specifically applied to the legal sphere, the basic dilemma for
the traditionalist states is that: "The 'new' countries are not so much concerned with ascertaining or restating existing international law doctrine
as with rewriting it; in effect, with legislating."[57]

---

52. Castañeda, *op. cit.*, pp. 41–42. Great Britain has more recently proposed that
the issue of Gibraltar's status be submitted to the International Court, which Spain
has rejected in turn.

53. Anand, *International and Comparative Law Quarterly*, p. 73.

54. Arthur J. Goldberg, "International Law in the United Nations," USUN Press
Release 304 (Dec. 29, 1966), p. 8.

55. Max Huber, "The Roles of International Law," Carnegie Endowment for International Peace, *Perspectives on Peace: 1910–1960* (Praeger, 1960), p. 158.

56. Robert L. Friedheim, "The 'Satisfied' and 'Dissatisfied' States Negotiate International Law: A Case Study," *World Politics*, Vol. 18 (October 1965), p. 36.

57. McWhinney, *op. cit.*, p. 31.

A second hazard to the rapid development of new, generally acceptable rules has received less attention, namely, that the delegates of many new states are made cautious by a combination of their suspicions of the former imperial powers and their relative lack of training and experience. For example: "The dissatisfied states [at the law-of-the-sea conferences] constantly feared that their agreement to a detailed proposal would create obligations for them that their negotiators could not perceive. . . ."[58] More, and more imaginative, diplomacy and adaptability on the part of the "old" states might help to overcome both those difficulties and result in faster advance toward an acceptable common meeting ground.

CONFLICT IN KIND

Controversy between communist and noncommunist states, over the role of law in settling disputes and in controlling force, is more basic and therefore becomes infinitely more difficult to resolve through agreement on common rules. The ideological conflict is reflected especially in their differing interpretations of the legitimate use of force under the Charter and in their attitude toward the use of third-party settlement procedures.

On the one hand, communist governments raise almost to the point of absoluteness (for themselves) the principle of national sovereignty and the concomitant domestic-jurisdiction reservation—which safeguards them from intervention by, or even the claims of, other governments. On the other hand, they pick and choose their Charter obligations toward other states. "Marxists have recognized, and still do recognize, only wars of liberation, wars that are just," Khrushchev declared on one occasion; and "condemn wars that are predatory and imperialistic." Among those "just" wars, he welcomed the "sacred struggle of the colonial peoples against the colonialists and for their liberation." And the Chinese communists go even further in praising force as a legitimate instrument of national policy, and revolutionary wars as "holy."[59] Thus by definition their "wars of liberation" do not constitute intervention. All use of force, in short, is defensive against the inherent aggressiveness of the capitalist-imperialist system. It is no wonder that it has been as impossible to reach

58. Friedheim, *op. cit.*, p. 31.
59. Khrushchev quoted in Richard P. Stebbins, *United States in World Affairs 1959*, Council on Foreign Relations (Harper, 1960), p. 332; Mao Tse-tung quoted in A. Doak Barnett, *Communist China and Asia: A Challenge to American Policy* (Harper, 1960), p. 75.

agreement on a definition of "aggression" in the United Nations as under the League of Nations.[60]

The same self-judging interpretations also apply to communist attitudes toward peaceful methods of settlement. Without compulsory jurisdiction for the International Court, of course, there is nothing illegal in Soviet or satellite refusal to accept any suit brought against them before the judicial organ. But it is otherwise with refusals to observe settlement procedures in treaties accepted by them. When Hungary, Rumania, and Bulgaria were charged by the Western signatories with violation of the human rights provisions in the peace treaties, for example, they refused to designate representatives to the commissions prescribed in those treaties to settle such disputes.[61]

Similarly, in political, as well as legal, aspects everything is done to keep out of the United Nations framework all disputes involving states of the communist group. Any effort by outsiders to bring them before the Organization is always strongly resisted. Whether the proposed machinery is judicial or political, the use of third-party agencies for decision, or even for fact-finding or mediation, is normally opposed when communist states are involved.[62] Their emphasis on negotiation as the only acceptable

60. After some years of failure to achieve any progress toward a definition, the Assembly set up a Committee on the Question of Defining Aggression (A/Res. 1181, XII), in 1957, to consider when the plenary body should discuss the matter again and to report its recommendations to the Secretary-General. After periodically deciding the time was not ripe and then adjourning for two years, the committee met again in April 1967. The decade of futility led the United States and Bolivia to propose that the committee adjourn until a majority requested the Secretary-General to reconvene it. Czechoslovakia and Hungary proposed to recommend, on the other hand, that the 22nd Assembly resume work on a definition. Vietnam and the increasingly tense situation in the Middle East reduced the committee discussion to polemics. In the end, it adjourned for consultations. Although a compromise resolution draft was offered by Cyprus and Ecuador (to report the stalemate to U Thant) when the committee reconvened on May 26, the Middle Eastern situation led only to "an exchange of charges." Finally, the committee adopted the chairman's proposal to adjourn to "a date to be set," to enable further study of the three drafts. It had not met again by August. UN Monthly Chronicle, Vol. 4 (May 1967), pp. 51–58; (June 1967), pp. 79–81.

61. The General Assembly, concerned at these refusals, asked the Court in October 1949 for an advisory opinion on whether the disputes came under those provisions. The Court declared that they did; that the states were obligated to nominate representatives to the settlement commissions; but that, when they failed to do so, the Secretary-General was not thereby authorized to appoint the "third" member of each commission.

62. The Soviet Union has not been wholly consistent in this. On isolated occasions, when not directly involved, it has not opposed suggestions that other communist states should submit their disputes to international adjudication. It abstained, for example, in the U.N. recommendation that the Corfu Channel dispute be taken by Great Britain

means of settlement reflects their theoretical emphasis on national sovereignty.

There is, clearly, little basis on which to reconcile so radically opposed an approach with Western understandings of the principles of international law and the concomitant obligations of states as written into the Charter. As Dean Acheson has pointed out, when "disagreement on values is wide, no agreement seems likely on how opposing values can be pursued in an orderly way."[63] Yet the Soviet Union, in recent years, has energetically sought to promote the formal acceptance of "peaceful coexistence" as "a qualitatively new and higher stage" in the development of international law and interstate relations—a stage that it compares with the coexistence of states in the past, "which incorporated war and peace as constantly alternating relationships between states."[64]

PEACEFUL COEXISTENCE AND FRIENDLY RELATIONS

In 1961, the Sixth Committee recommended that the next Assembly consider the "principles of international law relating to *friendly relations and cooperation among states in accordance with the Charter of the United Nations.*" The original proposal, initiated by communist members, had referred simply to principles relating to "peaceful coexistence"; but they accepted the italicized phrase as an amendment that, presumably, did not alter their intention. The "legal aspects" of peaceful coexistence, they had argued, ought to be codified, "if possible," which would then "direct all other work of codification towards the essence of coexistence." Against this, it was argued that the expression had no generally accepted meaning; that if it was not simply a political slogan, it was certainly primarily a political subject, not lending itself to codification. Eight delegations (including the United States) therefore proposed that a better way to develop international law would be through rules giving practical effect to the principles of cooperation in the Charter.[65] In 1962, the

---

and Albania to the Court; and it supported a Cuban proposal (1962) that the Court be requested for an advisory opinion on the legality of the OAS exclusion of Cuba. See Higgins, *op. cit.*, pp. 153–55. It even accepted the Assembly decision on the disposition of the Italian colonies, although rejecting any United Nations involvement in Korea.

63. Acheson, *op. cit.*, p. 9.
64. Higgins, *op. cit.*, p. 102.
65. U.N. Doc. A/5036, Dec. 15, 1961, pp. 8–10.

Assembly accepted the proposal to study such principles, listing seven as directly relevant:

(a) [The duty to] refrain from the threat or use of force against the territorial integrity or political independence of any state, or in any other manner inconsistent with the purposes of the United Nations;

(b) [The duty to] settle international disputes by peaceful means;

(c) The duty not to intervene in matters within the domestic jurisdiction of any state;

(d) The duty of states to cooperate with one another in accordance with the Charter;

(e) The principle of equal rights and self-determination of peoples;

(f) The principle of sovereign equality of states;

(g) The principle that states shall fulfill in good faith the obligations assumed by them in accordance with the Charter.[66]

The principles are not, in fact, essentially different from those expounded by communist proponents of peaceful coexistence, which derive historically from the "five principles" (or Panch Shila) first contained in a 1954 Indian-Chinese agreement and reaffirmed more elaborately by the Bandung Conference in 1955.[67] As described by Premier Khrushchev: " 'Peaceful coexistence' is not merely the absence of war, a temporary unstable truce between wars; it is the existence of two opposite social systems based on mutual renunciation of a resort to war as a means of settling disputes between States."[68] That is, it refers to relations between nations, while revolution means the overthrow of the oppressors as a class by the oppressed within each country. Thus support of national liberation movements is not incompatible with adherence to peaceful coexistence between communist and imperial states. On the other hand, intersocialist relations do not seem to require the same standards:

The tacit [Soviet] argument appears to be that revolutionary leaders are operating in conditions too far short of a tolerable *modus vivendi* for peaceful coexistence to be possible; and relations between socialist states are too perfect for peaceful coexistence to be necessary ... [They are, rather,] based on "prole-

66. A/Res. 1815 (XVII), Dec. 18, 1962.

67. These were: (1) mutual respect for territorial integrity and sovereignty; (2) mutual nonaggression (often redrafted as "renunciation of war as a national instrument"); (3) mutual noninterference in internal affairs; (4) equality and mutual benefits; (5) peaceful coexistence. The last became also the concept resulting from all the principles, especially after the 20th Soviet Communist Party Congress (1956) adopted them as the foundation of peaceful relations among all states.

68. Quoted in Higgins, *op. cit.*, p. 105.

tarian internationalism." This is regarded not as a mere political slogan, but as a judicial principle.[69]

Western governments, therefore, have suspected the Soviet Union's continual proclamations of its "peaceful coexistence" intentions, believing that most of the principles represent nothing more than long-accepted law, being neither "new" nor "qualitatively higher" norms. Others are either unclear as to legal scope (for example, self-determination) or lack legal content (for example, free exchange of cultural ideas). The concept of peaceful coexistence is, in this view, no more than a military armistice, giving Moscow time to gain strength for the inevitable battle in accordance with its real Marxist beliefs.

There has also been another aspect of this debate, which has received less attention than the Soviet-Western theological controversy. That is the attempt by the "new" countries to make of the concept (however named) "an intellectual ideological base for a rewriting or reordering . . . of old international institutions and old international law doctrine." The "neutralist, uncommitted countries" were impatient and dissatisfied with

all the slowness and procedural cumbersomeness and simple obstructionism in the U.N. Sixth (Legal) Committee and the General Assembly, and with the seeming unimaginativeness, even timorousness, of the International Law Commission, which too often perhaps in the eyes of the "new" countries, has appeared to be preoccupied with the petit-point needlework of international law rather than to be concerned with the imaginative reshaping and rewriting of international law to meet new conditions in international society.[70]

They were therefore active, after the Assembly accepted the seven principles of friendly relations (as the cumbersome description inevitably became known), in supporting the establishment of a Special Committee in 1963, to study them in greater depth.[71]

69. *Ibid.*, p. 124. The Yugoslav version of coexistence, on the other hand, stresses its importance as a principle in relations with the Soviet Union also; while Chinese communism rejects the idea of peaceful transition to the ideal social system, arguing that "the whole of communist history shows that the imperialists will only 'coexist' under compulsion; the realization of peaceful coexistence can only be won by struggle. . . . 'Until the imperialist system and the exploiting classes come to an end, wars of one kind or another will always occur.' " Quoted in *Ibid.*, p. 131.

70. McWhinney, *op. cit.*, pp. 2–3. The author thinks these initiatives "may hardly have been anticipated by either of the original protagonists in the great debate."

71. In 1962, the Assembly assigned principles 1, 2, 3, and 6 (see above) to Committee VI for study. In 1963, the Special Committee on Principles of International Law concerning Friendly Relations and Cooperation among States was set up to report

When the committee met in Mexico City in 1964, the "new" states (often in cooperation with the communist delegations) sought more than a "mere statement of the international law *status quo*"; they wanted "a more affirmative venture in the political rewriting of international law" in terms of contemporary needs "as they themselves . . . might define those needs." They did not succeed in achieving that aim, but the debates were important in signaling the areas where pressures for change are strongest.[72] The Western states, however, continued to see the committee's task as that of codification. In 1966, therefore, they still "sought to establish the meaning of the principles without changing their traditional connotation. On the other hand, the developing nations, frequently supported by the East European delegations, . . . stressed their revision and reformulation, rather than codification." On both sides, moreover, there was a tendency to offer legal arguments that "reflected more often than not immediate political concerns rather than long-term policies directed toward the creation of a stable legal order."[73] On the principle prohibiting the threat or use of force, for example, the legal debate has been especially "political" in view of its central importance to both coexistence and friendly relations, by any definition.

Writing in 1965, McWhinney found the time "ripe for a change in basic Western tactics" of primarily and defensively resisting the Soviet campaign for an immediate act of codification. "It would be a pity," he concluded, if the "originally legitimate and methodologically valid Western response" were to be interpreted as only a stratagem for defeating the aspirations of the new countries. He therefore urged "the West to take part in the dialogue with *elan* and imagination," projecting the inherent capacity of "our own revolutionary legal tradition" to adapt traditional international law "creatively."[74]

After its 1966 meetings, however, the committee had made so little progress toward any sort of adaptation that it could only report to the

---

on that study, while Committee VI was assigned the remaining three principles. (A/Res. 1966 [XVIII], Dec. 16, 1963.) In 1965, the Special Committee was reconstituted as the 1966 Special Committee on Principles of International Relations and Cooperation among States to study further all the principles. A/Res. 2103 (XX), Dec. 20, 1965.

72. McWhinney, *op. cit.*, p. 3. Pages 7–29 contain an analysis of the debate on the four principles considered at Mexico City.

73. Carnegie Endowment for International Peace, "Issues before the Twenty-first General Assembly," *International Conciliation*, No. 559 (September 1966), p. 189.

74. McWhinney, *op. cit.*, pp. 29–30.

Assembly certain limited points of "consensus" (incomplete as definitions) on two of the seven principles: (1) peaceful settlement of disputes
and (2) sovereign equality.[75] The Assembly, in turn, continued the committee, requesting it to complete the task of formulation and to submit to
the twenty-second session a draft declaration "which will constitute a
landmark in the progressive development or codification of those principles."[76] Unfortunately, it seems much more likely to continue "tied up
with items over which no real basic agreement is possible in the foreseeable future."[77]

Prohibitions on the Use of Force:
The International Controversy

Their emphasis on national sovereignty leads communists not only to
favor direct negotiations as the best method of settlement, but also to
stress the importance of treaties as *the* source of international law, while
demoting the significance of international custom, which is equally
stressed by the West.[78] The Soviet view is, in general, that contemporary
international law is treaty law. At the same time, in order to avoid the
need to uphold treaties that are awkward to its political objectives (such
as the Panama Canal Treaty or other unequal "imperialistic" accords),
Soviet doctrine asserts that the only valid treaties are those compatible
with the basic rules of international law—naturally, as those rules are
identified by the Soviet Union. This reliance on treaties also underlies its
attempt to "codify" the elements of peaceful coexistence within a single
United Nations instrument, as just noted. In addition, Moscow has
sought to promote more specific accords on individual phases of the general principles, the most important being a proposal by Khrushchev at the

75. U.N. Doc. A/6230, June 27, 1966.
76. A/Res. 2181 (XXI), Dec. 12, 1966, adopted 86–0–2 (United States and
France).
77. Higgins, *op. cit.*, p. 169.
78. "The basic reason underlying this attitude is the Soviet view of itself as a
completely new entity appearing upon the world stage in 1917. The body of international rules . . . was [then] largely customary in origin . . . in the main the result of
the consensus between the Christian European nations of the West. . . . The Soviet
Union was reluctant to accept the entirety of this body of law. At the same time, in the
post-1917 world, it has been, in bodies where a majority vote obtains, in a minority
position. . . . [It therefore] found in treaties a safeguard against the imposition of
unacceptable majority views by the outside world." *Ibid.*, p. 142.

end of 1963 for an international agreement renouncing the use of force in settling territorial disputes.

In December 1963, a few days after reiterating once more that "peaceful coexistence" was inapplicable "between oppressors and oppressed,"[79] Khrushchev underlined the selective Soviet doctrine on renunciation of force in a formal New Year's message to all heads of government. Calling for an international agreement against force in the settlement of territorial claims and frontier disputes, he noted that: "Of course, territorial claims and disputes between States are not all alike."[80]

One class of such claims—the "demands of the revanchist circles in certain states which were the aggressors in the Second World War"— constituted "a special class" that must be "emphatically rejected" as incompatible with peace. Other types, having nothing to do with the "just postwar territorial settlement," would in general come under the agreement "not to resort to force to alter the *existing State frontiers.*" The emphasis is added to point up the basis on which the Soviet proposal managed to justify simultaneously exempting a whole series of territorially based disputes from its prohibition against settlement by forcible means:

[Some] are associated with the completion of the liberation of this or that people from colonial oppression or foreign occupation . . . not all the young national states by any means succeeded, immediately after becoming independent, in liberating from the power of the colonialists all the territories that are theirs by right. Taiwan is the most obvious case in point. . . .

All this, of course, also applies without qualification to the territories of the peoples . . . still suffering colonial oppression . . . [and] striving to win their freedom and independence by peaceful means, [which are not always] adequate. . . . In such cases, the oppressed peoples have no other choice than to take up arms. . . .

Similarly, military bases established in foreign territories wrested from States concerned should be liquidated. And no one should be misled by arguments that the lands on which such bases are sited and foreign troops are stationed were conceded under some past treaty or agreement. The manner in which such agreements were concluded . . . is no secret, . . . the stronger imposed his will on the weaker. . . . Yet another problem . . . is to some extent associated with the territorial question—that of the unification of Germany, Korea and Vietnam. . . . It goes without saying, however, that the question of

79. *Soviet News*, No. 4934, Dec. 23, 1963, p. 156.
80. Text in U.N. Doc. A/5740, Oct. 9, 1964.

reunification must be settled [peacefully] by the peoples of these countries and their Governments themselves, without any outside interference or pressure and, in all cases, without foreign military intervention or occupation such as actually exists, for instance, in South Korea and South Vietnam. . . .

With these "interpretations," Khrushchev could then declare: "In our day there are, and can be, between existing States no territorial disputes or unresolved frontier issues which it is permissible to resolve by the use of armed force." Seemingly favoring the settlement of such issues by direct negotiation, the Premier also acknowledged that the use of good offices or of assistance from international organizations was possible—although he did not regard the United Nations "in its present form as an ideal instrument of peaceful cooperation between States. . . ." The main provisions of his agreement would cover:

FIRST, a solemn pledge by the States parties to the agreement not to resort to force to alter existing State frontiers;

SECOND, recognition that the territory of States should not, even temporarily, be the object of any invasion, attack, military occupation or other measure of force directly or indirectly undertaken by other States for political, economic, strategic, frontier or other reasons of whatsoever kind;

THIRD, a firm declaration that neither differences in social or political systems, nor denial of recognition or the absence of diplomatic relations, nor any other pretext may serve to justify the violation by one State of the territorial integrity of another;

FOURTH, an undertaking to settle all territorial disputes exclusively by peaceful means, such as negotiation, mediation, conciliation and also other peaceful means at the choice of the parties concerned in accordance with the Charter of the United Nations.

In September 1964, the Soviet Union formally requested the Secretary-General to place the subject on the Assembly's agenda, explaining that:

The Soviet Government proceeds from the belief that the undertaking by states of a commitment to settle territorial disputes only by peaceful means will further develop the principles of the United Nations Charter . . . particularly the principle stating that all members . . . shall refrain in their international relations from the threat or use of force against the territorial integrity or political independence of any state, or in any other manner inconsistent with the Purposes of the United Nations.[81]

Discussion in the stalemated nineteenth Assembly was, of course, impossible. Although the identical topic was not reintroduced in the twentieth Assembly, the Soviet Union submitted a new item, "The inad-

81. Text of letter in *Soviet News*, No. 5038 (Sept. 25, 1964), p. 1.

missibility of intervention in the domestic affairs of States and the protection of their independence and sovereignty."[82] This approached the same subject from a slightly different angle. Rather than attempting to ostracize Western policies—such as military aid (including bases) in foreign countries or refusal to accept certain postwar territorial dispositions as final—by means of an agreement selectively prohibiting force, the new attack focused on the charge of intervention per se. Events in Vietnam and the Dominican Republic undoubtedly provided the excuse for this agenda submission; but events in the twentieth Assembly gave it an unexpected turn, from the Soviet point of view, in part because many other states shared at least some of the United States objections to the original Khrushchev letter.

UNITED STATES POSITION ON INDIRECT AGGRESSION

Washington's underlying political concerns were indicated in a reply by the President in January 1964, which sought to widen the prohibitions on the use of force to cover the Soviet exceptions. Where the Soviet note would legitimize aid in support of "liberation" movements, Washington's reply sought to extend the prohibition on force to cover subversive activities and civil war, as well as to safeguard its own programs of military aid in terms of self-defense under Article 51. President Johnson therefore proposed "guidelines" to implement Khrushchev's renunciation-of-force principle, "even broader and stronger than your own."[83] These were:

FIRST, all governments or regimes shall abstain from the direct or indirect threat or use of force to change:
International boundaries;
Other territorial or administrative demarcation or dividing lines established or confirmed by international agreement or practice;
The dispositions of truce or military armistice agreements; or
Arrangements or procedures concerning access to or passage across or the administration of those areas where international agreement or practice has established or confirmed such arrangements or procedures.
Nor shall any government or regime use or threaten force to enlarge the territory under its control or administration by overthrowing or displacing established authorities.

82. Agenda Item #107, assigned to the First (Political) Committee.
83. Letter of Jan. 20, 1964, U.S. Department of State, *Bulletin,* Vol. 50 (1964), pp. 157–58. Similar points were also made in answer by Prime Minister Pearson of Canada in a letter of Feb. 7; see *Canadian Weekly Bulletin,* Vol. 19 (Feb. 19, 1964), pp. 3–4.

SECOND, these limitations shall apply regardless of the direct or indirect form which such threat or use of force might take, whether in the form of aggression, subversion, or clandestine supply of arms; regardless of what justification or purpose is advanced; and regardless of any question of recognition, diplomatic relations, or difference of political systems.

Third, the parties to any serious dispute should also seek a peaceful solution by means of their own choice. Fourth, continuation of the proposed obligations would depend on their "quite general" observation; and, "in any event," the inherent right of self-defense under Article 51 would "remain fully operative."

DECLARATION ON NONINTERVENTION

When the Soviet nonintervention item came up in the Assembly in 1965, Ambassador Goldberg reminded a press conference that:

In 1949, the General Assembly adopted, at United States initiative, a resolution entitled "Essentials of Peace," which called on all states "to refrain from any threats or acts, direct or indirect, aimed at impairing the freedom, independence, or integrity of any state, or at fomenting civil strife and subverting the will of the people in any state." The Soviet Union voted against this resolution. If the new Soviet item means the Soviets have changed their approach on this problem and are genuinely against interference in the affairs of other states, such as Peiping is now carrying on across Asia, we shall be the first to welcome this change of heart.[84]

The First Committee considered draft declarations of the Soviet Union, of a Latin American group, and of an Afro-Asian group of states, along with numerous proposed amendments. Communist spokesmen sought support for the original Soviet draft, which concentrated on armed military intervention and was aimed in particular at United States policy in Vietnam and the Dominican Republic. But many nonaligned states, as well as the United States and Great Britain (which had submitted extensive amendments to the Soviet draft), were critical of its omission of subversion, terrorism, and other indirect intervention. In the end, a working group prepared a draft declaration that included most of the points in all the proposals. It was sponsored by fifty-seven countries.

Some delegations felt that the subject should have been referred to the Special Committee on the Principles of International Law, but the composite draft was adopted as a Declaration on the Inadmissibility of Intervention in the Domestic Affairs of States, by a vote of 109–0–1. United

84. U.S. Department of State, *Bulletin*, Vol. 53 (1965), p. 683.

States and Soviet delegates both found that it supported their respective positions. Great Britain abstained, arguing that there was little value in a resolution that would mean different things to different governments and thus serve only as a basis for further propaganda attacks. Malta did not participate in the Assembly vote, on the ground that the declaration was being openly violated by several states that voted for it in committee and that were not likely to modify their policies in accordance with the declaration—a sage observation, regardless of how one identified the "violators."[85] At the twenty-first Assembly, a similar resolution was passed under the title of "Status of the implementation of the Declaration on Inadmissibility" of the previous year.[86] It urged all states to refrain from armed intervention, subversion, terrorism or other indirect forms of intervention to change an existing system or to interfere in civil strife in another state.

An additional approach to the subject was made in the 1966 Assembly, this time combining the prohibition of the use of force with the right to self-determination. An initial proposal by Czechoslovakia (for direct discussion in plenary because of the deteriorating international situation) was revised in a compromise with two competing drafts.[87] It ended up as one

85. A/Res. 2131 (XX), Dec. 21, 1965. An ironic aftermath of the Non-Intervention Declaration came in February 1966, when the OAS Council adopted a resolution denouncing the "Tri-Continental Solidarity Conference" in Havana that had proclaimed support for revolutionary subversion in the Latin American states and had established a permanent committee to provide assistance to the "national liberation fronts." The 18 states voting for the OAS resolution (Chile and Mexico abstained on the legal ground that the Council was not authorized to issue such a denunciation) transmitted it to the Security Council, for distribution to the United Nations, as a protest against "the open participation at the aforesaid Havana Conference of official or officially sponsored delegations" of U.N. Members that voted for its action "in violation of the principles of the Charter . . . and of Resolution 2131 (XX). . . ." (Council of the OAS, Doc. OEA/Ser. G. III, C–sa–594, Feb. 2, 1966). The Soviet Union had been present at Havana. It claimed the letter and the OAS resolution were attempts "to divert attention from the real acts in violation of the U.N. Declaration of Non-Interference . . . by the United States, which is committing armed aggression in South Vietnam. . . ." Text of Soviet letter to Security Council in Soviet News, No. 5247, March 1, 1966.

86. A/Res. 2225 (XXI), Dec. 19, 1966. The resolution followed the same procedure as that of 1965 also, being introduced by the Soviet Union and then amended by Latin American and African-Asian groups, and being found to meet the positions of all sides of the debate. It was adopted, 114–0–2 (Malta and Great Britain).

87. Czechoslovakian draft (Nov. 11), with 13 co-sponsors, would have the Assembly declare that military force and political or economic pressure by one state against another was a gross violation of international law, and that forcible action against peoples struggling against colonialism was in flagrant violation of the Charter. A Costa Rican-United States draft (Nov. 16) would call on all states to facilitate the right of

more resolution on the subject that, as the British delegate rightly described it, papered over differences and disagreements and took refuge in deliberate ambiguity.[88] It was then sent, with the record of debate, to be considered by the Special Committee on Friendly Relations.

International Law and the Use of Force: The United States Controversy

The political and military conflicts in, and over, the divided countries are paralleled by the legal controversy. Vietnam is seen by Peking as *the* test case of its interpretation of the communist theory that "wars of liberation" are inevitable and must inevitably succeed against even nuclear capitalist powers. The United States has taken that Chinese criterion as justifying American intervention on behalf of Saigon.

THE OFFICIAL POSITION

South Vietnam, Ambassador Goldberg told the General Assembly, is the stage where "apostles" of the violent Chinese doctrine

are today attempting to transform the country . . . into a proving ground for their theories. This challenge must be met, not in the interests of any single nation but in the interests of each member of [the United Nations]. It must be met in particular in the interests of the smaller nations who cherish their right to choose and follow their own path of national development.

The United States goals, moreover, are "plain and simple" in this situation:

We seek only to insure the independence of South Vietnam, with freedom from attack and the opportunity for its people to determine their own future. We seek no territory for ourselves, no preferential position, no permanent military presence. We stand ready to withdraw our forces when Communist

---

self-determination (not prevent it by armed force) and renounce doctrines advocating use of overt or covert force or terror against other governments. An eight-country draft (Nov. 17)—sponsored by Canada, Chile, Denmark, Iceland, Italy, Japan, Madagascar, Norway—would have the Assembly recommend that the two principles should receive priority in further study by the Special Committee on Friendly Relations.

88. A/Res. 2160 (XXI), Nov. 30, 1966, adopted 98–2 (Great Britain and Portugal)–8. For text and a summary of the debate, see *UN Monthly Chronicle*, Vol. 3 (December 1966), pp. 55–63.

aggression has ended and South Vietnam is left alone to determine its own destiny in its own way by principles of self-determination. And, above all, we seek a peaceful solution. . . .[89]

American officials contend in general that whereas the United States wants political change, even "revolution," to be effected by peaceful and democratic evolution, communists (whether Soviet or Chinese variety) rely on subversion, terror, and wars of liberation against the wishes of the majority of the population. Washington's military interventions are considered by the communists to be hypocritical violations of peaceful coexistence on the pretense of communist interventions, or even merely of indirect communist influence; but the United States sees the communist position as equally hypocritical. One official put it: "The way the Russians seem to mean 'peaceful coexistence,' it is intended to rule out large-scale wars in which they are at a relative disadvantage, but permit any kind of subversive local actions. It would be much more realistic if the Communists would rule out all violence in trying to bring about social change."[90]

Secretary of State Rusk translated the administration's position into Charter terms before the American Society of International Law.[91] The limitations of Article 2(4) on the employment of force as an instrument of national policy, he said, sought to apply a lesson of the interwar period, namely, that the use of force feeds on success: "The exceptions to the prohibitions were expressly set forth in the Charter. The use of force is legal: as a collective measure by the United Nations, or as action by regional agencies in accordance with Chapter VIII . . . or in individual or collective self-defense." Referring to communist efforts to legitimize "wars of liberation" as another exception, the Secretary noted that they have increasingly stressed such wars as the risks of overt aggression, whether by nuclear or conventional military means, have become increasingly evident:

International law does not restrict internal revolution within a state, or revolution against colonial authority. But international law does restrict what third Powers may lawfully do in support of insurrection. It is these restrictions which are challenged by the doctrine, and violated by the practice, of "wars of liberation." It is plain that acceptance of the doctrine of "wars of liberation"

89. U.S. Department of State, *Bulletin*, Vol. 53 (1965), pp. 581–82.

90. An "American official" quoted in Peter Grose dispatch from Moscow, *New York Times*, Aug. 20, 1965.

91. *Proceedings* (1965), pp. 248–55. A more formal brief on "The Legality of U.S. Participation in the Defense of Viet-Nam," is in U.S. Department of State, *Bulletin*, Vol. 54 (1966), pp. 474–89.

would amount to scuttling the modern international law of peace which the Charter prescribes.

Vietnam is thus "a clear current case of the lawful versus the unlawful use of force," since the insurgency in the South is not "truly indigenous and self-sustained." In resisting "the aggression against it," the republic was therefore exercising its right of self-defense; and in responding to Saigon's call for assistance, the United States and other nations were exercising the right of collective self-defense.[92] That assistance now "encompasses the bombing of North Vietnam . . . to interdict, as far as possible, and to inhibit, as far as may be necessary, continued aggression" against the South. When the aggression stops, the collective defense measures will cease, the Secretary declared. But he added, within a wider framework:

> It is true that we are committed to general principles of law and procedure which reject the idea that men and arms can be sent freely across frontiers to absorb a neighbor. But underlying the general principles is the harsh reality that our own security is threatened by those who would embark upon a course of aggression whose announced ultimate purpose is our own destruction.

The legal adviser of the Department of State made an equally unequivocal defense, in the name of international law, of the United States intervention of 1965 in the Dominican Republic. While inveighing against "fundamentalist views of international law"—presumably including the charge that the intervention violated Articles 15 and 17 of the OAS Charter—he invoked the declaration of Punta del Este (January 1962) to justify United States action. That meeting of Foreign Ministers, he pointed out, had declared Marxism-Leninism "incompatible with the Inter-American system," and had urged OAS members:

> to take those steps that they may consider appropriate for their individual or collective self-defense, and to cooperate, as may be necessary or desirable, to strengthen their capacity to counteract threats or acts of aggression, subversion, or other dangers to peace and security resulting from the continued intervention in this hemisphere of Sino-Soviet powers, in accordance with the obligations established in treaties and agreements, . . .

such as the OAS Charter and the Rio Treaty.[93] The situation in Santo Domingo, he argued, was "the very kind of threat" referred to in that

92. Moreover, the Secretary said on another occasion, "Article IV [of the SEATO treaty] binds each party individually; it does not require a collective finding." U.S. Department of State, *Bulletin*, Vol. 54 (1966), p. 929.

93. Leonard C. Meeker, address before Foreign Law Association, U.S. Department of State, *Bulletin*, Vol. 53 (1965), p. 62. See Chap. 6 above, pp. 180–82, for the inter-American reaction and comment at the time.

declaration: "In the context of Cuba only a few miles away, and of the announced drive of the Communists to expand their control in this Hemisphere, external threat to the Dominican Republic was by no means fancified. . . ." And in relation to the regional organization, he maintained:

The OAS . . . exists to assist the American States to maintain their rights, to defend their integrity, and to provide for their preservation and prosperity. The action of the United States gave the organs of the OAS the essential time in which to consider the situation in the Dominican Republic and to determine means of preserving the rights of that country under the Inter-American System.[94]

THE LEGAL CONTROVERSY

The official position has its supporters in both Congress[95] and legal circles; but it has also been strongly criticized by both sources. Because it reflects fundamental political, as well as legal, differences of approach to the problem of developing order in a disorderly world, the controversy as highlighted by two outstanding international law experts is worth summarizing here in conclusion.

Professor McDougal, declaring that the "prohibitions of aggression in the Charter apply to every kind of external attack, direct or indirect, and even to indigenous civil war when it threatens to spread," also argued:

The fundamental policy which underlies the right of self-defense, the principle that one state may come to the aid of the established government of another state, and the Charter provisions about self-determination are one and the same: that the people in a given territorial community should be accorded, and protected in, a genuine freedom of choice about their form of government and social order.

.   .   .   .   .   .

The Charter prohibits the employment of coercion against the territorial integrity or political independence of another state. Given the lack of effective

94. *Ibid.*, p. 62. For a different viewpoint, see "Differences between Intervention and Collective Action," report of the Inter-American Juridical Committee (January 1966), especially pp. 17–22. OAE/Ser. 1/VI. 2, CIJ–81.

95. The House of Representatives, for example, passed the Selden Resolution (Sept. 20, 1965), 312–52, which in effect constituted endorsement of the unilateral use of force by this or any other Western Hemisphere country to prevent a communist takeover of any other American state. Its sponsor declared that it merely restated U.S. obligations to itself and the Hemisphere in terms of the new menace of internal subversion, the same intent as the OAS resolution of 1962. (*Congressional Record*, Vol. 111, Pt. 18, 89 Cong. 1 sess., pp. 24348, 24364.) Passage of the resolution was followed by immediate and violent attacks from numerous Latin American countries.

international organization, it is all the more important to protect the historic competence of particular states to act in the interest of world order. In the exercise of self-defense, both individual and collective, particular states have long made preliminary decisions and taken action, and these decisions and actions have then been subjected to appraisal by the general community. The United States need not be embarrassed over its actions as long as they serve the purpose of maintaining the freedom of the people of South Vietnam.[96]

He would presumably agree with the legal adviser that the United States, "in the tradition of the common law, . . . did not pursue some particular legal analysis or code, but instead sought a practical and satisfactory solution to a pressing problem."[97]

On the other side, the most thoughtful protest against the United States position from a legal point of view is that by Professor Friedmann, who has declared that:

The Legal Adviser's argument is one of policy, not of law, and it seeks to justify what is patently, by standards of international law, an illegal action, in terms of the ultimate policy objectives of the United States. By using the language of legal rather than of political justification, the argument comes unintentionally close to the attempts made by Nazi and Communist lawyers to justify the interventionist and aggressive actions of their respective governments in terms of a legal order of the future. . . . Surely, the legal as well as the political style of the United States should remain unmistakably different from that of its totalitarian opponents.[98]

Noting that "certain types of conflict have never come effectively within United Nations purview"—those between major Member states or involving a major nonmember state; "open-ended" or "intermediate" conflict situations "not clearly covered by the traditional distinctions between peace and war" (the Cuban missile crisis, for example); and cases of civil war—he points out:

In principle, civil war situations threatening international peace and security are within the purview of the Charter, and the United Nations did intervene in a civil war of such character in the Congo operation. But this venture also showed the precariousness of this type of intervention, at least where it leads to action favoring one or the other side in civil war. . . .

96. Myres S. McDougal, in American Society of International Law, *Proceedings* (1965), p. 79. See also Ambassador Goldberg: "The U.N. is certainly the preferred policeman, but where it cannot act, individual states must accept the responsibility— as the United States and others are doing in Vietnam today." U.S. Department of State, *Bulletin*, Vol. 54 (1966), p. 940.

97. Meeker, *op. cit.*, p. 64.

98. Wolfgang Friedmann, "United States Policy and the Crisis of International Law," *American Journal of International Law*, Vol. 59 (October 1965), p. 869.

Granted the multiplicity and increasing importance of civil wars with international implications, the inability of the United Nations to control these situations is certainly a serious matter. But this state of affairs is implicit in the still very precarious organization of mankind. A large proportion of the world's states are subject to continuous upheavals and revolutions which, because of the renewed intensity of the political "Cold War" between the Communist Powers and the West, and the revolution in modern transportation, often pose threats to peace.[99]

He challenges the particular arguments used by the administration "to vindicate its military intervention" in Vietnam and the Dominican Republic, in particular, as they apply to the American claim that, in today's world, "the old distinction between 'civil war' and 'international war' has already lost much of its meaning."[100] Friedmann argues that:

In the absence of any international body such as the United Nations, a commission of inquiry or an international judicial authority, the decision whether a particular conflict is essentially a phase of civil war or of foreign aggression, is one that cannot be objectively determined and therefore rests with the Powers directly concerned. . . . This, [whatever it may be called,] is in fact a return to unmitigated national control over the use of force. The degree of discretion is further heightened by the leeway which Communist theory has long accorded to intervention in wars of "national liberation," and by the counterpoint theory, now tentatively adopted by the United States, . . . that the involvement of Communists . . . in an internal revolution implies of necessity intervention by a foreign (Communist) Power, and therefore justifies counter-intervention.

In his view, it would be "a better if negative service" to international law to acknowledge a deliberate departure from its obligations if, "in the considered judgment of this country's responsible policy-makers and of students of international affairs, international tensions have become too great to make the observance of international law compatible with elementary interests of survival. . . ." "The survival of states is not a matter of law," he "sadly" agrees with former Secretary of State Acheson, even when, as in the Cuban missile crisis, accepted legal principles influenced a course of action "consistent with ethical restraint."[101]

Whatever one's view of the theoretical legal arguments, it is difficult to disagree with Professor Friedmann's conclusion that it is policy, not law, that determines the *actions* of states with respect to intervention in civil

99. *Ibid.*, p. 865.

100. President Johnson, address at Baylor University, May 28, 1965, in U.S. Department of State, *Bulletin*, Vol. 52 (1965), p. 991.

101. Friedmann, *op. cit.*, pp. 866–67, 870–71.

wars or "indirect-aggression" cases. In effect, the quotations above, alike from official and unofficial advocates of United States policy, admit as much. Unless and until international agreements and procedures for maintaining peace and order are more willingly adhered to, as well as subscribed to, the minimum of "coexistence-law" will continue to prevail, rather than the desired maximum of "cooperative-law" that is the aim of the United Nations system. And if greater agreement is not reached on restraints in the use of national force according to rules of international law, the unprecedented expansion under the United Nations of international cooperation in many other fields of international law and organization, such as physical communication and economic and social welfare, is not likely to survive in the long run.

In these terms, greater success in expanding the degree of political cooperation is essential to any significant improvement in the degree of legal cooperation. The "rule of law" in the critical field of international security can advance only in harness with political cooperation. Expansion of neither the judicial structure, the total of legal instruments in force, nor the number of "interpretations" and definitions accepted by "United Nations majorities" will in itself eliminate the need for an improved political community to undergird the law in matters of peace and war.

CHAPTER NINE

ORGANIZATIONAL PROBLEMS:
FINANCING AND MEMBERSHIP

United States security policies in relation to the United Nations were considered in Chapters 4–8 primarily from the point of view of the substance of the policies concerned. To complete the picture, the role of the Organization itself, as a continuing body, must also be considered in relation to national policy determination.

The institution's role could not be a central one under the conditions of conflict that have dominated the other relationships of its independent-state Members. As an agency to promote cooperative policies, the very weakness of the United Nations institutional authority in relation to its Members has, on the other hand, served to keep it from foundering on the rocks of their conflicts. The open-endedness of many Charter provisions, which reflected that lack of organizational authority, also gave the United Nations sufficient flexibility to adapt to many unforeseeable and contentious developments.

By the nature of the relationship between the members and the Organization, national policy regarding the institution itself must always be secondary to policies concerning the substance of national foreign and security interests. As a "center for harmonizing the action of nations" to attain those common purposes as set forth in the Charter,[1] the role of the Organization becomes more important as the policies of the nations become more cooperative and therefore more susceptible to harmonization through its channels. The Organization may develop its role in two ways: as the collectivity of the Member states acting through its machinery and procedures, it may develop and supervise joint international policies; and as the organ of the Secretary-General and his staff, it may act to carry out such of those joint policies as are of a continuing or operational nature. Considering the United Nations in the latter context, it should hardly be

1. Art. 1(4).

necessary to point out that when the Secretariat becomes the executive of the Organization, it becomes so only to the extent delegated.

The "executive capacity" of the Secretary-General is not something that can be separated from the effective will of the Member states; and because the Members granted only the most limited mandatory authority to the Organization (and that, under even more limiting voting procedures to control its use), any extension of organizational "authority" must be based on the effective consent of the Member states. Chapter 2 briefly surveyed the extraordinary increase in such authority granted to the Secretariat under the United Nations, as compared to the League of Nations; but the chapters in Part 2 also illustrated the political restrictions that have accompanied the use of that wider authority.

It has become a commonplace of political rhetoric in the United States to refer to the United Nations as a cornerstone of American foreign policy. Washington has indeed been the strongest supporter of the Organization in general, both financially and in promoting the development of the Secretary-General's executive capacity. In the peacekeeping field in particular, these two aspects were brought together in an attempt to extend the assessment authority of the Assembly in connection with highly contentious operations being carried out by the Secretariat. In face of the active opposition of the Soviet Union and France, however, the legal position supported by the United States could not be implemented without unduly endangering the future of the Organization. As a result, policy with regard to the institution itself became at that point an issue predominating over the substantive policies concerned, to the extent that the United States retreated from its insistence on forcing the issue of Article 19 sanctions.

On the whole, Washington has found the standards of the Charter in line with United States interests, and was for long in the happy position of having a majority of Members on its side in both of the major organs and on most of the major issues. The Soviet Union was then on the other side, and when regularly in the minority, interpreted the Charter's standards to fit its own ideological and political interests. In general, for the first decade and a half, those were usually shared only by the few other communist Members. In that situation, Moscow sought to safeguard its position in the Security Council by means of the veto and fought to restrict the development of the Assembly in the direction of any independence of action, as in broad assessment authority or in the authorization of peacekeeping operations. When in its view it then found the

Secretary-General usurping functions that belonged only to the Security Council, it fought also to restrain the development of any independent executive authority. Those issues came to a head in the Congo operation, at a time when the anticolonial states and the United States were on the same side and successfully supported the activities of the Secretary-General. When the main point at issue changed from the Secretary-General to the question of financial assessments for those activities, the majority of Members, although continuing to accept the general principle of collective responsibility, refused to join the United States in forcing the particular case to a showdown.[2]

Both superpowers have thus been frustrated on occasion by the Assembly majority; and each has sought in different ways to operate through that body when it thought the majority would be on its side.[3] The United States on occasion has opposed positions taken by the Secretary-General, as have most Members when his views seemed at variance with their national interests. However, only the communist states under Soviet leadership have sought in principle to destroy the independence of the Secretary-General and even to eliminate his office in favor of a three-man executive, in their effort to establish a "troika" system of Secretariat organization. A three-way division of Secretariat authority would, in effect, paralyze the organ whenever the implementation of contentious Assembly decisions was at stake. Consequently, especially as the proposal was made at the time of greatest controversy over the Congo operation when the majority of the smaller states supported the Secretary-General, the "troika" plan was defeated.[4]

2. See above, Chap. 6, pp. 198–209 for the constitutional and pp. 333–54 below for the financial developments.

3. For a brief survey of some similarities and differences between U.S. and Soviet approaches to the U.N., see John G. Stoessinger, *The United Nations and the Superpowers: United States–Soviet Interaction at the United Nations* (Random House, 1965), especially Pt. 1.

4. Space does not permit their consideration here, but less direct methods of attack on the Secretariat's independence and competence have also been resorted to by the Soviet Union through efforts to increase the proportion of "fixed term" to career appointments (which Moscow is interested in for its nationals) and through encouraging the newer Members to demand faster widening of the geographic distribution of Secretariat personnel to include more from their countries. The desire of the newer states to increase their own "representation" on the Secretariat (regardless of U.N. career-service requirements or of their own lack of competent candidates) has led many of them to support this approach of the Soviet Union. See Sydney D. Bailey, *The Secretariat of the United Nations*, 2d rev. ed. (Praeger, 1964), for the original system and later changes, pp. 63–64, 70–72, 80–83.

Although failing in this direct attack, the Soviet Union succeeded by indirect means in eventually achieving much of its objective of curtailing the activities of the Assembly and the Secretary-General in the peace and security field. It was able to do so when the United States allowed peace-keeping activities to become dependent on financial support from opponents of those operations, which was what happened as the Article 19 crisis evolved. The United States thus found itself in the weakest possible negotiating position, since the Soviet Union and France literally needed to do *nothing* to obtain what they wanted. They had only to let the financial crisis continue.

Development of the Financial Crisis

The financial problem that confronts the United Nations Members is embodied in the fact of a relatively large cash deficit. But that is only the outward sign of an inward political conflict over the direction of the Organization's development. The pattern of failure to pay the assessed portions of expenses for UNEF and ONUC or to make up the deficits by voluntary contributions began with the first year of UNEF. By April 1961, the resultant gap between United Nations income and expenditures had reached a point where the Assembly recognized that some way would have to be found not only to continue financing current operations but also to deal with future peacekeeping activities in a more satisfactory manner. It accordingly set up a Working Group of 15 to examine the whole problem. Aside from recommending that the Assembly ask the International Court for an advisory opinion on the applicability of Article 17 to the financing of UNEF and ONUC, the Group had little new to contribute when it reported the following November.[5] It did, however, identify the major questions to be settled if the financing problem was to be met, although it could agree on no recommendations to that end.

THE BOND ISSUE, 1961–62

By December 1961, as a direct result of the mounting costs of ONUC, arrears in the payments of assessments and shortfalls in voluntary contributions were threatening the United Nations with insolvency. The

5. The Working Group was established by A/Res. 1620 (XVI), April 21, 1961. Its report is in U.N. Doc. A/4971, Nov. 15, 1961.

Assembly, therefore, with strong support from the United States, autho-rized a $200 million bond issue as an emergency measure to meet the current crisis while efforts were being made to collect arrears and to find a longer-term solution. The Soviet delegate had denounced the bond pro-posal as illegal, along with the peacekeeping activities it was designed to sustain; but most Members felt that the Assembly could legitimately raise funds by methods other than assessment.

The Soviet Union raised another point, however, that found support from France and a number of other noncommunist states: namely, an inconsistency between the resolution to finance ONUC for 1962—which kept those expenses apart from the regular budget—and the proposal to pay interest and amortization on any bond issue out of the regular budget, although its proceeds were clearly intended to pay the Congo costs. The bond issue was adopted nonetheless, but by a vote of 58–13–24–9 (ab-sent), the large nonvoting proportion indicating considerable doubt among the membership.[6]

In January 1962, President Kennedy sent a special message to the Con-gress requesting an appropriation of $100 million to purchase half the authorized issue. The question unfortunately arose at a time when there was already rising congressional criticism of the United Nations on various points: aspects of the Congo operation, increasing conflict with the Soviet Union over many other issues, a general malaise with the rising influence of so many small new states in the Assembly, whose voting voice often seemed in inverse ratio to their economic and political weakness. All these brought to a head latent dissatisfactions with the Organization and crys-tallized a widespread congressional feeling of being "put upon" by govern-ments that took American financial generosity for granted but felt neither inhibited from criticizing the United States nor inspired to follow its financial example.

In the circumstances, one of the points on which the administration persuaded Congress to authorize purchase of $100 million of the bond issue (but only on a matching basis with purchases by other states) was the provision for interest and amortization payments to be included in the regular annual budget, which was allocated among the entire member-

---

6. A/Res. 1739 (XVI), Dec. 20, 1961. The negative votes included France, Bel-gium, and the 11 communist states. The bonds were to pay 2% interest and were repayable in 25 annual installments, beginning in 1963. For further discussion of the bond episode, see John G. Stoessinger, *Financing the United Nations System* (Brook-ings Institution, 1964), pp. 124–33.

ship. The United States theoretically would save money by this device, since it would then pay only its apportioned 32.02 percent share of the funds from the bond issue used for ONUC, instead of the nearly 40 percent it was currently paying with its additional voluntary contributions. The compelling effect of this device was doubted by some legislators even then; and in retrospect it appears somewhat naive to have judged that governments so adamantly refusing to pay far larger peacekeeping assessments would meekly hand over small payments on a bond issue they had voted against.[7]

In any event, both the Soviet bloc and France withheld from their 1963 (and subsequent) budget contributions the specific amounts assessed against them for those bond charges. The Soviet bloc countries also withheld payments on four other "peacekeeping" accounts in the regular budget: the Korean Commission, the U.N. Cemetery (Korea), UNTSO, and the Field Service. Thus the peacekeeping dispute began for the first time to affect the integrity of the regular budget.[8] General subscriptions to the bond issue also fell short of the desired total. Even with an extension of time for subscribing, only some $170 million were finally taken.[9]

FINANCIAL DEVELOPMENTS, 1962–65

In 1962, the Assembly reestablished the Working Group, with an increased membership of 21, to report on methods of financing peacekeeping operations to a special session of the Assembly called for May 1963. The purpose was to provide for essential financing of UNEF and ONUC until the end of the year.

7. Congress took its own safeguarding measures in authorizing the bond purchases by providing that amounts equal to the United States share of principal and interest receipts should be deducted beforehand from its annual budget contribution.

8. It was not, however, the first Soviet protest against the use of regular budget funds for peacekeeping activities which began in 1947. After unsuccessfully opposing the sending of UNSCOB to Greece, Moscow declared that no portion of its budgetary contribution should be used to defray UNSCOB expenses. The earlier protest did not lead to similar follow-up action, however.

9. As of Dec. 31, 1964, $169,910,923 were subscribed by 64 nations, with the United States purchasing $76,263,276. It was authorized to purchase up to the same amount as other governments (with $100 million limit), but chose not to do so in view of the development of the financial problem in the United Nations. See also *United Nations Financial Situation: Background and Consequences of the Article 19 Controversy over the Financing of U.N. Peacekeeping Operations*, H. Rept. 1564, 89 Cong. 2 sess., App. 3, p. 66.

There were four major positions in the Group: (1) The communist states continued to contend that only the Security Council could impose assessments for peacekeeping operations. (2) Delegations from the poorer states urged a special scale for expenses beyond an initial $5 million, which would be assessed normally on the full membership; beyond that, it was proposed that from 50 to 90 percent of costs be assessed against the industrialized countries only. (3) Great Britain suggested that up to $10 million should be assessed on the regular basis, to cover the second half of 1963, with 50 percent reductions for the developing countries if they paid promptly, and with the resulting deficit to be covered by voluntary contributions from the industrialized countries. (4) The United States opposed any special scale of assessments for the rest of 1963 (which would probably increase its share beyond its regular 32.02 percent). It argued its position formally on the grounds that the regular scale made ample adjustments for low-income countries and that needs for the rest of 1963 should be raised by some ad hoc method that would not necessarily provide a pattern for the future. More important in fact, no doubt, was its situation under a 1952 law that prohibited the delegation from committing the United States to accept more than one-third of any total budgetary assessment by the Assembly without specific legislative authorization.[10] More will be said of this law shortly.

The Working Group was unable to agree on a proposal for the special Assembly, which continued to argue these conflicting positions. It finally decided, in June 1963, to authorize expenditures for UNEF and ONUC during the rest of the year on the basis essentially of a compromise between the industrialized and developing countries, except for France and the Soviet bloc which continued their adamant opposition. A minor part ($2.5 million for UNEF, $3 million for ONUC) of the estimated costs for the period were assessed on the regular budget scale for 1963; the remainder of the appropriated amounts ($7 million and $30 million, respectively) was then apportioned similarly but with each "economically less developed country" (all but twenty-six members) assessed only 45 percent of its regular rate. That is, it was actually granted a 55 percent reduction, while the twenty-six developed countries were "recommended" to make additional voluntary contributions to finance the resultant shortfall from the total authorized expenditures.[11]

10. P.L. 495, July 10, 1952, 66 Stat. 550.

11. UNEF, A/Res. 1875 (S-IV) and ONUC, A/Res. 1876 (S-IV), both passed June 27, 1963. Use of the voluntary contributions was made contingent on payment by the developing countries of their discounted assessments. The 26 "developed" coun-

The compromise brought in enough contributions to maintain the peacekeeping operations for the time being; but it elicited nothing from the Soviet Union and France,[12] both of which began also to make their contributions to the regular budget on a selective basis, as already noted. The Working Group of 21 was continued and instructed to consider again the problem of "a special method for the equitable sharing of the cost of future peacekeeping operations involving heavy expenditures to the extent not covered by agreed arrangements."[13] But the basic problem did not change, nor the opposing great-power viewpoints which remained unreconciled while the new Assembly session progressed. The financial situation continued to deteriorate: the Assembly voted another assessment for UNEF and ONUC in 1964, much of which was not collected; and Members failed to respond to their own resolutions, repeatedly urging additional voluntary contributions. The point was reached, moreover, where the threatened "confrontation" over Article 19 was avoided, in 1964, only by procedural devices that allowed the constitutional crisis to be temporarily postponed.

Although the retreat of the United States from its demand for the application of Article 19 sanctions allowed the twentieth Assembly to return to normal operation in 1965, it did nothing to eliminate the accumulated financial deficit of the Organization. Meanwhile, since 1962, the interminable haggling over financing methods for UNEF and ONUC had begun to assume an air of unreality as new peacekeeping missions were authorized, but paid for by voluntary means almost wholly outside the United Nations budgetary system: either by the parties in dispute dividing the costs (UNTEA, Yemen, and Malaysia), or by the participating governments sharing with other voluntary contributors (UNFICYP). The Special Committee on Peacekeeping Operations, successor to the Working Group, made another appeal for voluntary contributions to what had come to be called the "rescue fund." Then, shortly before a special session of the Assembly was held in San Francisco in June 1965, to

---

tries included: Australia, Austria, Belgium, Byelorussia, Canada, Czechoslovakia, Denmark, Finland, France, Hungary, Iceland, Ireland, Italy, Japan, Luxembourg, Netherlands, New Zealand, Norway, Poland, Rumania, South Africa, Sweden, Ukraine, the Soviet Union, the United Kingdom, and the United States.

12. France continued to pay its assessed share for UNEF, which it claimed was a voluntary contribution, but rejected the assessment for ONUC.

13. A/Res. 1880 (S-IV), June 27, 1963. It was to report to the 19th Assembly.

commemorate the twentieth anniversary of the signing of the Charter, Great Britain opened the subscription list with a $10 million contribution. It was followed promptly by Canada, the Scandinavian countries, and a few others.

Early in the twentieth Assembly, U Thant estimated that some $100 million was needed to liquidate outstanding obligations and to restore the Working Capital Fund to its authorized $40 million level.[14] Little more than $23 million had been contributed by 23 countries to the rescue fund by February 1967, and some $18 million of that had been given as the initial gifts noted above.[15] Most Members, including the Soviet Union, France, and the United States, continued reluctant to contribute to the fund. The latter, of course, owed nothing to the Organization and had already made large voluntary contributions directly for peacekeeping operations. But it was unwilling to make an additional voluntary gift in the spirit that animated the first contributors to the rescue fund, none of which was in arrears either.[16] The United States, in fact, displayed a certain ambivalence in its policies toward the financing of peacekeeping operations as compared with those toward the financing of other undertakings by the Organization. This stemmed immediately from its rigidly legal case for mandatory peacekeeping assessments; but it had a deeper background, which is illustrative of some of the hazards of American foreign-policy-making methods.

AMBIVALENCE OF UNITED STATES POLICIES

Originally the use of international military forces by the United Nations was thought of solely in terms of the application of military sanc-

14. U.N. Doc. A/C. 5/1037, Oct. 11, 1965, p. 10.

15. Pledges to the United Nations Rescue Fund, by early 1967, were as follows: Canada, $4,000,000; Denmark, $1,000,000; Finland, $600,000; Ghana, $20,000; Greece, $50,000; Iceland, $80,000; Italy, $1,500,000; Jamaica, $10,000; Japan, $2,500,-000; Kuwait, $500,000; Liberia, $8,000; Mali, $5,000; Malta, $9,000; Nigeria, $20,-000; Norway, $698,324; Sudan, $100,000; Sweden, $2,000,000; Tunisia, $5,000; Uganda, $19,000; United Arab Republic, $50,000; United Kingdom, $10,000,000; Yugoslavia, $100,000; Zambia, $14,000. (Information supplied by the U.N.) See also "Budgetary Financial Practices of the United Nations," ST/ADM/L. 4 (Jan. 14, 1966), p. 123, and H. Rept. 1564, p. viii.

16. According to columnist James Reston, the fact that he published beforehand President Johnson's plan to announce at the San Francisco twentieth anniversary commemorative meeting of the Assembly in June 1965 a U.S. contribution to the rescue fund as part of a plan to end the crisis, led the President to cancel the proposal and order his speech rewritten. See "The Press, the President and Foreign Policy," *Foreign Affairs*, Vol. 44 (July 1966), p. 565.

tions, and the question of financing procedures was left open-ended.[17] It was assumed, however, that the permanent members of the Security Council would, whatever the method of sharing, bear the major financial and other burdens of applying collective sanctions, which was one of the reasons for granting them their privileged position within that organ.

When the first and only sanctions operation was undertaken in Korea, no attempt was made to obtain agreement to any form of collective financial responsibility. That approach would clearly have been unrealistic in the circumstances. In any event, the United States wanted no controlling international supervision of its conduct of the military conflict, such as could have been implied by any collective assumption of its financial costs. Nor was such a system suggested in the Collective Measures Committee discussions of means to improve future sanctions actions.[18]

The early United Nations field operations involving a few military personnel were partially paid for through regular budgetary allocations among the membership, in spite of Soviet objections. When the costs of larger, later peacekeeping forces mounted and became more contentious politically, Moscow's objections increased. In 1960, in a Committee of Experts to Review the Activities and Organization of the Secretariat, the Soviet expert proposed that three budgets be used in future: (1) the regular one, with a net ceiling of some $50 million, to include only administrative expenses; (2) a separate account for "extraordinary" and other expenses "directly connected with the maintenance of peace and security"; and (3) an operational budget for technical assistance and various welfare programs.[19] Separate agreements would then be drawn up with interested Members for the latter categories, thus allowing any state to opt out of obligations it did not wish to assume. The system was not recommended by the committee; but for all practical purposes, the Soviet Union began applying it to itself, in 1963, when it refused payment for some budgetary accounts.

The United States was not only willing to pay by far the largest share of all budget allocations, but made the largest voluntary contributions as

17. The anticipated Article 43 agreements might have included specific provisions for sharing the financial burden of enforcement; or an ad hoc approach might have been followed, leaving decisions on sharing to be negotiated in connection with each operation, through some adaptation of traditional alliance financing methods.

18. See Chap. 5 for discussion of Korea and the Collective Measures Committee.

19. U.N. Doc. A/4776 (XIV), June 14, 1961. The proposal adopted, in effect, an argument which had had considerable support in the debates on UNEF financing—that extraordinary operations (recognized as such by being handled in special accounts rather than in the regular budget) should not be treated as normal operating costs.

well. Washington, however, had its own argument with the Assembly over budget allocations. From 1946, when the Committee on Contributions wished to assess the United States nearly half the budget on a capacity-to-pay basis, the latter strongly objected to such a heavy apportionment as making the Organization too dependent on one Member. In immediate postwar conditions, it was willing to accept an assessment of nearly 40 percent; but it continually sought to reduce its share. It succeeded, by 1954, in reaching the one-third it considered should be the upper limit for any state; and by 1966, it was paying just under 32 percent. Moreover, it persuaded the Assembly in 1948 to accept the principle that in normal times no Member should pay more than one-third the annual expenses; and in 1958, to reduce the desirable limit to 30 percent.

Meanwhile, Washington left the matter neither to chance nor to the Assembly. In 1952, Congress reinforced the Executive's diplomatic hand by passing the law earlier noted, requiring specific authorization before acceptance of any international organization's budgetary allocation over one-third the total.[20] Thus, in principle, Congress made it clear that it considered the final decision on amounts to be paid by the United States rested with the United States, not with the Assembly. The 1952 law, of course, did not necessarily mean that the Congress would not have accepted particular assessments at a higher rate; and in practice it often offered to accept up to 40 percent of total contributions to voluntary programs. The history of the annual congressional conflicts over foreign-aid appropriations provided sufficient political warning, however, against any systematic effort to raise the regular allocation to the United States.

When United Nations expenses were greatly increased by the larger peacekeeping operations, the principle of collective responsibility would logically have seemed to call for adoption of something like the graduated income tax principle in the form of a special scale, but such a practice was strongly resisted by Washington. Any special scale would inevitably have raised the United States share above the one-third limit, and the Executive branch preferred to rely on voluntary contributions alone to make up the shortfalls, rather than to test the willingness of Congress to accept a higher obligation.

By 1964, not only were peacekeeping procedures at issue, but the increasing demands of the less-advanced countries for greater amounts of assistance (in both financial and technical terms) culminated in the United

20. Inter-American agencies alone were excepted, a limit of two-thirds being set for them. In practice, the United States generally pays about 60 percent.

Nations Conference on Trade and Development (UNCTAD). There, the industrialized nations as a group were outvoted on various issues by the "seventy-seven" (the developing country majority). One objective of the latter, as noted in Chapter 2,[21] was to establish a capital development fund under the Assembly, since they were dissatisfied with both the amounts of capital available through the World Bank and the conditions under which it was loaned. Moreover, the Bank's weighted voting system automatically gives the United States a dominating voice; while Washington's usual 40 percent contribution to the voluntary development program similarly gives it a heavy voice in their direction.[22] Under either arrangement, Washington was able in practice to control its outlay according to its own determination.

The United States has always feared that a special capital development fund under the Assembly might make excessive demands (even if contributions were to be voluntary).[23] It has also been concerned that such a fund might authorize large expenditures in communist countries and might lower standards required of fund-receiving countries.[24] That Congress would resist any such open-ended, large-scale fund was a foregone conclusion. The delegation in 1966, thus voted against the establishment of the fund and made it clear that contributions would not be forthcoming.[25] Even the relatively minor amounts involved in the Special Fund programs have given rise to some congressional criticism when a small proportion of that total has been used for projects in Cuba.[26] How much

21. Pp. 38–40.

22. The two voluntary programs within the U.N. framework—for technical assistance and for pre-investment projects—were combined in 1965, in a single U.N. Development Program.

23. See USUN Press Release 5044, Dec. 21, 1966, for Ambassador Goldberg on U.S. position on funds.

24. See, for example, statement of U.S. policy in Richard N. Gardner, *In Pursuit of World Order* (Praeger, 1964), pp. 119–21.

25. It also opposed actively a move to include the administrative costs of the fund in the regular budget—an interesting position in view of Washington's stand in favor of including the interest and amortization payments on the bond issue in the regular budget, as noted above.

26. In 1961, for example, the United States opposed a Special Fund grant for a Cuban agricultural research project. Not wishing to jeopardize the 97 percent of the fund's projects for that year which were favored by the United States (as the State Department feared might happen since its position was opposed by most of the fund's Governing Council that passes on the year's projects as a group), it entered its objections in the (closed) official record at the time. The Cuban project did not become operational (and hence public) until 1963, in the aftermath of the Cuban missile crisis. This led to a congressional outcry and a special subcommittee hearing by the

greater would be the outcry were development projects in communist countries to be approved for full financing by the Capital Development Fund, to which the United States would be expected to contribute the largest amount, but without the protection of weighted voting. The government has accordingly emphasized its view that large majorities are sterile unless they include those states which must furnish the resources.

In addition, the record also shows one occasion (in 1954) on which the House of Representatives passed a resolution declaring that no United States funds paid to the United Nations should be used for a specific purpose.[27] This was for certain compensation payments to a number of former Secretariat employees of United States nationality, who were found by the U.N. Administrative Tribunal to have been illegally dismissed from their positions as a result of refusing to answer questions by a subcommittee of the Senate Judiciary Committee during the period of Senator Joseph McCarthy's attacks on the State Department. The resolution was binding on neither the Executive nor the United Nations; but, according to one student of the subject, domestic pressures "exerted on the Executive Branch made it necessary to urge the Secretary-General to give in to the demands."[28]

The record can thus not be said to be one of unequivocal support by the United States for the principles of mandatory Assembly determination of

---

Senate Foreign Relations Committee. On the ground that separate accounts are kept of the various national contributions to the fund, the State Department assured the senators that: "No U.S. dollars, personnel, materials, or services will be used in the project." Since that meant that more American resources went to other projects, the system struck Senator Symington as "ridiculous." The device certainly violated the spirit, if not the letter, of the supposedly nonpolitical international administration of the fund's resources, free from national interference. See *United Nations Special Fund*, Hearing before the Senate Subcommittee on International Organization Affairs, 88 Cong. 1 sess., pp. 16–17, 25–30.

In 1966, a somewhat similar case developed in connection with a single proposed Cuban project (out of a total of 82 for the year), which the United States opposed. (See *Washington Post*, Jan. 20, 1966.) During hearings in March-April by a House subcommittee of the Foreign Affairs Committee on the general financial situation of the United Nations, Congressman Fascell again raised the issue of the nonuse of U.S. resources by the Special Fund. Congressman Gross thought it "unconscionable that a single dime of money should go from the U.N. to Cuba." See H. Rept. 1564, p. 138.

27. H. Res. 262, 83 Cong. 2 sess. (1954).

28. Stoessinger, *The United Nations and the Superpowers*, p. 47. The dilemma presented to Lie by this situation was resolved on a technicality: compensation was paid out of the Staff Equalization Fund (which relates to taxation of Secretariat members and is funded by them, not by the Member States), rather than out of the regular budget.

national budgetary contributions and of nonpolitical administration of all international funds. Although the official position continued to be that Assembly assessments for part of the larger peacekeeping operations were in fact mandatory, there were always minority voices which pointed out that the United States itself could hardly be imagined as paying similar Assembly assessments for some future peacekeeping force that it opposed politically, that it might even have previously vetoed in the Security Council.[29] There were even some who felt that the State Department's insistence that economic development financing was an entirely different issue could not be sustained; and that, if the United States succeeded in getting its position on peacekeeping assessments accepted, the Assembly would soon begin levying assessments for a capital development fund.[30] They argued that Congress would never accept such assessments for the United States and that therefore the official position should not be pressed to a showdown against the Soviet Union and France.

Within the Congress, however, as within the State Department, the "hard-line" legal case for mandatory peacekeeping assessments prevailed. It was sustained, presumably, by the judgment that, if the major delinquents were not sooner or later persuaded to change by the pressures of the majority that favored the principle of collective financial responsibility, they would eventually pay up rather than find themselves losing their Assembly votes.

FINANCIAL CONTROVERSY, 1964–66

By 1964, however, it began to be apparent that Washington was not going to be able to mobilize the necessary support in the Assembly for its position on Article 19, which seemed increasingly likely to result in a Soviet walkout and certain to fail to bring in the disputed funds. Although maintaining its legal position, the United States began to show more flexi-

29. A recent advocate of this viewpoint is Senator Frank Church (a member of the U.S. Delegation to the 21st Assembly). See his report to the Senate Foreign Relations Committee: *The United Nations at Twenty-One*, 90 Cong. 1 sess. (February 1967), pp. 24–25.

30. For a discussion of this issue, see the separate opinion of Judge Fitzmaurice in the *Certain Expenses* advisory opinion of the International Court of Justice in *I.C.J. Reports*, 1962, pp. 198–215. The Justice did not feel that such "permissive" economic and social activities created the same obligation on Members as the political peacekeeping activities; but he also noted the difficulty of drawing hard and fast lines and the fact that "changing concepts are also involved."

bility in its attitude toward special procedures for large peacekeeping expenses. It suggested officially that a special standing finance committee might be established by the Assembly, including the permanent members of the Security Council and other heavy contributors to the budget, with voting weighted to give them a heavier influence, though not a veto, in the determination of the method for financing future operations. A special scale of assessments above a specified minimum to be allocated on the regular scale was recognized as one method the finance committee might recommend for operations involving the use of military forces.[31]

Meanwhile, informal consultations were proceeding that led eventually to an Afro-Asian proposal based on a different type of compromise—one that sought to balance an undertaking to eliminate the financial deficit through voluntary contributions, against agreement that the applicability of Article 19 would not be raised (although positions of principle would be retained). But the compromise fell through at the beginning of the nineteenth Assembly, evidently over the terms of the request for the necessary voluntary contributions.[32] If such contributions by the major states in arrears were large enough to restore United Nations solvency, they would incidentally reduce the formal deficits owed by those states below the size where the Article 19 penalty came into question. Washington therefore apparently insisted that these voluntary contributions would have to be sufficiently large by each state concerned to achieve that practical result, and would have to be made *before* the Assembly could return to normal voting procedures. The Soviet Union was equally adamant in refusing to announce a contribution *until* the Assembly definitely shelved the Article 19 issue. The stalemate resulted in the establishment of the Special Committee on Peacekeeping Operations in early 1965, as noted in Chapter 6, and its inconclusive discussions leading, so far as the financial issue was concerned, only to the consensus in June that the current difficulty should be solved through voluntary contributions.

In August, the United States conceded to the majority view on the immediate Article 19 issue; but that part of the Special Committee's consensus (that, to permit the Assembly to return to normal procedures, "the

---

31. See U.S. memorandum of Oct. 8, 1964, "The United Nations Financial Crisis," U.S. Department of State, *Bulletin*, Vol. 51 (1964), pp. 681–90.

32. See subsequent discussions of the 1964 issue in U.N. Doc. A/AC.121/SR.2, April 22, 1965; SR.4, April 27, 1965; SR.5, April 29, 1965; and SR.6, May 6, 1965. See also Philip van Slyck, "Conversation with Adebo," *Vista*, Vol. 1 (July-August 1965), pp. 38–39.

question of the applicability of Article 19" would not be raised with regard to UNEF and ONUC) was not formally conditioned on its other point of accord (that the current financial difficulties should be solved by voluntary contributions).[33] At the twentieth Assembly, which began immediately thereafter, normal voting procedures were accordingly restored, but neither the Soviet Union nor France made any financial contributions. The latter hinted that it would probably do so if its proposal for a study to improve the general budgetary procedures of the entire United Nations system was adopted. This was done,[34] and an *Ad Hoc* Committee of Experts reported in March 1966 on the immediate financial problem, but without touching on any of the politically difficult issues.[35]

However, continuing disagreement within the committee over the official size of the Organization's deficit meant that the financial controversy merely took a new turn. On the assumption that the states in arrears would not be likely to make substantial payments thereon in 1966, the committee split over the amount of voluntary contributions necessary in the current year to restore United Nations solvency. The argument became whether the sum needed (as of March 1966) was some $53 million or only $32 million.[36] The difference was accounted for by the excess of authorizations over actual expenditures in the accounts of UNEF and ONUC. Assistant Secretary of State Joseph J. Sisco explained the situation to a subcommittee of the Committee on Foreign Affairs:

We are in favor of the larger figure simply because of the fact that we think these credits are still due to the members. The Russians and the French are in favor of the smaller figure because they say there is no such thing as a surplus account, there are no such things as credits . . . because . . . this larger figure

33. U.N. Doc. A/5916, Aug. 31, 1965.

34. A/Res. 2049 (XX), Dec. 12, 1965. It provided for an *Ad Hoc* Committee of Experts to Examine the Finances of the United Nations and the Specialized Agencies, to consider: (1) a complete statement on the financial situation to be submitted by the Secretary-General by March 1966; and (2) "the entire range of budgetary problems" of the United Nations and specialized agencies, submitting to the 21st Assembly, "without prejudice to the terms of reference of the Special Committee on Peacekeeping Operations," recommendations to secure better utilization of available funds and to ensure that any expansion of activities takes into account both the needs intended to be met and the resulting costs to Members. The committee members were: Argentina, Brazil, Canada, France, Hungary, India, Italy, Japan, Nigeria, Senegal, the Union of Soviet Socialist Republics, the United Arab Republic, the United Kingdom, and the United States.

35. U.N. Doc. A/6289 and Add. 1, March 28, 1966; also Add. 2, March 31, 1966.

36. These figures took into account voluntary contributions made before the date of the committee's report of March 28, 1966.

takes into account the UNEF expense as well as the ONUC expenses. The Russians claim the assessments are illegal, and therefore they say that you cannot figure moneys going to pay the costs of UNEF and ONUC in the so-called surplus accounts.

It was apparent that the purpose of the Russians and French . . . was to try to get the Committee to come out with a judgment that this was the absolute minimum . . . needed over the next year in order to bring the U.N. to solvency. The reason they wanted this small figure was twofold. One they wanted either directly or indirectly for this expert committee's judgment to appear to be a writeoff of the past debts. Secondly, [decision on] the lowest possible figure . . . would presumably have permitted the Russians and the French to make the smallest possible symbolic voluntary contribution and then say it is up to the United States to make up a substantial part of the difference. Of course, we didn't fall into this trap.[37]

The committee therefore left the short-run issue unsettled. It listed the full amount of money needed in the long run, not only for peacekeeping debts as of 1966, but also for the replenishment of the Working Capital Fund and the regular budget requirements, not writing off either past debts or the 1961 bond obligations.

Meanwhile, in the twentieth Assembly, the United States had made known Washington's interpretation of the August 1965 "consensus": its own willingness to contribute to the "rescue fund" would depend on similar contributions forthcoming from "a substantial number of other states," inasmuch as it had "paid its share—and considerably more—of all United Nations expenses [almost $2.5 billion] ever since this Organization was established."[38] At the same time, when speaking of other aspects of peacekeeping than financing, Ambassador Goldberg exhorted the Members to act so that United Nations effectiveness would not be "determined by the level of support coming from its least cooperative Members."[39]

FINANCING UNEF, 1965–66

Peacekeeping expenses for ONUC had ceased with its termination in 1964; Cyprus continued to be financed voluntarily but with great difficulty; and the expanded observer group in Kashmir in 1965 was paid through the regular budget by special agreement of the Security Council. There remained, however, the question of financing UNEF for 1965 and

37. H. Rept. 1564, pp. 114–15.
38. U.S. Department of State, *Bulletin*, Vol. 54 (1966), p. 210 (Ambassador Nabrit, Dec. 17, 1965) and *Ibid.*, pp. 73–74 (Rep. Frelinghuysen, Oct. 19, 1965).
39. *Ibid.*, Vol. 53 (1965), p. 454.

1966 (the two-year requirement resulting from the inability of the nine-teenth Assembly to adopt a formal budget). The Assembly approved a total expenditure for the Force of $33.9 million. It was to be apportioned among the Members on a special scale and as "an ad hoc arrangement" without prejudice to the Members' "position of principle" on the financ-ing of peacekeeping operations.[40] Fifteen million dollars for each year was to be allocated on the basis of $800,000 among all the economically less developed nations, and $14.2 million among the twenty-six "developed" members (of the 1963 classification). In each case, the individual con-tributions were to be in the relative proportions of the regular budget scale. In addition, the latter group would pay 25 percent more than their regular assessments to cover "reserve requirements," that is, the expected shortfall due to continued refusal to pay by the states in arrears.[41] This pat-tern of distribution for the first time apportioned $6.8 million, nearly 40 percent of the total, to the United States, which was in line with the total share it had actually paid in the past, adding voluntary contributions to its assessment of about 33 percent.[42]

In December 1966, a similar resolution was passed appropriating $14 million for UNEF operations in 1967, again apportioning the amount as an ad hoc arrangement, which it hoped would "not need to be repeated in future years and that the General Assembly will be able to reach agree-ment on an acceptable method for the equitable sharing of the cost of peacekeeping operations involving heavy expenditure." (The unexpected withdrawal of UNEF in May-June 1967 met the first hope at any rate.) The less developed countries were allocated $740,000, the developed twenty-six, $13,260,000 plus 25 percent additional "to meet reserve requirements."[43] Ambassador Goldberg spoke approvingly of this exten-

40. The wording of the resolution was vague in avoiding the issue whether the allocation should be considered an "assessment" in the pre-1965 sense.

41. A/Res. 2115 (XX), Dec. 21, 1965.

42. The resolution passed by the curious vote of 44–14, with 46 abstentions. The United States delegation abstained, citing the 1952 congressional limitation on its acceptance at that time, but indicating that Congress would be requested to appropriate the funds if the resolution passed. See Rep. Frelinghuysen's statement, in U.S. Depart-ment of State, *Bulletin*, Vol. 54 (1966), p. 296. The request was subsequently pre-sented to the Congress as part of the foreign-aid appropriations request, used regularly for voluntary contributions, rather than within the annual State Department appropria-tion, normally used for assessed contributions.

43. A/Res. 2194 (XXI), Dec. 16, 1966, adopted 56–11–25–30 (absent). The United States voted for the resolution this time, subject to the necessary congressional approval of the funds for its contribution.

sion, which he noted provided for cost-sharing "along the line of the model scale of assessments embodied in the Canadian resolution," in the postponed Report of the Special Political Committee.[44]

There also continues to be a smaller, cumulative deficit of some $2.4 million annually, resulting from items in the regular budget (the bond-issue payments and the smaller peacekeeping costs) that are not paid by the Soviet Union, France, and a number of other members.[45] No proposals have yet been made to meet this problem. Presumably, its resolution will depend on what happens in the more major peacekeeping controversy. The only encouraging note in this rather sorry tale occurred when the Special Assembly opened in April 1967. Five Members—Bolivia, Congo (Leopoldville), Yemen, Haiti, and the Dominican Republic—in arrears more than two years, without counting UNEF and ONUC assessments, stayed away to avoid the Article 19 issue. Subsequently, all paid enough to avoid any question of the sanction.[46]

THE IRISH RESOLUTION

The twentieth Assembly, as anticipated, also continued the Special Committee on Peacekeeping Operations, instructing it to report to the next session and reiterating the call for voluntary contributions to the rescue fund. The committee was assigned for special consideration a proposal by Ireland on the financing of future peacekeeping operations.[47]

The Irish resolution reasserted the Assembly's "right" to recommend a peacekeeping operation when the Security Council is unable to take "prompt and effective action" to maintain peace; then "invited" the Special Committee to consider (a) criteria for distinguishing between peacekeeping operations and enforcement measures under Chapter VII, (b) means of harmonizing the respective responsibilities of Council and Assembly in these matters, (c) the implementation of peacekeeping resolutions, including making personnel and facilities available to the Organization, and (d) the preparation of a special scale for "the equitable appor-

44. USUN Press Release 5044, Dec. 21, 1966, p. 6. See Chap. 6, pp. 207–08 for action on the committee report.

45. See U.N. Doc. A/6289 (March 1966).

46. *New York Times*, April 26, 1967.

47. A/Res. 2043B (XX), Dec. 14, 1965, adopted 93–1–7. The Irish draft resolution was also sponsored by Ceylon, Costa Rica, Ghana, the Ivory Coast, Liberia, Nepal, the Philippines, and Somalia. Text of the proposal is in *UN Monthly Chronicle*, Vol. 3 (January 1966), pp. 33–34; summary of the debate on the proposal, pp. 30–31.

tionment of" peacekeeping costs among the Members. Meanwhile, until some comprehensive financing arrangement might be adopted, it proposed that expenditures not otherwise covered should be apportioned on the following basis:

(a) (i) As to 5%, among the group of economically less developed Member States;

(ii) As to 25%, among the group of economically developed Member States other than the permanent members of the Security Council;

(iii) As to 70%, among the ... permanent members ... to be assessed only on those permanent members who vote in favour of the operation, provided, however, that no Member shall be assessed for more than 50% of the net cost of the operation and that any balance unassessed by reason of this proviso shall be added to the sum apportioned on the group of Members in sub-paragraph (ii);

(b) Within each group the amount to be paid by each Member shall be in proportion to its capacity to contribute relative to the other members of the group as determined by the scale of assessments for the regular budget;

(c) Any Member of the United Nations or other State or organization may make voluntary subscriptions to reduce the amount to be assessed on any or all of the groups.

In the Special Political Committee, Ambassador Goldberg reiterated the United States belief in "full collective responsibility [as] the first choice"; but as that was not achievable for the time being, he declared Washington ready "to accept such an opting-out arrangement for permanent members as an interim measure if that is the wish of the majority." While not opposing the principle of a special scale, the Ambassador did object to the idea of "a fixed scale [for] all operations regardless of their size" or special circumstances. He supported, "in accordance with the practice of the United Nations," using the regular budgetary scale for "relatively small peacekeeping operations and for a small proportion of larger operations" (that is, as in financing UNEF and ONUC in 1962–64). And he added:

The United States also has reservations about a proposal that one country might have to pay as much as 50% of the costs of any operation for which it cast an affirmative vote. Under existing legislation, the United States delegation is not authorized to vote for an assessment in which the United States share is more than 33⅓ per cent....[48]

The United States is hardly likely to accept anything like the Irish-proposed scale, since in principle it has so far not been willing to accept

48. Statement in the Special Political Committee, Nov. 24, 1965. Text in U.S. Department of State, *Bulletin*, Vol. 54 (1966), pp. 97–99.

the political reality that, if some permanent members of the Security Council refuse to pay their allocations for peacekeeping operations, few besides the other permanent members can be expected to make up the deficit so caused. In practice, this seems to many Americans to mean only that the United States would be "paying for the deadbeats in the U.N."[49] Nor has the Executive Branch been prepared to ask the Congress to adopt the viewpoint of Representatives O'Hara and Frelinghuysen (after their service as delegates to the twentieth Assembly), that "the United States should not tie its hands by insisting on rigid financial limits on U.S. contributions," specifically the $33\frac{1}{3}$ percent limit on assessments:

In our view [they continued], the United States should be prepared to contribute financially whatever is required to support United Nations peacekeeping operations of which it approves; for example, operations like UNEF, ONUC, and UNFICYP. Certainly we should be willing to support such operations up to the 50 percent level. It follows, of course, that the United States should be able to 'opt out' of operations to which we object, as do the Soviet Union and other major contributors now. . . . The United States, in other words, should not be frightened by high-contribution percentages when the absolute dollar amounts are small, or take the line that we must refuse to contribute because the Soviet bloc or others do not pay their shares.[50]

In addition, many smaller states have indicated opposition to accepting even their proposed minor burdens without the same privilege of opting out of operations they do not favor. Also, the Soviet Union has continued to hold to its "position of principle," namely, that the whole Irish approach is "contrary to the Charter, since it was designed to bypass the Security Council, the only organ entitled to take actions involving the use of armed forces in the name of the United Nations."[51] In view of these attitudes, it is not surprising that the Special Committee, in spite of its mandate, did not formally discuss the Irish formula in its meetings during

49. Congressman Frelinghuysen thus described the attitude of those insistent on attempting to make the delinquent Soviet and French governments pay their arrears. See H. Rept. 1564, p. 120.

50. *The Costs of World Peacekeeping*, Report by Barratt O'Hara and Peter H. B. Frelinghuysen, H. Rept. 1404, 89 Cong. 2 sess. (March 1966), p. 17.

51. Summarized in *UN Monthly Chronicle*, Vol. 3 (January 1966), pp. 30–31. The Irish opting-out proposal for the permanent members, it might be noted, would not allow the Ukraine or Byelorussia legally to escape their assessed shares of the 25 percent allocated to the other developed nations. This provides another reason for continued Soviet opposition, even though it would not itself be bound.

1966. It had to report to the twenty-first Assembly that it had not resolved any fundamental issues of the peacekeeping controversy. The Special Political Committee returned to the fray but the Assembly postponed action on its recommendations until the Special Assembly called for April 1967.[52] The most pertinent point here was the withdrawal in plenary of a new version of the Irish resolution, which, however, maintained the mandatory allocation element that had been adopted in the Special Political Committee by far less than the two-thirds majority required for plenary adoption.

By the spring of 1966, the United States saw its interest in trying to maximize support for any future peacekeeping operation that it approved and voted for. That would mean, for example, that when Soviet-American interests are parallel, as in the 1965 Kashmir outbreak, the operation can probably be financed on the basis of the regular budget; but that when differences exist, as Assistant Secretary Sisco explained to a House sub-committee, it will be necessary to rely on those who favor the operation in question:

Those of us who think that a peacekeeping operation is politically desirable and support it politically, and want to support it financially will have to do it basically in one of two ways: either by a pure and simple voluntary contribu-tion [as in Cyprus]; or by getting a group of like-minded states to decide, as we did in the resolution on [UNEF], to apportion the cost among the 40 or 50 countries who support that particular peacekeeping operation politically.[53]

He was also frank to recognize the broader implications of the situation, noting on another occasion that: "As long as there are fundamental dif-ferences between the U.S.S.R. and the United States about the role of the U.N. in the peacekeeping field, it will be difficult to make real progress toward a more reliable system of financing or authorizing future peace-keeping operations."[54]

This was not only an accurate forecast of the lack of progress in the twenty-first Assembly—the pattern has been maintained into 1967. The Committee of 33 again proved unable to agree on recommendations to the Special Assembly, which met in late April. And its discussion of the financial issue took on an increasingly open tone of asperity. Ambassador

52. A/Res. 2220 (XXI), Dec. 19, 1966.
53. H. Rept. 1564, p. 120.
54. U.S. Department of State, *Bulletin*, Vol. 54 (1966), p. 649.

Goldberg, having "regretted" at the end of the Assembly in December 1966, that neither the Soviet Union nor France had yet made "the substantial voluntary contributions which were contemplated in the consensus arrived at last year,"[55] became even more explicit in the Committee of 33 a few months later. He noted that:

When a way was being sought to end the deadlock over Article 19 many delegations came to the United States Delegation and assured us that, if we would not press for application of the Article 19 voting penalty, then the members who had refused to contribute to certain peacekeeping operations would make substantial voluntary contributions to reduce the deficit of the Organization. In spite of these assurances, I am obliged to note that more than a year has passed and no voluntary contribution has yet been made by any of those countries . . . particularly the major ones.

Now, some have suggested that the United States also should make a voluntary contribution. . . . My country took the initiative in breaking the deadlock over Article 19. Now it is for others to take the initiative by doing their part in the interest of U.N. solvency. . . . But I again repeat the assurance that I have given before, that, once the promised substantial voluntary contributions have been made by those who we have been assured would make such contributions, the United States will not be found wanting in support of the UN's needs and requirements.[56]

The Soviet Union and France responded to this by, in effect, chastizing the United States for not having made a contribution to the rescue fund itself and for "advancing groundless and unacceptable conditions" before it would do so. France declared that, at the time of the 1965 consensus, it had never undertaken "any commitment whatsoever" or "recognized the principle that the payment of a voluntary contribution could constitute a type of counterpart offered to those Member States which had envisaged . . . the application of Article 19."[57] The Soviet representative "confirmed that the Soviet Union, which was always true to its word, would make a voluntary contribution . . . in accordance with the understanding [of 1965]. . . . The resolution on voluntary contributions, moreover, was not aimed in any one direction but applied equally to all States, including the United States . . . [which], unlike the Soviet Union, refused to make its intentions clear. . . ."[58] The French representative later also

55. USUN Press Release 5044, Dec. 21, 1966, p. 6.
56. USUN Press Release 28, Corr. 1, March 22, 1967, pp. 4–5.
57. U.N. Doc. A/AC. 121/WG. A/PV. 3, March 29, 1967, p. 12.
58. U.N. Doc. A/6654 (May 17, 1967), pp. 38–39. See also, *New York Times*, April 13, 1967, on the Soviet-U.S. exchange.

declared "once again" his government's intention "to take its share of the collective effort through which the industrialized countries as a whole have undertaken to settle this problem by paying national contributions. The French Government, of course, cannot determine the modalities for this unless the decisions to be taken are coordinated and are made concurrently."[59] The United States found these views incredible, considering its over-all financial contributions to both United Nations peacekeeping and economic-social activities—which were "some 25 times greater than those of the Soviet Union"—and it continued to remain, as Ambassador Goldberg said, "content to rest on the record of our performance and leave it to the judgment of the members whether others have fulfilled their obligations under the consensus."[60] It did not appear that any of the major contenders would heed the reminder of the Swedish representative that, nearly two years after the 1965 consensus, which had not been implemented, it would not be unreasonable to expect, particularly on the part of the great powers, a "gesture of generosity."[61]

As the present study goes to press, neither Moscow nor Paris has made its generalized commitment specific; and they will no doubt continue to insist that other developed countries—meaning the United States—must make similar payments under the Assembly resolutions in order to "prove" that their own contributions are not made to compensate for their unpaid peacekeeping assessments. Moreover, since neither government wants the Organization to expand its field activities, the continuing financial difficulties provide a good rationale for opposing any program they do not favor. The United States, on the other hand, may also continue to adhere to its own position to prove the point it has been so insistent upon. Washington, at the same time, remains a strong supporter of continuing and improving the capacity of the United Nations to deploy peacekeeping forces under Secretariat direction and financed by "viable and equitable" arrangements, "faithfully implemented."[62]

The end result, as noted earlier, was that the Assembly once more continued the Committee of 33 with the same instructions, to review "the whole question of peacekeeping operations in all its aspects, in particular

59. U.N. Doc. A/6654, Annex III, p. 67.
60. *Ibid.*, p. 40, and U.S. Department of State, *Bulletin*, Vol. 56 (1967), p. 896.
61. U.N. Press Release GA/3371, May 22, 1967, Assembly Plenary.
62. U.S. Department of State, *Bulletin*, Vol. 56 (1967), p. 895.

those relating to methods of financing and to the provision of services and personnel by Member States."[63]

The Character of United Nations Membership

The constitutional and financial crises have been explained by Washington as due in major part to failure by the smaller Members to support the United States in upholding the principle of collective financial responsibility to the point of penalizing other great powers able, but unwilling, to pay their shares.[64] The problem came to a head during the years when the great increase of newly independent states was transforming the size and character of the Assembly. These states were pressing their anti-colonial and racial concerns with an intensity disturbing to the United States as well as to its NATO allies most directly concerned. Many of the particular issues on which their views tended to go too far too fast for Washington's comfort have been discussed in previous chapters, especially the southern African "hard core" cases where mandatory sanctions are impatiently demanded, and the remaining dependent territories where almost instant independence is indiscriminately proposed.

Egged on by the communist powers, this latter anticolonial drive became even more specifically related to security issues in the twentieth Assembly, in the resolution concerning removal of military bases. That was passed by a procedural evasion of the requirement of Article 18(2) that decisions on "important questions" (specified to include "recommendations with respect to the maintenance of international peace and security") be made by a two-thirds majority in the Assembly. Ambassador Goldberg formally declared the action to be "unconstitutional" and "of no effect."[65] The recommendation was nonetheless repeated in the twenty-first Assembly as noted in Chapter 7.

63. A/Res. 2249 (S-V), May 23, 1967.
64. See, for example, Ambassador Goldberg's statement of Aug. 16, 1965, in the Special Peacekeeping Committee, U.N. Doc. A/AC. 121/PV. 15, pp. 7–10; and a more recent statement by a senior delegation member, in USUN Press Release 25 (March 11, 1967), p. 3.
65. "If the Assembly," he said later to a subcommittee of the House Foreign Affairs Committee, "disregards its own constitution . . . it is taking an unconstitutional action and we will disregard it, and we have disregarded it and will continue to do so. . . . I think it is an absolutely sound position . . . as a matter of constitutional law." (H. Rept. 1564, p. 88.) At the time, the Ambassador warned the Assembly: "If the matter is an important question, and the Charter requires it be decided under a ⅔ rule, the

The conjunction of these and other episodes that to some indicate a degree of small-power "irresponsibility" has led to increased concern with what has come to be known as the "international apportionment problem." From the viewpoint of the United States, it is the problem of adapting "the decision-making procedures of the United Nations . . . to take adequate account of world power realities."[66] A second major problem involving the nature of the membership is that of the nonmember, or nonrepresented states, of which communist China is the most significant. But in relation to the security interests of this study, the other "divided states" are also important factors.

THE RELATION OF VOTING TO POWER

Increasing United States difficulties in obtaining strong support for its policies in the Assembly stem from two sources. One is the sheer dramatic increase in numbers, from 51 members in 1945 to 123 in 1967. The expectation is that Members will total 125–30 before many years. The large number of Members would in itself complicate the proceedings of the Organization even if its procedures were the most efficient possible. Given the traditions and requirements of international diplomacy, however, the Assembly's procedures will probably continue to be time-consuming and inefficient.

The problem of streamlining the plenary organ must be left to others to deal with. It should be noted in passing, however, that complaints about the Assembly's annual "talkathon" may be overlooking one of the more educational aspects of United Nations diplomatic experience for many of the newer nations. The procedural difficulties, nonetheless, are real enough and any improvements that will facilitate the more efficacious conduct of the Assembly's business are to be welcomed. Some use is already made of smaller, special ad hoc committees with appropriately representative membership, as seen throughout this study. Where differences are deep over the substantive issues before such committees, how-

Assembly is without competence by changing its rules of procedure to amend the Charter. Any resolution passed in violation of this provision . . . can only be null and void." USUN Press Release 4762 Dec. 17, 1965, p. 1. See also Press Release 4771, Dec. 20, 1965.

66. Richard N. Gardner, "United Nations Procedures and Power Realities: The International Apportionment Problem," *American Society of International Law, Proceedings*, Vol. 59 (1965), p. 233.

ever, their more representative make-up does not facilitate resolving the problem (as witness the Committee of 33). In spite of this, they perhaps offer the best promise of improving efficiency and of more closely reflecting the weight of influence of the several members. The recently increased size of the Economic and Social Council theoretically should enhance the acceptability of its actions as an organ representative of all the membership, and therefore serve to decrease the amount of "re-hashing" of its agenda items in the full Assembly. In practice, it will probably not make that difference.

The serious problem from the viewpoint of the United States, however, is not so much the inefficiency of the Assembly as what Washington sees as an eroding of its earlier influence in the plenary organ. This results less from the number than from the nature of the enlarged membership. Thus the concern of Secretary of State Rusk, that there be

some adaptation of procedures if the U.N. is to remain relevant to the real world and therefore effective in that world. Theoretically, a two-thirds majority of the General Assembly could now be formed by nations with only 10 percent of the world's population, or who contribute, altogether, 5 percent of the assessed budget. In practice, of course, this does not happen, and I do not share the dread expressed by some that the General Assembly will be taken over by its "swirling majorities."

But even the theoretical possibility that a two-thirds majority, made up primarily of smaller states, could recommend a course of action for which other nations would bear the primary responsibility and burden is one that requires thoughtful attention. . . . The plain fact of the matter is that the United Nations simply cannot take significant action without the support of the Members who supply it with resources and have the capacity to act.[67]

The logical extension of this conclusion was pointed out by another official:

The manifest disproportion between voting power and real power is now a central preoccupation of persons concerned with the future of the world organization. Unless we can find ways to allay the anxieties on this subject in the United States and in other countries, it will be increasingly difficult to use the United Nations in the years ahead for important tasks of peacekeeping and development.[68]

The most common procedural suggestion for meeting the situation is some sort of weighted voting in the Assembly and in the separate con-

67. Secretary Rusk, "The First Twenty-Five Years of the United Nations: From San Francisco to the 1970's," Dag Hammarskjold Lecture, Columbia University, Jan. 10, 1964. U.S. Department of State, Publication Series S, No. 17.
68. Gardner, American Society of International Law, *Proceedings*, p. 233.

ferences dealing with more specialized technical subjects. The United Nations system has had various forms of weighted voting built into its structure from the start: such as the permanent members' unanimity requirement in the Security Council; their normal membership in ECOSOC; the balanced membership of the Trusteeship Council; and the size of capital contributions in the specialized financial agencies. The one-state-one-vote principle of voting in the Assembly was based on the feeling that, in the United Nations proper, the smaller states would refuse to accept an "undemocratic" weighting of the voting system except in the limited area of the Security Council's predominance.[69] Any system of weighted voting considered for the future would have to be based on such criteria as population, wealth, technological advance, and so forth. Population alone would favor countries like India and China and would therefore be opposed by states that are powerful by reason of wealth and technology. Almost any combination of all the factors would tend to place the current major powers in favored positions in the Assembly as well as in the Council. This would, inevitably, be resisted by the less-favored majority. Moreover, when the State Department experimentally applied various possible formulas to important past votes:

It was found that, while they would have somewhat reduced the number of resolutions passed over U.S. opposition, they would have reduced much more the number of resolutions supported by the United States and passed over Communist opposition. The same conclusion was reached in projecting these formulas to 1970, having regard to further increases in membership.[70]

The voluntary intergovernmental character of the Organization makes it impossible to enforce contentious Assembly decisions against strongly resistant Members. In effect, therefore, where such resolutions serve to initiate field operations of any kind, they must necessarily be sustained materially and financially, as well as by the required votes of a majority

69. The principle was technically violated even in the Assembly, with separate seats and votes permitted to Byelorussia and the Ukraine. It was accepted as a matter of political necessity at the time of Yalta and San Francisco, partly because it did not, in effect, alter the minority position of the Soviet Union within the plenary organ. See Ruth B. Russell, A *History of the United Nations Charter, The Role of the United States 1940–1945* (Brookings Institution, 1958), especially pp. 433–37, 533–35, 631–33, 636–39.

70. Gardner, American Society of International Law, *Proceedings*, p. 238. See also pp. 237–44, for an excellent summary of various other approaches proposed, in addition to weighted voting, as possible ways in which "power steering" might be built into the U.N.: dual voting, bicameralism, selective committees, informal relations with the secretariats, and conciliation procedures.

(whatever its character) of supporting states. And where they require action only by particular states (as in the demand for removal of military bases from dependent territories), they must be acceptable to those states —unless adequate accord might be mobilized in the Security Council to support strong enough sanctions, on the ground that refusal to implement such a resolution constituted a threat to peace. Voting procedures in themselves, even the formal conciliation procedures of UNCTAD, will not make a resolution effective without greater conciliatoriness in fact on the part of both great and small states; nor without adequate political accord on the objectives of Assembly resolutions, whether in the field of peace and security or of economic development.

UNIVERSALITY AND MEMBERSHIP QUALIFICATIONS

The logic of universal membership is inescapable for any organization that aims to maintain world peace and security and to promote world prosperity and the advancement of mankind. Such universality was the ideal of most, if not all, of the founding fathers in 1945; but the establishment of the United Nations by the allied powers in the midst of World War II meant that original membership was impossible in any event for the enemy states. Given political sentiment at the time, moreover, it was not surprising that neutral states, too, were excluded from the list of those invited to San Francisco to negotiate the Charter and thus to become the 51 original Members.[71] Universality remained the ultimate objective, although criteria for the admission of new Members were written into Article 4(1): "Membership in the United Nations is open to all other peace-loving states which accept the obligations contained in the present Charter and, in the judgment of the Organization, are able and willing to carry out these obligations."

The "peace-loving" qualification was the result of historical accident[72]

71. Only 50 countries were actually represented at San Francisco because of the inability of the Big Three to agree on recognition of a single Polish Government at the time. See Russell, *op. cit.*, pp. 628–31, 636–39.

72. In October 1943, the "Declaration of Four Nations on General Security" first committed the major allies to establish a postwar international security organization, "based on the principle of the sovereign equality of all peace-loving states, and open to membership by all such states." At British suggestion, the doctrine of sovereign equality had been tempered to apply only to "peace-loving" countries in order to avoid any implication that the allies intended to admit the current enemy states at any early postwar date to a footing of equality with the victorious United Nations. See *ibid.*, p. 134. Text of Declaration, *ibid.*, pp. 977–78.

—unfortunately, since its chief virtue, when used in the Moscow Declaration of 1943, was as wartime propaganda, and in the years since it has served more to confuse than to help intelligent discussion of controversial membership problems.

The adjective was carried over without debate to the Dumbarton Oaks Proposals in 1944, which declared, simply, that the future organization should be based on "the principle of the sovereign equality of all peace-loving states."[73] Before the San Francisco Conference, the United States delegation agreed that the term was too vague as a qualification for membership, although its wartime currency was such that no suggestion was made to eliminate it from the Proposals. Rather, the group decided to propose that the Charter authorize the Assembly to "determine the qualifications of membership," leaving more definitive standards to be decided by the plenary organ itself. At San Francisco, however, the more specific requirements of Article 4(1) were added and "peace-loving" was also retained in the final Charter text. No delegation challenged its suitability as a legal qualification and, it would appear, most took for granted that the term was intended mainly to force the then-enemy states to "work their passage home" before qualifying for membership in the new Organization.[74] After twenty years' experience, "peace-loving" may be said to be what all states are, by their own definitions and on their own terms.

The "able and willing" criteria of Article 4(1) were more specific and capable of being judged as qualifications for membership. They have, however, been largely ignored since the early years of the Organization. In its first decade, only a handful of states were admitted to membership. The permanent Members on both sides of the cold-war front acted to keep out other applicants that each considered to favor the opposite side —a criterion not listed in the Charter. At the start, the United States supported the speediest possible achievement of universality by the new Organization. In 1946 it recommended that all eight initial applicants be admitted en bloc, despite "certain doubts entertained with respect to whether Albania and the Mongolian Peoples' Republic met the requisite qualifications."[75] The Soviet Union was not prepared to go along with this approach. Washington therefore abandoned it when it became evi-

73. Chap. II, Principles, in *ibid.*, p. 1019.
74. See *ibid.*, pp. 613, 844–45.
75. U.S. Department of State, *The United States and the United Nations: Report by the President to the Congress for the Year 1946*, Publication 2735 (1947), pp. 39–40. The other original applicants included Afghanistan, Iceland, Ireland, Portugal, Sweden, and Transjordan.

dent that Moscow would veto Ireland, Transjordan, and Portugal. Only Iceland, Sweden, and Afghanistan, consequently, were admitted in 1946.

Despite an advisory opinion by the International Court[76] to the effect that each application should be considered on its own merits, the mutual-boycott technique was followed until 1955, when a "package deal" was agreed to by the Soviet Union and the Western powers that admitted 16 states to membership. In the second decade, applications came primarily from states newly emerged from colonial dependency and the exclusion pattern was succeeded by an almost competitive "welcome-wagon" technique. Each side in the cold war was concerned to win the approval and support of newcomers in the Assembly. As a result, any idea that serious consideration should be given either to the credibility of an applicant's acceptance of Charter obligations or to its ability to carry them out was lost. Applicant political units were readily accepted as full-fledged Members, without discussion of whether their political and economic condition was adequate to sustain their undertakings.

Proliferation of small, politically unstable, and economically inviable states tends now to be seen by many as a primary cause of the Assembly's increasing unruliness and disregard of procedural norms in recent years.[77] It must not be forgotten, however, that the Assembly itself has always been split between its major "camps." The inexperienced newcomers entered, not only a "house divided," but a family where the older members had already set some fairly low standards of diplomatic conduct. The leader of one superpower, after all, still holds the record for shoe-thumping as a sign of dissent; nor has the straining of procedural rules been confined to small-state delegations. This is not to condone either bad habit,

76. Soviet opposition took the form of making its consent to "Western" applicants specifically dependent on the admission of communist applicants. In 1947, the Assembly (on Western initiative) requested the International Court to advise whether this "additional condition" to the requirements listed in Art. 4 was permissible. In 1948, the Court advised not, 9–6. It considered the requisite conditions for membership to be 5 in number: an applicant must (1) be a state; (2) be peaceloving; (3) accept the obligations of the Charter; (4) be able to carry them out; and (5) be willing to do so. The conditions in Art. 4(1) should be regarded "not merely as the necessary conditions, but also as the conditions which suffice." A member therefore was not juridically entitled to make its consent to admission dependent on an additional condition that other states be admitted simultaneously. *ICJ Reports 1948*.

77. For a discussion of some of the ways in which procedural rules have been upset, see Sydney D. Bailey, "U.N. Voting: Tyranny of the Majority?" *World Today* (June 1966), pp. 234–41.

but to point out that irresponsibility is not limited to small or new governments.

Be that as it may, the dissatisfaction of many older Members was reflected in 1965 by the United States and France, when their delegates for the first time formally raised some question about this previous lack of standards. The possibility of establishing "some agreed standards, some lower limits to be applied in case of future applicants for United Nations membership," was urged by the United States representative when the Security Council considered the admission of Singapore and the Maldive Islands. The French delegate also proposed that the Council consider setting up a special committee (under procedural rule 59, established by the original Council but not used) to review general problems and examine future applications.[78] The idea would be to find some special relationship for the small political units with the Organization, so its effectiveness would not be diminished, rather than to seek to exclude them from "the family of nations." Both delegates, however, voted for the admission of the two applicants in spite of these misgivings.

Their attitude was not supported by all Security Council members. China noted that: "The very first principle laid down in the Charter is the principle of sovereign equality of all its Members"; nor did smallness (as in the Maldive Islands) lessen the will of people "to independence and freedom." The Ivory Coast felt that "the smaller states are, the more they need the United Nations;" while the Soviet Union declared the provisions of the 1960 declaration on colonial independence were applicable "to all colonial territories, large and small, no matter what part of the world they may happen to be in."[79]

The 1965 move proved abortive. No committee was set up to examine the credentials of applicants, and in 1966 four more small new countries were admitted—Guyana, Barbados, Botswana, and Lesotho—all of which might have been questioned on the issue of capacity to fulfill their undertakings under the Charter.

By accident, rather than design, membership in the United Nations has become, in effect, a sign of legitimacy to practically all new governments,

78. U.N. Doc. S/PV. 1243 (Sept. 20, 1965), pp. 31, 26. Singapore is a 24 x 24 mile island with about 2 million population; the Maldive Islands include some 2,000 small islands and islets in the Indian Ocean, with less than 100,000 people living on about 115 square miles of land area (less than that of Andorra).

79. *Ibid.*, pp. 17, 13, 21. For further discussion of the problem in the context of decolonization see Chap. 7, especially pp. 283–87.

notwithstanding the few autonomous political units preferring not to apply for entry. The applications seem likely to continue coming in, therefore, especially with the Soviet Union in favor of making ever more new states out of the remaining old colonies. Moreover, since any permanent member of the Security Council could have denied admission to any smaller applicant by a negative vote, the Western powers are not in an especially strong position in regretting the results of their earlier inaction. From the viewpoint of complaining governments, about all that can be done at this stage is an extension of the relationship applied in generally similar ways between New Zealand and the Cook Islands and between the United States and Puerto Rico.

Since the imperial powers were unable to maintain their former political control of the territories that are now the new states, they might have sought to make better use of the United Nations as a potential framework within which to develop more orderly new relationships in place of the disintegrating old ones. That it was not so used to greater advantage is, as indicated, due as much to the failure of the older states as to the fault of the newer. The general refusal of the colonial powers even to seek to use the Trusteeship Council and Assembly in some collective endeavor to bring dependent peoples to independent status in a more gradual and systematic fashion was not compensated for by either willingness or ability to use some other unilateral, bilateral, or multilateral channel more effectively for the purpose. An inevitable result of the decolonization experience and of this attitude toward the United Nations was to weaken any possibility that the Assembly might "take constructive action in the troubled aftermath" of the colonial struggles for self-determination.[80]

The proliferating small countries affect the character of the United Nations and, from the viewpoint of some of the large ones, endanger world peace and security by reason of the general international instability they contribute to, as well as because of the particular problems they create or complicate. The effects of the decolonization movement on the problems of military bases, of racial conflict, and of economic development, are all examples of this. The other group of states, which creates a membership dilemma for the United Nations, is related even more directly to international security problems. These are the "divided countries," Germany, Korea, Vietnam, and (though its division is not the result

80. Ernest A. Gross, "Shifting Institutional Patterns of the United Nations," Francis O. Wilcox and H. Field Haviland, Jr., eds., *The United States and the United Nations* (Johns Hopkins Press, 1961), p. 84.

of a recognized armistice arrangement) China. Whether their divisions resulted from World War II or from postwar upheavals, their status reflects still unresolved conflicts between great-power antagonists—originally the Soviet Union and the United States, but now with Communist China as a political (if not yet military) third, at odds with both the others and simultaneously one of the split countries itself.

THE DIVIDED COUNTRIES:
GERMANY AND KOREA

Germany and Korea were divided into occupation zones by the allies after World War II and eventually organized into separate, independently functioning units.[81] As former enemy territories, they came under the provisions of Article 107 of the Charter, which recognized the right of those "Governments having responsibility" for the treatment of enemy states to determine the postwar status.[82] The powers were able to agree on the methods and terms of reunifying Austria alone, and then only after ten years. The greater strategic importance of the other two as iron-curtain frontier countries precluded agreement to allow the United Nations to determine their final status, as was done with the former Italian colonies. Early attempts were, however, made by the Western powers to use United Nations channels for resolving both the situations.

By 1947, the United States-Soviet Joint Commission was deadlocked in its effort to set up a provisional Korean national government in accordance with its instructions. Washington took the problem to the United Nations in spite of Article 107, and the Assembly established the Temporary Commission on Korea to facilitate election of representatives to a national government and to provide for the early withdrawal of occupation forces.[83] The communist delegations refused to participate in the voting, which followed rejection of Soviet proposals to invite representatives from both the Korean zones to participate in the discussions. Moscow also unsuccessfully recommended simultaneous withdrawal of Soviet and American troops, leaving establishment of a national government to the Koreans

81. Although Austria and Japan were also occupied, they were never divided in the same way as the other two, and in any event they have become independent governments and U.N. Members.

82. The stiff phraseology of Article 107 reflected the fact that when the Charter was signed, the Soviet Union was not yet at war with Japan.

83. A/Res. 112 (II), Nov. 14, 1947.

themselves. Not surprisingly, the Soviet Union later refused to let the Temporary Commission enter its zone.

In May 1948, commission-supervised elections were held in the south; and in August a government was established in Seoul. In September, a separate government was set up in the north. In December, the Assembly recognized the Seoul government as the only lawful government based on free elections in the Republic of Korea. It also established a new Commission on Korea, to lend good offices in further reunification efforts and to observe the withdrawal of occupation troops.[84] In 1949, the commission having made no progress toward reunification, the Assembly assigned it the additional task of observing any developments that might lead to military conflict.[85]

The conflict occurred in 1950 and was only suspended by the 1953 armistice agreement that left the country still divided near the 38th parallel. The political conference held at Geneva, in 1954, likewise failed to achieve either a peaceful settlement or the establishment of a unified national government. Meanwhile, the earlier commission was succeeded in 1950 by another U.N. Commission for the Unification and Rehabilitation of Korea (UNCURK), which has continued to the present to pursue the elusive goal of unification. In answer to communist efforts to dissolve the commission and to order withdrawal of all foreign troops as "occupation troops" responsible for the continued division of the country, the Assembly once again, in 1966, reaffirmed its terms for peaceful settlement and reunification (as accepted by the noncommunist participants in the 1954 conference) and continued the commission's mandate. It also noted that governments with troops still in Korea were prepared to withdraw them whenever requested by South Korea or whenever the Assembly's conditions for a settlement were fulfilled.[86]

Germany has been the "enemy territory" of most concern to the cold-war antagonists, as the major wartime allies became, and as such there was less tendency for even the Western powers to look to the United Nations for action when four-power negotiations became stalemated. By September 1948, however, the Soviet blockade of surface transport to Berlin had raised international tensions to unprecedented heights, and the United States, Great Britain, and France brought the matter to the Security Council. The Soviet Union (and the Ukraine) first refused to participate

84. A/Res. 195 (III), Dec. 12, 1948.
85. A/Res. 293 (IV), Oct. 21, 1949.
86. A/Res. 2224 (XXI), Dec. 19, 1966.

in the discussion, and then vetoed a proposal by the nonpermanent members to resolve the situation. Informal efforts went on behind the scenes for months, involving the nonpermanent Council members, the Assembly President, and the Secretary-General; and a formal appeal was made by the Assembly to the great powers to compose their differences. These moves only managed to keep all parties talking rather than fighting until, in May 1949, the four powers reported that they had succeeded in agreeing among themselves to lift the Berlin blockade.

Subsequent instances of political hypertension over Berlin have not been brought within the United Nations framework even to this limited degree. In 1951, however, the three Western powers asked the Assembly, at the request of the German Chancellor (the Federal Republic having been established in Western Germany by that time), to appoint an international commission to determine whether conditions in the Republic, the Soviet Zone, and Berlin would permit free elections throughout the country as a step toward reunification. Although East German spokesmen declared such a commission would constitute domestic intervention, the Assembly set one up in December.[87] The Soviet Union maintained the United Nations had no authority in relation to Germany; but declared it would accept investigation by a similar commission formed by the four occupying powers.[88] Moscow also supports in principle the idea of both the Germans and the Koreans themselves reestablishing the unity of their respective countries, with the two parts in each case "negotiating" reunification. Any arrangement that does not provide for guaranteed free elections in the Western sense, supervised and carried out on the same basis through the entire country, has on the other hand been unacceptable to the Western powers. Stalemate has thus continued to the present.

OBSERVER STATUS AT THE
UNITED NATIONS

West Germany has had an observer at United Nations Headquarters since 1952.[89] It has also been an active member in various specialized

87. A/Res. 510 (Dec. 20, 1951). The commission was to include Brazil, Ireland, the Netherlands, Pakistan, and Poland, but the last refused on the ground that the resolution was illegal.

88. See *Yearbook of the United Nations 1952*, p. 312.

89. The development of observer status has been a pragmatic matter and the position has never been officially provided for by the Assembly. Governments with observers at Headquarters in 1966 included: Switzerland, Monaco, the Holy See.

agencies and a significant financial contributor to the United Nations technical assistance and Special Fund programs, the peacekeeping operations, and the bond issue. Its degree of participation, despite having no vote, has given it a sort of "back door" membership.

Bonn has not applied for full membership, although insisting that it is the only legitimate German Government, a position supported by the three Western occupation powers. That a peace settlement with a reunified Germany was prerequisite to German admission as a Member of the Organization was apparently accepted for years by both sides in the German dispute. In March 1966, however, the [East] German Democratic Republic, in a memorandum submitted through Bulgaria,[90] applied for membership. It suggested that the cause of peace in Europe would be served if both Germanies became Members.

The Bonn Government immediately rejected the possibility of a "two Germanies" policy, as did the United States, Great Britain, and France. The official Western position is that East Germany "is not a state within the meaning of Article 4(1)," not being recognized by the great majority of the world community; and that only the Federal Republic "is entitled to speak" as "the representative of the German people in international affairs."[91] This position is consistent with the position taken by the Western powers in opposition to Soviet policy on broader European security issues, and there is no sign of Western willingness to separate those issues from the question of United Nations membership.

The Soviet Union (also consistently with its position on European security aspects of the German question) wrote the Secretary-General, too, in support of East Germany's application. Moscow argued that the de facto situation had to be recognized as an irrefutable fact, and added: "When claims by States to represent the population of other countries—no matter who makes these claims—are put forward in the United Nations," they are intended to violate its principles.[92] This is an interesting

South Korea, South Vietnam, and West Germany. All are members of one or more specialized agencies, and contribute to the U.N. Development Program. They also have governments recognized by a majority of U.N. Members. See A. Glenn Mower, Jr., "Observer Countries: Quasi Members of the United Nations," *International Organization*, Vol. 20 (Spring 1966), pp. 266–83.

90. U.N. Doc. S/7192, March 10, 1966. Submission by Bulgaria got around the problem of having the memorandum accepted as a U.N. document.

91. U.N. Doc. S/7207, March 16, 1966, a joint letter to the Secretary-General. See also *Washington Post* and *New York Times*, March 4, 1966.

92. U.N. Doc. S/7259, April 20, 1966.

approach since it would imply acceptance also of a two-Chinas solution in Asia. That is not, of course, the official Soviet position, which recognizes the claims of Peking as the sole lawful representative of all China, including Formosa. Although other communist states also supported the East German move, no request was made for a Security Council meeting to consider the application. The Western powers could probably have prevented inscription of the item on the Council's agenda, which may explain the inaction.

South Korea and South Vietnam also have observer status at the United Nations. In 1949, South Korea's membership application was vetoed in the Security Council by the Soviet Union, and again in 1955 (when the mass admission "deal" was made), 1957, and 1958. In those last two years, North Korea was refused admission by majority votes. South Vietnam, similarly, was vetoed in 1952, 1955, 1957, and 1958; and North Vietnam failed to gain acceptance in 1948, 1952, 1957, and 1958, the application not even being circulated on the first occasion.

The Secretary-General has frequently expressed his concern that the Organization should "achieve universality of membership as soon as possible." In 1965, for example, he added:

Being aware of the political and other difficulties involved in bringing this about, I should like to renew the suggestion which I made in the introduction to my last annual report to the effect that, in the meantime, the countries not at present represented at United Nations Headquarters should be enabled to maintain contact with the world body. . . . I have no doubt that the true interests of peace would be better served if non-Member States were to be encouraged to maintain observers at . . . Headquarters so that they may be in a position to sense the currents and cross-currents of world opinion which are so uniquely concentrated in the Organization. . . .[93]

The lack of formal procedure for sending an observer to Headquarters, and the precedents set by the Vatican and Monaco, would enable the issue whether a political entity is a "state" to be avoided if the communist nonmembers should seek to send observers there. That does not seem likely, however, especially after the East German move toward full membership. Even observer status would probably be opposed by the Western allies for East Germany (and by the United States, at least, for the Asian governments) so long as Washington remains unwilling to separate the United Nations participation issue from its security policies, which stress isolation of the communist regimes. Those communist governments have

93. *Introduction to the Annual Report of the Secretary General on the Work of the Organization, 16 June 1964–15 June 1965*, U.N. Doc. A/6001/Add. 1, p. 11.

also been kept out of the specialized agencies, which could be cited on the basis of custom as grounds for not accepting their presence as observers at Headquarters.[94]

The most important divided country, in terms of participation in the United Nations, is China. It differs from the other three cases discussed in that its division is not formally recognized and that "China" has always been a Member of the United Nations. The issue within the Organization is therefore one of representation rather than admission, although that is not always recognized in the arguments of the contending sides. It is like the other cases, so far as the United States is concerned, in that Washington has treated policy on United Nations representation as a tactical issue in relation to its much broader strategic concerns. Those concerns were viewed in a different light, and consequently did not determine United States policy toward the Nationalist Chinese, when the Communists drove them from the mainland in 1949. To understand current United States policy it is therefore first necessary to consider the sea change it suffered in 1950.

China, the United States, and the United Nations

In November 1949, the Foreign Minister of the Central People's Government of the People's Republic of China informed the Secretary-General and the Assembly that the Chinese Nationalist delegation no longer spoke for China; and in January 1950, he notified the Security Council that the "illegal" Nationalist delegation should be expelled. The Soviet Union then proposed that the Council not recognize the credentials of the current Chinese delegate. When its proposal was rejected, the Soviet representative declared he would not participate in the Council's work until the representative of the "Kuomintang group" was excluded; nor would Moscow recognize as legal any Council decision made with the latter's participation. Thus began the question of Chinese representation in the

---

94. Observers must also be admitted physically by the U.S. Government. That might face Washington with an embarrassing predicament if a case developed where an observer's government was not recognized by the United States since he would not be covered by rules applicable to representatives with the diplomatic status equivalent to delegates to the United Nations. See Mower, *op. cit.*, p. 274.

United Nations. The Chinese representational problem for the United States, however, had begun well before then.

The Communists' success in China amounted to a painful defeat for United States policy as well as for the Nationalist Government, which this country had supported during the years of civil war. American assistance, however, had been primarily in the form of a large aid program rather than direct military support; and it had been accompanied by a vain effort to bring about a political settlement between Nationalist and Communist factions. As Secretary of State Dean Acheson reported to the President in July 1949:

A realistic appraisal of conditions in China, past and present, leads to the conclusion that the only alternative [to the above policies] open to the United States was full-scale intervention in behalf of a Government which had lost the confidence of its own troops and its own people. Such intervention would have required the expenditure of even greater sums than have been fruitlessly spent thus far, the command of Nationalist armies by American officers, and the probable participation of American armed forces—land, sea, and air—in the resulting war. Intervention of such a scope and magnitude would have been resented by the mass of the Chinese people, would have diametrically reversed our historic policy, and would have been condemned by the American people.[95]

In January 1950, in line with that appraisal, President Truman declared that the United States would not follow a course leading to involvement in the Chinese civil conflict and would therefore not "provide military aid or advice to the Chinese forces on Formosa."[96] And in more general terms Secretary Acheson reaffirmed the strategic "defensive perimeter" policy, which excluded further United States intervention both on the island and on the mainland.[97] Official statements thus appeared tacitly to accept Formosa as an integral part of China, though that may not have been their intention, as its legal position remained open in the United States view.

Formosa also represented an integral part of the Chinese domain to Peking, which therefore considered that "liberation" of the territory (and the offshore islands) was essential to the successful completion of the revolution. On the basis of the American declarations just noted, it might have been supposed that Washington would accept the political implications of its military position and accede to the Moscow-Peking claims to

95. U.S. Department of State, *United States Relations with China: With Special Reference to the Period, 1944–1949*, Publication 3573 (August 1949), pp. xv–xvi.
96. U.S. Department of State, *Bulletin*, Vol. 22 (1950), p. 79.
97. See above, Chap. 1, pp. 15–16.

China's seat in the Security Council. It even seemed that way in fact when the United States delegate, in January 1950, maintained that while his government considered the Nationalist representative's credentials to be valid, it would "accept the decision of the Security Council on this matter when made by an affirmative vote of seven members."[98]

By early 1950, however, Peking's seizures of American properties and citizens and its closure of United States consulates made Washington unwilling to give formal recognition to the communist government. With the cold war in full force, it may also have been influenced to oppose seating the Chinese Communists in the Security Council by Soviet sponsorship of them. A more important element, however, was the fact that domestic opinion in the United States had become roused to the support of Chiang Kai-shek. Secretary-General Lie was therefore violently attacked by the American press when he supported the seating of Peking in the Council. "It was *China* [his emphasis], not Chiang Kai-shek, that belonged to the United Nations," he had argued, and the issue should therefore be simply a procedural matter of credentials.[99] The Secretary-General was accused of "surrendering" to Moscow as well as of transgressing the limits of his authority in taking his position publicly. Washington succeeded in defeating Lie's effort at that time to find seven votes for seating a Communist Chinese delegate in the Security Council. The policy of "no recognition, no representation" was consistently adhered to thereafter by the United States.

INFLUENCE OF KOREAN WAR

Its arguments in support of that position in the United Nations—while made primarily in political terms related to the Organization directly— have in reality been determined since the Korean war by broader strategic concerns of the United States. That development altered the American military view of the Pacific and Asia: from the 1949 defensive-perimeter

98. Quoted in Lie, *op. cit.*, p. 252. See also U.N. Doc. A/AC. 18/62, June 5, 1948, Interim Committee Report on Voting in the Security Council, which had recommended that approval of credentials of representatives of Members of the Security Council should be by procedural vote (p. 12). The U.S. approved this position.

99. Lie, *op. cit.*, pp. 254, 256–57. On the basis of Washington's initial reaction, Lie later wrote, he expected "that the United States would refrain from exerting pressure against the seating of Peking. I was wrong. The State Department proceeded to take off on an entirely different course" and actively sought to prevent a favorable vote. *Ibid.*, p. 261.

policy of neutralism and withdrawal, the United States increasingly changed over to a Far Eastern version of its European policy of containing "international communism," now manifested most virulently in Peking.[100] As a result, not only was the relationship of Formosa to United States policy radically changed, but a steady expansion of American political and military involvement in the entire Pacific region logically followed.

Concurrently with sending help to South Korea, President Truman ordered the Seventh Fleet to "neutralize" the Formosa Straits (June 27, 1950); and, in related moves, increased military assistance programs to the Philippines and French Indochina. The extension of action to Formosa was justified to protect the flank of United States forces acting in Korea; but the official explanation of this move also reflected Washington's interpretation of the actions of all communist governments as integral parts of a single vast conspiracy regardless of the particular national source. The President thus declared that:

The attack upon Korea makes it plain beyond all doubt that communism has passed beyond the use of subversion to conquer independent nations and will now use armed invasion and war. It has defied the orders of the Security Council of the United Nations issued to preserve international peace and security. In these circumstances the occupation of Formosa by Communist forces would be a direct threat to the security of the Pacific area and to the United States forces performing their lawful and necessary functions in that area.

He therefore ordered the Fleet to "prevent any attack on Formosa" and to see that Nationalist attacks against the mainland from Formosa also ceased. These actions constituted forcible intervention in the Chinese civil war, although not so declared.[101] Moreover, the official announcement also pointedly raised the question of the legal status of the island, in

100. This extension had been resisted in fact when the Truman Doctrine was announced in 1947.

101. U.S. Department of State, *Bulletin*, Vol. 23 (1950), p. 5. The official view has been summarized in the following terms: "The corollary limitation on action by the Chinese Government on Formosa had originated . . . in the belief that, under the circumstances then prevailing, any other course would have amounted to direct intervention in China's unfinished civil war." See Richard P. Stebbins, *The United States in World Affairs*, 1953 (Harper, 1954), p. 24.

The most extreme argument against this interpretation of the nature of American action as constituting intervention in the Chinese conflict was stated by Admiral Arthur W. Radford (Ret.): "Except for Taiwan and the Pescadores, China is an *occupied* country, like the Ukraine, and the people captives of an alien regime." Foreword to R. A. Hunter and Forrest Davis, *The Red China Lobby* (Fleet Publishing Corp., 1963), p. vii.

announcing that: "The determination of the future status of Formosa must await the restoration of security in the Pacific, a peace settlement with Japan, or consideration by the United Nations."[102]

All of this was logical in terms of United States strategic concern to prevent Peking from succeeding in its announced intention to seize Formosa, and thus turn a safeguarding military flank into a hostile source of potential attack on American defense and communications lines from Alaska to the Philippines and Southeast Asia.[103] It incidentally had the fortunate result of serving to silence some of the domestic criticism of Washington's earlier "hands off" policy toward the Chinese situation. At the same time, however, it unilaterally widened the character of the United Nations action in Korea, by indirectly involving "Chinese" territory several months before the Chinese Communists directly entered the war in North Korea. Perhaps of most importance in the present context, it fed the emotional build-up of the American attitude toward Red China[104] which was a major factor leading to McCarthyism and preventing a more rational, unemotional approach to the problems of United States relations with both de facto Chinese governments.

U.S. TECHNIQUES OF EXCLUSION

The United States early sought to raise the question in the Security Council from procedural to substantive status. It protested Lie's argument

102. U.S. Department of State, *Bulletin*, Vol. 23 (1950), p. 5. The legal status of Formosa at that time rested on a pledge at the Cairo Conference in 1943 (U.S., U.K., and China) that Formosa and the Pescadores would be restored to China after the war, to which the Soviet Union adhered in the Potsdam Declaration of 1945; and on the allied decision that Chiang Kai-shek would accept the surrender of Japanese troops in the island. Nationalist authorities thereafter administered the island as an army of occupation, until the Nationalist Government retreated there in defeat from the mainland in 1949. By 1950, the island was in practice treated as a de facto part of Nationalist China.

103. One student of the subject has noted: "When the Joint Chiefs in late 1949 and early 1950, had taken the position that Formosa was not sufficiently important to American security to justify the use of American forces in its defense against Communist China, the commitment of American ground forces in Korea had not been envisaged. It is quite possible that the neutralization of Formosa was a condition set by the Joint Chiefs for their consent to the State Department's proposal to come to the assistance of the Republic of Korea with armed force." Leland M. Goodrich, *Korea: A Study of U.S. Policy in the United Nations* (Council on Foreign Relations, 1956), p. 111.

104. This was intensified to the point of obsession by the subsequent stalemating of the Korean action as a result of Chinese intervention.

in 1950 that the question was one of representation thus requiring only the lesser majority. In December of that year, it also succeeded in getting the Assembly to adopt a resolution declaring that, whenever a representation issue becomes "the subject of controversy," it is to be considered "in the light of the Purposes and Principles of the Charter and the circumstances of each case."[105] Then in February 1951, the Assembly found that Communist China, "by giving direct aid and assistance to those who were already committing aggression in Korea and by engaging in hostilities against United Nations forces there, has itself engaged in aggression in Korea." And it reaffirmed United Nations determination to "meet the aggression."[106]

For many years, however, it was unnecessary for Washington to use these resolutions directly in arguing against the seating of Peking as China's representative, because it managed to mobilize enough votes to apply what came to be known as "the moratorium" technique—that is, of getting discussion of the issue postponed (by simple majority), Assembly after Assembly. Indirectly, of course, it made its views clear. In brief, it emphasized that Peking did not meet the "purposes and principles" part of the 1950 resolution, and could not do so until it purged itself of the United Nations aggression charge (although without specifying what criteria, beyond the cessation of hostilities in Korea, would meet that requirement). Critics of these arguments either joined the communists in simply accepting the de facto authority of Peking as justification enough for its representation claim; or they placed their emphasis on the other point to be considered: "the circumstances of each case." With the end of active hostilities in Korea, this latter point acquired greater importance for many governments; and in voting to defer consideration of the issue in the Assembly, the percentage of votes in support of the United States position decreased steadily after 1953.[107]

105. A/Res. 396 (V), Dec. 14, 1950 (the month after Chinese intervention in North Korea).

106. A/Res. 498 (V), Feb. 1, 1951. The resolution also simultaneously affirmed the Organization's pacific intentions, however, declaring that "it continues to be the policy of the United Nations to bring about a cessation of hostilities in Korea by peaceful means." The section on Chinese aggression has accordingly been interpreted by some as the price paid by the majority for United States acceptance of the Assembly's strong desire to start political negotiations for settlement in Korea.

107. See tabulation of votes on the China question, 1950–63, in A. M. Halpern, ed., *Policies Toward China and Views from Six Continents* (McGraw Hill, 1965), App. B, pp. 503–07.

In the Security Council, where it had always been possible for Washington to muster the necessary majority against any change in Chinese representation, American officials nonetheless declared in 1954 that, if necessary, the United States would use the veto to prevent the seating of Peking in the Security Council[108]—thus reversing its earlier position.

A main reason for the hardness of the administration's policy lay in the even more extreme positions which, at that period, predominated in Congress. In 1953, for example, Senator Knowland of California (who was sometimes referred to as "the Senator from Formosa") introduced resolutions calling for the withdrawal of the United States from the United Nations if Communist China were seated. These were ultimately modified to the form of a declaration in the Mutual Security Act that opposed the seating of Peking.[109] The Senate Appropriations Committee also decided to recommend the termination of financial support for the Organization in the same event; and a unanimous House resolution reiterated that body's own opposition.[110]

While the extremity of these expressions of congressional feeling diminished somewhat in later years, resolutions were regularly passed (usually unanimously) reiterating the formal opposition of Congress to the seating of Peking, on "some twenty occasions" since 1950 in the House alone, according to Representative Reuss of Wisconsin in 1966.[111] Even the few who ventured to break the sound barrier against public criticism of the established policy, did so for long with great caution. Senator Fulbright in 1964, for example, spoke of "the elaborate vocabulary of make-believe" in both official and public discussion of China, partly a reflection of "the fear of many government officials undoubtedly well-founded that even the suggestion of new policies toward China and Vietnam would provoke a vehement public outcry." Yet the Senator at that time was against either recognition or the seating of Peking in the United Nations, as long as it continued its implacable hostility toward the United States.[112]

By 1961, in contrast, opinion in the newly enlarged Assembly was already clearly changing. Recognizing that it might not obtain another postponement of discussion (especially if the Nationalist representative in the Security Council again vetoed the application of Outer Mongolia for

108. Dulles statement in U.S. Department of State, *Bulletin*, Vol. 31 (1954), p. 87.
109. 68 Stat. 833 (1954).
110. H. Res. 627, July 15, 1954.
111. Quoted in *Washington Post*, March 24, 1966.
112. Quoted in A. T. Steele, *The American People and China* (McGraw Hill, 1966), pp. 213–14.

admission, as it had done in 1955),[113] the United States took a different approach that year. It succeeded in mustering support for a resolution that declared the issue of Chinese representation to be an "important question," thus requiring a two-thirds majority for decision.[114] In 1965, Washington felt it necessary to press for a "reaffirmation" of that decision, which it obtained by dint of much lobbying, but only by a scant majority vote of 56–49–11.[115] The standard draft resolution submitted in opposition to the United States position[116] was only rejected, moreover, by a tie vote: 47–47, with 20 abstentions and 2 "not participating."[117]

If Peking (along with its communist and neutral supporters) were not so adamant that Nationalist China must be expelled before it will take a seat in the Organization, it would probably have been offered that seat by the Assembly under a declared "two-Chinas" policy. It could thus achieve Assembly recognition as the accredited Chinese representative also entitled to the permanent seat in the Security Council—even though that would not guarantee the same action in the Council itself.[118] (The offer might have been refused, since Peking violently rejects that policy; but it also might have been accepted, since actions do not always follow the words of governments.) Combined with the communist use of force against Tibet (1959) and India (1962), however, this factor enabled the

113. If Mongolia was vetoed, the Soviet Union was ready to veto Mauritania's pending application. The twenty-plus African states would in that case be likely to retaliate by voting Communist China into the Assembly at least. The Kennedy Administration was prepared to recognize Mongolia in 1961 to demonstrate that U.S. policy in Asia was not so completely rigid as it was accused of being; but the storm raised by supporters of Nationalist China when feelers in that direction became known soon led the State Department to announce that negotiations to establish relations had been suspended. See Roger Hilsman, *To Move a Nation: The Politics of Foreign Policy in the Administration of John F. Kennedy* (Doubleday, 1967), pp. 205–97. In the Security Council, China and the United States abstained in the vote on Mongolia's membership application, which was approved.

114. A/Res. 1668 (XVI), Dec. 14, 1961. The decision whether a question should require a two-thirds majority is made by simple majority in the Assembly. Art. 18 (3).

115. A/Res. 2025 (XX), Nov. 17, 1965.

116. Recognizing Peking as "the only lawful representative of" China in the United Nations and expelling "forthwith" the Nationalist representatives.

117. The draft resolution was in A/L. 469, voted Nov. 17, 1965.

118. Myres S. McDougal and Richard M. Goodman argue that giving the Assembly "principal responsibility for settling the . . . question would be almost to guarantee that different 'China' delegations will sit in different organs of the United Nations." "Chinese Participation in the United Nations: The Legal Imperatives of a Negotiated Solution," *American Journal of International Law*, Vol. 60 (1966), p. 721.

United States to maintain enough support to keep Peking out on grounds of its aggressiveness, though India favored its seating, notwithstanding.

In 1966, the situation looked uncertain as the twenty-first Assembly approached; but the United States maintained its earlier position, feeling that it could once again muster the necessary votes for reaffirmation of the "important question" issue and more than the essential one-third plus one in the vote on the standard procommunist resolution. In part because of the extraordinary development of the "great cultural revolution," which made many states question the desirability of seating Chinese Communists in the United Nations until the situation on mainland China clarified, a renewed resolution reaffirming the decision that any proposal to change the representation of China is an important question was passed by a safe 66–48–7.[119] The procommunist resolution to oust Nationalist China was once more defeated, also by a clear majority, the vote being 46–57–17.[120]

The twenty-first Assembly, in addition, saw two other moves to "unfreeze" the China problem in the United Nations. Italy proposed a resolution to establish an Assembly committee to study the issue, in particular to ascertain officially Peking's attitude toward the Organization and the question of compliance with the Charter's obligations. Although framed so as not to prejudice the outcome of the proposed study, the resolution failed of adoption (34–62–5). Pro-Peking delegates claimed it was a mere time-wasting device. Ambassador Goldberg, although announcing United States support for the Italian initiative, added so many questions of his own as to cause "much critical comment" that he was "transforming a proposal for an inquiry into a demand for an inquisition."[121] More significant for the future, perhaps, was a Canadian proposal, which the Secretary for External Affairs later described as "an interim solution." On the ground that it was "wrong to continue the essentially negative policy" which had marked United Nations discussions for years, he told the Assembly that until Taiwan and Peking could settle their jurisdictional claims, both should be represented at the United Nations; and, as he later commented: "I also suggested that we might further face up to the realities by offering Peking the permanent seat on the Security Council."[122] This pro-

119. A/Res. 2159 (XXI), Nov. 29, 1966.

120. Draft resolution in A/L. 496. See also Ambassador Goldberg's gratified statement after the voting: USUN Press Release 4995, Nov. 29, 1966.

121. *New York Times*, Nov. 27, 1966.

122. Department of External Affairs (Canada), *Canadian Weekly Bulletin*, Vol. 22, March 15, 1967, p. 2.

posal went much too far for Washington. The Canadians, as one reporter wrote, "because they [wanted] to keep their concept alive," did not therefore put it to a vote, "although they might have done so had the United States given its approval."[123]

Within the United States, moreover, A. T. Steele found that, by 1965, in spite of the unchanged official position:

In fact, . . . there is considerably less harmony [in congressional policy declarations] than meets the eye. In conversations with members of Congress one soon discovers that a fair number of them have private reservations regarding our present policy but feel that political expediency demands conformity with the majority view. . . .
[Among the] reasons for congressional caution . . . is the pressures involving China policy to which [members] are subjected. These pressures come in part from the Committee of One Million and its allies and in part from organizations of the extreme right with a penchant for letter-writing. . . . The fact is that most members of Congress have been maneuvered into a position where they are heavily committed on the China question through their affirmative votes on repeated resolutions opposing the admission [sic] of Communist China to the United Nations.[124]

And in 1966, for the first time in years, a serious nonemotional public discussion of the problem was initiated by two congressional committees: the Senate Forcign Relations Committee, under its Chairman, Senator Fulbright, and a Subcommittee on the Far East and the Pacific, of the House Foreign Affairs Committee, under Chairman Representative Zablocki.[125] Although advocates of policy reappraisal and change (with respect to both recognition and representation in the United Nations) drew forth the usual defenses of the established policies, the whole atmosphere was calmer and more open-minded than had been the case earlier. In the context of this study, only the possibility of a two-China policy in the United Nations will be considered below;[126] but much of the argumentation applies equally well to overall United States policy toward China.

123. Drew Middleton, "The China Debate is Over—for this Year," *New York Times*, Dec. 4, 1966.
124. Steele, *op. cit.*, pp. 210, 219.
125. *U.S. Policy with Respect to Mainland China*, Hearings before the Senate Foreign Relations Committee, 89 Cong. 2 sess., March 8–30, 1966; *United States Policy Toward Asia*, Hearings before the Subcommittee on the Far East and the Pacific of the House Foreign Affairs Committee, 89 Cong. 2 sess., (January–February 1966).
126. The shorthand of "two-China policy" is used here to cover either that policy or the alternative of recognizing an independent Formosa in a "China-Formosa" policy. While the legal and political implications are different in respect to the island and to procedural requirements within the United Nations, they are much the same in respect to U.S. policy toward Communist Chinese representation in the Organization.

THE TWO-CHINAS ARGUMENTATION

The United States has consistently opposed the possibility of seeking a resolution of the China dilemma by means of accepting the de facto two-Chinas situation. In relation to the United Nations, one way suggested for doing this procedurally would be by an Assembly resolution recognizing that two successor states have emerged in China and that both are entitled to seats in the Organization. Or, if the acceptance were to be in terms of a China-Formosa solution, an independent Formosa might be recognized after some act of self-determination under United Nations auspices. The logic of the situation would give Peking the Chinese seat in the Security Council, as Canada recognized; but for political reasons (and to safeguard Taiwan's future), proponents of two Chinese seats in the Assembly often leave the issue of Security Council seating open.[127] (It forms something of a separate issue in any event, both because of the Chinese veto in the Council and because each organ interprets its own rules.) In view of the difficulties inherent in this procedural confusion, it has also been suggested that the participation issue be settled by advance negotiations.[128]

The proposal is supported by many who are concerned to find an effective way to avoid an eventual Assembly recommendation to accept the communist proposal instead—namely, that the seating of Peking be accompanied by expulsion of the Nationalist Chinese and the acceptance of Formosa as an integral part of one communist-governed China.

Before examining the official American case against a two-China solution, it may be well to reiterate that, behind the political argumentation in the United Nations, the significant determinant of United States policy is the Pacific strategic situation. That was considered important in 1950, and events of recent years have multiplied the significance attached by military officials to retaining Formosa in anticommunist control. Even before the greatly increased military involvement of the United States in Vietnam, Formosa's general military importance (given United States strategic views) was enhanced by the build-up of the island as an air base and by the development of Chiang Kai-shek's armed forces viewed as a reserve against possible involvement in war with mainland China.

At the same time, the United States has combined its support of Chiang Kai-shek as president of all China with a consistent refusal to support him

127. See, for example, UNA–USA National Policy Panel, *China, the United Nations, and United States Policy* (United Nations Association of the United States of America, 1966), pp. 39–40.
128. McDougal and Goodman, *op. cit.*, p. 724.

in his persistent aim to return to the mainland. Washington has periodically obtained statements from Chiang to the effect that he contemplates doing that by peaceful means only; but then, presumably for his domestic political reasons, they are followed by renewed declarations of belligerent intent.[129] Washington evidently has some fear that Chiang might make a "deal" with Peking as a lesser evil than losing United States support for the legal fiction that the Nationalists represent all China. Or it may be concerned lest he start a suicidal attack of his own on the mainland with military forces built up by United States aid, but wholly inadequate to such a purpose, in the expectation that Washington, despite its formal disapproval, would then be forced to back him up rather than permit his defeat. These possibilities become the more significant in light of United States relations in southeast Asia and of its declared policy to avoid further expansion of the conflict there. They also underline the importance in the American view of avoiding a conflict with the Nationalists in, or over, Formosa.

Washington's official response for years, however, was to stress that neither China would accept the two-Chinas solution—and, indeed, it is almost the only thing on which the two governments do agree. But if taken at face value, this position allowed United States policy to be determined by the interests of both those governments, rather than by its own. Proponents of the two-Chinas approach therefore argued that even if rejection by both Chinese factions meant a continuation of the existing unsatisfactory situation in the United Nations, it would at least take the onus off American shoulders and put it where it belongs. There are many who feel that the time has long since passed when the United States should have taken "steps to make clear beyond cavil that Formosa and the Pescadores constitute an independent state. . . . Such a course would seem to be in the clear interest of the United States and the people of Formosa and the Pescadores, including the Chinese Nationalists who have found a home there and have contributed significantly to its development."[130]

129. In the Generalissimo's latest inaugural speech in 1966, for example, he saw no other course but "putting into effect our plans for an all-out offensive against the Communist-occupied mainland." *New York Times*, May 21, 1966. See also Mme. Chiang's advocacy of bombing mainland China's nuclear installations, in *Washington Post*, March 19, 1966.

130. Benjamin V. Cohen, *The United Nations: Constitutional Developments, Growth, and Possibilities* (Harvard University Press, 1961), p. 55. See also pp. 47–56 for a discussion of the legal status of Formosa and the Pescadores. Both the Japanese peace treaty (1952) and the U.S.-Nationalist defense treaty (1954) carefully avoided finding that the islands are an integral part of China.

Such recognition would also improve relations with many allies and neutrals which share Washington's view, that it "would be unthinkable and morally wrong to expel" Nationalist China from the United Nations at Peking's demand;[131] but which, unlike Washington, draw therefrom the conclusion that legal separation is the best hope for eventual peaceful adjustment.

Washington no longer contends, as it did through the Eisenhower Administration, that the Peking regime is but "a passing . . . phase";[132] but it still rejects the argument that it is unrealistic to exclude from the world Organization the authority that governs such a large proportion of the human race. Some contend, Ambassador Goldberg noted in November 1965:

that Peiping must be represented here so that the United Nations will be closer to the goal of universality. But, we have to ask ourselves, would this in fact be a move toward universality? Many of those who strongly advocate the seating of Peiping just as vociferously call for the expulsion of the Republic of China. And Peiping itself clearly opposes membership for all sovereign states. . . . Peiping's representation here would run contrary to the only true principle of universality for which this organization should strive . . . [that which] is envisaged in Article 4 of the Charter. . . .

"How," he asked rhetorically, "can this Assembly even consider" meeting the Communist demand for the expulsion of the Nationalists?

The Republic of China [he continued] is a founding member of the United Nations. It participated in the consultations and conferences which led to the adoption of our Charter, and it is a signatory to and named in the Charter itself. Its control over mainland China was taken from it by force of arms, but who can deny that the Republic of China continues to exercise the responsibilities of a sovereign state? It exercises effective control over approximately 14,000 square miles of territory—more extensive than the territories of at least 18 members; and it exercises control over and governs 12 million people— larger than the populations of 83, or more than two-thirds, of our member states.[133]

To many, these facts seem to argue more for insisting that "China on Formosa" stay in, than that "China on the mainland" be kept out.

The United States also maintains that Peking cannot be seated because it does not meet "the requirements clearly set out in Article 4 of the

131. William P. Bundy speech, Feb. 12, 1966, U.S. Department of State, *Bulletin*, Vol. 54 (1966), p. 316.

132. John Foster Dulles, address at San Francisco, June 28, 1957, U.S. Department of State, *Bulletin*, Vol. 37 (1959), p. 95.

133. Text in *ibid.*, Vol. 53 (1965), pp. 946, 941.

Charter for participation in this Organization."[134] But China, as Mr. Lie pointed out in 1950, is already a Member; and those criteria are not proposed as a reason for reexamining whether the Soviet Government (because of Hungary), or the Egyptian Government (because it refuses to make peace with Israel), or Cuba (because of its subversive revolutionary activities), or any other Member government (because, according to United States belief, it does not meet the requirements of Article 4) should be denied further right to participate. On the contrary, Washington has argued strongly against African moves to expel South Africa from the United Nations and the specialized agencies, although South Africa has violated Charter purposes and principles (even if not the same ones Peking flaunts), and it has been roundly condemned by the United Nations (even if not on the same basis as Peking). Its argument in that case is, roughly, that it is better to have the sinner within reach and hopefully more subject to the political pressures of the Organization.

When the same argument has been used as a reason to encourage the participation of Peking, however, Secretary Rusk (as Secretary Dulles before him) has dismissed it with the remark that "the United Nations is not a reform school." Perhaps not, but it is the nearest approach to one that is available to governments that wish to avoid a solution by force.

That is not to say, as American spokesmen frequently imply, that those who advocate seating Peking necessarily do so in the expectation that that violently suspicious and xenophobic government will soon be brought to a more benign political condition. Most do so, rather, because of the feeling that the very violence of the Communist regime makes it necessary to use every available approach to break down the by now largely self-imposed isolation of Peking. Some naive persons may expect to see a reformed Red China within a short period. But surely most Americans who criticize administration policy for seeking to maintain the exclusion of Peking from the international community do so with a more sophisticated appreciation of the difficulties ahead. The initial one is that the Communist government at this point is as adamant as Washington and Taipei in refusing to accept the status quo on some such basis as here discussed. Professor Doak Barnett put the opposition viewpoint as follows:

We should accept the fact that the Chinese Communists are going to be in the United Nations, because in the long run it is desirable and in the short run it is unavoidable, and try to work toward a formula that would be the best

134. *Ibid.*, p. 950.

possible formula from our national interest point of view, which would be one which preserves representation for the Chinese regime in Taiwan.[135]

And he made the point even clearer in a subsequent prediction:

Unless we soon evolve a new and sounder policy on this issue, we are likely to be defeated in the General Assembly, and then our entire policy of isolation of Peking will begin to unravel as the result of a major political defeat, even before we can, on our own initiative, begin to redefine our posture.[136]

Such an event would no doubt be widely considered a major political defeat for the United States, if for no other reason than because so many Americans, official and otherwise, have so often announced that it would be. Such reiterated pronouncements become eventually self-fulfilling prophecies. Americans have also declared that Peking could not be allowed to "shoot its way into the United Nations" (that is, via Korea, its attacks on the offshore islands, and its threatened attacks on Formosa). In view of the attainment of nuclear status by Peking largely by its own efforts, it will be ironic if the communists succeed psychologically in "bombing" their way in instead.

Another argument begs the issue by urging a continuation of the exclusion policy because Peking is likely to disrupt the Organization. As one official queried, for example:

Had Communist China been in the United Nations could there have been a cease-fire resolution on the India-Pakistan conflict in September [1965] and could Secretary-General U Thant have received any mandate to bring that conflict to a halt? Peiping's critical comment on the Tashkent proceedings is a clear answer. We are dealing with a nation that, at least as far as we can now see, will attempt as a matter of principle to put a monkey wrench into every peace-making effort which may be made in the world.[137]

The answer to the specific question is that, had the political will of the other powers to halt the fighting in Kashmir been as great as it was in the actual circumstances, a Chinese veto in the Security Council would no doubt have been followed by another resort to the General Assembly

---

135. *United States Policy Toward Asia*, Hearings, *op. cit.*, Pt. 1, pp. 63–64.

136. Quoted in *New York Times*, March 10, 1966. A decade earlier Professor Barnett already was advocating transformation of the Nationalist regime "from a claimant to rule over all China, which is unattainable and unacceptable to most of the world, to a stable local regime." See A. Doak Barnett, "The United States and Communist China," in *The United States and the Far East* (The American Assembly, Columbia University, 1956), p. 167. See also his *Communist China and Asia: A Challenge to American Policy* (Random House, 1960), pp. 472–74.

137. Bundy, *op. cit.*, pp. 316–17.

or to action outside the United Nations. Moscow has been inconsistent in action before now; it would probably have been so again in the circumstances assumed. In more general terms, the answer is that undoubtedly Peking will be a disruptive influence; but if the general membership remains firm in its support of the Organization, there is no more reason to suppose that an obstreperous China will ruin the United Nations than an obstreperous Soviet Union did in the first years of the Organization. And if the membership is not strong in its support, it will not be merely Red China that destroys the institution.

Those who argue that the problem is how to bring Peking in rather than how to keep it out, also often foresee a period of possibly worse obstructionism than during the years of the Stalin regime. But, they ask, what is the alternative to seeking to involve the Communist Chinese in the world community if "solution" of the Chinese problem by forcible elimination of the regime is ruled out?[138] And if a difficult time must be lived through, the sooner it starts, the better. Certainly, from the viewpoint of the United States, no constructive initiative can be hoped for from Peking. Are others, then, to be equally obstinate?

Finally, while justifying American refusal to "abandon the 12 million people of Free China on Taiwan to Communist tyranny," and insisting that Peking show evidence of reform before entering the world Organization, United States officials have also echoed Secretary Rusk's declaration that: "When mainland China has a government which is prepared to renounce force, to make peace, and to honor international responsibilities, it will find us responsive."[139] Logically, that would seem to mean that in the event of Peking's decision to accept the reality of a separate government on Formosa, Washington would then recognize the "peaceful" Communist government or at least accept a two-Chinas solution of the United Nations problem. Curiously enough, that point seems not to have been raised in public until the spring of 1966, when, during a TV interview, the Secretary was asked whether such a statement meant that "if there were a change of heart, one that we could detect, in the attitude of Communist China, changing its policy of belligerency, would we be

138. See, for example, Rusk statement before House Foreign Affairs Subcommittee on the Far East and the Pacific, that: "Fifth, we should continue our efforts to reassure Peiping that the United States does not intend to attack mainland China." U.S. Department of State, *Bulletin*, Vol. 54 (1966), p. 694.

139. *Ibid.*, Vol. 50 (1964), p. 234. In his State of the Union message, January 1967, President Johnson also said: "We would be the first to welcome a China which decided to respect her neighbor's rights." *Ibid.*, Vol. 56 (1967), p. 162.

prepared as a nation to receive that change and make adjustments thereto?" Mr. Rusk replied:

President Johnson, President Kennedy, President Eisenhower, and President Truman, in this postwar period, have always left the door open to peaceful relationships. . . . Now, if there is any indication that Peiping is prepared to live at peace with its neighbors . . . to live as a loyal and decent member of the world community, then other possibilities do open up.

But I don't want to speculate on that unduly, because we see no indications from Peiping that they are prepared to be an active and loyal member of the world community.[140]

In short, the administration was formulating its policy from the short-run point of view, fundamentally banking on a continuation of Peking's attitude to enable it to continue mustering enough support to keep the Communist regime out of the United Nations for another year. The only noticeable change in administration statements on the question as 1966 advanced was a greater emphasis on the importance of maintaining Taiwan's right not to be expelled from the United Nations or taken over by mainland China. They apparently sought to meet increasing criticism of official policy as frozen and as aimed at "containment and isolation."[141] But they did not change the essence of the official position recognizing the Nationalist Government as that of all China and opposing the admission of Peking to the United Nations.[142]

140. *Ibid.*, Vol. 54 (1966), p. 568. In April, Ambassador Goldberg went further, when answering questions after a speech at the National Press Club: he said that "the minimum conditions acceptable to the United States to have Communist China in the U.N." were: (1) "A change in Peking's view that its price of admission is the expulsion of the representative from Taiwan"; (2) Withdrawal of its demand that the United Nations rescind the resolution condemning Peking's aggression in Korea (and pass one condemning the United States); (3) Withdrawal of its demand for reorganization of the United Nations, including expulsion of American "lackeys"; and (4) A promise to adhere to the Charter. Quoted in *Washington Post*, April 20, 1966. This off-the-cuff acceptance, in effect, of a two-Chinas approach did not, however, prove to be a forerunner of an official policy change.

141. Professor Barnett, in testifying before the Senate Foreign Relations Committee (March 8, 1966), recommended that the United States shift to a policy of "containment but not isolation," a phrase that immediately gained wide currency. *U.S. Policy with Respect to Mainland China*, Hearings, *op. cit.*

142. In a speech on July 12, 1966, for example, President Johnson stressed U.S. proposals for exchange of newsmen, scholars, and other professionals (all rejected by Peking), but did not even mention the political issues of recognition or U.N. admission. U.S. Department of State, *Bulletin*, Vol. 55 (1966), p. 161.

Shortly before, however, Secretary Rusk (on a visit to Taipei) had reiterated U.S. opposition to any proposal to "deprive the Republic of China of its rightful place in the U.N. and to seat the Chinese Communists in its place. . . . We recognize the Republic of China as the Government of China with all the implications that go with that." *Ibid.*, Vol. 55 (1966), pp. 176–77.

As the twenty-first Assembly neared, with the Chinese item on its agenda, the usual public statements were issued by groups supporting administration policy. The most important was the annual advertisement of the Committee of One Million[143] listing the endorsement of senators and representatives (324 in all, in 1966) for the committee's declaration opposing United States recognition or trade relations with Peking, its admission to the United Nations, and "any policy of accommodation which might be interpreted as U.S. acquiescence in, or approval of, Communist China's aggression, direct or indirect, against her neighbors." But something new was added in 1966. In December, Senator Javits of New York announced he was withdrawing from membership in the committee, and on the same day the committee secretary sent " a memorandum to all congressional members saying that [it] would discontinue the use of [their names] on letterheads and Committee publications."[144] Also, in the months following the House and Senate hearings early in 1966, a number of private statements were issued supporting the more flexible policies advocated at those hearings by opponents of the official position.[145] The anti-administration argument was succinctly summarized by one scholar as follows:

We should not continue to confuse a policy of trying to isolate Communist China, which has almost no real chance for success, with the necessary objective of limiting China's ambitions. We must continue to resist the efforts of the Chinese to upset the present world order by refashioning it to their own purposes, but the Peking government cannot and should not be excluded indefinitely from the normal channels of international contact.

.   .   .   .   .   .

As long as the United States recognizes the government on Taiwan as the government of China, we force ourselves to have only very limited and almost furtive dealings with the Peking government; and to support the Nationalist claim to be the only legal Chinese government, we are also compelled to do our utmost to prevent the Chinese Communists from being accepted into the world community. This policy of isolating the Peking regime has steadily been undermined. . . . The American position on this issue in the United Nations

143. After Eisenhower's election, in 1953 the China Lobby formed the "Committee of One Million against the Admission of Communist China to the United Nations" to collect a million signatures in opposition. In 1955, it was reorganized as the "Committee of One Million" to fight the possibility of recognition of Peking and its admission to the United Nations for the sake of peace. Committee's ad in *New York Times*, Oct. 31, 1966.

144. *Ibid.*, Dec. 18, 1966.

145. See, for example, the statement of 198 experts on Asian problems (March 21, 1966) and the report of the special panel established by the United Nations Association of the U.S.A. (Oct. 20, 1966), both in favor of a two-China policy in the United Nations. Text of statement in *New York Times*, March 21, 1966; report cited above.

and other international institutions will be unable to survive for long the mounting pressures for change on the part of other nations. . . .[146]

So far, then, as the divided countries are concerned "our guard is up" against all of them, but there is little sign of the "outstretched hand"—of those bridges the administration has declared it wishes to build across the political and ideological chasms between the communist states and ourselves. "There are many ways in which we can build bridges toward nations who would cut themselves off from us," declared Secretary of Defense McNamara, naming three: "properly balanced trade relations, diplomatic contacts, and in some cases even by exchanges of military observers."[147] Given United States strategic conceptions of both Europe and the Far East, it seems certain that the Secretary did not intend "diplomatic contacts" to include membership in the United Nations for the communist segments of the divided lands. That is not the only way in which the world Organization might be more actively used in the bridge-building effort, however, as the following chapter will consider.

146. Robert Blum, *The United States and China in World Affairs*, A. Doak Barnett, ed. (McGraw-Hill, 1966), pp. 268, 267.
147. U.S. Department of State, *Bulletin*, Vol. 54 (1966), p. 880.

RETROSPECT AND PROSPECT

CHAPTER TEN

THE PAST AS PROLOGUE

On accepting the Nobel Peace Prize a decade ago, Lester Pearson noted that: "While we all pray for peace, we do not always, as free citizens, support the policies that make for peace, or reject those which do not. We want our own kind of peace, brought about in our own way.... The grim fact is ... that we prepare for war like precocious giants and for peace like retarded pygmies." And he predicted: "We are, I think, in for a long, often depressing, exasperating and frustrating period of armed peace, or what passes for peace in this modern age, leading, we may hope, to a peace which will rest on something more enduring than arms."[1] So far, the first half of his prognosis is proving correct. This final chapter will reconsider the evidence of earlier pages in an attempt to judge whether, from the point of view of the United States and the United Nations, the world also seems headed toward that more enduring peace that Prime Minister Pearson hoped for.

The fall of 1967 is an especially difficult time in which to reach such a judgment. The shadow of Vietnam falls athwart United States domestic and foreign policy; and divided counsels on what should be done to better conditions at home are directly related to issues of American obligations, if any, to remote countries and to the costs and methods of applying declared policies concerning them. The relations of the superpowers are also affected by the Vietnamese conflict. Efforts to "build bridges" and otherwise thaw the cold war are hampered, on the communist side, by taunts and charges from Peking whenever there is any indication of cooperation from Moscow toward Washington; and on the United States

1. Lester B. Pearson, "The Four Faces of Peace," in Sherleigh G. Pierson, ed., *The Four Faces of Peace: The International Outlook* (Dodd, Mead, 1964), pp. 6, 14, 56.

side, by congressional rejection of administration moves toward economic or political liberalization of any kind in relations with states that aid or trade with North Vietnam. In the United Nations, the question has become so touchy that the Security Council refused to discuss Vietnam even after it was inscribed on the agenda. At the same time, the poison of the issue injects itself into the debates on numerous other matters, increasing the difficulty of making the Organization into that "center for harmonizing the actions of nations," which the Charter proclaims as one of its purposes. In the spring of 1967, when asking for a truce in the fighting to make possible direct talks among the parties in Vietnam, U Thant declared that: "As Secretary-General of the United Nations, I am distressed lest the prolongation of this war bring about a suffocation of this organization and in the end seriously affect the détente and cooperation among all nations."[2]

Nonetheless, this is not another book on Vietnam. Its effects on United Nations issues cannot be ignored. But certain assumptions will have to be made if this chapter is not to lose all perspective in looking to the future. United States policy is still declared to be that of seeking to bring Hanoi to the conference table to negotiate an honorable settlement on the general basis of the 1954 Geneva accords, which would leave South Vietnam an independent entity able to determine freely its future relationship with the North. Whether the air and naval war in the North will, in fact, result in the desired negotiations, the downfall of the Hanoi regime, or the ability to terminate the antiguerilla war in the South is an open question in September 1967. It is argued by many that current United States political and strategic policy in Vietnam is more likely to lead to the intervention of Communist China, or even to uncontrollable escalation into nuclear conflict with the Soviet Union.

That point of no return has not yet been reached, however. This chapter will assume that it continues to be held off, that the conflict does not widen beyond the Vietnams, and even that a diminution of hostilities permits political controls to be exerted over the fighting and negotiations to be started on some agreed basis. This much amelioration of the current situation would by no means automatically be followed by an improvement in the manifold other problems that hamper peaceful cooperation among the nations and that sooner or later seem to appear in the United Nations. But without that much progress toward an acceptable *modus*

2. *New York Times*, March 30, 1967.

vivendi in Southeast Asia, there seems little chance of constructive advance toward solving many other difficulties that keep the world in turmoil.

America's Quest for Peace

Some years ago, the diplomatic historian, Dexter Perkins, gave a series of lectures under the title "America's Quest for Peace" in which he analyzed three roads by which the United States has sought, over the years, to attain the objectives of a peaceful world: peace through law, peace through collective security (what this study calls collective enforcement), and peace through disarmament.[3] His surveys showed, of course, that none of these approaches to peace through institutionalized international relations has provided a final solution. At the same time, he rejected (with the "peacemongers") the notion of a fourth road: that of peace through power, as the nuclear deterrent school might be called. Nor did he consider one vital lesson that might have been drawn from the experience of the League of Nations and the United Nations, both of which sought to incorporate aspects of all three historical approaches in their efforts to bring world order out of the chaos of international affairs. This lesson would have been that peace through the politics of states is the only practical road to world order.

This has certainly been true in the United Nations. The extent to which it has succeeded in becoming the Charter's center for harmonizing national actions has depended basically on the policies of its Members, rather than on the machinery for organizing their interstate relations. Until governments can reach a level of political accord that will permit the development of a common system of values pertaining to the international politics of war and peace, they will continue unable to develop within the United Nations framework a viable system of ground rules for the conduct of peaceful international relations. That is what is meant by those who maintain that the development of political community is essential to progress toward world peace. The standards of law, the control of arms, and the collective use of them to enforce those standards, are at best but means to agreed ends—in international, as in national, affairs. "Our

3. Dexter Perkins, *America's Quest for Peace* (Indiana University Press, 1962). The lectures were given in 1959.

problem," wrote Walter Lippmann, "is that technics have established a rudimentary world community but have not integrated it organically, morally, or politically. They have created a community of mutual dependence, but not one of mutual trust and respect."[4]

The process of developing that community, however, is not the simple one it apparently seems to those who support the world-peace-through-world-law approach. To adapt a classification by Karl Deutsch,[5] they are the "optimistic Utopians," who see the end more clearly than the means —in fact, almost to the exclusion of worrying about the measures necessary to get there. If the analyses of the preceding pages have any validity, on the other hand, world law will have to continue its step-by-step development concurrently with the advancement of common interests and values that permit agreement on common standards of action. As such standards are accepted, the machinery and procedures can be developed that will make possible both the application of the rules on a universal basis and their enforcement against the occasional violator.

The assumption underlying the voting provisions of the Security Council remains valid today: unless the overwhelming support of the holders of great power is behind the standards of the Charter—and unless those standards are commonly understood in the same practical terms—the United Nations cannot function effectively to maintain world peace. A blueprint for a "disarmed" world and an "international" enforcement agency of practically irresistible power[6] must remain a utopian dream in a world of bitter and basic ideological and political conflict. The perfect becomes the enemy of the possible; the sincere believers are only deceiving themselves when they argue that modern weaponry has outlawed war and that only disarmament and supranational enforcement agencies can bring about a peaceful world. Their efforts would be more fruitful if directed to limited, but practical, steps toward effective community.[7]

4. "The Great Revolution," *UN Monthly Chronicle* (April 1965), p. 67.

5. Karl W. Deutsch, "The Future of World Politics," *The Political Quarterly*, Vol. 37 (1966), p. 9.

6. "To call such an arrangement 'disarmament' is about as oblique as to call the Constitution of the United States a 'Treaty for Uniform Currency and Interstate Commerce.' The authors of the Federalist Papers were under no illusion as to the far-reaching character of the institution they were discussing, and we should not be either." Thomas C. Schelling, *Arms and Influence* (Yale University Press, 1966), p. 251.

7. To some extent this is already being done, when disarmament and enforcement aspects can be isolated from more modest steps to develop world law. This was the case e.g. with two resolutions—appealing to all governments to accept compulsory jurisdiction of the International Court of Justice and supporting research to adapt international law to changes resulting from technological advance—adopted at the 1967 World Peace through Law Conference in Geneva. See *New York Times*, July 14, 1967.

The "practical" men at the other extreme, however, are little more realistic in their own proposals. They are, to borrow from Deutsch again, the "pessimistic Utopians," who see conflict so imbedded in the nature of Man that the maintenance of peace (from the American viewpoint) can only be secured through the maintenance of the greatest deterrent force. Without becoming involved in a philosophical discourse, it may be noted that it is not necessary to change the nature of Man in order to change the standards by which men react to situations. History shows repeated alterations in the nature of accepted political principles, over time and over the areas in which common standards can be applied. Such developments do not move "onward and upward forever"; but neither have the downward swings been permanent.

A more effective practical argument against the pessimistic utopians may be the observation that many of the assumptions concerning the security to be derived from a "stable deterrence" system, which underlie this school of thought, have been proven wrong in the course of the past twenty years. The original United States monopoly of atomic power was soon broken; and each stage of "superior" development since attained has been sooner or later threatened, or surpassed—and the endless chain continues to grow.

It has now reached the anti-ballistic missile (ABM) stage without achieving lasting security; indeed, the process has only made men feel more insecure than ever. Each step weakens the thread holding aloft the sword of Damocles and increases the potential of holocaust should it finally break. Nor is there any reason to think that the Soviet Union, and in time China, are likely to accept willingly the sort of military balance that satisfies the United States as meeting its security needs; not, in any event, while communist and American political objectives are so opposed and while Moscow and Peking are willing to strive to overcome the United States strategic lead.[8] Yet Secretary McNamara, when arguing against the introduction of an ABM system in the United States, pointed out that: "With our force, superior as it is in numbers, we do not have sufficient power to destroy them [the communists] without in effect destroying ourselves in the process."[9] To call the present national deterrent situation

---

8. As Secretary McNamara said on one occasion: "My position is a very simple one on disarmament or arms control: I think we should engage in such agreements if and when, and only if and when, we can do so without reducing our power advantage." Quoted in Arthur Herzog, *The War-Peace Establishment* (Harper & Row, 1965), p. 118. See also Thomas Schelling: "The most promising course is to get the Soviets to agree to a fairly expensive inferiority and taper off ourselves." Quoted in *Ibid.*, p. 52.

9. U.S. Department of State, *Bulletin*, Vol. 56 (1967), p. 442.

"peace and security," therefore, would be as great a travesty on words as that indulged in by those who urge a "disarmed" world with an over-whelming "international deterrent" force.

If the thinking of the "protracted conflict" warriors is utopian in regard to the objective of peace, they are much more realistic in regard to the feasibility of their proposed means than are the optimistic utopians. The achievement of an international treaty on even a significant degree of arms control (let alone on general and complete disarmament) or a reconstruction of the United Nations system into a world confederation is so far off in the future as to be left to the dreamers. But the question whether to make a commitment to the ABM spiral in the arms escalation is under serious debate as this study is being completed. The current situation in Vietnam also contains the possibility of escalating policy in Southeast Asia to the level desired by the containment-confrontation school.[10]

A clear-cut general policy on these lines is still not the government's position, however, even with the intensified war in Vietnam. Official policy remains, as it has been ever since the end of World War II, the pragmatic, somewhat bumbling, and inconsistent policy of keeping our nuclear "guard up," while seeking to "build bridges" with an "out-stretched hand." The stance has become ever more difficult to maintain, however, as recent events, both technological and political, have increased the complications of an already almost unbearably complex situation. Nonetheless, so long as the American objective remains to achieve a more peaceful state of containment-coexistence, the temptation must be resisted to adopt the psychologically easier way out in the short-run that is provided by the protracted-conflict approach. If there is to be any hope of a more peaceful world in the longer run, time must be bought during which to develop those common standards that alone can de-escalate contemporary political conflicts.

Within that framework, the role of the United Nations could be more important in the future than it has been, or been permitted to be, in the

10. See Secretary McNamara's statement to the Senate Armed Services Committee, Subcommittee on Preparedness Investigation, Aug. 25, 1967, opposing a wider and less discriminating bombing campaign in North Vietnam. He concluded: "The tragic and long-drawn-out character of [the] conflict in the South makes very tempting the prospect of replacing it with some new kind of air campaign against the North. But however tempting, such an alternative seems to me completely illusory." *New York Times*, Aug. 26, 1967, p. 4. The Secretary's position was later criticized in the Subcommittee report which supported the arguments of the Joint Chiefs of Staff in favor of an escalation of the bombing. Text in *Ibid.*, Sept. 1, 1967, p. 10.

recent past. If means of gradual improvement in the international situation are sought, the United Nations need be viewed neither as the center of a peace-through-law universe, nor as merely one more weapon with which to fight the protracted conflict in terms of an intensified cold war. Both these approaches, it is true, have the advantage of providing a clear-cut program for achieving the desired peaceful world, though its description differs markedly in each case. Both, curiously enough, are based on a touching faith in the ability of governments to control the weapons of holocaust: the one, through controlled and enforced national disarmament; the other, through control of the deadliest armaments.

But if general nuclear conflict can be avoided, accommodation is much more likely to proceed at a snail's pace; and the improvements at each stage will, according to their nature and extent, be the major determinants of what can be achieved in the succeeding stage. Men of goodwill will undoubtedly continue to disagree over the best procedures at each stage; those of ill-will may continue to oppose the whole endeavor in favor of promoting the dominance of one group over the peaceful relations of all. The best that can be done at this point, therefore, is to attempt to replace the "blueprints for peace" and the "strategies for settlement" with a consideration of some of the more limited possibilities of using the United Nations as one of the collective means to the declared end of all parties in the present conflict—even of that most bellicose-sounding of current governments in Peking.

As preceding chapters have shown, increased international cooperation will be essential to improvement in each of the aspects of a peaceful world, from the control of armaments to the development of international law and the machinery of the United Nations itself. These are, therefore, examined in turn below.

Arms Control and Disarmament

"Pronouncements about military power and disarmament," writes a British historian, "are still made by public figures of apparent intelligence and considerable authority with a naive dogmatism of a kind such as one finds in virtually no other area of social studies or public affairs."[11] The official

11. Michael Howard, "Military Power and International Order," *International Affairs*, Vol. 40 (July 1964), p. 407.

Soviet and United States plans for general and complete disarmament (GCD) fall within that class of "grandiose and improbable proposals" which are likely to "create more favourable political effects than [would] modest and negotiable ones." The fact that governments and individuals can solemnly advocate GCD (even as a long-term objective) in the world of today reflects inability to face the reality that, "in general, arms races arise as the result of political conflicts, are kept alive by them, and subside with them."[12]

The attitude being discounted here was defended by a leading British disarmament negotiator as follows: "It is easy to say that disarmament is Utopian. But if the choice is between Utopia and Nirvana, most of us would plump for Utopia."[13] But that is not the choice. Even if Nirvana is at one end of the scale, Utopia still remains unattainable and the search for it is no guarantee of escaping oblivion. Moreover, failure to find it will not necessarily mean oblivion, although the self-propelling tendencies of the arms contest in the field of advanced nuclear weaponry may well mean that failure to control even those arms will lead to Armageddon.

For all the GCD talk, it is in the narrower terms of nuclear controls that the only effective negotiations are taking place. And even there, little has been accomplished. In late August 1967, the Soviet Union and the United States, after many delays, submitted identical draft texts of a nonproliferation treaty to the Geneva Conference.[14] The drafts contained little more than reciprocal pledges of the nuclear-weapons powers not to transfer, and of the nonnuclear-weapons states not to receive or manufacture, such "weapons or other nuclear explosive devices." The inspection procedures could not be agreed upon, so the drafts contained a blank Article III. The nuclear powers would retain a veto on any amendments to the treaty; and they offered no concession to Brazil and others which complain about the prohibition on peaceful nuclear explosions by nonnuclear-weapons states. Moreover, although there appears to be wide agreement that some form of security guarantees will have to be given by the superpowers to the nonnuclear states, the drafts contain no provision for them. Nor do they impose any other obligation on the nuclear weapons states—such as a Swedish proposal that they should "cooperate" in gradually applying safeguards over peaceful nuclear activities on their own territories.

12. Hedley Bull, *The Control of the Arms Race* (Praeger, 1965), pp. 143, 148.
13. Sir Michael Wright, *Disarm and Verify: An Explanation of the Central Difficulties and of National Policies* (Praeger, 1964), p. 150.
14. Text in *New York Times*, Aug. 25, 1967, p. 12.

Clearly, a nonproliferation treaty is not yet assured. Even if achieved, it promises no degree of disarmament—and perhaps no cessation of proliferation, unless political relationships improve enough to reinforce any tenuous treaty guarantees for the nonnuclear states against nuclear "blackmail."

Nevertheless, because the stakes are so high, the effort to agree on at least some limits to the nuclear arms race must go on. To call even a high degree of success (which seems unlikely) in this effort "arms control" would be unrealistic. But at this stage any degree of nuclear crisis control or any weapons limitation beyond those in uninhabitable areas of earth and space would be encouraging. Yet the lengthy Soviet-Western discussions aimed to complete the ban on underground atomic testing have failed in the face of the drive for nuclear missile supremacy; and those for a nonproliferation treaty have still to be completed. Moreover, nothing has yet happened with regard to the proposed Soviet-American talks on the ABM situation, which may reflect the concern of both parties over the continued advance of Chinese nuclear achievements, as well as their own mutual suspicions and fears.

The latter are illustrated, in the United States, by military pressures for the introduction of a large-scale ABM system in spite of the view stated by Secretary McNamara: Such a system, he believed, would require an enormous investment, would "not significantly change the balance of power," and would not protect the American people; but would, on the contrary,

actually increase the risk to both of the parties [because] each of us . . . must, to the extent it is technically and financially capable of doing so, erect a deterrent against a potential strike by the other.

We have that deterrent today; in a very real sense the Soviets have it as well. We feel we must keep it. I don't know of any reason why they should think differently than we in this point. . . .

. . . Because we know our knowledge is uncertain, in effect we overreact, because we forecast the most extreme circumstances.[15]

To talk about significant arms control measures in these circumstances is to be unduly optimistic; and to discuss anything even remotely resembling a GCD treaty is sheer fantasy. Proposals for control or reduction (whether for Stage I of the GCD plans or as peripheral measures) are, in practice, aimed by both sides at improving and stabilizing the existing arms structure as part of their respective national security policies—not at seriously reducing national armaments. The most that can be hoped for

15. U.S. Department of State, *Bulletin*, Vol. 56 (1967), p. 442.

was pointed out by William Foster, the chief American negotiator: "No one will deny that there are uncertainties in maintaining the present rough balance of deterrence as arms continue to build up on both sides. The point to remember . . . is that it is possible to maintain military balance at a fixed level—or on a downward plane—rather than on an upward plane.[16] Even if the two nuclear giants at Geneva were able to agree on halting their race and on giving constructive leadership to effective control and reduction measures among most of the states, there would still remain the holdouts: France and Communist China.

The first may be important primarily as a reminder of what may happen if other near-nuclear states decide not to make the commitments required by the draft nonproliferation treaty. But China has already demonstrated that it will sooner or later become the producer of both medium- and long-range nuclear missiles—a prospect that can only be considered grim, unless some way can be found to mitigate the hostility with which Peking now views the rest of the world. The fact that no serious threat to the United States itself may develop until some time in the seventies is no consolation if, in the interim, Chinese political relations generally do not improve. The political fallout from China's scientific achievements has already been felt throughout the world; and the countries of Asia will become subject to nuclear blackmail long before the United States itself need worry. In the short-run, the destruction of Chinese nuclear facilities might be both feasible and a way to reduce that threat. Unless Americans were prepared to wreak havoc literally in China, however, it could be only a matter of more time before the threat was renewed. In any event, that is not declared United States policy (whatever some individuals might wish), both because the unforeseeable dangers of uncontrolled reactions are too risky and because such wholesale destruction, except in response to a direct threat to this country, goes against the American grain.

If there seems little hope for arms control at the top level, greater effort might bring more rewards at regional and local levels. The pattern of the Latin American denuclearization plan ought to provide a model for other regions and encouragement to them. But difficulties caused by the peaceful-explosion issue and by active opposition from a nonparticipating country (Cuba) are likely to be repeated elsewhere. At the same time,

16. *Ibid.*, Vol. 52 (1965), p. 661.

difficulties over the Geneva nonproliferation treaty may halt regional progress. In the area of conventional armaments, it seems unlikely, without improved political relations among the smaller states, that they will be easy to persuade to refrain from increasing their armaments, even as they condemn the great powers for refusing to control their own competition.

Moreover, the major military powers are themselves in great part responsible, as suppliers, for the arms race among the lesser states. This has been most obvious in the India-Pakistan and Arab-Israel conflicts since 1965. But lower-level threats to political stability, if not actually to peace, have been increased, if not created, by arms sales elsewhere. Once again, however, a greater degree of accord between the superpower suppliers seems a prerequisite to any effective measures of control among quarreling purchasers (or gift recipients). Another too little considered aspect of this problem has been pointed out by one expert:

> It is ironical that the industrial powers . . . Western and Communist, have in the past decade spent tens of billions of dollars in the attempt to stabilize the balance of power among themselves, but elsewhere have pursued policies leading to local arms races which, by committing [the industrial powers] increasingly to their client states have risked the destabilization of their own precarious relationship.

Other advanced industrial states are also involved in this situation—"20 non-African nations" are supplying "arms or military training to the 33 African countries," according to this same observer. Consequently, any effective control of such sales would have to have "active support" from all the Big Four powers and such other countries as Canada, Czechoslovakia, Switzerland, Sweden, and Italy; otherwise, any of them might replace those that had agreed to stop supplying arms, as France has stepped into Great Britain's place to supply South Africa.[17] Besides the economic aspects of the revolutionary rate of technological change, which makes obsolescent for the advanced powers much sophisticated equipment that is still highly serviceable elsewhere, there is always the tendency of governments to see in arms sales a source of influence politically. Although immediately outside the direct East-West conflict, such activities may all too soon become infected by the cold war as well. Thus, technical approaches to arms control in the Third World, as among the indus-

17. Alastair Buchan, "Arms Nobody Wants to Control," *New Republic*, Nov. 6, 1965.

trial powers, appear certain to be barren of results except as they become a part of improved political relations.

Collective Enforcement

During the past year, the United Nations advanced significantly toward the ultimate issue of forcible sanctions against both Rhodesia and South Africa. Had the majority of African states had their way, unlimited economic (if not military) sanctions would probably have been proclaimed against the Rhodesian, South African, and Portuguese governments. The decision of the International Court of Justice against judging the South West African case on its merits was a blow to those who had hoped that, in this instance at least, the issue of enforcement might be brought within a legal as well as a purely political framework.[18] The nature of the basic political problem has not been altered by the change in legal status of South West Africa according to the decisions of the Special General Assembly in the spring of 1967. Enforcement of United Nations decisions will still require both the necessary votes and adequate support from the Members that control the power (economic or military) essential to implement them.

In principle, none of the permanent members of the Security Council (save France) appears opposed to the possible eventual use of sanctions to force South Africa and the illegitimate Rhodesian government to conform to United Nations judgments on their policies. Both the United States and Great Britain, however, maintain that the situation does not yet constitute a serious enough breach of, or threat to, the peace to warrant such strong measures. In fact, neither Washington nor London—the two who count in connection with southern Africa—is prepared to enter upon the costly and highly uncertain path of a strong economic blockade, much less of outright military enforcement measures. Even if they were so prepared, experience of partial sanctions against Rhodesia has demonstrated the difficulties of obtaining results by that method alone. The British economic situation (especially in relation to its vast interests in South Africa), and United States involvement in Vietnam and its balance-of-payments difficulties, also militate against early overcoming of their

18. As Rosalyn Higgins has pointed out, however, much of the criticism of the Court for refusing to get involved in that highly political controversy comes ill from governments which have refused to grant the Court strong jurisdictional authority lest it become involved in their own political disputes. See "The International Court and South West Africa," *International Affairs*, Vol. 42 (October 1966), pp. 589–90.

reluctance to provide the kind of leadership that Washington gave in the case of Korea.

The Soviet Union's economic interests in southern Africa are unimportant in contrast; and Moscow was able for long to enjoy the best of both worlds. Standing to lose nothing economically, and profiting politically from the indignation of the African and other anticolonial states with the Western powers, it could be strong in verbal support for sanctions. When the chips were finally down on the South West African issue, however, Moscow, too, became a reluctant dragon. Communists can look to benefit, even so, from the continuation of generally disturbed conditions in Africa that hamper economic and political development and the evolution of more orderly international relations there.

These particular cases bring to a head the more general issue of whether it is possible for enforcement and conciliation to coexist institutionally. It seems certain that, while the nations remain as divided over fundamental political standards as they now are, it will not be possible to develop the degree of international accord necessary to unify the political will of the great majority of states and the military power of the leading governments through the enforcement machinery of the United Nations.

In 1945, the authority of the Organization in the field of settlement (related then to the conventional sort of international dispute) was deliberately limited to recommendation only. That was done, partly because the major powers felt that the smaller states would resist any extension of the privileged position of the permanent members of the Security Council beyond the limited field of action against aggression; and partly because they were unprepared to permit international arbitration of their own disputes except with their consent in each individual case. Nor could anyone then have envisaged the enforcement of peaceful change, which both the Rhodesian and South West African cases in their beginnings exemplified.[19]

In 1967, the same resistance by parties in conflict to the arbitration of settlement terms continued in relation to the more traditional type of interstate disputes, such as the Arab-Israel, India-Pakistan, Turkey-Greece-Cyprus, and Thai-Cambodian controversies. And the great powers remained so divided that, rather than using their influence to effect mediation, one or both often more or less openly sided with one party or the other in the Security Council and thus prevented any effective recom-

19. See Rosalyn Higgins on "the difficulty that the Charter fails entirely to provide for the enforcement of that peaceful change which justice requires." *The Development of International Law through the Political Organs of the United Nations* (Oxford University Press, 1963), p. 93.

mendations through that body. In that situation, the Council could hardly contemplate the enforcement of settlement terms it could not even agree on.

Nonetheless, in the one class of racial-decolonization conflict, there had developed over time a high degree of accord in principle, so that continued resistance to political adjustment and change in this single area had come to seem at least a potential threat to the peace. That accord in principle, however, has not yet extended to agreement on action.

Irony becomes irresistible, moreover, when it is realized that if the situation were carried to its logical conclusion, the attempt to enforce either settlement terms or political change on any significant scale would result, not in the maintenance of international peace but in the extension of military hostilities. Only when the degree of community is such that enforcement requirements become the exception to a general rule of reasonably peaceful relations will it become possible to maintain international peace, like domestic peace, through a system of collective enforcement.[20]

Peacekeeping and Pacific Settlement

While such a state of accord has clearly not been attained, on occasion violence has occurred in circumstances where the nuclear powers have been concerned lest its intensification involve them too directly. It has then been possible through the United Nations to agree on nonenforcement collective (including military) operations to help the parties maintain an agreed, if uneasy, suspension of the violence—usually obtained as the result of some political pressure from above on the states in conflict.

Such "military peacekeeping operations" represented an unusually high degree of international cooperation, in terms of their organization and deployment under executive authority delegated to the international Secretariat. As a result, they misled many into crediting them with greater and more independent political authority than they possessed. They could

20. See also Henry Kissinger: "An enforcement agency can contribute to . . . peaceful change only in a society where legal norms are generally accepted and where their observance is unchallenged by an organized minority. In such circumstances, violations will generally appear clear and unambiguous, enforcement becomes a technical problem of detecting the wrongdoer and assembling overwhelming power against him. In less stable societies, the police force is not considered nearly so benevolent." *The Necessity for Choice* (Harper, 1961), p. 235.

not, of themselves, lead to settlement of the underlying disputes that called them into being in the first place; and continuing conflict between the great powers remained serious enough to neutralize the influence the latter might otherwise have exerted on the parties to reach final settlement while the peacekeeping presence maintained quiet. Only in West Irian (where a lasting political settlement was reached before the international force came on the scene) and in Lebanon (where the controversy in effect ended with an accepted election) were the peacekeeping operations complete political, as well as technical, successes.

In other cases, the true nature of the United Nations military groups as part of the pacific-settlement machinery has been reflected in the same limitations that apply to more conventional political-civilian settlement efforts. Without fundamental accord among the great powers, there is no way for them to enforce an agreed settlement; and there is too much opportunity for the smaller parties in conflict to utilize the cold war situation to avoid settlement themselves.

Where the parties are basically desirous of settling their dispute, on the other hand, the machinery either of direct negotiation or of third-party mediation or arbitration, including the Security Council or International Court, as appropriate, has a good chance of achieving a solution. Even creaky machinery, in such a situation, tends to work effectively; and in any event, it would not be difficult to agree on means to improve it or extend its usefulness. The basic problem remains how to get the states to give more than lip service to the desirability of settlement. Since one government's "justice" is often another government's "oppression," settlement can only be achieved by compromise of some sort—a characteristic notable for its absence from the contemporary scene. Yet without such willingness to compromise, none of the proposals for "strengthening" the already available legal and diplomatic institutions of settlement is likely to be accepted —or to work if formal acceptance is somehow achieved.

The numerous proposals for strengthening the peacekeeping capacity of the Organization must be viewed against both this general background and the particular history of the stalemate over the question in the Committee of 33 and the General Assembly. In retrospect, it is clear, the misguided United States attempt to force acceptance of the procedures of peacekeeping on a strongly resistant Soviet Union and France undermined the real United Nations achievements in this field before the crisis developed. The still-deadlocked situation of 1967 equally clearly suits the purposes of the Soviet Union and France, neither of which wishes to see a more active United Nations. In this aftermath of the "disastrous confrontation" over Article 19, as one participant calls it,[21] it is therefore questionable whether anything is to be gained by continuing to reiterate the diametrically opposed positions aired in the Committee of 33. The debates have, however, shown that the majority of Members would support the basic guidelines for peacekeeping (as set forth by the committee in 1965) and a positive role for the Assembly in authorizing and financing such operations. But they will not support them at the price of defying Soviet and French intimations of vague but dreadful repercussions on the Organization should they vote those attitudes into an Assembly resolution. Since no resolution, passed by however large a majority, is likely to change Moscow's or Paris' position on the constitutional and practical issues involved, at least in the near future, it might be well to heed the warning U Thant gave in 1966 that:

Much could be gained if Members . . . represented in the organs concerned with peace-keeping would . . . [consider] possible new approaches to the task of solving disputes. This would be much more useful than holding inflexibly to their present positions . . . [on] peacekeeping, which can only result in inhibiting the capacity of the Organization to deal with threats or actual violations of the peace at a time when this capacity is needed most.[22]

Among other results flowing, partially at least, from the peacekeeping stalemate might be listed the scornful manner in which President Nasser withdrew Egyptian consent for the continuation of UNEF in May 1967, and the curious device of a non-resolution "consensus" that had to be used to place a small United Nations presence on the Suez Canal in July. In the circumstances, the United States might be better advised to accept the knowledge that a majority favor its general attitude and to refrain for the time being from pushing for endorsement of its specific proposals. These always include several elements that the Soviet Union and France will not

21. Charles W. Yost, "The United Nations: Crisis of Confidence and Will," *Foreign Affairs*, Vol. 45 (October 1966), p. 33. Former Ambassador Yost was a member of the U.S. delegation throughout the period of the developing crisis. He quotes from the Soviet-French declaration of June 1966 when General de Gaulle visited Moscow: "As concerns the UNO, note was taken with satisfaction of the progress made in the sense of realizing more exactly the role which belongs to the Organization in accordance with its Charter, and also of the efforts which are being undertaken for the introduction of greater financial and administrative strictness in its functioning." *Ibid.*, pp. 26–27.

22. *Introduction to the Annual Report of the Secretary-General on the Work of the Organization, 16 June 1965–15 June 1966*, U.N. Doc. A/6301/Add. 1, p. 5.

presently tolerate, even by implication, in a formal resolution.[23] They do not even favor strong international action through the Security Council alone, quite aside from the constitutional issue of the Assembly's role.

One way in which the debate on peacekeeping might make some progress in the near future would be for the Committee of 33 to look into the possibility of reviving the Article 43 approach. After the twenty-first General Assembly in 1966 and the Special Assembly session in the spring of 1967, Czechoslovakia once again drew the Security Council's attention to its 1964 offer to make a contingent of Czech troops available for United Nations use in compliance with the provisions of Article 43.[24] It then listed a series of twelve "principles" from which "the agreement [that] the Czechoslovak Government is ready to conclude . . . should proceed." A number of them would probably preclude adapting the Article 43 provision to cover preparations for noncombat, voluntary peacekeeping forces, as well as for contingents and facilities necessary to undertake enforcement measures. As examples:

(3) A military contingent made available to the Security Council in accordance with an agreement would be employed in whole or in part solely on the basis of a valid decision of the Security Council and only for a period necessary for the fulfillment of the tasks envisaged in Article 42. . . .

(9) The individual contingents of armed forces shall remain also during the employment [by the Security Council] under national command and jurisdiction. The contingents will retain their national character and will always be subject to rules and regulations in force in their respective national armed forces. In the event that the Security Council employs such contingents, the Military Staff Committee shall be responsible under the Security Council for their strategic direction.

There is, however, nothing inherently different *in principle*, in many respects, between preparations for peacekeeping and those for enforce-

23. Ambassador Goldberg on one occasion listed them as four "basic principles" the United States considers "among the minimum essentials of a solution": (1) Preservation of the U.N.'s capacity to deploy peacekeeping forces "promptly in an emergency." (2) "Viable and equitable financial arrangements . . . agreed upon, and faithfully implemented, to support this capacity." (3) Maintenance of the Secretary-General's "essential role" as executive head of the Organization. (4) "No single country, however powerful, can or should be permitted to frustrate by the veto a peacekeeping operation . . . properly initiated by an appropriate organ of the U.N." Statement in the Committee of 33, March 22, 1967, text in U.S. Department of State, *Bulletin*, Vol. 56 (1967), pp. 637–38.

24. U.N. Doc. S/7852, April 13, 1967, letter to the President of the Council. Quotations below are from this document.

ment, as the Czech memorandum made clear on certain other points, for example:

(5) The military contingent shall be made available [by a state] from among especially selected and trained units of national armed forces.

The differences would come in such practical details as the size of contingents and the nature of the special tasks the troops were to be trained for. The communist states have, moreover, even indicated some willingness to consider the adaptation of peacekeeping (as against enforcement) principles, for instance, the use of contingents only from countries other than the great powers.

It would thus seem feasible, subject to certain reservations safeguarding the noncommunist positions, to discuss in the Special Committee on Peacekeeping the possibility of requesting the Security Council to take up the issues involved, perhaps in an enlarged Military Staff Committee that would include all the Council members plus a number of other states now on the Committee of 33. It would, however, be essential to keep the political direction of the discussions under the control of the Council itself, and not allow even an enlarged Military Staff Committee to conduct the kind of autonomous, semisecret negotiations that, in 1946–47, in effect negated its supposedly subordinate advisory role to the superior political organ. Given goodwill, there would be no reason the possibility of agreements for making contingents and facilities available to the Council could not be discussed in terms of the requirements for both peacekeeping and enforcement tasks; and in terms of Council use for enforcement purposes, but not on a basis foreclosing any other use for noncombat tasks by collective agreement.

Present United States resistance to renewed negotiations within the Military Staff Committee appears based on the difficulty that such negotiations under Articles 42–43, interpreted as they were in 1946, would necessarily limit the talks to enforcement-type arrangements only. "Provision of forces under Article 43 agreements, therefore, would not necessarily meet the need for manning consent-type peacekeeping operations."[25] This is true; the only answer is that the article need not be interpreted in those same narrow terms today.

The necessary goodwill, unfortunately, seems likely to be lacking if such talks should begin, but even that would clear the air. The majority of present Member states have no idea of the type of difficulties encountered

25. U.N. Doc. A/AC. 121/WG. B/PV. 2, April 6, 1967, p. 15.

in the original Military Staff Committee negotiations. Even unsuccessful talks might be highly educational, therefore.

Success in changing the present rigid attitudes of the Soviet Union and France seems most likely to come as a result of urging by the nonaligned states that the two once more accept peacekeeping operations at least passively, as they did earlier. It is not, as some would charge, sheer "irresponsibility" that has kept the Afro-Asian states in particular from developing such a corporate approach. Some of the complexities that enter into this unsatisfactory situation are discussed later; but one of the factors is undoubtedly the way in which the other aspect of the peacekeeping stalemate itself has developed, that is, the financial controversy.

The United States has, in effect, insisted on the letter of the 1965 compromise—that its agreement not to try to enforce the Article 19 sanction against those in deficit on payment of peacekeeping assessments would be followed by voluntary contributions substantial enough to rescue the financial standing of the Organization; while the Soviet Union and France continue to stand on their position that they will make literally "voluntary" contributions, but only to help resolve the financial problem, *not* to acknowledge even tacitly or indirectly any obligation to pay for peacekeeping expenses. By reiterating that the understanding of 1965 was that "Members who had refused to contribute to certain peacekeeping operations would make substantial voluntary contributions to reduce the deficit,"[26] the United States kept the original controversy alive and allowed its two major opponents to turn the tables on it in the Special Assembly session in April 1967.

The Soviet Union and France, after repeating their interpretation of the voluntary nature of the contributions they intended to make (time unspecified), then pointed the finger at the United States for not making a contribution of its own. Ridiculous though the charge was, in view of the heavy proportion of both assessed and voluntary costs that Washington has always borne, it remains technically correct. And it served to demonstrate once more that Moscow and Paris have little interest in relieving the Organization's financial situation, which might allow it to become more active in various ways. Such bickering by leading Members of the

26. Ambassador Goldberg, statement in the Committee of 33, March 22, 1967, text in USUN Press Release 28 (Corr. 1), March 22, 1967, p. 5. See also, Ambassador Seymour M. Finger's reference to the Art. 19 compromise: "The delinquents voted unchallenged [thereafter]—with the understanding that they would make substantial voluntary contributions to cover the deficit brought on by their refusal to pay peacekeeping assessments." Address, March 11, 1967, text in *Ibid.*, 25, p. 3.

United Nations was not conducive to the development of more "responsible" attitudes by the lesser Members; nor could the final statement from the United States Mission in this latest round have inspired much eagerness for more valiant action on their part:

The position of the United States was stated by Ambassador Goldberg on March 22nd. As he indicated then, if those countries whose contributions toward the deficit are long overdue will now make appropriate, substantial contributions, the United States, which has led all countries in voluntary contributions to the UN throughout its twenty-one year history, will not be found wanting.[27]

The official United States tendency to press for agreement on certain principles of peacekeeping, in spite of the continuing obstacle of Franco-Soviet opposition, parallels, perhaps partly results from, a tendency of numerous congressional supporters of the United Nations to press for American action to forward plans for a permanent international peacekeeping force. As noted earlier, it is not clear that sponsors of the draft resolutions purporting to express congressional support for such a move always recognize the difference between "enforcement" and "peacekeeping" forces. At the same time, it seems only too clear that they do not appreciate the implications of the stalemate within the Organization when they advocate plans for a permanent force of any type, which the State Department rightly opposes as premature and impractical. None of these congressional enthusiasts has seen fit, on the other hand, to propose that the government demonstrate American backing of the United Nations in the form of a large contribution to the rescue fund—one action that might help move the sterile debate off dead-center.

In view of the efforts by some congressmen, led by Senators Mansfield and Morse, to bring the Vietnam issue before the Security Council for discussion (which were renewed with added vigor after the August 1967 escalation of bombing in the North), it is worth noting that over two years ago the Canadian Secretary for External Affairs, Paul Martin, tied that issue directly to the peacekeeping crisis—and that his judgment is unfortunately still valid. He said then:

If we look back over the past two decades, it would be difficult to think of many situations of the kind which is now confronting us in Vietnam in which the United Nations has not had some part to play. . . . But here we are, faced with a situation that is full of the gravest risks, . . . threatening to set back much of the patient progress we have made towards broadening the basis of inter-

27. *Ibid.* (unnumbered), April 28, 1967.

national cooperation, and the United Nations has been powerless to intervene
... to reverse the course of events in Vietnam, to bring the parties to the negotiating table, to prepare the ground for peaceful and honourable accommodation. It has been incapable of doing these things because some of the parties
concerned have refused to accept its credentials to act in this situation and
because it is itself engulfed in a crisis which has had the effect of paralyzing
the general will for international action. . . .[28]

Peaceful Adjustment and Political Change

Experience since 1945 has also made clear that, in the circumstances of
the age, it is probably too late for effective international settlement by the
time a quarrel between states has reached the stage of a serious dispute.
The Charter's provisions for international economic and social cooperation, for an evolutionary system of decolonization, for the promotion of
human rights, and for the development of international law concurrently
with those other activities were aimed at preventing the intensification of
such disputes by ameliorating the underlying causes of conflict and by
extending the area of international agreement on standards and machinery
for accomplishing the desired ends.

While a sometimes surprising amount of international cooperation has
developed in these various areas—as compared to the period before World
War II—it has been less than adequate to bring about an era of peaceful
adjustment and development. Although the majority of the more than
fifty new states that have emerged from colonial status since 1945 did so
without serious violence, the remaining hard-core decolonization-cum-
racial-discrimination cases have already developed to the enforcement
stage in Rhodesia and may eventually do so in South Africa and the Portuguese territories. And in the successor states to French Indochina, where
the process of decolonization became an integral part of the communist-
anticommunist conflict, the cold war has already become a hot war and
involves the great powers directly or indirectly, as well as the Vietnamese
factions. Because the Indo-Chinese situation developed as it did, and
because France always, and the United States for long, refused to bring it
to the United Nations, the smaller states have shown no desire for formal
action in the Organization, in contrast to their usual approach to such
issues.

28. Address, April 12, 1965, Department of External Affairs, *Canadian Weekly
Bulletin*, Vol. 20, April 14, 1965, p. 1.

It was natural that the new states would seek to use the United Nations to compensate, through the political pressure of their voting strength in the Assembly, for their lack of military and economic power against the resistance of the imperial states to speedy independence for all territories. They were encouraged and abetted, moreover, by the communist powers for their own ends—China and the Soviet Union remaining agreed on this, whatever else their differences. The specific and practical communist concern to eliminate Western military bases in many present or former colonial areas combined with the theoretical communist belief that the end of imperialism would mean the economic collapse of much of the capitalism sustained (in their view) to a great extent by colonial exploitation. Within the United Nations, in addition, Moscow's anticolonial stance provided a way to find "compensation for her isolation [in a weak minority position], as Britain did for her dissatisfaction with the Holy Alliance, by calling into existence a new world to redress the balance of the old."[29]

That the imperial powers failed to develop their dependent peoples in the arts and skills of self-government and economic management has become only too evident in the aftermath of independence; but it has become equally evident that it was largely a Marxist myth that the metropoles depended on continued exploitation of the colonies for their economic well-being. The shedding of colonies, on the contrary, was accompanied by unprecedented increases in the economic development and welfare of the major European colonial powers. "Neo-colonialism" has therefore been substituted as the Marxist interpretation of this unorthodox phenomenon. It provides a convenient explanation alike for the communists and for the weak, noncommunist governments beset by the trials of independence and their lack of resources or of the experience to develop those they have.

The failure of the Western colonial powers to utilize the possibilities of the United Nations in the decolonizing process, as discussed in Chapter 7, must be counted the great missed opportunity of the West, since neither did they develop any satisfactory system of postcolonial relationships outside the Organization's framework. Now they are unhappy with many of the actions of the increased United Nations membership, although its growth was an almost inevitable consequence of the end of colonialism. Yet, as the Secretary-General pointed out a few years ago:

29. J. Duncan Wood, *Building the Institutions of Peace*, Swarthmore Lecture, 1962 (London: Allen and Unwin, 1963), p. 72.

With just a little imagination, both the East and West could find in the building up of the United Nations authority a common platform with these newly emerging nations, for many of whom this would be the best guarantee of their independence. For the Western powers it would be the rational sequel in world politics to their renunciation of control over their far-flung empires. It would, moreover, pave the way for new techniques of international relationship within the framework of a growing United Nations.[30]

There is still insufficient détente between the major East and West powers to hope for the erection of that "common platform" in the near future. For that very reason, however, it is perhaps even more important that the leading Western states attempt to develop the Organization more effectively in cooperation with the newer states. The difficulties of doing that in current circumstances are not overlooked in making this recommendation. For one thing, there is a fundamental need for better understanding on both sides. Too many of the advanced Western states are inclined to see the newer governments as "over-emotionally concentrated on just two issues—colonialism and race";[31] while the latter tend to complain that "anti-communism obsesses the Western bloc to such an extent that it does not pay sufficient attention, nor give the interest that could be wished, to the evolution of the modern world."[32] The advanced states, being prepared to admit their superior position (even, at times, to claim an undue superiority) should also be prepared "to go further in accommodating" the new nations: "We have been inclined to see the United Nations as an instrument for security and stability. They see it as an instrument for peaceful change in the world. There must be a bridging between these two concepts if we are to give the new nations a firm stake in the United Nations."[33]

Tolerance on the part of the older states might be enhanced by recalling some of their own history. The young United States, for example, suffered half a dozen years of political and economic instability until, on a second try, it successfully established a national government; before the end of the eighteenth century, it engaged in an undeclared war against France, its chief ally during the Revolution; after three-quarters of a century of

30. Speech at Uppsala, Sweden, May 6, 1962. Text in U Thant, *Toward World Peace: Addresses and Public Statements, 1957–1963* (Thomas Yoseloff, 1964), pp. 138–39.

31. Francis T. P. Plimpton, "The U.N. Needs Family Planning," *New York Times Magazine*, Sept. 18, 1966, p. 99.

32. (President) Modibo Keito, "The Foreign Policy of Mali," *International Affairs*, Vol. 37 (October 1961), p. 433.

33. Martin, *op. cit.*, p. 4.

self-government, it fought one of the bloodiest civil wars in history; and Euro-Americans fought Indo-Americans in "tribal" wars until late in the nineteenth century.[34] While most of the great wave of new African states emerged from colonial status only some half-dozen years ago, a number of them have already discovered that neither "the political kingdom" (in Nkrumah's phrase) nor the promises of Marxism are automatic guarantees of successful government in terms of acceptance by their own people or of satisfactory internal development. Disenchantment internationally has also set in, as exemplified in the somewhat farcical events at the aborted "Second Bandung" conference in Algiers in 1965 (which was anything but a repeat performance of the original Bandung a decade earlier).[35]

Suspicion of "Western imperialism" has historical roots that will take long to eradicate, especially when it continues to be kept alive by communist encouragement; but suspicion of communist "imperialism" is beginning to balance out the situation somewhat, especially in the disillusionment of many African and Asian states with Chinese subversive or openly militant policies against their new nationalist governments. The question is whether the United States (and the other Western powers) are ready and able to make the most of the opportunity apparently opening up. In spite of what are to them the sometimes annoying actions of the less developed states, both within and without the United Nations, the game appears worth the effort for the long-run goal.

Washington has been seeking to "build bridges" of détente directly with the communist countries of Eastern Europe and has even indicated willingness to see increased contacts of an unimportant, unofficial nature with the Chinese Communists. In the long run, however, it might prove equally effective in increasing the cooperativeness of communist governments if those "new techniques of international relationship" advocated by U Thant could be developed through the United Nations by the West with the weaker states. Communist governments, including Peking before the irrationality of the current "cultural revolution," have responded in the past more from desire to influence the underdeveloped world than to

34. See also Dankwart A. Rustow, *A World of Nations: Problems of Political Modernization* (Brookings Institution, 1967), for numerous examples of instability and violence during the formative periods of older nation states.

35. See Guy J. Pauker, *The Rise and Fall of Afro-Asian Solidarity*, RAND Staff Paper, p.–3190 (August 1965). Boumedienne's seizure of the Algerian Government from Ben Bella was used as an excuse to liquidate a venture that had gone sour for other reasons. The Peking delegation failed to have the "postponement" of the conference attributed to "imperialist intrigues."

direct pressures from the anticommunist West. The Soviet Union, for example, eventually became a contributor to the United Nations' technical assistance program after initially castigating it as nothing but an economic sheepskin on the imperialist wolf. Communist participation may contain the seeds of disruption of programs so joined, but that should be no more of a hazard to them than communist opposition from outside. And participation at least lowers the level of polemical criticism. (Although only the United Nations aspect of this problem is under discussion here, there is an equal need for greater efforts and greater achievements in the many other bilateral and multilateral programs in this broad field, since all the experts seem agreed only on the fact that the gap between rich and poor nations has increased rather than diminished in recent years.)

There is more than sufficient justification in the development needs of the Third World to call forth such an effort; and the time, according to President George Woods of the World Bank, is more than ripe. Present policies, he has pointed out, are frustrating the trade potential of the less developed countries, and:

The amount of development finance flowing to [them] is considerably less than they could effectively employ and . . . than the industrialized countries could reasonably afford—even by their own standards of what is an appropriate basis for sharing a small part of their increasing wealth with the poor countries. . . . At a time when we should be making full speed ahead, development assistance is in the doldrums . . .

If the momentum of economic growth in the developing countries . . . is not speeded up, if leaders in these regions lose heart, then the prospect is for a rapid deterioration in world affairs that will inevitably become a matter of highest concern in the United States and other industrial countries. . . . What is needed now are firm political decisions to carry out an intensive, sustained and coordinated attack on under development, together with the political will and stamina to stay the course.[36]

There is little sign as yet of any such plan of attack on poverty and overpopulation.[37] Hazards in the way of the United States taking leadership of such a program are more domestic than international, and will be considered later in that context. The pertinent point here is that any plan, in which the United Nations and the specialized agencies would have a large

36. George D. Woods, "Finance for Developing Countries: A Time for Decision," Gabriel Silver Memorial Lecture, Columbia University, April 13, 1967, pp. 16–18.

37. At the opening of the 22d General Assembly, however, The Netherlands took a promising initiative in that direction, which could develop into such a plan. See "Memorandum submitted by The Netherlands on the Preparatory Work for the Second Development Decade," U.N. Doc. A/C. 2/235, Oct. 2, 1967.

role to play, would help to create those improved relations between the West and the Third World which were urged above. It would also meaningfully "strengthen" the United Nations in the only way in which that can be done—through using it.

For the United States and other noncommunist industrialized countries to give the necessary leadership to such an effort, however, they must see the need to change some of their own policies, as well as to urge changes on the governments of the less developed countries. They were unable, as a group, to do this in terms of developing a new relationship to take the place of the old imperial framework of political order and economic support. Nor are there signs that the new opportunity, in terms of development and modernization within a multilateral framework, is comprehended. Some such vision underlay the Decade of Development proposals, in the origin of which President Kennedy played a notable part. But with 70 percent of the decade almost over, the U.N. Development Program (UNDP) could muster only $170 million (of a modest $200 million goal) in pledges for 1967 activities; and the UNDP "is the world's largest multinational source of pre-investment assistance and technical cooperation."[38] Other assistance and financial programs have also fallen short of what should be done.

One reason for the reluctance of the industrial countries to meet the challenge more effectively is, of course, their preoccupation with military and other domestic expenditures that appear to them much more urgent, so long as the existence of vast numbers of destitute people is not seen as a threat to world peace. Yet President Woods points out that: "We see every day how [such conditions] may create vacuums of authority into which the great powers may be drawn in uneasy confrontation." And Pope Paul has declared in more general terms: "Development is the new name for peace."[39]

Another reason for their reluctance to act is the disenchantment of the industrialized countries because of the alleged inability of the poorer countries to make more productive use of aid, while they claim more assistance as of right, and because of their unstable and often revolutionary politics.

38. At the UNDP pledging conference in October 1966, Administrator Paul Hoffman emphasized the importance of reaching the $200 million target for 1967, and the need for increasing it to $350 million by 1970. Other voluntary U.N. programs were pledged only some $240 million additional for 1967. See U.N. Press Release M/1709, Dec. 31, 1966, pp. 16–17.

39. Woods, *op. cit.*, p. 4. Papal encyclical, "Populorum Progressio," March 26, 1967. Text in *New York Times*, March 29, 1967, pp. 23–24.

These issues, as noted earlier, have been important factors in United States political and military, as well as economic, policy thinking. There are few indications, in 1967, of official Western readiness to accept the advice of economist Robert Heilbroner that: "The initial premise of Western foreign policy toward economic development must . . . be an acceptance of its revolutionary potential [since] the tensions and disruptions of the developing world are by no means apt to diminish. . . ."[40]

For the United States, in particular, this would mean bringing itself to regard the turmoil apparently inherent in the modernization process as the manifestation of "a passionate nationalism . . . forced to rely on the resources and generosity of the old imperialists,"[41] rather than as "inevitably" leading to communism—a tendency which "makes the historical process the opponent of the United States rather than its ally."[42] Also, it leads to too great stress on military defenses against communism, which are not a solution to what is an essentially political problem even though it constitutes a major element in United States security. Secretary McNamara recognized this when he declared:

> The irreducible fact remains that our security is related directly to the security of the newly developing world. . . .
> The rub comes in this:
> We do not always grasp the meaning of the word "security" in this context. In a modernizing society, security means development.
> Security is not military hardware—though it may include it. Security is not military force, though it may involve it. Security is not traditional military activity, though it may encompass it.
> Security is development. . . .

Unfortunately, the Secretary did not make this break with tradition until 1966; and he prefaced the above declaration with the admission: "There is still among us an almost ineradicable tendency to think of our security problem as being exclusively a military problem—and to think of the military problem as being exclusively a weapons-system or hardware problem."[43] Circumstantial evidence would indicate that the tendency has not yet been eradicated from official thinking.

---

40. Robert L. Heilbroner, *The Great Ascent: The Struggle for Economic Development in Our Time* (Harper, 1963), pp. 176, 178.

41. Jahangir Amuzegar, "Nationalism versus Economic Growth," *Foreign Affairs*, Vol. 44 (July 1966), p. 653.

42. Herbert S. Dinerstein, *Intervention Against Communism*, Studies of International Affairs No. 1 (Washington Center of Foreign Policy Research, 1967), p. 37.

43. Robert S. McNamara, address before American Society of Newspaper Editors, May 18, 1966. Text in U.S. Department of State, *Bulletin*, Vol. 54 (1966), p. 877.

The adoption of even the most far-seeing plan, and its application with a minimum of inefficiency and a maximum of resources, will not guarantee automatically what President Kennedy called the fundamental task of creating "a new partnership between the Northern and Southern halves of the world."[44] Time and patience will be needed, for the task is one of enabling the weaker countries, not merely to raise their GNP and standard of living sufficiently to avoid social revolt, but to develop enough internal strength in their societies so that subversion and even indirect aggression become relatively profitless.[45] From what is now known of the problem, such "a new world stability" will also require that "the rich nations . . . be prepared to modify their economic policies in the interest of a broader sharing of opportunities."[46] Current attitudes on that question within the United Nations were put briefly in the following year-end summary of 1966 actions by the U.N. Conference on Trade and Development (UNCTAD):

The developing countries represented on the [UNCTAD] Board, in a joint memorandum . . . urged the developed countries to take action before the second UNCTAD session [February 1968] to conclude commodity agreements on cocoa and sugar; institute a scheme of general and non-discriminatory preferences; increase the flow of financial assistance to developing countries; alleviate the debt burden, and improve loan conditions.

Representatives of the developed countries indicated they shared the concern over the situation of the developing countries, but could not subscribe to the memorandum because it was not sufficiently balanced. Representatives of socialist countries of Eastern Europe expressed sympathy with the desires of the developing countries, stressed the growth of their countries' trade with the latter, and said normalization of world trade was impeded by political conditions.[47]

44. Message to Congress, *Ibid.*, Vol. 44 (1961), p. 509.
45. See, for example, David P. Mozingo on the Asian situation: "The fact is that China is assigned far more responsibility than she deserves for the disturbances that lie at the roots of American anxiety about Asia. . . . Local non-Communist elites themselves, not Peking, created the basic sources of internal discord in Laos, Vietnam and Indonesia. . . . Asian communism's greatest asset is . . . primarily the existence of incompetence and corruption and the lack of a genuine, socially progressive, nation-building ethic within the non-Communist elite in every country where communism has made serious advances." "Containment in Asia Reconsidered," *World Politics*, Vol. 19 (April 1967), pp. 373–74.
46. Gunnar Myrdal, *Beyond the Welfare State* (London: Duckworth, 1960), p. 169. See also Susan Strange on policies that would amount, in effect, to "a measure of progressive international taxation of the rich countries." "Debts, Defaulters, and Development," *International Affairs*, Vol. 43 (July 1967), p. 529.
47. U.N. Doc. PR–M/1709, Dec. 31, 1966.

If those negative attitudes are the best that the more developed countries, East and West, can do in the face of the critical economic, social, and political problems which continue to retard internal growth and moderniz- ation in the underdeveloped countries, and of the "insupportable burden of foreign debt"[48] accumulated in the course of the unplanned develop- ment process that President Woods deplored, then the outlook for the longer term is indeed gloomy.

Universal Membership

Two problems relating to the character of United Nations membership are important in looking to the future: one, the question of the limits, if any, that ought to be applied to the admission of "mini-" or "micro-states" as Members; secondly, and more directly related to security issues, the question of the divided countries.

The problem of micro-states, it should perhaps first be pointed out, is not fundamentally that of their sovereign status. Liechtenstein and Monaco, for example, have long been sovereign. League policy, however, was to consider such tiny states as not in a position to carry out all the international obligations imposed by the Covenant. As indicated above, the almost unquestioning admission of sovereign applicants to the United Nations nowadays has been a reflection of great-power competition, rather than of deliberate membership policy. It has also been a part of the heri- tage of colonialism, that so few new states have been willing to remain in any associated relationship with their former imperial rulers.

Somewhat late in the day, suggestions are now being made for develop- ing some sort of associate membership, or other limited relationship to the United Nations. The Organization itself might accept responsibility for the protection of such small territories, which could at the same time be self-governing in their internal affairs and legally independent. The inter- national economic relations of such political entities could be handled through some adaptation of multilateral economic programs, and they might even participate in the Assembly and other significant bodies, such as UNCTAD, but without voting rights. They might also adhere to the Statute of the International Court. The easiest way to have handled many of the small dependencies that could not become viable in and of them-

48. Robert E. Asher, *International Development and the U.S. National Interest* (National Planning Association, 1967), p. 24.

selves would probably have been through using the Charter's authority for the United Nations to assume the role of trustee. Unfortunately, as Chapter 7 showed, the original concept behind the provision to this effect in Article 81 became lost in the years of conflict over the rising tide of nationalism within the old empires. It is no doubt too late to revive the possibility now, but some adaptation of the idea might be useful in the short run.[49]

In the longer run, it is to be hoped that regional or smaller groupings of some of these mini-states might form out of their own needs and experience, through gradual steps such as the development of common services or common markets where those would fill a useful function. Great Britain, in particular, attempted to impose federal forms of association on colonial units that had no common experience and too little practice prior to independence in functioning even cooperatively (much less within a political harness of federation). While concepts of the benefits that would flow therefrom made theoretical economic sense in a number of cases, in practice they have proven unsuccessful. A federal or confederal keystone, at the end of an evolutionary cooperative experience, on the other hand, might result in economically and politically viable new entities capable of assuming full status as Member states. To start toward any such process of bringing the micro-states under the United Nations, however, the remaining colonial powers would have to prove more willing than heretofore to enter into cooperative relations with the Committee of 24: at the minimum, by accepting visiting missions; at the maximum, by jointly working out steps for the transition to their new status.

The second membership problem presents even more difficult adjustment problems for the major Western powers. The United States, in particular, would have to face the issue of the divided countries much more frankly than heretofore. In the long run, all of them will have to be brought into the United Nations if the Organization is to fulfill its function properly. But in the short run, the forces of opposition to admitting them as eight separate units appear too strong to be overcome; while the forces for either their unification or their peaceable agreement to remain separated are in each case too weak to achieve resolution of the United Nations problem as a consequence of prior resolution of the national problem. As a practical matter, therefore, universality in the near future

49. The Secretary-General recently made recommendations on this matter in his *Introduction to the Annual Report of the Secretary-General . . . 16 June 1966– 15 June 1967*, U.N. Doc. A/6701/Add. 1, p. 20.

would appear to be achievable only by the kind of package deal that, as noted in Chapter 9, enabled the objections of both communist and anti-communist governments to membership for various states to be balanced out in 1955.

Legal arguments will undoubtedly continue over whether the separate parts of the divided countries are really "states" or properly qualify for membership in the Organization. But these issues need not prevent their separate admission or seating if there is a general desire for that action. Precedents abound in United Nations history that can be used to sustain the argument for giving priority to universality over other considerations.

Neither India nor the Philippines, for example, was an independent state when the Organization was founded, yet they were included as original Members. The two Soviet Republics that hold seats in the Assembly along with Moscow provide precedents for more than one seat per divided country, given the necessary consensus, and without prejudice to the positions of other countries on recognition and acceptance as Members. Many states deal in the United Nations with representatives of governments they do not otherwise recognize diplomatically—the Soviet Union with Nationalist China and the United States with Byelorussia, for example. The division of single states (India into India and Pakistan) and the formation and "deformation" of federal unions by United Nations Members (the UAR) have been accepted by the Organization on the basis of the decisions by the governmental authorities concerned. There is even the precedent of two Members with practically the same name: Congo (Brazzaville) and Congo (Leopoldville).[50]

The countries under discussion here, however, are all involved in conflict of varying degrees of violence, between their two parts, over which government should represent the whole. What is perhaps more important, they are also all strategically located and intimately involved in the cold-war conflict between the major powers. Whatever their shortcomings as "states," on the other hand, all eight political entities in Germany, Korea, Vietnam, and China-Formosa are substantial in size and population, and have had established governments exercising traditional sovereign rights for a substantial period of time. This is especially true in comparison with many of the newly independent states with little political form or economic substance, which were accepted as United Nations Members without hesitation. The difficulty, then, lies outside the United Nations. There

50. The two are now formally known as the Republic of Congo and the Democratic Republic of the Congo.

is no doubt that the majority of Members would accept the divided states in any form if they could agree on presenting themselves for admission or seating.[51]

From the viewpoint of the United States, its insistence on excluding the communist halves from membership is logical only in terms of a security policy that leads to using the world Organization as an instrument of the cold war. The continuance of a rigid attitude of extreme hostility toward the admission of these governments to the United Nations, as well as in every other way, goes back to the belief of the protracted-conflict school that there is no hope of changing them through any policy of accommodation on the part of Washington. That view was made with reference to China, but could as well be applied to the other countries in question.

The United States recognizes the Nationalist Chinese and the Bonn Germans as the governments of all China and Germany, respectively, and originally hoped to foster the downfall of the governments in Peking and East Germany by policies of isolation. In Germany, moreover, the insistence that reunification must precede admission to the United Nations has persisted as part of a NATO policy which assumed that somehow, someday, the continued maintenance of a strong Western alliance would result in a solution of the German problem.[52]

In neither case did the approach work, and in practical terms the theoretical isolation has been breached at many points. With the NATO

51. Only Korea might present a possible legal issue within the United Nations itself about the admission of two members. However, A/Res. 195 (III), Dec. 12, 1948, recognized the establishment of "a lawful government" in effective control of the part of Korea where the UN Commission was able to observe the valid election of that government; "and that this is the only such government in Korea." The United Nations did not recognize any right by South Korea to extend its jurisdiction by force.

52. It is difficult to find plausible explanation of how this denouement is supposed to come about. The Austrian experience is sometimes used as an analogy, but it is a poor one both geographically and politically. One attempt to spell out a method of reunification by isolation was made by Professor Brzezinski. He advocated bridging the East-West barriers so far as the other East European Communist states are concerned as a means to bring agreement from the Soviet Union to a reunified Germany on a sort of confederal basis. Only the Western section would have German troops, and it would remain in NATO; while the East would be demilitarized and policed by United Nations (or even Soviet) troops. See Zbigniew Brzezinski, *Peaceful Engagement in Europe's Future* (Columbia University, School of International Affairs Occasional Paper, 1965).

See also Miriam Camps: "The assertion that [Western European unity] was a precondition to [German unification] was frequently made; but only relatively recently has the assertion come to be examined in any very serious way either in Germany or in the United States." *European Unification in the Sixties: From the Veto to the Crisis* (McGraw-Hill, 1966), p. 238.

alliance in some disarray and growing dissatisfaction among the Germans with things as they are, it might be supposed that this is a good time to seek ways to build bridges between East and West Germany as well as with the other East European countries. Similarly, when signs indicated that a more flexible stance on China policy might be feasible with respect to domestic American opinion, the promotion of a two-Chinas approach seemed not impossible in 1966. Yet, in 1967, the official United States position remained rigidly against recognition of either communist government and opposed to any move to bring them into the United Nations.

There is no inherent reason why unification, recognition, and admission to the United Nations need be treated as a single policy; but to treat the three elements separately would require United States willingness to consider its strategic and political objectives in somewhat different terms than heretofore. The containment-coexistence approach would clearly justify using the United Nations in this way as one of the "bridges" so much talked about. In the case of Germany, the move would have to be accepted by Bonn, given the history of reunification policy until now; but such acceptance might not be so impossible as it seemed in the past, if current stirrings mean anything.[53] The fear that the recognition attained by an East Germany admitted to the world Organization would inevitably mean the end of any possibility for reunification, seems exaggerated. No one now considers reunification possible in a short time in any event; and there is no logical reason to think that two Germanies within the United Nations would have a harder time agreeing on reunion than they are likely to have outside it if present circumstances continue.[54] That issue will depend basically on the Germans' attitudes and on the tolerance of the Soviet Union, not on the position of the two governments in or out of the United Nations. The arguments in the East German and Soviet memo-

53. See, for example, Welles Hangen, "New Perspectives Behind the Wall," *Foreign Affairs*, Vol. 45 (October 1966), pp. 135–47; and Theo Sommer, "Bonn Changes Course," *Ibid.* (April 1967), especially pp. 490–91. See also: Charles R. Planck, *The Changing Status of German Reunification in Western Diplomacy, 1955–1966* (Washington Center of Foreign Policy Research, Studies in International Affairs No. 4, 1967).

54. The unique problem of Berlin might be resolvable within a broader pattern for mini-states, such as proposed above, pending final settlement by agreement of the contending parties or by some resolution of the unification issue. The Chinese off-shore islands might be handled in a similar fashion. See also, Lincoln P. Bloomfield, *The United Nations and U.S. Foreign Policy* (Little Brown, 1967), p. 185, for a proposal for a non-dependent-territorial "protectorate" under the United Nations.

randa discussed in the preceding chapter might even be considered sensible, if only they had been made by noncommunists.

The case of East Germany may in time be made easier, in one fashion or another, by some degree of détente with the Soviet Union. But the case of Communist China has been made even more difficult by the continuing conflict in Vietnam. Failure to bring Hanoi to the conference table or to achieve more improvement in the political system and more rapid pacification of South Vietnam has been reflected in constant escalation of the bombing of the North. Although there were news reports, in July 1967, that President Johnson was apparently "trying to signal to the leaders of Communist China his revived interest in reducing tension between Washington and Peking"[55]—such as through talks on nuclear nonproliferation—in August, attacks were authorized to within ten miles of the Chinese border and two planes were shot down over China itself. The administration took the position that "these air strikes are not intended as any threat to Communist China. And they do not in fact pose any threat to that country. We believe Peking knows that the United States does not seek to widen the war in Vietnam. The evidence has been quite clear."[56]

Both the evidence and the confidence were challenged by many. Senator Fulbright was perhaps typical of them in declaring: "I don't know how they can be so sure Red China won't intervene in the fighting. They're pretty close to being in the war when they are shooting down our planes over their territory."[57] On another occasion he said: "Nobody knows what the Chinese will do, but I'm convinced their leaders believe the President is trying to get them involved so that he can destroy their nuclear installations."[58] Given the Communist Chinese emphasis on Marxist-Leninist ideology, their belief in the aggressiveness of noncommunist powers follows naturally. Given the history of United States support for the Nationalist regime, the ideological belief can only have been reinforced against Washington in particular. And given the fact that the United States has officially considered the use of atomic weapons against China on at least

55. New York Times, July 11, 1967.
56. President Johnson, Press Conference, Aug. 18, 1967, New York Times, Aug. 19. Under Secretary of State Nicholas deB. Katzenbach also declared that "no threat to China was involved and Peking understood that." Hence it would make no difference "whether bombs were dropped 10, 50, or 100 miles from the border." Ibid., Aug. 22.
57. Ibid.
58. Washington Post, Sept. 27, 1966.

two occasions,[59] and has rejected all proposals for a no-first-strike pledge, it is difficult to imagine the suspicious Peking Government accepting official American reassurances at face value.

Even if administration confidence is based more on an estimate that China will refrain from intervening directly in North Vietnam in order to avoid provoking an attack on itself, or because it would not thereby confront American and South Vietnamese forces, or even because its internal condition is too chaotic at this point to permit such external action, the resulting situation is not likely to lead to any lessening of tension between Washington and Peking. But if the United States really wants to see Communist China return to the community of nations, and if it wants the United Nations to be able to act as an honest broker or a channel of effective communication in connection with Vietnam, an effort to bring Hanoi and Peking into the world Organization would seem to be one of the logical preliminaries. While little success is likely to attend such efforts in the short run, in the longer run, as U Thant has pointed out, "the Organization cannot be expected to function to full effect if one fourth of the human race is not allowed to participate in its deliberations."[60]

The United States, however, still takes the position that all initiative toward an improved relationship must come from Peking: "Thus, the door to cooperation between ourselves and the people of mainland China could be opened—but the keys are in their hands."[61] Others feel, on the contrary, that even though the Communist Chinese "have seemed to relish their self-imposed isolation . . . it is wrong to continue the essentially

59. Two known occasions were: (1) In 1953, in connection with the Chinese delay in agreeing to the Korean truce, the new Eisenhower Administration let Peking know that unless terms were agreed without unreasonable delay, the United States would resume fighting without limitation geographically or on weapons used. (2) In 1958, in connection with the possibility that Peking would launch a determined attack against Quemoy-Matsu, Eisenhower and Dulles agreed in a memorandum of understanding that intervention to save Quemoy, if necessary, might face them with the necessity of using nuclear weapons to succeed. For (1), see Roscoe Drummond and Gaston Coblentz, *Duel at the Brink: John Foster Dulles' Command of American Power* (Doubleday, 1960), pp. 112–13; (2) Dwight D. Eisenhower, *Waging Peace: 1956–1961* (Doubleday, 1965), p. 295 and App. O, pp. 691–93. See also Morton H. Halperin for discussion of Peking's interpretation of American enmity and its feeling that the U.S. may launch a nuclear attack on China in "China's Strategic Outlook," *China and the Peace of Asia*, Alastair Buchan, ed. (Praeger, 1965), pp. 104–08.

60. *Introduction to the Annual Report of the Secretary General . . . 16 June 1965–15 June 1966*, U.N. Doc. A/6301/Add. 1, p. 14.

61. "China, the United Nations, and the United States," U.S. Department of State, *Bulletin*, Vol. 56 (1967), p. 695.

negative policy which has marked United Nations discussions of this fundamental problem for many years."[62] If representation in the Organization could be seen as an obligation rather than a privilege, the principle of universality might put the "key" in noncommunist hands. In the circumstances of 1967, the United States can do little itself to turn that key; but it could cease its opposition to practically all moves by others to begin to unfreeze the situation. The internal inconsistencies that mark its current China policy can only be described as providing an "unsolution," in terms of declared American policy objectives that are themselves confused.

If the conflict in Vietnam does remain limited, or is even brought to the stage of political negotiations, then a new emphasis on universality for the United Nations would also make it possible to propose the seating of both Vietnams pending the resolution of their own differences over unification. With respect to the divided countries, Washington's declarations have consistently been to the effect that it does not aim to destroy the communist governments. The military objective of American strategy in Asia was expressed by the Chairman of the Joint Chiefs of Staff in the following terms: "Balance of power . . . underlies our presence in Vietnam, as we try to determine where is the line that marks the balance of power in southeast Asia."[63] In broader terms, the political equivalent of that military strategy was once spelled out by Under Secretary of State George Ball in terms which, while not so intended, in effect lend support to the idea of bringing all the countries divided by a "balance of power line" into the United Nations separately, until such time as their peoples may decide to unite peaceably. The war in Vietnam, the Under Secretary declared, is:

a product of the great shifts and changes triggered by the Second World War . . . [which brought about] a drastic rearrangement of the power structure of the world . . . [and] a very uneasy equilibrium of forces. For even while the new national boundaries were still being marked on the map, the Soviet Union exploited the confusion to push out the perimeter of its power and influence in an effort to extend the outer limits of Communist domination by force or the threat of force.

That attempt was checked by the Marshall Plan and NATO. The later similar threat posed by the Communist Chinese victory, in 1949, also had

---

62. Secretary of External Affairs Paul Martin, "Aspects of Canadian and U.S. Foreign Policies," *Canadian Weekly Bulletin*, Vol. 22 (March 15, 1967), p. 2.

63. General Earle G. Wheeler, address, Department of Defense, Press Release 476–66, June 5, 1966.

to be met by "an effective counterforce." The first test, in Korea, Ball pointed out:

was fought from a central conviction—that the best hope for freedom and security in the world depended on maintaining the integrity of the postwar arrangements. Stability could be achieved only by making sure that the Communist world did not expand by destroying those arrangements by force and threat—and thus upsetting the precarious power balance between the two sides of the Iron Curtain. . . .

That conviction led to the creation of regional security alliances to prevent the communist powers in any part of the world from "violating internationally recognized boundary lines fixing the outer limits of Communist domination." This does not mean, the Under Secretary concluded:

that [those] boundaries . . . are necessarily sacrosanct and immutable. Indeed, some of the lines of demarcation drawn after the Second World War were explicitly provisional and were finally to be determined in political settlements yet to come. . . . But those settlements [Germany, Korea, South Vietnam] have not yet been achieved, and we cannot permit their resolution to be preempted by force . . .[64]

That general policy of containment, expressed in containment-coexistence terms, would seem logically to carry with it some obligation to accept the communist governments within those bounds—including the mainland Chinese, North Korean, and East German authorities, as well as the North Vietnamese; and, subject to their subscription to the Charter, to be willing to see them in the United Nations. If they could be brought in by this method, their obligations under the Charter would become an extra mite of influence against further effort to achieve reunification by force. If the communist governments continued to reject such an approach from their side, their absence would be more obviously of their own choice and in opposition to an offer that appeared reasonable to the majority of Members. Dissension might thus be lessened whether or not the offer was accepted.

The main difficulty, of course, is that the communist governments concerned have not, from the viewpoint of the United States, accepted either the general lines of demarcation laid down by Secretary Ball—"internationally recognized boundary lines"—or the rule against attempting to

64. George W. Ball, *The Issue in Vietnam*, U.S. Department of State, Publication 8043, Far Eastern Series 141 (March 1966). See also Secretary Rusk's statement of Feb. 18, for a similar analysis of "the problem in perspective." U.S. Department of State, *Bulletin*, Vol. 54 (1966), pp. 347–48.

alter them by force. While refraining since Korea from frontal assaults by organized military forces against the de facto boundaries, the Soviet Union (and later Peking) has sought through subversion or "wars of liberation" to achieve the same end. The differences over what are legitimate and illegitimate uses of force are still a fundamental part of the ideological conflict between communists and their opponents in the international sphere.

Prime Minister Pearson of Canada has also described the southeast Asian struggle as "basically an attempt to establish the principle that armed assistance from outside to 'wars of liberation' constitutes aggression and must be checked." How to do this should be the concern of the entire international community, he continued, because when a single power undertakes to do it, "there arises the danger of widening the struggle into general war."[65] But an international alternative cannot be developed until there is more accord on the basic principle—and that, as Chapter 8 showed, is the main bone of contention in the legal arguments which, like the political practices, are still so far apart.

The Development of Law

Failing to achieve such accord on the basic principle through the United Nations, the United States has asserted a right to enforce its own interpretation of the law in Vietnam. Ambassador Goldberg (after denying any American desire to be an international "policeman") once declared that:

> In the case of Vietnam, nothing would be more heartening and welcome than to have the international community—acting through the United Nations—accept the responsibility for the most immediate of our aims—that of checking the resort to violence against South Vietnam.
>
> .   .   .   .   .   .
>
> But to say that the membership of the United Nations is not yet prepared to accept the responsibility . . . is not to say that the responsibility can be shirked or ignored by those committed to the rule of law—and we do not intend to do so.

More recently, the Legal Adviser of the State Department has argued that United States actions in Vietnam, in these circumstances, themselves contribute to the creation of international law:

65. Lester Pearson, address March 5, 1965, excerpts in *Current* (May 1965), pp. 14–15.

If a government acts consistently with a series of coherent principles, it may make a contribution to the common law of nations. The United States Government has tried to do this in the case of Vietnam, both with respect to situations not envisioned by the Geneva accords and in giving practical interpretations and applications to the general rules laid down by the Charter. . . .[66]

The difficulty with this approach is that it is equally applicable to communist governments and communist principles—which leaves the development of international law by this method just where it was before.

The problem was illustrated in comments by President Kennedy and Premier Khrushchev after their 1961 meeting. The latter declared: "We in the U.S.S.R. feel that the revolutionary process should have the right to exist." The question of "the right to rebel, and the Soviet right to help combat reactionary governments . . . is the question of questions. . . . This question is at the heart of our relations with you. . . . Kennedy could not understand this." While President Kennedy reported on his talks: "We have wholly different views of right and wrong, of what is an internal affair and what is aggression, and, above all, we have wholly different concepts of where the world is and where it is going."[67] The United States feels that the Soviet-claimed right to assist, or even to participate with, indigenous forces seeking to overthrow an alleged reactionary regime is incompatible with a realistic concept of "peaceful coexistence." The Soviet Union (and other communist states) feel that the right claimed by the United States to assist, and even to participate with, the armed forces of a legitimate, but dictatorial, regime to suppress insurgency and rebellion is likewise incompatible with that concept. In a period of détente, it might be possible to work out acceptable new rules setting limits on the right to intervene in the affairs of another state, either on the side of the established government or of a rebel group, which both sides would consider compatible with peaceful coexistence. Tacitly accepted limits of this kind, for example, appear to have prevailed in South Vietnam until 1965. That is, Hanoi kept its level of infiltration low, sending only trained cadres of former southerners and relatively small quantities of supplies (although generally of key items); while the United States refrained from escalating its participation to the point of bombing the North. The problem would be to

66. U.S. Department of State, *Bulletin*, Vol. 54 (1966), pp. 610, 611; *ibid.*, Vol. 56 (1967), p. 59.
67. Khrushchev, quoted in Arthur M. Schlesinger, Jr., *A Thousand Days: Kennedy in the White House* (Houghton, 1965), pp. 366, 377; Kennedy statement in U.S. Department of State, *Bulletin*, Vol. 44 (1961), p. 993.

achieve accord on such new concepts of limited warfare and on appropriate changes in traditional international law.

Within the framework of the United Nations, the communists present the problem in the following terms: "Consistent adherence to the principle of unanimity is the chief legal guarantee of peaceful coexistence, for its purpose is to prevent the United Nations from becoming a vehicle for any policy pursued by any group of states."[68] Previous chapters have shown how frequently the Soviet Union is prepared to accept a considerably less rigid standard in practice; but in the foreseeable future, it is not likely to relinquish its insistence on the lowest common denominator for any formal agreement. It would not be necessary for the United States formally to accept such a confining interpretation of the possible area of collective international action. But if a policy of using the Organization to ameliorate conflict among the nations rather than to intensify it is to be pursued, then in practice Washington will have to accept the fact that, at least in great-power conflicts, the United Nations must be used for the time being as "a forum for adjustments, not an instrument for guaranteeing to either side security against the other."[69] This applies in the legal field as elsewhere, as demonstrated by the financial-peacekeeping controversy.

In the more formal approach to the development of international law, as through the Committee on Friendly Relations, it might also become possible to meet somewhere on common ground in defining the principles of coexistence (friendly relations) if the rigid positions earlier adopted by the Soviet and Western "camps" are mitigated in the interests of movement toward détente. It appeared to one observer that, during the 1966 committee session, "a serious quest seem[ed] to have begun for generally acceptable formulations of progressive interpretations and common ideals."[70] Greater and more deliberate efforts to use the potential of the law and the functions of the International Court, by isolating the legal aspects of political cases, might also serve in the longer run to strengthen both the content and application of legal norms.[71]

68. G. Morozov and E. Pchelintsev, *The U.N.—Twenty Years of Failures and Success* (Novosti Press Agency Publishing House, 1965), p. 13.

69. H. G. Nicholas, "Is Force Necessary? The Peacekeeping Experience of the League and the United Nations," *NATO Letter* (May 1966), p. 11.

70. Piet-Hein Houben, "Principles of International Law Concerning Friendly Relations and Co-operation Among States," *American Journal of International Law*, Vol. 61 (July 1967), p. 731.

71. See also: Bloomfield, *op. cit.*, pp. 236–38, for a proposal that the United States initiate a "legal community" of likeminded states, which, however, would require it to begin by repealing the Connally reservation.

The fact must be faced, however, that this is a highly political age, when the legitimacy of international law is widely challenged. In such an environment, the United Nations has already become, without deliberate intent, "a dispenser of politically significant approval and disapproval of claims, policies, and actions of states, including but going far beyond their claims to status as independent members of the international system." This function of "collective legitimization" results partly from "the Organization's incapacity for decisive intervention in and control of international relations," in a period when "statesmen exhibit a definite preference for a political rather than a legal process of legitimization." In this sense, it "represents a political revolt against international law."[72] And the extent of its effectiveness—in the area of decolonization, for example—is an indication that the shorter run is not likely to see any great extension of "the rule of law" in the more conventional sense.

Foreign Policy and Domestic Politics

In the fall of 1967, there seems little chance that the United States will undertake a serious effort, centered on the United Nations, to give as much weight to the positive security values that might result from ameliorating the underlying causes of conflict and unrest as it already gives to the more negative approach of strategic containment. Not only do the immediate pressures of Vietnam militate against such an effort; but shorter-run military measures, with visible results, are often psychologically more satisfying and hence politically more appealing. In this respect, they cannot be matched by any costly effort aimed at persuading a multitude of states to cooperate on long-term international measures that often give little apparent return in the short run. Nor are such multilateral measures subject to the same degree of national (or limited allied) control, even when the United States pays the biggest part of the bill. The lack of that psychological satisfaction so essential to continuing political programs has already become apparent in connection with the United States bilateral foreign-aid policies. And far greater commitment, without immediately visible returns, would be necessary to the eventual success of any national-development and broad bridge-building program aimed at the Third World as well as the communist states.

72. Inis L. Claude, Jr., "Collective Legitimization as a Political Function of the United Nations," *International Organization*, Vol. 20 (Summer 1966), pp. 367, 369, 372, 377.

Moreover, the Congress, as well as other governments, must be persuaded to cooperate in such a program—and at a time when many of its leaders are deeply at odds with the administration on both foreign and domestic policy matters. In such circumstances, any costly foreign expenditures proposed by the Executive outside the military sphere are likely to suffer, less because of any inherent faults than as a result of general domestic political discord. Although space does not permit detailed consideration of the effects of either the American temperament or the structure of government on policy development, a few outstanding characteristics of each should be noted because of their probable effects on the direction of United States policy in the future.

Americans, being notoriously pragmatic and in a hurry, tend to sacrifice long-run possibilities in favor of more apparent short-run results.[73] This tendency is reinforced by a political system requiring frequent elections, which lead to campaign promises of quick returns on policy investments. It combines also with what has been called an "engineering approach." This is reflected in undue emphasis on individual problems ahead of longer-term policy requirements; in discontinuity both in time (as related to the changing nature of problems over a period) and in space (as related to interactions among problems at any one time). It is also reflected in thinking that sees the problems of international relations in terms of "machinery"—that is, as "essentially organizational problems, matters to be regulated and, ideally, controlled by appropriate organizational structures."[74] Another result of this way of thinking has been aptly described, by a Swiss journalist returned from Vietnam, as "binary reasoning: whatever is not white is black. [Americans] reduce everything to a simple choice: it is the 'true and false' pattern of their university examination papers."[75] Individuals in both the Executive and legislative branches of government share these characteristics, as many of the conflicts over policy within and between the two branches illustrate.

73. "The absence of an ideological tradition has often made America respond to contemporary challenges in an extremely short-range and excessively pragmatic fashion; we have over concentrated on means and techniques at the expense of long-range perspectives. Yet, paradoxically we have also tended to become wedded to particular formulas and concepts once they were formulated and crystallized." Zbigniew Brzezinski, "Tomorrow's Agenda," *Foreign Affairs*, Vol. 44 (July 1966), p. 669.

74. Bloomfield, *op. cit.*, p. 100. See also: Stanley Hoffmann, "Restraints and Choices in American Foreign Policy," *Daedalus*, Vol. 91 (Fall 1962), p. 686.

75. Pierre Kyria, "The Defeat of the I.B.M.," in *Global Digest*, Vol. 3 (1966), p. 66. An interview with Fernand Gigon, Swiss journalist and expert on Indochina.

In the context of the present study, perhaps the most critical policy weakness that results from these tendencies is the continued failure, in practice, to realize the Clausewitz dictum that receives so much formal acquiescence: namely, that "war is a continuation of policy by other means." Too many officials, political as well as military, either do not know, or do not appreciate, the explanatory sentences that follow the General's more famous words: "It is not merely a political act, but a real political instrument, a . . . conduct of political intercourse by other means . . . for the political design is the object, while war is the means, and the means can never be thought of apart from the object."[76] Americans do, on the contrary, often think of "the means . . . apart from the object." That has been the basic criticism of policy in Vietnam by those who consider that the means of large-scale warfare being applied are unsuitable to the political object of simultaneously safeguarding and building a viable South Vietnam. But the "binary reasoning" syndrome then often tends to lead opponents of current policy to advocate the opposite extreme, of more or less unconditional withdrawal—which may equally ignore the suitability of means to ends.

At the time of Korea, it proved impossible wholly to reconcile earlier United States strategic thinking with the new official policy of using limited-war means to a limited political objective. General MacArthur's overenthusiasm for using the United Nations operation to enforce his version of United States objectives eventually resulted in bringing the Communist Chinese into the conflict and in a return to the original political strategy. Rather than providing military officials with an adequate political lesson, however, the Korean experience appears to have led to what one former official has called "the 'never again' school of thought in the Pentagon," which opposes "any limitation on the use of force, if force [is] to be used."[77] President Kennedy's warning to West Point graduates in 1962, that "the basic problems of the world today are not susceptible of a final military solution,"[78] has not yet been accepted by American military strategists generally. And the tendency remains for many still to see the

76. Edward M. Collins, ed., *War, Politics, and Power: Selections from "On War" and "I Believe and Profess,"* by Karl von Clausewitz (Henry Regnery, 1962), p. 83.

77. Roger Hilsman, *To Move a Nation: The Politics of Foreign Policy in the Administration of John F. Kennedy* (Doubleday, 1967), p. 534.

78. *Public Papers of the Presidents, John F. Kennedy, 1962* (U.S. Government Printing Office, 1963), p. 454.

only alternative to the nuclear deterrent approach to security in terms of disarmament and world government, whether they oppose or favor it.[79]

In terms of what would be required of Congress by a serious effort to evolve a long-term policy for using the United Nations in a conciliatory political and economic approach, while military strength maintains the guard against nuclear dangers, the problems of bridge-building and foreign aid serve to illustrate the hazards of developing broad policies under the American system of divided powers. In general, the governmental structure makes it easier for Congress to deny support to administration proposals than to develop a consistent alternative program to which it would be prepared to commit itself. Where the Executive branch seems sometimes made up of "semi-independent institutions with quasi-constitutional rights," which fail to share a common vision of policy requirements,[80] the congressional committee system, in tandem with party politics, results in a similar situation. The complex, interdependent issues of foreign and strategic policy are considered piecemeal in separate compartments by the Congress. These are normal structural defects of the American system, but strong leadership in both branches behind a widely accepted policy can overcome them, as happened with such programs as the Marshall Plan.

When, however, agreement is lacking on basic policy objectives and means, the disintegrative forces inherent in the system are likely to prevail. Thus, for some years, there has been division within the Congress, as elsewhere, on whether the government should follow a general containment-confrontation or containment-coexistence policy. As a result, particular policies—such as for increased foreign aid and trade liberalization—which would be necessary to full-speed-ahead in the latter direction have sometimes suffered defeat in Congress, sometimes not even been proposed by the Executive. In 1965, for example, Congress failed to act on an East-West Trade Relations bill that would have given the President discretionary authority to grant or withdraw nondiscriminatory tariff treatment

79. Alastair Buchan noted, in connection with NATO, another motivation for the tendency to extremes: "Occasionally, when statesmen or thinkers become too despondent about the problems of inter-allied cooperation, they turn to the idea of creating an Atlantic political federation." And he also pointed out: "Because political consultation and military planning are conducted in separate compartments, NATO has made virtually no contribution to the evolution of constructive arms control and disarmament proposals—a subject that is as central to its responsibilities as defense policy, and more complex." "The Reform of NATO," *Foreign Affairs*, Vol. 40 (January 1962), pp. 166, 173.

80. Walt W. Rostow, address, "West Point Conference on the New Nations and Their Internal Defense" (April 18–20, 1963), Final Report, p. 9 (processed).

to East European countries. In 1966, the administration was unable to ship requested surplus food to Yugoslavia under the Food for Peace Program, because a provision in the year's agricultural appropriation act prohibited such sales to countries exporting to North Vietnam while it remains communist. And in 1967, the Senate approved a consular treaty with the Soviet Union by only a three-vote margin, although its acceptance had been urged by the President as evidence of United States willingness to build bridges to the East.[81] Thus, although there is a strong element in favor of the policy of expanding contacts and exchanges with the communist states (especially with a state so unorthodox as Yugoslavia), there is still formidable resistance to the programs necessary to implement the declared coexistence aim.

The same basic difficulty applies to foreign-aid policy, but it is also subject to additional hazards in the way of both consistency and adequacy. Foreign aid has long been a whipping boy for dissatisfaction (partisan in nature or otherwise motivated) with administration policy. Being famous for "having no constituency," it suffers both from the competition of domestic demands for resources and from any and all irritations with the ways of foreign governments, allies or adversaries, recipients of aid or not. The result has been, for some years past, a decline in the size of the aid appropriations (relative to steadily increasing American GNP and, more recently, in absolute terms), while the need for development assistance has become recognized as greater than ever before acknowledged. An effort by the administration to obtain authorization for assistance programs on a slightly longer-term basis than the usual annual bill met resistance in almost all cases, both in 1966 and 1967. Objections, however, appear to have been due less to failure to understand the long-term character of the development process than to a desire for greater control over policy through annual congressional review.[82]

81. The treaty had been signed in 1964, but it was not brought before Congress earlier for fear that it might be defeated. The vote was 66–28.

82. Senate Foreign Relations Committee, *Report on the Foreign Assistance Act of 1967*, S. Report 499, 90 Cong. 1 sess. (1967), repeats approvingly a statement from the previous year's report: "The majority of the members . . . feels that there should be at least an annual review by the policy committees of the Congress, at least until the world situation stabilizes somewhat. Aid as a factor in United States involvement in Vietnam, use of American arms by both sides in [Kashmir], persistent overselling of aid as a 'cureall,' . . . balance of payment problems—these and other factors have had the effect of merging the thinking of members who previously held opposite views on the merits of long-term authorizations." P. 15.

By 1967, domestic problems on top of the Vietnam situation, and both added to longer-term dissatisfactions with foreign-aid policy, brought the Foreign Relations Committee to a tie vote on a motion to submit the aid bill to the Senate without recommendations. In the House of Representatives, a less critical report was followed by a near defeat of the authorization bill itself, which passed by a mere eight-vote margin. Summing up the major factors in its attitude, the Senate committee declared:

With the cost of the war mounting each day, from an annual rate of some $25 billion, plus; with the Federal Government facing its largest deficit since World War II; with the fabric of our society in danger of being torn asunder because of inattention to domestic problems; and with the threat to the dollar continuing without letup, it is hardly reasonable to expect the American people to be very enthusiastic over a proposal to increase foreign aid, while at the same time, they are being asked to pay a 10% war tax. Under these circumstances, there was a strong consensus among committee members for cutting back on the foreign-aid program.

Nonetheless, the committee concluded:

But in spite of the faults and frustrations of the program, . . . foreign aid remains an essential instrument of foreign policy, and is likely to remain so for some time to come. The richest, most powerful nation in the world has an inescapable obligation, as a member of the world community and in its own self-interest, to do something to close the widening gap between more- and less-developed countries. The question is not, 'Should we provide aid?'; it is, rather, 'How, what kind, and how much?'[83]

There is also the wider question whether the United States will decide it has an obligation to back the broader kind of international program discussed above, which would properly require an integrated approach to commercial, investment, and assistance policies. Neither the Executive nor Congress has yet contemplated any such improvement in its policy-making procedures, either for the broad purpose of speeding up the development process throughout the Third World, as Bank President Woods proposes, or for the generally beneficial domestic results that might flow from improved governmental procedures in both branches.

Within the aid program alone, there is also the question of American support for multilateral programs. In overall terms, these have received less criticism from the Congress than the much larger bilateral programs, and they have even increased in relative importance as the total program

83. S. Rept. 499, pp. 6, 15.

has been decreased. Recent years have also shown some disposition to favor additional multilateral programs of a regional or consortia nature, especially through regional development banks. But the total of United States support for all such programs still remains small in comparison with all its international expenditures, and minuscule in relation to needs if the race against poverty and population is to be won. Even a relatively large increase in assistance through multilateral channels would still be a small part of the total. Any effort to obtain such an increase, however, would undoubtedly be resisted. Besides the above arguments of the Foreign Relations Committee against general aid increases, there are some additional hazards when national funds are lost to national control. Continued congressional opposition to the use of any American funds on behalf of Cuba, for example, led to a proposed Senate amendment that would add the following paragraph to the act: "The President shall seek to assure that no contribution to the United Nations Development Program authorized by this Act shall be used for projects for economic or technical assistance to the Government of Cuba, so long as Cuba is governed by the Castro regime."[84]

However the 1967 assistance program finally comes through the obstacle course of authorization and appropriation, the criticism and attitudes indicated above augur ill for congressional willingness to undertake the far broader program through the United Nations that has been urged here. Moreover, the outlook is no better for necessary supporting policies in trade and investment matters. The day the President acclaimed successful conclusion of the Kennedy Round of tariff talks (June 30, 1967), for example, he also approved new restrictions on dairy-product imports.

The trade liberalization of those talks, moreover, applies mainly to products of the industrialized countries, rather than opening significant markets for exports from the underdeveloped world. Similarly, in talks among the Group of Ten (the world's leading financial powers) the plan contemplated for increasing international liquidity, which has been approved in principle, would apply mainly to industrial states.

While the economic prosperity of these advanced countries is necessary to the prosperity of the poorer lands, since they must provide both markets and financing, their own well-being is no automatic guarantee of adequate improvement in conditions in the underdeveloped areas. And the evi-

84. S. Rept. 499, p. 62. See note 26, pp. 341–42 for earlier hearings.

dence, as already noted, indicates little willingness on the part of the former deliberately to develop policies that will effectively hasten that improvement. In the trade field, in particular, the United States shows little inclination to give up the luxury it is rich enough to afford of continuing to provide protection to manufactures containing a high labor content, such as the cheaper cotton textiles, and to semiprocessed products, such as smelted ores, which developing countries can produce with relative efficiency and to the benefit of their general development.[85]

Any such program would require not only a greater amount of financial support from the United States, but also American willingness to accept a greater *share* of the larger total. The strong theoretical argument, that an international organization may lose its international character if it is financed (and hence by implication dominated) to too great an extent by a single member, becomes almost irrelevant in the circumstances. Given the altered membership of the General Assembly, in any event, Washington's long-run problem is to maintain a degree of political influence commensurate with its military and economic power. It will not "dominate" the Assembly even if it pays a larger part of the bill for desirable programs; but it should be more influential politically as a willing supporter than as a grudging one. Where political factors are strong enough to outweigh theory—as in inter-American agencies generally and in such particular cases as the Palestine refugees—the United States already pays much more than the 40 percent it has come to consider a "fair" share of the voluntary economic and social programs of the United Nations. To alter this limit now would require a degree of congressional consent that would be difficult to obtain. It would nonetheless be essential to success in any program for coping with the global race between population and development, which is presently being lost; and unless Congress can also be convinced of the need to commit itself to a long-term program, there is even less hope that a meaningful United Nations program could be sustained. For so long as it is so difficult for the richest country in history to see the need to expend money for the intangible political benefits

85. The United States is not alone in this attitude, as a report of a group at the Council on Foreign Relations made clear. See Harold vanB. Cleveland, *The Atlantic Idea and Its European Rivals* (McGraw-Hill, 1966), p. 103: "Wealthy industrial countries can afford a certain amount of inefficiency in agriculture and the older industries for the sake of domestic peace." Possible effects on the developing countries were apparently not considered.

of a possibly more peaceful world, it is clearly going to be even harder to stimulate relatively greater sacrifices from considerably poorer states.[86]

A selective list of criticisms, such as the above, inevitably exaggerates the deficiencies of Washington's policy-making. In comparison with most other countries, the United States role in, and in support of, the United Nations balances out on the credit side. As one not uncritical foreign observer has remarked: "If the language of American public pronouncements about the United Nations is sometimes inflated, the currency of American actions has on the whole been less subject to debasement than that of any other great power."[87] Unfortunately, comparative virtue is not enough to meet the challenges ahead. Even if American deficiencies are absolutely less than those of other peoples, the power position of the United States is such that its weaknesses have relatively much greater repercussions on the United Nations as an organization than do the failures of others. As the dominant power in the noncommunist world since World War II, the United States

has, on the whole, used its power prudently. It has shown a desire to work with other countries that is perhaps unique in the world's history; the initiative, the planning, and the money for most of the world's international organizations, both global and regional, has come preponderantly from the United States. Nevertheless, although the American belief in the advantages of collective action is plain, we have frequently lacked the incentives that would make it possible for us to give the collective approach as large a role as we profess to believe it should have.[88]

One reason for this may be the sometimes uncomfortable fact that on the United Nations stage, as nowhere else, the inconsistencies of American policy are highlighted by being forced into a single focus. The fragmented nature of Washington's policy-making has sometimes allowed contradictions of policy to go for long unnoticed, until they are brought

86. Some of the lesser industrial powers, it should perhaps be noted, already contribute a relatively larger share of their national product to foreign assistance and a relatively larger proportion of their trained manpower than the United States. President Johnson's message requesting congressional appropriation of little more than $3 billion in the 1967 Foreign Assistance Act (exclusive of the regional development banks) declared that: "This country . . . can well afford to devote less than 7/10 of 1 per cent of its national income to reduce the chances of future Vietnams. . . ." (Text in U.S. Department of State, *Bulletin*, Vol. 56, 1967, p. 385.) This was perhaps an unfortunate way to phrase the matter, since "involvement" in Vietnam is now blamed by many critics on earlier foreign aid to that country.

87. Herbert G. Nicholas, *The United Nations as a Political Institution* (Oxford University Press, 1959), p. 170.

88. Camps, *op. cit.*, p. 257.

into juxtaposition within the Organization. This can be very salutary in the long-run, if policy-makers make the most of the need to think in over-all terms; but it may also create short-run difficulties for those who, having taken a narrower view of some aspect of policy, resist the need to alter treasured postures. Such, for example, appears to have been the case with the policy on Article 19 enforcement in connection with failure to pay peace-keeping assessments. One of the reasons for the United States retreat in August 1965, from its earlier insistence on such enforcement, was the State Department's fear that the underdeveloped countries might some day try to assess a share of some large economic assistance program against this country if the principle of mandatory assessment was thus sustained.[89]

It should at the same time be recognized that, from the viewpoint of the United States, it is simply not possible to "resolve precisely what we want and disengage from paradox" with regard to basic policy directions.[90] The upraised guard combined with the outstretched hand is inherently para-doxical while containment-coexistence remains the only practical alterna-tive to containment-confrontation. Unavoidable inconsistencies will con-tinue to result from the mixture of means by which the consistently held end must be approached in the circumstances; but they will be supportable if the general direction remains steady in the long run. The difficulties become much less bearable, however, if basic policy direction swings from one objective to another, in which situation short-run policies are likely to

89. See Jonathan Bingham, "Article 19 Must Be Preserved," *Vista*, Vol. 1 (May-June, 1966), p. 55. A foretaste of a similar situation that may arise in the State Depart-ment, if the question of membership for the divided countries is ever seriously con-sidered, was shown in the report of a United Nations Association panel on the China problem. In referring to the possibility of bringing all of them into the Organization, the report declared: "But the German situation is politically very different . . . [and] would be likely only to complicate further the United Nations membership and repre-sentation problems." A demurrer was entered by a Far Eastern expert on the panel, Professor George E. Taylor, who felt that "the representation of Communist China in the UN is no more or less important than that of other States not now members. We should move toward the position that membership in the UN is an obligation of any people claiming to have an independent government. . . . Representation of Communist China . . . could be discussed if it is understood that the Republic of China as a legal entity is not negotiable and that all remaining States not now members should be invited to membership of the Assembly at the same time." UNA-USA National Policy Panel, *China, the United Nations and United States Policy* (United Nations Associa-tion of the United States of America, 1966), pp. 29, 44.

90. C. L. Sulzberger, "Foreign Affairs: The Have and Have-Not Policy," *New York Times*, June 13, 1965.

become schizophrenic. Thus, although the administration advocates a bridge-building policy with the Soviet Union consistent with its long-run aim of détente and coexistence, the Congress by no means supports such a policy objective when it rejects trade and aid liberalization measures toward Eastern Europe.

The Road Ahead

The United States, historically, has been fortunate in the extent to which it has been able to achieve its national objectives. Americans may, therefore, more than most other peoples (and governments) tend to identify their own policies with the moral law, especially in relation to the standards of the Charter. In the early years of the containment policy, for example,

> The commanding position enjoyed by this nation in the General Assembly, . . . the existing identity of interests between the United States and at least two-thirds of the members . . . seemed as good an insurance as could be expected that a similar identity would prevail between the dicta of the world's conscience and the necessities of American policy. Thus the doubt that might otherwise arise [over whether a given use of force conformed to the Charter and moral law] would be removed by the General Assembly.[91]

This was illustrated during the Korean conflict by a statement of John Foster Dulles (then a member of the United States Delegation to the General Assembly) when advocating the Uniting for Peace resolution. The Assembly, he declared, would "reflect better than any other body, the supremacy of 'law,' which in essence is the consensus of world opinion as to what is right."[92] First successes in Korea led to an effort to extend that international action beyond the original objective of simply throwing back the aggressor, and resulted in the march north to the Yalu in an attempt to impose a military settlement of the problem of reunification. Proponents of "strengthening" the authority of the United Nations, even in the face of opposition by a principal Member, supported the undertaking as the start of an ideal, "vetoless," collective-security system. Proponents of the protracted-conflict school supported it for what they saw as an occasion for the ultimate defeat of "international communism." Both were disillusioned by the failure to achieve either of their opposed aims. This first

91. Robert W. Tucker, *The Just War* (Johns Hopkins Press, 1960), p. 45.
92. U.S. Department of State, *Bulletin*, Vol. 23 (1950), p. 658.

drive to reshape the Organization nearer to American desires was then followed by a period of reaction when Washington largely ignored the United Nations in security matters, turning instead to expand its system of regional collective-defense arrangements.

After the Suez crisis in 1956 opened new possibilities for United Nations collective action to help maintain the peace, the expansion of peacekeeping operations led to a second effort to develop the Organization's authority beyond the point where the state of international cooperation could sustain it. Even before developments in the Congo peacekeeping episode opened the Article 19 drama, the United States suffered a setback by failing, in effect, to obtain international endorsement of its action in sending the Marines into Lebanon in 1958. At that time, Secretary of State Dulles found that the Assembly was "powerful when it reflects a genuine moral judgment"; but that its claim to represent humanity's aspirations to peace through law and justice would be impaired if it endorsed "a permanent double standard" or developed into a "system of bloc voting in terms of geographic areas or in terms of the 'haves' as against the 'have nots'."[93]

In the early sixties, the conflict over peacekeeping activities tended to center on the financial issue. The administration, considering such United Nations operations in the "national interests of the United States and the cause of peace,"[94] led the drive to "strengthen" the Secretariat's executive capacity for peacekeeping and the Assembly's authority to mount such undertakings and to finance them through mandatory assessments on all Members. Again, the operations could be supported by the protracted-conflict school as an additional security option in United States political-strategic capabilities; while the financial controversy was viewed as a means of forcing the Soviet Union and France to pay their share of the undertakings. Proponents of the development of enforceable international law and of greater independence for the Organization (through expansion of its executive capacity and its ability to levy assessments for controversial operations) could, on the other hand, view these same achievements as first steps toward the ultimate development of a true world authority.

When this second attempt foundered on the rock of Article 19, the United States retreated from its professed intention to push the issue to a showdown. Both schools, again for diametrically opposed reasons,

93. *Ibid.*, Vol. 40 (1959), pp. 758–59. See also Tucker, *op. cit.*, pp. 46–50.
94. Assistant Secretary of State for International Organization Affairs, Joseph Sisco, address April 2, 1966, U.S. Department of State, *Bulletin*, Vol. 54 (1966), p. 649.

deplored the "weakness" of the United Nations. Both tended also to ignore the fact that the United States itself was unready to accept unreservedly the full implications of the advanced legal position it had so ardently fostered to the point, as Congressman Bingham declared, where "we seemingly had become obsessed by the rectitude of our own legalistic arguments about the scope of Articles 17 and 19."[95] The government reaction was to criticize the smaller states by implication for not supporting the enforcement of the Assembly's power to levy mandatory assessments, and thus of the United States position against the Soviet Union and France; and it criticized the latter for not voluntarily contributing what they had refused to be assessed for. Washington, in short, was violating the sound political rule set forth by the Canadian Secretary for External Affairs to an international youth group: "Above all," he told them, "don't mistake a policy in the interest of your group, your country, or yourself for an immutable principle. To do so is to make . . . conflict inevitable."[96]

On the other hand, like its two opponents, the United States has laid increasing emphasis on stricter budgetary practices and financial conservatism: "Our support [for the many United Nations programs] cannot and must not be taken for granted," the Assistant Secretary for International Organization Affairs declared in the spring of 1966. And there has been no sign of any support from the Executive for the more generous suggestions of Congressmen Frelinghuysen and O'Hara, noted in Chapter 9, that the United States should cease to place limits (at least not below 50 percent) on the proportion of costs it might accept in future operations of which it approves. At the same time, the administration has officially recognized that: "as long as there are fundamental differences between the U.S.S.R. and the United States about the role of the U.N. in the peacekeeping field, it will be difficult to make real progress toward a more reliable system of financing or authorizing future peacekeeping operations."[97] Yet it has also continued to press for precisely that sort of system; and to criticize the Afro-Asian states in particular. Thus, Senator Case, a delegate to the twenty-first Assembly, ended his report on peacekeeping actions by that Assembly as follows:

95. Bingham, *op. cit.*, p. 55.
96. Paul Martin, address, Aug. 4, 1967, *Canadian Weekly Bulletin*, Vol. 22, Aug. 16, 1967, p. 2.
97. Sisco, *op. cit.*, p. 649.

If small, weak nations are to continue to look to the United Nations for their security, as they must, the General Assembly's capacity to respond quickly to appeals for help must be reaffirmed. Many of the smaller nations of Asia and Africa are naturally reluctant to become involved in what they look upon as only a great power dispute over peacekeeping. But if they expect the United Nations to help them, they must have the courage to help strengthen the United Nations. Sadly, this courage was lacking in the 21st General Assembly.[98]

Nonetheless, further progress will not necessarily be prevented by failure formally to systematize the peacekeeping procedures of the United Nations. It may be, however, by failure to reestablish the Organization's solvency and improve its financial fortunes; it certainly will be by continued failure to remove the dead hand of the past from American as well as from the Soviet and French attitudes in the United Nations. Although the United States has more than once urged other Members not to allow the effectiveness of the institution to be "determined by the level of support coming from its least cooperative Members,"[99] its own refusal to donate to the rescue fund contributes to that very end.

Canada, on the other hand, provides a good example of the kind of leadership required from states that want to "strengthen" the United Nations. In relation to its size, Canada has probably contributed even more than the United States to the Organization. In addition to supplying personnel and facilities to practically every peacekeeping operation under the United Nations, Ottawa has paid its assessed share of all budgets and has given generously to the voluntary activities. Yet it was still willing to join with Great Britain and the Scandinavian countries in June 1965 in contributing an additional sum of $4 million to initiate the rescue fund.[100] Currently, Ottawa's share of the regular U.N. budget is 3.17 percent and Washington's is 31.91 percent, or about ten times that of Canada. A comparable United States contribution to the rescue fund would on this basis come to some $40 million. If, however, the contributions were based more strictly on gross national product, the comparable United States contribution would be over $60 million since its gross national product is more

98. Clifford P. Case, The United Nations Peacekeeping Dilemma, Senate Committee on Foreign Relations, 90 Cong. 1 sess. (1967), p. 16.

99. Ambassador Goldberg, U.S. Department of State, Bulletin, Vol. 53 (1965), p. 454.

100. At that time, the following contributions were made: Canada, $4 million; Denmark, $1 million; Iceland, $80,000; Norway, $700,000; Sweden, $2 million; and Great Britain, $10 million.

than 15 times that of Canada.[101] Ottawa, in short, has not made its support of the United Nations contingent on better behavior by "the least cooperative Members." Why, then, has Washington been less willing to come to the rescue of the maiden it professes to find so fair?

Its reluctance in the past can be attributed only in part to administration distaste for tackling Congress over the necessary appropriation—although, by 1967, this motivation has undoubtedly become more important. While some members are angered at the thought that the United States should be expected once again to pick up the tab for the "dead beats," others with the same forward-looking attitude as Representatives Frelinghuysen and O'Hara might be mobilized behind an Executive request for funds. Whatever the reason, since the influence of the United States supported the operations that later resulted in the financial crisis, and since it pressed strongly for the resolutions that annually continued a system of financing which neither produced adequate funds nor served to overcome increasing resistance from certain Member states (although the Organization lacked effective means to enforce payment from them), Washington might seem to have some moral obligation to help rescue the Organization from the financial consequences of those policies.

Many of the smaller countries must have inferred that the persistent United States pressure to put across those annual resolutions implied a willingness, in case the endeavor to develop binding Charter law should fail, to accept that implication. Such, after all, is the penalty of misjudgment by a leading power. But the administration seems never to have contemplated any such consequential action; and articulate congressional members have generally been more concerned to levy blame than to levy taxes for the Organization. With domestic civil problems and the Vietnamese military situation reinforcing the resistance of the "hardliners" toward the United Nations, and with African actions (backed by the communists) upsetting procedural rules to the discomfit of the United States,[102] both branches of government apparently remain in a mood to

101. There were news reports during the twenty-first Assembly of a Secretariat suggestion that the other four permanent members of the Security Council might retrieve the financial situation by following the British precedent and contributing $10 million each to the rescue fund. The United States was said to consider that the proposal was inspired by the French or Soviet delegation; that it had already made its contribution; and that there was no reason it should now give more to encourage the other two to make some contribution of their own. (*New York Times*, Dec. 1, 1966.) See also official comment on the "surplus accounts" debate, in Chap. 9, pp. 345–46.

102. See the Plimpton article cited above for a number of examples.

decline any responsibility, beyond the United States normal large contributions, for the financial difficulties of an unappreciative Organization. This attitude is understandable, and there is undoubtedly support for it among the public. But whether that support, by both the Congress and the public, would be as unrelenting as some officials appear to think, is at least open to question.[103] So long as it persists, there is clearly no likelihood that the government will undertake the burdens of a strong political drive behind a policy to utilize the United Nations in the kind of fundamental program considered above. There may be greater willingness to promote, in the more strictly security field, its increased use for the limited function of "preventive diplomacy" (in the Hammarskjoldian sense), as a neutralizing function in the cold war. This, in Inis Claude's words,

involves the use of the Organization for politically impartial intervention into a troubled area peripheral to the Cold War [when the great powers want] to avoid a confrontation that might shift their relations from stalemate to showdown. . . . In principle, the Cold War makes preventive diplomacy necessary, and the existence of uncommitted Members makes it possible.[104]

That is essentially a prescription for "more of the same," better than inaction, but limited in effectiveness to picking up the pieces rather than positively acting to prevent the development of conflict in the first place. And it would mark a retreat from emphasizing the broad security concepts of the Charter to accepting the narrower concept of national policy primarily in terms of military strategy—an emphasis that has proven inadequate to bring about the kind of international peace and security that is the American objective. This is not good enough in a world dominated by the ever-increasing dangers of the nuclear arms race, which results from continuing inability to translate a universal interest in preventing nuclear war into agreed rules of the game for controlling political conflict and armaments and thereby maintaining world order.

There is no technical solution to the dilemma of decreasing security in the face of ever-increasing military power. Any successful political approach to the problem will have to be able to use the United Nations actively and constructively, if only because no other place exists where "all

103. The extent of congressional opposition, for one thing, is always partly a function of Executive ability to make a convincing case for its own position, or of Executive willingness to exert leadership in pushing a policy.

104. Inis L. Claude, Jr., "Implications and Questions for the Future," in Norman J. Padelford and Leland M. Goodrich, eds., *The United Nations in the Balance: Accomplishments and Prospects* (Praeger, 1965), pp. 476–77.

the varied interests and aspirations of the world [can] meet . . . upon the common ground of the Charter. . . ."[105]

Unfortunately, there is a widespread attitude, in Congress and outside, that can only be described as a second turning from the Organization such as followed the Korean episode. Senator Fulbright put his finger on it when George Kennan, former Ambassador to the Soviet Union, was testifying before the Foreign Relations Committee in January 1967. The Chairman noted: "Mr. Kennan, no mention has been made of the United Nations. Have you given up on that as having any future whatever?" Kennan answered that, so long as the cold war remained "the dominant reality in our world," the Organization could only be effective "outside of the realm of international security"—on such problems, that is, as "the purity of the seas, the preservation of fisheries, . . . the development of Antarctica. . . ." The Senator, however, was not so disparaging of the political possibilities of the agency. He said:

The United Nations might be the mechanism by which the United States or Russia or anyone else who likes, might come to compose their differences rather than simply through bilateral or trilateral agreements. I don't know. I just thought it was rather interesting that no one seems to take any notice of the United Nations any more in the discussions as to how we can arrange our political relationships.[106]

To urge an even more far-reaching kind of approach through the Organization in this current atmosphere will be considered too idealistic by nationally oriented realists. But, as the Secretary-General said in a somewhat similar context: "I put it to you that our present situation is unrealistic without even the benefit of being idealistic."[107]

The great difficulties of the longer-term task create some temptation to opt for the simplicities of a hard-line confrontation policy, especially in its extreme form which, in effect, proposes to resolve the main foreign-policy problems of the United States by eliminating the main communist adversaries. The sheer complexities of current events also reinforce the American tendency to a short-term approach. As one former official has commented, "The preoccupation of officials with current emergencies" means that "so much time is devoted to stamping out fires that not much is left

105. *Introduction to the Annual Report of the Secretary-General . . . 16 June 1956–15 June 1957*, U.N. Doc. A/3594/Add. 1, p. 9.
106. *The Communist World in 1967*, Hearing before the Senate Foreign Relations Committee, 90 Cong. 1 sess. (1967), pp. 64–65.
107. *UN Monthly Chronicle* (June 1966), p. 63.

over for fire prevention."[108] And prevention would be the essence of any serious endeavor to close the growing gap between the rich in the West and the poor everywhere else, between population and production, before the revolutionary potentials of overpopulation, economic frustration, and political instability are added to those of communist policies.

Times of military stalemate have traditionally given the political forces of diplomacy their opportunity. Never has the stalemate been greater, either in nuclear terms or in wars of liberation. It is high time for the United States, if it is to warrant its position of world leadership, to mobilize its resources of imagination and political courage in the service of an international diplomatic breakthrough.

108. Richard N. Gardner, *Blueprint for Peace: Being the Proposals of Prominent Americans to the White House Conference on International Cooperation* (McGraw-Hill, 1966), p. 8.

APPENDIXES

APPENDIX A

CHARTER OF THE UNITED NATIONS[1]

WE THE PEOPLES OF THE UNITED NATIONS
DETERMINED

to save succeeding generations from the scourge of war, which twice in our lifetime has brought untold sorrow to mankind, and

to reaffirm faith in fundamental human rights, in the dignity and worth of the human person, in the equal rights of men and women and of nations large and small, and

to establish conditions under which justice and respect for the obligations arising from treaties and other sources of international law can be maintained, and

to promote social progress and better standards of life in larger freedom,

AND FOR THESE ENDS

to practice tolerance and live together in peace with one another as good neighbors, and

to unite our strength to maintain international peace and security, and

to ensure, by the acceptance of principles and the institution of methods, that armed force shall not be used, save in the common interest, and

to employ international machinery for the promotion of the economic and social advancement of all peoples,

HAVE RESOLVED TO COMBINE OUR EFFORTS
TO ACCOMPLISH THESE AIMS.

Accordingly, our respective Governments, through representatives assembled in the city of San Francisco, who have exhibited their full powers found to be in good and due form, have agreed to the present Charter of the United Nations and do hereby establish an international organization to be known as the United Nations.

---

1. Source: *Charter of the United Nations and Statute of the International Court of Justice*, U.S. Department of State Publication 2368 (1945), pp. 1–20. For amendments to the Charter see p. 474.

Chapter I: Purposes and Principles

ARTICLE 1

The Purposes of the United Nations are:

1. To maintain international peace and security, and to that end: to take effective collective measures for the prevention and removal of threats to the peace, and for the suppression of acts of aggression or other breaches of the peace, and to bring about by peaceful means, and in conformity with the principles of justice and international law, adjustment or settlement of international disputes or situations which might lead to a breach of the peace;

2. To develop friendly relations among nations based on respect for the principle of equal rights and self-determination of peoples, and to take other appropriate measures to strengthen universal peace;

3. To achieve international cooperation in solving international problems of an economic, social, cultural, or humanitarian character, and in promoting and encouraging respect for human rights and for fundamental freedoms for all without distinction as to race, sex, language, or religion; and

4. To be a center for harmonizing the actions of nations in the attainment of these common ends.

ARTICLE 2

The Organization and its Members, in pursuit of the Purposes stated in Article 1, shall act in accordance with the following Principles.

1. The Organization is based on the principle of the sovereign equality of all its Members.

2. All Members, in order to ensure to all of them the rights and benefits resulting from membership, shall fulfil in good faith the obligations assumed by them in accordance with the present Charter.

3. All Members shall settle their international disputes by peaceful means in such a manner that international peace and security, and justice, are not endangered.

4. All Members shall refrain in their international relations from the threat or use of force against the territorial integrity or political independence of any state, or in any other manner inconsistent with the Purposes of the United Nations.

5. All Members shall give the United Nations every assistance in any action it takes in accordance with the present Charter, and shall refrain from giving assistance to any state against which the United Nations is taking preventive or enforcement action.

6. The Organization shall ensure that states which are not Members of the United Nations act in accordance with these Principles so far as may be necessary for the maintenance of international peace and security.

7. Nothing contained in the present Charter shall authorize the United Nations to intervene in matters which are essentially within the domestic

jurisdiction of any state or shall require the Members to submit such matters to settlement under the present Charter; but this principle shall not prejudice the application of enforcement measures under Chapter VII.

Chapter II: Membership

ARTICLE 3

The original Members of the United Nations shall be the states which, having participated in the United Nations Conference on International Organization at San Francisco, or having previously signed the Declaration by United Nations of January 1, 1942, sign the present Charter and ratify it in accordance with Article 110.

ARTICLE 4

1. Membership in the United Nations is open to all other peace-loving states which accept the obligations contained in the present Charter and, in the judgment of the Organization, are able and willing to carry out these obligations.

2. The admission of any such state to membership in the United Nations will be effected by a decision of the General Assembly upon the recommendation of the Security Council.

ARTICLE 5

A Member of the United Nations against which preventive or enforcement action has been taken by the Security Council may be suspended from the exercise of the rights and privileges of membership by the General Assembly upon the recommendation of the Security Council. The exercise of these rights and privileges may be restored by the Security Council.

ARTICLE 6

A Member of the United Nations which has persistently violated the Principles contained in the present Charter may be expelled from the Organization by the General Assembly upon the recommendation of the Security Council.

Chapter III: Organs

ARTICLE 7

1. There are established as the principal organs of the United Nations: a General Assembly, a Security Council, an Economic and Social Council, a Trusteeship Council, an International Court of Justice, and a Secretariat.

2. Such subsidiary organs as may be found necessary may be established in accordance with the present Charter.

ARTICLE 8

The United Nations shall place no restrictions on the eligibility of men and women to participate in any capacity and under conditions of equality in its principal and subsidiary organs.

Chapter IV: The General Assembly

Composition

ARTICLE 9

1. The General Assembly shall consist of all the Members of the United Nations.

2. Each Member shall have not more than five representatives in the General Assembly.

Functions and Powers

ARTICLE 10

The General Assembly may discuss any questions or any matters within the scope of the present Charter or relating to the powers and functions of any organs provided for in the present Charter, and, except as provided in Article 12, may make recommendations to the Members of the United Nations or to the Security Council or to both on any such questions or matters.

ARTICLE 11

1. The General Assembly may consider the general principles of co-operation in the maintenance of international peace and security, including the principles governing disarmament and the regulation of armaments, and may make recommendations with regard to such principles to the Members or to the Security of Council or to both.

2. The General Assembly may discuss any questions relating to the maintenance of international peace and security brought before it by any Member of the United Nations, or by the Security Council, or by a state which is not a Member of the United Nations in accordance with Article 35, paragraph 2, and, except as provided in Article 12, may make recommendations with regard to any such questions to the state or states concerned or to the Security Council or to both. Any such question on which action is necessary shall be referred to the Security Council by the General Assembly either before or after discussion.

3. The General Assembly may call the attention of the Security Council to situations which are likely to endanger international peace and security.

4. The powers of the General Assembly set forth in this Article shall not limit the general scope of Article 10.

ARTICLE 12

1. While the Security Council is exercising in respect of any dispute or situation the functions assigned to it in the present Charter, the General Assembly shall not make any recommendation with regard to that dispute or situation unless the Security Council so requests.

2. The Secretary-General, with the consent of the Security Council, shall notify the General Assembly at each session of any matters relative to the maintenance of international peace and security which are being dealt with by the Security Council and shall similarly notify the General Assembly, or the Members of the United Nations if the General Assembly is not in session, immediately the Security Council ceases to deal with such matters.

ARTICLE 13

1. The General Assembly shall initiate studies and make recommendations for the purpose of:

a. promoting international cooperation in the political field and encouraging the progressive development of international law and its codification;

b. promoting international cooperation in the economic, social, cultural, educational, and health fields, and assisting in the realization of human rights and fundamental freedoms for all without distinction as to race, sex, language, or religion.

2. The further responsibilities, functions, and powers of the General Assembly with respect to matters mentioned in paragraph 1(b) above are set forth in Chapters IX and X.

ARTICLE 14

Subject to the provisions of Article 12, the General Assembly may recommend measures for the peaceful adjustment of any situation, regardless of origin, which it deems likely to impair the general welfare or friendly relations among nations, including situations resulting from a violation of the provisions of the present Charter setting forth the Purposes and Principles of the United Nations.

ARTICLE 15

1. The General Assembly shall receive and consider annual and special reports from the Security Council; these reports shall include an account of the measures that the Security Council has decided upon or taken to maintain international peace and security.

2. The General Assembly shall receive and consider reports from the other organs of the United Nations.

ARTICLE 16

The General Assembly shall perform such functions with respect to the international trusteeship system as are assigned to it under Chapters XII and

XIII, including the approval of the trusteeship agreements for areas not designated as strategic.

ARTICLE 17

1. The General Assembly shall consider and approve the budget of the Organization.

2. The expenses of the Organization shall be borne by the Members as apportioned by the General Assembly.

3. The General Assembly shall consider and approve any financial and budgetary arrangements with specialized agencies referred to in Article 57 and shall examine the administrative budgets of such specialized agencies with a view to making recommendations to the agencies concerned.

Voting

ARTICLE 18

1. Each member of the General Assembly shall have one vote.

2. Decisions of the General Assembly on important questions shall be made by a two-thirds majority of the members present and voting. These questions shall include: recommendations with respect to the maintenance of international peace and security, the election of the non-permanent members of the Security Council, the election of the members of the Economic and Social Council, the election of members of the Trusteeship Council in accordance with paragraph 1(c) of Article 86, the admission of new Members to the United Nations, the suspension of the rights and privileges of membership, the expulsion of Members, questions relating to the operation of the trusteeship system, and budgetary questions.

3. Decisions on other questions, including the determination of additional categories of questions to be decided by a two-thirds majority, shall be made by a majority of the members present and voting.

ARTICLE 19

A Member of the United Nations which is in arrears in the payment of its financial contributions to the Organization shall have no vote in the General Assembly if the amount of its arrears equals or exceeds the amount of the contributions due from it for the preceeding two full years. The General Assembly may, nevertheless, permit such a Member to vote if it is satisfied that the failure to pay is due to conditions beyond the control of the Member.

Procedure

ARTICLE 20

The General Assembly shall meet in regular annual sessions and in such special sessions as occasion may require. Special sessions shall be convoked by the Secretary-General at the request of the Security Council or of a majority of the Members of the United Nations.

ARTICLE 21

The General Assembly shall adopt its own rules of procedure. It shall elect its President for each session.

ARTICLE 22

The General Assembly may establish such subsidiary organs as it deems necessary for the performance of its functions.

Chapter V: The Security Council

Composition

ARTICLE 23 [*This article has been amended; see note on p. 474.*]

1. The Security Council shall consist of eleven Members of the United Nations. The Republic of China, France, the Union of Soviet Socialist Republics, the United Kingdom of Great Britain and Northern Ireland, and the United States of America shall be permanent members of the Security Council. The General Assembly shall elect six other Members of the United Nations to be non-permanent members of the Security Council, due regard being specially paid, in the first instance to the contribution of Members of the United Nations to the maintenance of international peace and security and to the other purposes of the Organization, and also to equitable geographical distribution.

2. The non-permanent members of the Security Council shall be elected for a term of two years. In the first election of the non-permanent members, however, three shall be chosen for a term of one year. A retiring member shall not be eligible for immediate re-election.

3. Each member of the Security Council shall have one representative.

Functions and Powers

ARTICLE 24

1. In order to ensure prompt and effective action by the United Nations, its Members confer on the Security Council primary responsibility for the maintenance of international peace and security, and agree that in carrying out its duties under this responsibility the Security Council acts on their behalf.

2. In discharging these duties the Security Council shall act in accordance with the Purposes and Principles of the United Nations. The specific powers granted to the Security Council for the discharge of these duties are laid down in Chapters VI, VII, VIII, and XII.

3. The Security Council shall submit annual and, when necessary, special reports to the General Assembly for its consideration.

ARTICLE 25

The Members of the United Nations agree to accept and carry out the decisions of the Security Council in accordance with the present Charter.

ARTICLE 26

In order to promote the establishment and maintenance of international peace and security with the least diversion for armaments of the world's human and economic resources, the Security Council shall be responsible for formulating, with the assistance of the Military Staff Committee referred to in Article 47, plans to be submitted to the Members of the United Nations for the establishment of a system for the regulation of armaments.

Voting

ARTICLE 27   [*This article has been amended; see note on p. 474.*]

1. Each member of the Security Council shall have one vote.

2. Decisions of the Security Council on procedural matters shall be made by an affirmative vote of seven members.

3. Decisions of the Security Council on all other matters shall be made by an affirmative vote of seven members including the concurring votes of the permanent members; provided that, in decisions under Chapter VI, and under paragraph 3 of Article 52, a party to a dispute shall abstain from voting.

Procedure

ARTICLE 28

1. The Security Council shall be so organized as to be able to function continuously. Each member of the Security Council shall for this purpose be represented at all times at the seat of the Organization.

2. The Security Council shall hold periodic meetings at which each of its members may, if it so desires, be represented by a member of the government or by some other specially designated representative.

3. The Security Council may hold meetings at such places other than the seat of the Organization as in its judgment will best facilitate its work.

ARTICLE 29

The Security Council may establish such subsidiary organs as it deems necessary for the performance of its functions.

ARTICLE 30

The Security Council shall adopt its own rules of procedure, including the method of selecting its President.

ARTICLE 31

Any Member of the United Nations which is not a member of the Security Council may participate, without vote, in the discussion of any question brought before the Security Council whenever the latter considers that the interests of that Member are specially affected.

ARTICLE 32

Any Member of the United Nations which is not a member of the Security Council or any state which is not a Member of the United Nations, if it is a party to a dispute under consideration by the Security Council, shall be invited to participate, without vote, in the discussion relating to the dispute. The Security Council shall lay down such conditions as it deems just for the participation of a state which is not a Member of the United Nations.

Chapter VI: Pacific Settlement of Disputes

ARTICLE 33

1. The parties to any dispute, the continuance of which is likely to endanger the maintenance of international peace and security, shall, first of all, seek a solution by negotiation, enquiry, mediation, conciliation, arbitration, judicial settlement, resort to regional agencies or arrangements, or other peaceful means of their own choice.

2. The Security Council shall, when it deems necessary, call upon the parties to settle their dispute by such means.

ARTICLE 34

The Security Council may investigate any dispute, or any situation which might lead to international friction or give rise to a dispute, in order to determine whether the continuance of the dispute or situation is likely to endanger the maintenance of international peace and security.

ARTICLE 35

1. Any Member of the United Nations may bring any dispute, or any situation of the nature referred to in Article 34, to the attention of the Security Council or of the General Assembly.

2. A state which is not a Member of the United Nations may bring to the attention of the Security Council or of the General Assembly any dispute to which it is a party if it accepts in advance, for the purposes of the dispute, the obligations of pacific settlement provided in the present Charter.

3. The proceedings of the General Assembly in respect of matters brought to its attention under this Article will be subject to the provisions of Articles 11 and 12.

ARTICLE 36

1. The Security Council may, at any stage of a dispute of the nature referred to in Article 33 or of a situation of like nature, recommend appropriate procedures or methods of adjustment.

2. The Security Council should take into consideration any procedures for the settlement of the dispute which have already been adopted by the parties.

3. In making recommendations under this Article the Security Council should also take into consideration that legal disputes should as a general rule be referred by the parties to the International Court of Justice in accordance with the provisions of the Statute of the Court.

ARTICLE 37

1. Should the parties to a dispute of the nature referred to in Article 33 fail to settle it by the means indicated in that Article, they shall refer it to the Security Council.

2. If the Security Council deems that the continuance of the dispute is in fact likely to endanger the maintenance of international peace and security, it shall decide whether to take action under Article 36 or to recommend such terms of settlement as it may consider appropriate.

ARTICLE 38

Without prejudice to the provisions of Articles 33 to 37, the Security Council may, if all the parties to any dispute so request, make recommendations to the parties with a view to a pacific settlement of the dispute.

Chapter VII: Action With Respect to Threats to the Peace, Breaches of the Peace, and Acts of Aggression

ARTICLE 39

The Security Council shall determine the existence of any threat to the peace, breach of the peace, or act of aggression and shall make recommendations, or decide what measures shall be taken in accordance with Articles 41 and 42, to maintain or restore international peace and security.

ARTICLE 40

In order to prevent an aggravation of the situation, the Security Council may, before making the recommendations or deciding upon the measures provided for in Article 39, call upon the parties concerned to comply with such provisional measures as it deems necessary or desirable. Such provisional measures shall be without prejudice to the rights, claims, or position of the parties concerned. The Security Council shall duly take account of failure to comply with such provisional measures.

ARTICLE 41

The Security Council may decide what measures not involving the use of armed force are to be employed to give effect to its decisions, and it may call upon the Members of the United Nations to apply such measures. These may include complete or partial interruption of economic relations and of rail, sea, air, postal, telegraphic, radio, and other means of communication, and the severance of diplomatic relations.

ARTICLE 42

Should the Security Council consider that measures provided for in Article 41 would be inadequate or have proved to be inadequate, it may take such action by air, sea, or land forces as may be necessary to maintain or restore international peace and security. Such action may include demonstrations, blockade, and other operations by air, sea, or land forces of Members of the United Nations.

ARTICLE 43

1. All Members of the United Nations, in order to contribute to the maintenance of international peace and security, undertake to make available to the Security Council, on its call and in accordance with a special agreement or agreements, armed forces, assistance, and facilities, including rights of passage, necessary for the purpose of maintaining international peace and security.

2. Such agreement or agreements shall govern the numbers and types of forces, their degree of readiness and general location, and the nature of the facilities and assistance to be provided.

3. The agreement or agreements shall be negotiated as soon as possible on the initiative of the Security Council. They shall be concluded between the Security Council and Members or between the Security Council and groups of Members and shall be subject to ratification by the signatory states in accordance with their respective constitutional processes.

ARTICLE 44

When the Security Council has decided to use force it shall, before calling upon a Member not represented on it to provide armed forces in fulfillment of the obligations assumed under Article 43, invite that Member, if the Member so desires, to participate in the decisions of the Security Council concerning the employment of contingents of that Member's armed forces.

ARTICLE 45

In order to enable the United Nations to take urgent military measures, Members shall hold immediately available national air-force contingents for combined international enforcement action. The strength and degree of readiness of these contingents and plans for their combined action shall be determined, within the limits laid down in the special agreement or agreements referred to in Article 43, by the Security Council with the assistance of the Military Staff Committee.

ARTICLE 46

Plans for the application of armed force shall be made by the Security Council with the assistance of the Military Staff Committee.

ARTICLE 47

1. There shall be established a Military Staff Committee to advise and assist the Security Council on all questions relating to the Security Council's military requirements for the maintenance of international peace and security, the employment and command of forces placed at its disposal, the regulation of armaments, and possible disarmament.

2. The Military Staff Committee shall consist of the Chiefs of Staff of the permanent members of the Security Council or their representatives. Any Member of the United Nations not permanently represented on the Committee shall be invited by the Committee to be associated with it when the efficient discharge of the Committee's responsibilities requires the participation of that Member in its work.

3. The Military Staff Committee shall be responsible under the Security Council for the strategic direction of any armed forces placed at the disposal of the Security Council. Questions relating to the command of such forces shall be worked out subsequently.

4. The Military Staff Committee, with the authorization of the Security Council and after consultation with appropriate regional agencies, may establish regional subcommittees.

ARTICLE 48

1. The action required to carry out the decisions of the Security Council for the maintenance of international peace and security shall be taken by all the Members of the United Nations or by some of them, as the Security Council may determine.

2. Such decisions shall be carried out by the Members of the United Nations directly and through their action in the appropriate international agencies of which they are members.

ARTICLE 49

The Members of the United Nations shall join in affording mutual assistance in carrying out the measures decided upon by the Security Council.

ARTICLE 50

If preventive or enforcement measures against any state are taken by the Security Council, any other state, whether a Member of the United Nations or not, which finds itself confronted with special economic problems arising from the carrying out of those measures shall have the right to consult the Security Council with regard to a solution of those problems.

ARTICLE 51

Nothing in the present Charter shall impair the inherent right of individual or collective self-defense if an armed attack occurs against a Member of the United Nations, until the Security Council has taken the measures necessary to maintain international peace and security. Measures taken by Members in the exercise of this right of self-defense shall be immediately reported to the Security Council and shall not in any way affect the authority and responsibility of the Security Council under the present Charter to take at any time such action as it deems necessary in order to maintain or restore international peace and security.

Chapter VIII: Regional Arrangements

ARTICLE 52

1. Nothing in the present Charter precludes the existence of regional arrangements or agencies for dealing with such matters relating to the maintenance of international peace and security as are appropriate for regional action, provided that such arrangements or agencies and their activities are consistent with the Purposes and Principles of the United Nations.

2. The Members of the United Nations entering into such arrangements or constituting such agencies shall make every effort to achieve pacific settlement of local disputes through such regional arrangements or by such regional agencies before referring them to the Security Council.

3. The Security Council shall encourage the development of pacific settlement of local disputes through such regional arrangements or by such regional agencies either on the initiative of the states concerned or by reference from the Security Council.

4. This Article in no way impairs the application of Articles 34 and 35.

ARTICLE 53

1. The Security Council shall, where appropriate, utilize such regional arrangements or agencies for enforcement action under its authority. But no enforcement action shall be taken under regional arrangements or by regional agencies without the authorization of the Security Council, with the exception of measures against any enemy state, as defined in paragraph 2 of this Article, provided for pursuant to Article 107 or in regional arrangements directed against renewal of aggressive policy on the part of any such state, until such time as the Organization may, on request of the Governments concerned, be charged with the responsibility for preventing further aggression by such a state.

2. The term enemy state as used in paragraph 1 of this Article applies to any state which during the Second World War has been an enemy of any signatory of the present Charter.

ARTICLE 54

The Security Council shall at all times be kept fully informed of activities undertaken or in contemplation under regional arrangements or by regional agencies for the maintenance of international peace and security.

Chapter IX: International Economic and Social Cooperation

ARTICLE 55

With a view to the creation of conditions of stability and well-being which are necessary for peaceful and friendly relations among nations based on respect for the principle of equal rights and self-determination of peoples, the United Nations shall promote:

a. higher standards of living, full employment, and conditions of economic and social progress and development;

b. solutions of international economic, social, health, and related problems; and international cultural and educational cooperation; and

c. universal respect for, and observance of, human rights and fundamental freedoms for all without distinction as to race, sex, language, or religion.

ARTICLE 56

All Members pledge themselves to take joint and separate action in cooperation with the Organization for the achievement of the purposes set forth in Article 55.

ARTICLE 57

1. The various specialized agencies, established by intergovernmental agreement and having wide international responsibilities, as defined in their basic instruments, in economic, social, cultural, educational, health, and related fields, shall be brought into relationship with the United Nations in accordance with the provisions of Article 63.

2. Such agencies thus brought into relationship with the United Nations are hereinafter referred to as specialized agencies.

ARTICLE 58

The Organization shall make recommendations for the coordination of the policies and activities of the specialized agencies.

ARTICLE 59

The Organization shall, where appropriate, initiate negotiations among the states concerned for the creation of any new specialized agencies required for the accomplishment of the purposes set forth in Article 55.

ARTICLE 60

Responsibility for the discharge of the functions of the Organization set forth in this Chapter shall be vested in the General Assembly and, under the authority of the General Assembly, in the Economic and Social Council, which shall have for this purpose the powers set forth in Chapter X.

Chapter X: The Economic and Social Council

Composition

ARTICLE 61 *[This article has been amended; see note on p. 474.]*

1. The Economic and Social Council shall consist of eighteen Members of the United Nations elected by the General Assembly.

2. Subject to the provisions of paragraph 3, six members of the Economic and Social Council shall be elected each year for a term of three years. A retiring member shall be eligible for immediate re-election.

3. At the first election, eighteen members of the Economic and Social Council shall be chosen. The term of office of six members so chosen shall expire at the end of one year, and of six other members at the end of two years, in accordance with arrangements made by the General Assembly.

4. Each member of the Economic and Social Council shall have one representative.

Functions and Powers

ARTICLE 62

1. The Economic and Social Council may make or initiate studies and reports with respect to international economic, social, cultural, educational, health, and related matters and may make recommendations with respect to any such matters to the General Assembly, to the Members of the United Nations, and to the specialized agencies concerned.

2. It may make recommendations for the purpose of promoting respect for, and observance of, human rights and fundamental freedoms for all.

3. It may prepare draft conventions for submission to the General Assembly, with respect to matters falling within its competence.

4. It may call, in accordance with the rules prescribed by the United Nations, international conferences on matters falling within its competence.

ARTICLE 63

1. The Economic and Social Council may enter into agreements with any of the agencies referred to in Article 57, defining the terms on which the agency concerned shall be brought into relationship with the United Nations. Such agreements shall be subject to approval by the General Assembly.

2. It may coordinate the activities of the specialized agencies through consultation with and recommendations to such agencies and through recommendations to the General Assembly and to the Members of the United Nations.

ARTICLE 64

1. The Economic and Social Council may take appropriate steps to obtain regular reports from the specialized agencies. It may make arrangements

with the Members of the United Nations and with the specialized agencies to obtain reports on the steps taken to give effect to its own recommendations and to recommendations on matters falling within its competence made by the General Assembly.

2. It may communicate its observations on these reports to the General Assembly.

ARTICLE 65

The Economic and Social Council may furnish information to the Security Council and shall assist the Security Council upon its request.

ARTICLE 66

1. The Economic and Social Council shall perform such functions as fall within its competence in connection with the carrying out of the recommendations of the General Assembly.

2. It may, with the approval of the General Assembly, perform services at the request of Members of the United Nations and at the request of specialized agencies.

3. It shall perform such other functions as are specified elsewhere in the present Charter or as may be assigned to it by the General Assembly.

Voting

ARTICLE 67

1. Each member of the Economic and Social Council shall have one vote.

2. Decisions of the Economic and Social Council shall be made by a majority of the members present and voting.

Procedure

ARTICLE 68

The Economic and Social Council shall set up commissions in economic and social fields and for the promotion of human rights, and such other commissions as may be required for the performance of its functions.

ARTICLE 69

The Economic and Social Council shall invite any Member of the United Nations to participate, without vote, in its deliberations on any matter of particular concern to that Member.

ARTICLE 70

The Economic and Social Council may make arrangements for representatives of the specialized agencies to participate, without vote, in its deliberations and in those of the commissions established by it, and for its representatives to participate in the deliberations of the specialized agencies.

ARTICLE 71

The Economic and Social Council may make suitable arrangements for consultation with non-governmental organizations which are concerned with matters within its competence. Such arrangements may be made with international organizations and, where appropriate, with national organizations after consultation with the Member of the United Nations concerned.

ARTICLE 72

1. The Economic and Social Council shall adopt its own rules of procedure, including the method of selecting its President.
2. The Economic and Social Council shall meet as required in accordance with its rules, which shall include provision for the convening of meetings on the request of a majority of its members.

Chapter XI: Declaration Regarding Non-Self-Governing Territories

ARTICLE 73

Members of the United Nations which have or assume responsibilities for the administration of territories whose peoples have not yet attained a full measure of self-government recognize the principle that the interests of the inhabitants of these territories are paramount, and accept as a sacred trust the obligation to promote to the utmost, within the system of international peace and security established by the present Charter, the well-being of the inhabitants of these territories, and, to this end:

a. to ensure, with due respect for the culture of the peoples concerned, their political, economic, social, and educational advancement, their just treatment, and their protection against abuses;

b. to develop self-government, to take due account of the political aspirations of the peoples, and to assist them in the progressive development of their free political institutions, according to the particular circumstances of each territory and its peoples and their varying stages of advancement;

c. to further international peace and security;

d. to promote constructive measures of development, to encourage research, and to cooperate with one another and, when and where appropriate, with specialized international bodies with a view to the practical achievement of the social, economic, and scientific purposes set forth in this Article; and

e. to transmit regularly to the Secretary-General for information purposes, subject to such limitation as security and constitutional considerations may require, statistical and other information of a technical nature relating to economic, social, and educational conditions in the territories for which they are respectively responsible other than those territories to which Chapters XII and XIII apply.

ARTICLE 74

Members of the United Nations also agree that their policy in respect of the territories to which this Chapter applies, no less than in respect of their metropolitan areas, must be based on the general principle of good-neighborliness, due account being taken of the interests and well-being of the rest of the world, in social, economic, and commercial matters.

Chapter XII: International Trusteeship System

ARTICLE 75

The United Nations shall establish under its authority an international trusteeship system for the administration and supervision of such territories as may be placed thereunder by subsequent individual agreements. These territories are hereinafter referred to as trust territories.

ARTICLE 76

The basic objectives of the trusteeship system, in accordance with the Purposes of the United Nations laid down in Article 1 of the present Charter, shall be:

a. to further international peace and security;

b. to promote the political, economic, social, and educational advancement of the inhabitants of the trust territories, and their progressive development towards self-government or independence as may be appropriate to the particular circumstances of each territory and its peoples and the freely expressed wishes of the peoples concerned, and as may be provided by the terms of each trusteeship agreement;

c. to encourage respect for human rights and for fundamental freedoms for all without distinction as to race, sex, language, or religion, and to encourage recognition of the interdependence of the peoples of the world; and

d. to ensure equal treatment in social, economic, and commercial matters for all Members of the United Nations and their nationals, and also equal treatment for the latter in the administration of justice, without prejudice to the attainment of the foregoing objectives and subject to the provisions of Article 80.

ARTICLE 77

1. The trusteeship system shall apply to such territories in the following categories as may be placed thereunder by means of trusteeship agreements:

a. territories now held under mandate;

b. territories which may be detached from enemy states as a result of the Second World War; and

c. territories voluntarily placed under the system by states responsible for their administration.

2. It will be a matter for subsequent agreement as to which territories in the foregoing categories will be brought under the trusteeship system and upon what terms.

ARTICLE 78

The trusteeship system shall not apply to territories which have become Members of the United Nations, relationship among which shall be based on respect for the principle of sovereign equality.

ARTICLE 79

The terms of trusteeship for each territory to be placed under the trusteeship system, including any alteration or amendment, shall be agreed upon by the states directly concerned, including the mandatory power in the case of territories held under mandate by a Member of the United Nations, and shall be approved as provided for in Articles 83 and 85.

ARTICLE 80

1. Except as may be agreed upon in individual trusteeship agreements, made under Articles 77, 79, and 81 placing each territory under the trusteeship system, and until such agreements have been concluded, nothing in this Chapter shall be construed in or of itself to alter in any manner the rights whatsoever of any states or any peoples or the terms of existing international instruments to which Members of the United Nations may respectively be parties.

2. Paragraph 1 of this Article shall not be interpreted as giving grounds for delay or postponement of the negotiation and conclusion of agreements for placing mandated and other territories under the trusteeship system as provided for in Article 77.

ARTICLE 81

The trusteeship agreement shall in each case include the terms under which the trust territory will be administered and designate the authority which will exercise the administration of the trust territory. Such authority, hereinafter called the administering authority, may be one or more states or the Organization itself.

ARTICLE 82

There may be designated, in any trusteeship agreement, a strategic area or areas which may include part or all of the trust territory to which the agreement applies, without prejudice to any special agreement or agreements made under Article 43.

ARTICLE 83

1. All functions of the United Nations relating to strategic areas, including the approval of the terms of the trusteeship agreements and of their alteration or amendment, shall be exercised by the Security Council.

2. The basic objectives set forth in Article 76 shall be applicable to the people of each strategic area.

3. The Security Council shall, subject to the provisions of the trusteeship agreements and without prejudice to security considerations, avail itself of the assistance of the Trusteeship Council to perform those functions of the United Nations under the trusteeship system relating to political, economic, social, and educational matters in the strategic areas.

ARTICLE 84

It shall be the duty of the administering authority to ensure that the trust territory shall play its part in the maintenance of international peace and security. To this end the administering authority may make use of volunteer forces, facilities, and assistance from the trust territory in carrying out the obligations towards the Security Council undertaken in this regard by the administering authority, as well as for local defense and the maintenance of law and order within the trust territory.

ARTICLE 85

1. The functions of the United Nations with regard to trusteeship agreements for all areas not designated as strategic, including the approval of the terms of the trusteeship agreements and of their alteration or amendment, shall be exercised by the General Assembly.

2. The Trusteeship Council, operating under the authority of the General Assembly, shall assist the General Assembly in carrying out these functions.

Chapter XIII: The Trusteeship Council

Composition

ARTICLE 86

1. The Trusteeship Council shall consist of the following Members of the United Nations:

    a. those Members administering trust territories;

    b. such of those Members mentioned by name in Article 23 as are not administering trust territories; and

    c. as many other Members elected for three-year terms by the General Assembly as may be necessary to ensure that the total number of members of the Trusteeship Council is equally divided between those Members of the United Nations which administer trust territories and those which do not.

2. Each member of the Trusteeship Council shall designate one specially qualified person to represent it therein.

Functions and Powers

ARTICLE 87

The General Assembly and, under its authority, the Trusteeship Council, in carrying out their functions, may:

    a. consider reports submitted by the administering authority;

    b. accept petitions and examine them in consultation with the administering authority;

    c. provide for periodic visits to the respective trust territories at times agreed upon with the administering authority; and

    d. take these and other actions in conformity with the terms of the trusteeship agreements.

ARTICLE 88

The Trusteeship Council shall formulate a questionnaire on the political, economic, social, and educational advancement of the inhabitants of each trust territory, and the administering authority for each trust territory within the competence of the General Assembly shall make an annual report to the General Assembly upon the basis of such questionnaire.

Voting

ARTICLE 89

    1. Each member of the Trusteeship Council shall have one vote.

    2. Decisions of the Trusteeship Council shall be made by a majority of the members present and voting.

Procedure

ARTICLE 90

    1. The Trusteeship Council shall adopt its own rules of procedure, including the method of selecting its President.

    2. The Trusteeship Council shall meet as required in accordance with its rules, which shall include provision for the convening of meetings on the request of a majority of its members.

ARTICLE 91

The Trusteeship Council shall, when appropriate, avail itself of the assistance of the Economic and Social Council and of the specialized agencies in regard to matters with which they are respectively concerned.

Chapter XIV: The International Court of Justice

ARTICLE 92

The International Court of Justice shall be the principal judicial organ of the United Nations. It shall function in accordance with the annexed

Statute, which is based upon the Statute of the Permanent Court of International Justice and forms an integral part of the present Charter.

ARTICLE 93

1. All Members of the United Nations are *ipso facto* parties to the Statute of the International Court of Justice.

2. A state which is not a Member of the United Nations may become a party to the Statute of the International Court of Justice on conditions to be determined in each case by the General Assembly upon the recommendation of the Security Council.

ARTICLE 94

1. Each Member of the United Nations undertakes to comply with the decision of the International Court of Justice in any case to which it is a party.

2. If any party to a case fails to perform the obligations incumbent upon it under a judgment rendered by the Court, the other party may have recourse to the Security Council, which may, if it deems necessary, make recommendations or decide upon measures to be taken to give effect to the judgment.

ARTICLE 95

Nothing in the present Charter shall prevent Members of the United Nations from entrusting the solution of their differences to other tribunals by virtue of agreements already in existence or which may be concluded in the future.

ARTICLE 96

1. The General Assembly or the Security Council may request the International Court of Justice to give an advisory opinion on any legal question.

2. Other organs of the United Nations and specialized agencies, which may at any time be so authorized by the General Assembly, may also request advisory opinions of the Court on legal questions arising within the scope of their activities.

Chapter XV: The Secretariat

ARTICLE 97

The Secretariat shall comprise a Secretary-General and such staff as the Organization may require. The Secretary-General shall be appointed by the General Assembly upon the recommendation of the Security Council. He shall be the chief administrative officer of the Organization.

ARTICLE 98

The Secretary-General shall act in that capacity in all meetings of the General Assembly, of the Security Council, of the Economic and Social

Council, and of the Trusteeship Council, and shall perform such other functions as are entrusted to him by these organs. The Secretary-General shall make an annual report to the General Assembly on the work of the Organization.

ARTICLE 99

The Secretary-General may bring to the attention of the Security Council any matter which in his opinion may threaten the maintenance of international peace and security.

ARTICLE 100

1. In the performance of their duties the Secretary-General and the staff shall not seek or receive instructions from any government or from any other authority external to the Organization. They shall refrain from any action which might reflect on their position as international officials responsible only to the Organization.

2. Each Member of the United Nations undertakes to respect the exclusively international character of the responsibilities of the Secretary-General and the staff and not to seek to influence them in the discharge of their responsibilities.

ARTICLE 101

1. The staff shall be appointed by the Secretary-General under regulations established by the General Assembly.

2. Appropriate staffs shall be permanently assigned to the Economic and Social Council, the Trusteeship Council, and, as required, to other organs of the United Nations. These staffs shall form a part of the Secretariat.

3. The paramount consideration in the employment of the staff and in the determination of the conditions of service shall be the necessity of securing the highest standards of efficiency, competence, and integrity. Due regard shall be paid to the importance of recruiting the staff on as wide a geographical basis as possible.

Chapter XVI: Miscellaneous Provisions

ARTICLE 102

1. Every treaty and every international agreement entered into by any Member of the United Nations after the present Charter comes into force shall as soon as possible be registered with the Secretariat and published by it.

2. No party to any such treaty or international agreement which has not been registered in accordance with the provisions of paragraph 1 of this Article may invoke that treaty or agreement before any organ of the United Nations.

ARTICLE 103

In the event of a conflict between the obligations of the Members of the United Nations under the present Charter and their obligations under any other international agreement, their obligations under the present Charter shall prevail.

ARTICLE 104

The Organization shall enjoy in the territory of each of its Members such legal capacity as may be necessary for the exercise of its functions and the fulfillment of its purposes.

ARTICLE 105

1. The Organization shall enjoy in the territory of each of its Members such privileges and immunities as are necessary for the fulfillment of its purposes.

2. Representatives of the Members of the United Nations and officials of the Organization shall similarly enjoy such privileges and immunities as are necessary for the independent exercise of their functions in connection with the Organization.

3. The General Assembly may make recommendations with a view of determining the details of the application of paragraphs 1 and 2 of this Article or may propose conventions to the Members of the United Nations for this purpose.

Chapter XVII: Transitional Security Arrangements

ARTICLE 106

Pending the coming into force of such special agreements referred to in Article 43 as in the opinion of the Security Council enable it to begin the exercise of its responsibilities under Article 42, the parties to the Four-Nation Declaration, signed at Moscow, October 30, 1943, and France, shall, in accordance with the provisions of paragraph 5 of that Declaration, consult with one another and as occasion requires with other Members of the United Nations with a view to such joint action on behalf of the Organization as may be necessary for the purpose of maintaining international peace and security.

ARTICLE 107

Nothing in the present Charter shall invalidate or preclude action, in relation to any state which during the Second World War has been an enemy of any signatory to the present Charter, taken or authorized as a result of that war by the Governments having responsibility for such action.

Chapter XVIII: Amendments

ARTICLE 108

Amendments to the present Charter shall come into force for all Members of the United Nations when they have been adopted by a vote of two thirds of the members of the General Assembly and ratified in accordance with their respective constitutional processes by two thirds of the Members of the United Nations, including all the permanent members of the Security Council.

ARTICLE 109 [*This article has been amended; see note on p. 474.*]

1. A General Conference of the Members of the United Nations for the purpose of reviewing the present Charter may be held at a date and place to be fixed by a two-thirds vote of the members of the General Assembly and by a vote of any seven members of the Security Council. Each Member of the United Nations shall have one vote in the conference.

2. Any alteration of the present Charter recommended by a two-thirds vote of the conference shall take effect when ratified in accordance with their respective constitutional processes by two thirds of the Members of the United Nations including all the permanent members of the Security Council.

3. If such a conference has not been held before the tenth annual session of the General Assembly following the coming into force of the present Charter, the proposal to call such a conference shall be placed on the agenda of that session of the General Assembly, and the conference shall be held if so decided by a majority vote of the members of the General Assembly and by a vote of any seven members of the Security Council.

Chapter XIX: Ratification and Signature

ARTICLE 110

1. The present Charter shall be ratified by the signatory states in accordance with their respective constitutional processes.

2. The ratifications shall be deposited with the Government of the United States of America, which shall notify all the signatory states of each deposit as well as the Secretary-General of the Organization when he has been appointed.

3. The present Charter shall come into force upon the deposit of ratifications by the Republic of China, France, the Union of Soviet Socialist Republics, the United Kingdom of Great Britain and Northern Ireland, and the United States of America, and by a majority of the other signatory states. A protocol of the ratifications deposited shall thereupon be drawn up by the Government of the United States of America which shall communicate copies thereof to all the signatory states.

4. The states signatory to the present Charter which ratify it after it has come into force will become original Members of the United Nations on the date of the deposit of their respective ratifications.

ARTICLE 111

The present Charter, of which the Chinese, French, Russian, English, and Spanish texts are equally authentic, shall remain deposited in the archives of the Government of the United States of America. Duly certified copies thereof shall be transmitted by that Government to the Governments of the other signatory states.

IN FAITH WHEREOF the representatives of the Governments of the United Nations have signed the present Charter.

DONE at the city of San Francisco the twenty-sixth day of June, one thousand nine hundred and forty-five.

NOTE: Amendments to Articles 23, 27 and 61 of the Charter of the United Nations, adopted by the General Assembly on 17 December 1963, came into force on 31 August 1965. An amendment to Article 109, adopted by the General Assembly on 20 December 1965, is in the process of ratification by Member States.

The amendment to Article 23 enlarges the membership of the Security Council from eleven to fifteen.

The amended Article 27 provides that decisions of the Security Council on procedural matters shall be made by an affirmative vote of nine members (formerly seven) and on all other matters by an affirmative vote of nine members (formerly seven), including the concurring votes of the five permanent members of the Security Council.

The amendment to Article 61 enlarges the membership of the Economic and Social Council from eighteen to twenty-seven.

The amendment to Article 109 provides that a General Conference of Member States for the purpose of reviewing the Charter may be held at a date and place to be fixed by a two-thirds vote of the members of the General Assembly and by a vote of any nine members (formerly seven) of the Security Council.

ROSTER OF THE UNITED NATIONS
WITH DATES OF ADMISSION[1]

Afghanistan *Nov. 19, 1946*
Albania *Dec. 14, 1955*
Algeria *Oct. 8, 1962*
Argentina *Oct. 24, 1945*
Australia *Nov. 1, 1945*
Austria *Dec. 14, 1955*
Barbados *Dec. 9, 1966*
Belgium *Dec. 27, 1945*
Bolivia *Nov. 14, 1945*
Botswana *Oct. 17, 1966*
Brazil *Oct. 24, 1945*
Bulgaria *Dec. 14, 1955*
Burma *April 19, 1948*
Burundi *Sept. 18, 1962*
Byelorussian Soviet Socialist
    Republic *Oct. 24, 1945*
Cambodia *Dec. 14, 1955*
Cameroon *Sept. 20, 1960*
Canada *Nov. 9, 1945*
Central African Republic *Sept. 20, 1960*
Ceylon *Dec. 14, 1955*
Chad *Sept. 20, 1960*
Chile *Oct. 24, 1945*
China *Oct. 24, 1945*
Colombia *Nov. 5, 1945*
Congo (Brazzaville) *Sept. 20, 1960*
Congo (Democratic Republic of)
    Sept. 20, 1960
Costa Rica *Nov. 2, 1945*

Cuba *Oct. 24, 1945*
Cyprus *Sept. 20, 1960*
Czechoslovakia *Oct. 24, 1945*
Dahomey *Sept. 20, 1960*
Denmark *Oct. 24, 1945*
Dominican Republic *Oct. 24, 1945*
Ecuador *Dec. 21, 1945*
El Salvador *Oct. 24, 1945*
Ethiopia *Nov. 13, 1945*
Finland *Dec. 14, 1955*
France *Oct. 24, 1945*
Gabon *Sept. 20, 1960*
Gambia *Sept. 21, 1965*
Ghana *March 8, 1957*
Greece *Oct. 25, 1945*
Guatemala *Nov. 21, 1945*
Guinea *Dec. 12, 1958*
Guyana *Sept. 20, 1966*
Haiti *Oct. 24, 1945*
Honduras *Dec. 17, 1945*
Hungary *Dec. 14, 1955*
Iceland *Nov. 19, 1946*
India *Oct. 30, 1945*
Indonesia[2] *Sept. 28, 1950*
Iran *Oct. 24, 1945*
Iraq *Dec. 21, 1945*
Ireland *Dec. 14, 1955*
Israel *May 11, 1949*
Italy *Dec. 14, 1955*
Ivory Coast *Sept. 20, 1960*

1. As listed in U.N. Press Release M/1449/Rev. 11, Dec. 14, 1967.
2. Temporarily withdrawn between Jan. 20, 1965–Sept. 28, 1966.

Jamaica *Sept. 18, 1962*
Japan *Dec. 18, 1956*
Jordan *Dec. 14, 1955*
Kenya *Dec. 16, 1963*
Kuwait *May 14, 1963*
Laos *Dec. 14, 1955*
Lebanon *Oct. 24, 1945*
Lesotho *Oct. 17, 1966*
Liberia *Nov. 2, 1945*
Libya *Dec. 14, 1955*
Luxembourg *Oct. 24, 1945*
Madagascar *Sept. 20, 1960*
Malawi *Dec. 1, 1964*
Malaysia[3] *Sept. 17, 1957*
Maldive Islands *Sept. 21, 1965*
Mali *Sept. 28, 1960*
Malta *Dec. 1, 1964*
Mauritania *Oct. 27, 1961*
Mexico *Nov. 7, 1945*
Mongolia *Oct. 27, 1961*
Morocco *Nov. 12, 1956*
Nepal *Dec. 14, 1955*
Netherlands *Dec. 10, 1945*
New Zealand *Oct. 24, 1945*
Nicaragua *Oct. 24, 1945*
Niger *Sept. 20, 1960*
Nigeria *Oct. 7, 1960*
Norway *Nov. 27, 1945*
Pakistan *Sept. 30, 1947*
Panama *Nov. 13, 1945*
Paraguay *Oct. 24, 1945*
Peru *Oct. 31, 1945*
Philippines *Oct. 24, 1945*
Poland *Oct. 24, 1945*
Portugal *Dec. 14, 1955*

Romania *Dec. 14, 1955*
Rwanda *Sept. 18, 1962*
Saudi Arabia *Oct. 24, 1945*
Senegal *Sept. 28, 1960*
Sierra Leone *Sept. 27, 1961*
Singapore *Sept. 21, 1965*
Somalia *Sept. 20, 1960*
South Africa *Nov. 7, 1945*
Southern Yemen *Dec. 14, 1967*
Spain *Dec. 14, 1955*
Sudan *Nov. 12, 1956*
Sweden *Nov. 19, 1946*
Syria[4] *Oct. 24, 1945*
Thailand *Dec. 16, 1946*
Togo *Sept. 20, 1960*
Trinidad and Tobago *Sept. 18, 1962*
Tunisia *Nov. 12, 1956*
Turkey *Oct. 24, 1945*
Uganda *Oct. 25, 1962*
Ukrainian Soviet Socialist Republic
    Oct. 24, 1945
Union of Soviet Socialist Republics
    Oct. 24, 1945
United Arab Republic[4] *Oct. 24, 1945*
United Kingdom *Oct. 24, 1945*
United Republic of Tanzania[5]
    Dec. 14, 1961
United States *Oct. 24, 1945*
Upper Volta *Sept. 20, 1960*
Uruguay *Dec. 18, 1945*
Venezuela *Nov. 15, 1945*
Yemen *Sept. 30, 1947*
Yugoslavia *Oct. 24, 1945*
Zambia *Dec. 1, 1964*

3. Originally admitted as Malaya; named changed, Sept. 16, 1963 with addition of new territories.

4. Syria joined Egypt as the UAR between Feb. 21, 1958–Oct. 13, 1961; after termination of the union, Egypt continued as UAR.

5. Tanganyika became a Member on Dec. 14, 1961 and Zanzibar on Dec. 16, 1963. The two formed the United Republic of Tanganyika and Zanzibar on April 26, 1964, later changing its name to United Republic of Tanzania.

SELECTED REFERENCES

Official Sources

Debates and resolutions of the General Assembly and Security Council are contained in the *Official Records* of each organ. Reports of commissions, committees, the Secretary-General, and other United Nations officials are in collections of U.N. documents available in depository libraries. Some of the more important reports are also on public sale. Statements of United States delegates and pertinent correspondence and memoranda are often printed also in the United States Department of State, *Bulletin* or issued as press releases of the department or of the U.S. Mission to the United Nations.

Decisions and advisory opinions of the International Court of Justice are in the annual *I.C.J. Reports*.

Official summaries of United Nations activities are contained in the *United Nations Yearbook* and in the *UN Monthly Chronicle* (since 1964) and its predecessor monthly publication, the *United Nations Review*. In addition, the *Annual Report of the Secretary-General on the Work of the Organization* and a separately published *Introduction* to the report, present regular surveys of United Nations activities and problems. *Everyman's United Nations* (7th ed., 1964) covers briefly the "Structure, Functions, and Work of the Organization, 1945–1963." The Office of Public Information also issues various specialized surveys on U.N. fields of activity, such as *The United Nations and Disarmament, 1945–1965* (issued in 1967).

The U.S. Department of State *Bulletin* provides the best coverage of official U.S. statements and actions in the international field on a weekly basis. It not only contains a regular record of department activities, but also publishes major statements of the President and other Executive branch officials dealing with foreign policy issues. Executive statements also often appear in pertinent hearings of congressional committees. For purposes of this study, the hearings and reports of the Senate Committee on Foreign Relations and the House of Representatives Committee on Foreign Affairs (and their subcommittees) have been most important sources of congressional (and often public) views. Formal proceedings and actions of the legislative branch are contained in the daily *Congressional Record*.

In addition, periodical reports of special interest include the annual report by the President to the Congress on *U.S. Participation in the United Nations* (issued by the State Department) and the annual reports of the

477

Arms Control and Disarmament Agency (established in 1961) and its periodic collections of *Documents on Disarmament* (beginning with two initial volumes covering 1945–1959).

Books and Articles

Abel, Elie, *The Missile Crisis*. Philadelphia, Pa.: J. B. Lippincott, 1966.

Ahmed, M. Samir, *The Neutrals and the Test-Ban Treaty: An Analysis of the Non-Aligned States' Efforts Between 1962–1963*. New York: Carnegie Endowment for International Peace, Occasional Paper No. 4, 1967.

American Society of International Law, *International Legal Materials*, Vol. 6, May-June 1967. (Documents on the Withdrawal of the United Nations Emergency Force and the War in the Middle East.)

Anand, R. P., "Attitude of the Asian-African States toward Certain Problems of International Law," *International and Comparative Law Quarterly*, Vol. 15, 1966.

Annual Review of United Nations Affairs, 1949 through 1965–1966. New York: New York University Press. (The last volume includes a cumulative index of all fifteen volumes.)

Armstrong, Hamilton Fish, "The U.N. Experience in Gaza," *Foreign Affairs*, Vol. 35, 1957.

Bailey, Sydney D., "U.N. Voting: Tyranny of the Majority?" *World Today*, Vol. 22, 1966.

———, *The Secretariat of the United Nations* rev. ed. New York: Praeger, 1964.

Baron, Leo, "Rhodesia: Taking Stock—The 1961 Constitution and the Tiger Proposals," *World Today*, Vol. 23, 1967.

Beaton, Leonard, *Must the Bomb Spread?* New York: Penguin Books, 1966.

Bechhoefer, Bernard G., *Postwar Negotiations for Arms Control*. Washington: Brookings Institution, 1961.

Beedham, Brian, "Cuba and the Balance of Power," *World Today*, Vol. 19, 1963.

Blair, Patricia Wohlgemuth, *The Ministate Dilemma*. New York: Carnegie Endowment for International Peace, Occasional Paper No. 6, 1967.

Bloomfield, Lincoln P., *International Military Forces*. Boston: Little Brown, 1964.

———, *The United Nations and U.S. Foreign Policy*, 2nd ed. Boston: Little Brown, 1967.

Bourguiba, Habib, "The Outlook for Africa," *International Affairs*, Vol. 37, 1961.

Boyd, Andrew, *The United Nations: Piety, Myth, and Truth*. New York: Penguin Books, 1962.

Boyd, James, "Cyprus: Episode in Peacekeeping," *International Organization*, Vol. 20, 1966.

Briggs, Herbert W., "Confidence, Apprehension, and the International Court of Justice," *Proceedings*, American Society of International Law, 1960.

Buchan, Alastair, ed., *China and the Peace of Asia*. New York: Praeger, 1965.

Bull, Hedley, *The Control of the Arms Race: Disarmament and Arms Control in the Missile Age*, 2nd ed. New York: Praeger, 1965.

Burke, Arleigh, "Power and Peace," *Orbis*, Vol. 6, 1962.

Burns, Arthur Lee, and Heathcote, Nina, *Peacekeeping by U.N. Forces: From Suez to the Congo*. New York: Praeger, 1963.

Burns, E. L. M., *Between Arab and Israeli*. New York: Ivan Obolensky, 1963.

————, "Can the Spread of Nuclear Weapons Be Stopped?" *International Organization*, Vol. 19, 1965.

Calvocoressi, Peter, *Suez: Ten Years After*. New York: Random House, 1966.

————, *World Order and New States: Problems of Keeping the Peace*. New York: Praeger, 1962.

Castañeda, Jorge, "The Underdeveloped Nations and the Development of International Law," *International Organization*, Vol. 15, 1961.

Chayes, Abram, "The Law and the Quarantine of Cuba," *Foreign Affairs*, Vol. 41, 1963.

Clark, Grenville, and Sohn, Louis B., *World Peace Through World Law*, 4th ed. Cambridge: Harvard University Press, 1966.

Clark, Mark W., *From the Danube to the Yalu*. New York: Harper, 1954.

Claude, Inis L., Jr., "The OAS, the UN, and the United States," *International Conciliation*, No. 547, March 1964.

————, "Collective Legitimization as a Political Function of the United Nations," *International Organization*, Vol. 20, 1966.

Cohen, Benjamin V., *The United Nations: Constitutional Developments, Growth, and Possibilities*. Cambridge: Harvard University Press, 1961.

Cordier, Andrew, and Foote, Wilder, eds., *The Quest for Peace: The Dag Hammarskjold Memorial Lectures*. New York: Columbia University Press, 1965.

Cox, Arthur M., *Prospects for Peacekeeping*. Washington: Brookings Institution, 1967.

Crocker, W. R., *Self-Government for the Colonies.* London: Allen & Unwin, 1949.

Crozier, Brian, *Neo-Colonialism: A Background Book.* Chester Springs, Pennsylvania: Dufour Editions, 1964.

Dallinn, Alexander, *The Soviet Union at the United Nations: An Inquiry into Soviet Motives and Objectives.* New York: Praeger, 1962.

Dayal, Shiv, *India's Role in the Korean Question.* New Delhi, India; Chand, 1959.

Dean, Arthur H., *Test-Ban and Disarmament: The Path of Negotiation.* New York: Harper & Row, 1966.

Dreier, John C., *The OAS and the Hemisphere Crisis.* New York: Council on Foreign Relations, 1962.

Duffy, James, *Portugal's African Territories: Present Realities.* New York: Carnegie Endowment for International Peace, Occasional Paper No. 1, 1962.

Dulles, John Foster, "Challenge and Response in U.S. Policy," *Foreign Affairs,* Vol. 36, 1957.

Eban, Abba, "Reality and Vision in the Middle East," *Foreign Affairs,* Vol. 43, 1965.

Eden, Anthony, *Memoirs of the Rt. Hon. Sir Anthony Eden: Full Circle,* Vol. 1. Boston: Houghton-Mifflin, 1960.

Edwardes, Michael, "India, Pakistan and Nuclear Weapons," *International Affairs,* Vol. 43, 1967.

Eisenhower, Dwight D., *The White House Years: Mandate for Change, 1953–1956.* New York: Doubleday, 1963.

———, *The White House Years: Waging Peace, 1956–1961.* New York: Doubleday, 1965.

Eisenhower, Milton, *The Wine Is Bitter: The United States and Latin America.* New York: Doubleday, 1963.

Emerson, Rupert, *From Empire to Nation.* Cambridge: Harvard University Press, 1959.

Falk, Richard A., and Mendlovitz, Saul H., eds., *The Strategy of World Order,* 4 Vols.: (1) *Toward a Theory of War Prevention;* (2) *International Law;* (3) *The United Nations;* (4) *Disarmament and Economic Development.* New York: World Law Fund, 1966.

Finkelstein, Lawrence S., "Arms Inspection," *International Conciliation,* No. 540, 1962.

Foote, Wilder, ed., *Dag Hammarskjold, Servant of Peace: A Selection of the Speeches and Statements of Dag Hammarskjold.* New York: Harper & Row, 1963.

Foster, William C., "New Directions in Arms Control and Disarmament," *Foreign Affairs*, Vol. 43, 1965.

Friedheim, Robert L., "The 'Satisfied' and 'Dissatisfied' States Negotiate International Law: A Case Study," *World Politics*, Vol. 18, 1965.

Friedmann, Wolfgang, "United States Policy and the Crisis of International Law," *American Journal of International Law*, Vol. 59, 1965.

Frydenberg, Per, ed., *Peacekeeping: Experience and Evaluation: The Oslo Papers*. Oslo: Norwegian Institute of International Affairs, 1964.

Fulbright, J. William., *Old Myths and New Realities*. New York: Random House, 1964.

García Robles, Alfonso, *The Denuclearization of Latin America*. New York: Carnegie Endowment for International Peace, 1967.

Gardner, Richard N., *In Pursuit of World Order: U.S. Foreign Policy and International Organizations*. New York: Praeger, 1964.

————, *Blueprint for Peace: Being the Proposals of Prominent Americans to the White House Conference on International Cooperation*. New York: McGraw-Hill, 1966.

Goodrich, Leland M., *Korea: A Study of U.S. Policy in the United Nations*. New York: Council on Foreign Relations, 1956.

Gordenker, Leon, *The UN Secretary-General and the Maintenance of Peace*. New York: Columbia University Press, 1967.

Gordon, King, *UN in the Congo: A Quest for Peace*. New York: Carnegie Endowment for International Peace, 1962.

Gross, Ernest A., *The United Nations: Structure for Peace*. New York: Harper, 1962.

Gross, Franz, ed., *The United States and the United Nations*. Stillwater, Oklahoma: University of Oklahoma Press, 1964.

Gross, Leo, "Expenses of the UN for Peacekeeping Operations," *International Organization*, Vol. 17, 1963.

Haekkerup, Per, "Scandinavia's Peace-Keeping Forces for U.N.," *Foreign Affairs*, Vol. 42, 1964.

Hall, John A., "Atoms for Peace, or War," *Foreign Affairs*, Vol. 43, 1965.

Halperin, Morton H., *China and the Bomb*. New York: Praeger, 1965.

Halpern, A. M., "China, the UN, and Beyond," *China Quarterly*, Vol. 10, 1962.

Harris, Richard, *Independence and After: Revolution in Underdeveloped Countries*. London: New York: Oxford University Press, 1962.

Henkin, Louis, "International Law and the Behavior of Nations," *Recueil des Cours de l'Académie de Droit International*. The Hague, Netherlands, 1965.

Higgins, Rosalyn, *The Development of International Law through the Political Organs of the United Nations*. London: New York: Oxford University Press, 1963.

———, *Conflict of Interests: International Law in a Divided World*. Chester Springs, Pa.: Dufour Editions, 1965.

Hilsman, Roger, *To Move a Nation: The Politics of Foreign Policy in the Administration of John F. Kennedy*. New York: Doubleday, 1967.

Hilsman, Roger, and Good, Robert C., eds., *Foreign Policy in the Sixties: The Issues and the Instruments*. Baltimore: Johns Hopkins Press, 1965.

Hoyt, Edwin C., "The United States Reaction to the Korean Attack: A Study of the Principles of the United Nations Charter as a Factor in American Policy-Making," *American Journal of International Law*, Vol. 55, 1961.

Hyde, James N., "Peaceful Settlement Studies in the Interim Committee," *International Conciliation*, No. 444, 1948.

Inter-American Institute of International Legal Studies, *The Inter-American System: Its Development and Strengthening*. Dobbs Ferry, N.Y.: Oceana Publications, 1966.

Jacobson, Harold Karan, "Our 'Colonial' Problem in the Pacific," *Foreign Affairs*, Vol. 39, 1960.

———, "ONUC's Civilian Operations: State-Building and State-Preserving," *World Politics*, Vol. 17, 1964.

Jordan, William M., "Concepts and Realities in International Political Organization," *International Organization*, Vol. 11, 1957.

Kaplan, Morton A., ed., *The Revolution in World Politics*. New York: John Wiley, 1962.

Kaufmann, William W., ed., *Military Policy and National Security*. Princeton, N.J.: Princeton University Press, 1956.

Kay, David A., "The Politics of Decolonization: The New Nations and the United Nations Political Process," *International Organization*, Vol. 21, 1967.

Keohane, Robert O., "Political Influence in the General Assembly," *International Conciliation*, No. 557, 1966.

Khan, Mohammed Ayub, "Pakistan Perspective," *Foreign Affairs*, Vol. 38, 1960.

Lansdale, Edward G., "Vietnam: Do We Understand Revolution?" *Foreign Affairs*, Vol. 43, 1964.

Lash, Joseph P., *Dag Hammarskjold: Custodian of the Brushfire Peace*. New York: Doubleday, 1961.

Lefever, Ernest W., *Uncertain Mandate: Politics of the U.N. Congo Operation.* Baltimore: Johns Hopkins Press, 1967.

Legum, Colin, "What Kind of Radicalism for Africa?" *Foreign Affairs,* Vol. 43, 1964.

Leiss, Amelia C., ed., *Apartheid and United Nations Collective Measures: An Analysis.* New York: Carnegie Endowment for International Peace, 1965.

Lewis, I. M., "The Referendum in French Somaliland: Aftermath and Prospects in the Somali Dispute," *World Today,* Vol. 23, 1967.

Li, Thian-hok, "The Chinese Impasse: A Formosan View," *Foreign Affairs,* Vol. 36, 1958.

Lie, Trygve, *In the Cause of Peace.* New York: Macmillan, 1954.

Lissitzyn, Oliver, "International Law in a Divided World," *International Conciliation,* No. 542, 1963.

Martin, Laurence, ed., *Neutralism and Non-Alignment.* New York: Praeger, 1962.

Martin, Paul, *Canada and the Quest for Peace.* New York: Columbia University Press, 1967.

Mazrui, Ali A., "The United Nations and Some African Political Attitudes," *International Organization,* Vol. 18, 1964.

Mecham, J. Lloyd, *The United States and Inter-American Security: 1889–1960.* Austin, Texas: University of Texas Press, 1961.

Miller, Linda B., *World Order and Local Disorder: The United Nations and Internal Conflicts.* Princeton, N.J.: Princeton University Press, 1967.

Morozov, G., and Pchelintsev, E., *The United Nations—Twenty Years Of Failures and Successes.* Novosti Press Agency, 1965.

Mudge, George Alfred, "Domestic Policies and UN Activities: The Case of Rhodesia and the Republic of South Africa," *International Organization,* Vol. 21, 1967.

Nathanson, Nathaniel L., "Constitutional Crisis at the United Nations: The Price of Peace-Keeping," *University of Chicago Law Review,* Pt. I. Vol. 32, 1965. Pt. II, Vol. 33, 1966.

Nicholas, Herbert G., *The United Nations as a Political Institution* 3rd ed., London: New York: Oxford University Press, 1967.

———, "The U.N. in Crisis," *International Affairs,* Vol. 41, 1965.

Nielsen, Waldemar A., *African Battleline: American Policy Choices in Southern Africa.* New York: Harper & Row, 1965.

Nogueira, Franco, *The United Nations and Portugal: A Study of Anti-Colonialism.* London: Sidgwick & Jackson, 1963.

Nutting, Anthony, *No End of a Lesson*. New York: Clarkson N. Potter, 1967.

Osgood, Robert E., *Limited War: The Challenge to American Strategy*. Chicago: University of Chicago Press, 1957.

Padelford, Norman J., and Goodrich, Leland M., eds., *The United Nations in the Balance: Accomplishments and Prospects*. New York: Praeger, 1965.

Pearson, Lester B., "Force for U.N.," *Foreign Affairs*, Vol. 35, 1957.

Pélissier, René, "Spain's Discreet Decolonization," *Foreign Affairs*, Vol. 43, 1965.

Pelt, Adrian, *Libyan Independence and the United Nations: Planned Transition from Colony to Statehood*. New York: Carnegie Endowment for International Peace, 1968.

Perham, Margery, *The Colonial Reckoning: The End of Imperial Rule In Africa in the Light of British Experience*. New York: Alfred A. Knopf, 1962.

Perkins, Whitney T., "Sanctions for Political Change—The Indonesian Case," *International Organization*, Vol. 12, 1958.

———, *Denial of Empire: The U.S. and Its Dependencies*. Leyden, Netherlands: A. W. Sythoff, 1962.

Possony, Stefan T., "Toward Nuclear Isolationism?" *Orbis*, Vol. 6, 1963.

Posvar, Wesley W., ed., *American Defense Policy*. Baltimore: Johns Hopkins Press, 1965.

Power, Thomas S., (with Albert A. Arnhym), *Design for Survival*. New York: Coward-McCann, 1965.

Quaison-Sackey, Alex, *Africa Unbound: Reflections of an African Statesman*. New York: Praeger, 1963.

Rajan, M. S., *United Nations and Domestic Jurisdiction*. Bombay, India: Orient Longmans, 1958.

Rapacki, Adam, "The Polish Plan for a Nuclear-Free Zone Today," *International Affairs*, Vol. 39, 1963.

Ridgway, Matthew B., *The Korean War*. New York: Doubleday, 1967.

Rivkin, Arnold, *The African Presence in World Affairs: National Development and Its Role in Foreign Policy*. Cambridge: Massachusetts Institute of Technology, 1963.

Robertson, Terence, *Crisis: The Inside Story of the Suez Conspiracy*. New York: Atheneum, 1965.

Rosner, Gabriella, *The United Nations Emergency Force*. New York: Columbia University Press, 1963.

Rubinstein, Alvin Z., *The Soviets in International Organizations: Changing Policy Toward Developing Countries, 1953–1963*. Princeton, N.J.: Princeton University Press, 1964.

Russell, Ruth B., *A History of the United Nations Charter: The Role of the United States 1940–1945*. Washington: Brookings Institution, 1958.

———, *United Nations Experience with Military Forces: Political and Legal Aspects*. Washington: Brookings Institution, 1964.

———, "United Nations Financing and the 'Law of the Charter'," *Columbia Journal of Transnational Law*, Vol. 5, 1966.

Rustow, Dankwart A., *A World of Nations: Problems of Political Modernization*. Washington: Brookings Institution, 1967.

Salazar, António de Oliveira, "Realities and Trends of Portugal's Policies," *International Affairs*, Vol. 39, 1963.

Schachter, Oscar, "Dag Hammarskjold and the Relation of Law to Politics," *American Journal of International Law*, Vol. 56, 1962.

———, "The Relations of Law, Politics, and Action in the United Nations," *Recueil des Cours de l'Académie de Droit International*, 1963.

Schlesinger, Arthur M., Jr., *A Thousand Days: Kennedy in the White House*. Boston: Houghton-Mifflin, 1965.

Shamuyarira, N. M., "The Coming Showdown in Central Africa," *Foreign Affairs*, Vol. 39, 1961.

Sirc, L., "Changes in Communist Advice to Developing Countries," *World Today*, Vol. 22, 1966.

Stein, Eric, "Mr. Hammarskjold, the Charter Law and the Future Role of the UN Secretary-General," *American Journal of International Law*, Vol. 56, 1962.

Stoessinger, John G., *The United Nations and the Super Powers: United States-Soviet Interaction at the United Nations*. New York: Random House, 1965.

Stoessinger, John G., and Associates, *Financing the United Nations System*. Washington: Brookings Institution, 1964.

Stone, Julius, *Quest for Survival: The Role of Law and Foreign Policy*. Cambridge: Harvard University Press, 1961.

———, "The International Court and World Crisis," *International Conciliation*, No. 536, 1962.

Strausz-Hupé, Robert, "The Real Communist Threat," *International Affairs*, Vol. 41, 1965.

Strausz-Hupé, Robert, and others, *A Forward Strategy for America*. New York: Harper, 1961.

Tandon, Yashpal, "Consensus and Authority behind United Nations Peacekeeping Operations," *International Organization*, Vol. 21, 1967.

Taylor, Alastair, *Indonesian Independence and the United Nations*. Ithaca, N.Y.: Cornell University Press, 1960.

Taylor, Maxwell D., *The Uncertain Trumpet*. New York: Harper, 1960.

Taylor, Philip B., Jr., "The Guatemalan Affair: A Critique of U.S. Foreign Policy," *American Political Science Review*, Vol. 50, 1956.

Thant, U, *Toward World Peace: Addresses and Public Statements, 1957–1963*. New York: Thomas Yoseloff, 1964.

Thompson, Sir Robert, *Defeating Communist Insurgency*. London: Chatto & Windus, 1965.

Travis, Martin B., and Watkins, James T., "Control of the Panama Canal: An Obsolete Shibboleth?" *Foreign Affairs*, Vol. 37, 1959.

Tsou, Tang, *America's Failure in China, 1941–1949*. Chicago: University of Chicago Press, 1963.

Urquhart, Brian E., "United Nations Peace Forces and the Changing United Nations: An Institutional Perspective," *International Organization*, Vol. 17, 1963.

Van Der Kroef, Justus M., "The West New Guinea Settlement: Its Origins and Implications," *Orbis*, Vol. 7, 1963.

Van Der Veur, Paul W., "Political Awakening in West New Guinea," *Pacific Affairs*, Vol. 36, 1963.

Von Horn, Carl, *Soldiering for Peace*. New York: David McKay, 1966.

Wainhouse, David W., and Associates, *International Peace Observation: A History and Forecast*. Baltimore: Johns Hopkins Press, 1966.

West, F. J., "The New Guinea Question: An Australian View," *Foreign Affairs*, Vol. 39, 1961.

Whelan, Joseph G., "The U.S. and Diplomatic Recognition: The Contrasting Cases of Russia and Communist China," *China Quarterly*, Vol. 5, 1961.

Whitaker, Arthur P., "Protracted Conflict in Latin America," *Orbis*, Vol. 6, 1962.

Whiting, A. S., *China Crosses the Yalu: The Decision to Enter the Korean War*. New York: Macmillan, 1960.

Wilcox, Francis O., and Haviland, H. Field, Jr., eds., *The United States and the United Nations*. Baltimore: Johns Hopkins Press, 1961.

Windass, Stanley, "The Vitality of the United Nations," *Yale Review*, Vol. 53, 1964.

Wint, Guy, *What Happened in Korea? A Study of Collective Security*. Greenfield, Middlesex, England: Batchworth, 1954.

Wint, Guy, and Calvocoressi, Peter, *Middle East Crisis*. New York: Penguin Books, 1957.

Wohlgemuth, Patricia, "The Portuguese Territories and the United Nations," *International Conciliation*, No. 545, 1963.

Wolfers, Arnold, *Discord and Collaboration: Essays on International Politics*. Baltimore: Johns Hopkins Press, 1962.

Wright, Quincy, "The Goa Incident," *American Journal of International Law*, Vol. 56, 1962.

———, *International Law and the United Nations*. Bombay, India: Asia Publishing House, 1960.

Wurfel, David, "Okinawa: Irredenta in the Pacific," *Pacific Affairs*, Vol. 35, 1962.

Younger, Kenneth, "The Spectre of Nuclear Proliferation," *Pacific Affairs*, Vol. 42, 1966.

Zinkin, Taya, "Indian Foreign Policy: An Interpretation of Attitudes," *World Politics*, Vol. 7, 1955.

INDEX

Codification of international law, 138, 313, 316–17

Coercion vs. consent, 307, 310

Coexistence, peaceful, 313–18, 324, 427–28

Coexistence. *See* Containment-coexistence.

Coffey, J. I., 105n

Cohen, Benjamin V., 289n, 309n, 379n

Cold war (*see also* Communism: threat of), influence on: Art. 43 agreements, 120–21; colonial issue, 233, 252, 272; international law, 309–10, 328, 399; Southeast Asia, 409; U.N., 43, 170, 359–60, 370, 419–20, 444; U.S. aid programs, 227

Collective approach, U.S. policy, 408, 437

Collective enforcement: By U.N., 29, 43, 49–57, 70, 118–60, 332, 391–92, 400–02, 405–06, 440; defined, 179, 391; ICJ decisions, 300–02; Korea, 126, 128–29; Rhodesia (*see* Rhodesia); Suez proposal, 134–36

Collective Measures Committee, 131–33, 339

Collective security (*see also* Collective enforcement; Regional organizations), 52n, 102, 391, 439

Colombia, 110n, 111n, 158n, 170n, 235n, 277n

Colonial Independence, Declaration on, 34, 150, 153n, 254–59, 262–64, 267, 283, 285, 290, 361

Colonial issues: Great Britain, 31, 32n, 33, 255–59, 263–64, 266n, 286–87; Soviet Union, 31–32, 230–33, 252–55, 259n, 264, 272, 281–82, 289–90, 410; U.S., 255–83, 286–87, 290

Colonial (imperial) powers (*see also* Australia; Belgium; France; Great Britain; Netherlands; New Zealand; Portugal; South Africa; Soviet Union; United States), 246–52, 287, 410, 418

Colonialism (*see also* Anticolonialism; Dependent peoples; Dependent territories), 148–49, 226, 252, 254–56, 261–62, 265–72, 409–11; economic, 289–90; neo-, 287–90, 410

Commission on Cooperation in Technical Matters in Africa (CCTA), 247–48

Committee of Experts to Review the Activities and Organization of the Secretariat, 339

Committee of Experts to Examine the Finances of the United Nations and the Specialized Agencies, 345–46

Committee of 24. *See* Special Committee on Granting of Independence.

Committee of 33. *See* Special Committee on Peacekeeping Operations.

Committee of One Million, 377, 385

Committee on Information Transmitted under Art. 73(e), 250–52, 263

Common markets, 418

Communism: Anticolonialism, 230–33, 246, 248, 263, 287, 318, 322n, 354, 410; attitude toward use of force, 311; concept of change, 230–31; containment of, 228–30, 232, 367, 371, 420, 429, 439; expansion of, 424–25; Korea, 122–23; Southeast Asia, 17; threat of, 4–6, 8–11, 15–16, 20–22, 179–80, 182, 224–25; U.S. confrontation with (*see also* Cold war), 4, 266–67, 281, 415; use of subversion, 134, 160, 162, 180, 232n, 324–25, 412

Communist states (*see also* China (Peking); Soviet Union): Peaceful coexistence doctrine, 313–17, 324, 427–28; peacekeeping assessments, 336; policy re Secretary-General, 285, 332, 339; U.N. bond issue, 334–35; U.N. failure to involve, 167; views on international law, 317–20

Compulsory jurisdiction. *See* International Court of Justice.

Compulsory settlement of disputes, 302–04

Conciliation, 56, 168–69, 303, 319, 358, 401

Confrontation: Indonesia-Malaysia, 190

Confrontation. *See* Containment-confrontation approach.

Congo: Belgian resistance to U.N. competence, 251; Belgian withdrawal, 176, 267n; civil war, 327; effects of conflict in, 21, 186, 256–57, 332, 440; ONUC (*see* U.N. Force in Congo); payment to U.N., 348; Soviet tactics, 69, 148; U.N. difficulties re, 18, 161, 209, 211, 214; U.N. membership, 253n, 419

Congress, U.S. (*see also* Senate): Arms sales, 117; attitude toward U.N., 51, 52n, 443–45; China, 374, 377, 385; disarmament, 75; financing of international organizations, 340–43, 347n; foreign policy and domestic politics, 430, 432–36, 439; nuclear control, 95; Pacific Islands, 242–43, 245; Panama Canal Zone, 274–76, 278n, 279, 281; Rhodesia, 159; U.N. bonds, 334; U.N. peacekeeping proposals, 212, 213n,

TYPESETTING   Monotype Composition Company, Inc., Baltimore

PRINTING & BINDING   Garamond/Pridemark Press, Inc., Baltimore